CLARK'S

FOREIGN

THEOLOGICAL LIBRARY.

THIRD SERIES.
VOL. VIII.

Ebrard's Commentary on the Epistles of St John.

BIBLICAL COMMENTARY

ON

THE EPISTLES OF ST JOHN,

IN CONTINUATION OF THE WORK OF OLSHAUSEN.

WITH AN APPENDIX ON
THE CATHOLIC EPISTLES,

AND AN

INTRODUCTORY ESSAY ON THE
LIFE AND WRITINGS OF ST JOHN.

BY

DR JOHN H. A. EBRARD.

TRANSLATED BY
REV. W. B. POPE,
MANCHESTER.

WIPF & STOCK · Eugene, Oregon

Wipf and Stock Publishers
199 W 8th Ave, Suite 3
Eugene, OR 97401

Biblical Commentary on the Epistles of St. John, In Continuation of the Work of Olshausen
With an Appendix on the Catholic Epistles, and an Introductory Essay on the Life an Writings of St. John
By Ebrard, John H. A. and Pope, W. B.
Copyright © 1860 by Ebrard, John H. A. All rights reserved.
Softcover ISBN-13: 979-8-3852-1471-6
Hardcover ISBN-13: 979-8-3852-1472-3
eBook ISBN-13: 979-8-3852-1473-0
Publication date 1/25/2024
Previously published by T. and T. Clark, 1860

This edition is a scanned facsimile of the original edition published in 1860.

ST JOHN THE APOSTLE, AND HIS WRITINGS.

ST JOHN occupies a place so peculiar and prominent, among the disciples of our Lord as a person, and among the New-Testament writers as an author—and the writings which bear his name have always been the object of such various and conflicting discussion—that a comprehensive exhibition of his personal character, his life, his labours, and his literary activity may well be regarded as one of the most difficult undertakings. If, in the brief limits here prescribed to us, we are to succeed, we must enter upon the subject not analytically, but synthetically; that is, we must set out with the collective picture of the Apostle and his writings given in the New Testament, and then pass on to a general view of all the critical questions arising out of it. The personality of the Apostle himself, and the character of his writings, and their adjustment in the extant cycle of New-Testament literature, must first of all be viewed as a thesis; and upon that we may found a universal review of the critical questions which have been raised in relation to those writings.

Three of our Lord's Apostles stand out prominently from the general circle: St John, St Peter, and St Paul. The last was not in the number of the Twelve. Among them St James, the son of Zebedee and brother of St John, had been singled out by Christ to be the companion of St John and St Peter in the special distinction of witnessing His transfiguration and His deepest humiliation (Mark v. 37; Matt. xvii. 1, xxvi. 37); but St James soon followed his Master in a death of martyrdom (Acts xii. 2), and on that account is less known to us than the rest.

As compared with St Peter, St John exhibits to us a

calm and reflective nature, with a preeminent receptivity: every word of his beloved Master, which tends to solve to his heart the mystery which he pondered, he apprehends in his deepest soul, and holds it fast, and meditates upon it, blessedly losing himself in the contemplation of the glory of the Son of Man. In relation to all that Christ speaks or does, he does not seize the element of practical conduct; he does not ask, "What shall *I do?* shall I build tabernacles upon the Mount of Transfiguration? shall I draw my sword against Malchus?" —but, far from feeling the pressure of action and co-operation, he loves calmly to contemplate what passes, and asks, "What is this that *He* doeth? what is it that *He* saith?" He was lost in the pondering, affectionate contemplation of Jesus, as a bride in the contemplation of the bridegroom; in the most profound and purest love, he sank into the person of his Master (hence he was chosen as an individual *friend* rather than the others, John xiii. 23, etc.). And thus it is to be explained that in the soul and in the living remembrance of this disciple the very character of our Lord, in its most fine and characteristic traits, was retained so clearly and unconfusedly; and that so many long colloquies of Jesus with friends and foes remained in all their vividness, down to the minutest particulars. All the supreme and preeminent glory and dignity of Christ, which is exhibited in the Gospel of St John, did not certainly remain concealed from the rest of the disciples; but only St John was capable of being the instrument of reproducing the exhibition of it. Every man may *see* the ineffable beauty of an Alpine scene under the setting sun; but not every man can *paint* it. St John had the nature of a living mirror, which not merely received the full brightness of the Lord's glory, but could also reflect it back. The other Apostles and Evangelists have rather preserved those points of our Saviour's speaking and acting which produced the greatest effect, externally viewed, at the time. The Sermon on the Mount, delivered before a large assembly of the people upon a sunny height of Galilee, was to them, humanly speaking, for ever rememberable; the undemonstrative conversation with the woman of Samaria, or the controversial discourses of Jesus in the Temple at Jerusalem, would not make so deep an impression upon them, as not producing any striking immediate effect: St John alone was able to penetrate and discern the glory which radiated through such less apparently significant words. And, under the influence of the Spirit, he was able to do this, to retain and faithfully reproduce all, because his was a receptive and observant nature. For, this is the talent of a true observer : not to overlook the most minute trait, and to place it in its right position in the connection of the whole. But then St John was only an observer, not a poet or inventor. The first requisite of an inventive poet—the art of rounding, and making an artistic whole out of, the things narrated—is altogether wanting in him. Plainly, and altogether without artificial attractions—often, it might seem, wearisomely —he faithfully gives back " that which he had seen and heard" (1 John i. 1).

We are conducted to another side of St John's nature by the comparison with the Apostle Paul. In inwardness, St Paul is much more like St John than St Peter is ; but it is another kind of inwardness : in St Paul it is dialectic, in St John purely contemplative. St Paul views psychologically the becoming, St John the eternal being ; St Paul directs his regards to the appropriation of redemption, St John to the Founder of salvation ; St Paul to conversion, St John rather to the fulness of life in Christ. Hence St Paul's is a much gentler character than that of the υἱὸς βροντῆς (Mark iii. 17). St John, indeed, has often been called " the Apostle of love," because the word ἀγάπη often occurs in his writings as an important term in his doctrine. But this ἀγάπη occurs at least as often in St Paul's writings : in St Paul, in its relation to faith as its outward expression ; in St John, in its opposition to hatred and wickedness. St John has even been regarded by many as a sentimental man of feeling, and he has been painted as a youth with soft and effeminate features ; but thus his personal character has been most egregiously misconceived. On the other hand, the passage Luke ix. 51 seq. by no means justifies those who describe him as a man of violent *temperament*. Rather he was that which the French describe in their expression, "*il est entier;*" he had no mind or sense for relativities and mediating modes; and hence was not a man of middle courses. The ground of this, however, lay, not in a vehemence of his natural temperament, but in the peculiarity of his mystic-contemplative and deep insight, which everywhere and always pierced through to the last extremes. Irenæus (Hær. 3, 3; comp. Euseb. 3, 28; 4, 14) relates, as received from Polycarp, that St John, when he once met the Gnostic Cerinthus in a bath, instantly left the place; fearing that the building would fall down in which such an enemy of the truth was found. He was—even in his natural temperament—a man who was *altogether* that which he was; a man who could only have been altogether a Christian, or altogether a devil. In St John, grace celebrated a silent, and permanent, and decided victory over the natural corruption. He had never moved in contradictories. He had been from earliest youth piously trained; for his mother, Salome (Mark xvi. 1; Matt. xx. 20), belonged to the circle of those few souls who found their consolation as true Israelites in the promises of the Old Covenant, and who longed for the coming of the Messiah. Salome was one of those women who ministered of their substance to the Lord, who had not where to lay His head (Luke viii. 3); she did not leave Him when He hung upon the cross (Mark xv. 40); and it was her high distinction that the Saviour put her son in His own place, as the son and sustainer of His mother Mary (the bosom-friend of Salome). To such a mother was St John born—probably in Bethsaida,[1] at least in its neighbourhood—and trained up in the fear of God and hope of Israel. The family was not without substance; for Zebedee had hired servants for his fishing trade (Mark i. 20), Salome ministered to Jesus, St John possessed τὰ ἴδια, a dwelling (John xix. 17), and was personally known in the house of the high-priest (John xviii. 15).

As soon as the Baptist came into trouble, St John adhered to him with all the energy of his receptive inwardness. We see from John iii. 27–36, that the Evangelist had formed the peculiar style which distinguishes him from all the other New-Testament writers—a style strong, concise, clear, sententious, and ever reminding of the Old-Testament prophetic diction—under the express influence of the Baptist, that last and great prophet; not so much, however, appropriating the Baptist's to himself, as constructing his own style, under the Baptist's influence, in harmony with the intuitional Hebrew character of his

---

[1] Chrysostom and others mention Bethsaida with confidence as the place of his birth, resting upon the passages John i. 44, Luke v. 9. But those passages do not speak with absolute precision.

own mind, which rejected all dialectics and logical grammatical construction. For, that longer discourse of the Baptist—although in its substance altogether pre-Christian, and springing simply out of the distinctive position of the Baptist (and therefore, most assuredly, not composed by the Evangelist)—exhibits the same Hebraically-conceived construction of sentences, which was certainly natural to the Baptist, and which is everywhere reproduced by the Evangelist. As the Baptist was finally to prepare all Israel for Christ, so it was his specific vocation to prepare the ἐπιστήθιος μαθητής, to develop in him the related ("Johannæan") germs, to form him into a stamped and distinctive personality, into an instrument which would be capable of receiving into himself all the outbeaming glories of Christ. Thus no other disciple so clearly and effectually seized the kernel of the preaching of John the Baptist (John i. 26-36). His relation to the Baptist was analogous to that which he afterwards bore to Christ: he apprehended those profounder views of the preaching of John which were comparatively concealed from the others. The Synoptists dwelt largely on the Baptist's preaching of repentance; and added only a brief notice, that he pointed also to the coming Messiah. But this last point is taken up by St John as the centre of the Baptist's work; and he has preserved and recorded his prophetic discourses concerning the nature and the passion of Christ, which no other has preserved. From the Baptist he had further received the fundamental categories of his own subsequent doctrine—the antithesis of heaven and earth (John iii. 31), the love and wrath of God (ver. 36); and even the word in ver. 29 may have sounded afterwards in his soul as a prophetic note of his own relation to Christ.

But with the same decision of will and absoluteness of purpose with which he had joined himself to the Baptist, and at his command fully renounced all fellowship with the σκοτία, he now joined himself to Jesus, when to Him he was directed by the Baptist (John i. 35 seq.). This fixed decision, this absolutism in the best sense, manifested itself in his whole nature—so far as that nature was not yet entirely purified and shone through, or was still under the influence of erroneous views. When the inhabitants of a Samaritan village would not receive Jesus, his Jesus, he does not break out into reproach,—that would have been the reaction or vehemence of a hot temperament,—but he goes with his brother to *Jesus*, and *asks*—again purely receptive and self-resigning; but *what* he asks testifies to the *internal* absoluteness with which he apprehends the two perfect opposites—he asks whether he should not call fire down from heaven. In his *nature* and *temperament* he is everywhere and always *receptive*: not prominent, active, interfering, challenging; but expectant, observant, listening, and self-devoting. But in his internal distinctive *character*, he is always most fixed and decided. His is a self-devoting nature; but it is devoted only to one object, and to that altogether and absolutely devoted. And, because his nature was so self-devoting, therefore it needed such strong decision.

The same positive decisiveness, the same incapacity to tolerate vacillation and middle points, appears also in St John's views of the plan of salvation. St Paul views it as becoming, and pauses and lingers in the conflict between the old and the new man; St John beholds salvation as the simply perfected victory of light over the darkness: he who is born of God is light, and hath light, and sinneth no more. St Paul, in his writings, has more to do with sin *quà* weakness; St John, although he does not omit this aspect (1 John i. 8, ii. 1), yet has more to do with sin as wickedness. St John also well knows that the victory of light over darkness is won only by what seems to be a subjection, abandonment, and succumbing; as in the case of Christ Himself, who overcame death by dying, so also in every individual (1 John v. 4) in the collective Church (Rev. ii. 8, vii. 14, xx. 4). But he contemplates the victory, which in time is still future, as already decided from eternity (comp. 1 John iv. 4, " Ye are of God, and have overcome the spirit of Antichrist;" ch. v. 4, " Our faith is the victory which *hath* overcome the world;" and, in respect to holiness, ch. iii. 6 and 9). To St John there are only two postures of heart:—*for* and *against*. He knows no third; and the points of transition from the one to the other he brings not into consideration.

Such a nature, sanctified by grace, would never have been in a position to win the heathen world for Christ; never could St John have done the work which St Paul did,—who became a Jew to the Jews, and a Gentile to the Gentiles, and, with inexhaustible patience, entering dialectically into the relation of each Church, contended against its weaknesses and errors. But then such a character as St John's was needful, in order to preserve pure and to purify the Church already founded and established. That was his high vocation; he was an ambassador as much of the Judge as of the Saviour, called as he was by the Holy Ghost to prophesy of judgment and to publish the redemption,—to be alike an Apocalyptic and an Evangelist. As in the time of his Master's life he directed his gaze, not so much outwardly to the practical field of work, as inwardly to the contemplation of Christ, so he was called after the ascension to consecrate his energies, not so much to the conversion of the extra-Christian world, as to the perfecting and cleansing of the Christian Church. It was his to supplement the doctrine of the other Apostles, and so to consummate the διδαχὴ τῶν ἀποστόλων; and accordingly he added the topstone of the speculative mystery of the incarnation of the Logos, as well as of the mystery of the *unio mystica*—by communicating those utterances of our Saviour which contained these things, and which he alone has preserved in all their fulness and depth. He had to cleanse the Church from the worst primitive defilement, to exercise judgment upon Gnosticism: this he did by simply opposing to the Gnostic caricatures of the Saviour and His salvation the truth which he especially had received, by letting shine forth from himself that image of the true Son of Man, in His judicial Divine glory, which he had received into his inmost nature, and by placing it visibly before the eyes of the world in his *Gospel*. He had for all future ages to rebuke and condemn the abominations of the antichristian nature; and thus was called to lay down in the Apocalypse that prophecy of the future conflict of the σκοτία with the light, an everlasting test for the discrimination of all the shifting forms of corruption in the Church. In short, while his relation to Christ is altogether that of the softer and receptive nature, he shows himself to be altogether man, and like a consuming fire, against all antichristian error. The old hymn aptly describes him in the words, *Volat avis sine meta*, etc.

The consideration of St John's personality leads us now, naturally, to the consideration of his apostolical and specifically literary work.

His apostolical labour, during the first three decennia after the ascension of our Lord, was, in conformity with his personal characteristics, still and retired, and marked by no external demonstration. At the Saviour's final passion (33 Ær. Dion.), St John was the only disciple who did not forsake the Lord, but stood fearless under the cross, avowing himself the Saviour's friend and disciple. After His resurrection, St John remained with the other disciples in Jerusalem. But he does not appear to have assumed any *external* prominence among them. Were it not for the passage Gal. ii. 9, we should not have known that he, in connection with St Peter and St James, enjoyed any distinctive personal consideration in the Church. As it respects his work, he retired, during that period, into the silent background. In harmony with his apostolical vocation, he laboured like the rest; assuredly he did not keep holiday. But his work was not of the outward kind which attracted attention; and, unless we are altogether mistaken, he was much more occupied with the edification of churches already founded than with the conversion of new communities. It is hard to say how long he remained in Jerusalem. At the persecution following upon the death of Stephen, he remained in that city with the other Apostles (Acts viii. 1). When, on the other hand, St Paul came up, three years after his conversion, to Jerusalem (Gal. i. 18), in the year 40 Ær. Dion., he met there only St Peter, and St James the Lord's brother. It does not indeed follow from this, that the other disciples had forsaken Jerusalem, and settled themselves elsewhere. (The itinerant visitation-journey of St Peter, Acts ix. 32, was only a transitory one.) In the year 51 (Acts xv.), we find the collective Apostles again in Jerusalem; St Peter and St James taking the prominent place as their leaders in the Council. But, seven years later, in the year 58 (Acts xxi. 18), St James alone, with the πρεσβύτεροις, is present in Jerusalem. In the interval between 51 and 58 it seems that we must place the dispersion or removal of the remaining Apostles from Jerusalem. An ancient tradition relates concerning St John (Clem. Alex., Strom. vi. 5), that he left Jerusalem twelve years after the death of Christ (thus, as early as 45 Ær. Dion.). By no means did he then go *at once* to Ephesus, where unanimous tradition locates him during the closing term of his life. But

we are altogether without anything like precise account of his
residence and occupation during the intervening time. It is
true that a later tradition sends him to Parthia; but that owed
its origin simply to the spurious gloss (πρὸς Πάρθους) in the
superscription of his First Epistle. The supposition of Jerome,
that St John preached in India, is equally groundless. There
is much more internal probability in the hypothesis that he
betook himself, at the time of St Paul's first missionary journey
(46 Ær. Dion.), to the then second centre of Christendom,
Antioch, that he might fill up the chasm created by the departure of St Paul. As early as Acts xi. 22 (43 Ær. Dion.)
Barnabas had been delegated thither from Jerusalem; in the
year 44 (ver. 27), prophets came from Jerusalem to Antioch;
according to Gal. ii. 11, Peter was sent to Antioch (in the year
54?). This much we see, therefore, at least, that the Church
in Jerusalem held it to be a duty to exercise a special supervision over Antioch, and to take special pains to supply it with
worthy men. On the other hand, it is certain that St John
was at a later time, and a much later time, the successor of the
Apostle Paul in Ephesus. Certainly this did not take place
until about the time of St Paul's death (64 Ær. Dion.), or
after it; for, neither in the farewell address at Miletus (Acts
xx., anno 58), nor in the Epistle to the Ephesians (anno 61),
is there any trace whatever of St John's being in Ephesus.
But that he subsequently guided the Church of Asia Minor,
from Ephesus as a centre (comp. Rev. i. 12, ch. ii. iii.), is the
unanimous tradition of the Fathers—a tradition which has
been doubted by some, only because it stands in the way of the
theory, which has been set up, of the opposition between St Paul
and the Twelve. Polycrates, a bishop of Ephesus in the second
century (of an illustrious Christian family, to which seven
earlier bishops of Ephesus had belonged, Euseb. v. 24), says,
in a letter to Victor of Rome (ibid.), concerning St John: οὗτος
ἐν Ἐφέσῳ κεκοίμηται. Irenæus (Hær. 3, 3, 4, in Euseb. 4, 14,
comp. Euseb. 3, 23) says: ἀλλὰ καὶ ἡ ἐν Ἐφέσῳ ἐκκλησία, ὑπὸ
Παύλου μὲν τεθεμελιωμένη, Ἰωάννου δὲ παραμείναντος αὐτοῖς
μέχρι τοῦ Τραιανοῦ χρόνων, μάρτυς ἀληθής ἐστι τῆς ἀποστόλων
παραδόσεως. (Trajan reigned, as is well known, 98-117.)
So also Irenæus (ii. 22, 5), that St John lived with a circle of
disciples μέχρι τῶν Τραιανοῦ χρόνων in Ἀσία (Proconsular

Asia, of which Ephesus was the capital). And Irenæus is here all the more to be depended upon, because one of those disciples of St John, the martyr Polycarp, was his own teacher and spiritual father (Iren. 3, 3, Euseb. v. 20, 24 ; where παῖς ἔτι ὤν means " as *puer*, boy or youth"). Ignatius of Antioch also, and Papias, were among those personal disciples of the veteran St John (Euseb. 3, 22 ; Iren. in Euseb. 3, 39). Jerome (Vir. Illus. 9) places the death of St John 68 years after the death of Christ; therefore in the year 101 Ær Dion. Eusebius, agreeing in the main, places it in 100. (Polycarp, a Christian " for eighty years" at his death in 170, Euseb. 4, 15, had therefore enjoyed the instruction of the Apostle for ten years, 90–100.)

There is, further, a unanimous tradition that St John was banished to the Isle of Patmos by a Roman τύραννος. Clemens Alexandrinus (*Quis div. salv.*, cap. 42) relates the beautiful story of the deliverance of the young man who had fallen among thieves by St John, as a μῦθος οὐ μῦθος (an orally-re-received but yet true narrative), and marks the date thus: ἐπειδὴ τοῦ τυράννου τελευτήσαντος ἀπὸ τῆς Πάτμου τῆς νήσου μετῆλθεν εἰς τὴν Ἔφεσον. He speaks here of the exile in Patmos as of a circumstance well known to his readers, and to all the world. (He cannot, therefore, as Credner supposes, have *conjectured* from Rev. i. 9 that St John must have been banished to Patmos; more especially as in Rev. i. there is not a word spoken about *banishment*.) So also Origen (in Matt. iii., p. 720) : ὁ δὲ Ῥωμαίων βασιλεὺς ὡς ἡ παράδοσις διδάσκει (he again appeals to the predominant tradition, not to a conjecture) κατεδίκασε τὸν Ἰωάννην μαρτυροῦντα διὰ τὸν τῆς ἀληθείας λόγον, εἰς Πάτμον τὴν νῆσον. As subordinate, he then cites the passage, Rev. i. 9. Tertullian (Præs. Hær., cap. 36) thinks the Roman Church happy, where St Paul was beheaded, and from which St John was banished to Patmos, after he had been plunged into boiling oil, but was miraculously (comp. Acts xiv. 20, xxviii. 5; Mark xvi. 18) preserved. Irenæus (in Euseb. 3, 18) records with precision that St John had been banished to Patmos *under Domitian*. Even the contemporaneous heathen writers did not omit (according to Euseb. l. c.) to relate τόν τε διωγμὸν καὶ τὰ ἐν αὐτῷ μαρτύρια—those, that is, οἵ γε καὶ τὸν καιρὸν ἐπ' ἀκριβὲς ἐπεσημήναντο, to wit, the fifteenth year of

Domitian (95, 96 Ær. Dion.). In the succeeding year, when Nerva assumed the government, the return to Ephesus had been permitted to him. Jerome (Vir. Illust. 9) mentions the fourteenth of Domitian as the year of the banishment of St John; so that the banishment must be placed in the year 95. The Syriac translation of the Apocalypse (discovered by Pococke, and of the same character as the Philoxenian, consequently originating in the sixth century) mentions by mistake Nero instead of Domitian.[1] The passage Acts i. 9 serves only to confirm that report.

These notices concerning the sphere of the external activity of the Apostle John, sparing as they indeed are, throw, nevertheless, a welcome light upon his work, and specially upon his literary work. This work is divided into two parts: on the one side, we have the Gospel, with the closely-connected First Epistle; on the other, the Revelation. First, let us take a general view of the Gospel and the First Epistle.

His Gospel is at the first glance plainly distinguished from the three others—as in its chronological order, so also in the selection of its materials. As it regards the latter, St John has, it is well known, very much that is peculiar, and coincides with the Synoptists only in a few sections (ch. i. 21–27, vi. 5–21, xii. 1–15, and the main points of the history of the Passion). The omission of the narrative of the childhood distinguishes him from St Matthew and St Luke; the records of the journeys to the feasts in Jerusalem are peculiar to him, and not found in the Synoptists. That he has supplemented the matter of the Synoptists, is no more than simple fact; and the question whether it was his *design* to do so (comp. Luthardt), is a perfectly needless one, since it is no other than the question whether he wrote as he wrote, and what he wrote, *consciously* or not— a question which none will for a moment hesitate how to answer.[2] But there is another, much deeper, and more internal

---

[1] Recent critics have conjectured,—though, in the face of Irenæus' account, without any grounds,—that St John was banished to Patmos in the time of Nero. This conjecture is pressed into the support of a false interpretation of the five kings, Rev. xvii. 10, which understands by them the first five Roman emperors.

[2] It may indeed be questioned whether this design—that of supplementing—was the last object of his work, or whether it was only a secondary aim, subordinate to a much higher one.

sense in which he supplements or completes the Synoptists. It has been already observed that St John, according to his individual endowment and personal peculiarity, was the only one who was overruled to seize *and* retain certain individual aspects of the nature and the doctrine of Jesus. First, to wit, those utterances of our Lord concerning His eternal relation to the Father, and His eternal, pre-temporal and supra-temporal, oneness of essence with the Father (John iii. 13, 17, v. 17, vi. 33, 51, vii. 16, 28, viii. 58)—an aspect of the teaching of Christ which, in opposition to that which the Lord lays down concerning His historical work upon earth, and his historical relation to men, may assuredly with perfect propriety be described as "the speculative aspect," and to the apprehension of which a "philosophical" tone and culture of mind (using this expression, of course, in the widest sense) must be supposed.[1] But, secondly, also those sayings of our Lord concerning the *mystical* relation of unity and fellowship of life into which He would enter with His people through the Holy Spirit. (John iii. 8, ch. vi., ch. xiv. 16 seq., xv. 1 seq., xvii. 21–23.) The question now arises, whether the individuality and personal characteristics of the Apostle was the only factor in the case; whether it was this alone which prompted him to supplement and perfect the picture which the Synoptists had given of the person and teaching of Christ (mark, not that he invented or feigned anything new and unhistorical, but that he gave a representation of an aspect of the historical and real Christ which he alone had apprehended in all its depth and fulness),—*or* whether there was also co-operating, as the second factor, an actual *necessity of the Church*, which was beginning to be pressingly felt at the period when St John wrote.

He who should hesitate to admit this, must be prepared to deny that the providential wisdom of God had assigned to St John any peculiar and independent vocation in the joint apostolical work of founding the Church. St Peter and St Matthew had it for their vocation to found the Christian Church among the people of Israel, and to bear their testimony to Jesus as the Fulfiller of the prophecies; the same St Peter and St Mark had it for their vocation first to bear the tidings concerning

---

[1] Against Luthardt, S. 227.

Christ, the Son of God, over the borders of Israel towards the Gentiles; St Paul and St Luke had it for their vocation to establish the relations between Jewish Christianity and Gentile Christianity, and to oppose at all points that great error of legal-Jewish perversion which envied the heathen their privileges, and insisted upon reserving the prerogatives of the law:—as if Israel did not exist for Christ's sake, and Christ for the sake of all mankind; as if, consequently, men must first belong to Israel by the rite of circumcision and the observance of the law, and then, as subordinate to this, belong to Christ. Now, can we suppose that St John alone was without any analogous *specific* apostolical vocation?

"There was neither occasion nor room for the origination of any new doctrine *concerning* Christ; but only for the attestation and confirming in manifold and various ways of the one great and well-known fact of Christ Himself. But the *Church* of Christ had their history; and, in the degree in which the apostolical Church had a history, new views of Christian doctrine grew up to the Apostles in connection therewith." (Luthardt.) Or, more correctly, they perceived more and more clearly what *aspects* of the one history and the one truth of salvation must be made emphatic, in opposition to the heresies as they arose; and thus the Apostle John became conscious, in the last years of the first century, that now the hour was come when he must bring out the reserved treasure, which had been peculiarly his own and shut up in himself, for the salvation of the Church of his own time, and for the rule of the Church of all times.

For, the Christian Church had, since the death of the Apostle Paul, and especially since the destruction of Jerusalem, entered upon a new stage of her history. That time when the Twelve lived in the midst of the Jews, and according to Israelite customs, having as believers in the Messiah a place and membership in the corporate body of the people of the Covenant, and making it their first great business to bear witness to the identity of Jesus and the promised Messiah (a period, the literary monument of which is the Gospel according to St Matthew)—was now long and for ever past. Israel as a people had rejected that testimony; the Church of the Redeemer had withdrawn from Israel and from Jerusalem; the judgment had been poured out on Israel; from a nation it had sunk down to an exiled *diaspora*; Christianity had thenceforward no more to do with the *people of Israel*, but with the heathen *Roman state*, and with individual Jews only so far as these in their malice denounced the Christians to the Romans. But, at the same time, that period of Pauline labour was past, during which there was a necessity for warning against the errors and the labours of the παρείσακτοι ψευδαδέλφοι (Gal. ii. 4), who taught that Christ and His salvation was the monopoly of the Jews, that circumcision and the fulfilment of the law was the condition of fellowship in the Messianic hope,—thus bringing men back to a dependence on their works. In opposition to them, St Luke, the investigator (Luke i. 3), had collected together in his Gospel, under the Divine Spirit's guidance, all those events and those discourses in the life of Christ which showed that not only Israel, and not all Israel, had inheritance in the salvation of the Gospel. The destruction of Jerusalem had impressed the seal upon his testimony (comp. Luke xxi. 24).

But, all this notwithstanding, there were still found among the Christian communities, a circle of Jewish-Christian Churches which had so little understood the judicial acts of the Lord upon Jerusalem that they still clung with blind wilfulness to the preservation of the dissolved Jewish nationality, to the use of the Semitic (Aramaic) tongue, and the continuance of Jewish usages. These Churches were conducted by their ungodly traditionalism to a separation from the rest of the Church, being known first as *Nazarenes*; in the last stage of their perversion and apostasy they appear in history as *Ebionites*. They saw in Christ only a second Lawgiver—as might have been expected from their legal position and relations; using only the Aramaic Gospel of St Matthew, in which the declarations of Christ concerning His Divinity are not yet so prominent as in the other Gospels, Christ became contracted in their creed to the limits of a mere man. It cannot be demonstrated that this error had already in St John's time reached its final point of development; nor can it be established that St John, living in Ephesus, was brought into direct conflict with these heretics, or that a "refutation of Ebionitism" is to be sought for in his Gospel.[1] But it is certainly a *possible supposition*, that the gradual separation of the

[1] Jerome, Epiphanius, and, in later times, Grotius, thought that they perceived such a polemical aim in the Gospel of St John.

Nazarene communities from the living body of the Church (a circumstance which *could* not have been unknown to the Apostle) disclosed to his seer-glance—his own special endowment—the prospect of the spiritual dangers into which this self-limiting and cramped system *must* necessarily lead; and, therefore, that these manifestations were regarded by him as an intimation that the time was come for him to come forward with his testimony concerning the eternal Divine Sonship of Christ (attested by all His words and acts), and by means of this testimony to erect, once for all and *for all time*, an impregnable bulwark against all Ebionite and Ebionitish heresies and departures from the truth.[1] This was the appearance of *one root* of all heresy, just showing itself above the ground; and it might possibly have had some influence upon St John in the publication of his Gospel.

But simultaneously with that, there was the sprouting of a second root of heresy: *Gnosticism*. A system of speculation which was heathen in principle laid violent hold of Christian *dogmas*, without receiving them in Christian *faith;* aspiring, not to reconciliation with God and holiness, but only to γνῶσις, that is, the solution of the fundamental problems which offered themselves to knowledge, and using for this purpose those Christian dogmas, rich in the elements of presentiment and speculation, which it grossly wrested and perverted. And it was all the more dangerous, because it presented the appearance of a deeper than ordinary apprehension of Christianity; and seemed to give its proper satisfaction to a want which came with Christianity, and which indeed Christianity excited— the desire of γνῶσις in the true and proper sense. The first noted teacher of this kind

---

[1] The view that St John might have viewed the existence of congregations of *John's disciples* as an exhibition of Ebionite error (Hug), is not to be so absolutely rejected as Luthardt rejects it. Lucke rightly says, "The somewhat strongly emphasized passages, ch. i. 8 and 20, seem to favour that view," as intimating an antithesis of definite errors. If it had been written, "Christ was not the Father, but the Son of the Father"—who could have denied that it was a plain denial of Patripassian error?— Further, it must be remembered that Ephesus was, according to Acts xviii. 24, xix. 1, a seat of the community of John the Baptist's disciples; and, if we have no proof that this community existed on into the end of the century, and degenerated into a denial of the Divinity of Christ, we certainly have no proof of the contrary.

of error was Cerinthus. He taught (Iren. Hær. 1, 26 seq., comp. Euseb. 3, 28) that the world was produced into existence, not by the supreme God, but a power having its origin from God; that Jesus was a Son of Joseph and Mary; that the Æon Christ was united with Him at His baptism, and guided Him in teaching men to know the Most High God, hitherto not known; that the Æon Christ left Him again before His passion; and that it was the mere man Jesus who suffered. A related, and still older, heretical tendency was (according to Iren. 3, 11) that of the "Nicolaitanes" (Rev. ii. 15),—concerning which, however, Irenæus does not seem to have known anything beyond what is said in Rev. ii. Now the men were still alive in the time of Irenæus (as is evident from the words, εἰσὶν οἱ ἀκηκοό- τες, ch. iii. 3) who received from the lips of Polycarp, St John's disciple, the circumstance of St John's having met Cerinthus in the bath. Thus it is historically firm—unless we are content hypercritically to throw overboard all, even the most trustworthy, tradition—that this Apostle had to contend against the Cerin- thian gnosis; and that *this* form of Gnosticism contained as well Ebionite as Docetic elements, that is, an Ebionite man Jesus by the side of a Docetic Æon Christ. Nor will any reasonable person be able to deny that there could not be a more striking, demonstrative, and victorious refutation of this Gnostic heresy than that which we actually find in the utterances of our Lord Himself, which St John has handed down, concerning His pre- existence and eternal Godhead, and in the testimony of the Apostle that the Father created all things by the Word. (Com- pare only with that doctrine of Cerinthus the passages John i. 3 and 14, and 33, 34, and 49; ch. iii. 13, 14, v. 23, 26, vi. 51, 62, viii. 58, xiii. 23 seq., xvii. 1, 2, 16, 19, xviii. 6, 11, 37.) As it would be very hard indeed to persuade oneself that St John, who past all doubt had to contend against the errors of Cerin- thus, and who past all doubt declared the identity of Jesus with the Son of God, and the incarnation of Christ (1 John iv. 2, 3, v. 5) to be the corner-stone of the Christian doctrine, and the distinguishing test between Christianity and Antichristianity— as it would be very hard indeed to believe that this St John wrote down all those utterances of Christ without any conscious- ness of the force which lay in them as against the Cerinthian heresy—nothing remains but that we admit the conviction of

St John's having written all those sayings with this express design. For he must then have written them with will and purpose: he who knows what effect his act will have, and therefore acts, must design and purpose that effect. Thus it was assuredly and preeminently the appearance on the stage of the Cerinthian gnosis which taught the Apostle to discern that the hour was come for him to bring forth that peculiar treasure of remembrances of the life of Jesus which was his own, and publicly to confront with it the germ of lie which it would refute as a testimony. Or, in other words, he knew that the time was come when his entire specific endowment must become fruitful in his own peculiar vocation and work:—fruitful, not only for salvation in the time being, but for the placing of the topstone on the whole apostolical function, in the consummating of the *norma credendorum* for all succeeding ages of the Christian Church.

When, therefore, St John came forward with the testimony of his Gospel to oppose the Ebionizing and Gnostic fundamental principle of all heresy, and at the same time externally and internally supplemented the Synoptists, he was not influenced by a multiplicity of separate and independent aims. It was *one motive* which impelled him to write his Gospel (that is, the knowledge that he had in himself what would be sufficient for the refutation of the fundamental principle of all heresy, concurred with the knowledge that it was now *necessary* to bring out the fulness of his treasures); and there was but *one means* by which the various needs, which at that time were arising, could be all at once and entirely satisfied. The striving after gnosis—in itself justifiable, though now excited by a wrong element—must not be ignored, or altogether suppressed; it must be gratified, but in the right way. It must be shown that the true γνῶσις had its root, not in the vain curiosity of knowledge, and in philosophical gropings sundered from faith, but inversely in *faith itself;* and that to childlike faith the true depths of blessed knowledge and blessed insight into the deepest mysteries were opened up (and *therefore* St John so often lays stress upon faith, and would lead his readers " to believe that Jesus is the Christ, the Son of God," John xx. 31). The materials which he wrought up to this end were not of a kind which it was necessary that he should first arbitrarily select and arrange; he himself in his original endowment already prepared for this, so that, during the lifetime of Jesus, that had become fixed in his nature which would serve for the refutation of all these heresies. Because St John in his own person was the complement of the other disciples, therefore his writings also were in themselves the supplement of the writings of the Synoptists. And preeminently the internal supplement. To the doctrines of lying speculation which sundered Jesus and the Christ, he had to oppose the utterances and discourses of Jesus Christ concerning His eternal unity with the Father, His preexistence with the Father, the glorification of the Father in His sufferings, and the giving up of the Bread of Life unto death. To a dead *striving* after gnosis without sanctification, he had to oppose the sayings of the Lord concerning the mystical *life* of the Head in His members (John vi. 15, etc.). It was obvious that the Synoptists would be thus *externally* supplemented also, since the majority of these sayings were uttered in the feast-journeys to Jerusalem. And thus, finally, it was obvious that he must so construct his Gospel as to subserve the subordinate end also of giving a *chronological* supplement to the whole.

The most decisive proof of this systematic (in a good sense) and orderly-planned character of the Gospel (exhibiting in the unity of the great end a variety of subordinate designs), lies, as we have said, in the words of John xx. 31, where the Evangelist himself plainly announces his design: that is, not (as Luthardt says) "that ye may believe," but "that ye may believe that Jesus is the Christ, the Son of God;" which contains the clearest and sharpest antithesis to the doctrine of Cerinthus that can be conceived.

But we have another evidence in the First Epistle of St John. The pervasive relation which this Epistle bears to the Gospel, in language, and style, and tone, and ideas, and phraseology, has been generally and by all acknowledged; but we have to add the remarkable fact that the writer of the Epistle gives us, ch. ii. 12–14, a sixfold repetition of the design for which *he writes and had written*—before he had written anything substantial at all! For, in ch. i. 1 seq., we have only an *announcement* that he would declare what he had heard, seen with his eyes, touched with his hands, that which concerned

" the Word of life," and that he would write this (the Epistle) that the joy of the readers might be full. But, for an actual declaration of that which he had seen and handled, we look in vain throughout *the Epistle*. Presently, in ver. 4, he announces this as the substance of his ἐπαγγελία, that " God is light," and appends to that practical inferences. Then at once begins in the second chapter that repeated resolution of the several ends for which he writes and had written. We are involuntarily driven to the conclusion that this "writing and having written," of which he speaks in the Epistle as of something objectively present before his eyes, cannot be the Epistle itself, but another independent document connected with it; that is, in other words, that the Epistle was no other than a companion-document of the Gospel. For, in this Gospel he had, in fact, announced that which he had seen, and beheld, and handled with his hands; had announced all that which was to be announced concerning *that* Word which was no word of dead theory and speculation, but the revelation-Word of God, who was life and light to sinful humanity—and therefore a Word of life—a Word giving life, and itself a living, personal Word. That this view, maintained by Hug, Lange, and myself, admits not of absolute demonstration, may indeed be conceded; but certainly there is no absolute demonstration that it is wrong. The whole Epistle assumes a living and perfectly intelligible character, only when we regard it as a companion to the Gospel. But, whether it was a companion-document of the Gospel (which, according to Theophylact, was written in Patmos, and according to some Scholia thirty-two years after the death of Christ, that is, 95 Ær. Dion.), or stood in no direct connection with it, this much is absolutely certain from 1 John iv. 2 seq., that the Apostle had to withstand those who denied that Jesus was the Christ. And he wrote his Gospel in order to lead to the faith that Jesus is the Christ. John xx. 31.

If the Gospel of St John, together with the First Epistle, forms the first part of the literary remains of the Apostle, the other part is the Apocalypse. It bears the same relation to St John's Gospel which the Acts of the Apostles bears to St Luke's.[1]

---

[1] The Apocalypse will be treated in an independent article.

Thus the life, work, and writings of St John form one compact, organic, independent, and harmonious unity. And this congruity forms an evidence for the genuineness of the three great writings of St John, more powerful and convincing than any analytical criticism could furnish. Not that external evidences are wanting to establish the age and genuineness of these writings: no book in all antiquity is so abundantly vouched as these documents are.

The testimonies in favour of the genuineness of the Gospel and the First Epistle are very decided. As the author describes himself as an eyewitness of the life of Jesus (ch. i. 14, comp. 1 John i. 1), there could remain only the choice between genuineness and laborious conscious deception. If it is added, that the author everywhere seems designedly to avoid mentioning the sons of Zebedee (ch. i. 35 and 42, xiii. 23, xviii. 15, xix. 26, xx. 2);—that he invariably calls himself "the disciple whom the Lord loved" (that he thereby means one of the three favoured disciples, is plain from John xiii. 23, xix. 26; that he means, not Peter, but one of the sons of Zebedee, from John xx. 2; that the son of Zebedee who wrote the Gospel could not have been James, from Acts xii. 2);—that, while he always carefully distinguishes the two Judases (ch. xii. 4, xiii. 26, xiv. 22), and always gives Thomas his surname (ch. ii. 26, xx. 24, xxi. 2), yet, on the other hand, he always called the Baptist only ʼΙωάννης:—all these are things to be explained only by the fact that the Apostle John was himself the writer.

With this direct declaration of the Gospel itself is connected a strong, unbroken chain of external testimonies. In an age when it was not customary to quote the New-Testament writings with a statement of their authors and subjects, we find a large mass of reminiscences from St John, and allusions to him. When Ignatius (Philad. 7) abruptly says concerning the "Spirit of God:" οἶδεν γὰρ πόθεν ἔρχεται καὶ ποῦ ὑπάγει, his words can be understood only as referred to St John's figure of the Holy Ghost as wind. In the same abrupt manner, with the same evident allusion to the figures and sayings of the Evangelist John, whom he supposes to be well known and familiar to his readers, he elsewhere (Philad. 9; Rom. 7) calls Christ "the Door of the Father," the "Bread from heaven." Polycarp (Phil. 7) quotes expressly and literally the passage

1 John iv. 2 seq. Justin Martyr's writings are pervaded with Johannæan thoughts, ideas, and views: he describes Christ as the "Living Water," the "Word of God," the "Only-begotten;" he speaks of His σαρκοποιηθῆναι, of the Regeneration, and occasionally makes allusion to certain specific passages in the Gospel (Otto).

Marcion's polemic against the Gospel of St John (Tert. adv. Marc. 6, 3) proves that it was at that time received as genuine and canonical by the Catholics. Valentinus did not dare to call in question its genuineness, but sought by a subtle allegorical interpretation to extract his Gnostic system from its contents (Tertull. de Præscr. hær. 38; Iren. 3, 11, 7); and his disciple Heracleon, with this design, even wrote a commentary on St John's Gospel, of which Origen has preserved for us many fragments (see Iren. Opp., Paris 1710, Tom. i. pp. 362–376). Theodotus cites the passages John i. 9, vi. 51, viii. 56, and others. Ptolemæus (ad Floram) quotes John i. 3. That the Montanists acknowledged the Gospel of St John as an apostolical document is proved by this, that Tatian not only literally cites the passages John i. 3 and 5, but also constructed out of the *four* ecclesiastically-received Gospels an evangelical Harmony or Diatessaron (Euseb. iv. 29; Epiphan. Hær. 46), which (according to the testimony of Barsalibi, who had it before him in the Syriac translation) commenced with the passage John i. 1 seq. So also Theophilus of Antioch (about 169) wrote a commentary on the four canonical Gospels, which Jerome (cap. 53, Vir. Ill. 25) had himself read.

The heathen Celsus also was acquainted with four Gospels, and mentions the showing of the marks of the nails in our Lord, which is related only by St John.

Theophilus (ad Autol. 2, 22) cites the Gospel of St John with mention of his name. To him may be added Irenæus (3, 1), who not only attests the genuineness of the Gospel by the tradition of Polycarp, but also quotes it with close precision.

Three other independent evidences may be appealed to. First, the testimony of Hippolytus in the Book περὶ πασῶν αἱρέσεων,[1] which was discovered on Mount Athos, critically investigated by Bunsen, and acknowledged to be genuine by all.

---

[1] Especially B. v. and vi., with which B. x. cap. 32 may be compared.

Secondly, the famous Fragment of Apollinarius, in which he says, against the Quartodecimans : καὶ λέγουσιν, ὅτι τῇ ιδ´ τὸ πρόβατον μετὰ τῶν μαθητῶν ἔφαγεν ὁ κύριος, τῇ δὲ μεγάλῃ ἡμέρᾳ τῶν ἀζύμων αὐτὸς ἔπαθεν, καὶ διηγοῦνται Ματθαῖον οὕτω λέγειν ὡς νενοήκασιν· ὅθεν ἀσύμφωνός τε νόμῳ ἡ νόησις αὐτῶν, καὶ στασιάζειν δοκεῖ κατ᾽ αὐτοὺς τὰ εὐαγγέλια. The Gospels which seem to conflict with and differ from each other, can be only the Synoptists on the one side, and St John on the other. And this is therefore proof that in the second half of the second century the Gospel of St John was diffused throughout the whole Church, and everywhere received as genuine and canonical. Thirdly, and finally, Papias (Euseb. 3, 39) was acquainted with, and quoted, in his time, the First Epistle of St John, which was undeniably from the same hand as the Gospel (κέχρηται δ᾽ ὁ αὐτὸς μαρτυρίας ἀπὸ τῆς προτέρας Ἰωάννου ἐπιστολῆς).

These collective facts, which require to be appreciated, not only in their separate and individual character, but in their combination, cannot possibly be understood on the hypothesis that the Gospel of St John was composed after St John's death, and in the second century, by a forger. Only five or six decennia had passed after the death of the Apostle when we find this Gospel in the possession of all Christendom as a known, precious, and much-loved common property; and none insisted with more energy upon the sanctity and apostolical authority of the Johannæan writings than the circle which was formed around the Apostle, and trained under his influence,—the principal members of it being Polycarp and Irenæus.

The destructive criticism of Rationalism approached these writings very slowly and very timidly; and we are met by the singular fact, that in its earlier period doubt was directed rather to the Apocalypse than to the Gospel,[1] while the Tübingen school aimed their attack, out of the Apocalypse acknowledged genuine, against the Gospel. Both proceeded, however, from the common supposition, that the Apocalypse was so fundamentally distinguished from the Gospel in language and spirit that they could not possibly have sprung from the same author.

[1] De Wette, Credner, Lucke, and Ewald maintained that the Apocalypse could not have been written by the author of the Gospel; Bleek and Credner attributed it to the Presbyter John.

Nevertheless, that the *spirit* of the author is the same in both books,—that, among the New-Testament writers, the Apostle John alone had the internal capacity and adaptation to receive such a revelation,—that this revelation is essentially and internally related in spirit to the Gospel and Epistle,—has been already shown above. And the saying of Polycrates about the πέταλον does not lead us to the *Presbyter* John (as Lücke says), but testifies the identity of the Apostle and the seer of the Apocalypse. But, as it respects the difference in language (remarked by Dion. Alex.), I have endeavoured to maintain,[1]—against Hitzig, who attributed the Apocalypse to the Evangelist John Mark,[2]—that the greater part of those more striking Hebraisms which are common to the Apocalypse and St Mark's Gospel, are found also in the Gospel of St John; further, that the little remainder which are *not* reproduced in that Gospel are to be explained by the fact that the author wrote in the Apocalypse more after the manner of the Old-Testament prophetic language, and therefore more Hebraically, than he was wont to do in ordinary life; while, on the other hand, in the Gospel, and in the First Epistle, he took the greatest pains to write as good Greek (for Ephesian readers) as he possibly could: so that one may say that in the Apocalypse he wrote more Hebraically, and in the Gospel less Hebraically, than was the wont of his ordinary language. Moreover, the Gospel of St John coincides with the Apocalypse in many peculiarities of expression and thought which are quite foreign to the Gospel of St Mark. That the Apocalypse describes known persons (Christ, and likewise Satan) in figures, finds its natural and sufficient solution in the fact that it is recording visions: no argument one way or other can be derived from that. That the (falsely so called) "doctrinal idea" of the Apocalypse does not anywhere come into collision with the Gospel, I have striven, and I hope successfully, to show in the work quoted above.

This preliminary question being settled, the important historical testimonies for the genuineness of the two writings mutually support each other.

But, independently of this, the testimonies in favour of the

---

[1] Hitzig, *ueber Joh. Marcus und seine Schriften*, 1843.
[2] Ebrard, *das Ev. Joh.*, 1845. *Krit. der ev. Geschichte.*

Gospel are abundantly sufficient to establish its antiquity and genuineness, which has invariably come victorious out of all critical contests. The attacks of Evanson, Eckermann, Schmidt, Simpson, and others, have all been fairly met. Later assaults have all issued in yielding abundant demonstration that, in order to contend successfully against the Gospel of St John, the whole history of the Church and its literature in the first two centuries must be thrown away as rubbish. We shall not now enter upon the romantic hypothesis which has been spun, to the effect that the Gospel of St John was fabricated by a clever forger in the second century, in order to reconcile the previously separated Jewish and Gentile Christians.

That the two smaller Epistles, the Second and Third, were admitted only by some Churches into the number of the writings publicly read in the congregation (*canones*), is to be accounted for by their individual and occasional character. Thus they were regarded, when the traditional catalogues of individual Churches began to be compared, as *antilegomena*. But this circumstance is absolutely no impeachment of their genuineness. But, as the author terms himself ὁ πρεσβύτερος, and as there was notoriously another John, distinguished from the Apostle, and well known by the distinctive name of "the Presbyter" (Papias in Euseb. 3, 39; Dionysius in Eus. 7, 25), it is natural to suppose that these two Epistles belong to him; and this was the opinion of many in remote antiquity. (Euseb. 3, 25: καὶ ἡ ὀνομαζομένη δευτέρα καὶ τρίτη Ἰωαννοῦ, εἴτε τοῦ εὐαγγελιστοῦ τυγχάνουσαι, εἴτε καὶ ἑτέρου ὁμωνύμου ἐκείνῳ.) The similiarity in style between these two Epistles and the First Epistle of St John is not decisive against this view. That similarity, carefully examined, reduces itself to three citations from 1 John (2 John 5, 6, compared with 1 John v. 3; 2 John 7, compared with 1 John iv. 1 seq.; 3 John 11, compared with 1 John iii. 6), which are precisely of the same character as the citations from the Pauline Epistles (2 John 3 and 8, and 3 John 6 and 7, and 8 and 15); and thus these quotations or allusions are only new evidences of the genuineness and the age of the First Epistle. That the *Apostle* St John should have encountered such a contradiction (not of his doctrine, but of his authority) as this which is described in 3 John 9, is certainly not probable; while that the Presbyter should have encountered it, is not so very strange. On the whole, it is the most probable hypothesis, that the Second and Third Epistles sprang from the Presbyter John.

While, then, these two Epistles contain very ancient testimony to the genuineness of the First Epistle and Gospel (compare 3 John 12 with John xix. 35), the *Appendix of the Gospel* (John xxi.) furnishes the same kind of demonstration. This chapter was composed, according to ver. 24, and the whole style and treatment, by the Apostle himself, who did not, however, at once and in the beginning attach it to his Gospel. Not till he had been honoured by beholding the *Apocalypse*, and this had made it plain what the Lord meant by His mysterious words, " he should tarry till He come" (that is, till He should come in vision and appear to him, so that John, still living upon earth, should behold with prophetic eye Christ's coming to judgment, Rev. xxii. 20), was this independent record appended. Doubtless, it was the Presbyter John who added it (compare John xxi. 24 with 3 John 12); scarcely the Apostle himself (in which case the addition καὶ οἴδαμεν ὅτι ἀληθής ἐστιν ἡ μαρτυρία αὐτοῦ would not have been supplementarily inserted). He who added it attested the authorship of St John; and, as ch. xxi. is wanting in no manuscript, the appendix must have been added a very short time after the composition of the Gospel. It must certainly have been added before the Gospel itself was circulated beyond the neighbourhood of Ephesus.

CONTENTS.

THE FIRST EPISTLE OF ST JOHN.

INTRODUCTION.

	PAGE
§ 1. The Epistolary Form,	1
§ 2. Identity of Author and Evangelist,	6
§ 3. Genuineness of Epistle,	11
§ 4. Its Relation to the Gospel,	14
§ 5. Time and Place of Composition, and Circle of Readers,	34
§ 6. Diction and Spirit of Epistle,	40
§ 7. Literature,	41

EXPOSITION.

Exordium,	43
PART I. Centre of the ἀγγελία: God is Light,	77
PART II. Relation of Readers to the Light, as already shining,	133
PART III. The Children of God in relation to the Enmity of the World,	203
PART IV. The Spirit from God a Spirit of Truth and Love,	272
PART V. The Faith which overcometh the World,	313
TRANSLATION,	350

THE SECOND AND THIRD EPISTLES OF ST JOHN.

INTRODUCTION,	359
EXPOSITION OF SECOND EPISTLE,	379

THE THIRD EPISTLE OF ST JOHN.

	PAGE
EXPOSITION, ...	397
TRANSLATION OF THE TWO EPISTLES, ...	407
APPENDIX ON THE CATHOLIC EPISTLES, ...	409

INDEX.

I. Greek Words and Phrases Explained, ...	417
II. Passages of Scripture incidentally Explained or Illustrated, .	418
III. Principal Matters, ...	419

THE FIRST EPISTLE OF ST JOHN.

INTRODUCTION.

I. THE EPISTOLARY FORM.

THE New-Testament document which occupies a place in our Canon by the name of "The First Epistle of St John," not only does not bear on its front the name of its author, but also omits any introductory greeting at the beginning, as well as any benediction at the close. Hence, while hypercritics have doubted whether St John wrote the Epistle, intelligent critics, admitting the evidences of his peculiar style, have doubted whether it should be called an epistle at all. J. D. Heidegger (Enchir. Bibl. Tig. 1681, p. 986) led the way: "This book, though it seems to bear the stamp of an epistle, may rather be regarded as a short epitome of Christian doctrine, and, as it were, a succinct *enchiridion* of the Gospel written by St John, to which have been added certain exhortations appropriate to the general state of the Christian Church. For it does not, like the other Epistles, begin with an inscription and salutation; nor does it end with salutation and good wishes, or benediction." In essentially the same style wrote Bengel (Gnomon), who was followed by Lilienthal, J. D. Michaelis, Eichhorn, Storr, Berger, Bretschneider, and Reuss. These all hold this book—thus doubtful as to its scope—to be a kind of *treatise* or *essay*. For, the circumstance that the readers are personally addressed, does not of itself constitute an epistle: were it otherwise (observes Michaelis), Wolf's "Mathematical Principles" must be held to be an epistle.

The majority of expositors and critics have now, however, declared against this view of Heidegger and Bengel. Ziegler, in particular, has emphatically shown, in opposition to Michaelis, that there is more in the language of the writer than a mere apostrophizing of the friendly reader; that, in fact, he rather speaks as one who assumes a definite personal relation to those whom he addresses. This is the opinion of the great mass of more modern commentators, such as De Wette, Düsterdieck, Huther, and Sander.

And certainly it must be admitted that they went very much too far who argued, from the absence of the epistolary *form*, that this document was not addressed to any definite circle of readers, but that it was a general essay, or treatise, or book intended for universal literary publication within the Church. Against this it may be urged, positively, that the author places himself in an express personal relation to his readers (ch. i. 1 seq., ii. 27, v. 13); that he has in view a definite class of readers, whose faith he knows (ch. ii. 20 seq., iv. 4)—one congregation or more, whose history is in his immediate thought (ch. ii. 19; comp. the comment on this passage), and which he finds it necessary to warn against specific dangers (ch. ii. 18 and 26, iv. 1 seq., v. 16 and 21); and negatively, that the arrangement of the matter, however clear in itself, is not such as is *conformable to the style of a treatise;* for, "with all its regularity, there reigns throughout a certain easy naturalness, and that unforced simplicity of composition which harmonizes best with the immediately practical interest and paracletic tendency of an epistle" (Düsterdieck).

Thus the First Epistle of St John is undoubtedly a *production addressed to specific readers.* Yet the circumstance from which Michaelis and the rest deduced their false conclusion, has in it a very important element of truth, which demands further attentive consideration. Assuredly, there may be such a thing as a proper letter without greeting or benediction: St James ends his with a sentence which, instead of a benediction, contains in it a *promise* of blessing (Jas. v. 19, 20); St Jude closes his with a doxology, which (ver. 28) does indeed contain an *invocation* of blessing, but nothing more. Our Epistle closes, not with this, but with a pregnant exhortation; and why may not a real epistle wind up with such a climax, or terminate with such a *point*, as condenses all that had been said in one pithy word? It is much more strange, however, that the epistolary *form* is entirely wanting at the commencement. The author does not mention himself, nor does he specify his readers, nor does he address them with the greeting of peace. For the circumstance that St John wrote the Epistle, ch. i. 4, "that their joy might be full," is most assuredly not to be regarded as standing in the place of the epistolary χαίρειν: this was not recorded, as Düsterdieck thinks, "because St John had the customary χαίρειν in his mind" (compare the Commentary on this passage). Our Epistle is altogether destitute of the greeting. We have only one parallel case—that of the Epistle to the Hebrews. But we have seen (in our Introduction to that Epistle) that that production lacks in many other respects the stamp of a proper letter, and especially that free outpouring of thought which is essential to it; and therefore, that it must be regarded rather as a treatise designed for careful study and repeated perusal, than as a letter or communication in the ordinary sense. It may be added, moreover, that, in the case of the Epistle to the Hebrews, the absence of personal superscription and address has another explanation; viz., the fact—which hardly admits of doubt—that it was written only under the commission of the Apostle Paul, and not by his own hand. But none of these explanations can be applied to the First Epistle of St John: it was not, as we have seen, a production sent forth in the form of a treatise, but a thoroughly epistolary outpouring of thought and feeling; and then it was, as we shall see, absolutely and distinctively from the very hand of the Apostle himself. This makes the absence of introductory greeting doubly strange; and, in connection with *this* circumstance, the absence of every kind of benedictory greeting at the *close* will appear equally remarkable. For even the Epistle to the Hebrews, which in its character and design is very much more like a treatise, yet at least in the close introduces a twofold benediction (Heb. xiii. 20, 21, and 25) and greeting (ver. 24). But here everything of the kind is wanting.

We may therefore venture to say that the First Epistle of St John is of the *essence* of an actual epistle, but does not bear the *form* of one. This, however, needs its own explanation.

It must be held to be *possible* that an Apostle should send to a church, or to a circle of churches, an epistle, *without naming his own name, the name of the author.* There was not then a public establishment, as with us, to take charge of the passage of letters; such communications then reached their destination through the medium of private messengers, or private opportunities; and, whether the Apostle would deem it needful or needless to mention his name, would depend altogether upon the position and character of the person who was the bearer in each case, as well as upon the confidence which was reposed in him by those who should receive it. Certainly, if the runaway slave Onesimus had brought, on his return to his master Philemon, an anonymous letter of recommendation, with the mere *oral* assurance that the writer who recommended him, and begged consideration for his case, was no other than the great Apostle Paul himself, Philemon might well have thought it a very strange circumstance, and distrusted the whole matter. Therefore, St Paul did not fail to attach his name to the epistle. Nor does he neglect it in his other epistles, having been taught by old experience (2 Thess. ii. 2) that deceivers carried about supposititious letters bearing his name; yea, he was constrained by this on some occasions to add, at the close of the dictated epistle, a subscription in his own hand (2 Thess. iii. 17), or even to write an entire epistle himself (Col. vi. 11). Indeed, even when he sent an epistle to the Colossians (Col. iv. 7, 8) by the trusted and trustworthy Tychicus, he thinks it better to authenticate the bearer by the epistle, than to authenticate the epistle by the bearer. Similarly, when he wrote by Epaphroditus to the Philippians (Phil. ii. 25). Viewed in itself, it is quite conceivable that St Paul might, in these two last-mentioned cases, have omitted the mention of his name; but it does not appear natural that he should. It is ever the more obvious and natural course, that the author of an epistle should name himself; and when this is not done, we must seek the reason in circumstances peculiar to the case.

Now, if we suppose (what, meanwhile, is quite destitute of proof) that St John wrote his First Epistle in Patmos, at a time when a number of Ephesian elders—and possibly with them elders of other churches in Asia Minor[1]—had come to

[1] According to Estius, Calovius, Lucke, Dusterdieck, and Huther, 1 John i. etc. is "only a peculiar form of the usual preface to a letter." *Very* peculiar, indeed, since it contains nothing but an absolutely general annunciation ("We declare to you that which we have heard, seen,

him, and that he committed his communication to this circle of most eminent men, then we may easily understand that he would hold it unnecessary to mention his own name in the superscription, his authorship being already attested by such a cloud of witnesses.

But even this hypothesis does not help us to understand why *all greeting and benediction are wanting at the beginning and the end.* This circumstance requires some further explanation, and on a different principle. Even if he had committed his greetings to be delivered *orally* by the bearers of the Epistle (which, however, we cannot suppose St Paul to have omitted in the case of Tychicus and Epaphroditus!), yet the fact remains, that the document which he committed to them *had not the external form of an epistle.* One would think, that if an Apostle wrote an *epistle* to one or more churches, bearing upon it the characteristic stamp of the object of an epistle—that is, being the substitute for, and the representative of, oral communication—he would have adopted the universally customary form of epistolary writing. Now it is this which we find wanting here.

I think that this circumstance would be capable of a more easy explanation, if *our epistle could be regarded as having no independent character and object of its own, but as attached to something else.* According to its form, it bears the stamp of a *preface* or *dedicatory epistle.* The Apostle addresses himself to specific readers, and holds communion, person to person, with them,—in that we mark the *essence* of the epistle; but he does this on occasion of another communication, to which this is attached, and to which it refers; and therefore, in its *form*, it is no epistle, no simple and direct substitute of oral speech, but an address uttered *on occasion of the reading of another and different communication.*

We shall see in due course what other and independent

handled, etc., and write unto you this, that ye truly have fellowship with us"), but *nothing* of all that which makes the opening of a *letter* the *opening* of a letter. Or, is there actually in vers. 1–4 only a single word which would not be suitable in the *preface* of a book (*e. g.*, in a *preface* to the Gospel of St John, in case St John would have written any such)? Hence Œcolampadius is quite right in saying : Hic est mos Joannis evangelistæ, ut fere absque omni verborum ambage sua mox ab ipso auspicetur Deo. . . . . Idem porro agit in exordio hujus epistolæ, quod egit in evangelii sui principio.

supports this supposition rests upon. Let it suffice now to have established that those expositors who regard 1 John as an independent epistle of the ordinary kind, have too lightly despatched the absence of the *epistolary form*, and have not given sufficient reasons for that absence.

II. IDENTITY OF THE AUTHOR OF THIS EPISTLE AND THE EVANGELIST.

Although the writer does not mention himself, yet there was never a doubt within the circle of the Christian Church— nor could such a doubt ever reasonably prevail—that this Epistle *was written by the hand of the same man who composed the Fourth canonical Gospel*. But that this had St John for its author, has been satisfactorily established by Olshausen in the first volume of this Commentary, and has since been defended, against the objections of the Tübingen school, by myself and others. Regarding, therefore, the Johannæan authorship of the Fourth Gospel as established, it only remains for us to enter a little more at length into the question, whether the author of this Epistle and the Evangelist were one and the same.

If we begin with what is most external, the *style* and *construction* remind us most expressly of the didactic passages of the Gospel; *e.g.*, John i. 1–18, iii. 27–36, and others. For, we meet in the Epistle the same peculiar manner of thinking in *paratactic* periods, and of combining the individual members of the thought by καί (compare only, for example, ch. ii. 1–3, where St Paul would doubtless have used ἐὰν δέ instead of καὶ ἐάν, and certainly αὐτὸς γὰρ ἱλασμός ἐστι instead of καὶ αὐτὸς ἱλασμός ἐστι). We need only to observe the manner in which he, 1 John iii. 20, resumes the ὅτι which had just preceded, and compare it with the *anaphora* in John i. 33, iv. 6, etc.; and to mark his preference generally for the particle ὅτι, used in manifold senses (comp., *e.g.*, John xvi. 3, 4, 6, 17; comp. further, 1 John ii. 12, etc., with John xvi. 9–11), as well as the frequent use of the particles περί, ἵνα, ἀλλά. It is evident to every one, that the author of the Epistle is accustomed, like the author of the Gospel, to think in Aramæan, and to move in the narrow circle of the particles ו, כי or די, למען. To these may be added some other Hebraic kinds of construction and thought; *e.g.*, the paraphrase of the Gen. by ἐκ, 1 John iv. 13, comp. John i. 35, vi. 8 and 70, and the resolution of a relative in a conditional clause (ἐάν τις ... οὐκ ἔστιν ἐν αὐτῷ instead of ὅστις, κ.τ.λ.), 1 John ii. 15, iii. 17, comp. John vi. 43, etc. The resolution of a simple antithesis into a final or causal sentence dependent upon a word to be supplied (οὐκ ἦσαν ἐξ ἡμῶν ἀλλ' ἵνα ...), 1 John ii. 19, comp. John i. 8, iii. 28; the paraphrase of the instrumental Dative by ἐν, 1 John ii. 3, comp. John i. 26 and 33, xvi. 30; and, finally, the abundant use of θεωρεῖν and θεᾶσθαι, while of ὁρᾶν only the Perfect occurs, and of individual phrases, such as τὴν ψυχὴν τιθέναι, Θεὸς ὁ ἀληθινός, ὁ σωτὴρ τοῦ κόσμου ὁ Χριστός, κόσμος λαμβάνει, and of φαίνειν, τεκνία, παιδία, etc.

More important than these specialities is the similarity of the *circle of ideas* in both writings. The notions φῶς, ζωή, σκοτία, ἀλήθεια, ψεῦδος, meet us in the Epistle in the same broad, and deep, and essentially speculative meaning which they bear in the Gospel: so also recur the notions ἱλασμός, ποιεῖν τὴν δικαιοσύνην, τὴν ἁμαρτίαν, τὴν ἀνομίαν; and the sharply presented antitheses φῶς and σκοτία, ἀλήθεια and ψεῦδος, ζωή and θάνατος, ἀγαπᾶν and μισεῖν, ἀγάπη τοῦ πατρός and τοῦ κόσμου, τέκνα τοῦ Θεοῦ and τοῦ διαβόλου, ποιεῖν τὴν δικαιοσύνην and τὴν ἁμαρτίαν, πνεῦμα τῆς ἀληθείας and τῆς πλάνης. But this leads us to something still higher. It is *the same personality* which moves before our eyes in the Gospel and in the Epistle. It is that same disciple who, in relation to Jesus, exhibits the virgin-spirit of devotion and receptiveness, but, filled with the Spirit, became altogether man and even a son of thunder against all the enemies of Christ; who no longer had to do with the contrast between Jewish Christianity and heathen Christianity,—no longer with the *historical* relation of the Messiah to the circumcision and the uncircumcision,—but whose business it was to judge and overcome the false speculation of dawning Gnosticism by the true gnosis and holy speculation, while he treated of "the Æonian eternal antitheses and relations." It is that disciple whose nature was full of self-devotion and altogether *receptive;* yet whose character was that of absolute *decision,* so that he devoted himself only to one thing, or rather to One Person, but to that One most perfectly and undividedly,—

who, as the result of this specific combination in his character, was incapable of entering into the spirit of an intermediate and neutral position, and therefore never, like St Paul, makes the process of the warfare between the old and the new man the object of his exhibition, but contemplates salvation at once as the perfected victory of light over the darkness.

It cannot, then, be otherwise than that we must find the *dogmatic views* of the Epistle bearing the same form and stamp, down to the minutest statement, which they present in the Gospel :—not as the views of *St John*, but as what he received from the lips of his Lord and Master, yet exhibited under *that* aspect which *he*, by virtue of his own personal individuality, beyond others apprehended and appropriated to himself. Thus, for example (as Düsterdieck has excellently shown), " the ethic of the Johannæan doctrine concerning the final judgment at the coming of the Lord, in its connection with the doctrine concerning the Paraclete, is altogether the same in the Epistle as in the Gospel; and in the Epistle the notion of the Spirit as the Principle of judgment who prepares the way for the final Judgment itself, is no more wanting than the representation of the actual coming is wanting in the Gospel. According to the Epistle, believers have already actually passed from death unto life (ch. iii. 14), are already the children of God (ch. iii. 2), have everlasting life, because they have the Son and the Father (ch. ii. 23, etc., v. 11, etc.), and the Holy Spirit (ch. iii. 24)." And so far there is no more judgment awaiting them (ch. ii. 28, iii. 2, iv. 17). The future judgment will only "finish the consummation of the life which believers already have received, and maintained, and preserved upon earth, in fellowship with Christ, and in the possession of the Holy Spirit (ch. ii. 12, etc., iii. 9, v. 1). And as the judgment is already, in time, preparatorily accomplished upon unbelievers, through the power of the Holy Spirit exerting His influence upon the world (ch. ii. 8 and 19), so also believers have in their earthly life, from the same Spirit, the principle of their holy and saving development, which will be blessedly consummated at the coming of the Lord, from whom they have received the Spirit." With this compare John v. 24, vi. 39, etc., and other passages. The present existence of the last hour is presupposed in the Gospel (ch. v. 25, xii. 31), in the same manner as in the Epistle (ch. ii. 18). According to the Gospel, as according to the Epistle (1 John ii. 1), *Christ* is the Paraclete; for the Holy Spirit is exhibited by the side of Christ in the Gospel, ch. xiv. 16, as ἄλλος παράκλητος, *another* Comforter. Compare further John iii. 16 with 1 John iv. 9, 10; John xiv. 15 and 21, with 1 John ii. 6, v. 3; John xvii. 14 with 1 John iii. 1; John xv. 18 with 1 John iii. 13.

That the Epistle came from the same author as the Gospel, was, therefore, never questioned, until in these later times the crotchety critics of the young-Hegelian school found it for their advantage, in the interest of their other views, to deny the identity of authorship. But, in their endeavours to establish their point, it has happened that they have split into two opposite parties, which have zealously contended against each other. United in this, that the Epistle came from another hand than that which wrote the Gospel, they then separated diametrically. Baur and Zeller[1] maintained, that the Gospel was the relatively older document; and that the Epistle was the imitative production, altogether void of original substance, of a man who sought to have himself identified with the author of the Gospel, and therefore did his best to imitate his style. On the other hand, Hilgenfeld[2] admitted the originality of the Epistle, but assigned to the Gospel a later date, and the authorship of a different hand.

What these critics allege for the establishment of their common assertion—to wit, that the author of the Gospel and the author of the Epistle are not one and the same—is really very insignificant; and we shall content ourselves with referring those of our readers who are desirous to investigate their subtleties at length, to the fundamental arguments of Düsterdieck, in his Introduction to this Epistle. All others will be contented with the proofs given above of the identity of the author of the Epistle and the author of the Gospel; for our remarks have contained, in part at least, the refutation of the supposed dogmatical contradictions which have been thought to

---

[1] Zeller made a beginning, by representing it as "conceivable" that the two writings might have had different authors (Tub. Jahrb. 1845). Baur, in his treatise on the Johannæan Epistles (Tub. Jahrb. 1848), elevated this "conceivableness" into positive certainty.

[2] Das Evangelium und die Briefe Johannis nach ihrem Lehrbegriff dargestellt, Halle 1849.

exist between the Epistle and the Gospel. The contradictions which we have not referred to rest upon a perverted exegesis of individual utterances of the Epistle (for instance, ch. v. 6); and they will be considered at large in the commentary on those passages. But what Baur, in particular, has alleged in disparagement of the Epistle, and in proof that it was no better than an unhappy imitation of the style and spirit of the Gospel, has been already reduced to nothing by our common adversary Hilgenfeld. Baur says, that in the Epistle there is not one of the ideas, borrowed from the Gospel, which is stated in an independent manner, and developed in a profounder connection; that whatever it contains is but taken arbitrarily from the rich contents of the Gospel; that if the Epistle has any leading fundamental thought, it is extremely hard to detect or follow it anywhere; that its polemics are idle and empty (everything is to Baur idle and empty that is directed against a false pantheistic gnosis!); and that the Epistle has received from the Gospel its manner of representation,—the monotony of which, however, is more strange, because it is a mere form without its corresponding essence. But to all this we can only reply by giving the great critic our humble assurance, that the poverty of thought and spiritlessness which he alleges, does not lie with the author of the Epistle. If a wild Indian can find no relish in the Olympic Jupiter, the fault is not with Phidias. Hilgenfeld discerns in the Epistle "profound views," which the author of the Gospel, without disparagement to his own "grand originality of conception," appropriated in his production.

But every remaining doubt as to the identity of the Epistle-writer and the Evangelist must vanish, when we observe that the latter, like the former, represents himself to have been an eye-witness of the life of Jesus, and an Apostle (1 John i. 1–3, iv. 14); and that he refers to the beginning of the Gospel (1 John i. 1–4) in such a manner as to leave no reason for doubting that it is his *purpose* to describe himself as the same who had written the Gospel. We have therefore the option, *either* to attribute deception (!) to the man who declares the devil to have been the father of the lie, and every one who speaketh falsehood to be a child of the devil, and the spirit of lying to be the spirit of darkness and of antichrist,—a supposition, the possibility of entertaining which, argues either a very suspicious failure of the power of thinking, or a still more suspicious moral abandonment—*or*, to accept the two writings as the production of the Apostle St John.

III. GENUINENESS OF THE EPISTLE.

This result, obtained by internal investigations, will be perfectly confirmed by the *external testimonies in favour of the genuineness of the Epistle.* Polycarp (according to Iren. adv. Hær. v. 33; Euseb. iv. 14, v. 20, an immediate disciple of St John) writes (Phil. 7): πᾶς γὰρ ὃς ἂν μὴ ὁμολογῇ Ἰησοῦν Χριστὸν ἐν σαρκὶ ἐληλυθέναι, ἀντίχριστός ἐστι—an undeniable allusion to 1 John iv. 3 (compared with ver. 2). Polycarp quotes these words, too, as a warning against those οἵτινες ἀποπλανῶσι κενοὺς ἀνθρώπους, and even introduces the expression used by St John concerning the same false teachers (περὶ τῶν πλανώντων ὑμᾶς, 1 John ii. 26). And this passage is all the more important, as the expression ἀντίχριστος is not found in any of the Fathers of the second century, except St John's own disciples, Polycarp and Irenæus (Lücke). And the words which immediately follow in Polycarp (καὶ ὃς ἂν μὴ ὁμολογῇ τὸ μαρτύριον τοῦ σταυροῦ, ἐκ τοῦ διαβόλου ἐστίν) certainly contain another specifically Johannæan expression. Moreover, Polycarp elsewhere, and generally, moves in a circle of Johannæan phraseology and turns of thought and ideas (περιπατεῖν ἐν ταῖς ἐντολαῖς, ἀξίως τῆς ἐντολῆς, κατὰ τὴν ἀλήθειαν τοῦ κυρίου, ζῆν ἐν Χριστῷ): he often sharply defines brotherly love as the climax of righteousness, commands his readers to separate themselves ἀπὸ τῶν ἐπιθυμιῶν τῶν ἐν τῷ κόσμῳ (cap. v., comp. 1 John ii. 16), and to hold fast τὸν ἐξ ἀρχῆς ἡμῖν παραδοθέντα λόγον (cap. vii., comp. 1 John ii. 7, and 19–21).

Papias also (who, according to Euseb. iii. 39, had been Ἰωάννου μὲν ἀκουστής, Πολυκάρπου δὲ ἑταῖρος) used, that is, cited, in his writings (lost to *us*, but extant and well known to Eusebius, who gives us on this point his unsuspicious testimony) the first Epistle of St John. (Euseb. l. c.: κέχρηται δ' ὁ αὐτὸς μαρτυρίαις ἀπὸ τῆς Ἰωάννου προτέρας ἐπιστολῆς καὶ τῆς Πέτρου ὁμοίως.) Indeed, it would appear that the citations from 1 John in the writings of Papias were much more striking than those in Polycarp's Epistle to the Ephesians; for Eusebius, when he speaks concerning this latter Epistle, does not make any mention of the allusions to St John's Epistle.[1]

The *Epistle to Diognetus*—written about the time of Justin Martyr—is most certainly full of Johannæan thoughts: examine, *e.g.*, the following passage (p. 500): ὁ γὰρ Θεὸς τοὺς ἀνθρώπους ἠγάπησε, πρὸς οὓς ἀπέστειλε τὸν υἱὸν αὐτοῦ τὸν μονογενῆ (comp. with 1 John iv. 9, 10, and John iii. 16): οἷς τὴν ἐν οὐρανῷ βασιλείαν ἐπηγγείλατο, καὶ δώσει τοῖς ἀγαπήσασι αὐτόν· ἐπιγνοὺς δὲ, τίνος οἴει πλησωθήσεσθαι χαρᾶς; ἢ πῶς ἀγαπήσεις τὸν οὕτως προαγαπήσαντά σε (1 John iv. 10, 11). Ἀγαπήσας δὲ, μιμητὴς ἔσῃ αὐτοῦ τῆς χρηστότητος (John xiv. 15 and 21; 1 John v. 3; 2 John 6; and, especially, 1 John ii. 6). Or, the following in cap. xii.: οὐδὲ γὰρ ζωὴ ἄνευ γνώσεως, οὐδὲ γνῶσις ἀσφαλὴς ἄνευ ζωῆς ἀληθοῦς, which is no other than a short and compact summary of the process of thought contained in 1 John ii. 18-25, iv. 4-6, v. 6-12. The Epistle to Diognetus represents Christians as those who are not ἐκ τοῦ κόσμου (cap. vi.; comp. 1 John iii. 1, and John xvii. 14); as those who are hated by the world (cap. v.-vi.; comp. John xvii. 14, xv. 18; 1 John iii. 13), and who yet love this world, even as (cap. vii.) the Father sent the Son, not that He might condemn the world, but that He might show love to it (comp. John iii. 17). The Epistle to Diognetus acknowledges (cap. vii.), with St John, the future παρουσία of Christ to judgment; teaches, with St John, that God has planted His holy Logos into the hearts of Christians (ὁ Θεὸς ἀπ' οὐρανῶν τὴν ἀλήθειαν καὶ τὸν λόγον τὸν ἅγιον καὶ ἀπερινόητον ἐγκατεστήριξε ταῖς καρδίαις, since He did not send an angel, but αὐτὸν τὸν τεχνίτην καὶ δημιουργὸν τῶν ὅλων). Further, it here, and in Ep. xi., terms Christ τὸν λόγον and τὸν ἀπ' ἀρχῆς.

The *Epistle of the Church of Vienne and Lyons* (in Euseb. v. 1) also contains an undeniable allusion to 1 John iii. 16, in the words: ὁ διὰ τοῦ πληρώματος τῆς ἀγάπης ἐνεδείξατο, εὐδοκήσας ὑπὲρ τῆς τῶν ἀδελφῶν ἀπολογίας καὶ τὴν ἑαυτοῦ θεῖναι ψυχήν.

The circumstance, further, is very important, that the Gnostic Carpocrates—who lived at Alexandria in the beginning of the

[1] The whole body of then-extant Christian literature lay before Eusebius' eyes, and he was a *learned* reader and investigator of it.

second century—sought to pervert and bend to his purpose the passage of 1 John v. 19, "Mundus in maligno positus est" (Origen in Genesin, cap. i.).

Irenæus cites our Epistle, as is well known, with express mention of its author (adv. Hær. iii. 16, v. and viii.; the passages are 1 John ii. 18–22, iv. 1–3, v. 1); hence Eusebius (v. 8) writes concerning him (as concerning Papias): μέμνηται δὲ καὶ τῆς 'Ιωάννου πρώτης ἐπιστολῆς, μαρτυρία ἐξ αὐτῆς πλεῖστα εἰσφέρων· ὁμοίως δὲ καὶ τῆς Πέτρου προτέρας.— So also Clem. Alex. Pædag. iii. and Strom. ii. quotes the passages, 1 John v. 3 and 16, and with mention of the author. Similarly Tertullian, Origen, and the succeeding Fathers.

Thus it is not to be wondered at, that the First Epistle of St John everywhere appears in the ancient *Canones*, or Catalogues of the ecclesiastical books of instruction, and that as ὁμολογουμένη.[1] The Syrian Church received it in the Peshito; the Alexandrian Church is represented as receiving it by Clem. Alex. (see above), Origen (in Euseb. vi. 25), and Dionysius (in Euseb. vii. 25); for the African Church vouch Tertullian (de Idol. ii. de Fug. 9) and Cyprian (de Orat. Dom.); for the Gallican, Irenæus; and for the East, Eusebius, who reckons the Epistle among the *homologoumena*.

In the face of these witnesses, it must appear only ridiculous to hear the pseudo-criticism of the young-Hegelian school peremptorily uttering their dictum—in the service of their a priori construction of the history of the development of Christianity—that the Epistle harmonizes only with the second century, because it contains "post-Montanistic" elements, or because it has incorporated Gnostic ideas which were not unfolded till during the course of the second century. A thorough refutation of these arguments—based upon pure misunderstanding and perversion—may be found in the introduction of Düsterdieck. The kernel of this refutation lies in the golden

---

[1] When we find in the Canon Murat. mention of "superscripti Joannis duas," this does not refer to the first and second, but to the second and third, Epistle; both of which required to be established against the suspicion which might place them among hurtful and heretical writings. The author of that canon did not think it necessary to mention the First Epistle, in this connection and for this purpose: *its* canonicity was self-understood.

saying of this commentator: "Baur, misunderstanding or ignorant of the truth of the apostolical thoughts, has regarded the Montanistic [and the Gnostic] *caricature* of those thoughts as their *type*." For the rest, the next section will contain sufficient exposure of the hypothesis of Baur.

It is well known that as early as the second century there were men who, purely on internal grounds, were repelled by St John's writings, and therefore rejected them from the canon.[1] They were named ἄλογοι—a name which in every sense was quite suitable for them.

IV. RELATION OF THE EPISTLE TO THE GOSPEL.

It has been shown above, Sect. II., that in the Epistle we may discern the same style, the same manner and substance of thought, the same doctrinal individuality, the selfsame spirit and character—in short, the same individual and personal traits of authorship—which meet us in the Gospel. But, beyond this general identity, there may be traced a still more direct relationship between the two writings, in respect to the similarity of the state of things to which they owe their origin, and the similarity of purpose which they were meant to subserve. In these respects they are more closely allied to each other than to the Apocalypse, which was written by the same author, but under totally different impelling circumstances. In style, also, the Epistle more nearly approximates to the Gospel, than either does to the Apocalypse.

That the Gospel of St John did not owe its origin to any mere impulse to write in the author, but also to an historical, practical necessity for it existing in the Church, I think I have already established in opposition to my friend Luthardt. It is most certain that St John received from the Lord a calling, and a circle of influence, as real as that of any of the other Apostles; and we know that it was his especial vocation (John

---

[1] The patristic notices of them are arranged in Kirchhofer's Quellensammlung zur Geschichte des N. T. Canons, ii. S. 425–432. But, as the opposition of the Alogi was mainly directed to the Gospel and the Apocalypse, we may here the more briefly dismiss this most uncritical demonstration of heresy.

xxi. 22) to remain until the Lord should come. He was to outlive the other Apostles; he should live to behold the *parousia*,—which he attained to, not indeed in external reality, but in the visions in which the Lord came to him, Rev. i. 9, etc., and gave him to see His coming to judgment, Rev. i. 7, xxii. 20. Thus, the vocation of this Apostle had an essentially *eschatological* character. When he came forth from his earlier comparative retirement to play an active part upon the scene of the history of the apostolical age, the perfected judgment upon Jerusalem had abolished the ground of the previous controversy between Jewish and Gentile Christianity,—the controversy which had enlisted the energies of St Paul (and with which the contest between the Papacy and the Reformation is analogous). But, instead of this, other powers of seduction and perversion had sought to force themselves into the doctrine of the Christian Church,—powers in which both Jewish and heathen elements of falsehood combined in wildly confused league *against* the Truth, while bearing the *guise* of truth and wisdom (and with which are analogous the powers of negative and destructive wisdom which have come forth in our day since the Deists and Encyclopædists). Of the Jewish Christianity there remained only that Nazarene element which still clung, in godless and naked traditionalism, to the observance of the ceremonial law, and the use of the national language, after the Lord had laid low in destruction both temple and nation; and which, as the result of this spiritual obstinacy, was suffered to sink into the lowest stage which was exhibited as *Ebionitism*, capable of viewing Jesus only from the legal point of view, as a new lawgiver, and therefore as no more than a mere man. It had not, in the Apostle's days, reached that stage; although that extreme development, to which the then existing separation of the Nazarenes from the organism of the Church must necessarily lead, could not possibly be concealed from that prophetic glance which was St John's special endowment.

Now, whether St John, in his so emphatic testimony to the eternal Divine Sonship of Christ, had in view the Nazarene element and its results, or not; whether it was his conscious *design* to interpose a barrier to one of the two fundamental principles of all heresy, or not; whether or not the strongly asserted sayings of the Gospel, ch. i. 8, 20, with which 1 John

v. 6 is connected, were directed against an Ebionizing school of John's disciples (which, according to Acts xviii. 24, and xix. 1, had continued in existence long after the Baptist's death as a school or sect);—thus much is clear, and historically established beyond possibility of doubt, that the same error, otherwise termed "*Ebionite*," did confront the Apostle from another point, and that as combined with the second root of all the heresies—*docetic*-pantheistic Gnosticism.

Gnosticism generally had in this its distinguishing mark, that it regarded Christianity not as having to do primarily with the salvation of the soul (as in Acts xvi. 30), but with theoretical wisdom. It appropriated many—and in some instances truly-apprehended—elements of Christian doctrine; but it sundered them from their *organic* connection with the centre of the Gospel, and wrought them into the complex of its problems and systems, making them do nothing better than minister to the enlargement of those problems and systems. And these questions of the older Gnosticism assume various forms in history. For example, in Marcion it was a problem of natural ethics, how the law was related to individual personal freedom:—solved by taking the ground of a no longer moral Antinomianism. Among the Ophites, it was a problem of the philosophy of history, how the Old-Testament limited national development was related to the New-Testament universality:—solved by the theory which wildly denied the truth of the Old-Testament revelation, and perverted it into a revelation of Satan. With Valentinian it was a problem of pure abstract speculation, how spirit was related to matter, and so forth. All these problems bear evident marks of their forced and artificial origin; we perceive that Christianity had not only imposed itself upon their originators as a power with which they must, in some way or other, place themselves in relation, but that they, in all their attempts at solution, set out with the principle and design, to assign the highest place to Christianity (that is, to what they could find good for their purpose in Christianity); yea, even to secure for their systems, by artificial, allegorical exegesis, the appearance of being founded upon Holy Scripture.

But, with such forced and artificial systems the spiritual movement of Gnosticism could not possibly have had its rise.

The first exhibition of the Gnostic nature—in itself very rough and unformed—within the Christian Church we see in Simon the Magician (Acts viii. 9, etc.), who before his conversion made himself honoured as an emanation of God (ἡ δύναμις τοῦ Θεοῦ ἡ καλουμένη μεγάλη), and brought over into Christianity, if not the *doctrine*, yet the general view, that the Christian mysteries, like all others, were an instrument and a means for the obtaining of money and fame (vers. 18, etc.). *So far* there was some element of truth in the old saying which made Simon the father of Gnosticism; he had in himself at least, in his moral and religious position and character, the material of a Gnostic.—But the most ancient actual Gnostic, who brought out a Gnostic *theory*, was *Cerinthus*. That he lived in Ephesus at the same time with St John, and that St John regarded him and shunned him as "the enemy of the truth," is attested by Irenæus with the express remark that he had received his information from Polycarp, the immediate disciple of St John.[1] His doctrine is given by Irenæus in the following words (i. 26): *Et Cerinthus autem quidam in Asia non a primo Deo factum esse mundum docuit, sed a virtute quadam valde separata et distante ab ea principalitate, quæ est super universa, et ignorante eum, qui est super omnia, Deum. Jesum autem,* subjecit, *non ex virgine natum* (impossibile enim hoc ei visum est) fuisse autem eum *Josephi et Mariæ filium simpliciter ut reliqui omnes homines,* et plus potuisse justitia et prudentia et sapientia ab hominibus. Et post baptismum *descendisse in eum* ab ea principalitate, quæ est super omnia, *Christum* figura columbæ; et tunc annunciasse incognitum patrem et virtutes perfecisse; in fine autem *revolasse iterum Christum de Jesu, et Jesum* passum esse et resurrexisse; Christum autem impassibilem perseverasse, existentem spiritualem.[2]

---

[1] Iren. adv. Hær. 3, 3, 4: Καὶ εἰσὶν οἱ ἀκηκοότες αὐτοῦ (τοῦ Πολυκάρπου) ὅτι Ἰωάννης ὁ τοῦ Κυρίου μαθητής, ἐν τῇ Ἐφέσῳ πορευθεὶς λούσασθαι, καὶ ἰδὼν ἔσω Κήρινθον, ἐξήλατο τοῦ βαλανείου μὴ λουσάμενος ἀλλ' ἐπειπών· Φύγωμεν, μὴ καὶ τὸ βαλανεῖον συμπέσῃ, ἔνδον ὄντος Κηρίνθου, τοῦ τῆς ἀληθείας ἐχθροῦ. So Euseb. H. E. 3, 28.

[2] What, on the contrary, Gaius and Dionys. Alex. say about Cerinthus (in Euseb. 3, 28) is of no moment. For Gaius, a fanatical anti-Montanist and anti-Chiliast, condemns Cerinthus as being the true author of the Apocalypse, which he invented in the Chiliast interest. But Dionysius (whose words in Euseb. 3, 28 are imperfect, but are quoted at length in 7, 25) relates of the *Alogi*, that *they* condemned Cerinthus for holding a sensual Chiliasm.

B

Thus there are two points in which the doctrinal system of Cerinthus culminates. First, he teaches that the Creator of the actual visible world was a *Demiurgus*, different from the supreme God, the Sender of Christ, a lower Æon who possessed no knowledge of God, and did not communicate to his creatures any such knowledge:—that primal and fundamental position of Gnosticism, which, under various modifications, runs through *all* the succeeding Gnostic systems. Second, he teaches that Jesus was a mere man, begotten of Joseph; that at his baptism an *Æon Christ* was united to him, sent down by the supreme God (the ἀρχὴ ἀνωτάτη), in order that he might lead the world, by the mouth of the man Jesus, to know Him, the Supreme God. Before the death of Jesus, however, the Æon Christ is represented as being again separated from him.

We see plainly enough glimmering throughout this system the problems which gave it its existence: the question of vain curiosity, how it was that God, supposing Him to have created the world, could have remained so long unknown to the world which He had made (the blame of this was not sought in *men*, who would not receive the light shining into the world, but was transferred from men to the world itself, and its δημιουργός!); and then the question of Rationalism, how the Son of God could have become man, and could have been conceived by a virgin. Hence, the *basis* of the system was not a Jewish-Ebionite error, which through an over-valuation of the *law* denied the necessity for the incarnation of Christ, but a rationalist philosophical error; although its *result* in relation to the person of Jesus concurred with the final result of (later) Ebionitism.

How, then, did the Apostle John bear himself in his attack upon this system of lies? A craving for γνῶσις had been excited; speculative thinking had been awakened, though in an un-Christian direction, to busy itself with such questions as these. This craving must be satisfied, but satisfied in the right manner: it must be shown that the true γνῶσις had its roots, not in the idle curiosity of a philosophical groping, altogether separate from penitent faith in the Saviour of sinners, but in that faith itself, and in that alone. And this is what St John has shown. The material which he had to use for this purpose, was not to be sought for anew, or laboriously to be constructed. He himself was prepared by his own original endowments: he had already, in the lifetime of his Master, viewed, apprehended, and retained especially those aspects of the nature and doctrine of Jesus Christ, which now served of themselves to bear victorious testimony against the Gnostic heresy. He, that is, alone among all the disciples, had been fitted to apprehend and lay up in his mind certain phases of the nature and doctrine of Jesus: to wit, first, the Lord's own declarations concerning His eternal relation to the Father, and His eternal, pre-temporal unity of nature with the Father (John iii. 13 and 17, v. 17, vi. 33 and 51, vii. 16 and 28, viii. 58, etc.); secondly, those utterances of our Lord concerning the profound mystical relation of unity and communion of life into which the Lord would enter with His disciples, through the Holy Ghost (John iii. 8, ch. vi., xiv. 16, etc., xv. 1, etc., xvii. 21-23). Because St John was, in his personal character, the complement of the other disciples, therefore it was obvious of itself that he would give the complement of their exhibition of Christ and His doctrine, by presenting, as soon as the occasion should arise, in doctrine and writing, that peculiar side of it which he had beyond others apprehended. And for that the occasion has now come. Merely taking a human view of the matter, and apart from all inspiration and enlightenment of the Holy Ghost, it must have now arisen to his consciousness that he had in his own internal self the living armoury against the new assaults of the spirit of lying! The Gnosticism of a Cerinthus must necessarily have awakened within him his holy indignation; for it directly contradicted all that which St John bore in his heart as the most sacred treasure from the lips of Jesus; and surely would he know that in these discourses of our Lord he had already received the refutation of Gnosticism, and the elements of a perfect victory over its errors. To the doctrinal statements of lying speculation which sundered the Father of Jesus Christ from the Creator of the world, he had to oppose the doctrine that the Father of Jesus Christ had created the world by the Logos;—to the lie that sundered the man Jesus from the Æon Christ, and separated them entirely before the passion of Christ, he had to oppose the doctrine of Jesus, the incarnate Logos, and of the glorification of the Father in His sufferings;—to the dead striving after dead knowledge, he had to oppose the discourses of Christ concerning the life of the Head in the members.

That he *did* set himself in opposition to them, is undeniable matter of fact. It has been questioned by some, whether he did so designedly and consciously: it has been asserted that, *without any reference to Cerinthus,* he purposed only "to make known to the collective One Church the whole One Christ, in His fullest and most perfect essential character, and universality of meaning for man;" and to show "in what way Jesus Himself knew or sought to create faith in Himself." But the Evangelist specifies his own *design* in the construction of his Gospel (ch. xx. 31): "These things are written, that ye may believe *that Jesus is the Christ, the Son of God;* and that believing ye *may have life in His name.*" And did St John write these words without at all thinking of that *enemy of the truth* who was living in the same city with himself, and who taught the precise reverse—that Jesus was *not* the Christ? If it was his design in the Gospel to lead His Church to a perfect faith, and to confirm them in that faith, that Christ was the Son of God, it was also his design, doubtless, to arm and prepare them against the cunning and subtile attacks of the Cerinthian Gnosticism, which was so nigh at hand.

And how aptly and specifically are the lying assertions of Cerinthus overthrown by individual passages of the Gospel! Cerinthus taught that the world was created by an inferior Æon, who did not know the Supreme God. St John writes: "The Word was to (with) God, and the Word was God. All things were made by Him; *and without Him was not anything made that was made*" (John i. 3). We must mark the polemico-negative repetition of the statement, which before was laid down in a positive form. Cerinthus taught that men before Christ had not the possibility of knowing the Supreme God, because the Demiurgus himself did not know Him, and could not therefore give the knowledge of Him to His creatures,—the Æon Christ having first made Him known. St John writes concerning the Word of God, who was Himself God, and through whom all things were made, " In Him was life, *and the life was the light of men:*" he thus writes that the supreme and only God had, through the Logos, given life from the beginning to men, and in this life the light of knowledge also. And, while Cerinthus ascribed the cause of human sin, blindness, and ignorance of God, to an increated impossibility, and that again to the Demiurgus, St John, on the contrary, writes, "And the light shineth in the darkness, *but the darkness received it not;*" and thereby throws the guilt of blindness where it should fall, on the wicked will of the creature, which is and abides dark because it *received not the light.* In ver. 9, he repeats once more, that the Logos was "the true Light, which enlighteneth *every man;*" and in ver. 10, once more, that "the world *through Him* existed, but that the world *knew Him not;*" and in ver. 11, that He, when He came to the world, came not into the strange province of a Demiurgus, but "*to His own,* though His own (creatures) *received Him not.*" Again, he charges the guilt upon the evil will of the creatures, while Cerinthus taught that the Æon Christ had come into the *alien* domain of an *alien* Demiurgus, whose creatures *could* not know the supreme *Principalitus* through an increate inability.

When St John had thus diligently opposed a barrier to the fundamental Gnostic assumption and presupposition of a Demiurgus, he could pass onward to the doctrine of the incarnation of the Logos, eternally one with God, in Jesus the Christ, and oppose it to the lying doctrine of Cerinthus concerning the mere man Jesus, and the Æon Christ only temporarily united to him (ver. 14): "The Logos *was made* flesh, and dwelt among us; and we *beheld* His glory, the glory as of the Only-begotten of the Father." To the lie of Cerinthus concerning the mere man and son of Joseph, he has to oppose that which he had seen with his eyes. And the eyes of no disciple had been so inwardly opened as his had been, to behold and apprehend the full and gracious outbeaming of the eternal glory of God manifest in Christ Jesus! "By *Jesus Christ* came grace and truth. No man hath seen God; the only-begotten Son, who is in the bosom of the Father, He hath declared Him (God)." Thus writes St John (ch. i. 17, 18); while Cerinthus was teaching that the Æon Christ, who brought to men the knowledge of God, was neither the Only-begotten in the bosom of the Father, nor one person with Jesus.

According to Cerinthus, it was *the Æon Christ* who descended, at his baptism, on the mere man Jesus, and communicated to him the "virtutes" of *prudence, wisdom,* and *righteousness.* St John relates (ch. i. 32, etc.) how the *Holy Ghost* came down upon Him, who Himself was already the

Son of God, and before the Baptist (vers. 30 and 31); and that He received the Holy Ghost, not that He might then and thereby become partaker of the Divine nature for Himself, but that He might be able (ver. 33) to baptize others with the same Spirit.

We shall not now go through the individual actual demonstrations of the Divine δόξα in Jesus which the Evangelist records. All we can do is to point to those individual utterances of Christ which the Evangelist cited for the confirmation of the doctrine laid down in ch. i. In ch. iii. 13, 14, we have the two things placed in close juxtaposition by Christ Himself— that the Son of Man came down from heaven, and is in heaven, and that the same Son of Man must be lifted up on the cross (while Cerinthus entirely sundered the Æon Christ, who came down from heaven, from the suffering man Jesus). Compare, further, ch. v. 23 and 25, where the Son, *Jesus* Christ, arrogates to Himself the same honour which belongs to the Father, and where He prophesies that He will raise the dead; and ch. vi. 51 and 62, where He again testifies that He came down from heaven. So also ch. viii. 58; and especially ch. xii. 23 seq. and xvii. 1 seq., where again *the suffering itself* appears to be the glorification of God in His incarnate Son; and, moreover, ch. xviii. 6 and 11 and 37, where the suffering appears as the counsel of God, and the end of the incarnation of the Son.

As certainly as St Luke, the companion of St Paul, wrote such passages and expressions as Luke xiv. 23, xv. 10 and 31, not without the consciousness of the immense energy which lay in those sayings as directed against a false legal Jewish Christianity, and, consequently, not without the latent intention to erect by their means bulwarks against this mischievous error, so certain is it that St John did not record the above-mentioned sayings of our Lord without the consciousness of the mighty witness which they would bear against the Cerinthian heresy, and, consequently, not without the design to put weapons in the hands of the Lord's people for their defence against that power of seduction and falsehood. Indeed, we must assume that this purpose and latent aim was much more distinctly conscious in the mind of St John, than in the mind of St Luke. When the latter wrote his Gospel, a false legal Judaism did not oppose itself in so concrete and concentrated a form as that with which Gnosticism confronted St Luke. That Jewish Christianity was, indeed, found everywhere, but especially in Palestine (Acts xv. 1 seq.; Gal. ii. 4), Galatia (Gal. i. 7, etc.), and Corinth (1 Cor. i. 12); certainly it was not so abundant, and it was not so vigorous, in the churches of Asia Minor which had been founded under the influence of St Paul, and for which St Luke wrote his Gospel. The contest with Judaism had been to St Luke, while he laboured by the side of St Paul, only an independent and general matter of interest; many years before, the conflict had been settled in his mind by those discourses, and parables, and acts of Jesus, which demonstrated that not only Israel, and not all Israel, would be saved, but only those who penitently believed, whether among the Jews or among the Gentiles. It is more *involuntarily* that he presents, in his Gospel especially, a selection of *those* portions which had *from the beginning* appeared to him to be pre-eminently important on the subject. With St John it was otherwise. He had not had previously—that is, *before* the rise of Gnosticism—any particular *external* occasion presented, which rendered it necessary that he should give prominence to that speculative side of the doctrine and the nature of Christ, which he beyond others had so deeply and inwardly apprehended; but now, when Cerinthus had begun in Ephesus to perplex the minds even of the members of the Church (1 John ii. 19), and to induce some of them to apostatize, the Apostle *must* have become distinctly conscious to what *end* and for what occasion the Lord had furnished him with his own peculiar talent of knowledge. That which he had long and faithfully retained in the inmost depths of his spirit, and pondered in his heart, he now comes forward prominently to declare, *in opposition to a concrete and locally concentrated lying power and influence,*—consequently, *with a directly polemical aim.*

We define Cerinthic Gnosticism to have been a "locally-concentrated" lying power, but not simply a "local" one. It was not a merely local and isolated occurrence, as was the heresy of Hymenæus and Philetus (2 Tim. ii. 17), which in Ephesus "spread like a cancer;"[1] but a lying power, which at

[1] It is not, however, denied that this spiritualism also was a symptom of a more general disease, nor that it was itself one of the earliest precursors of the Gnostic views.

that time had *its place in the air* (comp. Eph. ii. 2, vi. 12). Moreover, the history of Gnosticism in the second century teaches us what a widely extending growth was to spread from this root; and, that already about the end of the first century this root had put forth more than one stem, we are assured by the reports which the newly discovered Hippolytus gives us, in the fifth book of his φιλοσοφούμενα ἡ κατὰ πασῶν αἱρέσεων ἔλεγχος, concerning the Naassenes, Peratics, Sethites, and Justin the Gnostic.[1] Nevertheless, this power of the lie confronted St John in a *locally concentrated* form—that is, in the person and in the influence of Cerinthus. For, that St John had (as Bunsen thinks) the Naassenes and Sethites in his eye, is at least incapable of proof; and the manner in which these heretics interwove the Logos-idea into their systems, appears to assign them a place rather after than before the appearance of St John's writings.[2] That, on the other hand, Cerinthus lived at the same time with St John in Ephesus, and laboured for the subversion of Christianity, stands historically firm; and we have already seen how distinctly and sharply St John opposes precisely the *Cerinthian* doctrine (as explained to us by Irenæus) in his Gospel.

Thus the Gospel assumes a *concrete historical* place in a definite conflict with heresy.

But we find *that our Epistle has its place most clearly defined in the same conflict.*

Plainly and expressly the Apostle warns against "the liar who *denies that Jesus is the Christ*" (ch. ii. 22), and who thereby

[1] Compare Bunsen, Hippolytus i. S. 32.
[2] For they do not contain the Philonic Logos (the hypostatic reason in God, the world-idea, by which God created the actual world)—*that* notion of a creation of the universe is what they absolutely reject!—but a corruption of the *Johannæan* Logos, a Logos who descended for *redemption*, and (though indeed only docetically) *became man*. Bunsen himself, moreover, is constrained to admit (S. 33): "St John can have had in his eye, not so much the philosophical disciples of Philo, who abominated every notion of a personal union of the Logos with man, as the Christian heretics *who perverted that idea* in one manner or another." But, how could they have *perverted* the idea of the incarnation, if this idea had been nowhere *uttered and made prominent?* And where is there a single trace that it had been uttered before St John? Accordingly, the Johannæan writings must have *preceded* those heretics; and therefore were not composed for their refutation.

denies " the *Father and* the Son ; and in connection with this, he speaks of an already witnessed apostasy of some (vers. 18, 19), exhorting the readers to hold fast that which they had heard from the beginning (ver. 24). Nor do this warning and this exhortation stand here isolated and alone. It is not only that expressly analogous passages recur in the Epistle (ch. iv. 1–3 and 15, v. 1 and 5, and 10 and 20), which all exhibit the kernel and essence of truth to be the doctrine, that "*Jesus Christ came into the flesh ;*" that Jesus is the *Son of God ;*" that " Jesus is the Christ," and " the true God and eternal life,"—but *the entire Epistle, from beginning to end,* is constructed on this principle, to exhibit this opposition between the Christian truth and the Gnostic denial that Jesus was the Christ,[1] in its most intimate connection with the religious and moral opposition between truth and lie, righteousness and ἀνομία, love and hatred, and with the æonian opposition between the kingdom of God and the world, between God and Satan,—as will be made manifest in our explanation of these contrasts in the Commentary.

If, then, the Epistle thus originated in the same nature of things as the Gospel, we may at least consider this position as established, *that the Epistle belongs to the same period of time with the Gospel.* An attentive observation, however, will carry this position still further, and lead to the assumption that *the two documents were strictly simultaneous.* And in this case the Epistle must be considered to have been a *companion-document* to the Gospel, as it were an epistle dedicatory.

This view has been already defended by Heidegger, Berger, Storr, Lange, Thiersch, and others ; I have also in another work maintained it. Bleek, Düsterdieck, and Huther have recently opposed it, but by arguments which cannot be regarded as valid. Bleek rests mainly upon the insufficiency, which cannot be denied, of the arguments which I brought forward in the *Kritik der evangelischen Geschichte;* but even this he deals with partially, for he limits himself really to the question of the γράφω and ἔγραψα (1 John i. 4, ii. 12 seq.), which he supposes to refer, not to the Gospel, but to the Epistle itself.

---

[1] St John uses the formulæ, " Jesus is the Son of God," and " Jesus is the Christ," promiscuously and interchangeably. That this is to be explained only on the supposition of a definite opposition to Cerinthus, will be seen in the remarks below upon 1 John v. 1.

Düsterdieck asserts the same; and adds, that there is not throughout the Epistle any express reference to the Gospel. Huther goes somewhat more deeply into the subject; but it still needs a new and more thorough investigation.

It is in itself a significant circumstance, that Düsterdieck himself admits it to be very difficult to determine which of the two writings was the earlier written. This acknowledges that no *difference of time* is anywhere distinctly marked; in which case, we may assuredly venture to hold that they were written *at the same time.* Not, however, in the same hour: the one must have been written after the other. And here Düsterdieck follows Lücke in taking for granted that the Epistle was written after the Gospel. With this assumption we entirely agree, but not with the manner in which it is established. " The bearing of the Epistle, in its doctrinal and polemical positions, is such as to seem to presuppose that the development of them given in the Gospel *was known to the readers*," says Lücke. We cannot altogether assent to this; but hold rather, with Düsterdieck, that "the Epistle stands perfectly independent, and is self-contained;" and that it was quite intelligible in itself and alone, especially to readers who had already enjoyed the oral instruction of the Apostle John. Yet there is something of truth underlying the observation of Lücke. Ideas and trains of thought are repeated from the Gospel in the Epistle; and in such a way, that what is fully expanded or thrown out as opportunity required, is in the Epistle, not " abbreviated," as Lücke says, but yet *concentrated and formally condensed in summary.* But it is marvellous that any man should admit this, and then deny anything like a direct reference in the Epistle to the Gospel! It will not be required by any one that the Apostle should have " expressly," after the manner of modern authors, cited his Gospel, or written, " As I have already taught in my Gospel—"! Is it not quite enough that the Epistle, *as to its substance, rests upon the Gospel?*

But not only so, *it rests upon the Gospel in its very form.* For we have already seen that the absence of the *epistolary form* (the lack of address, greeting, and farewell benediction) is, in fact, then only intelligible when we assume that the document had no independent design as an *epistle* (the substitute of oral discourse), but rested upon something else. Now, if the

Epistle was a kind of dedicatory letter, or companion-document of the Gospel, its peculiar form is perfectly understood.

And that it was so, may be proved or supported by many of its individual passages. Düsterdieck, who denies any express reference in the Epistle to the Gospel, establishes, however, the priority of the Gospel, and says: " One may probably perceive in the profound exhibition of the commandment of love (1 John ii. 7), which is not new, which is old, and which yet is called new, an allusion to the written Gospel (ch. xiii. 34)." More important, and much less dubious,[1] is the passage 1 John i. 1–4. The similarity of the thought with that of the Gospel, ch. i. 14, might be explained by the mere identity of the author; but other things conspire to make the passage refer most expressly to the Gospel. The paragraph, vers. 1–4 (the construction and exposition of which will be treated more at large in the Commentary, where the exegetical establishment will be found of what is here anticipated), falls into two clauses, which are co-ordinated and connected by καί. The governing verb of the first sentence is the ἀπαγγέλλομεν of the third verse; the governing verb of the second sentence is the γράφομεν of ver. 4. The object of the first verb precedes it in ver. 1: "That which was from the beginning, that which we have heard, that which we have seen with our eyes, that which we have contemplated, and our hands have handled, declare we unto you." But to this object there is appositionally appended (not as dependent upon "handled," but as still dependent upon the governing verb "we declare") a closer definition and statement of it: "Concerning the *Word of Life* declare we unto you." In that St John announces that which he had seen and heard, that which he had beheld with his eyes and touched,—he makes announcement concerning "the Word of Life." And *these* words are again illustrated by the parenthesis of ver. 2: "And the Life hath appeared, and we have seen and bear witness, and declare unto you the Life, the Eternal Life, which was with the Father and hath been manifested unto us." The words of the parenthesis, "And we have *seen*, and bear witness and declare," which run parallel with the words of the first clause, "That which we have *seen* and heard, beheld and

---

[1] For, that " the commandment of love" is *not* meant in ch. ii. 7, see the commentary on the passage.

have handled, we *make known* unto you," and which contain a brief recapitulation of that clause, leave us no alternative but to interpret the "Word of Life" and "the Eternal Life" as referring to Something visible to the eyes, and to be touched with the hands;—not therefore to a Doctrine, not to an abstract Power, but only to the *personal Logos, who appeared in the flesh* (and who is personally the ζωή, and that the αἰώνιος; comp. John i. 4; and who is in 1 John v. 20 again expressly so termed); and it is a perfect confirmation of this, that it is said in the close of ver. 2, and that with undeniable backward allusion to John i. 1, 2: "Which was πρὸς τὸν πατέρα, and hath appeared unto us." Thus also, by this parenthesis, the περὶ τοῦ λόγου τῆς ζωῆς—ἀπαγγέλλομεν is more closely defined as an announcement of the Incarnate Logos as *beheld* by St John *qua manifested* (and not of an abstract idea, or of a doctrine); and this again serves for the closer definition of the first object—"That which was from the beginning, which we have heard, which we have *seen with our eyes*, etc." We perceive that St John would have us understand by that which he had heard, seen, and beheld, *not a complex of manifold experiences which he had attained unto concerning the nature and the power of Christian faith, and love, and walk*—or " the idea of the Gospel" (Düsterdieck)—but the *personal Christ*. And when he so declares or announces this Christ, as to make known " that which he *had seen with his eyes, and beheld*, that which *his hands had handled*," must he not necessarily mean by this an announcement of the *concrete manifestation of Christ, and His life?* He does not indeed write ὅν ἑωράκαμεν, κ.τ.λ.: " We declare to you *the Christ*, whom we have beheld and touched," so that the object of the announcement might be the person of Christ according to its abstract idea—the relative clause being then added for closer definition of this person, that it was actually beheld by St John (and not merely imagined and feigned),—but he writes ὅ, " *That which* we have seen, and beheld, and handled, we declare unto you." Thus that which St John had beheld in Christ and of Christ, forms itself the immediate object of the ἀπαγγέλλομεν.

But it may be reasonably asked, whether an announcement *precisely of this kind* does occur in the Epistle; and for any such we look everywhere in vain. For we learn in the Epistle, that

God is light, and that therefore we should not walk in darkness; that the light hath already appeared to us, since we have attained unto the forgiveness of sins, and that we therefore should not again apostatize; that we are the children of God, and that nevertheless, yea on that very account, we have still to bear the hatred of the world, which on our own part, however, we must repay with love; finally, that he who denies the identity of Jesus and the Christ, is antichristian, and belongeth to the darkness. We find pure developments of doctrine and direct dogmas, but never a plain announcement of Christ as such,—not to say any announcement of that which St John had beheld, heard, and handled with his hands!

And this first clause is immediately connected with a second in ver. 4: "And *this* we write unto you, that your joy may be full." The translation, or explanation: "And indeed we write unto you this (that which had been stated in vers. 1–3) on this account, that, etc.," is simply impracticable. Καὶ ταῦτα stands emphatically first, so that ταῦτα does not look back upon and recapitulate the contents of vers. 1–3, but is adjoined to the substance of vers. 1–3 as a *second and different matter*. That this ταῦτα refers to the Epistle is obvious, in the lack of any other specification of its meaning, and is acknowledged by Düsterdieck and Huther. But then the ἀπαγγέλλομεν of vers. 1–3 *cannot* refer to the Epistle, simply because the καὶ ταῦτα γράφομεν is plainly added to that ἀπαγγέλλομεν as something *new* and *different*. So we must rather assume that the Apostle designs in vers. 1–3 to characterize his ordinary (oral) instructions generally to the readers—but how aimless would this have been!—or we must be content to conclude, according to the most obvious and natural solution of the difficulty, that *the words of vers. 1–3 refer directly to the transmission of the Gospel to their hands*, and that in ver. 4 the Apostle further states his purpose to add *this* additional, the Epistle, in order to help his readers to a perfect joy. For, in the Gospel, St John had actually declared that which "was from the beginning" (John i. 1, etc.), and that which the disciples had heard from the lips of Jesus (His discourses), and that which they had seen with their eyes (His miracles), and that which they had beheld (His person, in its Divine δόξα), and that which their hands had handled (His resurrection-body, John xx. 27). Thus much is clear, that, as soon as we refer the " declare we" of ver. 3 to the transmission of the Gospel, all in these verses which otherwise seems confused, and no better than as it were " a certain interweaving and interplay of notions concerning the person and concerning the history and doctrine of Christ" (Düsterdieck), immediately receives life, distinctness, meaning, and force. St John had written his Gospel, and sends it to the Ephesians with the accompaniment of another document; in that announces the former by the words, " That which was from the beginning, etc., we declare unto you;" and then continues : " And *this* (accompanying document) we write unto you, in order to make your joy full." A stricter description of the Gospel was not necessary; for it came to their hands in company with the Epistle; and the words, which were necessarily referred to the Epistle itself, " And *these things* we write," would of themselves lead to the conclusion, that " that which was from the beginning, etc., we declare," must be referred to the accompanying Gospel.

This being so, we may meet the argument which Huther brings forward, by making it prove the contrary of what he intends. He maintains, that " a distinction between the ἀπαγγέλλομεν of ver. 3 and the γράφομεν of ver. 4 is not intimated by anything in the text;" but presently afterwards we find that even he cannot hold the strict and absolute identity of reference between the two words. *Some* distinction he cannot but perceive in them : " ταῦτα refers neither to what precedes merely, nor merely to what immediately follows, but to the whole Epistle." But, we need only observe carefully the manner in which the καὶ ταῦτα γράφομεν is opposed to the ὃ ἀπ' ἀρχῆς, κ.τ.λ., ἀπαγγέλλομεν, to see plainly the necessary distinction between them in the writer's mind. Who would begin a letter with the words, " That which I have experienced, I declare ; and *this Epistle* I write, that, etc.,"—if he wrote at the same time nothing but this letter, and if, moreover, in this letter he actually made known *none* of those experiences? Huther goes on, indeed, to say *:* " ὃ defines not the *life*, but the *person* of Christ; and the question is not here of a *narrative*, but of a *testimony* and a *declarative announcement*." But this is simply contrary to the truth,—the opposite is the case. " That which we have seen with our eyes," etc., cannot indicate, as we have seen above, *the person according to its abstract idea*, but only *the person in its concrete life*. The closer definition of ver. 2 points out to us simply to what *sphere* the " that which was from the beginning, that which we have heard, that which we have seen, etc.," of the first verse refers,—that is, not to any other gracious experiences of St John generally, but to *such* experiences as he had enjoyed περὶ τοῦ λόγου, in reference to *Christ*. The idea of *experience*, however, remains : not *Him whom* we had seen, heard, handled, but *that which* we had heard, seen, and contemplated, concerning Him, we will " declare ;" and by this very characterization of the object the announcement itself is defined as a *narration*. But, that a " testimony," and not a narrative, is the matter here, is so far not true as the " bearing witness" is not in the main clause, but only in the parenthetical explanation ; and, even if the thought of this parenthesis runs parallel with that of the main clause, a thorough exegete like Huther ought not to question, in the face of such passages as John xix. 35, xxi. 24, whether μαρτυρεῖν in St John's phraseology could ever mean a narration ! Is not the μαρτυρεῖν of 1 John i. 2 attached to the ἑωρακέναι precisely as in John xix. 35 ? " He who saw this, beareth witness." "We have seen and bear witness."

To this passage, 1 John i. 1–4, must be added a second, in which we cannot fail to find an equally undeniable reference to the Gospel. I formerly (with Hug) regarded the oft-recurring γράφω and ἔγραψα of the Epistle as referring simply and exclusively to the Gospel;[1] but I must now so far concede to Bleek as to allow that this is not unconditionally and universally the case. But Huther's equally unconditional assertion of the direct contrary is equally erroneous : " We cannot understand why the oft-repeated γράφω and ἔγραψα should not be referred to the Epistle itself, but to another production." In ch. ii. 12, etc., the Apostle founds a triple γράφω upon essentially the same causal positions or arguments on which he founds an immediately-following triple ἔγραψα. " I *write* unto you, children, because your sins are forgiven for His name's sake.

[1] That ταῦτα γράφω, ch. ii. 1, refers to the *Epistle*, and indeed to ch. i. 5–10 primarily, I never denied, but, on the contrary, expressly affirmed (*Kritik der ev. Geschichte*, S. 837) ; and ch. ii. 12, etc., I referred not to the Gospel *alone*, but to " the Epistle and Gospel together."

I *write* unto you, fathers, because ye know Him who is from
the beginning. I *write* unto you, young men, because ye have
overcome the evil one. I *have written to you*, children, because
ye know the Father. I *have written to you*, fathers, because
ye know Him that is from the beginning. I *have written to
you*, young men, because ye are strong, and the word of God
abideth in you, and ye have overcome the wicked one." The
very fact, that in the several fundamental reasons for the several
classes of the clauses there is no essential difference, should drive
us to the conclusion that there must have been a *material distinction* intended in the change from γράφω to ἔγραψα,—unless
we suppose the Apostle to have fallen into an intolerable tautology, and an aimless repetition of his own words (a supposition
which no Christian, and no rational, expositor would entertain
for a moment). But, are Düsterdieck and Huther in a position, on their principle, to point out any such distinction? The
former rightly rejects the artificial supposition of Lücke, according to which the triple γράφω must be referred to the three
following individual exhortations, vers. 15–17, vers. 18–27, and
ch. ii. 28–ch. iii. 22, while the triple ἔγραψα must be referred
to the three preceding fundamental doctrines, ch. i. 5–7, i. 8–
ii. 7, and ii. 3–11. He also rejects (and with equal correctness, as will be shown in the Commentary) the view of Bengel,
who connects γράφω with all that follows, and ἔγραψα with all
that precedes, in the Epistle; and the similar one of De Wette
(followed by Huther), which refers the γράφω to what precedes
and what follows, and the ἔγραψα to what precedes alone.
But Düsterdieck himself—following Beza—explained the
change from γράφω to ἔγραψα by different points of view in
the writer. The object is the same in both cases—that is, the
whole Epistle: when St John writes γράφω, he writes from
the then present moment in which he has the pen in hand;
but when he writes ἔγραψα, he throws himself into the time
when his readers would have the completed Epistle as such in
their hands. Certainly, if the question were to account for one
and the same writer saying γράφω in one place (*e. g.*, 1 John
ii. 1), and in another *quite different* place saying ἔγραψα (*e. g.*,
1 John v. 13), it might be received as a sufficient reason, that
he in the one place wrote as from the present moment, and in
the other transposed himself into the time when his readers

would have the Epistle in their hands.[1] But that St John should have thus played with the tenses, and in *one and the same* passage so distinctly and formally varied the *same* thought, " I write unto you this Epistle, because" etc., as to say: " I am even now occupied, fathers, in writing to you this Epistle, because ye know Him who is from the beginning. I have (when ye read these lines) written this Epistle, because ye know Him that is from the beginning," etc.,—is a solution that we never could be persuaded to receive. De Wette, Brückner, and Huther do not in reality get over this same difficulty; for, according to their view, St John designs to say: " I write unto you this Epistle (the whole of it), because ye know Him that is from the beginning. I have written unto you (already the former part of this Epistle), because ye know Him who is from the beginning." Apart from the fact, that the notion of the making prominent of " *already* in the former part of the Epistle," in opposition to the following part, is not intimated by anything in the text, one cannot see what motive could have impelled the Apostle to say to the readers that he wrote not only that which was to follow, but that also which had already preceded, because they knew the Father and the Son, and had overcome the wicked one. Even supposing this to have been declared to be the aim of the *whole Epistle*, would it not have been self-understood that the first part also of the Epistle was composed to the same end?

Much better worth considering than these expositions— which, in fact, make St John say nothing—is that of Neander, who in the ἔγραψα finds simply a *confirmation* and *intensification* of what had just been stated ("I write unto you, because— As I have said: I have written unto you, because," etc.)—if only this explanation would stand the verbal and grammatical test. But it is necessary to such a confirmation, that what had been already said should be repeated *exactly in the same manner, and without any change of form*. St John must have written, Ὡς εἶπον ὑμῖν· γράψω, ὅτι, κ.τ.λ.; or, ὡς εἶπον ὑμῖν, πάλιν λέγω· γράφω, ὅτι, κ.τ.λ. (comp. Gal. i. 9). And why, finally, should these three particular thoughts have stood in need of such pressing confirmation?

[1] That St John, in ch. v. 13, uses the Aorist, is much more simply and better to be explained by saying that he is now conscious of having come to the end of his Epistle.

Here also all difficulty vanishes, as soon as (with Whiston, Storr, and others) we submit to refer the γράφω to the Epistle itself, and the ἔγραψα to the Gospel, which those who received the Epistle had then in their hands. Instead of an empty play upon words, we receive an equally substantial and solemn testimony of the Apostle, that he would no more have written his Gospel, than he would write this Epistle, to his readers, if he had not known and been able to take for granted that they (ver. 8) had pressed through the darkness to the light, and were firmly established in the light; that they had known the Father as they had known the Son; and that they stood victoriously *above* the temptations which the wicked one now (in the assault of Gnosticism) had prepared for them. Neither the pearl of the μαρτυρία concerning Christ's life in the Gospel, nor that of the paternal exhortation and instruction in the Epistle, was intended or adapted for the children of the world. To both the readers had a right, only as far as they in very deed *knew* the Father in Christ (in the Johannæan sense!), and had already internally conquered the wicked one.

Thus, this passage also indicates that the Epistle must be regarded as a *companion-document to the Gospel.*

V. TIME, AND PLACE, AND CIRCLE OF READERS.

The question as to the time and place of the composition of this Epistle is strictly connected with the same question concerning the Gospel; and we may therefore dismiss it cursorily here, referring to what has been said in an earlier volume.[1] That the Gospel by St John was written *at a later time than the three other Gospels,* has been made abundantly certain; that it was written *after the destruction of Jerusalem,* and even *long after that event,* must appear most clearly and unambiguously from the whole position and character of ecclesiastical matters, as exhibited in the Gospel and in this Epistle (see above, Sect. IV.). The entire contest against a legal Jewish-Christianity, which ruled the Pauline period, is past; and so entirely settled, that to the question concerning the relation of faith and works *to justi-*

[1] Compare, with Olshausen's Introd. to the Gospel, my Kritik der Evang. Gesch. § 140, 141.

fication, regard is no longer paid.[1] So also the entire question as to the relation of the Christian Church to the people of Israel is closed: Israel *has* rejected Christ; hence "οἱ 'Ιουδαῖοι," as such and simply, appear as enemies, in opposition to the Christian community; and of any hope, or obligation, to win Israel *as a people* to the Gospel, there is found absolutely no trace. On the other hand, the Christian Church is already most deeply affected by the threatening onset of that Gnosticism of which, in the time of St Paul, only the preparations and forerunners were seen, and the continuation and further development of which occupied the second century (compare above, Sect. IV.). All this constrains us to place the composition of the Gospel and the First Epistle in the last decade of the first century.

Some have thought that they had found passages in the Epistle and the Gospel which point to an earlier date. Düsterdieck, following Grotius,[2] Hammond, and others, detects in 1 John ii. 18 a reference to the impending destruction of Jerusalem; but with no more propriety than Benson discovered in 1 John ii. 13, etc. an intimation that Christians were still living who had seen the Lord in the flesh: compare, in opposition to both, the commentary on those passages. Huther finds, in the omission of any mention of the destruction of Jerusalem, an argument for the earlier composition of the Epistle; "since the impression which that event must have produced upon the Christians, could not have faded away when the Epistle was composed." But it was not the Apostle's task to mention all the impressions and influences which Christian people had received; and, moreover, there was space enough between A.D. 70 and A.D. 98 for the dying away of the impression even of

---

[1] The assertion of our modern critics, that "the old controversy about justification" is solved in St John's writings by his making "love equally valid with faith in the matter," co-ordinating faith and love in the sinner's justification, has been abundantly refuted by Dusterdieck. As *unjustified*, or *less justified*, even St Paul has never represented love (1 Cor. xiii. 1–3, and 13); as *justifying*, in company with faith, St John never exhibits love.

[2] Grotius has elsewhere (Opp. Tom. iv. p. 463) so far modified his assertion as to admit: "Nomen horae extremae modo totum humanum genus respicit, modo populum Judaicum." It is worthy of note (as Huther shows) that Ignatius (Ep. xi.), long *after* the destruction of Jerusalem, writes: ἐσχατοὶ καιροὶ λοιπόν· αἰσχυνθῶμεν, φοβηθῶμεν τὴν μακροθυμίαν τοῦ Θεοῦ, ἵνα μὴ ἡμῖν εἰς κρίμα γένηται.

the destruction of Jerusalem. Huther, further, discerns in the Gospel, ch. v. 2, positive proof that Jerusalem had not been destroyed when the Gospel was written—which, according to our conviction, was accompanied by the Epistle. He thinks it clear that "not only the pool of Bethesda, but also the five porches, and the sheep-gate of the Temple, were still remaining." We do not (with Meyer) oppose this argument by adducing the passages, ch. xi. 18, xviii. 1, xix. 41, in which various localities in and near Jerusalem (Bethany, Gethsemane, the sepulchre of Joseph of Arimathea) are introduced with $ἦν$. We acknowledge that in the later passages the Imperfect does *not* constrain us to the assumption, "that Jerusalem destroyed lay in the background of the Apostle's representation;" but that St John, relating past events in the Aorist, added also the explanatory notices concerning the localities in the Imperfect. But then we also, conversely, require it to be acknowledged, that if St John once makes use of the *præsens historicum, so very familiar with him,* in giving such explanatory notices, it ought not to be at once concluded that the place in question lay as yet undestroyed in the background of his representation. St John narrates in an entirely objective manner, thinking altogether and only of the occurrence which is to be recorded, and not at all reflecting upon the state of things at the then present moment of his writing. He who denies this in relation to John v. 2, must also, to be consistent, deny it in relation to chs. xi. 18, xviii. 1, xix. 41. For, *only on the ground of this objectivity in St John's point of view in historical narration* can we make the concession, that in *these three* passages the Imperfect tense cannot be the foundation of an argument that the destruction of Jerusalem had taken place. In the case of any other, less objective and more reflecting, author, such a conclusion would be amply justified. When Goethe (W. und D. I. Buch v.) writes: "The Court-house is a regular and handsome building, towards the Maine," we rightly conclude that, at the time when Goethe wrote, the Court-house was yet standing (as it is now standing); but when he elsewhere writes: "The locality was neither pleasant nor convenient, since they have forced," etc., or, "A turret-like flight of steps led up to unconnected chambers," every one must see at once that he is describing localities which, when he wrote, stood no longer in this form.

Goethe would never have written, concerning the afterwards altered house of his parents: "A turret-like flight of steps *leads* up to unconnected chambers," any more than he would have written, concerning the still standing Court-house: "The Court-house *was* a regular and handsome building, towards the Maine!" And if, in relation to ch. v. 2, an analogous style of writing is presupposed in St John, then, in relation to the passages xi. 18, etc., we must come to the conclusion that "St John would never have written ἦν, if Jerusalem had been when he wrote still undestroyed." But the very contradiction which is the result of forcing upon St John this exact style of writing, makes it evident that the one conclusion would be as wrong as the other, and that St John, in *both* passages, wrote without any reflection upon what, at the time of his writing, was still remaining or had been altered,—using now the descriptive Present, and now the descriptive Imperfect. The certainty that both Gospel and Epistle were written long *after* the destruction of Jerusalem, is, therefore, not at all affected by the passage, John v. 2.

And to this conclusion we are led by *patristic tradition* also. On the later, and somewhat ambiguously-worded, passage in Epiph. Hær. 51, 12,[1] we lay no particular stress. Most weighty is the account of Irenæus (Hær. 3, 1, in Euseb. v. 8): ἔπειτα Ἰωάννης, ὁ μαθητὴς τοῦ Κυρίου, ὁ καὶ ἐπὶ στῆθος αὐτοῦ ἀναπεσὼν, καὶ αὐτὸς ἐξέδωκε τὸ εὐαγγέλιον, ἐν Ἐφέσῳ τῆς Ἀσίας διατρίβων. He is followed by Chrys. and Theod. of Mopsuestia. And the tradition which was widely circulated among the Fathers, that St John wrote his Gospel in his exile in Patmos, does not contradict that evidence. Dorotheus of Tyre, and the author of the Synopsis printed with the works of Athanasius, remark alike[2] that St John *wrote* his Gospel when an exile in Patmos, and then published it in *Ephesus* by means of his ἀγαπητὸς καὶ ξενοδόχος, the deacon Gaius. This account has sufficient *external foundation;* since Theophylact and the pseudo Hippolytus, and a multitude of later MSS., mention Patmos as the place of its composition. It has also *great internal probability* on its side; for it is only the separation of St John from his flock which explains the necessity of a written compensation

---

[1] Compare Meyer, Comm. zum Ev. Joh., Einleit. § 5.
[2] See the passages in my Kritik der evang. Gesch. S. 871.

for his now-lacking oral μαρτυρία. But if St John wrote his Gospel in Patmos, and sent it by his confidential friend to the Church of Ephesus, it becomes perfectly intelligible, first, that he did not think it needful to mention his name in the companion-document; and secondly, how it was possible for Irenæus to say that the Gospel must be placed in the Apostle's residence at Ephesus (in opposition to his earlier abode in Palestine). That report of Gaius bears, moreover, the plain stamp of historical tradition, and not at all that of a mere conjecture or invention resting upon supposed grounds.

The exile in Patmos must be placed in the last years of Domitian, about A.D. 94–97.[1] In all probability the Gospel, together with our Epistle, was written at the outset of this banishment—when the need of a written compensation for the cessation of his oral instructions and pastoral care would be felt most vividly, both by the Apostle and the Church,—and in any case before the Apocalypse.[2] That the latter refers to the Gospel, has been shown in the Commentary on the Apocalypse. And the twenty-first chapter of the Gospel appears to speak in favour of this assumption. For it is internally probable that this chapter was *then* added—through the Apostle, or by his instruction to Gaius—supplementarily to the Gospel, when the prophecy, ch. xxi. 22 ("If I will that he tarry till I *come*"), which originally appeared to affect only St John *personally*, attained an importance for the Church; that is, *then*, when the Lord in His revelation "had *come* to St John," and His "*coming*" (Rev. i. 7, xxii. 20) had been by St John seen in vision. For in the words of John xxi. 22 were contained a preceding foreannouncement, and consequently an authentication, of the revelations contained in the Apocalypse.

The *readers* of the Epistle we consequently must seek in the Church of Ephesus, doubtless including the neighbouring churches of Proconsular Asia.

It is of no great moment that a solitary intimation of

---

[1] According to Jerome (Vir. Ill. ix.), St John wrote the Apocalypse when an exile in Patmos, in the fourteenth year of Domitian (95); and under Nerva (96-98) obtained permission to return to Ephesus.

[2] That the better Greek of the Gospel and Epistle (to which Olshausen appeals for the priority of the Apocalypse) is *no* argument against our supposition, has been shown in the Commentary on the Apocalypse.

Augustin[1] asserts our Epistle to have been written *to the Parthians*;[2] it is generally acknowledged that not much weight is to be attached to this single evidence.[3] Augustin himself nowhere else mentions, often as he speaks of this Epistle, this destination for the Parthians; so that we have only to inquire how these isolated words could have originated. Scarcely could they have come from Augustin himself. Clemens Alexandrinus (Fragm. Adum. Oxf. edit. ii. 1011) mentions that the Second Epistle of St John was written *ad Virgines* (πρὸς παρθένους): he understood the ἐκλεκτὴ Κυρία, 2 John 1, allegorically; and hence, also, allegorically interpreted τὰ τέκνα αὐτῆς, in the sense of Rev. xiv. 4, as παρθένους. This view was widely extended; for in some manuscripts 2 John bears the simple superscription, πρὸς παρθένους. It would appear that the meaning of this πρὸς παρθένους was soon entirely lost; and hence that the superscription was soon (as *e.g.* Cassiodor. de Instit. Div. Script. cap. 14) appropriated to all the three Epistles. But the word, being misunderstood, was soon further changed into *ad Parthos*. (Other less probable attempts to explain it may be seen in Düsterdieck.)

Not in Parthia, and not even in Palestine (as Benson thought), nor in Corinth (Lightfoot), but in Ephesus and the country around, are we to seek for the readers of this Epistle. This may now be accepted as the firm and certain result of critical investigation.

---

[1] Secundum sententiam hanc etiam illud est, quod dictum est a Johanne in epistola ad Parthos. (Quæst. Evang. ii. 39.)

[2] That is, to the Christians living, not under Roman dominion, but in the Parthian Empire, east of the Euphrates.

[3] Possidius, in his *Indiculum operum Augustini*, entitled the tractates of Augustin on 1 John as *de Ep. Joannis ad Parthos sermones decem*. Vigilius Tapsensis, Cassiodorus, and Beda, copied this *ad Parthos*. Grotius thought Augustin's notice worthy of credit (Opp. iii. 1126), and conjectured that St John omitted his name to avoid doing any injury to the Christians who lived in a state opposed to Rome (!). The Heidelberg Paulus imagined that, not the Apostle, but the Presbyter John, wrote the Epistle to Parthian Christians in order to oppose a "magian-Parthian Gnosis," of the existence of which he had been informed by cameldrivers (!).

VI. DICTION AND TONE OF THE EPISTLE.

As the peculiarities of style which mark this Epistle have been already in Sect. III. mentioned at some length, we have now only a few observations to make upon the Johannæan style of writing as it is specifically seen in this *Epistle* as such. St John's was not a dialectic, but a contemplative, nature. Hence he does not *logically* arrange, and deduce, and expand individual ideas, but takes a leading idea as the object of internal contemplation; and with it he connects, though without any logical medium, the consequences which flow from it for the Christian consciousness of experience. "Even the establishment and reason of an idea is in the simplest manner given, by referring it to a truth the authentication of which is in the Christian consciousness itself" (Huther). Often there is the semblance of the repetition of the same thought; but closer investigation shows that every new turn given to it brings to light some new element of its meaning: he lets the individual positions or truths, filled with life, sparkle in the light like precious stones, that the eye may penetrate to their hidden meaning. His own language itself is as simple as possible, but as profound as it is simple. "All his characteristic words, in all their simplicity of sound—*life, light, truth, love, righteousness, abiding in God*, etc.—who can perfectly fathom and expound the meaning which they contain? He who ventures upon them with only his analytical understanding, and merely philological learning, will find that they remain unintelligible hieroglyphics; their internal essence is disclosed to us in proportion as we experience in our own souls that of which they speak." (Huther.) And thus the Epistle itself reflects a mind penetrated through and through by the light of the Spirit of God. "Whether the Apostle is unfolding Divine truths in themselves, or speaking in exhortation and warning to his readers, his language always retains the same uniform repose and precision; he never betrays a disposition moved to passion; everywhere is reflected the stillness of a heart resting in sacred peace, and in which he is assured that the simple utterance of the truth is enough to secure an entrance for his words into the minds of his readers. At the same time, there reigns throughout the Epistle a firm and manly tone, the perfect opposite of all effeminate and sentimental enthusiasm.—It is also observable that while, on the one hand, he speaks to his readers as a father speaking to his children, on the other hand, he never forgets that they are no longer babes to whom he has something new to communicate, but that they are altogether equal to himself, possessed like himself of all the truth which he announces, and of all the life which it is not for him to create in them, but only to strive to preserve and increase." (Huther.)

The Epistle is "a work of holy love. It appears to the simplest reader, who only has an experience of Christian salvation in his heart, immediately intelligible; while to the most profound Christian thinker it is unfathomable. To both, it is equally dear and stimulating." (Düsterdieck.)

And thus the expositor, like the readers, hears the cry at the entrance: "Put off thy shoes from off thy feet, for the place whereon thou standest is holy ground."

VII. LITERATURE.

Among the commentaries of the Fathers upon this Epistle, those of Diodorus and Chrysostom are altogether lost, and those of Clemens Alex. and Didymus are preserved only in fragments; on the other hand, the Catenæ of Œcumenius and Theophylact, the *Expositio* of Augustin, and that of Bede, are still extant, and have been very diligently used by later expositors.

Of the period of the Reformation, we may mention, besides the *Adnotationes* of Erasmus, Luther's two expositions, and Zwingle's. More important exegetically are Bullinger's *In ep. Johannis brevis et catholica expositio;* Gignæus *Expl. Epist. Cathol.;* and the well-known commentaries of Calvin and Beza, which include this Epistle.

In the interval between the Reformation and the rise of Rationalism, much was done upon 1 John. The celebrated Arminian Grotius (*Annott. in Ep. Joan. primam,* and *Commentatio ad loca N. T. quæ de Antichristo agunt*) was opposed by the rigid Lutheran Calovius (*Bibl. N. T. illustrata*). Of commentators who explained the entire New Testament, and who are worthy of notice upon 1 John, we may mention Piscator, Hammond, Bengel, Whitby, Rosenmüller, Beausobre, to whom Benson may be added: among those who wrote commentaries upon the Catholic Epistles, may be named Aretius (1589), Alsted (1640), Hornejus (1652), J. B. Carpzov (1790). Whiston wrote a special commentary upon the three Epistles of St John (London 1719); and so also did Weber (Halle 1778) and Schirmer (Breslau 1780). Upon the 1st Epistle of St John alone, we have the commentaries of Socinus (Rakau 1614), Episcopius (Amsterdam 1665), Spener (Practical Exposition), Hunnius, and S. Schmidt.

Of the Rationalist time, we may mention Oertel (über die drei Briefe Joh.), Morus, S. G. Lange, Paulus (on the Three Epistles), and Semler (1 John). In the transition-period are Augusti (katholische Briefe, 1808) and Lachmann (k. Briefe, 1838), but especially Lücke (Evangelium und Briefe Johan. 1836). Of a more recent date are Neander (part of 1 John practically explained, 1851), Wolf, Sander; but especially the thorough, though sometimes too diffuse, work of F. Düsterdieck (Die drei Johanneischen Briefe, Göttingen 1852), which has been followed by the briefer commentary of Huther (as part of Meyer's Commentary on the New Testament, 1855).

EXPOSITION.

THE EXORDIUM.

Ch. i. 1-4.

THAT which we have already in Sect. IV. of the Introduction exhibited in its main points of importance, we shall now more fundamentally and at length expound.

The paragraph which forms the entrance to the Epistle, vers. 1–4, is—as far as concerns the construction of its former part, vers. 1–3—somewhat obscure and involved: it admits, viewed grammatically alone, of three methods of construing. That ὃ ἦν ἀπ' ἀρχῆς is the grammatical object, admits of no doubt; the only question is, What is the main verb on which that object hangs? *First*, it would be possible (with Paulus) to make χεῖρες the subject, and ἐψηλάφησαν the main verb: "That which was from the beginning, that which we have heard, that which we have seen with our eyes, that also our hands have handled." But no sane expositor would fall into this error; partly, because there is not in the sense any such contrast, as made prominent by καί, between the handling and the seeing, and, partly, because the succeeding περὶ τοῦ λόγου τῆς ζωῆς *cannot* depend upon the verb ἐψηλάφησαν, on which that explanation would make it depend, inasmuch as one may handle "an object," but not "in relation to an object."— *Secondly*, we might (with Erasmus and Carpzov) take the words of ver. 2, καὶ ἑωράκαμεν καὶ μαρτυροῦμεν καὶ ἀπαγγέλλομεν, κ.τ.λ., as the main verbs; and then περὶ τοῦ λόγου τῆς ζωῆς would still depend upon ἐψηλάφησαν, while the words καὶ ἡ ζωὴ ἐφανερώθη would form a parenthesis. This construction is the most unnatural of all: in that case the governing verb would receive *two objects*—the preceding " that which was, etc.," and the following " eternal life;" and we should be obliged to suppose that the author—constrained by the brief intervening parenthesis—took up again in a new form the object, which had been already so copiously unfolded. The only way of escaping from the difficulty, on that hypothesis, would be to place a colon after καὶ ἀπαγγέλλομεν, ver. 2, and to refer the first two verbs in ver. 2 backward to ver. 1, but the third forward to τὴν ζωήν—which, however, would be still more unnatural. Thus there remains only the *third* construction, which the immense majority of expositors defend, and according to which ἀπαγγέλλομεν, ver. 3, is the main governing verb, on which the object, ὃ ἦν, κ.τ.λ., depends. A difference which divides Winer and De Wette here, vanishes when closely looked at. Winer (in his Grammar, § 65) would begin the after-clause with περὶ τοῦ λόγου, κ.τ.λ.; he assumes that the Apostle had it originally in his mind to continue thus: περὶ τοῦ λόγου τῆς ζωῆς ἀπαγγέλλομεν ὑμῖν (in which case the words περὶ, etc., would be a brief compendium of ὃ ἦν, etc.), but that, having interposed the parenthesis of ver. 2, he was thereby laid under the necessity of resuming from the beginning, in ver. 3, the sentence begun in ver. 1. On the other hand, De Wette and others begin the after-clause first in ver. 3; and then, while the whole of ver. 2 (as in Winer's explanation) is a parenthesis still, the words περὶ τοῦ λόγου τῆς ζωῆς still belong to the relative clause. As it regards this last point, thus much is clear, that περὶ cannot possibly depend upon the verb ἐψηλάφησαν, or upon the verbs ἀκηκόαμεν, ἑωράκαμεν, ἐθεασάμεθα, and ἐψηλάφησαν together (against Theophyl., Œcumenius, Erasmus, Beza, Grotius, Bengel, etc.; comp. Luther, Winer, De Wette, Neander). Therefore, we must either assume that the words περὶ, etc., form a kind of *apposition* to the objective clause ὃ ἦν—ἐψηλάφησαν, " in order to define more closely the indefinite ὅ,"—or we must make περὶ immediately dependent upon the subsequent governing verb ἀπαγγέλλομεν in ver. 3 (" That which was from the beginning, which we have, etc.,—that is, concerning the word of life—we announce unto you"): but these two methods of construction are as little different from each other, as they are distinguished from that of Winer. The appearance of difference arises only from the needless question, as to where the after-clause begins; whereas, in fact, there is no antecedent and no after-clause, and therefore no line of distinction between them, but only one quite *simple sentence*, consisting of the *verb* ἀπαγγέλλομεν and the *object*, the τοῦτο latent in the ὅ, which contains in itself a chain of relative clauses (ὃ ἦν—ἐψηλάφησαν), and then is again summed up in the appositional addition περὶ, κ.τ.λ. Thus, the appositional clause, equally with the objective clause preceding it, depends immediately upon the ἀπαγγέλλομεν; consequently, St John had already in ver. 1 the ἀπαγγέλλομεν in his mind and in his meaning. After the long parenthesis, ver. 2, St John recapitulates the *main object*, ὃ ἦν ἀπ᾽ ἀρχῆς—ἐψηλάφησαν, but only in the abbreviated form ὃ ἑωράκαμεν καὶ ἀκηκόαμεν.

Having now settled the *construction of the sentence*, vers. 1-3, we can turn to the exposition of the individual clauses.

We begin with the main verb, ἀπαγγέλλομεν, ver. 3, in which the *subject of the proposition*, "we," is contained. Beausobre, Grotius, and Bengel suppose that the plural was used because the Apostle would unite the other Apostles with himself,—it being thought that the familiar style of the Epistle would not permit a rhetorical *pluralis majesticus*. Yet St John writes in ver. 4 ταῦτα γράφομεν, in the plural, where we cannot imagine him to refer to the collective Epistles of collective Apostles! So also, in the "we make known," he does not mean to refer to the general communications of the Apostles as a body, but to *his own* announcement; and the plural must here, as in the case of "we write," be regarded as a more solemn form of speech—strictly in harmony with the elevated and glowing language of the exordium. We must not class this plural with the common collective plural which we find in vers. 6, 7, 8, and often elsewhere, and in which St John by the "we" unites his readers with himself. But it is not on that account a mere rhetorical form. St John is speaking of *himself* and *his* announcement and writing (not of that of the other Apostles, comp. ver. 5); thus, however, he does not feel himself to be a fortuitous private individual—an isolated I over-against his readers—but an *authority*, armed and authenticated by Christ and the Holy Spirit,—an authority which, in the consciousness of standing connected with all the messengers and servants of Christ (Lücke), had a perfect right to address to the readers the "We" of full dignity and prerogative. (Compare the analogous plural, ch. iv. 14.) But the plural ἀπαγγέλλομεν is doubly intelligible, when we remember that the plurals ἀκηκόαμεν, κ.τ.λ., have preceded, in which St John includes himself in the number of all the eyewitnesses of the life of Christ.

The predicative idea of the ἀπαγγέλλειν is clear in itself; its more exact specification it receives from the *object*.

That object consists, as we already know, of the relative sentence ὃ ἦν—ἐψηλάφησαν. As the proper objective Accusative to the governing verb ἀπαγγέλλομεν, we must supply a τοῦτο, which is latently contained in the relative ὅ. But the relative sentence is itself composed of more members than one: it falls, indeed, into two divisions, as the ὅ is first the subjective Nominative with the ἦν, and then takes the place of the objective Accusative with the verbs ἀκηκόαμεν, ἑωράκαμεν, ἐθεασάμεθα, ἐψηλάφησαν. In the first clause is stated what or how the object is in itself; in the second clause, the relation in which St John stood to it.

Ὃ ἦν ἀπ' ἀρχῆς.—Here at once is seen most evident that peculiarity of St John's language which consists in his presenting in most simple, and apparently transparent, words an almost unsearchable substance of meaning. The words in themselves would bear the mere grammatical and lexical interpretation, "That which was from the beginning, we declare unto you:" these words, considered in themselves, may say all that it is possible to say; and yet, when they are isolated, they declare fundamentally nothing. A philosopher, who would exhibit a truth held from all time—a natural philosopher, who would exhibit a law of nature established from the beginning —a historian, who would exhibit the primitive history of the world and humanity,—all might, each in his own sense, commence with the words, ὃ ἦν ἀπ' ἀρχῆς ἀπαγγέλλομεν. But it is not right, on that account, with so many expositors, to raise the question at once, whether by the ὅ—that which was from the beginning—be meant *a dogmatic object* (Theoph., Œcum., Socinus: the doctrine that God was manifested in the flesh), or a real *substantial essence* (the ζωή, De Wette, Huther), or *the personal Logos or Christ* (Calvin, Beza, Luther, Calov, Bengel, Lücke, Sander). The words of themselves furnish no means for the settlement of this question. Indefinite, and obscure, and mysterious are the words with which St John *begins*, "That which was from the beginning;" only the following members serve to make it more and more plainly evident what is present before his spirit. Thus we must seek our instruction as to the meaning of this first clause from that which follows.

The second member, ὃ ἀκηκόαμεν, ὃ ἑωράκαμεν τοῖς ὀφθαλμοῖς ἡμῶν, ὃ ἐθεασάμεθα καὶ αἱ χεῖρες ἡμῶν ἐψηλάφησαν, falls into a fourfold distribution of sub-members. What strikes the eye immediately here, is the progress from the more general to the more specific and energetic—that elevation and increase of meaning which Bullinger so beautifully describes: "There is in the words a wonderful intensification. It was not enough that he said, *We have heard;* he adds, that which *we have seen;* and, not content with that, subjoins *with our eyes*: moreover, there is still something more weighty: *that which we have beheld;* and then, above all the rest, *and our hands have handled.* St John advances from the more distant relation to that which is nearer, straiter, and more internal: that which he has to announce was *heard of* by him (and his fellow-disciples); and, still more, *seen with the eyes;* yea, *contemplated;* and even *handled with hands.* Thus, most assuredly, he would oppose that which he announces—as an absolutely undoubted, and immediately *sure, true,* and *experienced* reality—to all that is merely imagined, speculated upon, and dreamed about.

But this general view of the climax lying before us, and its design, does not complete the exegetical comprehension of the words of the text. Still limiting ourselves for a while to the merely formal arrangement, we are struck with the fact, that the four members of the sentence move in a duplicate connection throughout. Ἀκηκόαμεν stands without any more direct appendage; the next member, ἑωράκαμεν, marks of itself a progression (since the hearing may be through a medium, but the seeing must always be immediate), but made still more emphatically so by the appendage τοῖς ὀφθαλμοῖς ἡμῶν, which gives prominence to the immediate character of sight. The third member, ἐθεασάμεθα, without any appendage, is once more parallel with the first; while the fourth, which advances from the seeing to the still more immediate touching, and therefore again does not leave unmentioned the χεῖρες, is parallel with the second. Thus these four members form a proper climax—a ladder of three steps. In the first pair of members, the writer advances from the first stage of *hearing* to the second and higher stage of *seeing with the eyes*. In the second pair, he takes his stand upon this stage of seeing, which nevertheless, by a delicate internalization of the idea, is described as a *beholding*, and rises from it to the third stage of *touching with the hands*.

And what is the material advantage, for the understanding of the meaning which St John connected with these words, gained by this observation? In itself it throws a considerable measure of clearness upon the whole. We learn that "that which was from the beginning," and which he "declares," was somewhat not only heard by him, but beheld with his own eyes, and even handled with his own hands. Had it been only something heard by him, we might have interpreted it (with Theophylact, Œcumenius, and Socinus) of a doctrine, a dogma, or a truth. Had it been only something seen with his eyes, we might have accepted the notion of De Wette, that the power of the new life implanted in humanity by Christ was meant,—a power which St John had not only experienced in himself, but the fruits of which he had seen with his own eyes. But, when he describes that which he announced to be also something which he had handled with his hands, and when it is certain that he is not referring to any allegorical meaning of a spiritual touch, which altogether destroys the climax—nothing remains but to admit that *Christ Himself manifest in the flesh* alone was the object which St John had in view in this sentence. For neither His doctrine, nor the life infused by Him, could be touched; but the disciples did handle with their hands *Him, the Incarnate One*. "Every pressure of the hands was a handling of Him who had actually become flesh" (Düsterdieck). The disciples touched the Lord, in conformity with His own command, Luke xxiv. 39 : ψηλαφήσατέ με καὶ ἴδετε. And who does not think of the passage, John xx. 27, where Thomas placed his *hand* in the side of the risen Lord?

If we now return back to the first main member of the relative clause, ὃ ἦν ἀπ' ἀρχῆς, it is plain that St John here also cannot have in his meaning a doctrine, or a reality of existence in fact, but no other than the personal Lord. For there are not two distinct objects of the ἀπαγγελια which he names (else they would have been connected together by a καί), but it is one and the same object viewed on different sides. The same object of announcement whom St John heard, and saw with his eyes, and beheld, yea, handled with his hands, is also He that was "from the beginning." It was Christ whom he saw and touched; of Christ, therefore, it is said, He was from the beginning. In what sense, we are taught by a glance at the Gospel, without the first chapter of which our passage would indeed present a very startling obscurity of expression. *As an allusion to John* i. 1, *etc., the words* ὃ ἦν ἀπ' ἀρχῆς *are perfectly clear.* There it had been said, that ἐν ἀρχῇ the λόγος was; and that as a Word which God "to God" spake, and which was Itself God, and by which God created all things; and that this Word became flesh, and appeared visible upon earth. That which was in the Gospel more diffusely expanded, in the development of all its main points, is here condensed in energetic brevity. The Object which St John declared was both these in one: it had been from the beginning, and it had been seen and touched as visible and tangible. Most assuredly the fundamental theme of the Gospel is here referred to,—that *identity* of the Eternal Logos with the visible Jesus which, in opposition to the Cerinthian gnosis,[1] formed the kernel and heart of revealed truth; a truth which was not, like the figments of Cerinthus, invented or dreamed of, but which had been seen by St John's eyes, when he looked upon and handled the Incarnate One as a visible man, and beheld and experienced in Him the eternal δόξα of the Father.

Thus the ἀρχή is here, as in John i., not the temporal beginning-point of history or chronology, either of our earth (as in Matt. xix. 4 and 8), or (as in Gen. i. 1) of the universe, but that *eternal* ἀρχή and primal being in which the λόγος is exhibited to have been a λόγος πρὸς τὸν Θεὸν ὤν (John i. 1 and

---

[1] The polemical reference of ver. 1 was evidently felt by Luther, who writes: "He heaps up words, and thus makes the matter as great and weighty as may be. We have, he means to say, carefully and with all diligence beheld and observed what we declare; we were not deceived, but are sure that there was no delusion. He says this because he would make his readers also sure of the matter."

2), before as yet (ver. 3) anything is said of a creation of the world (comp. John xvii. 5). The expression ἀπ' ἀρχῆς is not substantially different from the expression ἐν ἀρχῇ (John i. 1): ἀπ' ἀρχῆς is written here by St John, because he has already in his mind his own having seen and having touched the Incarnate Lord, transposes himself into the *subjective* position of his own experience, and from that point of view would declare that He whom he had beheld had already been *from the beginning*. In the Gospel, ch. i. 1, on the other hand, St John begins *objectively* to unfold the eternal being of the Logos, and therefore can write only, " *In the beginning* was the λόγος."

Accordingly, the Object of St John's announcement is *Christ*: thus much is gained by the examination of the individual members of the relative clause. But this is far from exhausting the exegetical investigation of this first verse. The question arises, whether then this relative clause, one and fourfold, is merely a *paraphrase of the idea* " Christ," so that the concise sense of the whole would be, " We declare unto you Christ ;" as a panegyrist upon Goethe might begin : " To him who was born at Frankfort, who as a youth began to spread the wings of his poetic fancy, who studied at Leipzig and Strassburg, who spent the greatest part of his long life at Weimar, whom Germany honours as her greatest poet—to him this hour is devoted." Do the individual members of the relative clause serve the purpose in any way of making known *who* is meant? Assuredly not. It cannot be the object of the climax to heap up marks and notes by which it may be discerned that St John intended to speak of Jesus Christ, and *of no other;* but, as we have already seen, that progression was designed to exhibit *that which* was to be declared concerning Christ as an absolutely certain and experienced truth. *And thus we understand why the author connected the members of the relative clause, not by* ὅς—ὅν, *but by the neuter* ὅ.[1]

[1] In opposition to the view of Socinus, who concluded from the neuter ὅ that not Christ, but a doctrine or an idea, must have been meant. Also to the assertion of Beza and Calovius, that by means of the ὅ the two natures of Christ were to be represented in their union (!). Huther says, quite erroneously, and in contradiction to his elsewhere-expressed views : "The neuter ὅ is explained by this, that it refers to ζωή, an idea abstract in itself." But where is there the shadow of a grammatical reference between ὅ and ζωή?

If he had written, "Him, who was from the beginning, whom we have heard, etc., we announce unto you," then might we, with some appearance of right, have thought of an abstract Christ-*idea* as the object of the ἀπαγγέλλειν, or of the Christ-*dogma* (that He, to wit, was to be declared as He who was at once eternal and incarnate, at once One who was eternal and One that became visible and tangible). The neutral ὅ forbids our adopting this notion. It is the Person, concerning whom both the ἀπ' ἀρχῆς εἶναι and the ὀφθῆναι κ.τ.λ. at once hold good, that is to be declared—*quoad* His person; but also that *Being* which was from the beginning was to be announced, and as that *which* St John had heard, seen with his eyes, and handled, in and concerning Him. Even Lücke—who originally, misconceiving the predicates ἦν ἀπ' ἀρχῆς, etc., represents the "Gospel" as the object of the ἀπαγγέλλειν—cannot avoid acknowledging, nevertheless, that "with the idea of the Gospel *the person of Christ*, and the person of Christ *in its entire history and work*, is combined." That the object of the announcement is not the idea of the Gospel, *but* the person of Christ, has been shown by the predicative ideas, "was from the beginning," "seen," "touched;" that this Person was to be announced not as *abstract*, but in its historical manifestation, is shown by the neutral subject and object ὅ. The one- and four-membered relative clause does not serve the purpose of giving marks by which the reader may know *who* is meant, but to tell the reader *what* was to be declared concerning Him. Hence, then, the members of the relative clause are summed up, not in the words τὸν λόγον τῆς ζωῆς, but in the words περὶ τοῦ λόγου τ. ζ.

This being so, the four members, ἀκηκόαμεν, etc., receive a new and living reference to *that which* St John had experimentally known in Christ, to the individual phases or sides of His manifestation in the flesh. The last member, "handled with our hands," obliges us at once to think of Luke xxiv. 39, John xx. 27. The "hearing" reminds us involuntarily, in the same way, of all that the disciples had heard from the lips of Jesus, of all His discourses. The "seeing with our eyes" suggests immediately all the miracles and wonderful works which they had witnessed; while the more internal θεᾶσθαι will refer of itself to the beholding and discerning of the "glory of the Father" which shone through His whole life. (Compare John i. 14, καὶ ἐθεασάμεθα τὴν δόξαν αὐτοῦ.) Thus, behind or beneath the climax of the *modus percipiendi* there glimmers another climax of the object perceived. The Being, which was from the beginning, which (to wit, His words) he had heard, which (to wit, His miracles) he had seen with his eyes, which (to wit, His Divine glory) he had beheld, which (to wit, His resurrection-body) he had handled with his hands,—that Being he declares, and therewith declares "*that which* he had heard, seen with the eyes, beheld, handled with his hands"—the acts and the life of this Being, the Person in its historical manifestation.

This way of understanding the previous words finds now its full confirmation in the appositional clause περὶ τοῦ λόγου τῆς ζωῆς, which again is laid open and developed in the parenthetical unfolding of ver. 2.[1] A proper apposition, in the strict grammatical sense, περὶ τοῦ λόγου τ. ζ. cannot be, since that only bears the name of "apposition" which stands in the same Case with what precedes. But it is an appositional clause, which in its meaning represents a strict apposition. "That which was from the beginning, that which we have heard, etc., we declare unto you; and thereby we declare unto you what concerns, or something about, the Word of Life." It has been already shown that περὶ could not possibly (Fritzsche) depend upon the four previous verbs. Ἀκούειν is the only one which could have περὶ following it;—but even this would be very unsuitable here, since St John is not saying that he had heard something concerning Jesus, *de Jesu*, but that he had heard Jesus Himself. The remaining verbs cannot consistently with their meaning have a περὶ depending upon them; and a partitive ἀπὸ (that *of* Jesus which we have seen, etc.) περὶ cannot possibly here represent. Consequently, περὶ must depend upon the principal verb ἀπαγγέλλομεν; and the περὶ τ. λ. τ. ζ.

---

[1] It is strange that Sander should represent the grand impression of the whole as weakened by the second verse being made a parenthesis. As if a clause, which, *grammatically considered*, holds the place of a parenthesis—since it does not syntactically depend upon any portion of the previous clause, but rests in its own isolation—could not by its own matter, and indeed in its very isolation, have a grandeur of its own! When Sander alleges a breaking down of the construction, and confusion introduced into the arrangement of the words, what is that but admitting the *grammatical isolation* of ver. 2?

must be regarded as a closer definition of the object, something added to the object in order to explain it.

But what, then, is the meaning of this defining sentence? The Genitive τῆς ζωῆς may, regarded in itself, be variously viewed. It may be the *Genitivus objecti*, according to the analogy of λόγος τοῦ σταυροῦ, 1 Cor. i. 18; λόγος τῆς καταλλαγῆς, 2 Cor. v. 19; and, in this case, the introduction of such an objective Genitive defines the idea of the λόγος as that of an *announcement or doctrine*. The word *concerning the* life would be equivalent to the doctrine concerning life, the preaching concerning life. Or, we may take the Genitive here as the Genitive *of the closer definition of the property* of the thing itself, as in Phil. ii. 16; John vi. 68; Acts ii. 28; and then the "word of life" would be equivalent to "the word which is living," or "the life-giving word, bearing in it and bestowing the power of life,"—the "word" being understood in the sense of "preaching." Or, we may finally take the Genitive as the *Genitive of the substance:* the λόγος, He in whom the life is (so Œcumenius, Zwingli, Calvin, Beza, Bengel, Olshausen, Lücke); in which case the λόγος must be understood in the supreme sense of John i. 1. What De Wette urges against this last view—that περὶ would be very inappropriate for the description of an object—does indeed press fatally upon the two former views. That is, if we understand by the λόγος τῆς ζωῆς the *doctrine* or *preaching* concerning life, or the vivifying *doctrine,* St John would have said that he announced *the* doctrine itself, and not *concerning* the doctrine; but if, on the other hand, we take λόγος as the personal Logos in the sense of John i. i, St John writes with perfect propriety: while he announces what he had heard, seen, and handled, he gives an annunciation *of* the Logos, *about* the Logos. This περὶ is strictly parallel with the neutral ὅ. As he did not design to write, "*Him whom* we have seen we announce to you," but "*That which* (in, on, and of Him) we have seen"—as he does not purpose to say that he announces Christ as an abstract single *idea,* but that he declares his own concrete historical *experiences* concerning Christ,—so now he continues, not "*the* Logos," but "concerning the Logos," we make annunciation to you.

But what speaks most loudly in favour of the λόγος being

the personal Word, is the undoubted reference which the *preceding words already contain* to the Introduction of the Gospel. We have indeed seen how the words, "That which we have heard—handled," constrained the reader to think of *Christ;* and that, accordingly, also the first "that which was from the beginning" must be understood of Christ in the sense of John i. 1;—so also, when he reaches the words, περὶ τοῦ λόγου τ. ζ., he cannot fail to have still in his mind the passage of the Gospel, ἐν ἀρχῇ ἦν ὁ λόγος; and are we to think that anything else can be meant by the Logos of the Epistle than that same Logos of the Gospel, ch. i. 1? And when in the Gospel the very same thing is said concerning the Logos which, in a more condensed form, is here said in the Epistle, Ἐν αὐτῷ ζωὴ ἦν, then truly He was in the beginning ὁ λόγος τῆς ζωῆς, yea, He was Himself *the* Life; for we read there, further, καὶ ἡ ζωὴ ἦν τὸ φῶς τῶν ἀνθρώπων, and this very φῶς is in John i., vers. 5 and 8, represented as the personal Logos Himself.

As, then, in the Gospel the Logos was already identified with the φῶς, and this again with the ζωή, it cannot seem strange that St John, in the parenthetical expression of ver. 2, does not go on to say, καὶ ὁ λόγος ἐφανερώθη, but καὶ ἡ ζωὴ ἐφανερώθη. The argument which De Wette makes this change furnish *against* our explanation of the λόγος, falls therefore of itself to nothing.

If now, before we pass on to ver. 2, we look back once more upon the whole combined substance and meaning of ver. 1, we derive confirmation, from a twofold consideration, of the correctness of our position in Sect. IV. of the Introduction; viz., that the Apostle has nothing else in view, when he writes ἀπαγγέλλομεν, but his written Gospel. (1.) He declares, not *Christ, who* was from the beginning, and had been seen and handled by himself—*the* Logos,— but *that which* was from the beginning, *that which* had been heard, seen, beheld, handled, in His coming into the flesh, by himself the Apostle. Thus he declares *concerning* the Logos: the object of his announcement is not the *dogma* about Christ, but *his experience* about Christ. And such an announcement as that is not contained in the Epistle, but only in the Gospel. (2.) St John at the same time expresses this conception in such a *form* as should remind us, word for word, and point for point, of the announcement in the beginning of the Gospel; so that he here concisely recapitulates and sums up the *material collective substance of the Gospel*, as it is in John i. 1 seq. *pre-announced*, and then, in the historical portion of the Gospel, John i. 19–xx. 31, *unfolded*.

Ver. 2. That no doubt may remain on the readers' minds upon the question, what they must understand by the λόγος τῆς ζωῆς, St John here expressly exhibits, in a parenthetical explanatory clause, the great fundamental truth which he had already uttered in John i. 14. (1) That ζωή, which constitutes the nature of the λόγος, *is made manifest;* (2) it is that life which *had been* πρὸς τὸν πατέρα, and then appeared unto us ; (3) this "ὃ ἦν ἀπ' ἀρχῆς, ὃ ἀκηκόαμεν," κ.τ.λ., this object which we announce, is that very ζωή itself. Thus by the ζωή it is not an abstraction which is meant ; but that substantially eternal personal Being, which was from the beginning with the Father, and then was made manifest and tangible on earth.

The three thoughts indicated above in order, which serve the purpose of showing us the *identity* of the Being named ζωή in ver. 2 with the object of the message described in ver. 1, as also the identity of the ζωή with the λόγος, or exhibit most clearly the substantiality and personality of the ζωή—those three thoughts appear, ver. 2, in the following connection. Presupposing the readers' understanding of the expression, ὁ λόγος τῆς ζωῆς, as explained by the Gospel, ch. i. 4—presupposing that they would also understand the Genitive τῆς ζωῆς, ver. 1, as a Genitive of substance,—St John first of all confirms this way of understanding it, by laying down the fundamental sentence of all announcement of salvation, *that this Life has been made manifest;* and thereby at the same time *explains* how "that which was from the beginning" could be "beheld and handled." Certainly these words, "the Life was manifested," *considered in themselves alone*, would themselves be still more or less indistinct and ambiguous. They might have been understood of an abstract ζωή, of some spiritual or physical *energy* of life ; and as only expressing the fact that this life-energy had in some way or other been manifested in a chain of revelations and developments—just as the physical energies of nature are brought into manifestation by the production of manifold successive organisms. But the first verse, connected with its plain reference to John i. 4, must have already led the readers' minds to think of that personal eternal ζωή, which was itself the λόγος, and, accordingly, to interpret the φανερωθῆναι in the sense of a becoming visible and tangible: that no doubt, however, may remain upon this point, St John appends the second utterance, "And *we have seen*, and bear witness, and declare unto you that eternal Life." That, namely, which he had *seen* (thus he sums up in brief the *hearing, seeing, beholding,* and *touching* of the first verse; for the *beholding* is in reality the centre and chief of all these kinds of observation and perception, and here in ver. 2 it was not necessary to repeat the whole climax)—the Object mentioned in ver. 1,—which he can therefore *bear witness* to and *announce, because* he had *seen* Him, is to be understood by the ζωή. And when he calls this "Life" here "eternal," he only recapitulates the important point which had been already expressed in "from the beginning," and gives it that predicate which it bears in ch. v. 20—in the second from the last, as in the second from the first, verse of the Epistle,—a passage in which it is expressly said that *Christ* is that *eternal Life.* Thus has St John here, in ver. 2, uttered concerning the ζωή itself that which in ver. 1 he had begun to say concerning "that which was from the beginning," and concerning the "Word of Life,"—namely, that it was the Object of his announcement; and this confirms the right interpretation of this "Life" as substantial and personal, and identical with Christ. After he has done this, and clearly defined the idea of this ζωή, he returns, *thirdly,* back to the first, the essential *kernel*-thought of ver. 2— "The Life hath become manifest"—and repeats this thought, which was there obscure, but which is here perfectly cleared up by his adding to the word "eternal Life" the relative sentence, "which was with the Father, and was made manifest unto us." And thus the "manifestation" is clearly defined, by the antithesis with "being with the Father," as *an entering into the sphere of time and space, into the sphere of visibility and historical existence.*

Thus we have here at the outset an example of the peculiar *Johannæan* manner of thought and expression, which often neglects in its progress the line of a strictly dialectic development, moving in a circle, or rather in a spiral, going round and round a thought, illustrating it on all sides,—thus all the time approaching its essence with more and more evident precision.

Having thus made the construction of thought in the second verse plain to our minds, we shall find that the individual words will present no great difficulty. The καὶ which opens the verse we are neither required nor warranted to take in the sense of γάρ (with Beza, Grotius, Rosenmüller, etc.). It is true that the main thought of ver. 2, "the Life was manifested," contains an element which may be placed in an explanatory and demonstrative relation to ver. 1; that is, the "becoming manifest" of the "Life" would show how One "from the beginning," who was eternally existent, could have been also visible and palpable, —and thus the "and" might be substituted by "for." But the *scope* of ver. 2 cannot be to unfold and solve that problem (upon which, indeed, as such, no emphasis is laid in ver. 1). The aim and purpose of the Apostle is simply to detach and isolate from the main thought, begun in ver. 1, "*We declare unto you* the Word of Life who was from the beginning, and who was *by us* heard, seen with the eyes, beheld, and handled," the objective idea involved in it, "That eternal Being *has* become manifest," and to make that objective idea independent in order to its *confirmation* (though not without a connection still maintained with the thought of ver. 1). Or, to make it still clearer: In the main period, vers. 1 and 3, the *scope* of the Apostle is to lay emphasis upon the *truth and certainty of this* ἀπαγγέλλειν; hence in it the grammatically ruling thought is this—Thus and thus *we declare unto you*, that is, a Being both eternal and *yet visible to our eyes*. Meanwhile, the idea that Christ was of an eternal nature, but that He had come into flesh and *become* visible, is only *latent* in the object of the clause. On the other hand, in the parenthesis, ver. 2, this latent objective, dogmatical idea or position is to be exhibited most formally as the great fundamental doctrine, and therefore is thus repeated with confirmation; hence here the dominant thought is this—*The life became manifest*. Meanwhile, that which in vers. 1 and 3 appeared as the chief thought, takes in ver. 2 a rather subordinate place: "And *we* have seen, and bear witness, and declare unto you—;" yet, in such a manner that this *subordinate thought*, which gives expression to St John's subjective relation, hastens back in its object to the objective dogmatical main doctrine of the parenthesis ("The eternal Life, which was with the Father, and hath become manifest").

The καί does not stand here in the sense of γάρ, which it never does; but this is an instance of that free, Hebraic conjunction of clauses, and members of clauses, which meets us everywhere throughout the writings of St John. The subject, ἡ ζωή, has received its explanation already on ver. 1. The opinions of those who have interpreted it as meaning *doctrina de felicitate*, or *felicity* itself, need scarcely be mentioned, much less refuted.

Ἐφανερώθη—*was manifested*—is not to be regarded (with De Wette) as simply equivalent to σὰρξ ἐγένετο, *was made flesh:* although it is the same act of incarnation which is here and in John i. 14 described, yet it is exhibited under a different aspect and relation. Φανεροῦσθαι is equivalent to φανερὸς γίγνεσθαι. The ζωή as such, as it is πρὸς τὸν πατέρα, *with the Father*, is not for us men φανερά, *manifest*, but concealing itself in the unsolved mystery of eternity. It has, however, become a φανερά, visible to the eyes, yea, tangible to the hands, inasmuch as it became flesh in Jesus, and thus entered into the conditions of time and visibility. The σὰρξ γίγνεσθαι, therefore, designates the objective process of the incarnation itself as such; the φανερωθῆναι, the result as it respects our capacity of perceiving and understanding it. The former tells us what the Logos became in His incarnation as it regards Himself; the latter, what He became for us.

The three verbs, ἑωράκαμεν, καὶ μαρτυροῦμεν, καὶ ἀπαγγέλλομεν, must evidently be united together[1] (Œcumenius, Zwingli, Lücke), having for their common object the words τὴν ζωὴν τὴν αἰώνιον. Huther would separate the ἑωράκαμεν, and provide for it an object αὐτήν out of the preceding ζωή ("And the Life is manifested, and we have seen it; and we, etc."). Fritzsche, De Wette, and Düsterdieck would separate off and divide the two verbs, καὶ ἑωράκαμεν καὶ μαρτυροῦμεν, supplying both of them with an αὐτήν, so that ἀπαγγέλλομεν would stand quite alone with its τὴν ζ. αἰών. This very uncertainty where the sentence is to be cut into, whether after "seen" or after "testify," betrays the forced character of the whole hypothesis. Certainly, μαρτυροῦμεν and ἀπαγγέλλομεν are in their ideas more closely related than both are with ἑωράκαμεν. On the other

[1] Cod. B. reads καὶ ὃ ἑωράκαμεν. But the spuriousness of this ὃ is admitted on all hands by critics.

hand, the ὁρᾶν and μαρτυρεῖν recur presently (compare John xix. 35), as a compacted pair of ideas; so that it would not be well done to separate the two verbs by a grammatical severance of the construction. Assuredly, it is the scope of the Apostle to say, not that he saw the one thing and testified the other, but that he testified that itself which he had seen; and this takes effect only if both verbs have the same object. But then, again, the ἀπαγγέλλειν is so closely connected in its idea with the μαρτυρεῖν, that after the μαρτυρεῖν also a grammatical severance is impracticable. And why should we interpose or supply an object, when one stands evidently before us? According to Lücke's and our construction, the great objective, "the Life was made manifest," stands in its own nervous independence; and the subordinate subjective thought, " and *we* have seen, and testify, and declare," appears in its own unconfused clearness. According to Fritzsche, on the contrary, the two members of the verse would be so ordered as to make the former contain, in connection with the objective doctrinal statement, one half of the subjective utterance:

A) And the Life hath appeared, and we have seen it, [and bear witness to it.]

B) And we [bear witness, and] declare the eternal Life;—which utterly confuses the whole sense. That, finally, at the end of the verse the ἐφανερώθη has a ἡμῖν connected with it, does not justify Düsterdieck's conclusion, that the first ἐφανερώθη too must have the καὶ ἑωράκαμεν connected with it, as it were in compensation of the ἡμῖν which it lacks. For, in the first member of the verse, the *objective* truth, that the Life had been manifested, is exhibited as such; in the second member, that subordinate thought, concerning the subjective relation of St John, is added, that he had seen this eternal Life, and bore witness, and declared it; and the third member,—that is, the relative clause dependent on "eternal Life,"—leads back again to the objective fundamental thought, yet so that *now*, in a very natural synthesis, the subjective side is touched, though slightly, by the ἡμῖν.

As it respects the meaning of the three verbs, ὁρᾶν, as we have seen, takes here the place of the whole climax contained in ver. 1, and indicates all that is included in eyewitness-ship and personal immediate experience. Μαρτυρεῖν and ἀπαγγέλ-

λειν both signify an active announcement (compare upon μαρτυρεῖν John xxi. 24); but the reference of μαρτυρεῖν is directed
to the truth and absolute certainty of the object announced,
while ἀπαγγέλλειν points rather to the knowledge of the readers
and hearers, which is to be increased. " We have seen, and
come forward as witnesses of it, and announce it unto you."
But that μαρτυρεῖν is used only in reference to dogmatic doctrines, and not in reference to individual historical occurrences,
is an assertion which has nothing to establish it, and which is
glaringly refuted by such passages as John i. 34, xix. 35, xxi.
24. The μαρτυρεῖν which is here spoken of, has, equally with
the ὁρᾶν and the ἀπαγγέλλειν, for its object the concrete historical manifestation of the ζωὴ αἰώνιος in the life, sufferings, and
resurrection of Christ.

That the " eternal life" is not to be understood of the *vita
per Christum nobis parta* (Calvin), or of " the true eternal life
to be appropriated by believers," but only of that personal ζωή
which appeared in Christ, is established by the relative clause
which is appended to it. By the attribute " eternal" the idea
of " that which was from the beginning" is simply repeated;
yet so that this idea now comes forward in a purely objective
form (" eternal"), while the " from the beginning," as we saw
above, is spoken rather from the subjective position of the be-
holder, St John. In ch. v. 11 Christ is called in the same sense
ζωὴ αἰώνιος,—a sense which is as different from the ordinary
meaning of the expression in the New Testament (*e.g.*, Matt.
xxv. 46; John iii. 15), as the meaning of the expression λόγος
(τοῦ Θεοῦ), John i. 1 seq., and 1 John i. 1 and Rev. i. 2, is from
the customary use of that word; for example, in Heb. iii. 12;
John xvii. 17; 1 Thess. iv. 15.

The relative clause is appended with ἥτις, not with the
simple ἥ. Marvellous things have been seen or fancied by the
expositors in this ἥτις. According to Düsterdieck, the predicative definition which lies in the relative clause is by this ἥτις
not merely attached in a relative manner to the subject, but contains at the same time an *explanatory and demonstrative* reference to the ruling sentence. " We have seen, bear witness,
and declare to you the eternal life, *which namely* (because it, to
wit) was with the Father, but hath appeared unto us." Sander
explains: " We announce to you the eternal life as *being that*

which, etc." Huther thinks that it marks out what is uttered in the following words as something *essentially* added to the preceding idea. (But to which idea? That of the seeing and witnessing? or that of the "eternal life"?). All this seems to me far-fetched enough. The classical Greek ὅστις has certainly the signification "whosoever," *quicunque;* and then, when it refers to a definite object, the meaning of *utqui*, "*as who*,"— the definite individual object being thereby carried back to a general idea lying at its foundation. And this "*as who*" divides itself again into these meanings: (1.) "*who, to wit*" (when the matter of the relative clause serves for the elucidation or establishment of the utterance in the main sentence); or (2.) "*who indeed*" (when the matter of the relative clause serves for the exposition of the nature of the already well-known *noun* on which the relative in question immediately depends). Now, it is by no means to be denied that there are traces, even in the New-Testament writers, of a consciousness of the distinction which holds good in classical Greek between ὅς and ὅστις. It is true that in the two passages, Luke viii. 3, Acts xxiv. 1, ὅστις appears to stand in a quite enfeebled meaning; on the other hand, Düsterdieck has correctly observed that in the passages, Matt. ii. 6, vii. 15, xx. 1, xxv. 1, Mark iv. 20, Luke vii. 37, Acts x. 41, Rom. xi. 4, 1 Cor. v. 1, Phil. ii. 20 (to which he improperly adds Rev. xvii. 12, xix. 2), ὅστις has the meaning of τοιοῦτος ὅς. To these passages we would add the following: Rom. i. 32 ("such people as"); Heb. ii. 3; Mark xv. 7 ("which such were, who"). Then we find our above-mentioned meanings 1 and 2 again in the following passages: (1.) "*who, to wit*," Rom. ii. 15; Gal. iv. 24; Heb. viii. 6 (where the relative clause introduces an element which serves for the demonstration of the thought expressed in the main clause): (2.) "*who indeed*," Rom. i. 25 ("who indeed changed"); Rom. vi. 2 ("we, who indeed are dead to sin"); Eph. iii. 13 ("in which indeed my glorying is"); Acts x. 47; and approximately also, Heb. xii. 5 and 2 Cor. ix. 11. In these passages the relative clause unfolds something which lies, and is already assumed to be known, in the nature of the noun on which it depends. Which, then, of these interpretations suits ὅστις in our passage? Of the meaning τοιοῦτος ὅς we must not think for a moment: that has most assuredly no place where the noun, which has a relative clause connected with it, marks out a distinctive individual being, but only where it stands for a generic idea (as in Matt. ii. 6, " Out of thee shall arise *such a ruler* as ;" Matt. vii. 15, " Take heed of that *kind* of false prophets, which"). When, therefore, Sander would explain it, " We declare unto you the eternal life *as* being such as," he introduces a perfectly strange element into the text,—one which does not belong to the ὅστις, and which is opposed to the whole process of the thought; for, the meaning of St John is evidently this, that the " eternal Life" had been with the Father, and had been manifested *actually and in Himself,* and not merely that *He was presented as such in the Apostle's annunciation.* The signification "*which, that is,*" appears to me equally unsatisfactory in this passage. The statement that the ζωή " was with the Father, and appeared unto us," could only *in its second half* serve the purpose of establishing the sentence that " we have seen it, and can bear witness;" but the two halves are so co-ordinated, that we are not justified in considering the first as a merely preparatory, subordinate element of the clause. Thus the only signification of ἥτις which seems suitable, is that of " *which indeed.*" This, however, must not be taken in the sense suggested by Huther, that the matter of the relative clause was to be exhibited as an element " *essentially*" added to the preceding thought; but in the sense that the matter of the relative clause is exhibited *as an already known (from ver.* 1), *and consequently admitted,* element of the preceding main clause, and the noun in it on which the relative clause depends. We can reproduce this, in the most exact manner possible to us, by the translation, " *which indeed* (as before said) was with the Father, and was manifested unto us."

The first member of the relative clause, ἦν πρὸς τὸν πατέρα, intimates *in the direction towards the Father;* altogether as in John i. 1, etc., it is said of the Logos, that He had ever been in the direction towards the Father: that is, not an action of God *ad extra,* towards the creature, but a Word in which the Father *spoke to Himself,* uttered His own existence *before Himself,* or Word of God to God. So also it is here said concerning the ζωή, that it was *towards the Father.* Thus, according to its eternal being and nature, it was not a life which streamed forth from God and towards the creature (to be produced, or already produced), in order to call that creature into existence, or to fill it with powers of development; but a life which did indeed flow forth from the bosom of the Father, but which did at once return back into the bosom of the Father, in the ceaseless flow of the inmost being of God. We do violence to the passage, and weaken away its force, when (with the old Scholiasts) we interpret πρός by ἐν—an interpretation against which Basil delivered his warning. But so, also, the translation "*bei,*" *with,* in the sense of παρά (John xvii. 5), is not precise enough; and even the passage, John i. 18, ὁ ὢν εἰς τὸν κόλπον τοῦ πατρός, is not perfectly analogous, since εἰς there, used in connection with a verb of *rest,* somewhat as in 1 Pet. v. 12,[1] defines the *basis of support,* and not, like πρός, the *direction.* We must leave this πρός here in the possession of its full signification, to which we are led by the analogy of John i. 1. Moreover, it is to be acknowledged that this πρός, used in connection with the ζωή, *would* present a great obscurity and the appearance of harshness, *if* the reference to these words, ὁ λόγος ἦν πρὸς τὸν Θεόν, did not shed its sufficient light over our passage. Considered in itself, to wit, it is more easily understood when spoken of the *Word,* than when spoken of the *Life,* that it had been "*to* God, *to* the Father;" since the *Word* contains already the idea of being spoken to a person, and therefore involves the notion of movement and direction, while this is at least not so clear in the case of the idea *life.* Here, however, we find new reason for holding fast the conviction of the strict and essential reference of this verse to the Introduction of the Gospel, on which it entirely *rests.*

As God here receives, in relation to that personal *Life* which afterwards was manifested to the disciples in Jesus Christ, the name of *Father,* we may, with Huther, assert that the Logos is in reality, and is termed the "Son," not simply from the time of His incarnation, and not only in relation to that incarnation, but already in respect to the mystery of His eternal existence in the Divine Trinity.

---

[1] Quite of another kind are the passages, Mark ii. 1, xiii. 16; Luke xi. 7, where εἶναι stands for βεβηκέναι, and εἰς expresses an actual motion: similarly, Matt. xxvi. 55, where the motion lies still in the ἐκαθεζόμην; and Matt. xiii. 56, where εἶναι certainly involves the idea of a continuous relation of intercourse.

The second member of the relative clause, "and was manifested to us," finds its explanation in that which has been already said upon the first ἐφανερώθη, as also upon the construction of the verse generally.

It only remains that the inexhaustibly rich idea of the ζωή itself receive a more thorough and penetrating examination. It is self-evident, from John i. 1, etc., that the Son of God is called "the Life," not merely as He presents Himself in His incarnate being to us men as the Way, the Truth, and the Life (John xiv. 6), redeeming us from death, and restoring to us our forfeited life, but also as He, in His primordial eternal existence, laid the ground of *all* life in the creature—all life, whether physical, or spiritual and ethical. But not in the sense that He, the Son, in contradistinction from the Father, had the ζωή as *His own* peculiar prerogative, so that to the Son the ζωή was appropriate, to the Father not (which has been most improperly deduced by some from "which was with the Father"); for against this John v. 26 most decisively speaks. The Father hath life in Himself, and hath given to the Son equally to have life in Himself. Thus the Son stands to the Father in the relation of an eternal Receiver; the Father to the Son in the relation of an eternal Giver. But it is an *eternal* giving and receiving, in which we cannot conceive any not-yet-having-received on the part of the Son, any no-longer-giving, or having-done-with-giving, on the part of the Father, and which would make the gift itself consist in no other than *the most proper essential possession* of life, most essentially communicated from eternity to the Son. For it is given to the Son so to have life *in Himself*, —in Himself, that is, as being His own substantial nature, even as it is in the Father,—in contradistinction to all creatures, which have their life communicated to them, not in themselves, and not in their proper inherent substance, but as something which they may lose, and (to speak scholastically) as an *accidens*. Indeed, this is what is precisely the idea of the creature,—the having life as something that is received, and that may be lost, in time. This being so, the deepest and most internal idea of life cannot be obtained by any process of abstraction applied to what is visible in the creature. In the creatures can be seen only, as it were, the reflection of some individual characteristics of that ζωή, which constitutes the eternal nature of God. The life of the growing and self-reproducing *organism*, in opposition to the rigidity of inorganic dead matter; the livingness of the *soul*, which still actuates its body, in opposition to the state of death, in which the soul, separated from the body, is found in ᾅδης and θάνατος; the life of the spirit, which consists in the fellowship of love and holiness with God, its Original, in opposition to the death of the spirit, which is for ever separated from God; finally, that eternal life, to which the children of God will attain, in opposition to eternal death ;—all these are only detached and several fragments of that eternal primitive life in God, of that essential ζωή, which *in eternity* had already manifested itself in its perfection through the *generatio filii æterna*, and which produced for itself a sphere of organic, psychical, and spiritual-moral life in which to move; which, moreover, in *redemption* has manifested itself (and still manifests), when He who ἡ ζωὴ πρὸς τὸν πατέρα ἦν devoted Himself to the opposite of the ζωή, unto death, in order to lead the personal beings who lay in death, together with the κτίσις συνωδίνουσα (Rom. viii. 22), out of death into eternal life.—The notion, or the idea, or the nature, or the substance, of that primal life, and wherein that *in itself* properly consists, is for ever withdrawn as a μυστήριον Θεοῦ from our dim mortal eyes, and our stammering human speech ; we can only utter our thought of individual elements of it, and these only approximately, and never adequately defined. For, in that primordial life of God is the source of all organic-physical life, with the source of all spirit and spiritual life ;—in it is the source of all *wisdom*, inseparably one with the inexhaustible eternal spring of that *love*, in virtue of which the *life* of God could give no higher manifestation of itself than this, that it, the *eternal* ζωή, should enter into the *not-eternal* sphere of time and sense, into the σάρξ— that it, the eternal ζωή, should enter into θάνατος, in order to approve itself by death as the true life which overcometh death (Acts iii. 15, ii. 24).—And thus we have, in the *person* of Him, who is the ζωὴ φανερωθεῖσα, the life, and the *source* of all life —spiritual, moral, psychical, and that which will awaken and glorify the body again. If we have *Him* in us, we bear within us eternal life itself implanted.

In ver. 3 the Apostle resumes the sentence which had been

E

begun in ver. 1, and interrupted by the parenthesis, in order to give it its completion. It is customary, after a long parenthesis, for the same member of the sentence, which before the parenthesis had been established and fully developed, to be once more repeated, though in an abbreviated form, and in its most important points (to serve which purpose, we usually insert "I say;" and the Romans had their "sed"). The *object* of the sentence had in this case preceded; the transitive verb, with the subject latent in it, is now to be expected; therefore the *object* must now be in some manner resumed. But the object consisted of three parts: that is, the two members of the relative clause, "that which was from the beginning," and "that which we have seen," etc.; and, moreover, added to these, the appositional clause, "concerning the Word of Life." Which, then, of the elements of this threefold object must be resumed, when the sentence is taken up again? The appositional appendage, "of the Word of Life," will of necessity fall away, since it was *that* which gave occasion to the parenthesis itself, and therefore was a diversion from the main clause; moreover, *that* had received its full development in the parenthesis, and was so clearly still before the readers' thought that it needed no reference or resumption. So also the first member of the relative clause, which furnished the object in ver. 1,—to wit, "that which was from the beginning,"—had been repeated already, so far as its meaning went, in the parenthesis; and *it* therefore needed not to be resumed. Thus there remains only the second member of the relative clause, to wit, "that which we have heard—handled." This member contains the expression of the *subjective* position which St John assumed, as an eyewitness, to the object which he has to announce; this *subjective* side it is which stands in the nearest actual relation to the governing verb, "we declare;" from this subjective side had the parenthesis, as we have seen, diverged to the *objective dogmatic* representation of the object itself; in ver. 2 the objective side had taken the ascendency, and the subjective side had retreated into a subordinate place. Now, therefore, this subjective side, which is the principal matter in the main statement of vers. 1 and 3, and which in the second member of the relative clause had been expanded into a full climax, must again be resumed and made prominent. This is done by the words, "that which we have seen and heard." For, it is easily understood that the whole climax is not to be repeated in its entire extent, but only in its quintessence. And this takes place in a precise and suggestive manner by the so-called chiasmus (or limitation). The climax had advanced from the mere "hearing" to the "seeing;" the recapitulation begins at once with this higher, more immediate evidence, the "seeing," and then follows the less direct "hearing:"[1] "That which we have (thus) *seen* and heard" (equivalent to, "not merely heard, but also seen").

Now follows the governing verb of the sentence, ἀπαγγέλλομεν καὶ ὑμῖν, which includes in itself the subject of the sentence. This is the reading of A.B.C., Syr., Vulg., Did., Aug.; and Lachmann and Tischendorf have done right to receive into the text the καί wanting in the Text. Rec. That this καί was introduced negligently, as from the καὶ ὑμεῖς which follows, is not a happy conjecture of De Wette. It is altogether in St John's style to mark such antitheses, as often as they occur, by the addition of a καί (comp. John xvii. 18, κἀγώ; ver. 19, καὶ αὐτοί; ver. 21, καὶ αὐτοί; ver. 24, κἀκεῖνοι, etc. Grotius also well compares the "abundantia" in the passage, John vi. 51). But, when De Wette urges against the reading καὶ ὑμῖν that St John must then have announced his message already to *others* (which, however, is nothing inconceivable in itself!), his argument rests upon a perfect misunderstanding of the καὶ ὑμῖν. Not in opposition to *others*, to whom he had already announced that "Word of Life," but in opposition *to himself the eyewitness*, he writes, "That which *we* have seen, we declare now *also to you*, that *ye also* may have fellowship with *us*." (Grotius: ut et vos ipsi non minus quam nos fructum inde percipiatis.) The καί before ὑμεῖς is certainly a stronger pleonasm than the καί after ἀπαγγέλλομεν. For, the idea of co-ordination and common participation which is expressed by καί before ὑμεῖς, is already perfectly expressed in the idea of "fellowship with us." *On that account the καὶ before ὑμεῖς would be, logically, perfectly unaccountable, if it were not simply an emphatic repetition of the preceding καί*

---

[1] De Wette misses this delicacy of the change when he suggests that the ὁρᾶν is used because the words ἐφανερώθη ἡμῖν had preceded in the close of ver. 2. The beginning of ver. 3 is not joined on to the parenthesis, ver. 2, but diverges from it and leads back again to ver. 1.

ὑμῖν. And therefore this καὶ between ἀπαγγέλλομεν and ὑμῖν must be genuine.

"That which was from the beginning, which *we* have heard, and seen with our eyes, and handled with our hands, that declare we *also to you.*" Since the *object* of this declaration is not the idea of Christ, but the *experiences* of the Apostle in relation to Christ; since he is speaking of an annunciation of *Christ in His historical manifestation*, the *act* of the ἀπαγγέλλειν cannot be made to mean *the act of writing the Epistle.* Sander, indeed, has tried to discover in ch. ii. 1, etc., ii. 18, iii. 1, etc., iv. 1–3, iv. 9, 14, and v. 6, "historical declarations;" yea, he is persuaded that our ἀπαγγέλλομεν itself "contains a very momentous historical announcement." But, when we find that the most zealous endeavours of those who *will* detect everywhere in the Epistle historical matter, can bring nothing more decisive to light than these examples, we can but be the more firmly persuaded that the Epistle does not contain *any such* ἀπαγγέλλειν as that of which vers. 1 and 3 speak. Our ἀπαγγέλλομεν is still more clearly seen *not* to refer to the Epistle, when we take notice of the καὶ ταῦτα γράφομεν, which actually describes the act of writing the Epistle, and which, standing by the side of the ἀπαγγέλλομεν, distinguishes the one from the other. And ver. 5 cannot shake our position: since there St John does nothing more than extract the kernel and quintessence of that ἀγγελία which he had announced to his readers *in the Gospel* (and that, obviously, taken from *that part* of this ἀγγελία which contains what the disciples had *heard* from the lips of Jesus), in order to derive from it practical and hortatory deductions. St John does not *introduce* in ver. 5 the ἀγγελία *promised* in ver. 3; but he *reminds* them in ver. 5 of that message which had been *brought* to them in his Gospel, and which had been *mentioned* as such in ver. 3.

Thus it is certain that in the ἀπαγγέλλομεν of ver. 3 *the act of writing the Epistle* is not intended. Several recent expositors (Lücke, De Wette, Düsterdieck) more or less acknowledge this; but then they persist in regarding the ἀπαγγέλλομεν as meaning an altogether universal description of the apostolical teaching generally, or at least of that of St John (oral, to wit) in particular. The former is absolutely out of the question; for the characteristics of that teaching, as given in vers. 1–3, do not at all fit the doctrinal work of the Apostles *collectively*, whereas they contain all the specific traits of the peculiar doctrinal system of St John in a very marked manner. But not only so: there is in the words—as these expositors admit in their exposition of the passage—such a significant allusion to the *Introduction of St John's Gospel*, that this alone, and of itself, would suggest the thought that the Apostle had in his mind, when he wrote the ἀπαγγέλλομεν, the transmission of his written Gospel. In this case the words of vers. 1–3 have a very definite practical scope: he introduces to them the Gospel which accompanied the Epistle, and then appends, in the "these things we write," the design and scope of his Epistle itself. The relation of the two writings, now lying before his eyes—the written Gospel and the Epistle to be written, which should accompany each the other—is the theme of vers. 1–4. But what end would, on the other hand, have been answered, if the Apostle had placed his Epistle, which he was about to write, over against his general oral teaching on other occasions, and established a relation between one and the other? If it had been his design to express the thought, that in *all* which he had *ever* preached to them— that is, in his teaching that Jesus was the Christ, or that the Logos became flesh—he had not preached dreams and inventions, but certain and experienced truth,—if that had been his object, he would not have *co-ordinated* the object of his preaching (that the Logos had become flesh, or that Jesus was from the beginning) with the sentence that he had experienced and known this experimentally (as he does, ὃ ἦν ἀπ' ἀρχῆς, ὃ—ἑωράκαμεν), but he would then necessarily have made the former the subject and the latter the predicate. ("That which we make known unto you, *that* Jesus was from the beginning, and hath appeared unto us, we have heard and seen with our eyes," etc.) Thus he does not write. But he places the declaration, "That which was from the beginning, that which we have heard, seen, etc., that *announce we unto you*," by the side of the second declaration, "And *these things we write* unto you;" so that, in the former, the ἀπαγγέλλομεν is the emphatic predicate of the whole clause,—and with this emphasis in ver. 3 (*after* the parenthesis) isolated and made prominent,—and thus is *that which he expressly designs to say concerning the Object*. But we can hardly suppose that he intends now first, in the

Epistle, to communicate to them the information or new intelligence that he *declared*, or was *wont to declare* (in oral teaching), that which was from the beginning, etc. On the other hand, these words have a very important significance if St John actually communicates to them what was new intelligence, that he transmitted to them, in company with this Epistle, the annunciation characterized in ver. 1, that is, his written Gospel.

So also the καὶ ὑμῖν receives, on this view, a strong and lively reference. "That which we Apostles have beheld and experienced, that ye also, who have not been eyewitnesses of Christ's life, shall experience." And this took place simply through the announcement and exhibition of the *concrete life of Christ*, as contained in the written evangelical narrative.

And now from the main clause—which begins in ver. 1 with "that which was from the beginning," and ends with "that declare we unto you"—depends a *clause of the design*: "that—Jesus Christ." This, again, consists of two members: there is a twofold end which St John would gain by the transmission of his written Gospel. The two members are (as Zwingli and Calvin excellently remarked) parallel with the two members of our Lord's petition in the High-priestly prayer, John xvii. 21:—

(a) Ἵνα καὶ ὑμεῖς κοινωνίαν ἔχητε μεθ' ἡμῶν·

(a) Ἵνα πάντες ἓν ὦσιν (καθὼς σὺ, πάτερ, ἐν ἐμοὶ, κἀγὼ ἐν σοί),

(b) Καὶ ἡ κοινωνία δὲ ἡ ἡμετέρα μετὰ τοῦ πατρὸς καὶ μετὰ τοῦ υἱοῦ αὐτοῦ Ἰησοῦ Χριστοῦ.

(b) Ἵνα καὶ αὐτοὶ ἐν ἡμῖν ἓν ὦσιν.

Thus the final and highest positive end which St John aimed to attain by his Gospel was this, that the High-priestly prayer of Jesus should have its fulfilment in his readers; that they (1) should grow as living members into that fellowship, the mother-stem and centre of which was the disciples themselves, —into that fellowship, the members of which *among themselves* were one, but the common unity of which (2) has its internal ground of life in the unity in which every individual stands *with the Father and the Son*. It is obvious, accordingly, that the two members of this final statement of the design do not simply stand side by side in external conjunction, but are most internally and livingly one. The latter specifies the internal living ground and principle of life, on which the former grows, and on which alone it can be brought to perfection. This relation of the two members is grammatically expressed by the δέ which is added to the particle καί. Καὶ δέ, *et vero*, intimates that the second member is not simply appended or added on to the former: the combination expresses at the same time the introduction of a *new turn*, or more distinct essential definition given, to the thought that preceded. Compare John vi. 51, where the thought, "I am the living bread," receives, through the added clause, "and the bread, which I will give, is *My flesh*," a new turn and more exact modification. (Otherwise in John viii. 17, xv. 27, where the καί is not the leading conjunction which connects the clauses, but δέ; καί referring, in the sense of *also*, to an individual noun in the sentence—in ch. viii. 17 to νόμος, in xv. 27 to ὑμεῖς—so that there we must translate "*but also*.")

The second member of our final clause has no verb, no copula; for, the reading καὶ ἡ κοινωνία δὲ ἡ ἡμετέρα ᾖ μετὰ τοῦ πατρὸς κ.τ.λ. is decidedly spurious—the ᾖ being found only in one lesser codex, and in some versions where it has no critical significance whatever. But, though the ᾖ does not stand in the text, it must be supplied; that is, we must regard the second clause as dependent still upon the ἵνα (Vulg., Aug., Beda, Erasmus, Zwingli, Œcolamp., Luther, Calvin, Grotius, etc). Other expositors (Episcopius, Bengel, Düsterdieck, Sander, Huther) would supply ἐστί. But this rends the second clause out of its natural reference to the first, and reduces it to a merely explanatory remark. No, it is the design of St John, in his ἀπαγγελία, that that prayer of Jesus should be fulfilled on both its sides: that his readers should enter into fellowship with the disciples, and that this fellowship should have its living principle of life in the fellowship with the Father and the Son.

Instead of the ἓν ὦσιν of John xvii. 21, St John substitutes the idea of the κοινωνία. And this receives light from John xvii. itself. It is not merely a *made* fellowship, as it were resting upon agreement; also, it is not a merely ethical fellowship, *resulting* from a previous community of disposition in the individuals; but it is a fellowship of *being and nature*, having its root in this, that those who partake of it are begotten of the same σπέρμα Θεοῦ (1 John iii. 9), and are penetrated by the same powers of a heavenly and glorified life. And on that very account *is* this *fellowship* of the members essentially, and in its root, a *fellowship* with the Father and the Son :—with the *Father*, who giveth His σπέρμα, that is, His Holy Spirit, and thereby draweth to the Son ; with the *Son*, in union with whom the regenerate soul groweth up through the Holy Spirit as a member with the Head. "Concerning what fellowship he speaks this, and what society he thereby understands, the words expound : not alone that peace, concord, and brotherly amity, by which men are joined to men ; but that by which there is an indissoluble union of men with God in spirit and soul by faith, and hereafter eternal life with Him. This is that for which Christ prays the Father, John xvii." (Zwingli.)

"That ye may have fellowship with us"—this is the formal statement here of the Saviour's "that they may be one." Christ prays absolutely that "they all" who "should believe on Him" (ver. 20) might be one. St John has to do with a number of specific individuals, who are to be incorporated into the body of that πάντες ἓν ὄντες. The already-existing body, into which they are incorporated, appears here as "we ;" it consists of the already-existing older generation of those who had been eye-witnesses of Jesus. Those to be incorporated, or in process of being incorporated, are the readers to whom he is writing : these are, by the words καὶ ὑμεῖς (the form of which is explained, as we have seen, by the preceding καὶ ὑμῖν), set over against the ἡμεῖς. They are to have fellowship *with* the "us ;" thus, are to be incorporated into the already-present κοινωνία.

"And that our fellowship (sc. may be, ᾖ) with," etc. "Our fellowship," naturally, is *not that fellowship* in which the eye-witness stood already, *alone and exclusive of the "you ;"* but the "our" is here used *in community of meaning*. "*Our* fellowship ; that in which *we* already stood, and into which *ye* are now to enter, and must more and more increase."

Ver. 4. The first longer and more complex portion of the introductory section is now followed by a second, shorter, and less difficult portion. With the first main sentence is now co-ordinated a second, closely connected with it by the particle καί.

"And these things we write unto you, that our joy may be full." But, first of all, we must establish the reading. Instead of ὑμῖν, Cod. B. has ἡμεῖς, a reading which is here certainly opposed to *internal* probability. For, although St John not seldom (*e.g.*, John vi. 51) adds the personal pronoun which was already contained in the verb, yet he does so only in cases where some additional emphasis requires it. But here an emphasized ἡμεῖς would be altogether out of keeping. It would only introduce again with new force the antithesis between ἡμεῖς and ὑμεῖς which met us in ver. 3, but which had been just done away by the common ἡμετέρα; and the thought of ver. 4 does not give any occasion for this, since here the contrast is prominent between καὶ ταῦτα and that which had preceded, but not between the "*ye*" and "*we.*" ("And *this* we write, that—," but not, "And this write *we*;" for that this Epistle was written by St John, and not by the readers themselves, was evident enough already.) These internal arguments against ἡμεῖς are so strong, that they would be decisive against the reading, even if it were supported by much stronger testimony than a single codex. The variations of the codd. are much more important at the end of our verse, between ἡ χαρὰ ἡμῶν and ἡ χαρὰ ὑμῶν.[1] Ἡμῶν is the reading of B.G., of a series of the lesser authorities, of some Fathers (Theoph., Œcumen.), and the Slavonic Version. Lachmann, therefore, received ἡμῶν into the text of his greater edition, as Mill had done before him. If ἡμῶν be genuine, the Apostle again resumes the common ἡμετέρα, "that our (common) joy may be perfected." Now it is obviously more probable that a transcriber should continue—whether involuntarily by oversight, or by design—the ὑμῶν after the ὑμῖν which had just preceded, than that he should correct a plain ὑμῶν into ἡμῶν on account of the ἡμετέρα of ver. 3. For this reason I am not disinclined to hold ἡμῶν, with Lachmann, as the true reading; and as such it throws a finer tone into the meaning. Even the origination of the reading γράφομεν ἡμεῖς seems to point that way. For it manifestly sprang from the (perverted) endeavour to introduce once more the antithesis between *we* and *you* in ver. 4, which had been done away in ver. 3; and, therefore, we may assume that the first codices, which had read γράφομεν

[1] A third reading, ἡ χαρὰ ἡμῶν ἐν ὑμῖν (only in the Syr. and Erpen. Vers.), owes its origin evidently to the wish to combine the two other readings.

ἡμεῖς, would read also χαρὰ ὑμῶν. And thus we have a double explanation of the spurious ὑμῶν. But this makes it all the more significant, that Cod. B., which received from those (now lost) codices the γράφομεν ἡμεῖς, nevertheless suffered the χαρὰ ἡμῶν (unsuitable with the former) to remain; evidently because this ἡμῶν was too well otherwise authenticated, or too generally acknowledged as genuine. For the rest, the variation yields no *essential* difference of thought.

"And *these things*" points manifestly to the Epistle. But when Düsterdieck says that it points "*not merely* to vers. 1–3 (to which Sander refers it!), but also to the *whole* Epistle," this is far from being the right manner of putting it. Strictly to vers. 1–3 the καὶ ταῦτα cannot refer, since "and these things we write" is introduced as a *second* and *different* clause, added to the "that which was from the beginning—we declare," and with a new and perfectly independent design (that your joy may be full). On the other hand, we cannot say (with Socinus) that καὶ ταῦτα refers to the remainder of the Epistle only, to the exclusion of what precedes in vers. 1–3. In fact, the καὶ ταῦτα refers to no individual passage or portion of the Epistle as such, but to *the Epistle as such* in contradiction to the Gospel, which had been referred to in vers. 1–3. *The one writing* is co-ordinated *with the other*, and not one part of the Epistle with any other.

The design with which the Apostle adjoined his Epistle to his Gospel is expressed in the words, "that our joy may be *perfected*." The point of the design is not in the idea of the *joy*, but in the *making perfect* of that joy. It is not that the *joy* is to be added to the *fellowship*, ver. 3, as something different and separable from it; but that joy which is presupposed, though not stated, to have been already imparted in the fellowship, is to be brought to its *consummation*. And this it is which shows most decisively the internal preferableness of the reading ἡμῶν. The *mutual* joy—first the comfort and confidence of faith in the *readers* after evil overcome, and then the joy of the *Apostle* in the faith and fidelity of his people, and this mutual, common joy connected with the *blessed joy of both in God*—must be brought to its perfection. In order to the accomplishment of this, he adjoins to his written *Gospel*, which contained the material for the overcoming of all Gnostic assaults, the present *Epistle*, in which he shows the application of that defensive material, and teaches his readers how to use their weapons,—opening up to them the abyss, but also unfolding to their eyes the glory of fellowship with Him who is *light*.

The idea of the χαρά, and also the order of words ἡ χαρὰ πληροῦται, point again for their origin to the Gospel of St John (ch. xv. 11, xvii. 13). As ver. 3 manifestly connects itself with ver. 21 of the High-priestly prayer, so also we are reminded by ver. 4 of the passage in ver. 13 of the same John xvii. And there we find the same participle, πεπληρωμένη, used which is used in our passage. Christ utters, before He goeth to the Father, and while He is still ἐν τῷ κόσμῳ with His disciples, ταῦτα (*His Farewell-Discourses*), ἵνα ἔχωσι τὴν χαρὰν τὴν ἐμὴν πεπληρωμένην ἐν ἑαυτοῖς—that they might have *His* joy *fulfilled in themselves*. And here the veteran St John would add to his Gospel this further Epistle, as a word of remembrance and farewell, in order that the joy—the joy of *victory* in the confidence of having overcome the world (for *this* is the kind of joy which is meant, as in John xvii. 9–16, so also in the scope of this Epistle, the final section of which, as we shall see, treats expressly of the "victory over the *world*," so that the climax of the whole Epistle is in this νική)—might be perfected in them, as it was perfected in him (hence the χαρὰ ἡμῶν, used in common, which strictly corresponds with the ἐν ἑαυτοῖς, John xvii. 13, and embraces both points in one).

It is therefore not quite right to view this joy (with Zwingli, Œcolampad., Düsterd., Huther, etc.) in a too generally dogmatic light, and make it simply the blessed experience of salvation flowing from fellowship with God, or the *tranquillitas conscientiæ*. This effaces the delicate antithesis between vers. 3 and 4, and disturbs the full meaning of the relation to John xvii. 13. The χαρά is here, what it is in John xvii., *that* joyfulness which is grounded on the assurance that the children of God, although *in* the world, yet are not *of* the world, and that the world can have no advantage over them, either inwardly through temptation, or outwardly through persecution. Practically considered, this χαρά is always present wherever that κοινωνία, ver. 3, is present (this is itself more fully unfolded afterwards, ch. iii. 10 and 14), and not present where that κοινωνία is wanting; therefore St John can (as we stated above) take it for granted as self-understood, that with that κοινωνία this χαρά will also be given. But as certainly as in practical reality these two are ever united, so certain is it that they exhibit *two distinct sides* of one and the same divine life. The κοινωνία is the *positive* relation to the brethren, and to the Father and the Son; the χαρά (understood in the sense of John xvii. 13) refers essentially to the *hostile relation of Christians to the* κόσμος.

And how plain does this make the connection of the two distinct *ends* of ver. 3 and ver. 4 with the *means* specified for their attainment! His *Gospel*, the positive historical ἀπαγγελία of the eternal λόγος in His historical manifestation, St John gives to his readers, in order that the High-priestly petition of John xvii. 21 might be fulfilled; that is, in order that the *positive* end might be attained, of incorporating them into that fellowship of the body of Christ which depends upon fellowship with its living Head. But St John appends to the Gospel his *Epistle*,—with its hortatory application of essential doctrine, with its distinction and diagnosis of light and darkness, with its exhibition of the relation of Christians to the κόσμος (ch. iii.), with its delineation of all the distinctive marks of the antichristian power of temptation, and earnest warning against it, with, finally, its final and conclusive triumph of νικὴ over the κόσμος,—in order that that other High-priestly petition, John xvii. 13, might be fulfilled, in the attainment of his readers to a consummate *joy of warfare and victory;* an attainment never possible save when the Christian, though still *in* the world, is really sundered *from* the world, saved from its seductions, and inaccessible to its ensnaring arts.

PART THE FIRST.

CENTRE OF THE ἀγγελία : GOD IS LIGHT.

Ch. i. 5–ch. ii. 6.

ST JOHN, in ver. 5, lays down the central point and kernel of that *message*, of which he had spoken in ver. 3, viz., of that which was contained in his written Gospel. He does not here *introduce* (as we have shown above)—he does not introduce in ver. 5 the ἀγγελία which was in view, ver. 3; but he *reminds* them in ver. 5 of the *message brought already* in his Gospel, *handed over* to his readers, and mentioned as such in ver. 3. For this was the strict relation of his Epistle to his Gospel, that in the Gospel he declared his *experimental knowledge* of the manifested Logos as such, objectively and historically; but in the Epistle he as it were dogmatically sets forth the individual sides of the revelation of the Logos, and of His nature, and draws from them their practical consequences, whether hortatory or polemical.

But he *begins* this development, ver. 5, with a declaration which does not contain one aspect simply, in connection with the rest, but is itself the *central point and source of all the revelation of God*, from which all the other truths are derived. Hence he can write at once: καὶ ἐστὶν αὕτη ἡ ἀγγελία ἦν, κ.τ.λ.: *the* message heard from Jesus Christ, and the whole message, is presented in the truth, ὅτι ὁ Θεὸς φῶς ἐστιν—*that God is* light. And thus we may explain the ἐστὶν which is so emphatically placed first in that sentence. For, the reading καὶ ἐστὶν αὕτη is authenticated by Codd. B.C.G., Theophyl., Œcumenius, and others; and the circumstance that St John elsewhere (ch. ii. 25, iii. 11 and 23, v. 11 and 14) writes καὶ αὕτη ἐστίν, so far from being an argument against the genuineness of the reading (as Düsterdieck thinks), confirms it very strongly; for, it is much more probable that a transcriber should have conformed our passage to those later ones (where, however, St John is developing only individual doctrines of the revelation of Christ, and therefore uses less emphasis), than that a transcriber should have arbitrarily violated St John's customary usage by placing the word ἐστίν in the forefront of the whole sentence. Thus he writes very emphatically: " And truly is *this* the message;" by placing the ἐστίν first, he stimulates the attention to the following αὕτη, and throws upon this word a stronger accent. Καὶ αὕτη ἐστὶν ἡ ἀγγελία, κ.τ.λ., would run in Hebrew וזֹאת הַשְּׁמֻעָה ; on the other hand, the καὶ ἐστὶν αὕτη, κ.τ.λ., would correspond to the Hebrew וְהָיְתָה זֹאת הַשְּׁמֻעָה. Instead of ἀγγελία the Text. Rec. reads ἐπαγγελία; but external testimonies (A.G. and the Fathers), as well as the internal argument that ἐπαγγελία everywhere occurs in the sense (here unsuitable) of " promise," decide in favour of ἀγγελία. The conjecture of Socinus and Episcopius, who would read ἀπαγγελία, has everything against it; for this word does not occur in any MS. of our passage, nor anywhere in the New Testament.

" The message which we have heard from Him, and declare unto you," is in its essence no other than that same ἀπαγγέλλειν which had been the subject of ver. 3, but now modified, and seen more closely under one particular aspect. That which he had heard, and seen with his eyes, beheld, and handled with his hands—his experimental knowledge of the Incarnate Logos— St John declares in the Gospel. Here also he speaks of the very same announcement contained in the Gospel: the quintessence and the radical principle of this annunciation, which he is now in the act of transmitting to the readers in the written Gospel, he will now in these verses of the Epistle concentrate and develop; he will exhibit that in which the announcement, received from Christ and delivered to the Ephesians, consisted, as viewed in its central principle. He therefore characterizes it according to those two several critical points which had been already brought forward in vers. 1 and 3; that is, (1) as one that had been derived from Christ, and (2) as by him communicated to his readers. Only he does not, as to the former of these points, repeat the *hearing, beholding,* and *handling;* here he specifies only the *hearing,* and that for a good reason. For, this supreme truth, which he will *here* specify by name as the *source* of all the other developments of the revelation of God in Christ, and therefore as the quintessence of all announcement concerning Christ—the truth that *God is light*—has preeminently in itself the character of a *doctrinal statement.* It came forward especially in the *doctrine* of Christ (although, like every other part of the revelation of God, actually manifested also in the person and life of the Redeemer); it was uttered, viz., in those discourses of our Lord in which He disclosed and opened up to His disciples His own nature, as also the nature of the Father (John xiv. 9), and thus the nature of the Triune God, and revealed to them that His nature was light (John iii. 19, etc., viii. 12, ix. 5, xi. 9, etc., xii. 35, etc., and 46; comp. Luke xi. 35, xvi. 8). Viewed in relation to this its ultimate source, the ἀγγελία appears preeminently as one that had been ἠκουσμένη, as one that had been received from the *lips* of Christ. Christ had announced to His disciples that God Himself, and He Himself the Son of God, was light; and St John announces it over and again, on his part, to his readers (this *re-*announcement is expressed by ἀναγγέλλειν, *renunciare;* comp. John xvi. 13–15, and Erasmus and Düsterdieck on this passage).

Thus in this verse the *central point* of the whole Johannæan ἀγγελία is introduced; and it certainly is not true that ver. 5 connects itself with ver. 4 as a " condition," under which alone the disciples must enter into the fellowship mentioned in vers. 3, 4 (a view which Huther, S. 14 of his Commentary, holds, while he mentions it in S. 15 as "incorrect").

That main position and central point of the message is now exhibited in the words: ὅτι ὁ Θεὸς φῶς ἐστι. With utmost emphasis the negative side is added: καὶ σκοτία ἐν αὐτῷ οὐκ ἔστιν οὐδεμία. As it respects the literal understanding of the phraseology, φῶς is the qualitative predicate, and says that God in His nature is *light;* not that He (as Luther's translation expresses it) is *a* Light among many. But, if we would penetrate into the deeper meaning of this saying, that God is light, we are encountered by the same difficulty which met us in the interpretation of the ζωή, ver. 1, and that in an increased degree. When Düsterdieck would explain the idea of the φῶς by that of "the believer's walk in light being a ray of the Divine light," he moves in a circle, and explains *idem per idem*; when he goes on to reduce the idea of light to that of holiness, blaming Calovius for understanding it at once of the holiness and the omniscience of God, and then presently afterwards assures us that the idea of light cannot be referred to mere abstract holiness, he altogether fails to make the matter in any degree more comprehensible. It will be more helpful to set out by reminding ourselves that the declaration, God is light, is not peculiar to St John alone, but is found throughout the Holy Scriptures: so in Ps. civ. 2, the creaturely light of the stars is represented as a *garment* of God; and to Ezekiel and Habakkuk God appeared visible as a light (comp. Rev. i. 14, and iv. 3), as in Dan. ii. 22 God is exhibited as light in reference to His omniscience; and in St Paul (Rom. xiii. 12; Eph. v. 8; 2 Cor. vi. 14; 1 Thess. v. 5; 1 Tim. vi. 16), St Peter (1 Pet. ii. 9), and St James (James i. 17), we find the opposition of light and darkness, with the declaration that God *dwelleth* in light, or is the *Father* of light. But the simple statement, that *God Himself* in His very *nature is* light, is strictly peculiar to St John. And, in penetrating its meaning, all those other passages serve indeed to point out the way; but they only lead us a few degrees nearer to the thing itself—they do not lead us into the very heart of it, and in fact receive more light from our present passage than they throw upon it. For, all that is here and there said concerning the contrast of *walking* in the light and *walking* in the darkness, only serves generally to show us this much, that the entire category has not merely a physical and metaphysical, but also and most especially an ethical side; but, in order to understand *wherefore* the walking in the Spirit of God is described as a walking in the light, we must first of all know wherefore God Himself is as to His nature described as light.

In order to perceive this clearly, we must remember in this case—as analogously in the case of the ζωή above—that all which we are accustomed to term "light" in the domain of the creature, whether with a physical or a metaphysical meaning, is only an effluence of that one and only primitive Light, which appears as the nature of God. But, in order to penetrate into this primal and incommunicable idea of light, it is necessary, before every other question, that we ask what there is in common between those various kinds of creaturely light. The starting point for this is found in the passage, Gen. i. 3. The beginning of the Divine creative energy, as directed to the lower domain of creation, designated as ארץ, and as yet confused and orderless, consisted in this, that He commanded, "Let there be light." Thus light—physical light, to wit—was not something brought down and added to the already prepared substances and organisms, enlightening them, and making them subjectively visible; but it was rather the supreme source of all cosmical organization, chemical separation, and organic development. But physical light is in itself a phenomenon of movement, a *life* in enlightening bodies which makes their minutest particles vibrate, so that these their life-vibrations communicate themselves in beams issuing in all directions to the surrounding (transparent) bodies; and thus the light is that life-action of shining bodies, by means of which *it is their nature to give intelligence outwardly of their presence*, to declare themselves, to speak of themselves to others, to make themselves and their own nature manifest to all around. It belongs to the essence of the shining body *to be for others;* the dark body is shut up in itself. Consequently the light—even the physical light—is, in its inmost essence, as *life,* so also *love;* and, since it is the laying open of its own being, it is also *truthfulness.* But the shining body does not manifest itself only,—it shines upon other dark bodies not its own, which in their own nature were shut up in themselves. Its beams strike upon their surfaces; and, as the vibrating life meets here with opposition, it rebounds back on all sides, and gives in every direction notice of the existence and the nature of the body dark in itself. In this lies an ascendency of light over darkness: that which is in itself dark is, in spite of itself, drawn by the light to the light, made manifest, and disclosed as it is. Yea, more than that: physical light is for organisms a condition of their life; the opaque body is not only enlightened by the light, but quickened also; as the light is life, so also it diffuses life. But it is manifest that this physical light is more than a mere parable or symbol of the metaphysical and ethical light; indeed, there exists between all three more than mere analogy or resemblance. *Physical light is for us creatures the real basis of metaphysical knowledge:* not only are all our abstract and general notions formed out of concrete perceptions of sense, but our *thinking* itself may almost be said to take place within the category of *physical light*. We cannot think without distinguishing; and cannot distinguish without thinking of A and B as in juxtaposition, for the intellectual representation of juxtaposition is the root of all creaturely thinking. But this is the intellectual representation of space; and the simplest dimension of space— the representation of a line, or a point, or, in short, of any demarcation in space, cannot be internally effected without the representation of a distinct colouring—that is, *enlightenment*— and consequently without physical light. The nature of physical light is inborn in the thinking soul. Light is *distinction* in its very nature; and it may be said to be more than a mere allegorical phrase, that an intellectual truth is brought to *light*, when it is made plain.

And thus it is more than a parable or allegory, and even more than an analogy, when, *in the ethical domain*, sin, the selfishness which turns away from God, and shuts itself against the neighbour, is represented as darkness, and the sentiment of love and truthfulness is represented as light. It is not a fortuitous and external thing that sin, in all its diversified forms and manifestations, as cunning, as murder, as theft, as uncleanness, etc., shuns even the *physical* light. It is not alone the fear of discovery and punishment which operates here: sin is in its essential *nature* an involution and shutting up in self—a turning away from all moral and physical relations and ordinances in the world of God's arrangement—a wilful and selfish negation of those orderly gradations of cosmical, physical, and ethical organization which were developed by the hand of God out of the creation of physical light, Gen. i. 3, as the further results of creation. And thus the ethical darkness of sin is most internally related to the lie, as light is to truthfulness. For holy love has this for its nature, to open itself and its nature, and make it manifest towards others; sinful selfishness closes and conceals itself, and all that is in itself. Now, to conceal that which is actually present, and not to make it manifest, is to "lie."

Seeing, then, that we find light thus supreme in the sphere of creaturely existence—light physical, metaphysical, and ethical being thus undeniably one in the essence of their nature;—seeing that physical light appears to be the producing, forming, quickening principle of all organization, in its essence self-communicative, and the stimulating principle of all physical organic functions of life;—seeing, then, that the thinking soul, the spirit of man, has essentially the same physical light for the generating principle of its thinking life;—and seeing, finally, that the disposition of mind and will which we term holy love is no other than the illumination of our own nature for the sake of others; and thus that the same great principle may be traced throughout all these,—it cannot be thought an overbold leap in thought, if we draw from this deepest fundamental principle and fundamental law of the physical, intellectual, and religious life in the *creature*, an inference with respect to the eternal inner nature of the Creator. The Creator, who made light the principle of all orders of creation, physical, intellectual, and ethical, must Himself in His *nature* be *light* (comp. Jas. i. 17; He is not merely the *Creator*, but the *Father* of light!). That life—uttering and diffusing itself in love, making all darkness manifest, and drawing it to the light—must be the life and nature of the Creator Himself. The individual kinds of light, which in the creature are exhibited in their distinct characters and separately, must have been in Him from all eternity in their primal unity. And if in man *thinking and self-consciousness* takes effect essentially under the category of *physical light*—that is, of *distinction*—we have in *thought, self-conscious of love and of a relation to God*, a dim symbol or reflection of the manner in which the nature of God unites all three characters of light eternally in one.

To the positive clause St John now appends the confirming and more closely defining negative side: *And there is no darkness in Him at all.* He writes ἐν αὐτῷ, not ἐνώπιον αὐτοῦ; and therefore does not mean to say that *between God and the creature* all is light unto God, that is, that the creature lies naked and manifest before the glance of God (which would be a one-sided interpretation, leading only to the Divine omniscience), but that in the *internal essence of God's own nature* there is no kind of darkness at all. *No kind* of darkness—οὐκ —οὐδεμία. All and every kind of darkness, whatever may in any sense be termed σκοτία, is excluded from the nature of

God. Hence Düsterdieck admits that it is not the *holiness* of God alone which is here meant (as it is not alone the darkness of *sin* that is denied in relation to God), but rather that the observation of the old Scholiast has something right in it: οὔτε γὰρ ἄγνοια, οὔτε πλάνη, οὔτε ἁμαρτία, οὔτε θάνατος, *neither ignorance, nor error, nor sin, nor death.* Sander well exhibits the comprehensive and almost inexhaustible sense of these words, and remarks with propriety, " that no philosophy hath found one God, who is a Light in which there is no darkness." In Pantheism (he says correctly), with its ever-becoming God, the difference between evil and good is only seeming; even with Schleiermacher, sin is an inevitable point of transition, conditioned by Divine necessity. Spinoza declares (Tract. Theol. Polit. 2, 8), that what is called evil appears such only to the individual being, which cannot grasp evil as a necessary element of the universe of things. Even Schelling cannot go beyond the " dark primal ground" in God; as Plato could not go beyond the ὕλη, and Jacob Böhme beyond the " dark wrath-nature" in the Divine Being. It is only the Sacred Scripture, the word of the living God alone, which in fact teaches us to know the true God, in whom there is no σκοτία *at all,* who in *His very substance* is light, who has that principle in His very *nature,* the reflection of which we see in physical, metaphysical, and ethical light; *the* God, who—in Himself eternally a *Spirit self-conscious, living, loving,* and, in virtue of His life of love, *self-distinguishing* (as the Trinity)—produced the creature into existence, in self-conscious free will, and with a perfect contemplation of the end which He purposed, and organized and appointed the crown of the creature, man, to a loving knowledge of God, to the κοινωνία or *fellowship* of the light.

This being the comprehensively profound meaning which lies in the words of ver. 5, there are particularly two aspects of this truth which we may discern in the relation of ver. 5 to vers. 6–8, and which we must regard as clearly presenting themselves to the mind of St John. First, the *material* truth, that in God there is no kind of darkness, no kind of sin;—and from this flows the consequence, vers. 6, 7, that he who would have fellowship with God, cannot on his part walk in ethical darkness. But also the *formal* side of this truth, that in God there is no kind of metaphysical darkness, no obscurity and ignorance; that He rather, as being in His own nature light, fashioned the creature as ever and fully penetrable to Himself;—and from this flows the consequence, vers. 7, 8, that he who has sin and conceals it, deceiveth only himself (and not God). Both sides of the truth, like the whole statement itself, bear thus also an undeniable *polemical relation to the Cerinthian gnosis;* that is, are aimed at the very root of all Gnosticism. For in this the God of Cerinthus was the direct opposite of the true God,—and the teaching of Cerinthus the direct opposite of the truth—that the God of Cerinthus *was not light*, but that the *darkness* was so absolutely in himself, that all the darkness and sin in the world must at last be charged upon this Cerinthian " primus Deus." For, this primus Deus, or this " principalitas" (Iren. i. 26), was most assuredly an impotent being, who did not himself *create* in self-conscious will, but was obliged to *tolerate* the separation and emanation from himself of a "virtus," which virtus created a world altogether ignorant of the *primus Deus*. In the place of the clear almighty will in God, was brought in a dark fatalist nature-process in God. And the producing agent employed upon the natural world is no longer the light (as in Gen. i. 3), but the darkness condensing itself into matter. According to Cerinthus, the world *in its very substance* was created in sin. According to the word of God, the world in its very substance was created of light, and in light and for light; and was appointed to the knowledge of the Eternal Light, and to walk in it.

Hence, how simple soever the clause, God is Light, may seem, it nevertheless contains, in fact, the entire Christian doctrine and revelation infolded germinally in itself; and therefore may rightly be exhibited by St John as ἡ ἀγγελία, as the epitome and substance of the *whole* Christian announcement. For, that *primal law* which immediately follows from the light-nature of God, forms the basis of the Christian redemption. God, in conformity with His own nature, so fashioned and organized the nature of man (who is the crown and end of the creation), that he can have his perfect satisfaction only by actual fellowship with God, the Light in Himself: He therefore so fashioned it, that there is for men a distinction between light and darkness, holiness and sin, good and evil, innocence and guilt, blessedness and misery. Upon this primal law rests the whole necessity of a redemption; apart from this primal law of human nature, there would be for men no distinction between good and evil; without this, there would be no guilt and condemnation, and no necessity therefore to be redeemed. But, as this primal law, and the necessity of a redemption resulting from it, rests upon the light-nature of God, so, in the second place, *the nature of the redemption itself* flows from the light-nature of God. As in the nature of God as the Light both elements are in principle one—the formal element of *truth and self-manifestation*, and the material element of *holy love and self-communication* (the former disclosing, laying bare, and condemning the darkness; the latter communicating life and overcoming death)—so also, in the fact of atonement through Christ, both elements are in principle united: that of the truth and self-manifestation, which, as confronting the sinner, is no other than the *judging righteousness* of God (who, in opposition to sin and darkness, demonstrates and asserts His own nature, His light, His holiness, making it actually manifest against evil); and that of the sacred self-sacrificing, self-imparting, love, which, as confronting the sinner, is no other than *saving grace*. The sacrificial death of Christ is the judgment of grace, the grace of judgment, the redeeming confirmation of judicial righteousness, the highest confirmation of absolute love, in the act of holy condemnation pronounced upon sin,—in the surrender of the Holy One to judgment for sinners, of the Prince of life to death (Acts iii. 15), of the eternal Light to the power of darkness (John xiii. 20; Luke xxii. 53). In the *death* of Christ, sin is condemned and guilt is expiated, the sin is judged and the sinner is saved. Thus, from the nature of atonement these two things follow: *the requirement of repentance, of the knowledge of sin, and of truth as against himself,* on the part of man; and *the assurance of love, grace, and adoption,* unto man. The interaction and combination of the two—of the truth which knows and confesses sin, and the love to God which overcomes it—leads to and constitutes *the walking in the light,* or holiness. And this combination is the same which is exhibited in the nature of light itself, and which even physical light illustrates: it is the combination of the manifestation of self and of life-producing self-impartation. For both the *conspicuum esse* to the beholding *look,* and the *eradiare,* the beam ing forth into others' *substance,* belong inseparably to the nature of light as such, even of physical light. All light exerts both a judicial and a quickening influence.

The two central points which constitute the *walking in light,* or *the appropriation of the redemption accomplished in Christ,* are now specifically developed and expanded by St John in VERS. 6–8 : in vers. 6, 7, the requirement of a holy walk ; in vers. 8, 9, the requirement of the knowledge and confession of sin. But, in relation to these, the Apostle opportunely gives expression to those two elemental truths in God which constitute *the nature of the atoning act itself,*—His actual truth or righteousness, and His love or grace. The former is indirectly brought before us, when it is said in ver. 8, that he who concealeth his sin deceiveth himself, and hath not the truth (of God) in him ; the latter is directly referred to at the close of ver. 7, and again in ver. 9.

If we take a general glance at THE CHAIN OF THOUGHT FROM CH. I. 6 to CH. II. 6, we find that the Apostle first of all draws, in ch. i. 6–10, the two conclusions which follow from those two characteristics of the light-nature of God as it respects man, the Christian,—to wit, first, vers. 6, 7, *the Christian may not sin ;* secondly, vers. 8–10, *the Christian may not conceal his sin.* Thus these two consequences are seen to stand in connection with each other, without anything as yet to mediate between them, and as it were in apparent contradiction. Hence, in ch. ii. 1–6, St John gives the truth *which reconciles the two.* For he shows in ver. 1 that the not sinning is always a requirement which, *as such,* is binding upon us, notwithstanding that our *actual condition* may not as yet be in harmony with that requirement ;—but that the means in order to compliance with it lie in the *propitiation through Christ,* once for all accomplished, which is offered at the same time that the requirement is enforced ; while this propitiation does no detriment to that requirement (vers. 3–6), inasmuch as it takes effect generally only for those who have known the nature of the light, and accordingly lay that injunction *upon themselves.*

VERS. 6, 7. The *first consequence* from the truth, that God is light, is this, that the man who would assert truly that he has fellowship with God, must confirm it by his own holy walk in the light. St John draws out this inference in two conditional clauses, ver. 6 and ver. 7, which, as to their essential meaning, run strictly parallel, though the second of them in its conclusion contains a transition from the first to the second inference. Both clauses begin with ἐάν. This particle does not introduce, as Schmid says, a *casus ex re non fortuitâ sed debitâ et moraliter necessariâ*; nor, as Winer affirms,[1] a "condition with the assumption of objective possibility." Ἐάν is used when the possibility is not merely an *assumed* one, but one which has a real ground in objective relations; hence then, in particular, when *only two* cases are possible, of which the one *or* the other must necessarily be the fact, and therefore when *it is expected that it will in reality be decided whether that which is stated as possible will be the fact or its opposite*. So here. The one case is, that we, while we profess to have fellowship with God, walk in darkness; the other, that we walk in light. *Tertium non datur*. (So ch. ii. 15, iv. 20.) That St John uses this turn of phrase precisely here, where he "will exhibit a *moral* law" (Düsterdieck), has its reason, not in the meaning of ἐάν, but in this, that St John has to do here with the matter, not of physical, but of ethical religious objects. Viewed in itself, the ἐάν may just as well be used for the representation of natural laws and conditions.

"If we say that we have fellowship with God:" the εἴπωμεν is quite analogous to the λέγῃ of Jas. ii. 14, being an assertion to which no reality corresponds. On that account we must not lay too much stress on the 1 Pers. Plur.: it serves only to express the general "one," and *only so far* represents the universal application of the saying announced in vers. 6, 7; not as if St John had meant to say, "Even if I, the Apostle, were to say this, and nevertheless walk in darkness, I should be a liar;" and, certainly, not that he, in "sparing delicacy," gave this declaration the form of a common Plural.

To have κοινωνίαν *with God*, means to have κοινωνία with Him *who is light;* and that word cannot otherwise be under-

---

[1] On the other hand, εἰ, cum Opt., according to Winer, expresses "a condition with the assumption of subjective possibility." But what can we understand by a "subjective possibility?" Only the subjective assumption of an objective possibility. But in that case Winer's distinction between εἰ cum Opt. and ἐάν falls to the ground.

stood than of that relation of life and fellowship of nature which had been mentioned in ver. 3, and as it is defined by John xv. 1, xvii. 21, etc. Now he who says that he stands in such a fellowship of life with God, the Light, as that of a member with the head, and nevertheless *walketh ἐν τῷ σκότει,* —*lies*. Περιπατεῖν signifies here, as in Rom. vi. 4, viii. 4, 1 John ii. 6, etc., not the internal disposition as such, but the confirmation and external assurance of that which man bears in himself as his nature—the moral deportment, so far as it is manifest before *human* eyes, and is discernible by *man*. This coming to manifestation in the whole round of our nature, lies in the περί itself. Περιπατεῖν is *to go round,* to *go on*. Ἐν τῷ σκότει does not, as the ἐν clearly shows, express the qualitative characteristic, but the *sphere* in which that walk, that exhibition of the life outwardly, is conducted. In the darkness he walks whose actions and demonstrations of character have their being in the sphere of sin, of untruthfulness, of death—of the sinful course of the world and its perishable lusts, its lies, its wickedness, and its vanity. Where this is the case, *where the life and aim and deportment* of a man runs in the *sphere* of the selfish, ungodly, worldly, fleshly nature, there the *internal nature* of the man cannot be standing in that fellowship with God. From the *sphere* which a man chooses for the exhibition of his internal nature, we may draw a sure conclusion as to the *character of that internal nature itself*. And he who serves darkness in the bent of his life as it is visible to the eyes of men, and yet would assert that in his *internal secret nature* he stands in fellowship with God, is a liar. *Such* a discord between the inner and the outer man cannot by possibility exist. Internal fellowship of life with God cannot do otherwise than reveal itself externally to man in the fruits of sanctification ; yea, the light which shines inwardly must of necessity so diffuse its glow of holy consecration over the whole life, that the eyes of men may see it. He who lives in fellowship with God, and is born of the light, cannot in his life and deportment conceal his high derivation.

He who saith that he hath fellowship with God, and yet walketh in darkness, lieth, however, not only in words : he not only *speaketh* not the truth; he *doeth* not the truth likewise. Καὶ οὐ ποιοῦμεν τὴν ἀλήθειαν. In this, that he saith he hath fellowship with God, he *speaketh* not the truth; in this, that he walketh in the darkness, he *doeth* not the truth. The contradiction between his pretension and his walk has a double aspect of lying; both in *word* and *deed* he denies the truth: in word he denies *that* truth, that he is an unregenerate child of darkness; in act he denies that substantial truth, in which the nature of God and the nature of light consists. The former is the opposite of the formal truthfulness against itself, of the knowledge and confession of sin as a present reality in self; the latter is the opposite of the material truth, of the substantive love to God, of the requirement which he, by saying that he has fellowship with God, admits as a requirement, while he in act denies it.—That τὴν ἀλήθειαν can mean only the substantial truth—that which in its nature is conformed to the nature of God the Light—ought never to have been doubted, after the standard of interpretation had been given in such passages as ver. 8, ch. ii. 21; John iii. 21.[1]

In ver. 7 the second conditional clause follows. The converse to that laid down in verse 6 is this, that *we walk in the light*. This walking in the light forms the *actual* contrast to the acts of those who *say* indeed that they have fellowship with God, but yet *walk in darkness*. The meaning of the expression, *walking in the light*, must be explained after the analogy of the former. Περιπατεῖν marks, as in ver. 6, the externally-shown exhibition of that which is in the man; and ἐν τῷ φωτί, as in ver. 6, defines the *sphere* in which that outer demonstration of the internal nature moves. Hence, the φῶς does not indicate the light as the substance of God itself, but that in the objective *world* which in character corresponds to the nature of God —that which is not sinful pursuit, selfishness, falsehood, wickedness, but love, truthfulness, salvation, and the holy heavenly nature. In the light he walks whose action and deportment runs in the sphere of those deeds, impulses, and relations, which in their objective scope and quality correspond to the nature of light—that is, to the nature of love, life, and truthfulness.

[1] Episcopius explains ποιεῖν τὴν ἀλήθειαν by *facere quod rectum est*, and regards it then as equivalent to *dicere veritatem*. Lachmann takes it as ἀληθεύειν, Eph. iv. 15; Socinus as *agere recte;* Grotius, *sincere agere;* Luther, Calvin, Beza, Bengel, after the analogy of Ezek. xviii. 9, עָשָׂה אֱמֶת, the performance of good words, that which is right.

But, having once used φῶς, ver. 7, in this objective *qualitative* meaning—not to define the Divine substance, but the sphere of the manifestation of the good and the Godlike—St John does not go on to say, "As He is light," but, in order to avoid confusion of ideas, "As He is in the light." Even of God it is said that He is *in the light*. That sphere of the good, the holy, the heavenly, the pure, is the sphere in which God (while as the Creator everywhere present in and to His works) has in an especial sense His dwelling-place; that is, in which He may disclose His nature concealed, and on which His eye rests with holy complacency. (The passage, 1 Tim. vi. 16, treats of something quite different from this, and is not applicable here.) But it is not said of God that He περιπατεῖ ἐν τῷ φωτί: He ἐστὶν ἐν τῷ φωτί—He *is*, not *walketh*, in light. The idea of περιπατεῖν can have no place in God in any sense: that antithetical relation between the internal and the externally visible, which subsists among men, cannot be predicated of God. God *is* in light—that is, He *dwelleth* in that sphere in which no sin, no falsehood, no death is, among the holy angels and the souls of men made perfect. Between this and our walking in the light there is an analogy. As God elects for Himself the sphere of the sinless and pure life of the angels and glorified men for His dwelling-place, and His perfect complacency rests there, and as He is everywhere upon earth, also, specifically present in His power and blessing where He is feared and loved, so also he who is born of God will approve the character of his internal nature by conducting all his acts and aims in that sphere in which God is feared and loved: not amid the vain and impure pursuits of the world, and of the flesh, with its evil thoughts and unholy imaginations; but in the sphere of holy external and internal surroundings, in the circles of the children of God, as in the circle of sacred thoughts and holy imaginations. The macrocosm as well as the microcosm, the outer world as well as the inner world, in which his willing, loving, and striving live and move, will be light, that is, corresponding to the nature of God.

That is "to walk in the light, as God is in the light."

Turn we now to the sequel of the sentence. What is it that is declared concerning those who thus walk in the light? In ver. 6 we heard, that if we say that we have fellowship with

God, and yet walk in darkness, we lie in word and act; that is, if we walk in darkness, we *have no* fellowship with God. Accordingly, we might now expect the bare, and as it were tautological, converse, that if we walk in the light, we *have* fellowship with God. In fact, the reading μετ' αὐτοῦ instead of μετ' ἀλλήλων—*with Him* instead of *one with another*—is found in Tertullian, Clem. Rom., Clem. Alex., Didymus, and the Æthiop. Vers.; and it appears also to have been the reading of Cod. A. But that reading has too little external support, and is too suspicious internally, to have much stress laid upon it. For it is only too clear that it owed its origin to the desire to make ver. 7 externally conformable to ver. 6, and thus to establish a simple logical antithesis. But it is not St John's manner to lay down such bare contrasts and antitheses as repeat in the second member the same thought in a negative form which the first contained. He always prefers to introduce in every new clause of the discourse some new aspect of the object. And so it is here, in the correct reading, "one with another." He has already declared, in ver. 6, that he who *saith* that he hath fellowship with God, and yet conducts his life in the sphere of the ungodly nature, lies in word and deed. And certainly the leading thought of ver. 7 is no other than this: He, on the other hand, that walketh in the light, does stand *really* in fellowship with God. But this leading thought is presented in such a form, and is arranged in such an order, that it contains at the same time a twofold progression to something new. *First*, that is, the idea of actual fellowship with God is resolved into its two great elements. That fellowship with God is, according to ver. 3 (as in John xvii.), a fellowship which approves itself in fellowship of love with the brethren (just as "walking in the light" is essentially walking in love, and in the first member of our sentence is characterized as walking in the *sphere* and the *living circle* of holy persons and holy interests). And again this brotherly communion rests upon no other ground than that of fellowship with God in Christ. Thus St John resolves this fellowship with God at once into its two main points: into the fellowship of *believers one with another*,[1] and the fellowship and common participation

---

[1] It is grammatically inadmissible, and a perversion of the meaning, to make (with Augustin, Socinus, Calvin) the κοινωνία μετ' ἀλλήλων mean

of a *Divine power of life*. " He who walketh in light, as God is in the light," he would say, " hath that true fellowship with God really in its two aspects: He standeth, *a*) in the fellowship of the children of God (that was already expressed in " walking in the light"); and, *b*) in the fellowship of God Himself and His purifying power. But, *secondly*, St John now characterizes this life-fellowship with God as the *cleansing from all sins by the blood of Christ*. This is joined to the "fellowship one with another" by the καὶ as a second element; and therefore it is doing violence to the text to regard the second member (with Œcumen., Theophyl., Beza, etc.) as furnishing the *reason* of the first: " We have fellowship one with another, and stand in love, *because* we have through Christ forgiveness of sins." This is simply to obtrude dogmatics into the exposition of the words. An expositor should be (as Bengel says) like the maker of a well, who puts no water into the source himself, but makes it his object to let the water flow without diversion, stoppage, or defilement. That forced view of the relation of the thoughts would not have been adopted, had it not been taken for granted that καθαρίζειν signified the *forgiveness* of sins, *justification*. We find this view adopted also by Calvin, Bullinger, Schmid, and Episcopius; although these do not regard the second clause as establishing the first, but rightly view it as a co-ordinate member. But, in later times, the more correct apprehension of καθαρίζειν, as meaning the *sanctifying, purifying* power of the blood of Christ, has been very generally adopted (Lücke, Neander, Olshausen, Düsterdieck). This is conclusively decided by the ninth verse, where the καθαρίζειν occurs in connection with ἀφιέναι as something *different*. And it is supported by the use of the Present tense, which marks the cleansing as not being an act accomplished once, the act of justification, but as a continuous process.[1] But, finally and especially, the analogy of faith, like the process and connection of the specific context, leads necessarily to the idea of the *sanctifying*

the fellowship which believers, on the one hand, and *God* on the other, have " with each other." Similarly Episcopius, Paulus, and De Wette.

[1] This reason is nevertheless less decisive, since it may be said that, in connection with daily sanctification, there must be also a daily new appropriation of the assurance of forgiveness,—and indeed lying at the root of the former.

power of God exerted upon believers. That the *walking* in light is represented as the *condition* under which we attain to the forgiveness of sins (ἐάν!)—is a notion which utterly contradicts the whole strain of apostolical teaching. The walking in light must indeed be the result, and therefore the note and sign, of the faith which exists; consequently, it will be the sign that the condition under which God has promised to forgive sins has been complied with. But this sign cannot *itself* be represented as the condition of forgiveness; *that* is, according to St John, as according to St Paul, everywhere only *faith as such* (comp. John i. 12, iii. 15, 16, and 18 and 36, v. 24, vi. 29 and 40, xv. 3, etc.); and even in our ninth verse St John requires, as the condition of the ἄφεσις, not the *walking* in light, but simply the truthful, sincere *confession* of our sin and misery—that confession which is the essential ground from which springs faith—coming to receive, and not to do or give. Now, as the analogy of faith forbids our referring the καθαρισμός, of which walking in the light is a condition, to the forgiveness of sins, so the chain of thought in the context constrains us to refer it to the sanctifying power of God. The antithetical relation between ver. 6 and ver. 7 must not be omitted from our view. The fundamental thought which runs through both verses is this, that a *walk* in darkness necessarily infers an inner nature full of darkness, which has *not* God's nature living in it; that, on the other hand, a *walk* in light gives testimony of that fellowship (ver. 3) which, in its manifestation, exhibits itself as the fellowship of love with the brethren, but which, in its root, is a fellowship and participation in the *nature* of God, the *Light*. The subject here must be this, that God's *nature* lives in such a Christian; not this, that he receives the forgiveness of sins. Thus καθαρισμός indicates the *purifying, sanctifying* energy of God living within him; and with this also agree the words ἀπὸ πάσης ἁμαρτίας. From all and every kind of sin he is cleansed by God, who is light, and who liveth and worketh in him.

That not God Himself as such, but τὸ αἷμα Ἰησοῦ τοῦ υἱοῦ αὐτοῦ,[1] is mentioned as the subject, does not by any means

---

[1] Instead of the simple Ἰησοῦ (Cod B.C., Syr., Arm., Sahid., etc), Cod. A. and Rec. read Ἰησοῦ Χριστοῦ. The latter word may certainly be explained as an interpolation taken from ver. 3, for the sake of conformity with ch. ii. 1, iii. 23, iv. 2, v. 20; while it is not to be imagined why a

interfere with this construction of the meaning. That by the αἷμα Ἰησοῦ we must understand the real blood of Jesus poured out upon the cross, and not, with Socinus, the *fidus novum,* or with Grotius, the *fides in passionem,* or with Episcopius, the *obedientia Christi,* or with Paulus, the "rational faith in the moral end of the death of Jesus," is as certain and self-understood, on the one hand, as it is, on the other, that it is not the matter or material substance of that blood in which a magical power lay, whether to forgive or to cleanse from sin. Not in virtue of its material constituents, or of any magical power inherent in these constituents, but in virtue of its *having been shed,* has the blood of Jesus the power to cleanse from sins. Hence in St John (John vi. 53; 1 John v. 6, comp. Heb. ix. 14, Rom. v. 9, 10) the blood of Christ is most certainly equivalent to the death of Christ. But this death of Christ, or His blood *as* poured out, has not less power to cleanse our hearts from sin than it had to furnish a propitiation and obtain forgiveness: the latter, because in the blood of Christ guilt was reckoned for, and grace obtained; the former, because in the death of Christ sin has been condemned. He who livingly believes in the atoning death of Christ cannot love sin—the sin which brought Jesus to the cross. Thus the blood of Jesus continues to exercise a purifying, sanctifying influence, until the heart is cleansed from all sin. And, indeed, the blood and death of *Jesus* has this power, because He was and He is *the Son of God,* in whom the nature of the Father was manifested; because in Him *the eternal Light* surrendered itself, by virtue of its light-nature, that is, love, to that darkness. Hence the apposition τοῦ υἱοῦ αὐτοῦ. In Christ ruleth, worketh, dwelleth the Father Himself. The fellowship of the blood of Christ is fellowship with the Father in its most concentrated concentration.

But when St John has drawn out to this point the *first inference* from the statement that God is light—to wit, the inference, vers. 6, 7, that he who stands in fellowship with God must himself walk in the light—he has already in effect gone beyond that first inference, and has touched another and a

copyist should have omitted Χριστοῦ, if that had stood in the text. There might be good reason why St John here, where he is speaking of the *blood* of Christ, should describe the Lord by the name of His humanity and humiliation alone.

second element of the question. If the blood of Christ cleanses us from all sin, it is taken for granted that we *need* such a cleansing, *that sin is still in us*, even in those who "walk in the light." The *requirement*, that we walk in the light, is confronted by the *fact*, that in us there still is sin and darkness.

And this has now internally prepared the way, and given a connection for, a *second inference*, VERS. 8–10; to wit, that *we must in truth and sincerity of mind confess the existing sin that is in us to ourselves and to God.* In the external dialectic form of the passage, this inference is not connected with ver. 7, to say nothing of ver. 5; but an internal bond connects it with both these verses. First of all, the concluding thought of ver. 7 leads over immediately to the thought of ver. 8 : "Cleansing from sin presupposes the presence of sin even in believers; the denial of that is self-deception" (Huther). Accordingly, vers. 8–10 might appear to be only a further unfolding of a point contained in vers. 6, 7, and consequently as a mere continuation of vers. 6, 7. But who does not see that this new point assumes at once an independent position, and one even apparently in opposition to vers. 6, 7 ? Who does not see that in this, its independent position, it stands in an *immediate* relation to the leading sentence, ver. 5 ? From the truth, that God is light and in Him is no darkness at all, follows, first, that fellowship with Him will approve itself by a walk in light; but secondly, and not less directly, that we, who are not like God in having no darkness at all, must needs confess in *truth* this our darkness. For truth is not less an essential element of the light-nature than holiness is, and love. *Nam ipsa veritas lux est,* remarks Augustin on the passage.—Even in the formal view, vers. 8, 9 assume an independent position in regard to vers. 6, 7; for the construction of the clauses is perfectly parallel.

VER. 8. Here again the thought is distributed into two conditional clauses, beginning with ἐάν, in which an alternative, a pair of possible cases, is represented to the reader.

The first case is, ἐὰν εἴπωμεν, ὅτι ἁμαρτίαν οὐκ ἔχομεν. Once more (as in ver. 6) an εἰπεῖν, a *saying*, to which no actual fact corresponds. There, it was the profession of having fellowship with God, while yet walking in darkness; here, it is the profession of having no sin, while yet the sin is present.

There, St John requires of the Christian that he walk in light; here, that he confess that he has sin. This relation of the thoughts of itself establishes, with logical necessity, that ἁμαρτίαν ἔχειν must be something different from ἐν σκοτίᾳ περιπατεῖν. For the latter, the walking in darkness, is assumed to be entirely excluded from the condition of a Christian, while the former must be acknowledged as present by every Christian (the 1 Pers. Pl.). But wherein the difference between these two consists, it is not so altogether easy to determine. The first glance shows the fallacy of the opinion of Socinus, Grotius, and Episcopius, according to which ἁμαρτία defines the *guilt* of sins contracted *before* conversion. The subject here, is that of an actual inward possession of present sin. But this having of sin must be something different from the walking in darkness; and therefore we cannot, with Bengel and De Wette, refer it without qualification to the contracting of new guilt by new sins. The expression is interpreted to mean *original sin,* or still-remaining *concupiscentia,* in opposition to *actual sins,* by Augustin, Luther, Calvin, Beza, Calovius, Neander; of sins which are committed against better knowledge and will, by Huther; of the condition which is the result of still-continued sinning, by Lücke and others. But the assertion that the Christian has still only *concupiscentia,* or original sin, and no longer commits *any* actual sins, would be most assuredly, according to the Apostle's meaning itself, a ἑαυτὸν πλανᾶν! as also that, in the sins which he commits, his will does not concur. But, as it respects Lücke's opinion, we have only to put it in the right form to hit the truth, or at least to approximate towards it. Not the condition *which* proceeds *from* the continuing to sin, but the condition *from which* the continuing to sin proceeds, and in which it takes place, might be defined as the ἁμαρτίαν ἔχειν. Meanwhile that fails to establish the sharp distinction between this and the "walking in darkness." To bring this out, we must not hazard a variety of speculations, but contemplate each of the two expressions steadily, in its own distinctive meaning. Περιπατεῖν ἐν τῇ σκοτίᾳ describes, as we have seen, a walk, deportment, and pursuit, observable by man, which *is conducted in the sphere of that which is* σκοτία. The περιπατεῖν is in the σκοτία; on the other hand, in the ἔχειν ἁμαρτίαν, the man is not in the ἁμαρτία, but the ἁμαρτία in the man. Now, it is undoubtedly true that every kind of ἁμαρτία belongs to the domain of darkness, and not to that of light; but there would be a great difference between ἡ σκοτία and σκοτία, between ἡ ἁμαρτία and ἁμαρτία, without the article; how much wider is the difference therefore between ἡ σκοτία and the simple ἁμαρτία without the article! Ἡ σκοτία is *the* darkness in *all* its characteristics, shut up and comprehending in itself all these characteristics (sin, lie, deception, rebellion, death, vanity, and so forth), placing itself in contradiction to the nature of God: ἁμαρτία is any particular deportment of a sinful kind, so far as it is a falling away from the true renewed nature of the man. In the domain of "the darkness" he has his conversation whose aims and acts[1] move in the sphere of *the life turned away from God*, whose scope of life is thus carnal and vain, whose maxims are unspiritual and worldly, whose imaginations are impure, whose affections are unholy, and whose favourite society is not that of the true children of God. On the other hand, the "having sin" may still be said of him whose internal ruling principle is the love of God springing from faith, whose *system* of life (in aims, tendencies, maxims, endeavours) is one that is regulated by the Spirit of Christ, according to the will of God and the rules of His kingdom, whose delight is among the children of God, in whose society he seeks his consolation and help. He walks no longer in *the* sin, not to say *the* darkness; the sphere in which his life revolves is that of the kingdom of Jesus Christ. But while he is no longer in sin, sin is still in him. Not only impulses and affections of sensuous desire and constitutional inclination in his physical-psychical soul-life; but also obscurities and dark places in his intellectual life, which still need to be overcome and enlightened away (such as lack of self-knowledge, undue sparing of evil, principles and views which seem to be born of the Spirit, while in reality they are born of the flesh); and, as the consequence of both, there is the confused wavering

---

[1] The περιπατεῖν leads, as we have seen upon ver. 6, not to the idea of the internal spirit and temper, but to that of the conduct as outwardly exhibited, and witnessed by men without in the world. Only we must not suppose that others can perceive nothing but the glaring external act. The dispositions, the tendencies, the fundamental principles, and, above all, the character of men's imaginations, are sure more or less to betray themselves to the observer.

of will, which leads to individual obliquities of a grosser or more subtle kind. It is obvious that this ἔχειν ἁμαρτίαν is infinitely diversified, according to the successive measure of the purification and development of the new man; even the Apostle St John does not exclude himself from the universal "If we say."

He, then, who disputes or questions to himself or other men this ἔχειν ἁμαρτίαν before God, *deceiveth himself*, ἑαυτοὺς πλανῶμεν. Πλάνη is "error;" not error, however, in the objective sense of a theoretically erroneous principle of doctrine, but error in the ethical sense. It is a way of error, in which man, whether through self-deception or through seduction on the part of others, has been led astray; comp. John iv. 6, and 2 Thess. ii. 11. Hence πλάνος, 2 John 7, and 1 Tim. iv. 1, is he who deceives others touching the truth, and thus seduces them to lie and to error. Πλανάω, accordingly, does not mean in the New Testament "seduce" in the ordinary sense,—that, namely, of enticing to anything wicked; but the fundamental idea remains, that of *a deceiving with respect to the truth*. Thus it is not seduction of any and every kind, but the specific misleading *into error and falsehood*, which is expressed by πλανάω: compare Matt. xxiv. 4 and 11; Rev. ii. 20, xii. 9, xix. 20; 1 John iii. 7; 2 Tim. iii. 13, and other passages. Hence it is wrong to translate, "We mislead ourselves;" and most certainly Huther has no ground for the assertion that the Mid. πλανᾶσθαι means to "go astray," while πλανᾶν ἑαυτόν means "to mislead oneself." That there is no difference in *meaning* between the Middle and the Active, we are taught most clearly by the passage, 2 Tim. ii. 13, and by a comparison of Rev. xviii. 23 with xix. 20, or of John vii. 47 with 1 John iii. 7. Πλανᾶν ἑαυτόν is no other than a kind of paraphrase of the Middle, peculiar to St John's Greek. Everywhere, in the Middle and Passive, as in the Active, πλανᾶν bears the same signification: that of deceiving concerning the truth, that is, seducing to a lying doctrine; never does πλανᾶν mean misleading in general, and without any qualification. The translation, "We mislead ourselves," would in this passage give rise to the false idea that the Apostle meant, "If we say we have no sin, we seduce ourselves to *commit sin*—so that we thereby sin all the more." True, that this thought would not be incorrect in itself, in as far as every non-perception and palliation of present sin and past sins absolutely involves a hardening of the conscience with respect to future sins; but that is not what the Apostle has it here in view to say—his meaning is something different. For, the meaning and the customary use of the word πλανᾶν does not lead to the idea of seduction to sin, but that of misleading to falsehood; and, moreover, our πλανῶμεν ἑαυτούς runs parallel with the ψευδόμεθα of ver. 6, as our καὶ ἡ ἀλήθεια ἐν ἡμῖν οὐκ ἔστιν runs parallel with the words of ver. 6, καὶ οὐ ποιοῦμεν τὴν ἀλήθειαν. But these two pairs of phrases are certainly not similar in signification, though they are analogous. In both, the Apostle says that there is as well a theoretical untruth, as an actual negation of truth in life; only he declares it in ver. 8 by other and still stronger expressions. He that saith he hath fellowship with God, without however walking in the light, *lieth* in so saying; he *lieth* towards *others*, as his εἰπεῖν would appear to be primarily directed to *others*. He, on the other hand, who saith that he hath no sin, *deceiveth himself*, as *this* εἰπεῖν would appear to be primarily a speaking to self. "To deceive self," however, is in its guilt more heinous, and in its consequences more perilous, than that former simple ψεύδεσθαι. In that case it is an unregenerate man who would make others believe that he is a Christian; in this case it is a Christian, who, against his better knowledge, in spiritual pride, again deceives himself concerning the truth that he had already apprehended. The ἀλήθεια ἐν ἡμῖν οὐκ ἔστι is similarly related to the οὐ ποιοῦμεν τὴν ἀλήθειαν. He who walketh in darkness, while giving out that he stands in fellowship with God, denieth in fact that substantial truth in which the nature of God, the nature of the Light, consists. He who deceiveth himself into the belief that he hath no sin—in him the power and energy of the light, which discloses all darkness, and draws all sin to the judgment, cannot be working, cannot be present; thus, while he denies his still-existing sin, he casts the substantial truth or light-nature, immanent in him before, out of himself; yea, he must already have cast it out, in order to have been able to "say that he hath no sin." Ἡ ἀλήθεια, here as in ver. 6, does not indicate the subjective disposition of truthfulness, but the objective essence of the Divine nature, which is light, and therefore truth and truthfulness. This nature of God he cannot have, dwelling and working in himself, who denies his sin.

In VER. 9 the second member of the general thought now follows, in a conditional clause which introduces the opposite side of the alternative. "If we confess our sins." St John avoids here also a mere tautological repetition. He does not write, "If we confess that we have sin;" but, when he is setting over against the negative denial the positive confession, he speaks not of the confession of a sinful condition generally, but of our definite, concrete, and individual sins. For this is the form which confession of sin must assume, if it ever becomes a practical and effectual reality. The mere confession *in abstracto* that we have sin, would, without the knowledge and the admission of our concrete individual sins, lose its truth and value, and soon degenerate into a mere phrase. It is much easier to utter a pious lamentation over our misery, and to speak rightly about repentance, than to see our unrighteousness, to confess it, and mourn over it, in the definite instance in which we have sinned. St John requires the latter. The question, whether the ὁμολογεῖν means a confession before God and one's own soul (Bullinger, Neander), or a confession before men, is in its ground an idle one. As the "saying that we have no sin," as far as it is called a "deceiving ourselves," appears first of all as a representation to self, so the "confession" must be intended first of a confession in the inner soul and before God; even as in fact the next clause, "He is faithful and just," points to a procedure between the Christian *and God*. But, as certainly as the "saying" of ver. 8 might very possibly be a speaking before men, appearing then to be all the more audacious a lie and glaring a self-deception, so certainly there may, and there will, be circumstances which require the ὁμολογία of the sins committed in the presence of men (for example, before a pastor, or a Christian friend, or in public confession before the congregation). As often as the general *question* is asked of a Christian, be it by whom it may, whether he have sin, he who admits this before God and himself would obviously not deny it before men; nor would he deny or palliate his individual sins, when individual sins are charged against him. But this does not lie in the words of our verse: the context points primarily to something passing between the Christian and his God; and those Romish expositors are as far as possible from the truth, who (as à Lapide) would argue from this passage the necessity of a private confession to the priest. God, not the priest, is mentioned as He who forgives sins.

Πιστός ἐστι καὶ δίκαιος, ἵνα, κ.τ.λ., is the supplementary clause. If we confess our sins, He—that is, God, who is the only subject of vers. 5–10, and to whom also the αὐτοῦ of ver. 7, in the words τοῦ υἱοῦ αὐτοῦ, referred—is faithful and just that He should forgive us our sins, and cleanses us from all unrighteousness. Instead of καθαρίσῃ in the Text. Rec., A. and H. read καθαρίσει—a reading which is not to be attributed, as has been alleged, to an "error of the ear," but which has rather itself been corrected into καθαρίσῃ through the anxiety of copyists to preserve grammatical correctness. It is a peculiarity of the Hebraizing idiom to connect with ἵνα the Future instead of the Subjunctive: St John does this frequently in the Apocalypse (ch. xxii. 14; and, in the true reading, also xiii. 12, xiv. 13, ix. 5); and so in the Gospel, ch. xv. 16 (where δώσει is decidedly and manifestly the right reading), with the οὐ μὴ also, as well as the ἵνα, ch. x. 5 (where A.B.D.E., Cyr., Chrys. read ἀκολουθήσουσιν), and vi. 35 (comp. Lachmann), and x. 28 (according to D.C.). But the passage, John vi. 40, is especially worthy of notice, where St John, after ἵνα, falls back again from the better Greek of the Subjunctive into the Hebraizing Indicative ἀναστήσω; so that the second member of the final clause as it were limps in its connection with the whole sentence. Suffice that the same thing is observable in our present passage. According to the *sense*, even καθαρίσει still depends upon the ἵνα; but St John has fallen back into his more customary Future, and consequently the member καὶ καθαρίσει, κ.τ.λ., is as it were sundered from its strict connection with the ἵνα. The thought is altogether Hebraic: לְמַעַן יְכַפֵּר עַל־חַטֹּאתֵינוּ וּכְבָס אֹתָנוּ מִכָּל־פֶּשַׁע. Ἵνα never stands, and it does not stand here, simply instead of ὥστε; yet it must be admitted that its original telic signification seems to be considerably weakened in such passages as this of ours. Where ἵνα occurs in its genuine original telic or *final* meaning, it declares that the act which the governing clause defines, is to be accomplished for the express end that the final clause specifies. Thus the sense would here come out: "God is faithful and just, in the design to forgive (to the end that He may forgive) our sins." But this yields no intelligible meaning. God is not faithful and just on account of any object external to Himself, but in His very nature. That He forgives our sins, follows from His fidelity and righteousness; but His fidelity and righteousness do not result from His design to forgive our sins. Thus we shall be compelled to acknowledge that the particle ἵνα has here a meaning very closely related to that of ὥστε. The idea of a design does indeed enter, in some sense, into it; it is not, however, a purpose on account of which the declared truth of the leading clause ("He is faithful and just") is evoked, but a purpose by which what the final clause declares is conditioned. "God is faithful and just, *so that* He hath (and doth effect) the will and the purpose to forgive our sins." Compare below on ch. iii. 1, as also the perfectly analogous passages, John iv. 34 (ἵνα ποιήσω = My meat is that I *should* do), vi. 29 (The work of God consists in this, that ye *should* believe) and 40, xii. 23 (The hour is come that, that is, in which the Son of Man *should* be glorified). Some similarity with this (though not a proper analogy) is seen in the use of ἵνα after θέλειν, ἐρωτᾶν, and the like (John xvii. 15 and 24).

If, after these observations upon the *phraseology*, we now enter into the *thought* of the final clause, we are met by one of those glorious *progressions* of which St John is so fond. If we deny our sin, we deceive our own selves, and the (essential) truth dwelleth not in us. If we confess our sin—the conclusion is not only this, that *we* then are true, but the incomparably greater and most surprising thought meets us, that—*God* then in act approves Himself towards us as true, as the πιστὸς καὶ δίκαιος. (Thus in ver. 7 we had, not merely the *logical opposite* of the charge ψευδόμεθα, κ.τ.λ., but the *real result* added, the walking in light.)

If we confess that which in us is still related to the σκοτία, that is, our ἁμαρτία,—if, therefore, we suffer the light of God to rule in us, so that it may bring to the light and condemn in us the darkness which still remains,—then does God approve to us in act and fact His nature as light. And this is demonstrated in relation to us, who *have sin*, under two great general aspects of manifestation—as *fidelity* and as *justice*. The idea of fidelity must not be reduced or confused by the introduction of strange elements; it must not be limited to the faithfulness of God *to His promises and declarations* (Bullinger, Sander, Huther, etc.). God's faithfulness is here spoken of as faithfulness *towards us*, fidelity to that nature of truth and light, related to His own essence, which rules in us in as far as we confess our sins. And, similarly, the notion of δίκαιος is not to be arbitrarily restricted by the dogmatic reflection, that God, when He forgives the sinner believing in Christ, performs only an act of faithfulness to Christ, who paid the penalty of sins, and thereby obtained a right to demand forgiveness on behalf of all who believe in Him. But it is still worse (with Grotius, Rosenmüller, Carpzov) to enforce upon δίκαιος the meaning of *benignus, æquus, lenis.* Δίκαιος means here and everywhere *justus.* But righteousness must here be viewed as denoting an immanent quality of the Divine nature, and that (as Œcum., Calvin, Beza, rightly discerned) in its strict internal connection with fidelity; both being derived from, and understood by, the light-nature of God. As God approves Himself *faithful towards us*, so He approves Himself also *righteous towards us* when He forgives the sins of those who confess their sins, and cleanses them from their ἀδικία, their unrighteousness. Not, indeed, by any means in the Romish sense; as if the confession of sins were a meritorious act, which God is under obligation, in virtue of His rewarding righteousness, to reward by the forgiveness of the sin. Such a "*meritum de congruo*" is a notion that in itself cannot bear the application of a merely logical test: a forgiveness which one might have merited would be no forgiveness; for the idea of forgiveness rests upon that of grace, the idea of meriting rests upon that of retribution and right. "To forgive" means to abstain from letting the deserved award take place; "to deserve forgiveness" would mean to deserve the withholding of what we had deserved: and thus it comes to the not deserving what we have deserved, which makes pure nonsense. And as this idea of a *meritum de congruo* is logically contradictory, so is the thing in itself futile. How can the mere sincere confession that we have sinned and deserve punishment be sufficient to atone for the guilt, and give a claim for the remission of the sentence? Merit has its place in the sphere of judgment and prerogative of right; forgiveness, in the sphere of redemption and grace: to assert any prerogative of right in the presence of the Redeemer—to think of deserving grace—would be the purest *contradictio in adjecto.* It can, therefore, never be the purpose of St John to say that God was obliged by His retributive righteousness to forgive the sins of the man who should confess his sins, or (which is the same thing) that he who should confess his sins would have a claim upon the retributive righteousness of God for his forgiveness. The idea of righteousness here, as closely connected with faithfulness, and flowing from the declaration that "God is light," must be a higher and more comprehensive idea than that of *judicial compensative* right. The passage, ROM. I. 17 SEQ., affords us some light upon the subject; since we find St Paul also using a loftier and more comprehensive idea of the δικαιοσύνη.

EXCURSUS ON ROM. I. 17 SEQ.

Expositors are wont to understand δικαιοσύνη Θεοῦ, in Rom. i. 17, as meaning that righteousness of man which is valid before God; but in this they are wrong.[1] The citation, ὁ δὲ δίκαιος ἐκ πίστεως ζήσεται, does not support that view; since the emphasis is evidently laid upon the words ἐκ πίστεως—the citation being intended only as a foundation for the preceding words, ἐκ πίστεως εἰς πίστιν. We must not read ὁ δίκαιος ἐκ πίστεως together, but ἐκ πίστεως belongs to the predicative idea contained in ζήσεται, as more closely defining it; and ὁ δίκαιος is used in the broad Old-Testament meaning which it has in Hab. ii. 4, that is, to describe the pious in opposition to bold mockers; and thus ὁ δίκαιος would not itself correspond to that idea of "righteousness before God," which it has been sought to find in the words δικαιοσύνη Θεοῦ. But if the citation from Hab. ii. 4 does not serve to maintain that interpretation, the verb ἀποκαλύπτεται serves to refute it. If this verb is to retain its proper meaning, we must assume an ellipsis, and interpret, "The way to attain righteousness before God is revealed;" although even then "hath been revealed" (ἀπεκαλύφθη, or ἀποκεκάλυπται) would be expected. But, further, it cannot fail to be seen that in ver. 18 the words, "the wrath of God is revealed," are strictly parallel in phrase with the words of

[1] Compare my treatise on "The Doctrine of Satisfaction." The most important points of my investigation of the passage in that treatise are condensed in the present text.

ver. 17, "for the righteousness of God is revealed." It is true that vers. 17 and 18 do not form a parallel in such a sense that δικαιοσύνη might be translated by "grace," as being the exact *opposite* of ὀργή; but yet ver. 18 is so strictly connected with ver. 17, and its references to it are so close and full, that we cannot conceive ἀποκαλύπτεται in ver. 17 to bear a meaning perfectly different to that which it bears in ver. 18. "To reveal," apart from this, does not bear so full a meaning as that of "show forth," nor as that of "work in act;" but it everywhere (1 Cor. ii. 10, xiv. 6 and 26; Gal. i. 12 and 26; Phil. iii. 15; 1 Cor. xiv. 30; Eph. iii. 3 and 5; further, Rom. ii. 5, viii. 18; Gal. iii. 23; 2 Thess. ii. 3 and 6; 1 Cor. i. 7) indicates that something shut up in the nature of God, and as such concealed from the creature, comes forth from God, and is manifested in a manner cognizable by the creature. The ὀργή existing in God is revealed upon the ungodly, when it is manifested in its work of judicial punishment. So also the δικαιοσύνη Θεοῦ must be, not a relation *of man* to God, but a definition of the nature *of God* Himself, which is in the Gospel revealed and manifested "from faith to faith." The prepositions ἐκ and εἰς mark the boundaries within which that revelation takes place (comp. 1 Cor. xvii. 5—אל, מן); it is a revelation which takes place *altogether within the sphere of faith.* Ἐκ denotes what had been the issuing-point of its being made manifest; εἰς denotes the goal to which it leads. From faith it was derived, and it leads to faith.[1]

But, wherein consists that revelation itself of the righteousness of God? Assuredly a certain contrast between God's ὀργή and God's δικαιοσύνη is expressed: though it is not a contrast of contradiction, as between hatred and love, wrath and grace; yet it is a relative contrast, as between amendment and cure, help and full salvation, that which is preparatory and that which is perfect. The wrath of God is revealed in punishing; the righteousness of God is revealed in the Gospel, and therefore evidently in redemption. But the Apostle must have had a good reason for referring redemption here, not to the grace of God, but to His righteousness. Grace would form an exclusive opposite to

---

[1] That is, from the πίστις Ἰησοῦ Χριστοῦ, ch. iii. 22: not from faith *in* Jesus, but from the faith *which Jesus exercised.* For He is indeed the Leader and Finisher of faith (Heb. xii. 2).

the wrath; but the Apostle will not name the *counterpart of wrath* as the ground of the plan of salvation, but *something that is higher than the wrath is*. He will not deny, either that redemption is grace, or that wrath is righteous; but he will intimate *that it is not the full essence of righteousness which finds its realization in wrath; and that it is not merely grace, but, as essentially, righteousness also, which is manifested in redemption.*

What he had to say concerning the worth of the Gospel reached its climax in the utterance of ver. 17, that God's *righteousness* was revealed in it, and that as demanding faith and leading to faith. God's *wrath*, that is—he goes on explanatorily—will be revealed from heaven (not, like the former, upon earth, through the incarnation of Christ) upon the ungodly; and then he brings in demonstration, from ver. 19 to ch. ii. 29, *that this wrath is not unrighteous*, but a δικαιοκρισία (ii. 5), as against the Gentiles (ch. ii. 14–16), so against the Jews (ch. ii. 17 seq.). In ch. iii. he teaches that the pre-eminence of Israel did not rest upon his greater sinlessness or righteousness, but in his relation to God, as the instrument of the preparation for the Gospel (ch. iii. 2), since to him the prophecies (λογία) had been entrusted. For, the unfaithfulness of the Israelites did not abolish (ver. 3) the faithfulness of God (in the fulfilment of the promises). But, on the other side (ver. 5, δὲ), man cannot by unbelief do any service to God; unbelief could never have a right to demand discharge of punishment, because by means of it the faithfulness of God had been manifested in a still brighter light (ver. 7); but God suspends over the ungodly His ὀργή righteously, *God's ὀργή is a righteous wrath* (ver. 5).

Thus has St Paul shown that the ὀργή *does not stand in contradiction* to the δικαιοσύνη. But similarly the full nature of the latter *does not find its full realization* in the ὀργή. The righteousness of God extends beyond the wrath, and embraces more than it.

St Paul, in ch. iii. 9 seq., deduces from all that had been said, ch. i. 18–iii. 8, the conclusion, that no man is righteous before God (ver. 11),—that is, that no man is righteous through the works of the law (ver. 20). He then goes on: " But now the *righteousness of God* is revealed, apart from the law, as it was witnessed by the law and the prophets; but God's righteousness (has been revealed) through the faith of Jesus Christ, for all and upon all them that believe." Christ went—a second and greater Abraham—the way of faith (in the sense of Heb. xii. 2), and thereby revealed the δικαιοσύνη Θεοῦ. But this "righteousness of God" is here, as in ver. 17, not the way in which man is justified before God, but righteousness as essential in the nature of God. For φανεροῦν denotes, like ἀποκαλύπτεσθαι, not a creation or working out of that which previously had not existed, but a making manifest of that which before had been concealed in God's unapproachable nature (comp. 2 Cor. ii. 14; 1 Cor. iv. 5; John xvii. 6). Δικαιοσύνη Θεοῦ denotes here the same as in ver. 5 and ver. 25. Thus we obtain the very same thought here as meets us in ch. i. 17.

Thus, that righteousness of God—with which, according to ch. i. 19–iii. 7, wrath stands by no means in contradiction—is manifested *not merely in wrath* (in which God appears as He who *is righteous*), but more highly and more fully in *redemption*, in which God appears as He who *both is righteous and makes righteous* (ver. 26). For, in ver. 26 it becomes perfectly plain, what idea St Paul connects with the δικαιοσύνη Θεοῦ. Righteousness is never simply and of itself equivalent to grace; it is through a *redemption* (ver. 24) effected, and a *propitiation* made, that we are justified and absolved. Righteousness is that characteristic of God as a *Judge*, in the exercise of which He requires right to be done to sin—that it be condemned and punished. But this judging and condemning act of God's righteousness does not exhibit the whole and entire essence of His righteousness. When God set forth Christ as a כַּפֹּרֶת, that He should cover the guilt of sins by *His* blood (כפר), the design of God was *not merely* that of revealing Himself as One who *was* righteous, that is, in punishing sin; His higher aim was, that He might approve Himself to be righteous, *and at the same time* to *make righteous*.

Here we attain to the highest and most comprehensive notion of the Divine δικαιοσύνη, in which it is not any longer merely the *conduct* of God towards the *creature* (as a retributive judging), but a definition and character of the Divine nature. To let sin go unpunished, would have been contrary to the righteousness of God—contrary to His retributive righteousness, which follows from the essential righteousness of His nature; to leave the sinner to perish in his sin, would have been also contrary to the righteousness of God,—not, indeed, contrary to His retributive judicial righteousness, but contrary to that higher righteousness of His nature. From this flows, in connection with the retributive dealing with sin, the redeeming work for the sinner. What then is the inmost essence of this righteousness of nature?

That God not only *is* δίκαιος, but also *makes righteous*; that is, that He not only bears in Himself the *norm* in virtue of which His retributive righteousness shows itself as a holy negation of sin, as judgment and condemnation of all evil,—or, in other words, that He not only, in virtue of His light-nature, draws the darkness to the light and condemns it,—but that He also seeks to make this His own *light-nature* effectual in His creature, in bringing the creature to a perfect *victory* over the darkness. Therefore, it was not enough to His absolute righteousness that He should have condemned the sin in men; therefore, it was His sacred counsel to redeem and deliver mankind from sin.

Let us now return to our passage in St John. We have derived, from an unbiassed exegetical examination of Rom. i. 17–iii. 26, a notion of essential righteousness in the nature of God which is different from, and exalted above, the idea of mere retributive dealing, and which is most internally and most straitly coincident with that of the πιστὸς εἶναι (comp. Rom. iii. 3), as well as with the primal truth ὅτι ὁ Θεὸς φῶς ἐστι. It is not an arbitrary assertion, when we say that our δίκαιος, 1 John i. 9, stands for the designation of the same idea:[1] it *must* be the same δικαιοσύνη Θεοῦ; for in both passages the righteousness of God appears as the source in God from which flows His redeeming, sin-forgiving, and sin-destroying dealing with man.[2] It is that righteousness in which God, as being the Light, not only condemns the darkness, but gives to light a *real* victory

---

[1] That 2 Cor. iii. 10, v. 21, also present the same idea of the δικαιοσύνη Θεοῦ, I have elsewhere endeavoured to show.

[2] So Olshausen also remarks on our passage· "δίκαιος, not merely inasmuch as in Him perfect harmony reigns, but because, also, He reduces the discord to harmony; thus δικαιῶν, *making righteous.*"

over the darkness. God demonstrates Himself towards His creatures to be δίκαιος in this sense, or rather πιστός and δίκαιος: 1. faithful to His own light-nature, and to all in whom this light-nature works and rules; and, 2. δίκαιος, as not only being righteous, but also making righteous, and giving light the victory over the darkness, when we testify by the confession of our sins that His light is exercising its dominion within us. Towards him in whom the light so far exerts its influence that he brings with a true and sincere mind his darkness to the light, not sparing, but confessing and suffering the judgment of that darkness, God approves Himself as the Faithful and Just, who is not contented with an as-it-were one-sided judgment of the σκοτία existing in that man, but who acknowledges His own φῶς already working in his soul, and aids that to get the perfect victory.

But that victory is a twofold victory: first, the forgiving us our sins; and, secondly, the cleansing us from all iniquity. These two members cannot be tautological, as if by πᾶσα ἀδικία only the *guilt* of sin must be understood (against which the πᾶσα itself testifies!), and by the καθαρίζειν nothing but the ἄφεσις in another form; for such a tautology is without example in St John. But ἀδικία is *sin as such* (compare Luke xiii. 27, xvi. 8, xviii. 6; Heb. viii. 12; John vii. 18; Acts viii. 23; Rom. i. 18, iii. 5, vi. 13; 1 Cor. xiii. 6), while, on the other hand, ἀνομία is the term which expresses unrighteousness in relation to its guilt (Rom. iv. 7; Tit. ii. 14; Heb. viii. 12). And, indeed, St John defines sin here with delicate precision as ἀδικία—that is, as being the precise opposite of that essential δικαιοσύνη in God. From all that in our souls which does not correspond with that internal nature of God, He will cleanse and purify us, and thus in every sense *make us righteous*: that is, 1. by justifying and setting us free from guilt (ἀφῇ τὰς ἁμαρτίας); and, 2. by making us free from sin (καθαρίσει, κ.τ.λ.), in order that in each and in every relation the light may bear away the victory over the darkness.

The artifice of Romish theologians, who would establish their purgatory by the concluding words of our verse—introducing into the text surreptitiously the idea that the καθαρίζειν is not accomplished till the state after death—may be mentioned only as a curiosity of interpretation.

In VER. 10 St John repeats, with special emphasis and special keenness, the thought of ver. 8. There are those who think that ver. 10 contains, in relation to ver. 8, something entirely new,—to wit, that ver. 8 is directed against such as deny that they are still affected by sin, while, on the other hand, ver. 10 contends against an altogether extreme tendency of those who maintain that they have never committed sin in their life (even before their conversion). But, in that case, ver. 10 ought to have stood before ver. 9, by the side of ver. 8: first, that the progression from ver. 8 to ver. 10 might plainly be expressed; and, secondly, because ver. 10 would then, in connection with ver. 8, form the one negative member, and ver. 9 the other positive member, of the thought. Then, too, we should have expected that the characteristic of the error contended against in ver. 10—that is, the assertion of *never* having sinned —would be made emphatically prominent: instead of the simple οὐχ, an οὐδέπω (John vii. 39), or an οὔποτε, οὐπώποτε being used. Finally, we cannot understand, on the one hand, how St John could represent that which is said in ver. 10 with the 1 Per. Plural, as a case that might possibly be supposed of every Christian; nor can we comprehend, generally, how people who could assert that they had never committed sin should have wandered into the Christian community.—Equally perverse is the related view of Socinus and Grotius, that ἡμαρτηκέναι must be referred to sins *committed before conversion*. Resting upon this false interpretation of ver. 10, they explain also the ἁμαρτίαν ἔχειν of ver. 8 simply of the guilt of the sins committed before conversion. But there is nothing in the words of ver. 10 or ver. 8 which leads to or justifies such a restriction. The Perf. ἡμαρτηκέναι is sufficiently explained, as Lücke remarks, by the consideration that, at the critical point when a man comes to confess or deny any definite concrete sins, these sins are already perfectly accomplished acts (*perfecta*). And *single concrete* sinful acts are here (as also in the words ὁμολογῶμεν τὰς ἁμαρτίας ἡμῶν, ver. 9) the subject; and no longer the general condition of ἁμαρτίαν ἔχειν, as in ver. 8. After ver. 8 has once led the thought to concrete, definite, individual sins, it still adheres in ver. 10 also to these individual *committed* sins (thus to the ἡμαρτηκέναι).

He who denies that he "has sinned," that is, that he has

committed definite concrete sins (after as well as before his conversion)—*makes thereby God a liar.* These words, ψεύστην ποιοῦμεν αὐτόν, are an intenser and higher expression of the ψευδόμεθα, ver. 6, and the πλανῶμεν ἑαυτούς, ver. 8. It is not only a saying which contradicts the objective and actual state of the case, a ψεύδεσθαι,—not only a guilty self-deception, a sinning against one's own soul, when one deceives himself touching the truth, a πλανᾶν ἑαυτόν,—but it is also an impiety against God, whose word and revelation is thus daringly contradicted. For God says in His word (comp. Rom. iii. 10-23), as also by the actual revelation of the great act of Redemption by grace (comp. John ix. 41 ; Luke v. 31), that all men are sinners, and sin in many ways : he then who declares himself to be without sin, charges God with lying. But, as in ver. 6 and ver. 8 there was associated with the charge of a *theoretical* untruth (of the ψεύδεσθαι and πλανᾶν) the charge also of an *actual* want of participation in the power and nature of the *substantial* ἀλήθεια ("we *do* not the truth," and " the truth is not in us"), so also here there is associated with the charge, that we daringly contradict the revelation of God, the second charge, that we practically have no part in this revelation, that its power and essence do not dwell in us. Ὁ λόγος αὐτοῦ, that is, τοῦ Θεοῦ, is no other revelation than that which convicts us of sin, and which declares him to be a liar who will not confess his sin. Thus, according to this connection, ὁ λόγος does not indicate the Logos in the sense of John i. 1, but the revelation of God in general ; but, on that very account, the question whether the λόγος here means the Old-Testament revelation (Œcum., Theoph., Grotius), or the New-Testament revelation (Rosenmüller, Huther), or both revelations (Socinus, Calovius, Lücke, Neander), is no better than an idle one.[1] It is the collective revelation of God, not merely indeed that which is contained in the written words of the Old and New Testaments, but the entire self-annunciation of the nature of God, who is light :—and this revelation viewed as *one and sole*, which has revealed itself as well in the

---

[1] Huther is even of opinion that the Old Testament cannot be included, because the subject is the sinning of *Christians.* As if Christians did not acknowledge the Old Testament also as the word of God! As if even a *Christian* would not make God a ψεύστης if he should contradict the *Old-Testament* passages cited in Rom. iii. 10 seq.

Old- and New-Testament revelations of word as in their revelations of fact, and whose internal organic centre is assuredly the revelation of the Word of redemption, the "Word" which personally was manifested in Christ κατ' ἐξοχήν; so that the *collective* revelation of God in word and act is absolutely no other than the revelation of God in Christ, the personal λόγος. This revelation, as one great whole, convicts man of sin; this revelation, as a whole, is first dishonoured and charged with lying *by* him—and, secondly, it therefore dwells and rules not as a power of life *in* him—who denies that he had sinned. (Thus the λόγος of John i. 1 is not excluded from the λόγος of 1 John i. 10, but forms the centre of that revelation generally which is here indicated by λόγος. But it would be wrong to limit the broad and comprehensive idea of our λόγος in ver. 10 to the dogmatically-fixed and precise idea of the λόγος in the sense of John i. 1.)

St John, then, has repeated in a more rigorous expression the thoughts which had already been unfolded in vers. 8, 9, according to their two aspects. It is blasphemous denial of the collective revelation of God, and it betrays that a man has no part in that revelation, to say *that he has not sinned;* that is, if the individual sins which he has committed, or still commits, are either placed theoretically in question, or in the concrete instance are not confessed, or are proudly vindicated:—whether it be, that the theoretical denial of having sinned proceed so far as the wilful delusion (seldom or never exemplified, however) of asserting that he has *never* sinned; or whether it be, that by any artifice of false philosophy the sinfulness of sin is theoretically philosophized away, or only in practice a true confession of the individual sins is lacking. For, every instance—even every *individual* instance—of unconfessing impenitence is a blasphemy against the word of God, and also an evidence that God's judging and regenerating word of revelation does not effectually rule in the heart.

Thus the Apostle has deduced at large, from the ἀγγελία· ὅτι ὁ Θεὸς φῶς ἐστι, the two following cardinal consequences:

1. That *he who walks not in the light*, is a liar; and,
2. That *he who does not confess that he is a sinner*, is a liar.

But thus the two clauses stand side by side as yet *without a*

H

mediation between them, and as apparently contradictory. That they do not really contradict each other, has been already seen in the examination of the ideas "walking in darkness," and "having sin." But this reconciliation between them is as yet a latent one. St John has laid down the one requirement, "Ye must walk in the light," and the other, "Ye must confess that ye have sin, and so darkness, in you, that ye commit, and have committed, sins," as two *absolute* requirements, as it were harshly connected together; and therefore the reader feels the want of a *mediating explanation*. For there is, after all, no kind of "sinning" which is not in some way related to the "*walking* in darkness," and therefore belonging to the *sphere* of that walking. There is, in other words, no sin *in* the man by which he does not in some sense place himself again in the *domain* of the sinful impulse and the darkness. Consequently, it is necessary—in spite of all notional distinction between the "having sin" and the "walking in darkness"—that the double statement, 1. that we must simply not walk in darkness at all, and, 2. that we must simply confess our having and committing sin, should receive an explanation which may mediate between them, and resolve the seeming contradiction.

This reconciliation the Apostle gives in CH. II. VERS. 1–6.[1]

And he commences it from a *practical* point of view. He tells them *to what end* he had written to them ταῦτα, these two cardinal declarations, ch. i. 6–10. It is most instructive to observe how the Apostle here scorns and discards all notional dialectic operations for the solution of the difficulty. He does not say what a subtle and keen *understanding* might and would say concerning this intricate question. He says what his *conscience* would say to a simple and plain Christian upon the matter. To the sincere and conscientious—with whom the

---

[1] This relation of the thoughts Calvin alone has recognised. Bullinger and Lucke refer ch. ii. 1, 2 one-sidedly to ch. i. 8 and 10, as if St John had only in view to oppose a misapprehension that sin was inevitable. Augustin, Zwingli, and others, refer ch. ii. 1, 2, with equal one-sidedness to the forgiveness of sins assured in ch. i. 9: St John would show *commentatione gratiæ divinæ non præberi licentiam peccandi.* (But how do the words, "And if any man sin, etc.," suit this view?) Still more astray are those expositors who refer ταῦτα γράφομεν, not definitely to what precedes, but to "all that precedes and follows," or (Bengel) only to what follows. The true explanation speaks for itself.

ἀλήθεια of God has to do—the practical conclusions which St John here draws are in themselves and absolutely right, shining convincingly in their own light.[1] How far in this way the true reconciliation of those two apparently contradictory cardinal sayings is given, will appear from a strict exegetical examination of our verses themselves.

VER. 1 is divided into two main thoughts, which are connected together by καί. The governing verb of the first is γράφομεν, on which the clause expressing the design, *that ye sin not*, depends. The second main proposition no longer depends *grammatically* upon γράφομεν; at the same time it must be admitted that St John, if a complex construction of sentences had not been so alien to his nature, would certainly have made the second thought dependent upon the " we write," and have said: καὶ ἵνα εἰδῆτε, ὅτι, ἐάν τις ἁμάρτῃ, παράκλητον ἔχομεν

---

[1] Would that this great and simple rule were observed and followed in the treatment of other and analogical dogmatic problems! How simple, for example, is the position which the question concerning predestination assumes, when thus looked at! Here, also, two apparently contradictory truths are placed in juxtaposition. On the one hand, the truth to which the internal experience of every Christian bears witness, that he has experienced any victory of the good in himself, either before, or in, or after, his conversion—any victory of penitence over the pride of sin, of faith over doubt, of the love of God over sinful lust, of the new man over the flesh—in relation to which he is not constrained to acknowledge that in *him* there had been an inexplicable opposition, and that the decisive influence which made the good pleasant and possible to him was an influence of *free grace proceeding from God*, without the ὑπερπερισσεύειν of which he would have gone on for ever to resist. On the other hand, the truth that the final decision which determines whether the man be lost or be saved, cannot possibly be without the man, so that he should be only the passive creature of a power having the decisive control over his fate, and all his willing be wrought in him without his own self-decision. That first truth, further unfolded into all its consequences, leads inevitably to absolute predestination; this latter to a kind of Semipelagianism. A theoretical dialectic reconciliation of the two is infinitely difficult, and probably never to be attained in a perfectly satisfactory manner. But if, with St John, we ask our *conscience* what it has to say in the matter, it will answer: Hear *both* these truths, in order that " *ye may work out* your salvation with fear and trembling ;" and when it is wrought out, know " that God it is who worketh both in you, the willing and the doing, after His good pleasure."

—"And that ye may know that, if any man sin, we have an Advocate."[1] Thus much at least is certain, that *in fact* the two thoughts, 1. "We *should* not sin," and 2. "*If* we sin, we have an Advocate," are co-ordinate and parallel; and that both in their juxtaposition serve to make plain the internal relation of the two cardinal statements of ch. i. vers. 6, 7, and vers. 8, 10.

St John introduces these two clauses by the address τεκνία μου; the same recurs, vers. 12 and 28, iii. 7 and 18, iv. 4, v. 21. St Paul (Gal. iv. 19) grounds this address upon his relation as the spiritual father who had spiritually begotten the Galatians, and must a second time give them birth: with St John the expression seems rather to be a customary form; though it has its foundation in the same relation of a spiritual paternity, associated, however, in his case with the idea of his physical age. The diminutive form in τεκνία is that of affection: in our passage it is in full, "My little children," τεκνία μου. This appellation or address does not serve to "indicate a new section;" as some preachers are wont to begin every new head of their sermons by their "dear hearers." But it has an internal reason: for the Apostle, after he had been hitherto laying down objective doctrinal statements, turns now to the consciences of his readers; he appeals by the address τεκνία μου to their consciousness of their personal spiritual relation to himself, the Apostle, as if he would say: "Ye know me, who and what I am, how I am related to you, and who and what ye are; and thus it must be plain to you with what meaning and design I have written these statements unto you."

The first declaration is now: "*This I write unto you, that ye sin not.*" (Parallel with the personal address, there now enters, instead of the earlier apostolical 1 Pers., ch. i. 1–4, the individual 1 Pers. Sing.) If we go no further than this declaration itself, we may long contest the point to which of the preceding clauses the ταῦτα refers, whether to the words of ver. 9, "He is faithful," etc., or to the words of ver. 10, "If we say," etc. In the former case, we must assume (with Augustin) that the Apostle's purpose is to obviate the misconception that the forgiveness of sins gives license to sinning. But if the Apostle,

---

[1] A deeper reason why he does not use this expression will be seen in due course.

when he wrote "these things," had the concluding words of ver. 9 in his mind, and designed to meet that objection, he would manifestly have been obliged to say, "These things I do not write unto you, that ye may sin," or at least, "These things I write unto you, but not that ye might sin"—οὐ γράφω ἵνα ἁμάρτητε, or ἀλλὰ μὴ ἵνα ἁμάρτητε. He cannot have written the sentence which rendered the misunderstanding possible— to wit, the sentence that the sins would be forgiven—*to the end* that he might *guard* them against sinning. If we will entertain any such view, we must not understand by the "these things" the thought, "He is faithful and just," etc., but some other thought which the Apostle appended in order to obviate a misunderstanding of ver. 9. But where do we find any such thought? In vers. 1, 2 we seek it in vain: vers. 3, etc., would in themselves serve for the prevention of such a misunderstanding; the sentiment of those verses is not introduced as a correction, but as a new and independent thought, so that the Apostle's "these things" could hardly have referred to the following ver. 3.—There remains another supposition, that the Apostle's design was not directly to obviate an abuse of the forgiveness of sins, but only to lay down an as-it-were paradoxical statement; that he writes what had been said at the conclusion of ver. 9 concerning the forgiveness of sins with the design to set their hearts free from the desire to sin, and to fill them with abhorrence of sin. But perfectly true as the sentiment is *in itself*, that a living faith in the forgiveness of sins through Christ leads to an abhorrence of sin, the limitation of the generally-expressed "these things" to the individual and isolated thought of ver. 9 is perfectly arbitrary.

More natural, as allied to this, is the explanation of Bullinger and Lücke, according to which, "these things" must be referred to the *immediately-preceding* thought, that we must confess that we have sinned. St John does not write this declaration, concerning the absolute presence of sin, with the design that we should regard sin as something inevitable, and yield ourselves unresistingly to its lusts. "Ista vero non in hoc scripsi, ut ad peccandum incitarem"—is Bullinger's interpretation. But here returns in a strengthened form the same objection, that St John must then have written ταῦτα οὐ γράφω ἵνα ἁμάρτητε—*These things I write not that ye may sin*.

For, the statement that we are sinners cannot, to the extent that the doctrine of forgiveness can, be applied as a positive bulwark against sin.

For our part, we refer the ταῦτα most decidedly to the *entire* preceding exhibition of truth; that is, to the double-proposition vers. 6–8 and vers. 9, 10. The double-proposition, 1. that he who professes to have fellowship with God, and yet walks in darkness, speaks and acts a lie; and 2. that he who (professes to have fellowship with God, and) denies that he has sin, is a liar—this double-statement, that fellowship with God is conditioned by an actual denial of the σκοτία, and a positive acknowledgment of the really present ἁμαρτία—St John wrote *to the end* which he now in ver. 1 proceeds to express. But it is a *twofold* end; for, although the ἔχομεν does not grammatically depend upon the ἵνα, it is yet so internally bound up with the appeal to the *mind* and *conscience* in the address τεκνία μου, that it forms with the "that ye sin not" a *pair of antithetical clauses;*—as indeed this antithetical relation shows itself in the way in which the words "and if any man sin" are connected with the words "that ye sin not."

Thus in ver. 1 St John places two *practical* deductions over against the two *theoretical* propositions of ch. i. 6–10. "We should not sin" is the one. "*If* any man sin, we have an Advocate," is the second. But in what manner do these practical consequences flow from the theoretical propositions above?—The proposition, vers. 6, 7, that he who has fellowship with God *must* walk in light, leads to the conclusion that we ought not to sin; the second position, that we must confess our sins in order to obtain forgiveness, leads to the practical conclusion that we, if we have sinned, *should* think of this, that we have an Advocate in Christ. And it is in this very change from the thetical "must" to the ethical "should" that the semblance vanishes of an unexplained, and as it were inexplicable, contradiction between the two theoretical propositions. Here, upon the ethical domain of the inward life of the soul in Christ, those two doctrinal propositions reappear; but they appear again as changed, the one into a *requirement*, the other into a *consolation:*—and this diverse internal character of the two gives us, it may be observed, the reason why St John has not connected the second by ἵνα with the γράφομεν, but has placed it as an independent message and declaration by the side of the other.

The proposition, that fellowship with God excludes the walking in darkness, is exhibited, as transferred to the region of the inner life, in the form of a *requirement*, which every true Christian every moment presents to his own mind, that he must not sin. This is an injunction of his *conscience*, imposed upon his *will;* and in this respect, therefore, he has a power within himself which is higher and holier than his will. For, the will may set itself in opposition to that requirement, and follow the impulses of the flesh and of the old man. But, when that takes place, the new man—with the higher divine will of the conscience, enlightened and made free through Christ (Rom. viii. 14-16), and therefore endowed with the spirit and power of a new law unto a new life—rises up against the sinful will, and judges and condemns it. Accordingly, the sin that has been committed is not vindicated or softened away, but known and confessed to be sin; and thus, within the domain of internal life, that second cardinal proposition, ch. i. 8-10, is seen to be, not in contradiction to, but in most living harmony and identity with the first, ch. i. 6, 7: It is the same power of the conscience, christianly sanctified in the new man, which forbids and denies the sin of the old man, and on that very account does not cloak but confesses the sin which has been actually already committed. But it is the conscience which has been set free through Christ from the burden of guilt and all slavish fear, being invested with filial freedom; and therefore we have at once, by the side of that one aspect of the second cardinal proposition, ch. i. 8-10,—to wit, that we must confess our sins,—the other aspect of it appended, to wit, ch. i. 9, that we have in Christ an Advocate for the sin which has been committed and known and confessed.

In this way the clause, ch. i. 6, 7, is metamorphosed into the *requirement*—"We should not, and we may not, sin;" and the clause, ch. i. 8-10, is metamorphosed into the *message of encouragement*—"And if any man sin, we have an Advocate." Accordingly, it is self-evident that $\dot{a}\mu a\rho\tau\acute{a}\nu\epsilon\iota\nu$ is used in both cases—in $\mu\grave{\eta}$ $\dot{a}\mu\acute{a}\rho\tau\eta\tau\epsilon$ as well as in $\dot{\epsilon}\acute{a}\nu$ $\tau\iota\varsigma$ $\dot{a}\mu\acute{a}\rho\tau\eta$—with the same meaning. That sinning itself, which in fact still exists, and for which we need the propitiation, is, by the testimony of our conscience, declared to be absolutely forbidden and denounced. (The senseless explanation of Socinus, which makes ἁμαρτάνειν here also the sin of unbelievers, and specially the sin of unbelief itself, needs no refutation.)

The encouragement itself consists in this, that we have a παράκλητον πρὸς τὸν πατέρα. "*We* have," he says, and thus includes himself among those who need the intercession, placing himself on the same level with all the members of the churches, and all them on the same level with himself. Augustin remarks here that he did not exhibit himself, or any other of the holy Apostles, or any other saint in the Church, as an intercessor; but sets forth Christ as the only Advocate, of whom all are alike in need, and who is near to all alike. He terms Christ παράκλητος, Advocate, not in contradiction to John xiv. 16 and 25, xv. 26, xvi. 7, where the Holy Spirit is thus designated; but, in perfect harmony with those passages, where the Holy Spirit is placed, as the "*other* Paraclete," by the side of Christ as the first. Only, it must not be overlooked, that the idea παράκλητος is here modified by the context, and defined in a somewhat different meaning from that of the Gospel: there it was similarly predicated of Christ and of the Holy Spirit, and of both in their relation to the disciples; here, it is used only of Christ, and that in His relation to the Father (πρὸς τὸν πατέρα). The word παράκλητος is at once the translation of the Heb. מְנַחֵם (Sept. Job xvi. 2), and also in classical Greek the designation of a proxy or attorney in law. (Comp. Euseb. Hist. Ecc. v. 1.) In the former application it has an active meaning, and denotes him ὃς παρακαλεῖ, who utters consolation or exhortation; in the second it has a passive meaning, and denotes him ὃς παρακαλεῖται, who is appealed to as an advocate in law (*advocatus*). It is plain that in the Gospel, where our Lord is speaking of the Holy Spirit who should thenceforward comfort the hearts of the disciples in His place, the word is used in the former sense; in our present passage, on the contrary, where Christ is our advocate with the Father, it is used in the latter sense. And it speaks of that High-priestly *intercessio*, the notion and nature of which is explained in Rom. viii. 26; Heb. v. 15, vii. 25.

Christ receives the predicate δίκαιος, *just*, not (as Grotius and Calovius explain) because He is "merciful and gentle," for that is not the meaning of δίκαιος; but neither does He receive it because (as the majority of expositors assume) He on His part is perfectly sinless. Δίκαιος stands here in an analogously wide meaning as in ch. i. 9, and has also its explanation in the passage, Rom. iii. 26. As there to the Father, so here to the incarnate Son, that highest righteousness is attributed which not only is righteous, but also makes righteous. Because Christ is, first, Himself sinless; and because, secondly, He shares that righteousness of the Father which, while not standing in opposition to righteous retribution, yet rises also high above it, and which will in a righteous manner justify the unrighteous— because He also, the Son, is in this comprehensive sense δίκαιος —therefore is He suitable and prepared to be a παράκλητος πρὸς τὸν πατέρα; and so far Bede is right when he finds in the δίκαιος the guarantee that Christ, as a *justus advocatus*, will not undertake any *res injusta*. For, the justification of the believing sinner through His intercession is in very fact not an *injusta causa*, but one that is in harmony with the highest righteousness of God, and indeed has its origination in that supreme δικαιοσύνη Θεοῦ of Rom. i. 17, iii. 26.

VER. 2. The nature of this intercession of Christ has its *reason assigned* in ver. 2. For, though St John does not attach ver. 2 to ver. 1 by γάρ, yet the fact itself shows that ver. 2 does give the ground of what is said in ver. 1, and by no means, as many say, presents a mere progressive addition —that Christ is not only our Advocate, but also Himself the ἱλασμός. For, in truth, the intercession of Christ has lying at its *foundation* the fact that Christ is the ἱλασμός, and this latter is by no means appended, as something extraordinary and specific, to the intercession. Thus, when St John passes from the one declaration, that we have an Advocate in Christ, to the other declaration, that He Himself in His own person is the propitiation, on the ground of which the intercession rests, he is passing in reality from the result to the cause. He says that Christ's intercession has its basis, not in another's, but in His own propitiatory act. The καί, therefore, has the logical meaning of " and that."

The idea ἱλασμός (comp. iv. 10) does not present any peculiar difficulty. The ἵλεως εἶναι of God is the pure antithesis of the ὀργή. The δικαιοσύνη of God forms, as we have seen from Rom. i. 17, no exclusive antithesis to the ὀργή, though it goes far beyond it. Even the χάρις, as such, is one and reconcileable with the ὀργή; for, while God, in virtue of the χάρις, had determined the redemption of the fallen human race, He manifests nevertheless towards the still unredeemed His ὀργή; yea, it is an element essentially consistent with His grace, that He should not leave the sinner as such to himself, but should utter *His own* yea and amen of fact to the condemning voice of the sinner's conscience. On the other hand, the ἵλεως εἶναι is excluded from the ὀργή, and then first enters in when the soul has found its propitiated Father. The ἵλεως εἶναι is that demonstration of the Divine χάρις, in which it offers itself to be tasted by man in its unconcealed character as χάρις and εὐδοκία: it is the positive evidence of the *graciousness* of God (*clementia*). This relation of God towards us men has been rendered possible by Christ, through His having as a sacrifice offered satisfaction to the *judicial retributive* righteousness of God, and thereby having turned away from man the ὀργή, the expression of that judicial righteousness, and thus having manifested that higher δικαιοσύνη (Rom. iii. 26). Thus did He effect the act of ἱλάσκεσθαι, Heb. ii. 17, Luke xviii. 3 (*clementem reddere*), that is, the ἱλασμός. But the Apostle does not say merely that He *accomplished* the ἱλασμός, but that He *Himself is* the ἱλασμός, or propitiation. To give to this word the meaning of ἱλαστήρ (Grotius), is inadmissible; and the signification " sin-offering" (Bengel, De Wette) is unjustified and unnecessary. " Christ is Himself exhibited as the propitiation, because that exists actually in His own proper person" (Düsterdieck). Because that propitiation was not generally a mere individual act, which might be considered as separate from Him, but He was with His whole being and life no other than the personal present propitiation; and because, finally, this act accomplished in Himself is still a reality, for ever continuing its effect in His person (comp. 1 Cor. i. 30; John xiv. 5; Heb. x. 20).

He is the propitiation (not the atonement, which is καταλλαγή, and modifies the idea) περὶ τῶν ἁμαρτιῶν ἡμῶν. This says nothing but what was previously contained in the idea of ἱλασμός itself; for it is already self-evident, that we need the ἱλασμός, not in view of (περί) our excellence, but in view of our sins.

But the Apostle expressly adds these words, because they form a preparation for the appended clause : οὐ περὶ τῶν ἡμετέρων δὲ μόνον, ἀλλὰ καὶ περὶ ὅλου τοῦ κόσμου. (This *breviloquence*, the words being instead of περὶ τῶν ὅλου τοῦ κόσμου, needs no explanation; compare John v. 36). *What* the Apostle would say by this is much more plain than *why* he makes the addition. As it regards the former question, the antithesis between " us" and " the whole world" cannot be referred, keeping the Ephesian readers in view, to the contrast between the Jewish and the Gentile Christians (Cyril, Œcumenius). Nor can it be that between believers and unbelievers as such; as if the Apostle (according to the exposition of Arminian and Lutheran commentators) purposed to announce the dogma, that Christ made satisfaction not merely for the *elect*, but also *sufficienter* as well as *finaliter* for the reprobate also—a sentiment which the context shows to have been far from the Apostle's thoughts at this moment. The antithesis must rather be that between the (as yet) little company of those who were already at that time Christians and the whole human race to which, and as far as to it, the Gospel was yet to be preached. This is essentially the explanation of Calvin and the Reformed expositors; but they also are in error when they restrict the antithesis to those who were already believers and those who should *become believers* in the future, with express *exclusion* of the reprobate. But the question upon which St John would pronounce here, is not whether Christ merely *sufficienter* or also *finaliter* suffered for all. It is not his aim to define to whom alone the power of the atoning work of Christ extends, but to declare, that for no man in the whole world is there any other way of being reconciled than that of the propitiation of Christ. For the whole world is appointed *this* way of coming to the Father and attaining peace. This—no more and no less—lies in the words. And thus the second question finds already its answer: the question, to wit, for what purpose St John adds this reflection. We cannot find in the immediate context anything which would supply an answer to this question; for in ver. 3 St John leaves this subordinate thought, and returns back to the main subject, which had been pursued from ch. i. 5 onwards. On the other hand, we shall see hereafter how this apparently fortuitous reference to the universal design of the redeeming work of

Christ forms a point of departure for that which St John has to say in a later section concerning the relation of Christians to the world.

VER. 3 continues the train of thought begun in ver. 1. A first mediation between the seemingly contradictory propositions of ch. i. vers. 6, 7, and vers. 8–10, had been given in ch. ii. 1, where these two propositions are changed, and exhibited in their immediate unison and perfect harmony—as the *requirement* of the Christian conscience, on the one hand, and, on the other, as a *consolatory message* to the conscience. In the Christian, the conscience of the new man, enlightened, and at the same time freed from guilt, stands above the will; it demands that the man shall not sin, and thereby and therefore judges and condemns the sin which is still present, while it knows the Advocate who is our ἱλασμός. A second mediation between these two propositions follows now in ver. 3 ; an intermediate consideration, which is not in substance different from the former, but is fundamentally only its counterpart, or a direct deduction from it. From the presence of this energy of the conscience, at once demanding and condemning, and from that alone, can we conclude the presence of the new man, and the reality of a state of grace. But that energy is described by its *visible fruits:* " If we keep His commandments." This expression is not at once and of itself to be regarded as of similar signification with that of ch. i. 7, " If we walk in the light." This latter is deeper, broader, more comprehensive; the "keeping of the commandments" is more limited, but is on that account more appropriate as a *distinguishing mark.* Even the believing Christian, earnestly occupied with his sanctification— although the soul of his endeavour and aim moves in the sphere of that which is conformable with the nature of God, and therefore light—will yet find much, not only in his actions, but especially in his thoughts and motives, which belongs not to that sphere of light; and he might, therefore, in hours of internal conflict, easily fall into doubt whether he actually stood in a state of grace, and whether the conscience were really performing its office within him. Therefore the Apostle points here, where the question is of the *marks* of a state of grace, to a sign which may be known with greater security and confidence. It will be in every Christian the sure and certain fruit of that double activity, described in ver. 1, of the conscience both awakened and pacified in Christ—that is, of rigorous conscientiousness and the confidence of sonship—that such a Christian will, by that twofold necessity, *keep the commandments*. In the *commandments* of God he has an objective and certain standard for his spirit and walk; and an objective and certain test, therefore, of his real religious state. If he should ask only about the quality, and character, and tone of his internal disposition and feeling, he might easily mistake and be deceived. But if he asks whether he is keeping the commandments of God in his outward life, and at once discerns and condemns as sin, according to God's laws, every sin into which he may have fallen, and also finds in himself a vehement striving to live for the future after God's corresponding commandments (for all this lies in the τηρεῖν, which is by no means equivalent to the πληροῦν; comp. Deut. iv. 2, xxxiii. 9; Ps. cv. 45, cxix. 34; Prov. vi. 20, xxviii. 4; Job xxiii. 12; Mal. ii. 7)—then this testing of himself by the objective norm of the commandments is a certain confirmation that he " hath known God." Ἐν τούτῳ γινώσκομεν ὅτι ἐγνώκαμεν αὐτόν, κ.τ.λ. It is obvious of itself that the little clause with ἐάν, here as in John xiii. 35, serves for the development of the τούτῳ (as elsewhere ὅτι, ch. iv. 13, or ὅταν, ch. v. 2). But this ἐάν, or the related ὅταν, is not simply equivalent to ὅτι. If ὅτι be used, then γινώσκομεν is the leading proposition : " We know by this (fact)—that He hath given to us His Spirit, that He is in us." If ἐάν, on the other hand, be used, γινώσκομεν is a kind of conditioned conclusion : " *If* we keep His commandments, we know *thereby* (by this keeping of the commandments) that we have known Him." In the former, it is a simple inference from the actual present result to the cause of it; in the latter, it is a test—something from the presence or absence of which one may perceive the presence or absence of another thing. More difficult is the question, whether the object αὐτόν with ἐγνώκαμεν refers to Christ or to the πατήρ. The older expositors were misled to adopt the former view by the vicinity of ver. 2 (Augustin, Zwingli, Luther, Bullinger, Grotius, Bengel). But the position of the whole context obliges us to refer the αὐτόν to God (Calvin, Beza, Lücke, De Wette, Düsterdieck). We have already seen, in ch. i. 9, how St John referred back by the pronoun αὐτόν to God. And so it is here. Ver. 2 is a subordinate thought; and ver. 3 does not connect itself with ver. 2 as a consequence, but stands parallel with ver. 1, and with similar independence. The words in ver. 4, καὶ ἐν τούτῳ ἀλήθεια οὐκ ἔστιν, are analogous to the words ch. i. 6 and 8, and point most assuredly to the relation to the *Father*. So the idea of "commandments" points to commandments *of the Father*, not of the Son; for it is here the work of the Son, not to give commandments, but to propitiate for transgression of the commandments. But, finally, and this is most decisive, St John in ver. 6, when he speaks of *Christ*, leaves the hitherto-used αὐτός, and defines Christ by the pronoun ἐκεῖνος, so that Christ is distinguished from the subject indicated by αὐτός.

By our keeping of the commandments of God, therefore, we know that we *have known* God. Ἐγνώκαμεν cannot possibly —as used, too, in immediate connection with γινώσκομεν—bear the foreign and unusual signification of "*love*," which Carpzov and others have endeavoured to force upon it, with inexact appeal to the meaning of the Hebrew ידע. For ידע, while it is used in a sexual signification, never expresses the feeling of love as such. It is an actual *knowing* which is indicated here by the ἐγνώκαμεν; only not a merely theoretical apprehension of a divine *doctrine* (Socinus, Episcopius), nor a theoretical knowledge of the nature of God, which should have as its necessary accompaniment the feeling of love towards God (Calvin, Lücke). Zwingli's was a more correct judgment on the point: "That which he had above expressed by *having fellowship*, he here expresses by the word *know*." For it is not the knowledge of certain doctrinal statements concerning God which is here in question, but the knowledge of God Himself. But what is the signification generally of *knowing*? When the thinking spirit knows a truth, or doctrinal proposition, it is penetrated by that truth, and so takes it up into its own thinking, that that proposition becomes as it were an integral portion of its own thinking substance. Analogously, when a personal being knows a personal being, the former must receive the latter into itself. The phraseological use of ידע, *rightly apprehended*, leads to the same notion. In the highest energy of the mutual influence of the powers of the soul, both become one; the inmost life is disclosed to each other. And in that spiritual knowledge, of which St John here and elsewhere speaks, the *person* discloses to the *person* its substantial nature. To know God, means to enter into *the fellowship of life with God;* to have known God, means to stand in the fellowship of life with God. It is to disclose the inmost internal being to God, and to be penetrated and shone through by the φῶς—judging and quickening,— and thus to *know by experiencing* in ourselves this influence of the Light. Hence this knowing God is a being known, that is, being shone through, by God, and presupposes the εἶναι ἐκ Θεοῦ (1 John iv. 5, 6; 1 Cor. viii. 3, xiii. 12; comp. John x. 14); it is essentially connected and one with love (1 John iv. 7 seq.; 1 Cor. viii. 3); and identical also with eternal life (John xvii. 3).

In VERS. 4–6 the Apostle returns to the same sentiment, and with it closes the section, which had formed in ch. i. 6, 7 the starting-point of the subject; viz., the thought that he who says he has known God (that is, stands in fellowship with God), but keeps not God's commandments, is a liar. Now, after vers. 1 and 3 have given the internal reconciliation between this thought and the evangelical consolatory message concerning the ἱλασμός, St John can return to it, and state it once more, thus defined, thus established, and thus explained, in a most emphatic and impressive form. We gather, indeed, from the fact that he so expressly closes the section with *this* thought, that the *practical scope of the whole section tends to this conclusion*. If St John had set before himself a merely didactic aim, the two mediating thoughts, vers. 1 and 3, would have themselves formed the natural close. But that this is not the case, shows plainly that the Apostle *writes with a practical, and indeed a polemical, aim*. It is the Gnostics against whose deadly poison he warns his Christian people; those Gnostics, who boasted of the deepest ἐγνωκέναι τὸν Θεόν, while they daringly revolted against, or set themselves above, "His commandments." His readers must learn, before all things, from the Gospel sent to them, and from its central point, "that God is light" (ch. i. 5), that he who places himself above the commandments of God is also devoid of the true γνῶσις τοῦ Θεοῦ.

The *fourth verse* runs so closely parallel with the sixth verse of the first chapter, that no further specific explanation of it is here necessary. Instead of the κοινωνίαν ἔχειν, we find substituted—with designed allusion once more to the "Gnostics"—the ἔγνωκα introduced by ver. 3, and which also involves the κοινωνία. (The ὅτι is wanting before ἔγνωκα in some less important MSS., but it stands in A.B. and the Fathers; it was scarcely borrowed from ch. iv. 20, but is most probably genuine in this passage as well as in that). Instead of the περιπατεῖν ἐν σκοτίᾳ, we have μὴ τηρεῖν τὰς ἐντολὰς αὐτοῦ, which was prepared for by ver. 3, and is much more significant as a test. Ψεύστης ἐστίν is still more substantial and stronger than ψεύδεται: it condemns not merely the conduct as such, but the whole man in his whole spirit and nature. Ἐν τούτῳ ἡ ἀλήθεια οὐκ ἔστιν has already been explained, upon ch. i. 8.

As we found in ch. i. 7 the negative side followed and supplemented by the positive, so it is here, and in a very similar manner, in our *fifth* verse. To the lying nature of the Gnostics the Apostle opposes the true and truth-honouring deportment of Christians. But we are not met here, any more than in ch. i., with mere tautological repetitions. With new turns and applications he brings new sides of the object before the view. In the place of the τηρεῖν τὰς ἐντολὰς αὐτοῦ comes now the τηρεῖν τὸν λόγον αὐτοῦ. It is certain, as appears from the antithesis introduced by δέ between the fifth and the fourth verses, that ὁ λόγος means essentially the same as αἱ ἐντολαί; and we should certainly be in error if we were to refer λόγος to the evangelical message, or the requirement of faith, instead of the commandments themselves. Nevertheless, ὁ λόγος αὐτοῦ is not perfectly synonymous with αἱ ἐντολαί, but denotes *the revelation of the Divine will as one whole;* that is, primarily, the revelation of His Divine will as establishing the distinction between good and evil, but this revelation of His commandments *in its united reference to His will of grace.* It is the commandments of God as they are exhibited *to the Christian,* as comprised in that one word which the Father hath in Christ spoken to the world; the commandments, not as individual and hard injunctions, but as expressing the holy will of Him who so loved the world that he gave His only-begotten Son, and who bestows upon His people the power and the desire to fulfil them all. Hence, St John now says of him who keepeth this word of the Father, that "*in him is verily the love of God per-*

fected." Setting aside the feeble interpretation of Episcopius, according to which the "love of God" is the love which God *commands and requires*, there are three explanations of this expression which deserve notice. The first understands the *love of God to us;* the second, maintained by Luther, Calvin, Beza, Grotius, De Wette, Lücke, *our love to God;* the third, represented by Zwingli, Bullinger, Bengel, Olshausen, interprets it as the *mutua amicitia et conjunctio between God and the Christian*—that love of God to us which in us also has become a power. The first explanation has the ἀληθῶς against it; the second, the τετελείωται. Ἀληθῶς is never in St John a mere formula of affirmation, "truly," but has the meaning of a *qualitative* adverb, which not merely expresses the actual existence of a thing, but its existence in a manner most absolutely corresponding to ἀλήθεια. (Compare the Gosp., ch. xvii. 8; in the passage, ch. vi. 55, ἀληθῶς is certainly a spurious reading.) In our passage, to wit, it forms the antithesis to ψεύστης ἐστὶ καί, κ.τ.λ.; but here, as in ch. i. 6, it is not only said that the reality does not correspond to the profession of having known God, but that those transgressors of the commandments also have not the substantial ἀλήθεια in them. To both these ἀληθῶς forms a contrast; it is therefore to be regarded as not only a formal affirmative assurance, but as defining the quality and nature of the thing assured of. But such an ἀληθῶς can be expressed only of an act which might possibly have been accomplished in a manner *not* corresponding to ἀλήθεια. Now, on this account, it cannot be said of the love *of God* to us, that it was ἀληθῶς perfected: that is self-understood.—But neither can we assert the τετελείωται of *our* love to God. For it will not help us, to take refuge in the assertion that St John speaks from "an ideal standing-point;" for he is (as the following words, ἐν τούτῳ, etc., show plainly) giving a thoroughly real sign whereby it may be known who stands in a state of grace, and who does not. Now, it cannot possibly be said of a Christian, who keeps the word of God, that in him love to God has already "*been* perfected." For τετελείωται denotes, not an attribute (which τελεία ἐστίν would have expressed), but an accomplished act. Thus, then, the sense of the passage cannot be this: "He that keepeth God's commandments stands truly in a state of perfected love to God," or, "The fulfilling of the command-

I

ments bears witness to a perfected love of God."—We get rid of all these difficulties when we keep in view the antithetical parallelism between ver. 5 and ver. 4. What did the Gnostics assert, while they nevertheless kept not the commandments of God? That they *had known* God. This St John denies to them in the words, ψεύστης, κ.τ.λ. What, then, will he attribute to those who keep the word of God? Manifestly this, that in them that act of the *having-known-God*, which is at the same time a *having-been-known-of-God*—that actual union with God—has been brought into effect. Thus the interpretation of those who understood the ἀγάπη τοῦ Θεοῦ of this *conjunctio cum Deo*—of this establishment of a *mutual* relation of love between God and the Christian. (Olshausen refers very appropriately to 1 Cor. viii. 3.) This interpretation gives its appropriate force to the ἀληθῶς, as well as to the τετελείωται. The former is then suitable, because love is not now regarded as a feeling or action of *God*, but as that mutual condition of *communio* and *societas* and *conjunctio*, in the establishment of which, man having his own distinctive part, the ἀληθῶς is no longer a superfluous remark. So also τετελείωται is perfectly suitable; since it is not *our feeling* of love towards God which is spoken of, but the mutual *relation* of love between Him and us. For, where we behold in the conduct of a man that he is keeping the commandments of God, it is quite appropriate for us to draw the inference, that in him that relation of love with God has been brought to a consummation. And thus that translation of the τελειοῦν which Beza, on his view incorrectly, gives —that is, *mettre en exécution*, establish, give effect to—may be rightly applied; not as if the word τελειοῦν had here a different meaning from that which it elsewhere bears, but because the perfecting of a *relation* is no other than the full establishment or confirmation of it. And that mutual *relation* of love, or fellowship of love, *was*, in fact, at the moment of the believing surrender of the soul to Christ, *closed and perfected;* while, on the other hand, the *sentiment* of love in us is never perfect, but always admits of growth.

And thus the further thought is appended, strictly and connectedly, to the conclusion of ver. 5: ἐν τούτῳ γινώσκομεν, ὅτι ἐν αὐτῷ ἐσμέν (already the third form in which the thought that forms the practical aim of the whole section is expressed).

Ἐν τούτῳ does not refer to the words "truly perfected,"—since these words, as we have seen, do not contain allusion to the sentiment of love in us, consequently do not contain any distinguishing mark,—but to ὃς δ᾽ ἂν τηρῇ αὐτοῦ τὸν λόγον. By this, that we keep His commandments (and consequently experience the relation of love to God as one that is perfected in us), we know (the further and greater truth) that we *are* in Him. The being known of God, and the having known God, St John has more profoundly defined as a being loved of God and loving Him; and this is now again more profoundly defined as a *being in God*, as the actual fulfilment of that word which our Lord spoke, John xiv. 20, where He also, ver. 21, added the keeping of the commandments as a mark or token. But, how the being known and being loved of God involves an actual *being* in God, is not difficult to understand, when we compare the passages John xiv. 20 seq., xv. 4, xvii. 10 and 21 and 23. The Father is in Christ, and Christ in His people (ch. xvii. 23); His people are again in Christ (ch. xv. 4), and with Him in God. Not only does that light of the eternal ἀλήθεια shine, judging, enlightening, and quickening, into them (on which the "being known" and the "knowing" rest), but, through the incarnate Son of God, who is in them, God also *dwells* substantially *in them* (John xiv. 23); and, consequently, they have on their part their being *in God*, since they are received, by His indwelling, into the sphere of His specific *saving* presence (which is to be distinguished from His creating omnipresence).

But St John repeats in the *sixth* verse, by a fourth and final turn given to the thought, his practical hortatory main topic. That ἐν αὐτῷ μένειν of which our Lord had spoken in the farewell discourses (John xiv. 23, in μόνην ποιεῖν according to the sense; in ch. xv. 4 and 7 in the same words), and which is not essentially different from the ἐν αὐτῷ εἶναι,[1] cannot be conceived of without the known and consciously-accepted *obligation*

---

[1] This is plain from a comparison of those passages. It is not that St John in ver. 6 passes over from the *entrance* into a state of grace to the *preservation* of it, as another object; as if the keeping of the commandments was set forth as a *sign* of the entrance into that state, but the περιπατεῖν καθὼς κ.τ λ., the *means of retaining* it. This περιπατεῖν is most certainly exhibited, not as the means for the maintenance of a state of grace, but as an *obligation* (ὀφείλει) necessarily resulting from that state.

(ὀφείλει, *debet*) of walking even as Christ also walked. He that saith he dwelleth in Him, is *bound* to walk as Christ walked. This is the point to which converges the hortatory warning against the Gnostic-Antinomian lie. And with this the thought formally returns, as to ver. 4, so to ch. i. 6; and the section appears to be perfectly rounded off.

To walk as Christ walked: in this concrete view is conclusively and most clearly exhibited what is meant by walking in light (ch. i. 7); and by keeping the commandments, ch. ii. 3. For, in Christ the eternal Light itself has become flesh, and the eternal Will of God has become a person. Christ is Himself the Light (John i. 5 and 9); and walked in the light, not as in a sphere out of Himself, but as in His own nature. Christ is the incarnate accomplished Law of the Father; in His person and in His walk we see perfectly exhibited what the will of God is. He, then, who makes pretension to being and dwelling in God, assumes the *obligation* so[1] to walk as Christ walked: mark well, the *obligation*. When St John is speaking of the *marks* of a state of grace, he does not mention the walking as Christ walked. For no Christian could say that of himself (comp. ch. i. 8, 9), that his walk was like that of Christ—sinless! But the *obligation* to copy the example of Christ every true Christian must for ever place before his eyes, in unweariable fidelity and unweariable conflict with the old man. He who does not that, has no right to call himself a Christian.

---

[1] The οὕτως before καὶ αὐτός, in ver. 6, is wanting in A. and B., and is spurious (Comp. ch. ii. 27, iii. 3, iv. 17.) But the sense is obviously the same.

PART THE SECOND.

THE RELATION OF THE READERS TO THE LIGHT, AS HAVING ALREADY APPEARED AND NOW SHINING.

Ch. ii. 7–29.

THE verses which now immediately follow, ch. ii. 7–11, are generally regarded by expositors as a kind of *appendage* to vers. 1–6. The requirement that we should walk even as Christ walked, is regarded as being more strictly defined by the commandment of *brotherly love*, which St John lays down in vers. 9–11, after he had previously shown, vers. 7, 8, how far this commandment was an old one and yet new.

But the expositors who hold this view diverge so widely in the particulars, and are in many points so utterly at a loss, that this of itself should make us pause before we accept their interpretation. If we look more narrowly into the text, *keeping primarily only vers. 7–11 in view*, we encounter most formidable obstacles to its reception. For, in the first place, it must appear strange, on the supposition that the Apostle speaks already in vers. 7, 8 of the commandment of brotherly love, that he should assume his readers to have *understood* his subtle meaning in those verses, and to have interpreted them of brotherly love without a word being said about that precept till ver. 9. If his readers read the Epistle from beginning to end, and not from the end backwards to the beginning, they could not possibly, in vers. 7, 8, have guessed that St John had brotherly love in his thoughts; and the words, " which thing is true," etc., in ver. 8, could certainly give them no definite idea related to that subject. But granted that St John might have purposed in this mysterious way to stimulate their attention to greater intensity, yet there rises another difficulty that must make us pause. The words of ver. 8, ὅτι ἡ σκοτία, κ.τ.λ., are generally supposed to be a kind of subordinate observation, by which the words ὅ ἐστιν ἀληθές, κ.τ.λ., are to be explained or established; while these latter words themselves are again only an explanatory bye-thought—intended either to show how far the ἐντολή of brotherly love might be called a "new" one, or to say that brotherly love, as well in Christ as in believers, finds its true realization. Ver. 9 is then regarded as the main proposition, around which all has hitherto in reality revolved: this it is that sheds light upon the readers' perception of *what ἐντολή* was referred to in all the declarations of the two preceding verses. *But now it were to be expected that this ἐντολή would occur in an independent form.* Instead of this, it presents itself in such a form as to be *internally* dependent upon the (imaginary) bye-thought, ὅτι ἡ σκοτία, κ.τ.λ. "He that saith *he is in the light*, and hateth his brother, is *in darkness until now*"—thus means, that for him the ἡ σκοτία παράγεται, "the darkness is past," avails not. The sentiment of ver. 9 is thereby placed in such *dependence* upon the words, ver. 8, ὅτι ἡ σκοτία, κ.τ.λ., as to make it at once unimaginable that ver. 8 is a subordinate, and ver. 9 the leading, thought.

If now, in the third place, we examine more carefully the relations of the thoughts in vers. 7, 8, the concluding words of the eighth verse will be seen to be most decidedly the proper centre of the whole meaning of the Apostle. He begins the section by declaring to his readers that he wrote no new commandment, but the old commandment which they had possessed from the beginning. He then explains fully *what* the old commandment is; it is (so he says) ὁ λόγος ὃν ἠκούσατε—*the word which ye* have heard. In these words he gives *the substance* of the παλαιὰ ἐντολή, not restricting it to brotherly love, but exhibiting it as being generally the word which he had announced to his readers concerning Christ. Parallel with this introductory explanation stands now the declaration, ver. 8, that he again writes to them a *new ἐντολή*, "that which is true in Christ and in you: that the darkness is *past*, and the true light *already shineth*." According to the parallelism of the two verses, the words, ὃ ἀληθές ἐστιν, κ.τ.λ., ὅτι, κ.τ.λ., ought to contain an announcement of the substance or matter of the "new commandment." And, so regarded, how admirably all is harmonized! The *old* commandment was the λόγος announced to them from the beginning: the collective subject of this λόγος ἀκουσθείς St John had comprehended in the word, "*that God is light*, etc.," in ch. i. 5 (where that word is defined also as "the message which we heard from Him and declare unto you"—thus in sense as "the word which ye have heard"). The *new* ἐντολή is this: "that the darkness is past, and the true light now shineth." St John utters no word to describe the two ἐντολαί as identical; but he says of the ἐντολή dealt with in ch. i. 5-ii. 6, that it is not a new one, but one that had been declared to the readers from the beginning; and then he announces that he is about to declare to them *another*, a *new* ἐντολή. New it is, 1. as one distinguished from the former: for the definite modification now enters, that the eternal light was one *already shining*—ἐν αὐτῷ, inasmuch as in Christ the light had objectively risen on the world and overcome the darkness; and ἐν ὑμῖν, inasmuch as the light had also subjectively risen on the readers, and they had subjectively passed from darkness to light. But not only so, it is new, 2. in relation to the *readers*, because the consequences which are unfolded from it in vers. 9–25 are now for the first time impressed in all their rigour, and in this manner, upon the Ephesians.

This simple, clear, and harmonious relation of the thought would not have escaped so many expositors if they had not exposed themselves to error by a false notion of the word ἐντολή. They have mostly supposed that nothing but a requirement expressed formally as a commandment could be signified by that word. But when the Apostle himself specifies the "word which ye have heard" as the matter and substance of the "old commandment," he plainly enough shows in what sense he would have the ἐντολή understood. For, to restrict this "word which ye have heard" to the injunction of ver. 3 and ver. 6, is no better than purely arbitrary. "The word which ye have heard" is no other than what had been referred to, with the same generality of expression, in ch. i. 5 as "the message which ye have heard." It is the announcement that *God is light;* and that announcement St John can term an ἐντολή, inasmuch as it is not a mere doctrinal statement, but assumes the form and aspect of a specific and direct moral-religious requirement (ch. i. 6–10). Similarly, the *new* announcement, that the darkness is *past*, and the light *already* (as in the world, so also "in you") *shineth*, is not a mere theoretical doctrinal position, but assumes the form and aspect of a direct ἐντολή to the readers, and therefore is also, and in the same sense, termed a "commandment."

The words, "that the darkness is past, etc.," consequently run parallel with the words of ch. i. 5, "that God is light," and contain the *centre and leading* thought of the new section: vers. 9 seq. being the same development of the individual practical inferences as takes place in vers. 6–10 of the first chapter, after the fundamental position that God is light, ch. i. 5. Even in their very form vers. 9–11 of ch. ii. are perfectly parallel with vers. 6, 7 of ch. i. Thus, in vers. 9–11 it is shown how far the proposition, "that the darkness is past, etc.," might be defined as a "commandment."

And it is plain at the outset why it is no other than *brotherly love* that is exhibited as the first practical inference from the new ἐντολή, ver. 8. From the fact that God is in His eternal nature light (ch. i. 5), it was evident that he who would abide in fellowship with God must be, like Him, light, and not walk in darkness. From the fact that in Christ light is risen objectively on the world, and, in consequence of that, a church is formed of those in whom the light has also subjectively risen, it is evident, that these last must of necessity love one another as brethren.

Hitherto, we have limited our observation to the passage, ch. ii. 7–11. But, all that we have concluded from a consideration of these verses is most abundantly confirmed when we enlarge our circle of view, and include within its sweep the whole section down to ver. 25. How difficult, nay impossible, do those expositors who make the καινὴ ἐντολή of ver. 9 the commandment of brotherly love, and brotherly love the subject of the whole section, find it to discern or point out any kind of internal connection, or orderly transition, between vers. 7–11 and vers. 12–25! The scarcely-begun section concerning brotherly love abruptly comes to a stop in ver. 11. St John passes with emphasis, in vers. 7, 8, to brotherly love as a "new commandment," but only to fly off from it again immediately to quite different topics—not returning back to a proper exposition of that commandment till ch. iii. 11 seq.! Between vers. 11 and 12 no connection is even sought; a broad line of demarcation is drawn in thought between the two verses, and refuge is taken in the notion that a new sub-section—though without any point of connection—here begins.

On the contrary, as soon as we discern the correct relation of ch. ii. 8 to ch. i. 5, and perceive that the clause, "because the darkness is past, etc.," ver. 8, contains the theme of the new section, we become sensible of an exquisite harmony in the whole train and sequence of thought. Throughout, down to ver. 25, this is and must be acknowledged to be the predominant fundamental thought: *that for the world objectively, and for the readers subjectively, the light hath appeared, and the darkness hath passed away.*

A twofold practical consequence is seen at once to flow from this fundamental position; one part of it positive, and one part of it negative. First, the positive conclusion in vers. 9–11, that he in whom the light has arisen must *love* the others who, *like him,* have already passed from the darkness to the light. Secondly, a negative conclusion in vers. 12–25, which, however, is distributed again into two requirements. That is, the main thought, that the readers have already passed into the light, is at first in vers. 12–14 unfolded in a twofold direction: They have known the Father; and, They have overcome the wicked one. Therefore, because this is the case, St John can write to them his Epistle; therefore, because this is the case, he has been able to write to them his Gospel. It follows thence, first, that they should not let their affection rest on the world (vers. 15–17); and, secondly, that they should abide faithful to the doctrine received, and avoid the (Cerinthian) gnosis as apostasy and anti-Christianity (vers. 18–27). Hence, in vers. 9–11 is regulated their positive deportment towards the church of light, and in vers. 15–25 their deportment towards that which is σκοτία. Vers. 28, 29 form, as we shall see, the transition to the following section.

Thus the whole section regards the light as having historically entered into the world. The subject is no longer the light, as being the eternal nature of God, but the light in this relation, that a community has been founded upon earth, through Christ, of those who are delivered from the darkness, and have entered into fellowship with God, the eternal Light.[1]

[1] And this paves the way immediately for the third section (ch. iii.), where the subject is the enmity of the darkness against these children of light, and the position of these in opposition to that enmity.

After these general preliminary remarks, let us now pass to the explanation of the individual clauses.

VER. 7 seq. With the address ἀγαπητοί, *Beloved* (for this is the reading, according to the best testimonies, and not the Text. Rec. ἀδελφοί), St John begins the new section. It is his manner to begin new sections, or sub-sections, by addresses of this kind, which stimulate the minds of the readers to new attention. (With ch. ii. 1 compare ch. iii. 2 and 7, and 18 and 21, iv. 1 and 7 and 11.)

Οὐκ ἐντολὴν καινὴν γράφω ὑμῖν. Here rises a difficulty, which has very much divided the interpretations of expositors. Augustin, Bede, most of the Greek Fathers, Luther, Calvin, Grotius, Bengel, De Wette, Neander, and others, refer the idea of the ἐντολή forwards to that which St John *has it in intention to say,* ver. 9 : "It is not a new commandment, but the old which ye had from the beginning; yet again, in a certain sense, a new one *(what I now write to you) :* He who saith that he is in the light, and hateth his brother, is in darkness even until now." But this view requires, after what has been said above, scarcely any refutation. Others, such as Zwingli, Bullinger, Beza, Socinus, Piscator, Episcopius, Calovius, Lücke, and Fritzsche, felt the unnaturalness of referring ἐντολή forwards to ver. 9, and therefore referred it backwards to ver. 6. Accordingly, the Apostle is obviating the objection that he introduces a new doctrine, when he exhorts to the walking after the pattern of Christ. " When I exhort you to innocency of life, and propose to you the holy example of the Son of God, I set before you nothing new, but only that which ye have had from the beginning of religion. That word, that is, that preaching which ye have heard from the beginning through the law and the prophets, is the same as that very precept which we now set before you" (Bullinger). But, on this view also, the limitation to ver. 6 results in a very great indistinctness of idea. No Jew would ever have objected to the Apostles, that the exhortation to purity of life was a new one ; and no Christian would have ever objected that the walking after Christ's pattern was a new exhortation : to obviate the first objection was absolutely unnecessary ; to obviate the latter was at least quite needless to Christian readers. The entire assumption of an *apologetical* tendency in these words is therefore wide of the mark. Καινή and παλαιά do not refer to what might appear to Jews or to Christians as new or old; but simply indicate the opposition between that which *had been* already announced from the beginning to the readers (ch. i. 5 seq.), and that which was now *to be* announced as new. The idea of παλαιά St John himself explains by ἣν εἴχετε ἀπ' ἀρχῆς. Now he who understands by the ἐντολή the commandment of brotherly love, and, as the result of this, explains the old ἐντολή as *identical* with the new, falls here into inextricable confusion and difficulties. Calvin, Lücke, De Wette, Düsterdieck, and Huther refer ἀπ' ἀρχῆς to the beginning of the Christian life in the readers: "From the time that ye have been Christians the commandment of brotherly love has been announced to you, and so far it is an old commandment. But it is also a new commandment; that it is so, is proved to be true in Christ (inasmuch as He first by word and example exhibited it), and in you (inasmuch as ye first received it with the faith)." But whence arises, according to this explanation, the idea of the contrast between the παλαιά and the καινή? The commandment then would be old, in as far as Christians had had it *since their conversion*,—new, in as far as they had not had it *till their conversion*.[1] But this is mere playing with the thought: the *terminus a quo* would be the same for the old as for the new; it would be as if one were to say: "You are already old, because you are already forty years old; but you are still young, because you are only forty

---

[1] Compare Dusterdieck, S. 206: "The whole pith of the Johannæan oxymoron rests only upon this, that the reference, according to which *the same* ἐντολή is seen from *the same* standing-point ἀπ' ἀρχῆς, changes. If from this position I look out into the Christian time of the readers, the ἐντολή seems one which had been long known,—the readers had heard it from the beginning as the essential commandment. On the other hand, if from that position I look at the times before that beginning to the readers, the same commandment necessarily appears as a new and essentially Christian law, beginning as to the readers with that new commencement."—So Dusterdieck. But it is obvious that if the Apostle's reflection had been directed backwards simply to the time beyond the conversion of the readers—to the time when they were still heathens, he would not have been able to define the period of their conversion by the absolute expression ἀπ' ἀρχῆς. He can use that expression only as he *altogether keeps out of view* the pre-Christian time of their life.

years old." Nor would it be even objectively correct that Christ had first given the commandment of brotherly love "by *word* and act" (Huther). A glance at the Pentateuch (*e.g.*, Ex. xxiii. 4, 5) teaches the contrary.—*If* we must understand the ἐντολή of the commandment of brotherly love, then ἀπ' ἀρχῆς must refer to *the time before Christ*.

But now arises the new difficulty, that the readers were mainly heathen Christians, of whom it could not be said that they already before their conversion, as heathens, had possessed the commandments of the Pentateuch which refer to brotherly love. Those expositors who, like Lücke, refer ἐντολή to ver. 6, or generally to the requirement of *innocentia vitæ*, understand ἀρχῆς of the times before Christ, inasmuch as already in the Old Testament God had required the walking in His commandments, and in the Prophets even the walking according to the type of the Messiah. But here the difficulty arises anew, that St John wrote to heathen-Christian readers.

All becomes smooth when we admit that the old and new commandments are *not one and the same*—not the commandment of *brotherly love;* when we accept the old ἐντολή as that which St John in ver. 7 expressly *terms* the substance of the παλαιὰ ἐντολή, and, as we have already seen, no other than the ἀγγελία (ch. i. 5), which is both in its kernel and comprehensive summary, the statement "that God is light;" and when we understand by the new ἐντολή *that which St John in ver. 8 intends to connect with it as a new addition.*

How far, then, can he call that the παλαιά, and this the καινή, commandment? "Not a new commandment write I unto you, but an old commandment which ye had from the beginning. The old commandment is the word which ye have heard."[1] By the λόγος ὃν ἠκούσατε we must explain the εἴχετε ἀπ' ἀρχῆς. But the "word which ye have heard" is "that message (ch. i. 5) which we have heard from Him, and declare unto you;" it is the communication which is summed up in the word that God is light, and drawn out into its consequences, ch. i. 6–ii. 6, and which had been made known to Christians from the beginning. These all were truths which the readers had known ἀπ' ἀρχῆς, that is, *from the time of their conversion to Chris-*

---

[1] The words ἀπ' ἀρχῆς, standing in the Rec. Vers. after the words ὃν ἠκούσατε, are decidedly, and by general acknowledgment, spurious.

tianity.—But, while St John impresses upon them the old truth, he finds occasion to impress upon them further a new ἐντολή, *not yet brought home to them* (a new truth, immediately involving in itself practical requirements). The latter is *not one and the same* with the former, though it is identical with it, and grows out of it. It is the truth, *that the darkness is past, and the light now shineth.* Viewed as a dry doctrinal proposition, this truth was not to the readers a novelty; but St John understands by the " ἐντολή," ὅτι ἡ σκοτία, κ.τ.λ., not a *doctrinal proposition,* but that truth *so far as it resolves itself into practical requirements*—that truth *with* and *in* the requirements which spring out of it. And, thus regarded, this truth is assuredly one that is *new* for the readers. It involves the new exhortations and warnings, which for St John's time were specifically necessary, and which, as something *new,* must now be unfolded : the warning, not to forsake their first love; the exhortation, to hate the works of the Gnostics. (Compare Ephesus, Rev. ii. 4 seq.)

VER. 8. The πάλιν is, by all the expositors who regard the " new commandment" as *one and the same* with the " old," incorrectly and ungrammatically referred to the καινήν, instead of to the verb γράφω : " Again a new," and not, " Again I write." According to the view of those expositors, St John meant to say : " That one and the same commandment which I write as an *old one,* I write also as again a *new one ;*" but this is not what he says, and even De Wette is frank enough to confess, " It does not expressly say, Again I call it a new commandment ; but the silent assumption makes this commandment the same which had been spoken of before." Indeed the silent presupposition of De Wette, but not that of the Apostle ! St John rather distinguishes in the plainest manner between the two ἐντολαί, as it respects their substance. Concerning the παλαιά, he had said in ver. 7, that it was ὁ λόγος ὃν ἠκούσατε. On the other hand, he gives the substance of the καινή in these words, " That which is true in Him and in you,[1] that the darkness is passing, and the true light now shineth."

The words ὅ ἐστιν ἀληθές, κ.τ.λ., furnish endless difficulties

[1] Cod. A reads ἡμῖν ; B.C., Œcum., and others, ὑμῖν. The latter reading is therefore better authenticated, and must be held genuine. The other is quite irrelevant to the sense.

to those expositors who identify the two ἐντολαί, and understand them of brotherly love. They, and not they alone, take the clause ὅτι ἡ σκοτία, κ.τ.λ., as an appendage, which gives the reason of the words ὅ ἐστιν ἀληθές, and accordingly translate ὅτι, not by "that," but by "for" or "because." Then they are under the necessity of finding in the words, "that which is true, etc.," *such* a thought as might find its *reason* in the proposition with ὅτι, "because the darkness, etc." The strange and arbitrary notion of Erasmus and others, who hold the words ὅ ἐστιν—καὶ ἐν ὑμῖν for a parenthesis, and translate "quod in illo verum est, id etiam in vobis verum est," we may dismiss at once, as unworthy of refutation. And that of Lange is not much better: "*quisquis verus est*, that is, every true Christian, is to be united with Him and with you." According to Socinus, Flacius, Morus, De Wette, Lücke, and Neander, ὅ is an apposition latent in the preceding words : " This ἐντολή is also a *new* one." If, indeed, the preceding words have been falsely interpreted, "This *same* commandment I write unto you as *one that is again new*," then certainly the judgment does lie in them, "This commandment is a new one," and to this supposed latent judgment in the preceding words the ὅ is now made to refer as in apposition. "The proposition, that the commandment (whether the commandment, ver. 6, or brotherly love, ver. 9) is a new commandment, is a true proposition, and approves itself true in Christ and in you;" that is, in Christ, inasmuch as that commandment "did not already exist before Him, but He first laid it down by word and example," and also "in you believers, inasmuch as ye did not previously possess it, but received it first in and with your faith" (Huther). For the establishment of this interpretation, Huther appeals mainly to the fact that ἀληθής in St John denotes "constantly" the correctness of a "declaration."[1] That the direct contrary is the truth, that ἀληθής is always in St John the actual realization of a thing, or requirement, or idea, we have seen above upon ver. 5, where ἀληθῶς forms the contrast to the words ψεύστης ἐστὶν, καὶ ἐν τούτῳ ἡ ἀλήθεια οὐκ ἔστιν. And so also it is an assertion more bold than true, that the precept of brotherly love (or, according to some, the τηρεῖν τὰς ἐντολὰς τοῦ Θεοῦ !) "did not

---

[1] Huther incorrectly quotes Calvin as holding this view.

exist before Christ." Somewhat more plausible is the second explanation, defended by Œcumenius, Luther, Zwingli, and many moderns, according to which ὅ is not an appositional addition, but a relative clause, which refers to the *subject* of the καινὴ ἐντολή. The true matter of the commandment is realized and fulfilled in Christ and in the readers. But the objection which Lücke urges against this, that it should in that case have been ἥ ἀληθής ἐστιν, is not set aside by saying that it is not the ἐντολή as such, but the subject of it, which is a reality in Christ and in Christians. For, "that which the ἐντολή enjoins," is no other than the very ἐντολή itself. The *injunction itself* is realized in Christ, when its subject-matter is realized in Him. How unnatural this ὅ would be, is best seen in the forced paraphrase to which Düsterdieck has recourse in order to make it clear: " In writing to you this commandment, *I demand of you a walk in love*, which is true in Him and in you,—true on that account, because already (even in you also) the darkness is passing away, and the true light already shineth." The best of this must simply be supplied here. Nor can we perceive why the more definite clause, " The life of love has become already a reality in Christ and in believers," was to be established by the more indefinite clause, " The darkness is past, and the true light already shineth."

As soon as we have thoroughly seized the true relations of the whole train of thought, all these difficulties vanish of themselves. Ὅτι is not to be translated " because," but " that ;" and it introduces the *matter* of the " new commandment." Even as the " old commandment" was no other than " the word which ye had heard," that is, the truth ὅτι ὁ Θεὸς φῶς ἐστιν, *that God is light*, so the " new commandment" is the clause ὅτι ἡ σκοτία παράγεται, καὶ τὸ φῶς ἤδη φαίνει, *that the darkness is past, and the light now shineth.*" The little relative sentence with ὅ does not depend upon the ἐντολή, but upon the following clause, ὅτι, κ.τ.λ., to which it bears the relation of a prefixed apposition. " Again I write unto you a new ἐντολή, that, namely, which hath its truth in Him and in you : *that the darkness is in act of passing, and the true light already shineth.*" The reference to the light as the eternal nature of God, was the παλαιὰ ἐντολή ; the reference to the *relation of a victorious warfare commenced, of light against darkness, which had appeared in time and upon earth*, is the new commandment (which in its practical hortatory significance had not yet been exhibited to the readers) now to be written by St John.

The darkness *passeth away, is passing, is in the act of vanishing away.* On the Midd. παράγεσθαι compare ver. 17 and 1 Cor. vii. 31: παράγεσθαι, like παράγειν (but which latter St John uses only concerning physical passing-by; John viii. 59, ix. 1; comp. Matt. ix. 9 and 27), constitutes in itself the antithesis with the idea of eternal continuance; it thus marks (as, *e.g.*, in ver. 17) the idea of transitoriness as a quality of nature. But in our passage it receives, through the parallel ἤδη φαίνει, an emphatic *Present* meaning. It is intended to be said, not that the darkness was something in its nature transitory, but that it was in the present time already in the act of yielding and vanishing away. Parallel with this is the declaration that the light *already shines.* God is in Himself *eternal* Light; but upon earth it was not yet light, because the darkness received and admitted not the light of God into itself (compare John i. 5). But now it has become changed: the light, and indeed "the true light," the essential and real light, has already begun to shine upon earth. To what extent? That becomes plain in the member of the proposition which was placed first, ὅ ἐστιν ἀληθές, κ.τ.λ. The proposition, that the light already shines, has a twofold sphere, in which it is a true one (that is, not a theoretical truth, but an actually realized truth, and one which approves its ἀλήθεια). First *in Christ*—for to Him, who was in ver. 7 introduced with ἐκεῖνος, the ἐν αὐτῷ must in its meaning be referred; since it is not God the Father, but the incarnate Son, in whom the light began historically to appear upon earth[1]—thus first in Christ, inasmuch as He it is whose manifestation in the flesh was *objectively* that ἀνατολὴ ἐξ ὕψους (Luke i. 78), the brightness of which shone in upon the darkness of this world. But, secondly, it is also ἐν ὑμῖν, in the Ephesian readers themselves (and also in all Christians then living, as in all true and living Christians, who should ever read the Epistle); since in every one who had apprehended Christ in penitent faith, the night is *subjectively* past, the darkness is receding, and the true light already a shining reality. Thus the light which

---

[1] Even under the erroneous assumption that the clause ὅ ἐστιν, κ.τ.λ., refers to brotherly love, most expositors explain ἐν αὐτῷ of Christ.

shone into the darkness of this world, also makes those who believe, themselves the children of light.

Thus this is the *new*, to which St John will now turn the thoughts of his readers, *that at that point of time a crisis between the light and the darkness had already begun upon earth*, the beginning and issuing-point of which was Christ's manifestation in the flesh, but in which they, every one in his degree, must have their own part. As a theoretical dogma, indeed, this, as has been already remarked, was not absolutely a new thing to his readers; but, as an ἐντολή, as a living truth which shaped itself into practical injunctions and requirements, it was assuredly new:—as those requirements show, which are here unfolded, vers. 9–25, from this ἐντολή. For this exhortation to brotherly love, *constructed as it is here*, is one that does not belong to St Paul's, or St Peter's, or St James' circle of doctrine, but is quite specifically *St John's;* it belongs, in this form, properly to that disciple who is represented by trustworthy tradition as having summed up in his veteran age his whole testament in the words, "Little children, love one another." And, in fact, the warnings against the antichristian spirit of the Gnostics would not have been possible in an earlier period. Therefore St John describes the proposition of ver. 8, with its consequences, as a καινὴ ἐντολή: not that it was to the readers something that they had never heard before; not that St John had never orally declared anything similar; but because it bore in itself the *specifically Johannœan* message which was certainly, in comparison with that which the churches of Asia Minor had heard from St Paul in earlier decades (ἀπ' ἀρχῆς), a *new* commandment. It was the *new* precept which St John particularly was called to append to the old message, and to develop from it its consequences; and which he now—although he may previously, when opportunity served, have developed them by word of mouth —first exhibited in its written scriptural concentration, and in its full testamentary force, for the whole of Christendom.

After this positive exhibition of the thought of ver. 8, it is not necessary to enter polemically into the chaos of the various interpretations of its several words.[1]

[1] Grotius, Hunnius, Calovius, Semler, and others, incorrectly explain the παράγεται as a Perfect, and refer it indeed to the abolition of the law

VERS. 9–11. Just in the same way as in ch. i. ver. 6 was connected with ver. 5, ver. 9 is here connected with ver. 8. There the proposition preceded, that "God is light"—God was the subjective, and light the predicative, idea,—and the immediate consequence resulted, that to profess the enjoyment of fellowship with God, the subject must be confirmed by the evidence of a participation in this predicate and essence. Here in our passage the proposition comes first, that "the light already shineth"—here τὸ φῶς is the subject-idea,—and it therefore follows that he who appropriates to himself this subject-matter, that is, he who saith that he is in the light, must confirm his profession by love to those who are, equally with himself, in the light.

In the proposition, τὸ φῶς ἤδη φαίνει, it is tacitly declared that already, *historically upon earth*, there is a sphere existing within which the light has demonstrated itself as an enlightening, and life-bringing, and transforming power; and therefore a church of those in whom the fact ὅτι τὸ φῶς ἤδη φαίνει has become an ἀληθές. Now he who says that he belongs to this sphere and to this church, that he in the historical present stands, not on the side of the σκοτία ἣ παράγεται, but ἐν τῷ φωτί, must—and this follows as a most absolute necessity—approve his assertion to be true by doing actually that which he speaks of; that is, by consummating his fellowship with the members of this fellowship; and this is no other than love. For, the opposite of love is the opposite of fellowship. With him whom I hate, I do not stand in fellowship on the same side.

The members of this community of light are termed "brethren," because they are collectively and individually *begotten* of the light; because they are "children of light," as Luther says. The being begotten of the light is, however, essentially nothing but the being begotten of the "incorruptible seed" (1 Pet. i. 23) of the word and Spirit of God, in consequence of which we have God for our Father (Rom. i. 7; 1 Pet. i. 17; 1 John v. 1), and are His children (1 John iii. 1).

with its shadows! De Wette and others point to Rom. xiii. 12, where, however, the nearness of the *coming* of Christ is the subject. Calvin, who also makes the Present a Perfect in its meaning, one-sidedly understands by the σκοτία the obscuration of saving knowledge; but St John uses σκοτία as a much broader and deeper idea than that, as is clear from ch. i. 6.

He now that saith he is in the light, ἐν τῷ φωτί, that he is on the side of that community which was founded by Christ, and yet hateth those who, being also members of this community, must be loved—he that hateth these his brethren (thus denying fellowship with them in fact),—of him it is not true that he is in the light; rather he is ἕως ἄρτι, *until now*, in the darkness; he belongs, even to the present moment, to the opposite sphere. The words ἕως ἄρτι point undeniably back to ver. 8; it is here manifest how the *historical relation in time* between the kingdom of light begun with Christ, and the kingdom of darkness which concurrently continues, forms the basis, from ver. 8 onwards, of the whole of the individual thoughts which follow. It is the question whether for him, who in ver. 9 is introduced as speaking, the ἡ σκοτία παράγεται, κ.τ.λ., has already become an ἀληθές.

The tenth verse is analogous to the sixth verse of the first chapter: he adds the positive aspect of the thought to the negative. He that loveth his brother, abideth, or *dwelleth*, in the "light." Here, as always in such cases, St John does not content himself with laying down the bare logical opposite of that which he had previously laid down as a negative member; but he *surpasses* in his positive declaration the thought of the preceding negation. (As in ch. i. 7.) He that hateth his brother, doth not as yet belong to the light at all; he that loveth his brother, not only demonstrates thereby that in him the darkness is past, and that he is already actually in the light, but—what is still more—he also *abideth* in the light. The exercise of brotherly love is of itself a means of strengthening and confirming the new life; from the communion of brotherly love the new man derives plentiful invigoration and quickening for his faith; the fibres by which his religion roots itself more and more firmly in the fellowship of his brethren, nourish also the growth of the new man in God. Thus, this verse is in exquisite harmony with ch. i. 7 as its counterpart. There it was said, that if we walk in the light, fellowship with the children of God would result: here it is said, that the exhibition of this fellowship of love with the brethren retains us in the fellowship of light, that is, of God.

But, as the Apostle had in that passage added this further, that the blood of Christ cleanseth him who walketh in light from all sin (not from the guilt of sin; see above on ch. i. 7), so here also he appends the analogous reflection, καὶ σκάνδαλον οὐκ ἔστιν ἐν αὐτῷ—*there is no occasion of stumbling in him*. Recent interpreters (to wit, Lücke, Neander, De Wette, Olshausen, Düsterdieck, Huther) follow Calvin, Luther, and Bengel, in giving these words the meaning, "there is in him nothing present which might lead *him* to fall;" but this interpretation not only misses a delicacy in the construction of the thought, but also does violence to the grammatical use of the word. It is true that σκάνδαλον is the translation of the Heb. מִכְשׁוֹל and מוֹקֵשׁ; but in every case it depends upon the connection in which this word stands, whether it signify a snare laid for others, or one in which a man falls himself. When it is said in Ps. cxix. 165, concerning the righteous, וְאֵין לָמוֹ מִכְשׁוֹל (LXX. καὶ οὐκ ἔστιν αὐτοῖς σκάνδαλον), the meaning naturally is, that for the righteous there is no snare, which should entrap *them*. But in our passage we do not read αὐτοῖς, but ἐν αὐτοῖς, "there is *in* them or *about* them no snare or offence." To explain this ἐν by allusion to Judith v. 1 (ἔθηκαν ἐν τοῖς πεδίοις σκάνδαλα) is no more appropriate than to say at once with Grotius: ἐν *abundat*. No more can ἐν αὐτοῖς stand, as Lücke suggests, instead of ἐν τοῖς ὀφθαλμοῖς αὐτῶν; and all the less, because the thought, that "in the eyes" of these Christians there would be no stumblingblock, would after all say nothing more—to wit, nothing more than this, that they subjectively should count nothing as a *snare*. And the ἐν cannot have the meaning which Neander demands for it—*with* them, at their feet. Düsterdieck finds himself constrained to admit, that "in the expression ἐν αὐτῷ, the thing itself has fallen into the customary Biblical figurative language elsewhere: nothing should be in the soul of those αὐτοί which might become a snare to them."

But, even if we could understand and accept this artificial explanation of the words, would even then the resulting thought be a true one? Can this be said of one who simply loves his brother, that there is nothing any longer in him which might bring him into a snare? But Düsterdieck is obliged to weaken away the explanation which has been so laboriously obtained, by the remark, that "the occasion of falling and stumbling is even in believers always existing;" and on that account he reduces the proposition, that in his soul there *is* no longer any occasion of falling, to the proposition that he "is certainly assured of the sanctifying blood of Christ, which ever more and more removes whatever might be a σκάνδαλον."

And thus Düsterdieck at last, after many shifts, seems to reach a goal, which is much more simply and naturally reached by leaving to the words (especially the ἐν) their obvious and unforced signification. Σκάνδαλον is now and then used for the translation of מוֹקֵשׁ and such other words, but it means *generally* in the New Testament *offence*, in a spiritual and moral sense (Matt. v. 29, xviii. 6, 7, ix. 42, xxiv. 10, xxvi. 31; John xvi. 1; Luke xvii. 1; Rom. xiv. 13, xvi. 17; 1 Cor. i. 23; 2 Cor. vi. 7); so that it does not commonly denote the figure, but at the same time the thing itself, that is, conduct through which one gives offence to another. When it is said that " there is no offence in them," it means simply that there is nothing in them by which they would give offence to their brethren, or at which their brethren might take offence. (So Bullinger interprets: Vita sua nemini est offendiculo.) St John intends to express the twofold sentiment, first, that he who loveth his brethren confirms himself in the faith, and then that he gives no offence to the brethren which might be a stumblingblock to their " abiding in the light." Thus the idea is perfectly parallel with that of ch. i. 7. He who abideth in light, has (it was said there) fellowship with the brethren, and experiences the sanctifying power of the blood of Christ. Here it says, that he who perfects the fellowship of love with the brethren, abideth in light (this is the counterpart of the first member of ch. i. 7), and gives to others no offence (this is the counterpart of the second member of ch. i. 7: the sanctifying power of Christ is so shown in him, that he becomes a blessing and a helper to others, and not a stumblingblock to them).

In VER. 11 the thought of ver. 9 is repeated in a stronger manner (just as in ch. i., ver. 10 repeated in a stronger manner the thought of ch. i. 8). He that hateth his brother *is*, first, still in darkness—this is a repetition of what was said in ver. 9: he belongs still, in his inner nature, to the sphere and circle of those who have yet no part in the light which through Christ has risen upon the world; he stands still without the congregation of the children of light. But, secondly, he *walks* also in darkness; and here there is reference made to the category introduced in ch. i. 6.[1] It is said that hatred against the brethren bears the characteristic stamp of belonging to that course, and tendency, and end of action which is pursued in the sphere of the sinful nature turned away from God. Both are true: first, he that hateth the brother belongs not in his *person* to the kingdom and the community of light; in the second place, his *walk* pertains to that species of περιπατεῖν which is in its characteristic quality opposed to the nature of God. But a third, and a fourth, thing follow. The third is, that he οὐκ οἶδεν ποῦ ὑπάγει. This forms the antithesis to the μένει ἐν τῷ φωτί, but in an intensified degree. Nothing can be said in his case about *abiding* in the light, since he *is* not yet in the light; but not even is there any reference to the question whether he might not in the future attain to the light. "He knoweth not whither he goeth." (For the signification "whither" ποῦ with ὑπάγειν has here, as in John xiii. 33, xvi. 5, and elsewhere, often *e.g.,* Matt. iii. 20; hence Luther, Bullinger, and others have rightly translated *quo.*) But we must not (with Luther) assign to it the meaning that they know not that they are going to hell: this gives a definiteness to the words which they do not really possess. The sentiment is the more general one, that they still are groping in the darkness, and, in spite of their proud "saying that they are in the light," they have not even as yet known the way by which they might attain to the light. They do not as yet see even so much as to make them know that their hatred and lovelessness is ungodly and sinful.

A practical criterion, of the utmost possible importance, as to who has true and genuine faith!

"For"—this is the fourth thing—"the darkness hath blinded their eyes." We must not think (with Lücke) of any "figure" here (*they walk in the darkness like the blind*); but ἡ σκοτία is the darkness in the full, substantial, Johannæan sense —that primitive archetypal darkness, of which physical darkness is only a faint symbol. The power of darkness, opposed to the nature of God (and which is self and death, as light is

---

[1] It is quite wrong when Lucke interprets περιπατεῖν ἐν τῇ σκοτίᾳ as a "figurative" expression, but εἶναι ἐν τῇ σκοτίᾳ as a "proper and unfigurative" expression. We have, in ch. i. 5, seen that Φῶς is in St John something more than what one is accustomed to call a "figure." Φῶς is in both cases *properly* used, and so are εἶναι and περιπατεῖν.

love and life), hath made their eyes blind, so that they cannot discern their sin to be sin. For this is the first influence of light in us and upon us (compare above on ch. i. 5 and 8, and ii. 21), to make us discern and know the darkness existing in us *as* darkness; the sin, selfishness, and lovelessness—the "hatred" of God and the brethren—which ruleth in us, *as* sin, and blackness, and darkness. On the other hand, it is the nature of that spiritual darkness so to oppress the eye with blindness and fantasy, that that which is σκοτία, or darkness, shall appear to be light. (Comp. John ix. 41.) Thus, he who imagines that he may still hate his brother—with whatever subtle disguises his hatred may be softened—and thinks that this may be reconciled with the "being in light," shows thereby only that the darkness still rules his soul, and makes him ignorant and confused about the condition of his soul (ποῦ ὑπάγει), as also about the character of his deeds.

VERS. 12–14. The thought which follows in the twelfth verse, "because your sins are forgiven you for His name's sake," bears precisely the same internal relation to the preceding thoughts of vers. 9–11 which the second thought of ch. ii. 1 bears to the first, or which ch. i. 9 bears to ch. i. 6, 7. By the side of the *requirement* that we *should* not sin and walk in darkness (which requirement is contained in vers. 9–11, though under a specific modification of form), we have here again the announcement that we receive forgiveness for the sins which we have committed (Neander). Thus, it will appear at once from the matter of it, that ver. 12 begins a new group of ideas, a new *sub-section*. It assumes that character, also, in the address τεκνία, which is perfectly analogous with the address of ver. 1, and of the same signification. That is to say, it is obvious that the readers, if they read the Epistle from the beginning, and not backwards from the end, could not have understood the τεκνία otherwise than in ver. 1, to wit, as a common address to the whole body, and not as a special address to those who were in age or in religion little ones, or young.

Thus a new sub-section begins with ver. 12; but it is a *sub-section*, which is strictly subordinate to the second section begun in ver. 7—that is, to the theme laid down in ver. 8. And so we find that the announcement of the forgiveness of sins appears in this passage under a modification of form which perfectly corresponds with the theme laid down in ver. 8—the *temporal* relation of the readers to the *temporally and historically* established kingdom of the light. That is, there are two points in the clause ὅτι ἀφέωνται, κ.τ.λ., which strike our attention. *First*, the Perfect. The Apostle does not say, as in ver. 1, "But if any man should have offended against brotherly love, this sin *will be* forgiven him;" or, "He has an Advocate, through whom it *may* be forgiven him;" but he says, "Your sins *are* forgiven you:" he refers to the *already-effected entrance* of the readers into the state of grace, to the fact that "the darkness is past, and the true light now shineth—in you." And on that very account, *secondly*, he places the forgiveness of sins in a different relation to the requirement, vers. 9-11, from that which it bore above in ver. 1 to the requirement of ch. i. 6 seq. There it was said, "We *should* not sin; but *if* any man sin, we have an Advocate." Here it is said, "Ye *should* love the brethren; this I write unto you, *because* your sins *are* forgiven you."[1] That, namely, the ὅτι does not supply the matter of the γράφειν, but is added as giving the reason of the act of writing, and consequently is to be translated "because," and not "that," is undeniably evident from the analogy of the two following verses. (Compare Calvin, Beza, Grotius, Lücke, De Wette, *against* Socinus, Bengel, Paulus, Neander, who translate ὅτι by "that," and against Luther and Bullinger, who translate it in ver. 12 by "that," and in vers. 13, 14, by "because." See on this last point below.) Γράφω has, accordingly, no expressed object after it. The subject-matter of the γράφω is defined by what precedes; here primarily by vers. 8-11. The proposition that it "in you as in Christ is a truth, that the light already shines," with the inferences and obligations deduced from it in vers. 9-11—and especially the latter—the Apostle can and may write on the ground of the fact that the readers have already received the forgiveness of sins, and are already found in a state of grace. It is, indeed, the forgiveness of sins which disposes the heart to forgive the sins of others. He to whom much is forgiven, loveth much (comp. Luke vii. 47; Matt. xviii. 33). But, although we may regard the writing as having

---

[1] As it respects the words διὰ τὸ ὄνομα αὐτοῦ, compare Olshausen on John i. 12.

primary reference to what immediately precedes, we must not limit it to that: St John writes, not as in ver. 1, ταῦτα γράφω, but absolutely and generally, γράφω; and we shall see how in vers. 13 seq. also the γράφω and ἔγραψα refer quite generally to *all that he writes*. The readers must *primarily* have thought of what directly preceded, and this forms as it were the transitional link; *but the thought contained in the* γράφω *assumes at once a generalized character.*

But to understand this aright, we must first of all take a view of the entire construction of vers. 12–14. As it respects the text, at the outset, the variations of reading are only inconsiderable, and critically of no moment. The Text. Rec. reads in the third member of the proposition, ver 13, γράφω instead of ἔγραψα, but is not supported by any other critical authority; for A.B.C. read with one consent ἔγραψα, and this alone is suitable to the whole paragraph, since a triple ἔγραψα corresponds with the triple γράφω. In a single modern codex of the fourteenth century the first member of ver. 13 is wanting, and in the Vulgate the first member of ver. 14; but these are to be accounted for by the negligence of individual copyists or translators. So the variation of Cod. B. in ver. 13: τὸ ἀπ' ἀρχῆς instead of τὸν ἀπ' ἀρχῆς, may be regarded as a mere error in transcription; especially as Cod. B. in ver. 14 reads τὸν ἀπ' ἀρχῆς. The text is critically certain, as Tischendorf presents it.

And now the address τεκνία is followed by an address to the πατέρες, then by one to the νεανίσκοι; and all three times the words γράφω ὑμῖν ὅτι are used. To these three members correspond three other clauses; where, instead of the τεκνία, we have παιδία; followed again by πατέρες and νεανίσκοι; but, instead of the triple γράφω, a triple ἔγραψα. We have already seen that the τεκνία, ver. 12, could not be understood by any reader otherwise than in ver. 1; so the analogy of the passages, ch. iii. 7, v. 21, shows that τεκνία *is a general address to the collective body of the readers* (the Greek Fathers, Calvin, Luther, Beza, Calovius, Wolf, Lange, Morus, Bengel, Neander, Düsterdieck, Huther), and does not denote a special class in age (bodily or spiritual) by the side of the πατέρες and νεανίσκοι. But now, further, the third member of the second triad, " I have written unto you, young men, because—and ye have overcome the wicked one," is so entirely parallel, and in matter so similar, to the third member of the first triad, "I write unto you, young men, because ye have overcome the wicked one;" and, especially, the second member of the second triad, "I have written unto you, fathers, because ye have known Him that is from the beginning," is so parallel and similar to the second member of the first triad, "I write unto you, fathers, because ye have known Him that is from the beginning,"—that we must needs assume that the first members of the two triads, "I write unto you, τεκνία," and "I have written unto you, παιδία," must also correspond with each other. And so they actually do as to their subject-matter; for the having received forgiveness of sins, and the "having known the *Father*," are, essentially, not very widely distinguished. Nevertheless it is premature and rash to regard (with De Wette, Olshausen,[1] Düsterdieck) παιδία also as a common address to all classes of age collectively. Παιδία never occurs in this sense (not even in ver. 18 : see below), *and the Apostle must have had an internal reason why he thus changed the expression.* He repeats the πατέρες and the νεανίσκοι ; and he would certainly have repeated the τεκνία too, if he had wished the address to have been again understood in its universality. But he has in ver. 13 passed over from the address to all his "children" to an address to particular classes of age. He does not abandon that idea any more, in order to return to the general address ; but, after he had made the transition from the *universally*-applied τεκνία to the special classes of the fathers and young men, he continues in the discrimination of the classes of age ; and hence in the second triad he sets over against the *universal* address, τεκνία, the address παιδία, which turns its application to a special class of age. And this is confirmed by the appended clause, "because ye have known the Father." For, although essentially the having received forgiveness of sins is identical in meaning with the having known God as the Father, yet St John must have had a reason on account of which he does not

---

[1] Olshausen, when he mentions the opposite view, appends the marginal note : "Right in the main, but not to be carried out." And again he says that ἔγραψα was not used touching the παιδία, but only γράφω, because "these had just begun their course, and St John had not written to them before." Thus, then, Olshausen must have understood by the παιδία the *little ones in age.*

here, as in the second and third member, repeat the same words, either exactly or with some enlargement, but substitutes another turn of thought. But precisely for the *age of childhood* (whether the physical or the spiritual) the state of grace does assume the specific characteristic of a " having known the Father." While the forgiveness of sins in general characterizes Christians as such, the Christianity of the child (as to bodily or spiritual age) takes the specific form of a having known the *Father;* as the Christianity of the young man bears the character of a victorious conflict with the wicked one, and that of the old man bears the character of having known God as Him who is ἀπ' ἀρχῆς. The Christianity of the παιδίον reduces itself to this, that the child has God as a reconciled Father; the old man in Christ knows God as One who was from the beginning and from eternity, and Who has approved Himself in history as a whole, as also in his own specific experience, as ὁ ἀπ' ἀρχῆς ; the young man stands in the contest, and has as a *Christian* youth the victorious conflict as a settled matter already behind him. *Thus we must, with the great majority of expositors, take* παιδία, *in contradistinction to* τεκνία, *as an address to a specific class of age.* Only we must not connect together the members,

γράφω ὑμῖν πατέρες, κ.τ.λ.,
γράφω ὑμῖν νεανίσκοι, κ.τ.λ.,
ἔγραψα ὑμῖν παιδία, κ.τ.λ.,

as a triad,[1] to which triad, in fact, there would then be only a dualism to correspond; but the three members with ἔγραψα form together a triad, which corresponds to the first triad. Thus the order is this:—

First Triad.	Second Triad.
γράφω.	ἔγραψα.
1. τεκνία = all readers.	1. Children (in age).
2. Fathers.	2. Fathers.
3. Young men.	3. Young men.

[1] Many expositors who do so (Augustin, Calvin, Luther, Beza, Calovius, Bengel, Neander, and others) were misled by this into preferring the reading γράφω ὑμῖν παιδία. But we have already seen that that reading is critically worthless. Probably it owed its origin to such a false system as this of grouping the members.

That St John in the second triad does not advance from the children through the young men to the fathers, but springs from the children to the fathers, and then returns back to the young men, has its ground in the very construction of the first triad. But the beautiful contrast between the "ye have known the Father" of the children, and the "ye have known Him that is from the beginning" of the fathers, is brought thereby into very suggestive prominence. And so the third member of the first triad leads over to the first member of the second triad, in a very unforced and interesting manner.

But now there is another question to be answered, whether St John had in view the stages of physical or of spiritual age.[1] The latter was the view of Clemens Alexandrinus, Grotius, and à Lapide; the former is that of the great majority of expositors. The view which refers it to spiritual age seeks its support in the passages, 1 Cor. xiii. 11, 12; Heb. v. 13; Eph. iv. 13, 14; but in all these places, not παιδίον, but νήπιος, is used to designate the neophytes who had made only small advance in the faith; and it is not probable that St John would have addressed newly converted adults by the endearing term παιδία. This expression, as also the tender "ye have *known the Father*," suggests at once the idea of Christian children in physical age; and, analogously, the νεανίσκοι and πατέρες of young men and fathers in physical age. Moreover, physical age involved (at least in normal development, and as the rule) the corresponding spiritual age—but not conversely.

Another question now rises, *how the ὅτι is to be interpreted.* The Greek Fathers, Socinus, Schott, Paulus, Neander, and others, translate it by "that." And Sander defends this translation by the assertion, that it "certainly is not superfluous to remind those who have obtained forgiveness that they possess that forgiveness"—referring to Lücke's reason for preferring "because." But such assertions have no exegetical force. That St John *could* have once more written to the Christians the well-known message concerning the forgiveness of sins, is indubitable from vers. 1, 2. But with equal certainty he *might*

---

[1] Augustin's view, that the Apostle meant by all and each of the three descriptions *all* Christians in common, is manifestly a perversion. St John in that case called them children, *quia baptismo renati sunt;* young men, *quia fortes sunt;* fathers, *quia Christum patrem agnoscunt!*

also have given a reason for the exhortations of vers. 9–11 by referring to their received forgiveness of sins. All such abstract possibilities lead to no definite conclusion; nor does the assurance of Calvin and Düsterdieck, that the translation " because" yields " a better meaning." For neither of these exegetes has shown *how far* the resulting meaning would then be a better one. All these were led rather by an indefinite feeling, than by a clear insight.

But, decisive for the translation " because" is what follows. If we translate " that," the clauses with ὅτι furnish the *subject-matter* of the γράφειν. In this case, the members, " I write unto you, fathers, that ye have known Him that is from the beginning," and " I have written unto you, fathers, that ye have known Him that is from the beginning," are perfectly of the same meaning; while the members, " I write unto you, young men, etc.," and " I have written unto you, young men, etc.," are, essentially at least, of the same meaning; and consequently, *the change from γράφω to ἔγραψα sinks down to a mere play of words.* But if, on the other hand, we translate ὅτι by " because," the clauses with ὅτι only give the reason why the Apostle writes; but the subject of the γράφειν is another matter, and *then remains the possibility of assuming a real distinction between γράφω and ἔγραψα.*

And this distinction *must* be accepted. That St John should have so tamely repeated one and the same thought, with only a change (not thoroughly harmonious with the thought itself) in time, is an unreasonable assumption, which so troubled Calvin, that he took refuge from it in the conjecture that the fourteenth verse might be spurious! That was bold, but honourable; it was cutting the knot, but acknowledging at the same time that a knot was there; it was therefore better than Lachmann's supposition, that this meaningless change slipped from the Apostle as an unpractised author! Düsterdieck, following Beza, satisfies himself that γράφω and ἔγραψα refer both to one and the same thing, that is, to the writing of the Epistle as such; but, " while the Present is spoken from the standing-point of the act of writing, the Aorist is used as from the position of the readers when they read the previously written Epistle." According to this, the subtle meaning of our passage would be as follows: " I am at present engaged, young men, in writing to you an Epistle, because ye have overcome the wicked one; but, when ye read these lines, I *shall have* already written this Epistle, because ye have overcome the wicked one." But, we cannot help asking, was there any rational reason why St John should have first placed himself in the position of his present writing, and then suddenly have transposed himself into the time when the Epistle should be read? Would the thoughts which he wished to express to the readers gain anything in clearness by his placing himself in these two different positions? Better than this would be the view of Neander, who thinks that St John would express by the ἔγραψα this—that it must remain, and be so, as I have written. But this requires the ὅτι to be translated " that ;" and, moreover, even then this strong affirmation would have been expressed, not by a simple Aorist, but by ὃ γέγραφα, πάλιν γράφω ὑμῖν (comp. Gal. i. 9); the expression of such a confirmation is always effected by opposing the Present to the Perfect, not the Aorist to the Present.

By far the majority of expositors have been wise enough to admit a material distinction between the γράφω and the ἔγραψα. But they have not been so unanimous in seeking it where it is to be found. According to Grotius, Calovius, De Wette, Huther, and others, the ἔγραψα should be referred to the previous part of the Epistle (or to ch. 1), while γράφω must be referred to that which follows (or also to the whole Epistle). But, between the preceding and the succeeding portion, or between the first part and the whole, there is absolutely no such distinction and contrast of matter; and vers. 13, 14 do not form any such boundary line between two materially different parts of the Epistle, as to prevent the opposition between γράφω and ἔγραψα from being, even on this supposition, a mere repetition or play of words. What in the world could induce the Apostle to say, "I have already written the preceding, because ye have overcome the wicked one, etc.; and I now go on to write, because ye have overcome the wicked one?" Or, "I write to you this Epistle, because ye have overcome the wicked one; I have already written to you the two previous pages, because ye have overcome the wicked one?"—Still more forced is the hypothesis of Rickli and Lücke. It is, that the threefold γράφω looks forward to the three exhortations, vers. 15–17, vers. 18–27, vers. 28–ch. iii. 22 ; and that the threefold ἔγραψα, on the contrary, looks backward to ch. i. 5–7, ch. i. 8–ch. ii. 2, ch. ii. 3–11. But we have seen that in ch. ii. 3 there is not the beginning even of a sub-section; that in ch. i. 8 no section commences; that, on the other hand, the starting-point of a main part of the Epistle falls within ch. ii. 3–11. The threefold ἔγραψα cannot then possibly refer to three sections, which, in fact, do not yet exist. When we mention that Lücke makes the Trinity the basis of his twice-three sections (ch. ii. 15 seq. urging love to God the Father; ch. ii. 18 seq., remaining in the Son; ch. ii. 28 seq., sanctification by the Spirit!), we can understand why this view has never found supporters.

Γράφω and ἔγραψα—I *write*, and I *wrote*—must needs point to two different *acts* of writing: the present act of writing refers to the letter in hand; the past act of writing must refer to another previous document. But this does not require us to assume the existence of earlier and lost Epistles. What the writer meant, was that Scripture to which he had most undeniably alluded in the introductory verses of this Epistle, viz., *the Gospel*, which, at the time he wrote, lay before him as an already-finished, and as it were past, production. Of this, and of no other, would the readers themselves also think.

And now the whole passage receives a clear and living meaning. The darkness is already in the act of passing; the light has through Christ already entered into the course of human affairs as an historical power: this thought (ver. 8) forms the starting-point and the basis for this whole part of the Epistle. The first requirement, in which this idea took the form of an ἐντολή, was this (vers. 9–11), that he who professes himself subjectively to belong already to the community of the light, must exhibit and approve this by love towards his companions in this kingdom of light. By the side of this *requirement* there now enters (according to the analogy of ver. 1) another element, an element derived from the reassuring mercy of God's message. The Apostle can lay down this injunction only on the ground of this, that the readers have already been made partakers of the forgiveness of sins. But, coming to this, he generalizes the idea. Not only does he impose that requirement on the ground that the readers already stood in a state of grace, but he tells them generally all that the Epistle contains, only on the ground of his assurance that in them it was a realized *truth*

that the darkness had passed, and the true light shone—or, in
other words, that they already stood before God in a state of
grace and forgiveness of sins. Therefore he does not say ταῦτα
γράφω, but generally and unrestrictedly, γράφω (by which, however, the specific and primary reference to vers. 9–11 is not excluded, but contrariwise included all the more obviously). The
essential idea which governs in ver. 12, is the ἤδη φαίνει, hath
already appeared, the Perfect ἀφέωνται, *are* forgiven. The
Apostle's business is the *individual* position of his readers in
relation to the *historically*-manifested salvation;—the question
whether his readers are now actually already in the light. Only
on the assumption that they are, can he write to them,—as well
the requirement of vers. 9–11, as all else that he writes. His
Epistle is not intended for the children of the world; as addressed to people who still belong to the σκοτία, it has no point
or aim. This thought then he dwells upon, and resolves it into
a few special applications to special classes of age. To the
fathers of the community, to those who were mature in physical
and in spiritual age, he writes, and to them he can write,
" because they have known Him that is from the beginning"—
Jesus Christ, who ἀπ' ἀρχῆς (ch. i. 1 and 2) was with the
Father, light of light, and in the fulness of time appeared in
the world.[1] For this it is that must be demanded of the aged,
that they be mature in knowledge, and familiar with that eternity
in which He is whose nature is eternal. But to the *young men*
he writes, and can write to them, because they "have overcome
the wicked one," that is, Satan—comp. Matt. xiii. 19 and 38
seq.; 1 John iii. 12, v. 18 seq.; Eph. vi. 16—who, by means
of suggestions within, and powers of enticement from without,
labours to keep men fast bound in the slavery of sin and darkness, or to bring them again under it, if they have escaped.
For, it springs from the very nature of youth, that it has still
to contend, and to endure its own specifically hot temptations,
whether of the flesh and its lusts, or of the lie and its sophistries:
for youth must ever be in conflicts, theoretical and practical.
To such young men as had endured this conflict, and conquered
in it, and who had thus fought their way to assured certainty
of faith and to a joyful consecration of heart to Christ—to

[1] In contradiction to ch. i. 1, Grotius understood by ὁ ἀπ' ἀρχῆς, God
the Father.

such, and only to such, he writes his Epistle.—But not the Epistle alone. The Epistle was only a companion-document to the Gospel, as we have already seen on ch. i. 1 seq. Therefore he extends and generalizes his position still further. "I *have* written to you," he says, in easily-intelligible allusion to the already-finished Gospel which lay under his eye. But now he turns to the *little ones*, the παιδία, not only for the external reason that he may set three other corresponding members over against the three preceding members—for the specific παιδία does not precisely correspond to the general τεκνία—but because, when he is alluding to his Gospel-document, he bethinks himself that *this* is a precious and seasonable food even for the youngest (while the Epistle was manifestly to be understood only by the adults); and, therefore, in his tender love, he appropriates what he *had* written—the Gospel, to wit—specially and primarily to the *little children*, because they "have known the Father." But then he turns from the little ones, the children, to the fathers (by natural transition; for obviously the fathers are the most direct antithesis to the children), and declares that his Gospel, not less than his Epistle, was applicable because, and only because, they had known Him that was from the beginning. And so likewise to the young men he declares that his Gospel, like his Epistle, was written to them only on the ground of this, that they "were *strong* (comp. Heb. xi. 34; Matt. xii. 29), and the word of God remained or *dwelt* in them, and they had overcome the wicked one, Satan." He adds here to the victory already won in conversion, the habitual Christian ἰσχυρότης also,—that invigoration and daily renewed strengthening of the new man in daily new conflicts, which is the absolute condition under which alone the living word of salvation can *abide* in man.

VERS. 15-17. To this *condition*, which St John has here mentioned, is appended immediately a further *exhortation* or *requirement*. In this requirement we have really only a resolution of the substance of the ἰσχυρὸς εἶναι into its component parts. At the same time, this exhortation assumes the form of an independent train of reflection and of a separate sub-section, just as every organic germ of a plant takes the form of an independent branch. And thus this exhortation, although it

L

primarily grows out of that which was said to the young men, holds good not for young men alone (as Bengel says), but for every Christian.

As, in vers. 9–11, from the historical manifestation of the light upon earth, the *positive* requirement of love towards all fellow-partakers in the light followed as an immediate consequence, so here, from the mention of the internal conflict and victory the requirement follows, that the Christian should still further show himself strong and victorious, that is, in manfully renouncing that which is σκοτία, the κόσμος and its ἐπιθυμίας. *This* side of the σκοτία is here (vers. 15–17) first and preeminently prominent : it is *the σκοτία* as it was already present in the world (especially the heathen world), not yet under the full influence of Christ ; the common, fleshly, vain pursuits of this life, the κόσμος as such,—for κόσμος denotes simply the sinful world, not yet redeemed, as it is. Thereupon follows, in a particular paragraph which is appended (vers. 18–25), the reference to the σκοτία, as, in its opposition to the already manifested light, it already assumes the form, and will again and yet more assume it, of anti-Christianity.

In ver. 15, therefore, the subject in question is, first of all, the κόσμος. But he that has laid hold on Christ has renounced this "world," and its sinful, God-forgetting courses. He who will abide in Christ must, however, continually guard himself, and take heed that love to the world do not anew find place in his heart. For the world is not merely without us : a residue of the worldly nature is, indeed, as the old man, still in us ; in that the external world has a representative and deputy to do its work. Hence the solemn warning is ever and for all needful : "Love not the world, nor the things in the world." Ὁ κόσμος is the sinful world, the *extra-Christian* world, as such, as yet internally untouched by Christ—the mass and multitude of those who are still unregenerate, contemplated in their characteristic kind and impulses.[1] But τὰ τοῦ κόσμου are all the

---

[1] This conception of the κόσμος approves itself at once, when we have rightly understood ver. 8 as the basis of the whole division of the Epistle. The κόσμος stands in *opposition* to those who are addressed and characterized in vers. 12–14 ; it is thus the mass of those in whom the passing away of the darkness and the shining of the light has not yet become an ἀληθές. Thus κόσμος is the world ruined by Adam's fall, so far as it is *still* world,

lusts, inclinations, and pursuits of men which in their characteristic quality correspond with that world. As κόσμος does not designate the creature as such, but the ethical idea of the world of sinners as yet unpenetrated by the light of Christ, that is, the *extra-Christian world*, so also by τὰ ἐν τῷ κόσμῳ are not meant creaturely objects (such as gold, honour, etc.), either in themselves, or so far as they may become *objects* of sinful lust, but *kinds of sinful pursuit, or aim, or conduct* (*e.g.*, avarice, ambition, pleasure, etc.). "Love not the world, nor the impulses and pursuits of the world," is the sense of the apostolical exhortation.—Τὰ ἐν τῷ κόσμῳ are found not only in the κόσμος itself, not only among the multitude of those as yet strangers to a state of grace; but they may be also found even in the sphere of Christians, because these have still something of the world in them. Τὰ ἐν τῷ κόσμῳ include all that which *in its nature* corresponds to the nature and pursuits of that κόσμος, be it found in whom it may. We should, 1. not love the world itself, not directly cast our furtive regards at it and its ways; but, 2. we must not make the individual kinds of worldly lust and worldly spirit and pursuit, *as they are in the world, and are cultivated in it*, the objects of our longing, loving, and pursuit. How ὁ κόσμος and τὰ ἐν τῷ κόσμῳ are distinguished, may be most clearly seen in the example of those individuals and families which hold in great abhorrence really worldly pleasures, dancing, etc., but within their rigid Christian circle tolerate ambition and vanity and avarice, which have their genuine and fit place, not in Christian circles, but ἐν τῷ κόσμῳ, and hence belong to τοῖς ἐν τῷ κόσμῳ, to the things which make the world's pursuits.

Strangely has the question been raised and replied to, how this exhortation not to love the world is to be reconciled with the declaration of St John, ch. iii. 16, that God so loved the world as to give His only-begotten Son. The unity and perfect harmony of the two passages is clear enough to every one who (with such places as Rom. ix. 1–3 in his eye) remembers that we

and *still* bears Adam's sinful nature in it, and *not yet* is transformed into the kingdom of Christ. Κόσμος is thus, here, neither the creation (Neander), nor the *major pars hominum* (Grotius), nor the things by which the lust of sense is excited (Luther), nor *omne genus corruptelæ* (Calvin), nor original sin (Schmid), nor the world of men as such (Dusterdieck), nor the antichristian world (Storr).

not only *may*, but that we *must*, love *that* world of which John iii. 16 speaks with *that* love which in us is analogous to the love there mentioned. For not only the idea of the ἀγαπᾶν (as Düsterdieck thinks), but also that of the κόσμος, is entirely different in the two passages respectively. In that, the ἀγαπᾶν is the *merciful, holy* love, which wills not the death of the sinner, while it abhors the sin, and which therefore loves the sinner *in spite of* his sin; here, it is the *unholy lusting* which does not aim to save the sinner's person, but to share his sin,—which seeks not to deliver the sinner from his sin, but to place itself in the slavery of sin, and which therefore loves the sinner *on account of* his sin. *There* (John iii. 16), ὁ κόσμος is not (as Beza says) the *number of the elect* alone; but neither is κόσμος in our passage the sinful world of men as such (as Düsterdieck says). Rather is κόσμος in John iii. 16 the fallen world of mankind as such, as being, viz., the object of the Divine counsel of redemption, and contemplated as *capable of being redeemed*: in our passage, on the other hand, κόσμος is (as is perfectly plain from ver. 8, as also from vers. 12–14) the sinful world of men, so far as it forms a contrast to those who have already overcome the wicked one; and therefore it is the multitude of those who at any assignable moment *still belong to the darkness*. And therefore the κόσμος comes under contemplation here in its moral character and aspect, as opposed to the character of the children of God.

In the second half of the verse, that which was laid down in the first part as an exhortation takes the form of one of those negative and exclusive sentences which we so often meet with in St John (ch. i. 6 and 8 and 10, ii. 4 and 9 and 11). *If any man love the world, the love of God is not in him.* Τοῦ Θεοῦ is the reading of Codd. A.C., of the Coptic and the Æthiopic Versions, of Cyril and others. The reading of the Text. Rec., and that which is commonly adopted, τοῦ πατρός, is found only in Cod. B., the Vulgate, and a few of the Fathers. Düsterdieck gives the reading τοῦ πατρός the preference, "because it seems absolutely necessary on account of ver. 16;" but that only explains how it came to pass that the copyists corrected Θεοῦ into πατρός. For certainly it is more probable that it was thought necessary in ver. 15 to read πατρός, on account of the harmony with ver. 16, than that a Θεοῦ was inserted from the distant ver. 17 instead of the original πατρός.—The sentiment itself is clear. The world is the sinful world of men, so far as it is not yet penetrated by the light in Christ, and therefore is not itself light, not yet analogous to the nature of God (ch. i. 5), but rather in its characteristics opposed to that nature. Consequently, he who loves this world, and its God-opposed nature, shows that the "love of God" does not dwell in him. Ἡ ἀγάπη τοῦ Θεοῦ denoted, in ver. 5, neither one-sidedly the love of the saved to God, nor one-sidedly the love of God to the saved, but the mutual *love-relation* between God and man. In our passage we may indeed think of this relation of mutual love, yet the contrast between the "loving God" and the "loving the world" would constrain us to interpret it here preeminently of its one aspect, the human side; and therefore it is more natural, with the majority of commentators, to understand by the "love of God," in *this* connection, *the love of men* to God.[1]

Ver. 16 connects itself, by means of an argumentative ὅτι, with ver. 15. In ver. 16 it is more clearly illustrated to what extent the nature of the world is contradictory to the nature of God.

Πᾶν τὸ ἐν τῷ κόσμῳ is, as most expositors have seen, nothing but a strengthened repetition of the preceding τὰ ἐν τῷ κόσμῳ. This last expression denoted, as we have seen, not the individual external objects which exist in the created world, the creature (as in Acts xvii. 24)—for it is not the creature that is here described as κόσμος, nor individual objects and things, so far as they are or may become objects of sinful desire; but τὰ ἐν τῷ κόσμῳ must be understood of all that which has its place, as it respects its moral characteristics, *in the world*—that is, in mankind as not yet enlightened by the light of Christ, and still wandering in unchecked sinful pursuits,—and which therefore has not, or should not have, any place among Christians. Thus the expression denoted, not things, but *kinds* of deportment, and thought, and endeavour, and action. And all this is meant by πᾶν τὸ ἐν τῷ κόσμῳ; only that the Apostle here lays emphasis upon this, that *all things* which in this sense find their place ἐν τῷ κόσμῳ—all things without exception—are opposite to God. For he is now about to reckon the *individual species* into which

---

[1] It is altogether wrong, with Luther and Calov, to refer this expression here to the love of God to Christians.

the generic idea, τὰ ἐν τῷ κόσμῳ, is distributed.—Thus, first, the distinction vanishes, according to which τὰ ἐν τῷ κόσμῳ are the actual creaturely objects of sinful lust, and πᾶν τὸ ἐν τῷ κόσμῳ the internal moral nature of the world (Huther: the second here is correct, but the first incorrect). And, secondly, we are not under the necessity of assuming (with Düsterdieck) a "change from the notion of the objects of worldly lust into the appositional notion of subjective lust itself"—he referring both the phrases to the *creaturely objects* of sinful lust.

Three individual kinds of sinful worldly propension are named by the Apostle. But how these three kinds are related to each other,—whether one includes the other, or whether the one is a particular species of the other;—whether the whole forms a systematic and perfect distribution, or the three are only isolated examples individually;—how, finally, each of the three conceptions is to be defined and characterized;—on all these points there is endless confusion among the commentators. One main reason of this may be the fact, that expositors generally (especially in the domain of practical-ascetic Bible-explanation, which has never failed to exert its influence upon scientific exegesis) have been determined to find in our verse a distribution *of sin generally,* or of *original sin;* while the Apostle here has to do, not with sin as it is a power in the subjective inner man, but *with sin as it exhibits itself objectively in the external deportment and common life of the children of the world,*—in short, with the individual departments of the *world's pursuit.* (Bullinger: *studium mundi.* So also Calvin, Grotius, Wolf, Lücke, De Wette, Neander.) And this at once obviates and sets aside the views of those who discern in the three members a progression and climax: the lust of the flesh indicating gross actual sins; the lust of the eye indicating and condemning the more subtle sin of the desire, the lustful contemplation of the eye; and the pride of life similarly condemning even the sin of the thoughts of the heart (with which, however, the Gen. τοῦ βίου cannot be made very well to harmonize). So also is excluded the theory of those who (as Neander, De Wette, Düsterdieck) take σάρξ in that general sense according to which it forms the antithesis to τὸ πνεῦμα (as in John iii. 6; Rom. viii. 4–9), and all and every sin (even that of self-righteousness, Gal. iii. 3) falls under the idea of the σάρξ.

If we set out, as it is always the duty of the exegete to do, with the explanation of the individual words, we find that two of the notions involved in the idea of ἐπιθυμία are distinguished by the names ἐπιθυμία τῆς σαρκός and ἐπιθυμία τῶν ὀφθαλμῶν, while ἀλαζονεία enters as the third member of the idea, having the Gen. τοῦ βίου connected with it. But all the three members are united by the uniform καί, and thus exhibited as co-ordinate. 'Επιθυμία denotes, etymologically, every longing desire (Luke xxii. 15; Phil. i. 23; 1 Thess. ii. 17); but it is commonly used in the specific sense of sinful inclinations: sometimes these sinful desires are, as it regards their *objects*, described by ἐπιθυμίαι (thus in John viii. 44, Rom. vii. 8, Col. v. 16, etc., the fulfilling the lusts is accomplishing *that for which* we lust); sometimes the ἐπιθυμίαι denote the *impulses themselves* (2 Tim. iii. 6; Tit. iii. 3; Rom. vi. 12; Jude 18, etc.). Accordingly, a twofold view of the Genitive is here possible. If ἡ ἐπιθυμία denotes the impulse of desire as such, the Genitive may be a Genitive of the object; then ἡ ἐπιθυμία τῆς σαρκός would be " the desire after the flesh," that is, for fleshly enjoyment, and ἡ ἐπιθυμία τῶν ὀφθαλμῶν would be the desire after the eyes, that is, for the gratification of the eyes. So Huther says: "It is not the lust which is excited by looking, but the lust which seeks its own gratification in looking, and has its object in the satisfaction of the eye." But this view of the matter is in two ways erroneous. For, first, although we may admit that the Genitive τῆς σαρκός may assuredly be taken as the Genitive of the object (σάρξ, however, elsewhere commonly denotes, not the fleshly *after which* man lusts, but the flesh which lusts, and a Genitive of the object never does occur after ἐπιθυμίαι elsewhere in the New Testament), yet, on the other hand, it will appear too bold to accept οἱ ὀφθαλμοί in a double tropical sense as "the satisfaction which the beholding with the eyes secures." But, secondly, it is in itself at the outset improbable that St John would here, where the subject is the objective forms and manifestations of the worldly spirit, mention the subjective excitement of the desires. Hence we shall do better to take ἐπιθυμία in the sense which it bears in John viii. 44, etc., where it denotes *the desire according to its matter*, that *after which* man lusts, thus " the lusts." Then the Genitives are not Genitives of the object; for the object of the lust cannot have the object of the lust as a Genitive after it. They are then *either* Genitives of the subject, *or* Genitives of the kind and relation. (Genitives of the latter sort are found in Eph. iv. 22 and 2 Pet. ii. 10 connected with ἐπιθυμίαι.) Taking them in the former sense, ἡ ἐπιθυμία τῆς σαρκός would be the kind of lust which has its source in the flesh, carnal and sensual desires; but ἡ ἐπιθυμία τῶν ὀφθαλμῶν would be the kind of lust which springs from the eyes, that is, from beholding. But how could we then keep the two asunder, since in all sins of the flesh the external eye of the body, as also the internal eye of the fantasy, are usually as active as the proper fleshly impulse itself?[1] In the latter sense, ἡ ἐπιθυμία τῆς σαρκός would be that kind of desire or lust which has its existence in the domain of the σάρξ; but ἡ ἐπιθυμία τῶν ὀφθαλμῶν that which finds place in the domain of the *seeing*.[2] Now σάρξ may not here, as has been already shown, be understood in the broader sense, as the creature, or humanity, or mankind found in a state of opposition to God; rather must it be here used in the narrower sense in which it occurs 1 Pet. iii. 18 and 19 and 21, iv. 1, where by σάρξ and πνεῦμα the antithesis of body and spirit is designated. And thus ἡ ἐπιθυμία τῆς σαρκός is here that species of sinful desire which is preeminently directed to sensual, that is, sexual enjoyments. (So Augustin, Bullinger, Grotius.)

But what does the ἐπιθυμία τῶν ὀφθαλμῶν mean, in contradistinction to this? The expression in itself would be indistinct and vague, if it had not a plain stamp upon it which is derived from the Old-Testament use of the phrase. Luther, Socinus, Grotius, Bengel, and others, have not incorrectly referred to such passages as Prov. xxiii. 5, xxvii. 20; Eccles. iv. 8, v. 10; Luke xiv. 18, 19; and therefore understood the expression to mean *avarice*, or lust of having. Only this idea is too restricted. We must also bear in mind such other passages as Ps. xvii. 11, liv. 9, xci. 8, xcii. 12; Prov. vi. 17, etc. The eye

---

[1] Lucke and De Wette in fact identify ἐπιθυμία τῆς σαρκός with ἐπιθυμία τῶν ὀφθαλμῶν. The former is the desires of the sensually-excited lust; the latter, "what the eyes see, and that by which the sensual lusts are excited."

[2] Thus Olshausen seems to have taken the meaning of the expressions, when he explains ἐπ. τ. σαρκός of "fleshly, carnal enjoyment," and ἐπ. τ. ὀφθαλμῶν, on the contrary, of "dissipation through external or internal relations."

of the natural man looks at others' possessions with complacency, but also sees its own happiness in the calamity of one who is an enemy. The whole sphere of the desires of selfishness, of envy and of covetousness, of hatred and of revenge, is indicated by ἡ ἐπιθυμία τῶν ὀφθαλμῶν.[1]

And now remains the ἀλαζονεία τοῦ βίου. Our explanation above gives us this advantage, that we are able to take the first two Genitives in the same sense as the third, that is, as Genitives of the kind and respect. Ἀλαζονεία τοῦ βίου is ἀλαζονεία in the βίος, in the manner of life. Βίος, that is, means, first, the life itself (= ζωή, Septuagint, Job viii. 9, x. 20; Isa. liii. 8; comp. 1 Peter iv. 2); secondly, the sustenance of life (Luke viii. 43, xv. 12; 1 John iii. 17); and, finally, also the conduct of life, the direction, tendency, and manner of life (2 Tim. ii. 2 and 4; Luke viii. 14). Some expound it here according to the second of these meanings—βίος then being about equivalent to πλοῦτος, riches, and ἀλαζονεία τοῦ βίου, the magnificence of riches; but βίος means only the provision needful for the sustenance of life, and this can scarcely become the object or ground of vain boasting. Most expositors, however, are agreed in expounding βίος according to the third of these meanings (direction and manner of life), and that the ἀλαζονεία of the clause is *in* the regulation of life: it remains only that we define a little more precisely the idea of the ἀλαζονεία itself. Ἀλάζων is etymologically ἐν ἄλῃ ζῶν, a vagabond, or puffing mountebank: hence it is, according to Hesychius and Suidas, equivalent in meaning to πλάνος, ψευδής, ὑπερήφανος. Ἀλαζονεία is, accordingly, first of all, the prating and boastful nature, referring to the kind of people who make loud pretensions before others. Thus it is not simple pride,—the consciousness of one's own value and one's own superiority; nor presumption of heart,—which groundlessly exalts the personal I in one's own thoughts over all others, the selfishness which thinks lightly of all but self; nor scorn (ὕβρις), which tramples ruthlessly under foot all the claims of others; nor arrogance,—*eum quis nimium sibi aut verbis aut factis assumit* (Bengel); nor, finally, that presumption against God which trusts in the possession of earthly goods. But it is that *vanity, which in the eyes of others* will make a great display,

---

[1] Augustin and Neander arbitrarily refer it to the satisfaction of the eye in *spectaculis*. But this rather belongs to the ἀλαζονεία τοῦ βίου.

and which is therefore dependent upon the judgment of others, even the vilest—*the lust of shining and making a boasting display.* Thus in Wisd. v. 8, πλοῦτος μετὰ ἀλαζονείας denotes riches connected with the idle vaunting of luxury (on the other hand, in ch. xvii. 7 it has its original signification of loud boasting; and so also in 2 Macc. xv. 6). In Rom. i. 30 and 2 Tim. iii. 2, it is distinguished from ὑπερηφανία and also from ὕβρις, as something different from both. It is evident, therefore, that pride, in the sense of loftiness of spirit, does not correspond to the idea of ἀλαζονεία; but that it is a word which denotes worldly *luxury*, so far as that is connected with the spirit which is set upon surpassing others in magnificence of life, and thinks the better of self in proportion as others are excelled in dress, food, and expenditure of all kinds. Ἀλαζονεία τοῦ βίου does not signify pride of spirit, so much as pride of life, the desire to shine and outshine others. (So also in classical Greek : compare Raphelius Polyb. S. 709). The idea of *luxury* most perfectly answers to the expression. Political economy, indeed, from its position, understands by "luxury" something that is allowable and profitable, since it subserves the making of money and the interests of commerce; but that is only so far as that science has an extra-Christian ground. Morally viewed, "luxury" is not a *vox media*, but a word of disapproval. There are physical necessities of life, which even the savage satisfies; there are necessities of culture, the gratification of which is right and permitted; but where the means used to that end go beyond this end, and are subservient to the immoral purposes of vanity, and foolish ostentation, and the desire to outshine others, luxury begins; and so does prodigality, where there is waste without any purpose at all. But the spirit which desires to shine before others in splendour of dress, habitation, furniture, is a fundamental characteristic of the unchristian course of this world; and we must not think, because so many "Christians" of the present day have blunted consciences in this respect, that St John has no word of condemnation for this unchristian disposition, which in truth is the wretched source of untold public as well as private evil.[1]

[1] To provide classics, musical books, and the like, is not luxury, but the gratification of a necessitude of culture. To have them bound, not merely decently and carefully, but magnificently—for display on the table

After we have learned to understand individually the three kinds of worldly pursuit to which St John gives a name—the lusts of sensuality; the passions of hatred and vengeance, envy and selfishness; the luxury of the economy of life—the question arises, whether these are examples fortuitously selected, or constitute a distribution which sums up all the manifestations of the spirit of the course of this world in their several aspects, and in their whole comprehensiveness. The latter is in itself more probable; and we should not be justified, unless indeed there could be found in the nature of things absolutely no ground for the distribution, in taking St John's words (with Calvin, Lücke, Neander, and others) as giving us a mere exemplification of the spirit of the world. The internal and complete principle of distribution, such as embraces the whole round of the course of this world, lies near at hand. *Man in relation to his own bodily nature* and life of sense—*man in his personal opposition to his fellow-men*—and *man in his relation to them, and commerce with them,*—these are the three aspects of the subject, and a fourth added to these can hardly be imagined. There is, in fact, no form of the manifestation of the extra- and un-christian course of this world, which may not have its definite place assigned to it under one of these three heads.

Among the other principles of distribution which expositors have discerned or invented, those necessarily fall to the ground which rest upon an erroneous explanation of the three ideas individually considered: that, for example, of Bengel, who supposes that the lust of the flesh refers to the *sensus fruitivi*, taste and feeling; but the lust of the eye to the *sensus investigativi*, sight, hearing, and smell; and ἀλαζονεία, finally, being ambition and pride of place. Equally inapplicable are the views

—is luxury. When Lucullus ordered a dish of singing birds, it was extravagant prodigality. All these ideas must take their character from the relation of means to an end first, and then from the character of the end itself. Quite distinct from this is the question as to the relation of expenditure to the means at our disposal. That which oversteps our means, is morally blameworthy, but may not in itself be luxury or profusion. (For instance, more books may be bought than our income permits, though for an absolutely good end.) So, on the other hand, our expenditure may be regulated by our income, and yet there may be both luxury and prodigality. " So long as there is distress and want still in the world, no Christian man has a right to live in luxury " (Gerstner).

of all those who think they find here a distribution of sin generally and as such. So also is the view of those (Lücke and Düsterdieck) who do not regard the three ideas as co-ordinated, but think that the lust of the flesh includes the desire of the eye as a more subtle form of itself, and the pride of life as its extreme climax. Those, finally, who think of $\dot{\eta}\delta ovaί$, $πλοῦτος$, and $τιμή$, as the main objects of sinful desire, coincide, indeed, though not very exactly, with the three worldly vices named by St John, so far as the lust of the flesh is a kind of $φιληδονία$, and the $φιλαργυρία$ a kind of lust of the eyes, and the vanity of luxury is at least connected with the desire of honour in the sight of others. But they are altogether wrong who imagine that St John had *in his view* any such combinations, here and there occurring in profane writers, as $ἐπιθυμία\ \mathring{\eta}\ χρημάτων,\ \mathring{\eta}\ δόξης,\ \mathring{\eta}\ \mathring{\eta}δονῆς$ (Philo ad Decal. Opp. ii. 205), or of $φιληδονία$, $πλεονεξία$, $φιλοδοξία$ (Pythagoras, Clinias). St John had nothing in his eye but the things themselves, and all he did was to characterize the spirit of the world according to its three fundamental tendencies. But these fundamental tendencies are everywhere so marked, that even heathen writers could scarcely fail to seize them.[1]

We have now considered the *subject of the proposition. All that is in the world*, that is, all those vicious tendencies and sins which are in vogue in extra- and un-christian humanity — as well the sensual desires, as selfishness in avarice, and hatred,

---

[1] Bede and à Lapide push the matter to the verge of caricature, when they not only arrogate for St John the Pythagorean tripartite distribution of sin, but refer them to the three Persons in the Trinity (sensuality in relation to the Father, lust of possession in relation to the Son, ambition in relation to the Holy Spirit), and, moreover, place them in *contrast* with the three vows of the cloister (chastity, poverty, obedience), and in *parallel* with the threefold temptation of Christ. This last often reappears in ascetic literature, but without any propriety. Christ was not tempted to the abstract sins of sensuous enjoyment (to which the satisfaction of hunger does not belong), ambition, and pride of possession; but His temptation referred to the definite individual aspects of His coming mediatorial work. The sin contemplated by Satan in the first temptation was not the satisfaction of hunger, but the application of His power of working miracles to an end which lay beyond His Messianic vocation; that in the second was not the desire of honour, but the carnal method of collecting around Himself a Messianic body of adherents; that in the third was not the desire to have possessions, but apostasy from the Father.

and pride in the pursuits of life (luxury)—all this *is not of the Father, but is of the world*. This is the predicate, which is expressed concerning that subject. Ἔστιν ἐκ denotes, not merely similarity of kind and relation of nature, but their origin, as in ver. 21 and John viii. 44. On that very account the predicate is not tautological, as if it were said, " That which belongs to the world, belongs to the world;" nor is it any mere repetition of the sentiment of ver. 15, but a genuine establishment of the *ground* of that. The world itself, in its substance, was created by God; this human race which is fallen into sin, and has not yet yielded to the light from Christ, was, with all its creaturely powers and capacities, and with all the relations (*e.g.*, of family, of civil community, and of the state) in which it lives, and with all the possessions and natural objects in which it finds the substratum of its life, and action, and enjoyment, created by God. On the other hand, its pursuit and course, its desire for sensual, fleshly enjoyment, its self-seeking thirst for self-enrichment and advantage over the neighbour, its perversion of earthly possessions to purposes of vain ostentation, was not increased in it, and does not come from God the Creator and *Father* of all things (who on that account is *here*, ver. 16, with good reason called πατήρ), but has its origin in the sinful will of the creature; the *course* and pursuit of the κόσμος, of the extra- and un-christian world, is a *product* of the κόσμος, and that of the κόσμος *as it is* opposed to God. *Therefore* (ver. 15), " the love of the world, and the things in the world," and " the love of God," mutually exclude each other.

Now, as in ver. 16 the second half of ver. 15 has been established upon its grounds, so in ver. 17 the exhortation in the first half of ver. 15 finds its *further motive*. The first motive to our not loving the world lies in this, that love to the world cannot be reconciled with the love of God; and a second in this, *that the world with its lust is passing away*. But, it will be observed that this second motive is not placed externally *by the side* of the first; it grows internally and organically out of the reason of the first.

Καὶ ὁ κόσμος παράγεται: this is essentially the same παράγεσθαι, or passing away, which we had in ver. 8; but here it appears under another point of view, and therefore with a modifying difference. That which is here said of the κόσμος is, when looked at carefully, a consequence of that which had been there said concerning the σκοτία. The σκοτία—*the darkness*— is now, at the present time, in the act of passing away; the true light already shineth: the great crisis, therefore, or judgment between light and darkness has begun upon earth, and can self-evidently end only with the victory of the light. Hence it appears manifest, at once, that the sphere of those who stand in this conflict on the side of the σκοτία, on the *dark side*,— that is, the κόσμος, or world, in the sense of vers. 15–17,— cannot escape the destiny of one day vanishing, passing away, and ceasing to be. There *must* come a time when this κόσμος shall be no longer existent upon earth, and shall no longer oppose and thwart the congregation of the light. And this will enable us to perceive in what manner the sense of παράγεται is modified here in ver. 17. There, in ver. 7, it was said of the *present* time, that *already now*, ἤδη, in the time of St John, the σκοτία was in the act of vanishing: here it is declared concerning the κόσμος, that it is involved in its very *nature* that it must *one day* pass away. Here, therefore, the παράγεται does not express a present procedure as such (as Meyer maintains), but a characteristic quality, or, more correctly, a distinction of nature and necessity. The κόσμος is invested with the attribute of being under the necessity of passing, of having no eternal continuance. And with it comes to an end also ἡ ἐπιθυμία αὐτοῦ, its course as described in ver. 15, its sensual lusts, and lusts of the eye, and pride of life—all that in which it found its happiness.[1]

In opposition to this, it is expressed concerning him who doeth the will of God, that he μένει εἰς τὸν αἰῶνα. The subject, "he that doeth the will of God," furnishes no difficulty: τὸ θέλημα τοῦ Θεοῦ is the simple opposite of that which was designated by "all that is in the world." The course of the world is diametrically opposite to the will of God; the perfect opposite

---

[1] Here then it is plain, that ἐπιθυμία denotes, not the *excitement* of the desire, but the desire in its *matter*. But it is not by any means necessary to refer ἐπιθυμία to the *objects* of the desire (money, etc.). St John does not say that these *things* have an end, but that the *pursuit* of the world has an end. For, by the κόσμος itself he understands, not the *creation of God* embracing these *things*, but *unchristian humanity*, which has produced that *pursuit and spirit* out of itself: comp. ver. 16, "All that is in the world—is of the world."

of the course of the world,—to wit, that we love not the world, but God; that we deny ourselves all sensuality, all selfish greed, and pride of life; consequently, that we live purely and chastely, loving our brethren in self-denial and self-restraint, and humbly contenting ourselves with that which is necessary, our daily bread,—is therefore the will of God. He who doeth this will of God, *abideth εἰς τὸν αἰῶνα*. But what does this mean? Not, as Düsterdieck perverts the sense, that "the love to the Father abideth to all eternity:" it is not said of the love that it, but of him that shows it, that he, abideth for ever. This *μένειν εἰς τὸν αἰῶνα* cannot possibly, however, denote the mere naked *continuance without end:* this, indeed, is not a distinguishing attribute of the children of God; for does the Scripture any-where teach the annihilation of the unbelieving and ungodly? But no more can we understand why De Wette substitutes for the words, " abideth for ever," the unqualified words, " hath eternal life;" since the idea of "life" is not in any way expressed, and our words are used in direct opposition to *παράγεται*. A *continuance*, in opposition to a passing away, is certainly meant, but the kind of this continuance must needs be more closely defined; and the words *εἰς τὸν αἰῶνα* cannot possibly serve merely to repeat the idea of the continuance thereof, or to append to it the mere attribute of *endlessness*. It is generally a widely-spread but very great error of our exegesis, that the Biblical *αἰών* is made to refer so unconditionally to the metaphysical idea of " eternity," whether as endless duration, or as extra- and super-temporal. When it is said concerning God, or concerning Christ, that He is and that He abides the same *εἰς τοὺς αἰῶνας τῶν αἰώνων* (Ps. xc. 2, ciii. 17; Rev. i. 18), or that the kingdom of Christ will abide *εἰς τοὺς αἰῶνας τῶν αἰώνων* (Rev. xi. 15, xxii. 5; comp. xx. 10; Heb. xiii. 21), it is assuredly involved in the words that God is one who is *above* the change of all times and Æons, and that Christ's kingdom is an eternal and endlessly-continuing kingdom (because bounded by no future Æon). But the simple *εἰς τὸν αἰῶνα* cannot express simply the same thing; since the idea of endless continuance does not lie in the word *αἰών* as such. *Αἰών* is always *a definite large period of the world's history:* thus we have frequently mention made of *αἰὼν οὗτος* and *αἰὼν μέλλων* or *ἐρχόμενος* (Luke xvi. 8, xx. 34; 2 Cor. iv. 4; Eph. ii. 2; compared with

Luke xviii. 30; Eph. ii. 7); and so ἀπ' αἰῶνος (Acts iii. 21; John ix. 32) means "from the beginning of the world;" therefore, of the present Æon of the world, but not "from eternity." It is true that there is not a μέλλοντα connected with αἰῶνα in our passage; but it is obvious from the μένει εἰς τὸν αἰῶνα of itself, that neither any past Æon nor the present Æon is meant, but the future, and the nearest future;—the Æon which will begin with the visible establishment of Christ's kingdom upon earth in glory. Thus apprehended, the words form a really true and logically-correct antithesis to the words ὁ κόσμος παράγεται. The *world*—the unchristian world which in opposition to the Church of Christ in time still continues—must one day pass, and all the pursuits in which it now finds its happiness, its carnal lust, its lust of the eye, its luxury, will then have with it an end. In this is involved that the individual members of the κόσμος must behold the downfall of their party and all their glory; but, on the contrary, he who doeth the will of God will abide to the establishment of the kingdom of Christ, and it will be his to see the victory of that kingdom.[1]

In VERS. 18–21 begins a new subdivision, which goes on continuously down to ver. 25. The exhortation to fly the pursuits of the *extrachristian and unchristian* "world" had been closely connected with the address to the νεανίσκοι. Now follows a warning against all *antichristian* aims, that is, against the σκοτία, as it is not only a darkness yet untouched by the light, but as it has placed itself in *direct and conscious antagonism* to the light. This exhortation is opened by the address and appellation, τεκνία. This term of address has been thought by some to furnish proof that παιδία above in ver. 13 cannot denote a specific class of age, that is, children; but that it has the same meaning as τεκνία in ver. 12, and is an address to the whole Church. For, in our ver. 18—so they think—the whole community is most manifestly addressed. However, even in that case, it is not absolutely necessary to explain the former verse by the

---

[1] Not "He abideth *living upon earth* until the establishment of the kingdom of Christ:" this is not involved in the μένει. But only this is contained in it, that he will be a witness of this victory, and will stretch forward his existence into that victorious kingdom. *How*—we are told in the passages, 1 Thess. iv. 14–17; Rev. xx. 4, 5.

latter; in ver. 13 the change of expression *may* not be without purpose and aim; it would have been an unnatural harshness in the style not to repeat τεκνία also with the πατέρες and νεανίσκοι, if St John had intended to address the very same τεκνία. The *change* in the expression, occurring in such close proximity to the repetition of the others, shows incontrovertibly that there was also some change in the idea intended. If this be established, then our παιδία in ver. 18 may be referred to the same class of children in age which was denoted by παιδία in ver. 13. And so far from vers. 18–25 being unsuitable as addressed to children, all that these verses contain yields its living and subtle significance only when regarded as directed to the young rising generation of the Church. That is to say, while the antichristian element had already appeared in its beginnings, its full unfolding is contemplated by St John as future, and as to take place in a period when he should no longer be able as a faithful pastor to defend the Church: it is then quite natural that his provident foresight should take care for the babes and little ones especially (Bengel); and hence he seeks to excite the attention of those in particular, the spiritually weak and helpless, to the coming danger, and, by a word of fatherly warning, to arm them against it. And this he does precisely in such a manner as was adapted to the case of these *little ones*. (When, further on—addressing the whole Church —he comes to speak again of the Antichrist, he speaks in a very different manner.) He places himself and the Church as ἡμεῖς over against the little ones addressed; he brings to their mind (what every child might be able to understand) that the false teachers who had been separated from the Church, were externally separated only because they had not in their spirit and nature belonged to the Christian community; finally, he says (what was suitable expressly and only to children) that he writes this to them as presupposing, not that the truth was as yet unknown to them, but that they (although παιδία) knew the truth already,—for that the whole truth was comprised in the simple proposition, that Jesus is the Christ.[1] What the

---

[1] Sander correctly remarks, that the specific prophecy touching the Antichrist was not withheld from the children, even as St Paul, during the few days of his sojourn in Thessalonica, communicated it to the newly-converted Thessalonians.

words of ver. 21 should mean, as addressed to adults, or how St John should say to adults, "I have not written to you, because ye have not known the truth," can scarcely be understood. Addressed to adults, this declaration would be altogether superfluous. Sander is quite right when he sees in the παιδία, ver. 18, and the οὐκ ἔγραψα ὅτι, ver. 21, a member of the connection of thought which is *analogous* to the members of vers. 12–14.[1]

Thus we regard this παιδία (with Bengel, Sander, Besser, and others, against Lücke, De Wette, Düsterdieck, Huther) as an address to the class of children in literal age in the Church. To them the Apostle cries: ἐσχάτη ὥρα ἐστίν (where the article is wanting, as it is frequently with ὥρα alone, *e.g.*, Mark xv. 25 and 33; Acts xxiii. 23; comp. Winer Gr. § 18). The "last hour" must not (with Œcumenius, Bullinger, Carpzov, Rosenmüller, and others) be softened down to the vague idea of *tempora periculosa*. The only question which arises, is whether the expression is of the same import, or at least analogous, with "the last days" (Isa. ii. 2; Mic. iv. 1; Acts ii. 17; 2 Tim. iii. 1; 2 Pet. iii. 3), or "ὕστεροι καιροί" (1 Tim. iv. 1), and therefore takes a dogmatical meaning here; or whether it must be referred to the state of old age and the impending death of St John. Against this latter view the concluding part of the verse most decisively speaks: it was the rising up of *many antichrists*, by which it should be known that it was already the last hour. The expression has therefore a dogmatical meaning; but now arises the question, *What* period is indicated by it? In Isaiah, Micah, and Acts ii. 17, as also in 1 Pet. i. 20, the Messianic age as such appears, in contradistinction to the Old-Testament age, as אַחֲרִית הַיָּמִים; similarly, in Heb. i. 2, the subject is concerning the ἔσχατον τῶν ἡμερῶν τούτων, in opposition to the old covenant. On the other hand, it is quite evident that in 2 Pet. iii. 3, 1 Tim. iv. 1, 2 Tim. iii. 1, the last

---

[1] But he is wrong when, in spite of external authorities, he reads in ver. 13 γράφω ὑμῖν παιδία; thus making ver. 12 a general sentence,— ver. 13 containing the first triad, and ver. 14 with vers. 18 and 21 the second triad, the two first members of which are contained in ver. 14, the third coming after in vers. 18 and 21. The thought begun in ver. 12 *is closed in ver.* 14. Vers. 15–17 is a first *practical deduction*, vers. 18–25 a second. Only this is right, that in ver. 21 a thought occurs which is *analogous* to that of vers. 12–14, and reminding of it.

times of the present temporal dispensation (World-Æon) are meant,—the last times before the coming of Christ, in opposition to the time when St Paul and St Peter wrote those predictions. In our passage St John speaks of the ἐσχάτη ὥρα as of one already present (ἐστίν); but we cannot therefore conclude (with Calvin) that he uses the word, according to that first meaning, concerning the New-Testament age; for, the token that the ἐσχάτη ὥρα had already come, he derives, not from the incarnation of Christ, but from the appearance of the "antichrists." But, he cannot mean the final interval before the destruction of Jerusalem (Grotius), which, when he wrote, had undoubtedly already taken place; and those commentators are right who refer the ἐσχάτη ὥρα to the final period *preceding the return of Christ.* That St John, like the other Apostles, expected the coming of Christ as nigh at hand, is a certain fact; but not a fact which requires any apology in regard to him. Concerning the time of the Lord's coming, nothing specific had been revealed to the Apostles; the signature of those decennia, in which the awful corruption of Gnosticism suddenly appeared in the heart of Christendom, justified them in expecting Christ's return in the immediate future; and the word of the Lord, John xxi. 22, imperatively required them to do so, until the Lord had come to St John in the visions of the Apocalypse. This particular coming first rendered it possible to understand the ἔρχομαι of John xxi. 22, not of the objective coming of Christ to judgment, but of His coming to St John in vision; and that obliged him and all Christians, guided by the revelations of the Apocalypse, to assume that between the then-existing sixth Roman universal empire (Rev. xvii. 10) and the coming of Christ there must be interposed a seventh universal empire, and that not till then would arise that eighth one, the empire of the personal Antichrist. But the Gospel and our Epistle were written before the Apocalypse: it is therefore equally in order and propriety that St John should, like the other Apostles, expect the coming of Christ as immediately near; just as it was quite in keeping that the Old-Testament prophets contemplated together, and in one glorious future, the incarnation of Christ and His final return. It would have been, not in harmony with, but contrary to, the order of the Divine economy of revelation, if any prophet or any man of

God had attempted to anticipate or hasten the progression of the Divine revelation by any subjective knowledge of his own. At the time in which St John wrote his Epistle, it would have been possible only to a thoughtless child of the world to expect the coming of Christ otherwise than as immediately near.

Καὶ καθὼς ἠκούσατε, κ.τ.λ. The words καὶ νῦν ἀντίχριστοι, κ.τ.λ., form the sequel to which καθὼς refers; the καί, however, not being a copula, but meaning "even," and expressing the agreement of the existing fact with the prophecy which they had heard. (Calvin, Bengel, Lücke, Neander, Düsterdieck, Huther, etc., hold this against Luther, who unnecessarily assumes an *anacoluthon* here.) "And as ye have heard that the Antichrist is to come" (ἔρχεται, not like Luke xii. 40, where the Present stands for the Future ἐλεύσεται, "will come;" but like ch. iv. 3; Matt. xi. 3; John xvi. 13; Rev. i. 9, where in the notion of the ἔρχεσθαι itself the idea of futurity is contained, "is to come," = will one day appear), "so even now (in fact) many antichrists are come, by which we know that it is the last hour." By means of this καί St John gives such strong prominence to the consistency between the present fact of the *many* antichrists which had appeared and the prophecy given concerning *the* Antichrist, that many expositors have been misled into the supposition that St John did not, like St Paul, 2 Thess. ii. 3, expect *one* definite ἄνθρωπος τῆς ἁμαρτίας, but that he understood by ὁ ἀντίχριστος a collective whole. This was the interpretation of all those old Protestant exegetes who understood by "*the* Antichrist," not an individual, but the institution of the Papacy, and then all and every antichristian kind generally; and it is held also by Bengel, Lange, Besser, Huther, and others. They appeal, but improperly, to 1 John iv. 3, where, however, St John says only that it is τὸ πνεῦμα τοῦ ἀντιχρίστου which already is at work in the world; and, further, to 2 John 7, where the sentiment is perfectly analogous with 1 John iv. 3 and our present passage.

It is simply *impossible* that St John did not hold, or could have doubted, a doctrine which is so plainly unfolded by the Prophet Daniel, and which was so definitely preached by the Apostle Paul (2 Thess. ii. 5). St John refers to the doctrine which was *known* to his readers (ἠκούσατε), just as St Paul does there; and the church to which these readers belonged was founded by St Paul. The doctrine which he assumes to be well known to his readers can therefore be no other than that which had already been preached by St Paul; but we cannot, of course, admit, with John xvi. 13 before us, that St John convicts his apostolical predecessor of error, and is correcting the views of the Ephesians! Simply because St John could presuppose as well known the doctrine concerning the personal Antichrist, it was not necessary for him to expatiate at length upon the *distinction* between the already-existing πολλοῖς ἀντίχριστοις, and the ἀντίχριστος still to come, and expressly to say that those πολλοί were only πρόδρομοι and forerunners of the One. His object here is not theoretical, but practical: to impress most earnestly upon the hearts of his readers the *analogy* and *identity* of nature between the already-existing πολλοῖς and the One still to come; and to excite their attention to this, that it was not simply an *un*-christian kind which manifested itself in the appearances which they saw, but no other than the antichristian element itself. Hence Calvin, Lücke, De Wette, Neander, and others, were right in assuming that St John did not intend to be understood as meaning by πολλοῖς ἀντίχριστοις altogether the same as he meant by ὁ ἀντίχριστος, but that he referred to preparations and forerunners of the Antichrist (Calvin: Proprie loquendo nondum antichristus extabat, sed arcanum suæ impietatis clam moliebatur), laying the emphasis, however, not upon this particular element of distinction, but only upon the likeness of nature. The element of distinction is in the πολλοί, and the ὁ *hinted at*, or rather *taken for granted*.

Ἀντίχριστος is not (as Grotius thought) formed after the analogy of ἀντιβασιλεύς, vice-king, ἀνθύπατος, proconsul, as if it designated one who set himself *in the place* of Christ, therefore a pseudo-Christ. For, in the idea of "placed in the stead," there is not contained the element of an *unjustified* substitution in the place of another; as the word ἀντιβασιλεύς does not suggest a usurper who unlawfully takes the place of the rightful king. But ἀντίχριστος is formed, rather, after the analogy of ἀντιφιλόσοφος, opponent of philosophy, and ἀντίθεος, enemy of God, and signifies an antichrist in the sense of "*Christ's* enemy." The word ἀντίχριστος, etymologically considered, does not involve the idea that this enemy of Christ will demonstrate his enmity by giving himself out to be the true Christ in opposition to Jesus: that aspect of the matter would have found its expression in the definition ψευδόχριστος, as in Matt. xxiv. 24. In fact, it is never taught in Scripture that that "Antichrist," or "Man of Sin," who immediately before the coming of Christ will urge his cause and set up his kingdom, and of whom Jesus by His coming will make an end (2 Thess. ii. 8; comp. Isa. xi. 4), will represent himself to be a χριστος, an anointed of God, or the Χρίστος promised in the Old Testament, the Messiah and Redeemer. The erroneous view, that the Antichrist would give *himself* out to be a "*Christ*,"[1] owed its origin to the confusion of the older Protestant expositors, who confounded the spotted beast of the Roman power, or "Babel," enduring the half year-week from the ascension of Christ to His coming, with the blood-red beast of the last half of the apocalyptic day-week—the empire of superstition with that of open unbelief. The Revelation of St John, as also the passage, 2 Thess. ii. 1 seq., teaches us precisely the contrary. The Antichrist, the enemy of Christ, will place himself in the stead of *God*, will have himself, though man, honoured as God, and tyrannically put an end to all worship of God; but especially he will accomplish God's judgments upon Babylonish pseudo-Christendom (Rev. xvii. 16, xviii. 2), and make an end of it. His own kingdom, however, will bear upon it, not the semblance of a kingdom of Messiah, but the signature of the open and absolute apostasy, of open and daring rebellion against God and His Son (Rev. xix. 19).

And of this tendency and direction of thought St John saw in his own time the beginnings. The two great fundamental tendencies of the lie, which afterwards exhibited themselves formally in the course of Church-history, had already in the apostolical time their pre-formations. A legal Judaism had been withstood by St Paul, and had received its death-wound in the destruction of Jerusalem. Analogous to that is papistical Judaism, that power of Babylon, which will receive its death-wound in the destruction of Babylon the great (Rev. xviii.). But now, in the time of St John, the daring and essentially

---

[1] So Grotius, who then understands by the πολλοῖς Jewish pseudo-Messiahs! Sander includes in the ἀντίχριστος both ideas at once, that of enmity to Christ, and that of pseudo-Christianity; but this is out of the question.

heathenish Gnosticism had appeared within the Christian sphere, and consequently as an apostasy. It has its antitype in that power of infidelity and rebellion against all Divine and human order which appeared just at the end of the eighteenth century as a great power in human affairs, which in modern Pantheism (well termed by J. P. Lange "homunculo-theism") created a theory of religion for the educated, and in Materialism one for the mass; which will repeat its assaults upon all Divine and ungodly historical rule, accomplish God's judgments upon Babylon, but be ineffectual to hurt the Church of Christ (Rev. vii., and xix. 7 seq.); which will establish the Christ-opposed tyrannical empire, and then be hurled into the abyss by the Lord's final coming.

Not erroneously, therefore, but rightly, St John discerned in the Gnostics of that time the beginnings of this *Christ-opposed* characteristic. That its full development would be checked and restrained for well-nigh two thousand years, was not as yet revealed to him, but was revealed afterwards in the visions of the Apocalypse. Hence he could perceive, as we saw above, with perfect prophetical propriety, by the signs of the times then present, ὅτι ἐσχάτη ὥρα ἐστίν—that it was the last time.

In VER. 19 St John utters expressly the reflection, perfectly clear in itself, that those Gnostic false-teachers who had fallen from the churches (who, according to ver. 22, denied that Jesus was the Christ:—compare what was said in the Introduction concerning the gnosis of Cerinthus), gave proof by their apostasy[1] that they had never truly belonged to "us," to the company of Christians. For, if they had been ἐξ ἡμῶν, they would have remained μεθ' ἡμῶν. The Aorist ἐξῆλθαν (for this unusual form is the genuine reading, attested by A.B.C., and the variation ἐξῆλθον, on the other hand, is a mere correction) is a second Aorist with the termination of the first Aorist (as in the Septuagint, 1 Sam. x. 14 εἴδαμεν, 2 Sam. x. 14 ἔφυγαν, and other places; compare Matt. xxv. 36; Luke vii. 24: see Winer, § 13). Concerning the Præter-pluperfect without the augment, μεμενήκεισαν, compare Winer, § 12; and see Mark xv. 7, xvi. 9;

---

[1] For, the οὐ μεμενήκεισαν shows that ἐξῆλθαν is, not *prodierunt*, but *exierunt*.

Luke vi. 48. The ἵνα depends upon an ἐξῆλθαν or οὐ μεμενήκασι to be supplied after the ἀλλά. The ἀλλά does not mean "but," in the sense of laying down the contrast, " they went out, that," in opposition to the proposition, " they were not of us :" it must be strictly connected with " they would have remained." " Had they been of us, they would have remained with us ; but (they have not remained) that," etc. Ἵνα stands here again, as in ch. i. 9, not in its strict telic sense; for it is not *their* design in going out which is mentioned, but only a design which should be accomplished according to *God's* counsel, *ipsis invitis,* by their ἐξέρχεσθαι. In the proposition with ἵνα, two ideas are mingled together : 1. That *they* might become manifest, that *they* were not of us; and 2. that it might be evident that *not all* (who were with us, μεθ' ἡμῶν) were of us (but only those who remained with us). This little incorrectness of expression, or involution of meaning (which, indeed, often occurs in and out of the New Testament), induced some translators (the Syriac) and Fathers to omit πάντες. But the very fact that it is there, tends to assure us of its genuineness. Οὐ πάντες we are not justified in translating by *nulli,* as Socinus did (" that none of them were of us"). This would have required ὅτι πάντες οὐκ εἰσιν ἐξ ἡμῶν.

On this verse, among others, Calvin, Beza, and the other predestinarian divines, found their argument, that true faith is *inamissibilis,* indefectible, and that the man who falls from faith could not have had a true faith at all, but only its semblance. But they have no ground for this. We are not justified in regarding this proposition, uttered by St John here with reference to definite individuals, as a universal law. St John does not say ὅστις ἄν— ; or that whosoever shall fall from faith, can never have had true faith at all. But he speaks of those who, by the seduction and sophistry of *Gnosticism,* had suffered themselves to be brought to apostasy. The being seduced to *this decided and palpable lie,* could be possible only in the case of those who, in their true character, had been previously averse from Christianity, and strangers to its influence. Thus, we might, for example, say of those who in our times have suffered themselves to be led away by Ronge and Dowiat from the Christian Church into strange and heretical sects, that they had not been previously of us, otherwise they would have remained with us (and not have allowed themselves to be entangled by *such* spirits of error). But this certainly does not exclude the possibility that *others*, who stand now in a true faith, might in *other* ways " make shipwreck of faith" (for instance, through letting the good seed be choked by the foul growth of bosom sins and lusts); compare Heb. vi. 4 seq.; 1 Tim. i. 19.

In VERS. 20, 21, the Apostle, by means of καὶ ἡμεῖς, places the addressed παιδία in opposition to the ἀντίχριστοις, who "were not of us," and therefore " went out from us;" and says that those have the χρίσμα of the Holy One, and therefore suffer not themselves to be thus deceived by wicked seducers. He would not have been able to write to them, the παιδίοις, even his Gospel (in order to the faith that Jesus is the Christ, John xx. 31), if they also had not already known πάντα (ver. 20), that is (ver. 21) τὴν ἀλήθειαν, that truth which is comprehended in the one simple proposition (ver. 22), that Jesus is the Christ. Thus, in these verses there is only a recurrence of the old statement of ver. 8, *that it had become in the readers an* ἀληθές, *that the light already shines*.[1] But it recurs with a remarkable intensification; to wit, that even the παιδία already know πάντα, because they have the χρίσμα, and that they, these little ones, are already armed by this " anointing" against the most concentrated power of the lie, the antichristian power. This noble elevation of the meaning is lost, with all its delicacy, if we take παιδία as, like τεκνία, a general address to all the readers in common.

Καὶ ὑμεῖς, says the Apostle, and uses the καί just in the sense of a simple copulative particle (Huther), but for the appendage of an antithetical thought, as in ch. i. 4, ii. 4 (καὶ τὰς ἐντολάς, κ.τ.λ.) and 9 (and also in the Gospel). This is certainly in the Hebrew style of thought and phrase, and so far is an (unintentional) Hebraism. But, we must not go so far as to say, with Beza, Wolf, and De Wette, that this καί is to be translated " but," or that it stands here instead of δέ. The Apostle places the antitheses one by the side of the other, with-

---

[1] The view of Calvin, Semler, and others, that St John as it were apologizes in ver. 20 seq. that he had so anxiously warned them in ver. 18 seq. against the false teachers·—he did it not under the supposition that they were to be regarded as *rudes ignarique*.

out giving prominence to their antithetical relation; there lies the Hebraism of the conception, but not in this, that he purposed to make prominent that antithetical relation, and to that end used the καί instead of the customary δέ. "And ye have anointing from the Holy One," says St John. Χρίσμα, although without the article, must not be translated "an anointing," since neither several kinds nor several consecutive acts of anointing are here presupposed as possible; but neither is it "the anointing," since χρίσμα never can, and nowhere does, denote the act of anointing. Χρίσμα means (as in the Septuagint, Ex. xxix. 7, and everywhere) *anointing-oil;* it does not express the act of anointing, but the material with which the anointing is effected, and on that account the article is omitted from the expression. "Ye have anointing from the Holy One." Ἀπό does not depend upon χρίσμα (Carpzov says, *Unguentum a Christo compositum*), but from ἔχετε, which therefore is equivalent in meaning to *accepistis* (that is, *unctione accepistis oleum = oleo uncti estis*). The ἅγιος can be only Christ, and not the Holy Ghost (who is the χρίσμα itself, for which Olshausen rightly appeals to Ps. xlv. 8; Heb. i. 9; Matt. xxv. 3 seq.) or the Father: this is evident from the antithetical relation between χρίσμα and ἀντίχριστος. It is undeniable that χρίσμα does form the opposite of ἀντίχριστος (Bengel). He who has received the unction from the Holy One, is himself an anointed person, and essentially related in nature to the Anointed κατ᾽ ἐξοχήν, the Χριστός (Acts x. 38; John i. 33, iii. 34); such an one cannot possibly be seduced to go over into the camp of those who are enemies of the Anointed. Anointed were, as we all know, kings, priests, and prophets; but it is not appropriate to assume a special reference to any one of these offices (say the prophetic, on account of the "knowing all things"). St John has not here to do with the individual offices of Christ, but with the contrast between those who are anointed from Christ and like Christ, and those who are the enemies of the Anointed. The παιδία are men of whom the Apostle can say, "Ye know all things," not as the result of a special prophetic endowment, but as the result of their general Christian anointing with the Holy Ghost. The deep and glorious meaning of this πάντα is weakened away by those who (like Bullinger, Luther, and others) restrict it to *omnia ad salutem necessaria,* or (like Calvin, Beza,

Grotius, and others) "that which is necessary for distinguishing between truth and the antichristian lie," or (with Wolf, Bengel, and Neander) to both of these together. Still worse is the Syriac translation, "Ye know all these false teachers," and the explanation of Schmid, "Ye have already heard from my lips all that concerns these heretical teachers." It is no other than an oxymoron, when St John says of the little ones, the children in the Church, that they "know *all*." How he means this, ver. 21 shows. He who knows this one thing, that Jesus is the Christ, knows already in that *one* thing *all*: there is no most distant height or depth of truth, which is not contained or involved in that simple proposition for children's minds.

VER. 21. "I have not written unto you, because ye have not known the truth,"—that is, on the presumption that ye know it not,—"but on the presumption that (= because) ye know it." The clause may be grammatically resolved into two members: 1. οὐκ ἔγραψα ὑμῖν, ὅτι οὐκ οἴδατε τὴν ἀλήθειαν; 2. ἀλλ' (ἔγραψα ὑμῖν) ὅτι οἴδατε αὐτήν. But the οὐκ before ἔγραψα obviously is not to be connected with the latter, as if it was the writing itself which was to be denied ("I have *omitted* writing to you, because," etc.); but it belongs to the little clause ὅτι, κ.τ.λ., and it is this clause which is the matter of negation. "I *have* written unto you"—that is sure—"but not for the reason that ye knew not the truth (even the Attics would have used the Indicative here), but because ye know it."—In this, then, lies implicitly the thought, that if they did not know or had not known the "truth," he would not have been able to write unto them; or, that he had written to them, only because and as far as they knew the "truth." This thought is, as has been already remarked, quite analogous to the group of thoughts in vers. 10-14. Nor does anything in this hinder us from regarding the Gospel-document as the object of the ἔγραψα here again (as in ver. 13 seq.). That Gospel was, indeed, written with this design, "that ye might believe that Jesus is the Christ" (John xx. 31); St John had already in ver. 13 expressed the fact, that he wrote *it* even for the παιδία also; and the warning against the liars who denied that Jesus was the Christ must necessarily have brought to his thoughts afresh that writing and its design, giving him occasion to repeat what was said in ver. 13—only in a modified manner, as now more strictly defined by the context. The *children* already have received an anointing from Christ, and in that the pith and essence of all truth, enabling them to know the lie to be a lie. It was on that very account, because they possessed this knowledge of the truth, that St John could include them in the design for which he wrote the Gospel.

St John terms that ἡ ἀλήθεια which he had previously described by the word πάντα—but it is now viewed under another aspect. In ver. 20 he had laid down a simple statement, startling in itself, that they, because they had received the anointing, already knew *all things;* in ver. 21 he mentions "the truth" in definite contrast to the "lie" of the false teachers. This contrast appears most plainly in the concluding words, καὶ ὅτι πᾶν ψεῦδος ἐκ τῆς ἀληθείας οὐκ ἐστι. This ὅτι is not strictly parallel (Neander's construction so represents it) with the ὅτι twice before used, as if it depended also on the ἔγραψα; for, how could the fact, that all lie is not of the truth, have been made a motive for writing? Still less does our ὅτι form an antecedent to the question following in ver. 22. But the proposition ὅτι πᾶν ψεῦδος forms, together with the ἀλήθειαν, a second object of the verb οἴδατε. "Because ye know the truth, and know that every lie is not of the truth." The παιδία already know both: first, the centre and kernel in which the truth itself, and *all* truth in it, is contained; secondly, the proposition, self-intelligible to every child, that all that which is lie cannot have its origin in the truth, cannot be derived from the truth.

In vers. 22, 23, St John opposes to each other materially the lie and the truth, each of them in its simplest, and therefore most complete and comprehensive formula. He writes here in the perfect catechetical style, for children; but in the style of *perfect* catechism, which gives matter for pondering to the oldest and most mature. There is no passage in all the Scriptures in which, to the same extent as in this, the well-known adage finds its application:—A stream in which the infant may wade, and the elephant may swim.

The centre and kernel of all truth lies in the clause, ὅτι Ἰησοῦς ἐστιν ὁ Χριστός—*that Jesus is the Christ.* To lead his readers to a clear perception of this truth, and so to confirm their faith in it, had been the design of the Gospel which he had written: with the statement of this great truth, *that Jesus is the Christ*, he closed that Gospel; this fundamental theme hovers before his thoughts still, while he is engaged in writing the Epistle. It hovers before him as the concentrated bulwark of antithesis to the Gnostic lie; it necessarily hovered before him already in vers. 13, 14, where he spoke of the fundamental presupposition on the ground of which he could write, as this Epistle, so also his Gospel,—but that passage, vers. 13 seq., was not the place for the more developed utterance of that great proposition. But *to that* now tends the entire and full expansion of his thought: from the warning against the *unchristian* world and its nature (vers. 15–17) St John passes over to the *Christ-opposed* nature of Gnosticism; and now he can lay down the central point of his Gospel, "that Jesus is the Christ," in its sharp and rigorous antithesis to the central point of Gnosticism, "that Jesus is not the Christ." (So Olshausen also.) In this *dogmatic* antithesis to Gnosticism the second part of the Epistle (ch. ii. 7–29) finds its climax and goal; as the first part found it in the *ethical* antithesis to Gnosticism (ch. i. 10, ii. 6). For, by the immorality of their principle, and their fundamental propositions, the Gnostics offended against the eternal nature of God, who is light (which was the theme of the first part, ch. i. 5); but, by their dogmatic denial of the identity between Jesus and Christ, they blasphemed against the fact of the manifestation of the light upon earth (which is the theme of the second part, ch. ii. 8).—It is unspeakably glorious that St John here gives the refutation, or rather the triumphant demolition, of this dogmatical lie, not in the form of a dialectical exposition addressed to adults, but in the form of a catechism addressed to children. That lie was so frenzied and perverted, that its frenzy and perversion might be made intelligible in few words to every παιδίον.

Τίς ἐστιν ὁ ψεύστης, εἰ μὴ, κ.τ.λ., is the catechetical question with which St John begins. "Who is the liar, but he who denieth that Jesus is the Christ?" The article before ψεύστης has misled some into the opinion that St John here introduces *the* liar κατ' ἐξοχήν,—that is, *the* Antichrist, of whom he had spoken in ver. 18 (ἠκούσατε ὅτι—ἔρχεται),—and from this they would infer that St John did not mean by "the Antichrist" any individual being, but a collective manifestation or nature. But this is a total misapprehension of the whole chain of thought in vers. 18–25. The design of the Apostle is not in these verses to instruct the readers as to what they must apprehend by the Antichrist who should come; but warningly to testify to them that the πολλοί who were appearing in the present time, who denied the identity of Jesus and Christ, were in their character like the nature of the ἀντίχριστος ἐρχόμενος, and bore in themselves, in fact, the same nature. It had been said, in ver. 21, that the children could already distinguish the truth from the lie. Resting on this opposition between the ἀλήθεια and the ψεῦδος, St John directs now his question to the children, τίς ἐστιν ὁ ψεύστης; This question cannot possibly in this connection have the meaning, "What or who is understood by the Antichrist, who is to come?" but this meaning alone: "On what side is then the lie?" On whose side is the lie, and on whose side the truth? Is not he the liar (that is, he that standeth on the side of the lie), who *denieth* that Jesus is the Christ? That is equivalent to saying, Is not the denial of this identity the lie, the acknowledgment of it the truth? *Εἰ μή* here has not the signification which singles out from a *multiplicity* of imaginable cases, or existing persons, *one individual* (as if, for example, one should say, τίς τούτων ἐστὶν ὁ βασιλεύς, εἰ μή, κ.τ.λ.), for there is no multiplicity in the context; but there are *two* dogmatical tendencies opposed to each other, and the question is, Which of the two belongs to the lie?—εἰ μή having simply and literally the sense of *nisi*, "but," or "if not,"—which (of the two) is the liar? which, if not he who denies the identity of Jesus and Christ? (Bengel: ὁ vim habet ad abstractum, v. 21,—*i. e.*, quis est illius mendacii reus?)

For, as in the simple proposition, that Jesus is the Christ, is contained implicitly all truth, and the whole truth in all its relations, so in the converse proposition, that Jesus is not the Christ,[1] is implicitly contained *all* lie (of every kind contrary to Christianity). All the lying tendencies of unbelief which have even from time to time exhibited themselves, held either

---

[1] The pleonasm in ἀρνούμενος, which word already contains in itself by anticipation the negation which lies in the clause with ὅτι (comp. Luke xx. 27), is an elegant Greek form of speech. (Comp. Winer, § 67.)

a Jesus who is not the Christ (a mere man, a model of virtue, a prophet, teacher, or pattern, and so forth), or a *Christ who is not Jesus* (a Christ-idea, to which the individual Jesus was only fortuitously related, and which finds its true development, not in this individual Jesus, but in collective humanity). The former includes the Rationalist tendencies, which represent sin, in the true Pelagian style, as a little infirmity on the outside of the man, which he may be aided, by suitable instruction and by the influence of good example, to shake off. The latter includes the Pantheistic tendencies, which hold sin to be something which indeed penetrates the inmost nature of man, but which was essentially bound up with that nature as a necessary transition to the good; and therefore regard redemption as a necessary process of development, so that in man as such the *idea* of redemption—that is, of development—is realized and exhibited in fact. Cerinthus, master of heresy, knew how skilfully to combine the two sides of the lie. The denial of sin as involving *guilt* before God was common to both sides. Thus they play over into each other: on the one hand, there is an Ebionite Jesus, who is a mere man; and, on the other, a supermundane Æon Christ, who descended temporally into Jesus, and wrought in Him, but in like manner may exert his energy in every other man.

St John adds: οὗτός ἐστιν ὁ ἀντίχριστος, ὁ ἀρνούμενος, κ.τ.λ.: he thus says, concerning him who denieth that Jesus is the Christ, that he is the antichrist, but manifestly not in order to teach *who* is the antichrist, but *what* the denial of that identity is. Certainly, the predicative idea[1] has the article here, and stands in the singular; but this form has its sanction, and is pointed out, in the preceding ὁ ψεύστης. As it had been the question, which of the two was the "liar" and which

[1] The "predicative *idea*" we say cautiously; not forgetting that, according to the grammatical construction of such a sentence as οὗτός ἐστιν ὁ———, the Greeks always treated οὗτος as the grammatical predicate, even when it is not said, concerning the ὁ———, *who he* is, and that it is *this* one, but of the "this one" *what* he is. So in ch. IV. 5 it is not declared concerning the νικῶν τὸν κόσμον that he is "this one" (this or that individual); but, concerning him who believes, that he is an overcomer of the world; that is, that it is *he* to whom the predicate ὁ νικῶν, κ.τ.λ., belongs, therefore the predicate νικῶν is referred to him, declaring *what* he is.

the "true," so here the question is again, which of the two is the "enemy of Christ," and which the Christian. And therefore we may simply say, that ὁ ἀντίχριστος stands here in its *purely appellative* signification. Quite analogous is the fifth verse of the fourth chapter, where ὁ νικῶν is not a dogmatically-fixed term, but rather a purely appellative idea, like ὁ ἀντίχριστος in our text.

The words ὁ ἀρνούμενος τὸν πατέρα καὶ τὸν υἱόν are not an attributive definition of the οὗτος; but οὗτος refers back to the preceding ὁ ἀρνούμενος ὅτι Ἰησοῦς, κ.τ.λ. The words in question are, on the contrary, an appositional appendage to ὁ ἀντίχριστος; and an appendage by means of which the thought is *carried further*, a new declaration being introduced by it. The sense is precisely as if it was said, "*And truly* he denieth the Father equally with the Son."

This new thought, that *with the Son the Father also is denied*, is now developed in ver. 23. Υἱόν St John calls Christ here, and at the close of ver. 22, not because he would ascend from the "representation" of His Messiahship to that of His eternal Godhead, but simply because he would show how the denial of Christ is also a denial of God the Father, and because he therefore must mention Christ by the term which specifies His relation to the Father, that is, by the term "Son." By the denial of the Son, therefore, nothing assuredly is meant but the denial "that Jesus is the Christ;" that which in ver. 22 had been treated of and unfolded, is in the brief word ὁ ἀρνούμενος τὸν υἱόν shortly recapitulated, that Cerinthian gnosis being again intended by the latter.[1] Concerning this ἀρνούμενος, St John had said, at the close of ver. 21, that he *denies* also the Father. In ver. 22 he heightens this judgment into the declaration that that ἀρνούμενος *has not* the Father. (Compare the similar heightening in ch. i. 6, and ch. i. 8 and 10, and ch. ii. 4, where in each instance there enters, by the side of the charge of subjective lie, the judgment of an objective non-possession.) The foolish explanations of Grotius, Socinus, and others, that πατέρα οὐκ ἔχειν means *veram opinionem* or *cognitionem de Deo non*

[1] This admission naturally involves no acceptance of the Socinian exegesis, which makes this passage the ground of the trifling assertion that the idea of the υἱός is in itself synonymous with that of the Messiah, and goes no further than that.

habere, need no refutation. The best commentators, Zwingli, Calvin, Luther, Calovius, Bengel, and others, rightly perceive that the ἔχειν here signifies the most proper *possession* of the Father. Nor does it simply say that he who denies the Son has not the Father *as a Father;* but there is no limitation: "*he hath not the Father;*" he is not a *partaker* of God, and His nature, and His fellowship.

The internal *ratio* of both utterances it is not hard to find. He who denies that Jesus is the Christ, he who denies the *becoming*-man of the Son of God,—and on the one side retains a mere man Jesus, on the other, a mere docetic Æon or a mere Christ-idea—stands altogether without the sphere of the *Christian* life of faith, and essentially upon the Christ-*opposed* side. Thence follows, first, that he *theoretically denies* also the Father; that is, that his view and teaching concerning the Father is nothing worth, but fundamentally false (as was most strikingly seen in Cerinthus himself, in his doctrine that God was not the Creator of the world, and had not given Himself to be known by the world which the Demiurgus created, and therefore was Himself to blame for the blindness and sin of men; and, as always did and always must inevitably result from all Gnostic, and from all analogous antichristian, systems),—that therefore the God in whom he believes is not the true God, but an imaginary God; and from this springs, secondly, that, as he does not even know the true God, he can by no means be partaker of Him and of His nature. For, in order to be a partaker of the nature of God, which is light, the first step of all is to admit the penetration of the light which shows God to be the Holy One, and a man's self to be the sinner. (Comp. ch. i. 5 seq.). But the second step is to lay hold of the reconciliation with God effected in Christ. How then can he who has not yet Christ, but rather denies Christ and the true nature of Christ, ever become a partaker of the Father?

In opposition to this, the Apostle now says, "He that confesseth the Son, hath also the Father." This utterance will be clearly understood in the light of its contrast. The meaning of the Apostle is, obviously, not that a mere external lip-acknowledgment of the Son, and of the doctrine connected with Him (that Jesus is the Christ), is sufficient for the possessing the Father; nor must we, on the other hand, press into the ὁμολογεῖν (with Bede) the ideas of the *confessio cordis, oris, et operis*. Ὁμολογεῖν forms here the simple antithesis to ἀρνεῖσθαι, and denotes the (internal as well as external) condition generally of those who, in opposition to the fallen Gnostics, remain faithful; and it describes that contrast by this particular *sign*, that those deny the Son (in the sense of ver. 22), but these confess Him.

The little clause ὁ ὁμολογῶν, κ.τ.λ., is altogether wanting in the Text. Rec., but its genuineness is sufficiently guaranteed by A. B. and C. That τὸν υἱόν depends upon ὁμολογῶν, and not (as in 2 John 9), together with καὶ τὸν πατέρα, upon ἔχει (in which case ὁμολογῶν would stand absolutely),—is obvious from the preceding words, to which these form the antithesis.

In VERS. 24-27 the Apostle builds upon what had been said, the exhortation *to abide in the doctrine which had been heard from the beginning*. This exhortation, also, he addresses still to the παιδία, spoken to since ver. 18, for he continues in the same ἡμεῖς as before: it is the rising generation which specially needs the exhortation to remain faithful to the doctrine received. In ver. 28 he first applies himself again, with the general address τεκνία, to the whole Church—briefly repeating for all the members of the community the exhortation which had been given to the παιδίοις.

Ὑμεῖς he places emphatically first, as a vocative. That ὑμεῖς does not belong to ἠκούσατε—having been separated from it by trajection (Beza, Bengel, De Wette)—is clear, since the ἠκούσατε needed not such an emphatic ὑμεῖς. For, the distinction between those addressed and the false teachers—a distinction emphasized by means of the ὑμεῖς—did not consist in their having heard, but in their remaining true to what they had heard. While those have fallen away—St John would urge —or, if others still should fall away, *ye* must remain faithful. Ὑμεῖς, therefore, in its meaning, belongs strictly to the injunction, ἐν ὑμῖν μεινέτω. It is not necessary to assume, as some do, an anacoluthon or a change in the construction, as if St John had originally meant to say, ὑμεῖς ὃ ἠκούσατε ἀπ' ἀρχῆς, τοῦτο φυλάττετε; but ὑμεῖς is simply a vocative address, which may stand in connection, not only with an actual imperative of the second person, but equally well with a third person of the imperative, if this *in its meaning* involves an exhortation directed to those addressed.

"Let that which ye have heard ἀπ' ἀρχῆς" (in opposition to that which false teachers had said, or might say in the future) —the truth "that Jesus is the Christ"—" abide in you:" that is, not *with* you (παρ' ὑμῖν), as Luther and Theophylact interpret; but St John would say that the doctrine received should abide *in* them, as a power of life.

If this doctrine abideth in you, ye also abide in the Son and in the Father: thus continues the Apostle. The internal *ratio* of this utterance is, in itself, also not difficult to discover. This doctrine is in itself no dead theory, but, as had been before remarked, a *power of life* in him who maintains and preserves it; that man's faith is no mere adherence to a doctrinal proposition. "In faith, man receives not a mere revelation concerning the life which hath appeared in Christ, but that life itself as his own personal possession: the believer enters into personal relations and intercourse with the Son and the Father; the Father giveth Himself to him in the Son, John xvii. 23" (Düsterdieck).

Ver. 25. As in ver. 17 St John had appended to the warning against worldliness, as a first motive, the ungodliness of the course of the world, and, as a second motive, the transitoriness of the world and all its pursuits; so, analogously, he appends here to the exhortation to hold faithfully the doctrine received, as a first motive, the proposition, ver. 24, that this doctrine leads to fellowship with God, and as a second motive, ver. 25, the glory which is promised to all who abide faithful. Hence, we need not supply any thought between ver. 24 and ver. 25, to make up the connection; the connection already exists, though it is, as in ver. 17, an internal connection, involved in the thing itself, and not stamped upon the external arrangement of the chain of thought. (Even Düsterdieck supplies an artificial connection, when he says that the possession of life in God is something already present, and yet again an object of hope. This reflection is true, but it is alien to the text; which, from the analogy of the order and relation of thought traced by us in ver. 17, needs no such link.) It is quite wrong to take αὕτη (with Œcumenius, Sander, and others) as pointing backwards in its meaning ("And this, that we should abide in the Son and in the Father, is the promise which He hath given us"); for in this case the words τὴν ζωὴν αἰώνιον would stand disconnected and lost; and, even if they are regarded as an apposition to the *subject*-idea supposed to be found in the αὕτη, that is, to the idea τὸ μένειν ἐν τῷ υἱῷ, κ.τ.λ., the attraction and the accusative would still be intolerable. Αὕτη points rather (as all the best expositors have felt) forwards: "And this is the promise which He Himself (αὐτός) hath given us—eternal life." The accusative τὴν ζωήν is now easily explained. The proposition is thus conceived: "And this (what follows) is the promise, which He hath promised us—He hath promised us eternal life." Compare John iii. 16, v. 24, vi. 40 and 54.

In ver. 26 St John formally closes the exhortation given to the παιδίοις in the words, ταῦτα ἔγραψα ὑμῖν περὶ τῶν πλανώντων ὑμᾶς. By these obviously are meant the "many antichrists" of ver. 18, against whom they would have in the future to be on their guard; and by the πλανᾶν is self-evidently not expressed the actual result or success of their seduction, but only the design which they have in the attempt,—for the ὑμᾶς follows directly as the object.

But the Apostle cannot close this exhortation without once more repeating in condensed recapitulation, *ver.* 27, the substance of vers. 20 to 25. Such a style of recapitulation is nowhere else found in St John: it is to us a new demonstration that he addressed this whole section to *actual children*, before whom, like a gracious, faithful, and loving teacher, he recounts one by one the individual main points of his instruction, that they may understand everything and forget nothing. Καὶ ὑμεῖς is his personal vocative address to them here again, as in ver. 24; and even this style of address is appropriate to a colloquy with children. "The anointing, which ye received, abideth in you:" here he recapitulates the thought of ver. 20 (the reading χάρισμα in Cod. B. has no external support to make it worthy of notice), but in such a manner as to gather up and include with it the quintessence of what had been said, vers. 24, 25.

The Indicative μένει is not an "admission" (Düsterdieck) that the unction received may have remained in them, but expresses his certain assurance. Indeed, this Indicative bears a sort of imperative, or at least insinuating, power, as if St John should say: "Is it not so, then? this is the case, because ye faithfully preserve the anointing received!" In the same way must be explained the following words, "and have no need that any one teach you;" in which the thought of ver. 20, "and ye know all things," and of ver. 21, is recapitulated. "And thus it is not needful to you that any man should teach you,—is it not true, that ye are not dependent upon any other man's diligently teaching you on what side the truth lies?"

'Ἀλλ' ὡς τὸ αὐτό, κ.τ.λ. Here arises the question, where the concluding clause begins. Luther, Bullinger, Calvin, and others, regard the words καὶ ἀληθές ἐστιν, κ.τ.λ., as the conclusion; Œcumenius, Theophylact, Lücke, and others, take those words as a parenthesis, and καὶ καθὼς ἐδίδαξεν ὑμᾶς as a resumption of the antecedent. But this view is opposed, on the one hand, by the fact, that the resumption of the earlier part of a sentence after a parenthesis must, even in the most lively style, involve a strict repetition of the former words (in which case we should have had ὡς ἐδίδασκεν ὑμᾶς); and, still more emphatically on the other, by the consideration that the antecedent, "ἀλλ' ὡς τὸ αὐτό, κ.τ.λ.," contains a point in the words περὶ πάντων to which the supposed resumption of the clause stands in no relation. The former reason would render it more advisable to take the words καὶ ἀληθές ἐστιν καὶ οὐκ ἐστι ψεῦδος as the consequent ("And as that anointing teaches you concerning all things, so is it true and no lie"); but the scruple here also arises, that περὶ πάντων, which yet is manifestly a recapitulation of the important καὶ οἴδατε πάντα, ver. 20, must be reduced to a negative element ("As the anointing teaches you concerning every object, so is it true"), or stand in no relation whatever to the consequent. With this is connected another difficulty, that the καί at the beginning of the supposed consequent clause does not explain itself; for, to take it in conjunction with the following καὶ οὐκ ἐστι ψεῦδος in the sense of an *et—et* is not practicable, since only distinct and antithetical, and not identical, utterances may be connected by καί—καί. (To say, "This is as true as it is no lie," is intolerable.)

Hence I am of opinion that our ὡς does not form an antecedent premiss, but that it still depends upon the ἔγραψα of ver. 26. If we hold fast that the Apostle is here recapitulating, and that before children in a style adapted to *them*, this lax and lighter style of phraseology presents nothing startling. "This I have written unto you concerning those who seduce you; and ye—the anointing which ye have received from Him abideth in you; and ye have no need that any man teach you: but now the same anointing teacheth you concerning all things (sc. I have told you); and it is true, and no lie; and as it hath taught you, abide in Him." In the words ἀλλ' ὡς τὸ αὐτό, κ.τ.λ., St John recapitulates the words of ver. 20, οἴδατε πάντα, and of ver. 21, οἴδατε τὴν ἀλήθειαν. In the following words, καὶ ἀληθές ἐστιν, καὶ οὐ ψεῦδος, he recapitulates the thought of ver. 21, καὶ ὅτι πᾶν ψεῦδος ἐκ τῆς ἀληθείας οὐκ ἐστιν. Χρίσμα is the subject of ἀληθές ἐστι: "And it (the anointing with its διδάσκειν) is true, and is no lie;" he reminds them that truth and lie *exclude each other*, that the Divine teaching of the Holy Spirit cannot be a lie, and that the lie cannot spring from God and the truth. Finally, in the words, καὶ καθὼς ἐδίδαξεν ὑμᾶς μένετε ἐν αὐτῷ, he recapitulates the exhortation of vers. 24, 25. Ἐν αὐτῷ is not a resumption of the idea lying in καθώς (" abide in *that which*, as it = what it hath taught you"). Ver. 28 does not agree with this; the αὐτός is God. "As the anointing hath taught you, so (conformably) abide in Him."

In VERS. 28, 29, the Apostle turns again—after having thus, in perfect childlike tone, formally closed with the παιδίοις —to the whole Church, and ends the second part of his Epistle. This he does by addressing the three short words of exhortation given to the children, μένετε ἐν αὐτῷ, to the whole Church; but, as addressed to the whole Church, such motives are annexed as show conclusively that he here speaks to *adults*, even as the tone of vers. 18–27 reveals almost in every word that he is speaking to the children. For it is not only that the style rises now to a rounded construction of periods, but the thoughts also of vers. 28, 29 are of a more solemn kind. He directs his regards to the coming of Christ (concerning the then justifiable expectation of the near approach of which, compare the observations upon ver. 18): those who are addressed in ver. 28 are to take heed that they be not then put to shame. Such an exhortation, however, is more suitable to adults than to little children, the παιδία. It is the nature of the child to live in the present, or, *if* its glance is directed to the future, that glance is directed to the final and conclusive goal. Thus St John, in vers. 18–27, had warned the children against false teachers upon earth; and, when he pointed them (ver. 25) to the future, he set before their eyes at once and most simply the ultimate end of all, eternal life. Had he also referred them to the coming of Christ—to them, the children—that could have to them appeared only an object of joy and cheerful hope. As an object of solemn anxiety it could appear only to the adult, occupied in the earnest contest with sin; only in his mind could the pressing question arise, Shall I be able to stand, when the Lord shall come? And so the injunction, ver. 20, to practise τὴν δικαιοσύνην, is one strictly adapted to the position of the adults.—These are delicate and subtle traits; but they ought not to be overlooked: they serve fully to confirm us in believing that the vers. 18–27 were actually addressed to the class of the παιδία in literal age.

Καὶ νῦν is not to be taken with reference to time ("even now already," as Paulus and Semler translate); for nothing had been said previously which would make the exhortation to fidelity refer to the future. But neither does καὶ νῦν serve to deduce the exhortation μένετε as an inference from the present relations; and it must not therefore be translated by *igitur*. But its object is to lead over to a new reflection, to introduce a new turn of thought. So in John xvii. 5, where Jesus passes by καὶ νῦν from that which He had done to that which He prays for ("And now pray I Thee"). So in Acts x. 5, where from an explanation there is a transition to a command: similarly, ch. vii. 34, iii. 17. What the strict meaning of the expression is, must in each case be determined by the context. The transition in our passage is not the exhortation μένετε, for that exhortation had immediately preceded: the new element can be only in the τεκνία, which is stamped as such by the turn καὶ νῦν. By means of the address τεκνία, which the Apostle was accustomed to use in relation to the whole Church, and which therefore would be in that sense understood by them all, he turns away from the specific class of the παιδία in age, and again addresses himself to the whole circle of his readers. To mark this turn is the proper service of the καὶ νῦν. As we must complete John xvii. 3 by "And now pray I Thee," and Acts x. 5 by "And now I command," and Acts xxii. 16, "And now I ask thee,"—so here, "And now I turn to you, children," or, "And now I exhort you all, little children."

The exhortation itself, μένετε ἐν αὐτῷ, is of the same kind with that which had just preceded: "Abide in Christ." The motive for this exhortation is given in the words: ἵνα ἐὰν φανερωθῇ ἔχωμεν παρρησίαν, κ.τ.λ. The Rec. reads ὅταν instead of ἐάν; but this last is guaranteed by A.B.C., and ὅταν is manifestly no other than a supposed improvement. (By ἐάν, "*if*," it might be supposed that the coming of Christ was exhibited as only possible, and consequently as dubious; whereas ἐάν does not express any pure conditionality at all, but a condition with the expectation of a speedy decision of the question in the affirmative; and it is therefore so closely related to ὅταν as to be often used interchangeably with it: *e.g.*, Rom. xiv. 8; 1 John iii. 2; John xiii. 20, xiv. 3. In all these passages, it is not the event itself, but only the time of its occurrence, which is questionable, and viewed as undetermined.) Instead of ἔχωμεν (Codd. A.C.), Cod. B. reads σχῶμεν—a manifest error of the copyist, which the similarity of the letters will explain. As it respects the meaning of the words, the idea of παῤῥησίαν ἔχειν (compare ch. iv. 17) presents no difficulty: He who cometh to set up His kingdom, but to judge His enemies, is regarded with joyful confidence as coming, only by him who belongs to the children of His kingdom, and has not been a companion of the "antichrists." Καὶ μὴ αἰσχυνθῶμεν ἀπ' αὐτοῦ intimates the same in a negative form; ἀπό is not equivalent to ὑπό ("put to shame by Him," Meyer), nor is it equivalent to *coram* (Luther), but it stands here as in Ecclus. xxi. 22 (αἰσχυνθήσεται ἀπὸ προσώπου): "Be put to shame, away from His face." Thus αἰσχύνεσθαι has a pregnant sense: to be put to shame, and, as a consequence, to flee away from Him in terror and disgrace. The idea of the παρουσία is involved as well known.

But the exhortation "Abide in Him" is changed, ver. 29, into the more general exhortation to ποιεῖν τὴν δικαιοσύνην.[1]

---

[1] This is the simple and natural relation between vers 28 and 29. But it is not the mention of the future *judgment* which leads St John by association of ideas to the idea of righteousness. It was not the judgment which was mentioned in ver. 28, but the coming of Christ for the setting up of His kingdom.

"If ye know," ἐάν: two cases are supposed possible, that of knowing, and that of not knowing. "If ye know that *He* is righteous, know ye also" (γινώσκετε in the Imperative, with Zwingli, Bullinger, Luther, Calvin, Grotius, Lücke, against Beza and Bengel, because it stands between the Imperatives μένετε and ἴδετε) "that every one who doeth righteousness is born of Him." The καί (which is wanting only in B., is found in A.C., Syr., Vulg., and is the right reading) serves, as in ch. ii. 19, to make prominent the congruity of the inference with the premiss. By αὐτοῦ He only can be meant concerning whom it had been said, ὅτι δίκαιός ἐστι; else the entire *vis conclusionis* would escape. Hence it is untenable to refer δίκαιος to Christ, while ἐξ αὐτοῦ is referred to God. Either both must be interpreted of Christ (Bengel), or both of God (Zwingli, Bullinger, Luther, Calvin). Since the expression γεννᾶσθαι ἐκ Χριστοῦ never occurs, and in ch. i. 9 the δίκαιος εἶναι was attributed to the Father, the latter interpretation is to be preferred.—And even in vers. 27 and 28 it is not necessary to refer ἐν αὐτῷ specifically to Christ: it corresponds with what is said in ver. 24, ἐν τῷ υἱῷ καὶ ἐν τῷ πατρὶ μένειν: the idea is this—Through the Son to abide in the Father.

Τὴν δικαιοσύνην ποιεῖν is analogous with the τὴν ἀλήθειαν ποιεῖν, ch. i. 6. It means, to accomplish that which is and that which corresponds to the nature of God. For the δικαιοσύνη is here, in virtue of the ὅτι δίκαιός ἐστι, not righteousness *before* God; certainly not the complex of *works* through which man effects a righteousness before God; but it is righteousness as the inner, eternal nature of God, and that in the sense explained upon ch. i. 9, as *holiness which will bring the creature also to freedom from guilt and holiness.* That St John adduces the accomplishment of this righteousness, not as the cause of the being born of God, but as the effect and mark of the having been born of God, is plain from the simple Perfect γεγέννηται. If we know that God in His nature is δίκαιος, we must admit that he only can say that he is born of God who accomplishes that δικαιοσύνη which is God's nature—that is, *himself walks in holiness, and seeks to lead sinners to salvation* (comp. above on ch. i. 9).

St John has thus struck out a new theme: these words form the transition to the Third Part of his Epistle, where he views *the position of Christians as opposed to the enmity of the unbelieving world.* But it is not well to regard this verse, which contains only the transition to the Third Part, as being already the beginning of that Part, and to introduce a section between vers. 28 and 29 (De Wette). Ver. 29 is the conclusion of the Second Part; but it is in such a manner the conclusion, that it contains the organic germ out of which the following Part is developed.

PART THE THIRD.

THE CHILDREN OF GOD IN THEIR RELATION TO THE ENMITY OF THE WORLD.

Ch. iii. 1–24.

THE plan and construction of the Third Part is as follows:—
The idea of *righteousness*,—which is a definition of the nature of God (ὅτι δίκαιός ἐστι), but as such must have its perfect accomplishment in us and through us,—contains in itself *implicite* (comparing ch. i. 9) all those essential important points which are now to be unfolded in the Third Part. For we have seen reason, in our exposition of ch. i. 9, to come to the conclusion that St John terms God righteous, 1. as being holy and righteous in Himself; and, 2. as He helps the sinner in Christ to the attainment of righteousness. (In harmony with Rom. iii. 26, εἰς τὸ εἶναι αὐτὸν δίκαιον καὶ δικαιοῦντα τὸν ἐκ πίστεως Ἰησοῦ.) Accordingly, and consistently with this, the righteousness which we must perfect includes in itself these two elements, and exhibits these two aspects: 1. *We* must be holy in *our* walk—this being our distinction and difference from the children of the world; and, 2. we must not hate and repel those who yet know not salvation, but, so far as in us lies, should strive to lead them to the knowledge of Christ as a Saviour—this being our mission to the world. And, this being so, we might say at once, with Huther, that the last verse of the second chapter contains the *theme* of the section which now follows, and that its proper superscription would be, "The *righteousness* of the children of God in their relation to the enmity of the world." Not only is the first of these two points developed in vers. 2–12, to wit, our distinction from the world; but, if we adopt the right

meaning of ver. 16, the second also, to wit, our vocation and mission to the world.

Meanwhile, these two critical points are only *implicitly*, and, indeed, *very* implicitly, involved in the idea of that "righteousness." St John attaches the development of ver. 2, etc., not to the idea of "righteousness," but to that of "the being born of God;" for he places the idea of the τέκνον Θεοῦ, ch. iii. 1, first, and makes that the starting-point for what follows. To the idea of the δικαιοσύνη he returns only briefly and fleetingly in the course of the first sub-section—that is, in ver. 7. But, having expressed at the outset the notion of the "children of God," he lays down in ver. 1 a *formal theme* of a twofold character, which, not merely *implicitly*, but *explicitly*, contains the two elements which in fact make up the subject of the Third Part; to wit, (1) that we are the *children* of God; and that (2) on that account the *world knoweth us not*, because it knoweth not God.

As we have then in ch. iii. 1 an expressed and independent theme of the Third Part, we cannot assign that position to ch. ii. 29; that verse can be regarded as only the internal transition to the theme, that is, as the *germ* out of which the *theme*, ch. iii. 1, is unfolded. For, as we have already observed, it is not with ch. ii. 29 that the subsequent process of thought connects itself, but with ch. iii. 1. *We* are *the children of God:* that was the first element in the theme, ver. 1; and in ver 2 the Apostle takes up the word literally (νῦν τέκνα Θεοῦ ἐσμεν) and develops from it the whole process, vers. 2–12,—how we must, as *distinguished from the world* (comp. vers. 8 and 10), purify ourselves in hope of future glory, and be holy. The world *knoweth us not:* that was the second element of the theme in ver. 2, and to this element the Apostle passes over in ver. 13; he shows that the hatred of the world should not be cause of astonishment, since hatred is grounded in the nature of the world, even as brotherly love is rooted in the nature of God's children.

In ver. 1, therefore, the Apostle expresses the *theme* of this new section. He begins with ἴδετε; this time without any address (such as τεκνία ἀγαπητοί) being previously inserted, for he had already (ch. ii. 28) begun the introduction to it with such an address. Ἴδετε, ποταπὴν ἀγάπην δέδωκεν ἡμῖν ὁ πατήρ, ἵνα τέκνα Θεοῦ κληθῶμεν καὶ ἐσμέν. Instead of δέδωκεν (B.C.) Codex A. reads ἔδωκεν; but the former reading, as it is the better authenticated, so it is the more internally appropriate. The present relation of the matter, that we are called and are children of God, rests upon the fact, also accomplished and real in the present time, that God hath *bestowed* upon us such love. An historical tense would not suit here. The words καὶ ἐσμέν are wanting in no authentic sources of the text: it was Erasmus who first declared it to be a spurious addition, after the Vulgate had translated it wrongly—*et simus.* He was followed by Luther, Bullinger, Calvin, Beza, and the Textus Receptus. Lachmann and Tischendorf have, however, restored this indubitably correct reading to its right place.

The theme is first expressed in the form of an *injunction*: "*Behold*, what manner of love the Father hath given us." Ποταπός is the later correlative form of the old ποδαπός, which seems to have sprung from ποῦ—ἀπό, after the analogy of ἀλλοδαπός from ἄλλου—ἀπό, and therefore to mean, "from whence born." The bye-form ποταπός, however, occurs always only in the sense of *qualis, of what kind.* It is therefore quite incorrect to translate it, or to explain it (with Socinus, Episcopius, Lücke, De Wette, Sander), as bearing the additional meaning, *quam magnum amorem,* "how great love." St. John exhorts his readers to ponder, not the greatness, but the kind and nature of the love which God hath bestowed on us. But we must not at once infuse into the expression ποταπήν (with Calvin) the correlative idea of "how *undeserved* a love." For, it is not the kind and characteristic of the love to which the Apostle gives expression; he only demands that that love be made the object of contemplation and pondering. If we must define more closely the quality of that love (which, however, lies beyond the province of mere exposition of the text of Scripture), its critical characteristic, as that of being undeserved, that of holiness, or that of its wisdom, mercy, or greatness, must be excluded; for it is no other than that love in which the whole nature of God has been exhibited to the soul of man.—The depth of the thought is greatly qualified, if we explain ἀγάπη (with Beza, Socinus, Episcopius, Grotius, Spener, Neander, and others) by "*evidence of love.*" God hath given to us not only a proof of love, but His love itself: but in what and by what means? If we are to listen to the philological pedantry of those who insist upon giving the Johannæan ἵνα everywhere, and here, the *final* signification which the classical ἵνα bears, the question will remain, and force itself upon us, *by what means and wherein* God hath bestowed upon us His love,—a question which receives no answer. The translation in that case takes this form : " Behold, what kind of love God hath approved or demonstrated towards us, with the design that we should be called His sons ;" and that love is then arbitrarily explained, either of the sending of Jesus Christ, or of the outpouring of the Holy Spirit, or of both. On this view, however, we are at a loss to determine what is after all the essential element of the thought. Is it St John's purpose to give his readers an enigma to solve, when he challenges them to consider *what species* of love *that* love was which God bestowed upon us, in the design that we should be called His children? But this, in fact, is the goal at which finally all the love of God aims, and the clause with ἵνα would then be altogether superfluous: the Apostle would have then said only, " Behold, what kind of love the Father hath demonstrated towards us." Or, is the chief emphasis to be placed upon the final clause? Is it St John's design to lay the stress upon *this*, that God bestowed His love upon us *to the end* that He might make us His children? But, why then does he clothe what should then have been laid down in a simple thesis, in the guise of a question, or of a requirement which involves a question (ποταπήν)? It is manifest that such a kind of construction is altogether untenable. The requirement ἴδετε ποταπήν, κ.τ.λ., involves a problem, and this must have *its solution in the text*. Hence the great majority of ancient and modern expositors assume, correctly, that the clause with ἵνα serves to specify *wherein* this δεδωκέναι ἀγάπην consists. It is true that the ἵνα then stands in a weakened sense (*eo ut*, thereby that); the idea of a " should" does indeed remain (compare on ch. i. 9), but not properly in the ἵνα, rather in the κληθῶμεν. As in the passages, ch. i. 9, John iv. 34, vi. 29 and 40, so also here, there is a *design* involved in the clause; but not a design through which the thing asserted in the main proposition (ἀγάπην δέδωκεν) should be called into act, but a design by which the clause with ἵνα is conditioned. We must here again, as in ch. i. 9, complete the sentence thus: ποταπὴν ἀγάπην δέδωκεν ἡμῖν ἐν τῷ βούλεσθαι ἵνα τέκνα Θεοῦ κληθῶμεν. And so far Düsterdieck is right, that the ἵνα κληθῶμεν is, certainly, by no means absolutely equivalent to ὅτι καλούμεθα. We must resolutely acknowledge, on other and independent grounds, that, in the circles and at the time in which St John wrote, the signification of ἵνα had been weakened, and its use generalized: and this was probably owing to the influence of the Latin tongue, then already extended over the whole world; since ἵνα had come to express, as well the *eo ut* as the *eo consilio ut* (though not the *ita ut*). In the later Greek the use of ἵνα was still more extended; in modern Greek the *να* expresses every kind of "that." The Greek Fathers (Œcumenius, Theophylact) did not think of apprehending this ἵνα differently: both explain, ἔδωκεν ἡμῖν τέκνα αὐτοῦ γενέσθαι. Thus, the meaning results: "Behold, what a (kind of) love the Father hath bestowed upon us, by this, that we should be called the children of God,"—to wit, in this, that it is the Father's will that we should be called the children of God.

Thus viewed, the main point of the thought is essentially this—that we are called *God's sons;* and the injunction "Behold" only prepares the way for this main point, by giving prominence to the reflection, what kind of love was manifested in the will of the Father, that we should be called the children of God. Τέκνα Θεοῦ St John says designedly, after having before said ὁ πατήρ. For, the greatness and the marvel consisted in this, that we, *men*, should be called "sons *of God:*" in this expression there must be expressed the opposition or contrast between us, who are *men*, and the relation to God into which we have entered. The words must needs be τέκνα Θεοῦ: πατρός would have been only a tautological repetition of the idea already independently involved in the τέκνα. On the other hand, in that member of the clause, ποταπήν, κ.τ.λ., God is called ὁ πατήρ, because He demonstrated Himself to be our Father by this, that He made us His children.

The idea of the τέκνον Θεοῦ is explained by the words of the preceding verse, to which it is attached, that is, by the words ἐξ αὐτοῦ γεγέννηται, *born of Him*. The question, whether the τέκνον Θεοῦ involves rather the idea of the being reconciled (that we have God no longer as a Judge, but as a Father), and therefore of what God is now in relation to us—or rather involves the idea of the regeneration (that we are now begotten of Divine seed, ver. 9, and of the Spirit, ch. iv. 13, John iii. 3–7, and are partakers of the Divine nature), and therefore of what we have become in relation to God—is in reality an unnecessary question. For, the two cannot be separated: the relation of children is necessarily a reciprocal relation; and its glory consists as much in the victory granted to us over sin, as in the freedom from guilt and punishment vouchsafed. The γεγεννῆσθαι ἐκ Θεοῦ, that is, regeneration—which, however, must not be confounded with gradual sanctification, but must be conceived as the translation from an unbelieving man into a believer, as the apprehending of Christ and the being apprehended of Christ, comprising in itself the once-for-all completed reconciliation, together with the initial point of the gradual sanctification—forms the foundation or cause of the adoption: the adoption, the τέκνον Θεοῦ κληθῆναι, forms the state, become a reality in regeneration; and accordingly embraces, 1. the finished reconciliation through the atonement; and 2. the being endowed with the powers of a new life.

But the Apostle appends further the words καὶ ἐσμέν. The Vulgate translates *et simus*, regarding the ἐσμέν as still dependent upon ἵνα. Certainly, there is in reality a difference between "being called" and "being;" so that between κληθῶμεν and ἐσμέν there is a real progression. That God calls us His children (for we must in thought connect with the word ὑπὸ Θεοῦ, and not ὑπὸ τοῦ κόσμου), is supposed to be one point, and that we in our nature are God's children the other point, which St John intended to express; the κληθῶμεν intimating God's relation to us, or the element of reconciliation, and the ἐσμέν our relation to God, or the element of our change and renewal of nature. But the question arises, whether the Indicative ἐσμέν can be dependent upon the ἵνα. Many expositors assume it as a settled point that it cannot; they are right on strictest grammatical principles, but wrong on St John's grammatical principles. We have already shown, upon ch. i. 9, that the Apostle, in Rev. xxii. 14, and, according to the true reading, ch. ix. 5, xiii. 12, xiv. 13, and further, in John xv. 16, lets the ἵνα be followed by a Future Indicative. But, particularly striking is the passage, John vi. 40, ἵνα—ἔχῃ καὶ ἀναστήσω,—a passage which is in this analogous to our present verse, that the ἵνα does not specify the design, but (strictly as here, ch. iii. 1) the *matter* of what is said in the leading proposition ("*In this* consists the will of God, *that* every one should have eternal life, and that I should raise him up"). Certainly, St John in all these passages uses the Future (related to the Subjunctive); but that he could not have used ἐσόμεθα in our present passage, is clear, since the relation of sonship was to be and is exhibited as something already existing. Whether, therefore, we say that ἐσμέν depends directly upon ἵνα, or that, as in John vi. 40, the syntactically-begun clause limps in its correctness, its second member breaking off, this much is certain, that, according to the logical meaning, καὶ ἐσμέν is to be conceived as included in the dependent and connected clause, and that it is by no means an independent member, uttering the triumphant exclamation— And truly *we are* such children! For, this explanation would make the κληθῶμεν, in opposition to the consequent "actual being," a mere *being called*—which we cannot here admit. But, if we conceive the καὶ ἐσμέν as internally dependent still upon what precedes, that is, as belonging to the definition of that wherein the love shown by God consists, then κληθῶμεν and ἐσμέν express the beautiful antithesis which we have exhibited above: 1. We are called, and are acknowledged as, children by the Father; and 2. we are in our own proper nature born of God, and filled with the Divine nature.

And thus is laid down the one positive side of the theme of the now following Third Part. But out of this positive side is developed at once the negative or antithetical side: Because *we* are the sons of *God*, therefore the *world* knoweth us not; for the nature of the world consists in this, that it knoweth not God, and consequently cannot know us, who are of God. Διὰ τοῦτο refers to what had been before said: "Therefore, because we are *the sons of God*" (De Wette, Bengel, Huther, Lücke, and others, in opposition to those who refer τοῦτο forwards to ὅτι οὐκ ἔγνω αὐτόν; by which, however, all connection with the first half of the verse is lost). Ὁ κόσμος οὐ γινώσκει ἡμᾶς, The world *knoweth* us not: the children of God are a mystery to the children of the world; their whole nature, *as* children of God, is to the κόσμος—that is, to the world of still unredeemed sinners—sealed and incomprehensible: hence, it appears to them not only perverse and ridiculous, but also in the highest degree offensive and hurtful; it disturbs them in their false peace, as every uncomprehended spiritual power has in itself something most disturbing; and hence follows then the hatred of the world (ver. 13) against the children of God. That οὐ γινώσκει ὑμᾶς does not mean *non agnoscit nos pro suis* (Grotius), is self-evident; but no more does it mean *non diligit nos* (Carpzov), or *non approbat* (Socinus). The γινώσκειν must be left in its deep and proper significance.

The little clause, ὅτι οὐκ ἔγνω αὐτόν, scil. τὸν Θεόν, serves for the explanation of the inferential connection between the διὰ τοῦτο and the οὐ γινώσκει ἡμᾶς: it is intended to illustrate how far and wherefore from τοῦτο, that we are the children of God, the manifest fact, that the world knoweth us not, follows. Thus the clause with ὅτι contains an explanatory minor between the proposition of the first half of the verse, and that of the latter half. Because the world knew not God, it follows from our being children of God, that the world knoweth us not also. To him who hath not known the Father, the Father's children, who bear His nature in themselves, must also be a mystery.—The Aorist ἔγνω stands, as in 2 Tim. ii. 19, in the sense of a Perfect, after the analogy of the Latin *novi*. We must translate, either "has known," or "knoweth." The *essential* idea of the knowledge is obviously the same in ἔγνω as in γινώσκει.

In VER. 2 begins the unfolding or development of the theme, which is externally also marked off as such by the new address "Beloved;" compare ch. ii. 7. The Apostle opens up, vers. 2–12, the first, positive thought of the theme—the proposition that we are God's children,—and what that means, what it involves for ourselves (apart from the enmity of the world), and what the obligation is which it imposes. He contemplates the children of God, first, VERS. 2–6, in their thetical relation to the Father and to Christ; but this is a relation of *hope*, a relation which has not yet received its highest seal and full perfection, but which is laid down first as a beginning that tends towards a future goal; and from this follows directly the obligation of an absolute and unceasing progress, of an ever more complete accomplishment of all that is involved in the relation. But, while this requirement assumes the definite form of an injunction to live after the objective norm of the Divine law, that which is enjoined becomes defined, in vers. 7–12, as a characteristic distinction between the children of God and the world; and the contemplation of this leads to the second main thought of the theme, the enmity of the world to the children of God.

"Now are we the sons of God; and it doth not, etc." The καί—*and* it doth not—serves here also (as in ch. i. 6, ii. 9, ii. 21, etc.) the purpose of setting opposite thoughts over against each other (Beza, Grotius, Spener, and others). For νῦν—*now are we*—forms the most manifest antithesis to the οὔπω—it doth not *yet*; and therefore must not be interpreted as merely confirming the καὶ ἐσμέν of the first verse (Lange), nor as having the meaning of an inferential οὖν (De Wette), but in the genuine temporal sense of *now*. "Now already are we the children of God, and (still) it hath not yet been revealed what we shall be." Φανερωθῆναι may in itself have these two meanings: first, that of the being actually made manifest, exhibited in itself as a reality (ch. ii. 19); or, secondly, the being revealed to knowledge. In the former case, the sense would be this: Until now, the state which we shall hereafter attain to hath not been manifested,—that is, hath not yet appeared, or become a manifest reality:—and this has been the interpretation of most; it was that of Olshausen, and of Düsterdieck also among others, although he had just before cautioned the reader against the "coming into actuality." In the second case, this is the sense: Until now, it hath not been revealed to us by God, no intelligence hath been communicated, as to what our future condition will be, and in what it will consist. Apart from the fact that the former of these two interpretations borders on tautology—"our future condition is still in the future"—it is not grammatically tenable. It is not said οὔπω ἐφανερώθη ὃ ἐσόμεθα, but τὶ ἐσόμεθα. Not—That which we shall be in the future has not yet become manifest; but—It hath not yet been revealed *quid futuri sumus*, what we shall be. As governing a question, φανερόω can have only the meaning of *revelare*, of manifesting in the sense of a theoretical revelation. The antithesis which St John lays down is not this, that, whereas now we are already the children of God, a still higher something that we shall be hath not yet been manifested in fact; but this, that, while we are already God's children, we are nevertheless yet *in the dark* as to the nature of our future condition. (For what will be the nature, and what the enjoyment, of future blessedness, we have no adequate notion in the present time.) The question is then, in what manner the following words connect themselves with these. To answer that question, it is first necessary that we examine them carefully one by one. (The Rec. reads after οἴδαμεν a δέ, which is wanting in A.B.C. and other old sources and versions, and is nothing but the interpreting correction of a copyist.) Οἴδαμεν, ὅτι, ἐὰν φανερωθῇ, ὅμοιοι αὐτῷ ἐσόμεθα: ἐάν certainly has the same meaning here which it has in ver. 28 of the preceding chapter. Φανεροῦσθαι might indeed be taken in the same sense as in ver. 28, that is, as referring to a visible manifestation, and in that case Χριστός must be its subject (Calvin, Bullinger, Beza); but then also our φανερωθῇ must be separated, in a manner scarcely tolerable, from the immediately-preceding οὔπω ἐφανερώθη. It is manifestly better, therefore (with Augustin, Socinus, Grotius, B.-Crusius, Paulus, De Wette, Lücke, Olshausen, Sander, Düsterdieck, Huther), to supply the little clause τὶ ἐσόμεθα, "what we shall be," as the neuter subject of the φανερωθῇ—"We know, that, when it hath been revealed (that is, what we shall be), we shall be like Him." The relation of these words to those which precede, may now be conceived of under a twofold aspect. Nearly all expositors assume between οὔπω ἐφανερώθη and οἴδαμεν an antithesis (so Düsterdieck, who in S. 58 understood ἐφανερώθη of an *actual* revelation of glory, but in contradiction therewith assumes in S. 61 an "adversative relation" between οὔπω ἐφανερώθη and οἴδαμεν). The idea would be this: At present it hath *not been revealed* to us what we then shall be (= at present it is unknown to us); but *thus much at least we know*, that, when it shall be revealed to us, *we shall be like* Him. Thus it would be silently presupposed that the question, "what we shall be," should not otherwise be solved, and answered, and made plain, than by the *actual* coming of that which we shall be. Against this view of the relation of the thoughts speaks the absence of the δέ after οἴδαμεν—the δέ being, as we have seen, decidedly spurious. It is true that St John's way is to express the adversative relation after the Hebrew manner by καί[1] (of this we have had many examples), but then he never leaves it entirely out. And

---

[1] Of course he often employs δέ itself (ch. i. 7, ii. 5; John x. 2).

even that καί we find only in *pure antitheses*, which in themselves are plainly such; not in those which, as here, would introduce the second member as a mere *restriction* or *limitation* ("but so much we know already"). In this case the δέ would be indispensably needful. The δέ, however, being wanting, the logical relation of the words in question to those which precede must necessarily be another—not adversative, but *confirmatory, explanatory,* and *giving the reason*. It hath not yet been revealed to us, that is, made known to us, *quid futuri simus*. We know (we know, indeed), that *when* it shall be revealed to us, or made known, we shall be (then already) like Him. The emphasis lies upon the juxtaposition and *simultaneousness* of the theoretical "made known" and the actual "we shall be like"—as that simultaneousness is established by the ἐάν and its clause. It is on the whole as good as if St John had written: We know that *then first* will it be made known to us, when we (already in fact) shall be like Him. St John, however, has good reason for not giving the thought that turn, but for placing the "we shall be like" prominently in the after-clause: from that "being like" he has further consequences of practical importance to draw. Thus he writes: We know that, when once this shall be known to us, we then (already *in fact*) shall be like Him.—This view, moreover, is supported by the additional advantage, that the φανερωθῇ is apprehended strictly in the same sense which the ἐφανερώθη (on account of its relation to the "what we shall be") has and must have; that is, in the sense of a theoretical announcement. But especially we may say that the concluding words of the verse, "because we shall see Him as He is," come thus into their clearest light.

Expositors diverge in the interpretation of these words. Some of them (as Calvin, Rickli, Huther) find in the clause "because we shall see," not the *real cause* of the "we shall be like," but the logical reason: the "seeing Christ" is a *consequence* of the "being like Him," and therefore the seeing Him will necessarily imply that we have become like Him already; it gives the reason, not so much for the "being like," as for the "*we know* that we shall be like." "Thus much we know already, that we shall be like Him: we know this, for we shall then see Him as He is; but that would not be *conceivable* without a certain *being like Him*." "If our nature had not been made spiritual, and clothed with immortality, it could not draw nigh to God" (Calvin). Compare Matt. v. 8. It must, meanwhile, be confessed that there is something artificial in this explanation: a series of mediating thoughts must be interposed between the expressions of the text.—Others (such as Spener, Beausobre, B.-Crusius, De Wette, Neander, Düsterdieck) take the ὅτι ὀψόμεθα, "because we shall see," as the *real cause* of the ὅμοιοι ἐσόμεθα, "we shall be like," referring to 2 Cor. iii. 18; and this beyond all question is more profound, and certainly more in harmony with St John's style of thought. We need not adopt Beausobre's tame rendering of the process by which we become like God:[1] "The full knowledge of God will make us love Him supremely; and this love will effect, as its consequence, a perfect conformity with Him." Better is it to remember all that St John has said in ch. i. concerning the light-nature of God. Of that we shall be *really partakers*, in consequence of our being shone through and enlightened by it. We cannot be partakers of *light* otherwise than by *beholding;* it is by the *eye* that light enters into us. He becomes light himself who receives the light into himself; and this takes place through the beholding of the light. In our perfection we shall be irradiated and interpenetrated by all the fulness of God, the Light (that is the seeing Him as He is); and, as the consequence of that, we shall be ὅμοιοι *to Him*. And this of itself explains how we are to interpret the ὅμοιος. The question, whether ὅμοιος signifies "like, *i.e.* equal," or "similar," is of no moment. The notion of "similarity," in the ordinary sense of the term, has no place save between finite natures.[2] Here the ὅμοιος—remembering the standard for the interpretation given in ch. i.—can be no other than *like in nature*. But it is equally plain from ch. i. that that nature of God which we are to be like, is to be regarded as His *light-nature*[3] in the sense of His *qualita-*

[1] Augustin, Aretius, and others, are quite wrong in referring the ὅμοιοι αὐτῷ to *Christ;* τέκνα Θεοῦ has preceded.
[2] When, *e.g*., the Homoiousiasts attributed to the Son a ὅμοιος τῷ πατρὶ εἶναι in the sense of similarity, this was at the very outset unmeaning and vapid.
[3] Schmidt and Dusterdieck arbitrarily introduce the idea of God's *righteousness*. Righteousness is not received by beholding, but light is. They were misled by their false notion that ch. ii. 29 contains the theme of the Third Part.

tive moral nature; not as His absoluteness, His independence, His omnipresence, omniscience, omnipotence, and so forth : in short, we must not think of that by which God in our conception is *distinguished as God* from the creature, but of that *moral character* which it is His will to communicate to His own. Hence, and on that account, St John uses ὅμοιος, which expresses likeness of quality, and not ἴσος, which would express likeness of being.

"We know that when it shall be (theoretically) revealed to us (τί ἐσόμεθα), we then (in fact and already) shall be essentially like Him, *because* we shall see Him as He is." Thus the last member gives the whole clause its finish. This is what St John will *make prominent* (not merely silently taking it for granted, as they assume of necessity who supply, at least in thought, an adversative particle after οἴδαμεν),—this, I say, St John makes prominent, that there *will be* no *merely theoretical* revelation of our future glory. When it is made known to us what we in our perfection shall be, then that perfection, the being essentially like God, will be already present; for that being like unto God will indeed be *effected* by the beholding of God. And thus it is the ὁρᾶν τὸν Θεὸν καθώς ἐστι on which all at last depends. Our future glory is *no object of curiosity*, no object on which our speculative thought may spend its vain energy; in the degree in which we are now pervaded and penetrated by God the Light, we obtain some presentiment and anticipation of what we shall be hereafter. *Therefore* it is not yet revealed to us what we shall be, because we in our moral character *are* not yet through and through light, we do not as yet *see* God as He is. Future glory and blessedness is assuredly not something external, which might be added or imparted to a man as it were from without : it is no other than the perfected consummation of the "being sons of God;" when the light-nature of God is perfectly *born into* us, then first shall we know τί ἐσόμεθα,— that is, then first shall we know what glory and blessedness is contained in the τέκνα Θεοῦ εἶναι, the being God's children, itself.

From what has been said, it will further be self-evident that they are in error who (as Augustin, Aretius, J. Lange) refer the ὅμοιοι ἐσόμεθα to the glorification of the body. This is not spoken of here, since αὐτῷ does not refer to Christ, but to God as such.

In VER. 3 an ethical obligation is deduced from what has been said in ver. 2; but this ethical duty (like all obligations of an analogous kind in St John) occurs here not in the form of a legal injunction, but in the form of an internal necessity of nature. It is, as Huther rightly says, "the moral influence of the Christian hope:" nevertheless, not operating with the invariable necessity of *nature*, but after a *moral* necessity; as an operation therefore that *should* be felt,—consequently, it is an internal *requirement*. Πᾶς ὁ ἔχων τὴν ἐλπίδα ταύτην looks back to the ὅμοιοι Θεῷ εἶναι. This, that we shall be essentially like God in the sense of ver. 2, that is, that we shall be sinless, is to the Christian an object of ἐλπίς, of hope (and not of fear, therefore), and consequently of longing and pursuit. But as ἐλπίς is here connected with ἔχειν, it does not indicate the subjective disposition or bias of the soul, but the objectively-expected matter of the hope. Compare Acts xxiv. 15, where ἐλπίδα ἔχειν alone occurs, and certainly is not equivalent to ἐλπίζειν. The Apostle does not mean to say there, "As I hope that God will raise the dead;" but, "As I possess this hope towards God, and expect itself (its fulfilment) that there shall be a resurrection." So also here ἐλπίς is *that which a man is objectively justified in hoping for*. And as there, in the passage of the Acts, εἰς τὸν Θεόν is connected with it, so here ἐπ᾽ αὐτῷ: by ἐπὶ, with the Dative, it is defined to be a hope which is founded in God. (Comp. 1 Tim. vi. 17, iv. 10; Rom. xv. 12.) He to whom this (objective) hope, this object of hope (it is almost the same as "promise"), is given by God—he who possesses this ἐλπίς, based upon God, that he shall be one day in nature like God—he *purifieth himself*, ἁγνίζει ἑαυτόν; he cannot, he may not, do otherwise. Since the being sinless is set before him as the goal of his blessed hope, he must set all his powers towards the attainment of this object; his constant position must be that of one who is in the act of repelling and putting away his sin. The opposite of this, the loving and holding fast sin, or willing to do so, would be no other than a casting away of the ἐλπίς given to us by God, a rejection of the object of hope given us by Him. It would be no other than to say to God: "I will not have that jewel which Thou hast set before mine eyes in all its preciousness, and hast promised one day to give me; to me, the being delivered for ever from sin is no priceless jewel."—Ἁγνίζειν is distinguished from ἁγιάζειν, as ἁγνός is from ἅγιος. In classical Greek, indeed, there is no difference between ἁγνός and ἅγιος; the tragic poets use ἁγνός where Herodotus and others used ἅγιος. Both words serve to define priestly holiness, and therefore also virgin purity. But in the LXX. a distinction is firmly fixed: ἁγνός is used only for the translation of טהור (Ps. xix. 10; Prov. xv. 26) and זהב (Prov. xx. 9), never for the rendering of קדוש; similarly, ἁγνίζω is used for the translation of טהר (2 Chron. xxix. 16 and 18), and only then of קדש (Ex. xix. 10; Num. xi. 18; Josh. iii. 5, vii. 13; 1 Sam. xxi. 9; 1 Chron. xvi. 12; 2 Chron. xxix. 5, xxx. 3; Isa. lxvi. 17) when קדש refers to the restoration of Levitical purity. Ἅγιος, accordingly, is that which is permanently withdrawn from profane use and the profane sphere, and consecrated to God (and therefore itself may lay claim to reverence in the use of it); but ἁγνός is that which is accidentally in a Levitically pure condition, that of which the impurity is done away. The opposite to ἅγιος is *profane*; the opposite to ἁγνός is *impure*. The same phraseology, with the same distinction, is found in the Apocrypha (2 Macc. xii. 38), although in 2 Macc. xiii. 8 ἁγνός occurs in the sense of קדוש. The usage of the New Testament is perfectly in harmony with that of the Septuagint: ἅγιος is he or that which is withdrawn from the profane world, and has entered into the kingdom and service of the Lord. Hence all Christians *as such* are called ἅγιοι (Rom. i. 7; 1 Cor. i. 2; comp. 1 Pet. ii. 9), and the act of ἁγιάζειν is no other than that of a believing consecration to Christ: ἡγιασμένοι are we through *faith* (comp. 1 Cor. i. 2; Eph. v. 26; 1 Cor. vii. 14). On the other hand, ἁγνός describes a condition purified from sin,—that of holiness or *purity*, 1 Pet. iii. 2; Jas. iii. 17; Phil. iv. 8; 2 Cor. viii. 11; and specifically chastity, 1 Tim. v. 22; Tit. ii. 5; 2 Cor. xi. 2, vi. 6; and, in conformity with this, ἁγνίζειν defines the act of purification from sin, 1 Tim. iv. 12; 1 Pet. i. 22; Jas. iv. 8. (So ἁγνός and ἁγνίζω occur in the Old-Testament meaning of the Levitical purification and cleansing, Acts xxi. 24, xxiv. 18; John xi. 55.)

Thus he who possesses this hope founded on God—the hope of being one day perfectly and for ever sinless—comes under the ethical obligation of continually aspiring to that object now, and ever cleansing himself from all sin, καθὼς ἐκεῖνος ἁγνός ἐστι. Ἐκεῖνος is here, as in ch. ii. 6, different from αὐτός; ἐπ' αὐτῷ refers to Θεός, ἐκεῖνος to Christ (Düsterdieck and others, against Aretius, Estius, and Calvin, who refer both to Christ, and to Lyra, who refers both to God). In the clause, "as that One (Christ) is pure," a new relation is introduced into the general strain of thought. Hitherto only the promised future essential likeness in nature to *God as such* was mentioned as the motive to the ἁγνίζειν; now comes in also our relation to the Incarnate, to *Christ*. But in what manner this takes place is questionable: the words "as He is pure" present a difficulty, and are accordingly capable of being variously accepted, as the embarrassment of expositors bears witness. The difficulty lies in this, that the ἁγνός ἐστι which is asserted concerning Christ, is by the καθώς placed on a parallel with the ἁγνίζειν enjoined upon us. "*To be pure* from sin," and "to *purify* oneself from sin," are very different things; and it is not easy to see how it can be said that we should *purify* ourselves from sin, even as Christ *is* pure from sin. Among our recent expositors, Huther does not allude to this difficulty; Düsterdieck despatches it with few words, without seeming to be conscious that two very different methods of explaining the matter offer themselves. The first method is, to hold fast the *comparative* significance of καθώς; then, however, the *action* of the ἁγνίζειν cannot be placed on a level with the ἁγνὸς εἶναι of Christ, but only the *result* of that action, the being pure. And in that case the ἁγνίζειν is to be resolved in thought into ἁγνὸν ποιεῖ, the sense being this: Quisquis hanc spem habet se ipsum *tam purum* reddit, quam purus ille est. The clause "as He is pure" serves then to denote the *kind* or the *degree* of holiness which St John has in his mind when he uses ἁγνίζει; or, secondly, καθώς may be taken in the sense of expressing a *motive*, "even as also" (quandoquidem, comp. Winer, § 57, and the use of καθώς below in ver. 23); and then the perfect *being* pure of Christ is adduced as a (second) motive wherefore we must *become* pure. The latter of these views we regard as the right one. For John cannot possibly here, when he so plainly distinguishes the future perfect ὅμοιος τῷ Θεῷ from the present gradual ἁγνίζειν, lay it down, as the object of this latter gradual purification, that we should be now already *as* pure and *as* sinless as Christ was. Thus the clause "as He is pure" serves not for the definition of the ἁγνίζει, but only as a further motive in trying it.

Nevertheless, this further motive is not to be simply distinguished from the first motive, "the having this hope;" it is not placed side by side with it, but is developed internally from it. The future likeness in nature to God the Light, which is promised to us men, is not simply and only future, but one that has already become visible and historically real. In the Incarnate One, in Christ, there has already appeared a Man who exhibited in Himself, in its absolute perfect realization, that consummate goal which it must be our ceaseless object to aspire to, and which thus we must attain. And, as all our relations to God lead through Him, and are defined in Him, so also this relation of hope, ὅμοιος Θεῷ εἶναι. In Christ, the Sinless One, who is throughout and only Light, we possess the hope and the assurance that we also shall be partakers of the light-nature of God, filled and pervaded with light, and without any darkness at all. Thus, all our endeavours after purification from sin, as they flow from that hope of "being like God," so also they flow from our beholding of Christ, in whom the "being like God" was from the beginning a perfect reality.

In VERS. 4–6 this same *internal moral necessity of the ἁγνίζειν ἑαυτόν*, as it is defined both by our *relation to God* and our *relation to Christ*, is further developed.

Πᾶς ὁ ποιῶν τὴν ἁμαρτίαν, καὶ τὴν ἀνομίαν ποιεῖ, καὶ ἡ ἁμαρτία ἐστὶν ἡ ἀνομία, is the reading of A.C. and other Codd., while B. omits the article before ἁμαρτία. But this omission obviously sprang from an endeavour to make the sentence grammatically exact, since in classical Greek the predicate can have no article. But the transcriber's anxiety was useless, as it was a mistake to make ἁμαρτία the predicate.—The relation of thought between ver. 4 and ver. 3, as well as the precise meaning of the terms ἁμαρτία and ἀνομία, have given the expositors infinite trouble. We refer him who would understand the chequer-work of interpenetrating views to which they have given rise, to the commentary of Düsterdieck. For ourselves, we hold the cause of all the obscurity and confusion, here and everywhere, to lie in this, that expositors have busied themselves too much about the text, and have too little thrown themselves into it; that they have brought to the subject too many questionings of their own, and have not been anxious enough to observe calmly the still and subtle process of the connection of the thought in the text itself.—It is quite undeniable that *two motives* have been already named in ver. 3, which impel to the "purifying ourselves" by an internal ethical necessity: one being the hope *of being* ὅμοιοι *unto God;* and the other, the view of *Christ*, who is already pure from sin. The words πᾶς ὁ ποιῶν τὴν ἁμαρτίαν are so strictly parallel in their form with the words πᾶς ὁ ἔχων τὴν ἐλπίδα ταύτην, as to constrain one at the outset to assume that St John designs, after his ordinary manner, to set over against the positive clause of ver. 3 its negative counterpart in ver. 4. But it is also at the same time plain that the turn of the expression in ver. 4 is the opposite of that in ver. 3. In ver. 3 he said: "He that hath the hope of being like God, purifieth himself." In ver. 4 he does not introduce the bare tautological antithesis (and this again is his manner): "He that hath not this hope, purifieth himself not;" but he sets out with the opposite of that thought which in ver. 3 formed the predicative idea, and makes *it* the subjective idea. In ver. 3 he says, concerning him who "hath this hope," that he purifieth himself; in ver. 4 he says something also concerning him who purifieth not himself, but "doeth iniquity." But *what* is it that he says concerning him? Manifestly, something that shall be in some sense internally opposed to the "having this hope." If every man that hath the hope of being sinless and enlightened through and through, purifieth himself, then concerning him who purifieth not himself, but committeth sin, the *inference* must be valid, that in him the impulse and desire to be like God is not present. And it is this which the predicative idea, τὴν ἀνομίαν ποιεῖ, alleges, and nothing else. For ἀνομία, in such a *distinction* from ἁμαρτία, and yet in such *comprehensive identification* with it,—thus with such variation in the *substance* of the idea, and such identity in the *compass* of the idea,—can only indicate and define *sin as that which runs counter to the uttered law of God's will;* while, on the other hand, "committing sin" marks the simple opposite to "purifying himself." "Committing sin," therefore, defines sin in its immediate qualitative existence or character, and that in contrast with the "purifying" (hence, we must refer it, not to original sinfulness, but, as the "committing" of itself shows, to deliberate and voluntary sin, to sin as loved and cherished); ἀνομία, transgression of the law, on the other hand, defines sin *in its relation of opposition to the uttered will of God.*

Thus the τὴν ἀνομίαν ποιεῖ forms really an internal opposite to the disposition of heart in those whose hope it is to be one day like God, and perfectly free from sin. But, the question still remains, why that antagonist relation to the will of God is at once exhibited as opposition *to the law.* The answer to this question lies in the relation of the fourth verse to the fifth. To the first motive urged in ver. 3, the "having this hope," was appended the second, most internally allied with it, "as He is pure;" that is, the reference to *God* was followed by a reference to *Christ.* And, as in ver. 4 the first motive is developed, so likewise in ver. 5 the second motive is developed. *Sin appears in ver. 4 as what runs counter to the Law; in ver. 5 it appears as what runs counter to the Gospel.* In ver. 4 it is contrary to the eternal injunction of God's will as expressed in law; in ver. 5 it is contrary to the nature of the revealed redeeming will of God as exhibited in act in Christ. Thus the two critical points of ver. 3 are resolved and clearly developed in ver. 4 and ver. 5; and there is no need that we should (with B.-Crusius) hold ver. 3, etc., for an "intermediate thought," nor (with Luther, Calvin, Grotius, Spener, Lücke, De Wette, Neander, and others) regard ver. 4 as the main idea, and ver. 5, etc., as "arguments connected," nor (with Œcumenius, S. Schmidt, and, approximately, Düsterdieck) assume that vers. 4–6 look back upon the (imaginary) main idea of ch. ii. 29. Piscator comes nearest to the true view, when he says that vers. 4 and 5 contain two grounds on which St John warns against sin : ver. 4, because it is ἀνομία; ver. 5, because it is opposed to the end of the incarnation of Christ. A clear exhibition, however, of the manner in which the two critical points of ver. 3 are resolved and laid bare in vers. 4 and 5, we seek vainly in Piscator.

After this general investigation of the relation of the thought as a whole, it is necessary that we should give some further attention, though briefly, to the individual words. Τὴν ἁμαρτίαν ποιεῖν forms, as we have said, the opposite of the ἁγνίζειν ἑαυτόν, and is to be understood in the light of this contrast. It is not said ὁ ἔχων—he that *hath,* but ὁ ποιῶν—he that *committeth;* it is not ὁ ποιῶν ἁμαρτίαν, but ὁ ποιῶν τὴν ἁμαρτίαν—*the* sin. The former difference distinguishes it from the " having sin" of ch. i. 8 : it does not, like this latter, indicate a *state* in which man—though the whole character of his life is regulated by the Spirit of Christ according to the will of God and the laws of the Gospel, and he no longer walks in sin—yet has sin still in himself as the remains of unsanctified affections and the carnal mind, and as working in a mind not yet fully illuminated, and in the still impure impulses of his will (see on ch. i. 8) :—this state, according to ch. i. 8, would not in itself form a contrast to the " purifying of himself," inasmuch as it co-exists with this purifying; but ποιεῖν τὴν ἁμαρτίαν —*committing* sin—marks a *conduct* in regard to which the Christian is absolutely and in every sense *responsible,* since the new life bestowed upon him has given him sufficient strength to walk otherwise, that is, to " purify himself." But then, secondly, it is not ποιεῖν ἁμαρτίαν, but τὴν ἁμαρτίαν ; and this is not fortuitous (as Düsterdieck would wrongly deduce from vers. 6 and 9) :—the former expression would not (although generally synonymous with the ἁμάρτητε of ch. ii. 1) give us a sharp and defining antithesis to the " purifying himself." For, even he who " purifieth himself" will, in consequence of the condition of being which is designated as ἔχειν ἁμαρτίαν, ch. i. 8, have moments in which he fails, and *doeth* that which is sinful (comp. ch. i. 10); and, although such moments will be then interruptions and transitory negations of the ἁγνίζειν, yet are they viewed as only possible *transitory and partial* negations of the ἁγνεία : on the other hand, the perfect *opposite* of the ἁγνίζειν ἑαυτόν appears as the ποιεῖν τὴν ἁμαρτίαν, the committing of sin generally, that is, the doing what is sin. Here, the idea of the ἁμαρτία is by the article bound essentially and not fortuitously with the ποιεῖν : it does not mean, to perform such actions as have, among other notes, that of sin connected with them ; but it means, to commit that which is in its very nature sin. Thus, it denotes a sinning in spite of knowledge and conscience ; and therefore conduct which can be explained only by a love of sin, conduct which shows that the man will not abandon and renounce sin. This conduct, as it forms the sharp contrast to the " purifying himself," so it is such as the Christian is unconditionally responsible for. In the new life which is implanted in him, he possesses the power to which St John points in the words ἁγνίζει ἑαυτόν; and the neglect, misapplication, and disuse of this power it is, which has for its result the ποιεῖν τὴν ἁμαρτίαν.

He, then, who in this manner committeth that which is sin, committeth therefore that which thwarts the uttered will of God's law. (For all expositors agree that ἀνομία does not here, like ἄνομος in 1 Cor. ix. 21, indicate a mere ignorance, and unacquaintance with the law.) St John adds explanatorily,[1] καὶ ἡ ἁμαρτία ἐστὶν ἡ ἀνομία : that which is sin, is no other than that which is opposed to the will of God's law. The two ideas so perfectly cover each other, that he who would give a definition of the idea of sin could not otherwise define it than as "that which thwarts the will of God." Thus, it is self-evident that ἀνομία is not an intensification of the idea of ἁμαρτία (as B.-Crusius asserts) ; to say nothing of the notion that by ἁμαρτία the *peccatum mortale* in the Romish sense is to be understood (as Estius and other Romish expositors discover !). But it is also plain from the above exhibition of the connection and sequence of thought, that in the *word ἀνομία as such* there is not contained any polemical reference to antinomian Gnostics; although the pervading emphasis thrown upon sanctification throughout the whole Epistle (compare above on ch. i. 10) is to be explained by the Apostle's polemical pastoral relations, as confronting and withstanding the antinomian Gnostic false teachers and seducers.

VER. 5. After St John has shown that the "committing sin," this opposite of the "purifying himself," runs counter to the *Law*, he goes on to show that it also runs counter to the *Gospel*: the nature of the Father, and the nature of the incarnate Son, *alike* conduce to the internal moral necessity of holiness, according to ver. 3 : καὶ οἴδατε ὅτι ἐκεῖνος ἐφανερώθη, ἵνα τὰς ἁμαρτίας ἄρῃ, καὶ ἁμαρτία ἐν αὐτῷ οὐκ ἔστιν. (The reading ἡμῶν before ἄρῃ, from Cod. C., is decidedly spurious : it is wanting in A.B. and Vulg., and internal argument is strongly against it. For, the *end* of the incarnation of Christ could be

---

[1] We cannot say that καί is used here in the sense of "for;" but we may say that St John here, as often elsewhere, connects by the lax καί a clause which assumes an explanatory relation to what precedes.

laid down as only the *taking away of sin absolutely*, the *overcoming* of sin; and the restriction to the result in us, contained in the ἡμῶν, would be most inappropriate here.) Ἐκεῖνος stands, as in ver. 3, for the designation of Christ; ἐφανερώθη indicates here (according to the analogy of ch. ii. 28, and as distinguished from ch. iii. 2) the *actual* becoming-manifest of Christ in the flesh, as is self-evident. In the first clause, St John refers to the *end* of the incarnation of Christ, which was no other than the "*taking away of sin.*" In the second clause, he repeats essentially the thought of ver. 3, " as He is pure," while he refers to the *nature* of Christ as that of the Sinless One, who never *had* sin.

The former clause has indeed been differently understood. Relying upon John i. 29, Bengel, Hunnius, Piscator, Lücke, and De Wette took αἴρειν in the meaning of a vicarious bearing, propitiating, and atoning. Many others (as Estius, Luther, Bullinger, Calovius, Beausobre, Neander, Sander) thought that both significations, that of " atoningly-bearing" and " taking away," the *ferre* and the *abolere*, might be combined. But this is no better than an exegetical *monstrum*, since one and the same word cannot be used at once in two different significations. And the first explanation appeals in vain to John i. 29. It is true that in that passage, according to its context and the figure used in it, the subject is not the sanctifying, but the redeeming, work of the Lamb of God; not, however, because αἴρειν there signified anything other than " taking away," but because ἁμαρτία was used there tropically in the sense of נשׂא, that is, for the designation of the *guilt* of sin which was to be taken away. Αἴρειν has everywhere and without exception in St John the signification of *taking away* (John xi. 48, xv. 2, xvii. 15, xix. 31 and 38); and the Sept. translates נשׂא, where it means to bear, by φέρειν, but, where it means to take away, by αἴρειν. In our present passage, however, the context will not allow ἁμαρτία to mean the guilt of sin, but only that of sin itself; consequently, what is here intended is the " taking away of sin" (Calvin, Düsterdieck, Huther), and not the vicarious bearing of guilt. Neither would this last suit the context. Assuredly, it is true that the remembrance of the necessity that Christ should suffer under the guilt of our sin would present of itself a very urgent motive to our warfare against sin; but, if he had intended to make that prominent, St John must have laid the stress upon the point of the *suffering*, and made that the chief verb : he must have written, "And we know that He ἔπαθεν—that He *suffered*—to take away sins;" not, "that He ἐφανερώθη—was *manifested*." Moreover, if we interpret ἁμαρτίας ἄρῃ of the taking away of the *guilt* of sin,—that is, of the *propitiatory bearing* of sin,—the following words, "and there is no sin in Him," receive a meaning which, in *this* connection, would be altogether inappropriate. For, as appended to the thought of vicarious atonement, these words would only contain the *subordinate reflection*, that Christ bore sin, *although in Himself there was no sin*—a thought which, in *this* connection, manifestly would have no place.[1]

Therefore we must resolutely hold fast the explanation, " that He *might take away* sins." St John reminds us of this, that it was the final and most comprehensive design of the collective redeeming work of Christ, to make an end of the whole God-opposing power of sin, to abolish it altogether out of the world, *and to overcome the darkness*. In the closest connection with this, he reminds us—returning back to the final thought of ver. 3—of the truth, *that in Christ there was no kind of* ἁμαρτία, *that is, no darkness at all*. He appeared upon earth as man, that He might be the *Enemy of sin* in this twofold sense : He is the enemy of sin, inasmuch as in *His* nature He is altogether in conflict with it, as He is all and throughout light, all and throughout holy, and of Him the "having sin in himself," of ch. i. 8, can by no means, and in no sense, be predicated ; and He is the enemy of sin, inasmuch as in His whole *work*, and its results, He approves Himself the victorious foe of all iniquity, who hath come to make an absolute end of it, and to cast down the rebellion of the creature against the Creator, of the *darkness* against the *light*. From both there follows that which St John deduces in VER. 6 :

Πᾶς ὁ ἐν αὐτῷ μένων, οὐχ ἁμαρτάνει· πᾶς ὁ ἁμαρτάνων οὐχ ἑώρακεν αὐτὸν, οὐδὲ ἔγνωκεν αὐτόν. Thus St John returns back from the second motive, developed in ver. 5, to the *ethical law* laid down in ver. 3, and which finds its foundation in the mo-

[1] That ἐν αὐτῷ refers to Christ, and not (with Calvin) to the "body of Christ," that is, to all believers in Him, needs no demonstration

tives expanded in vers. 4, 5. He repeats this ethical law here in our sixth verse, naturally, in *the same* formula which it had received in its reference to the second motive (ver. 5), in its reference to *Christ*. But in doing this, he (after the analogy of ver. 3 and ver. 4) lays it down, first in a positive, and then in a negative, form.

" Every man, who abideth in Him" (on this μένων comp. above, ch. ii. 24), " sinneth not." Düsterdieck, as we before remarked, deduces from the ἁμαρτάνει, standing thus simply, that the article before ἁμαρτίαν above, in ver. 4, is fortuitous, and without significance, and that ποιεῖν τὴν ἁμαρτίαν means nothing more than ποιεῖν ἁμαρτίαν or ἁμαρτάνειν. An instructive and warning example, into what a man may fall when he moves in ὑστέροις προτέροις, explaining what goes before by what comes after, instead of the reverse! Our simple, and thus indefinite οὐχ ἁμαρτάνει, St John could use here, only because the preceding ποιεῖν τὴν ἁμαρτίαν, ver. 4, and its antithesis with ἁγνίζειν ἑαυτόν, had already defined clearly to the readers what kind of ἁμαρτάνειν was intended;[1] otherwise he would never have thus unconditionally, and without explanation, written, " He that abideth in Christ, sinneth not." But he has himself shown, in ch. i. 8–10, how and in what sense even he that abideth in Christ may still sin. He has, in ch. ii. 1, 2, set over against the requirement, " that ye sin not," the actual state, " and if any man sin." St John writes here, " sinneth not," only because ver. 4 has made it evident that he has in his mind that ποιεῖν τὴν ἁμαρτίαν which forms the opposite of ἁγνίζειν ἑαυτόν.

He who abideth in Christ, sinneth not in *this* sense,[2]—in this sense he cannot and may not sin ; he cannot wilfully, and against his better knowledge and conscience, do that which is sin ; he cannot love, and cherish, and entertain sin.[3] *Wherefore*

---

[1] In a similar manner he writes, ch. iv. 3, ὁ μὴ ὁμολογεῖ τὸν Ἰησοῦν, because in ver. 2 the more explicit ὁ ὁμολογεῖ Ἰ. Χ. ἐν σαρκὶ ἐληλυθότα had preceded. But who would think of explaining the more definite expression in ver. 2 by the less definite expression of ver. 3, instead of the reverse?

[1] Olshausen remarks on ch. v. 18, quite in harmony with our view: " The child of God *sinneth not at all*, that is, in a certain sense. He *has* indeed sin, ch. i. 8 ; but he *committeth* not sin, ch. iii. 4–8. He is not willingly overcome, he suffers not himself to be overcome, by sin."

[3] Huther violates the context by explaining ἁμαρτάνειν of the condition of those who are still members of the κόσμος, not yet having entered into

—it is easy to see. Because he who doeth this, abideth not in Christ; but, as the consequence of neglected purification, suffereth shipwreck of faith, and the good seed in him is choked among thorns.

And thus, then, the negative side also stands fast : He that (in this sense) sinneth, hath not seen Him nor known Him. ($Aὐτόν$ goes back here, as in ver. 5, naturally to the $ἐκεῖνος$, that is, to Christ.) St John advances his expression (after the manner of ch. i. 10) to this point, that such a Christian, who, instead of purifying himself, committeth willingly that which is sin, cannot be a truly regenerate man, cannot have attained to true, full, and genuine conversion of heart. True conversion presupposes full, perfect, and earnest repentance, that is, self-despairing hatred of sin ; and he who, thus self-despairing, has embraced Christ as his Saviour, has at the same time, when he came to behold and know Christ, cast away and renounced sin *with abhorrence.* He who has not done this, he who secretly entertains sin in his soul, has—it is frightfully solemn, but frightfully true : O that all preachers of the Gospel preached this sacred truth more distinctly and impressively than, alas, they commonly do!—" not yet beheld, and not yet known Christ :" he has not yet beheld Him who is throughout and altogether light, and the enemy of *darkness* and *sin ;* he has not yet beheld Him with the inner eye of the spirit, and not yet known Him in the inmost centre of his being; only with the superficies of the powers of his soul has he adhered to Christ, knowing only the fragmentary beginnings of the character of his Saviour, and not yet *Christ Himself.* He who has discerned in Christ *only* a consolation, and has not also embraced, and *loved,* and shut up in his heart the holy *Judge* of all $σκοτία$, has, according to the testimony of St John, " not yet seen and known Him " aright.

As Düsterdieck softened down the idea of $ποιεῖν\ τὴν\ ἁμαρτίαν$, ver. 4, by an unjustifiable reference to ver. 6, into the idea of sinning generally; so now in ver. 6, where he consistently understands $ἁμαρτάνειν$ in the same vague and general way, he introduces an exegesis which robs the Johannæan expression of

the number of God's children. But ver. 4 speaks of those who are Christians, but wanting in holiness. Not till the close of ver. 6 is it said, that and how far such Christians are not yet truly regenerated.

its precision and solemnity. He regards it as the "*ideal view of St John,*" that whoever "sins," in any sense whatever, has not yet rightly known Christ. According to this unjustifiable generalization of the idea of the ἁμαρτάνειν (which should rather be interpreted by ver. 4), St John's declaration certainly seems to be made more rigorous and emphatic than according to our exegetically-precise interpretation. In fact, it would be a frightful and most depressing utterance, that whosoever sins in any sense whatever, has no part in Christ. But this severity is abated by the expositor's notion that it is "St John's ideal way of viewing the matter, which leaves out of consideration the remaining sinfulness of believers;" and which, moreover, "in the case of those in whom the beginning of eternal life has not been followed by continuance, leaves out of consideration that beginning." That is no good divinity in which yea is nay and nay is yea. According to this notion, the sense would be: "Ideally viewed, that is, apart from the always-continuing sinfulness of believers, it may be said that whosoever sinneth, hath not yet known Christ. But, viewed in reality, that is, with due consideration of the fact that believers may still sin, we must say that one who sinneth, may nevertheless have known Christ." What, then, is there left in this whole utterance of St John? To do this interpretation the fullest justice, no more can be extracted from it than this seemingly ingenious but really empty declaration, that a Christian, *if* he commits a sin, approves himself in this—that is, *so far as* he commits this sin—not as one who has known Christ. But St John's words mean something very different from this, something fearfully solemn but equally true—a truth which must not be thus toned down and accommodated to the licentious Christianity of our days.

Ἔγνωκεν, as compared with ἑώρακεν, is not, as some think, an elevation of the idea; still less is it, however, an anticlimax, as others think. But ὁρᾶν is the beholding of Christ as of the light; γινώσκειν is the loving knowledge (comp. on ch. ii. 3) which contains the reception of the nature of Christ into our own selves.

Vers. 7–10. The contrast, established in ver. 6, between those who abide in Christ, and those who have not yet known Christ, leads of itself and immediately to a *comparing contrast* of the τέκνα Θεοῦ and the τέκνα τοῦ διαβόλου. By the hortatory appeal, "Little children, let no one deceive you," this new train of thought is separated from what precedes, while its meaning and substance is still strictly connected with it and developed from it. In vers. 7, 8, the thought is essentially a modified recapitulation of that which was expanded in vers. 3–6. The reflection of ver. 4 is repeated in ver. 7 in a positive form, and yet so that, not the "purifying of self," but the "doing righteousness," is opposed to the "sin;" for the Apostle here, from ver. 7 onwards, no longer speaks of Christians who intermit the care of their sanctification, but designs to oppose to the true and living Christians the *not-Christians as such*, the τέκνα τοῦ διαβόλου. Thus, the ποιεῖν τὴν δικαιοσύνην and the ποιεῖν τὴν ἁμαρτίαν stand in antithesis, as two absolute, complete, and diametrically opposed kinds of life. And thus there enters in the new modification, that presently in ver. 8 the idea of the ἐκ τοῦ διαβόλου εἶναι—as preparation for the conclusion of the strain, ver. 10—is introduced; and, conformably with this, there is a modification of the repetition of the idea of ver. 5, ἐφανερώθη ἵνα, κ.τ.λ.—Thus, on the one hand, vers. 7, 8 are attached to what precedes, while, on the other, they lead beyond to the main proposition of the new train of thought, expressed in vers. 9, 10,—to a contrasting juxtaposition of the children of God and the children of the devil.

Ver. 7. Τεκνία, μηδεὶς πλανάτω ὑμᾶς : this is the reading of Cod. B. and the Rec.; Mill, Wetstein, Griesbach, Lachmann, and Tischendorf, give this reading the preference. Codd. A. and B. (Copt., Syr., and Arm.) read παιδία, which Tischendorf prefers. But it is on internal grounds more probable that the παιδία was a correction introduced from ch. ii. 18 : there the section, vers. 18–26, began with the address παιδία, and ended with the words, "These things have I written to you concerning τῶν πλανώντων ὑμᾶς." Now, because a warning is found in this passage also against a πλανᾶσθαι, it might have been supposed that the passages were homogeneous, and that παιδία must be here also the true reading.

The warning, "Let no man deceive you," finds its explanation in this, that the Gnostic false teachers of that time actually maintained the assertion, that nothing could defile the ἄνθρωπον πνευματικόν, or, that the law did not proceed from the Supreme

God, and so forth, according to the various forms of their antinomian doctrine. These were the deceivers, whose seductions the readers were to withstand.

Ὁ ποιῶν τὴν δικαιοσύνην forms, as we have said, the contrast to ὁ ποιῶν τὴν ἁμαρτίαν. The latter was in ver. 4 placed in opposition to the ἁγνίζειν σεαυτόν; for there, according to the context, ver. 3, *Christians* were spoken of. To the conduct of those Christians who continually purify themselves from sin, a contrast was presented by the conduct of those Christians who "commit that which is sin," that is, do evil against their better knowledge and conscience, and wilfully. The Apostle has now uttered in ver. 6 the declaration that such Christians are not really Christians at all; and this leads him now, from ver. 7 onwards, to drop entirely the contrast between Christians and Christians (the genuine and the spurious), and to lay down instead the stronger antithesis between the children of God and the children of the devil. He has in vers. 2-6 viewed the idea of the τέκνον Θεοῦ as he is in himself; and has developed from it the opposition between what is consistent and what is not consistent with that dignity. Now, on the other hand, he places the idea of the τέκνον Θεοῦ in comparing contrast with the τέκνον τοῦ διαβόλου. Conformably with this, the opposite of ποεῖν τὴν ἁμαρτίαν assumes another form. Two complete and finished states of heart are opposed to each other, and that as exhibited in their actual and visible results. Here then the gradual ἁγνίζειν ἑαυτόν has no longer place; as opposed to the child of the world and the devil, the child of God is characterized, not by a gradual process of becoming pure, but by this, that he simply "doeth that which is righteous," while the child of the devil "doeth that which is sin." For, ποιεῖν τὴν δικαιοσύνην can mean, in such a contrast, no other than "the doing that which is right." Δικαιοσύνη denotes that which is, in its quality, δίκαιον, right.

Concerning him, then, who doeth that which is right, St John declares, δίκαιός ἐστι—*he is righteous*. A glance at the connection teaches that δίκαιος does not occur here in the sense of the Pauline doctrine of justification, and does not describe a justified state,—that of one who is able to stand before the judgment-seat of God, and is acknowledged to be free from guilt. For the question, Who may thus stand before God, and by what means he may thus stand? does not in the most distant manner enter into the subject here. Least of all is the δίκαιος εἶναι exhibited as the *consequence* or result of the ποιεῖν τὴν δικαιοσύνην. And with this falls to the ground the exegesis of the Romish expositors, who have perverted this passage into a refutation of the Protestant doctrine of justification. But we should not interpret it at once as meaning that he who doeth that which is right, demonstrates thereby that he has already attained to justification (in the Pauline sense) by faith. Nothing is said here about justification. But neither is anything directly said concerning regeneration. Δίκαιός ἐστι stands, first, in opposition to ἐκ τοῦ διαβόλου ἐστι; and, secondly, has the appendage καθὼς ἐκεῖνος δίκαιός ἐστι. This final clause must not, of course, be regarded as a mere repetition of that in ver. 3, καθὼς ἐκεῖνος ἁγνός ἐστι. In ver. 3 the clause καθώς, κ.τ.λ., serves to assign the motive for the requirement, "purifying self;" in our seventh verse, on the other hand, the καθώς is not connected with the subject-idea, involving the requirement, ὁ ποιῶν τὴν δικαιοσύνην, but with the predicate which is attributed to the doer of righteousness. Such a man is δίκαιος, as He (Christ) is δίκαιος. Here the καθώς cannot have the meaning of a motive (*siquidem*), but only that of comparison (*sicut*). He who doeth that which is right, is righteous, even as Christ is righteous; he who doeth that which is sin, is of the devil: this antithetical juxtaposition shows most plainly that the predicate-idea has no other aim than to attribute to him who doeth that which is right *a relation of nature*, or *likeness of nature, with Christ*. Not that such a man will be acknowledged, like Christ, to be guiltless before the judgment-seat of God, but that such a man *bears in himself the nature of Christ*, is what the Apostle would say. And so far our δίκαιός ἐστι has certainly some affinity with the ἐξ αὐτοῦ γεγέννηται of ch. ii. 29; that, however, must be interpreted, not by ch. ii. 29, but by the contrast contained in ver. 7. Nor does St John lay emphasis here upon the being born of Christ, but upon the consequence of that, the likeness of nature.—Δίκαιος therefore denotes here, not a man's position before God's judgment, but simply the character of his nature: the nature of Christ is one which corresponds to the will of the Father; so the nature of him who " doeth righteousness" is one which corresponds to the will of the

Father. And so far Calovius is right, that *this* idea of the *justus* falls not under that of *justificatio*, but under that of *sanctificatio*.

He who doeth that which is right, showeth thereby that the nature of Christ, conformed to the will of the Father, has become his nature: he who doeth that which is sin, showeth thereby that he ἐκ τοῦ διαβόλου ἐστι (comp. John viii. 44); that is, that he is a *child* of the devil, and that his nature and character[1] has been derived from him. For it is for ever the nature and character of the devil, to sin. This explanatory middle clause follows in the words, "For the devil sinneth from the beginning," which words plainly point to John viii. 14, and are by them to be understood. Ἀπ' ἀρχῆς is not to be referred, with B.-Crusius, to the beginning of the existence of the devil, as if he had never done anything but sin from the beginning of his existence; nor, with Bengel, to the period of his fall. The former contradicts the other teaching of Scripture; and the latter is an arbitrary and impossible interpretation of the words. But ἀπ' ἀρχῆς is the beginning of human history (Calvin, Lange, Semler); in comparison with the sin of men, the devil appears to be one who sinned ἀπ' ἀρχῆς.

Εἰς τοῦτο ἐφανερώθη, κ.τ.λ., is, in its substance, a repetition of the thought of ver. 5. In its form, this thought is here modified in two ways: first, Christ is not here, as there, designated by ἐκεῖνος, but, in marked contrast to the διάβολος, as the υἱὸς τοῦ Θεοῦ; and, secondly, in conformity with the previous train of thought, vers. 7, 8, the αἴρειν τὰς ἁμαρτίας is here described as a λύειν τὰ ἔργα τοῦ διαβόλου. These "works of the devil" are simply the ἁμαρτίαι; for, this is his work, that he sins himself and infuses sin into his τέκνοις; consequently, *the* ἁμαρτίαι which are committed by these children of his, are ἔργα τοῦ διαβόλου, works after the devil's kind, works which the devil works in them—thus in every view (in kind and origin) devil's works. Some expositors erroneously include death and all evil among the ἔργα τοῦ διαβόλου here mentioned; but this is against the context. Λύειν bears the meaning of cast down, destroy, abolish, as in John ii. 19, v. 18, vii. 23, x. 35; Eph. ii. 14.

---

[1] It is self-evident that we do not use these words in the sense of the scholastic "substantia," but designate by them the inherent moral character of the will.

In VER. 9 follows now the thought which Düsterdieck erroneously found in the words δίκαιός ἐστι, ver. 7. The Apostle has said, that he who doeth that which is (before God) righteous, shows thereby that he is partaker of the nature of Christ; but that he who doeth that which is sin, shows thereby that he is partaker of the nature of the devil. He has further repeated the declaration, that the whole scope of the incarnation of Christ is directed to this end, to make an end of the ἁμαρτία. Accordingly, he has shown that a child of God, a Christian, *may not* sin; or, more strictly, that he who would be, not a child of the devil, but a partaker of the nature of Christ, *may not* sin. He adds now the more inward truth, that he who is a child of God, born of God, *cannot* sin. That the ποιεῖν τὴν ἁμαρτίαν is a contradiction to the whole nature and work of Christ, has been shown in vers. 7, 8; it is now added in ver. 9, that the being born of God has for its essential and internally necessary and indispensable consequence the μὴ ἁμαρτάνειν.

The subject-idea, "born of God," finds its explanation in what was remarked upon ch. ii. 29. In the predicate ἁμαρτίαν οὐ ποιεῖ, St John could now omit the article, for the same reason which led him, in ver. 6, to substitute the bare ἁμαρτίαν for the ποιεῖν τὴν ἁμαρτίαν. The idea is sufficiently plain after what has gone before. The ποιεῖν, be it observed, is here repeated, in order that the reader may not think of a mere ἔχειν ἁμαρτίαν; afterwards he uses (as connected with δύναται) the mere ἁμαρτάνειν (as above, ver. 6), since it was no longer possible now to misunderstand his meaning. (Düsterdieck persists in doing so. He understands the ἁμαρτάνειν of all and every kind of sin, and explains the idea thus resulting, which is utterly opposed to ch. i. 8-10, as St John's "ideal view.")

He who is born of God, doeth not sin; that is, not with knowledge and will opposed to the will of God. Ὅτι σπέρμα αὐτοῦ ἐν αὐτῷ μένει: these words have been explained in two ways. Some (Bengel, and others) take σπέρμα in the sense of "child or progeny," and refer the αὐτῷ to God: "the progeny of God abideth in or with God,"—abideth faithful to Him, falleth not away. Nearly all other expositors understand σπέρμα of that same seed, in the spiritual sense, which the regenerate have received from God, and through which they have become new men,—that is, of the seed or germ of the new life; and, accordingly, they refer the αὐτῷ to men. "The seed of God abideth in them, in the regenerate men." The latter view is obviously to be preferred, because the words in question, on that view, contain a real argument; whereas, on the other view, they would be a tautological and weakened repetition of what had been said in ἁμαρτίαν οὐ ποιεῖ. Moreover, the designation of τέκνον Θεοῦ by the word σπέρμα would be here most inappropriate, and altogether out of keeping with the figure of the μένειν ἐν τῷ Θεῷ.

There has been much controversy as to what this σπέρμα refers to—whether the word of God (Augustin, Luther, Bullinger, Bengel), or the Holy Ghost (Calvin, Beza). It is (Episcopius, Œcumenius, Estius, Lücke) the germ of the new life implanted in us by the Holy Spirit, the germ of the new man in us,—that is, the Christ implanted in us. In him into whom this σπέρμα has been planted, it abides, μένει. This μένει is used, however, without any reference to the question whether a regenerate person might ever fall from faith; but with reference to the question, whether it be possible to him knowingly and wilfully to act contrary to the will of God. But, if the latter is with him an impossibility, certainly so much the more must the former be: if a ποιεῖν τὴν ἁμαρτίαν justifies us in coming to the conclusion that οὐχ ἑώρακε τὸν Χριστόν, how much more must a shipwreck of faith lead to the same conclusion? And *so far* Calvin and the Synod of Dort were right in saying, that he who falls away manifests that his faith had not been the true and genuine faith as to its *quality*; or that the *vera fides* has among its marks that of *perseverantia*.[1] But, to regard this

---

[1] In accordance with this, my remarks upon Heb. vi. 4, in the eighth volume of this work, must undergo some modification. Not that I can agree with Calvin, when he makes the γευσάμενοι there refer merely to those who had just begun to taste the blessedness of a state of grace. I must hold fast my affirmation, that it is not the scope of the passage to say that *the less* one had tasted of the enjoyments of grace the more easily he would be lost; but the contrary, that *the more* one had already enjoyed of the gifts of grace, the more irrecoverably would he be lost, if he should turn his back upon these blessings, and fall away from the confession of Christ. Only this must be added—from our present passage, 1 John iii. 9—that in the man who, in the sense of Heb. vi. 4, falls away again from *great* beginnings of the new life, a true and thorough regeneration cannot have

perseverance as a specific, as it were external and added gift, *donum*, is to go clean contrary to our present text.

But there is no essential connection between this whole doctrine and that of absolute predestination; for, the question whether the cause of a man's not reaching true regeneration lies in the will of man himself, or in a decree of God, is not at all touched by the teaching of our present passage—that *genuine* regeneration *cannot be lost*.

But there is another point of view in which this verse is dogmatically important. Nothing can be more absolute than its contradiction of the Romanist delusion, that regeneration is in some magical way effected in the baptism of children. *He who is born of God, committeth no sin.* He who committeth sin (in the sense of our context), that is, who willingly doeth, as an unconverted man, that which is sin, is not yet born of God, though he may have been twenty times baptized. The word of God cannot lie. *Little children, let no man deceive you.*

The Divine seed of the new life abideth in the regenerate man; and therefore it follows καὶ οὐ δύναται ἁμαρτάνειν, where ἁμαρτάνειν stands, as we have shown, in the meaning which alone the context marks out. To the regenerate man it is a thing impossible—by his very nature—to commit sin in that sense, to withstand and run counter to the commandments of God knowingly, and with deliberate will. For, sorrow on account of sin, and abhorrent abandonment of sin, lie at the foundation of his conversion; light and life derived from God, and love to Christ, are the very essence of the new life which is within him. Every true and genuine Christian gives testimony by his walk to the truth of this utterance of St John. He *hath* sin in him still (according to ch. i. 8–10); his constitutional dispositions and affections need constant grace and purification; and even in his maxims, and tendencies, and pursuits there may still be σκοτία, or perversion scarcely detected. Thus it may be that the σάρξ leads him into greater or lesser lapses; but this is contrary to the bent of his will, and his soul is affected with the deepest sorrow on account of the *slightest* fault. The sins which he commits bear in themselves most

taken place: the subsequent apostasy leads to the inference, that the preceding conversion had not been absolutely and in all respects sound. The inmost centre of the heart had not been pierced, and entirely changed.

decidedly the character of sins of infirmity, and are for the most part *peccata per accidens*. His anger, holy and justified as to its object and character, may, as a result of the temperament not yet fully sanctified, rise to sinful violence; the heat of conflict for truth may hurry him away to words and measures, the imperfect purity of which he may not at the moment perceive; and even the impulse of the flesh may, in a subtle manner, assault his fidelity, and involve him in hot conflict with himself;—yet, on the other hand, to the truly regenerate man it is altogether impossible willingly and wilfully to do that which he knows to be forbidden of God. He walks not as the world walks, ἐν τῷ σκότει (ch. i. 6); his endeavours and volitions move not in the sphere of that which is evil; and to perform deeds which as such are sinful, is to him in fact not possible: it is in the same sense impossible as it is, for example, impossible to a moral man, only partially conscientious, to do away with his enemy by poison or murder. As to a mere partially moral man the offer, " Give me so much, and I will poison your enemy," brings no temptation with it, because he is not capable of such a crime; so, analogously (though on other and higher grounds), the truly regenerate man is not capable of committing deeds which he knows to be contrary to the will and commandment of God,—such, for example, as the yielding to forbidden lusts, lying, depriving a neighbour of his goods, and whatever else may belong to the domain of the *peccata manifesta*. His walk is a holy and pure walk; and exhibits to every one who beholds as holy and pure. Let not thy high and most real boundary-line be obscured by any " ideal views."

In VER. 10 St John deduces from what had been said in vers. 7, 8, and ver. 9 (that a child of God *cannot* commit, and is not in his nature *capable* of committing, that which is sin), the final and conclusive reflection: *that thus in this* ποιεῖν *or* μὴ ποιεῖν δικαιοσύνην *is exhibited the difference between the children of God and the children of the devil.* Ἐν τούτῳ does not point backwards to what had been said, vers. 7–9, but forwards; and that to the words, " whosoever doeth not righteousness is not of God,"—which words are in reality the quintessence and concise formula of all that had been previously said. First, the additional words, " and he that loveth not, etc.," contain a progression in the thought, a transition to another train : in what manner conducted, we shall see. Φανερά ἐστι, are manifest, are as such quite comprehensible. Ὁ μὴ ποιῶν δικαιοσύνην, " who doeth not that which is right :" the article might here be omitted,[1] for the same reason as in ver. 9, before ἁμαρτίαν. Ἐκ τοῦ Θεοῦ εἶναι is synonymous with τέκνον Θεοῦ εἶναι, just as τέκνον διαβόλου εἶναι is with ἐκ τοῦ διαβόλου εἶναι, ver. 8.

Καὶ ὁ μὴ ἀγαπῶν τὸν ἀδελφὸν αὐτοῦ, St John now emphatically adds ; and by this thought, which is continued in vers. 11, 12, he forms the transition to the second sub-section, which begins in ver. 13. Indeed, he who cannot be brought to see that the idea of τέκνον Θεοῦ is the predominant idea of this whole Part of the Epistle,—he who persists in regarding ch. ii. 29, instead of ch. iii. 1, as expressing its fundamental theme,—will not be likely to discern the true relation of thought between ver. 10 and ver. 13. Thus many think (Düsterdieck) that throughout vers. 1–10 the subject has been the τέκνα Θεοῦ, simply as explanatory of the idea of the δικαιοσύνη ; while, conversely, the fact is that the ποιεῖν δικαιοσύνην, vers. 7 and 10 (which, moreover, the ἁγνίζειν ἑαυτόν, ver. 3, had preceded as no other than a co-ordinated idea), serves simply for the purpose of explaining the idea of the τέκνον Θεοῦ. These expositors suppose that in ver. 10 the Apostle passes over from the idea of the δικαιοσύνη to that of brotherly-love, and that ver. 10 therefore begins a new subordinate section which has brotherly-love for its subject; but they forget that in ch. iv. 11 there is the beginning of another section concerning brotherly-love, and that thus there would be two distinct and independent sections having the same subject and matter. But if, instead of this, we mark that the idea of τέκνον Θεοῦ is the predominant idea of this Third Part, and that the theme of this Part is contained in ver. 1, we cannot doubt for a moment that, not ver. 10, but ver. 13, is the beginning of the new sub-section, and that it treats, not of brotherly-love as such, but—in harmony with the words of ver. 1, " Therefore the world knoweth us not—of the hatred of the world in contrast with the mutual brotherly-love of Christians. After the Apostle has, in ver. 10, laid down the distinction between those who are born of God and those

---

[1] A. and C. read, moreover, τήν. But this variation seems to owe its origin to an endeavour to conform the verse with ver. 7.

who are not born of God, he passes over, in ver. 13, to the opposition and enmity manifested by the latter towards the former. The transition to this second sub-section is formed by the words from the conclusion of the tenth verse to the end of the thirteenth. That is, as St John has it in view to turn to the enmity of the world against the children of God, he singles out from the general μὴ ποιεῖν δικαιοσύνην the particular feature[1] of μὴ ἀγαπᾶν τὸν ἀδελφὸν αὐτοῦ, and makes it the object of special remark.

But here arises the question, what idea the Apostle connects with ἀδελφός. Düsterdieck is everywhere ready with the confident assurance that ἀδελφοί always means in St John those who are born of God, and that brotherly-love always means the love of those who are also born of God. And therefore he at once casts away the notion of Estius, Grotius, and others, who refer the ἀδελφός to the relation of men to men generally. But the matter is not to be despatched in so peremptory a manner. The Apostle is speaking of him who " is *not* of God," and says that his not being of God is manifested by this among other things, that he "loveth not *his* brother." Is then the unregenerate the brother of the regenerate in the sense assumed by Düsterdieck, that is, because both " are born of God?" Certainly not. Then, if the " loving his brother" be made to refer to the mutual love of the regenerate, founded upon their regeneration, it could hardly be alleged as a reproach against the unregenerate that he had no share in that love. Indeed, the words, " he who loveth not *his* brother, is not of God," would then, in consistency, be interpreted in some such absurd paralogism as this : " He that loveth not those who like himself are still unregenerate, is not of God." If St John had written ὁ μὴ ἀγαπῶν τοὺς ἀδελφούς, it would have been a different matter : then we might have taken the οἱ ἀδελφοί as an objective and absolutely stated idea, as the definition of those who are in the true and highest sense brethren, that is, of the regenerate ; and the meaning would then have been this, that he who has no part in this *love* of the brethren among themselves,

---

[1] Huther thinks that the ἀγαπή is not one part or specific trait of the δικαιοσύνη, but "the substance and nature" of it. That may be true of ἀγαπή as such (including love to God), but could not be said of love to the brethren.

must needs be still an unregenerate man himself. But St John does not so write; he makes it plain that the ἀδελφός, connected with the Gen. *αὐτοῦ*, is the brother of *him* who *does not love*, though he *ought* to love; that is, as a *relative* idea. The requirement "to love our brother" is presupposed to be one of *universal application* : When it is asked, who doth fulfil this? he who is proved to his own conscience not to fulfil it may be sure that he is not of God. *Accordingly, ἀδελφός is here taken in the widest sense, in the sense of πλήσιος,* Luke x. 36, etc., *denoting the relation of men to men generally.* In the passage, ch. ii. 9, the combination of thoughts was quite different: there, according to the context, the question was of members of the Christian Church who desired to be thought Christians; and when it was said of them, " and hateth his brother," the idea of "his brother" is defined by the context to be that of a fellow-member of this (visible) community— but by no means that of a fellow-regenerate, which would have been as little suitable there as here. The meaning was this : " He that *saith* he is in the light, and yet hateth him who (*as the result of this declaration*) must then be his brother in Christ, is still in darkness." In our present passage, on the other hand, the question is not of seeming and nominal Christians— at least not specially of such—but the subject has been, from ver. 7, the absolute and penetrating contrast between *all* who are " children of the devil" (and to them appertain preeminently the children of the world, without the Church of Christ), and *all* who are the children of God. Indeed, the Apostle has already purposed to concentrate the former in the expression ὁ κόσμος (ver. 13), and to contemplate them in their open, visible relation of enmity to the Church of Christ ; and the element of the "not loving his brother" must serve to give him the point of transition to the characteristic, "the world hateth us." Thus here, in the words, " he that loveth not his brother," we cannot possibly think of the conduct of those who *pretend* to be " brothers in Christ," but only of the general conduct of those who are unregenerate towards *their* neighbours. Thus a comparison with ch. ii. 9 adds confirmation to our view, that ἀδελφός, in the present passage, denotes the *relation of man to man.* But this is of great moment to the right interpretation of what follows in ver. 13 seq., especially of ver. 16.

VERS. 11, 12. Ὅτι αὕτη ἐστὶν ἡ ἀγγελία (ἐπαγγελία is the reading of Codex C.; but it is neither externally authenticated, nor internally suitable). "For this is the message which ye have heard from the beginning, that we ought to love one another." Γάρ stands here to show that what is said in ver. 11 is intended to explain why he who loveth not his brother is no child of God. To us, the children of God, this message was given from the beginning, that we should love one another. Ἵνα is used here again as in ch. ii. 27, iii. 1, etc. The clause with ἵνα does not specify the design in respect to which that which the main proposition contains took place; but the matter of the clause with ἵνα is itself exhibited as something that was contemplated.

"*This* is the message which ye have heard from the beginning:" αὕτη points, like ἐν τούτῳ, ver. 10, forwards, that is, to the clause with ἵνα. The substance of the message is the commandment that we should love one another. Thence follows, that our "message which ye have heard from the beginning" is *not* identical with the "old commandment," ch. ii. 7. For, there we saw that St John specifies as the substance of the "old commandment, etc.," "the word which ye have heard,"—that is, the whole word concerning Christ, announced to the readers. St John seems to have designedly avoided using the same word ἐντολή. Therefore, we must not explain the ἀπ' ἀρχῆς also of our verse by the ἀπ' ἀρχῆς of ch. ii. 7. In that passage the ἀπ' ἀρχῆς formed the antithesis to the new thing which St John had to say concerning the light " as already shining." In our passage there is no such antithesis as that existing. Hence ἀπ' ἀρχῆς is here to be taken, not in a relative, but in an absolute sense; not in the sense of "hitherto already" (in opposition to what was now first to be announced to them), but in the objective historical sense. The message, that we love one another, we have heard from the beginning, that is, from the beginning of history, as one that had been given from every beginning onwards. This is favoured also by ver. 11, where St John reminds them how and in what manner this ἀγγελία (though not in the form of ἐντολή—but this word St John has carefully avoided—yet in the one, actual Divine message) had already been sent to the past generations of men.

Οὐ καθὼς Κάϊν ἐκ τοῦ πονηροῦ ἦν, καί, κ.τ.λ. The grammatical connection is somewhat lax here. And if we would establish a logical relation in the sentences, we must certainly (though Düsterdieck denies it) supply something between them. The thought as a whole would run thus: ἵνα ἀγαπῶμεν ἀλλήλους, καὶ μὴ ποιῶμεν καθὼς Κάιν, ὃς ἐκ τοῦ πονηροῦ ἦν, κ.τ.λ. All other methods of supplementing the sentence are seen at the first glance to be forced.[1]

The thought itself is plain. Cain showed himself (according to ver. 8) to be ἐκ τοῦ πονηροῦ (=διαβόλου) by this, that he killed his brother (σφάζειν was originally used of the slaughtering of sacrifices, but in the Septuagint and in the New Testament, specially in the Apocalypse, of "killing" generally); but that was both a doing of what was not δικαιοσύνη, and the uttermost opposite of the ἀγαπή. Indeed, this very example shows how the "not loving his brother" and the "not doing righteousness" are inwardly related, the one leading to the other.—In the judgment which God's word pronounced upon Cain's act, lies the "message which ye have heard from the beginning."

But the Apostle does not merely in a general manner refer to this example of Cain: he also adds the words, "And wherefore slew he him? Because his own works were evil, and his brother's works were righteous." We catch the design of this additional clause only when we rightly view the relation of this verse to ver. 13. *The hatred of the world to the children of God* it is, to which St John would now lead on our thoughts. *Therefore* he has singled out from the "not doing righteousness," the "not loving his brother" for especial prominence; *therefore* he now makes it emphatic, that in Cain the *envy* of him who "was of that wicked one" and "whose works were evil" had shown itself against the "just."[2] Thus he passes over from the general "not loving" to the specific demonstration of this

---

[1] Grotius and Lucke supply: καὶ μὴ ὦμεν ἐκ τοῦ πονηροῦ, καθὼς κ.τ.λ.; but this forms, after all, no proper antithesis to ἀγαπῶμεν. Others have resorted to other methods.

[2] It is asked, how it can be known that Cain had previously done evil, and *therefore* hated his brother. This is not answered by saying that ἔργα πονηρά signify the whole disposition and condition of soul in general, which was exhibited afterwards in the act of murder; for the Apostle is speaking, not of a disposition, but of works, and not of such works as followed, but of such as preceded, the hatred. Better is it to say that St John deduced from this, that Cain's offering was unacceptable, what and

hatred, as it ever manifests itself on the part of those who are "of the wicked one" against the "children of God." The righteousness of the latter is in and of itself an object of hatred to the former; the nature which rules (compare above on ver. 1) in the children of God—their holy, righteous nature, conformed to the character of God—is to the children of the wicked one something displeasing and alien, hateful to them as God Himself is hateful. In their "wicked deeds" these are at peace and apparently happy, only so long as their consciences are undisturbed. The mere aspect, the mere existence of the children of God, who do τὰ δίκαια, disturbs them from their repose: they feel, though they may not confess it, that a power is reigning here which condemns them; and therefore they hate the τέκνα Θεοῦ.

Thus has St John now fully paved the way of transition to the second sub-section.

VERS. 13, 14. *The antagonist relation of the world to the children of God,* is, therefore, the subject of which St John now speaks. That which he has to say on this matter resolves itself into two things: first (ver. 13), that the Christian must not marvel at the hatred of the world (this is established in ver. 14); and, secondly, that the Christian must not return that hatred (vers. 15, 16).

The words of ver. 13 are in themselves perfectly plain. Concerning ὁ κόσμος, compare the remarks on ch. ii. 15: here again it is applied to the world as not yet penetrated by the light of Christ, still in bondage to the σκοτία, and therefore fearing and hating the φῶς. Εἰ is not used instead of ὅτι, nor for *etiamsi,* but in its own peculiar and genuine signification. Εἰ with the Indicative does not put the case as hypothetical, but represents what is said in the conditional clause as something which actually occurs; and asserts, that whenever or as often as such a case occurs, what is said in the conclusion will or should occur also. For example, εἰ βροντᾷ καὶ ἀστράπτει, "as often as it thunders, it lightens also," simply declares that the latter is conditional on the occurrence of the former, but without any

how evil his former works had been. It is not a single step that leads to murder. All points to this, that as Cain's spirit, so also his life and walk, had been altogether estranged from God.

further reference to the former being only *possible* or *uncertain*. So here: Whensoever it takes place that the world shows its hatred to you (and this assumes it to be well known that that often takes place), we must not wonder that it does occur. The conditional clause with εἰ specifies that state of things, or *the case in which* the injunction μὴ θαυμάζετε is to be binding on Christians. If it were ὅτι, the μισεῖ ὑμᾶς ὁ κόσμος would be exhibited as the *object* which was not to be wondered at. (As, for example, John iii. 7, iv. 27; where the εἰ would have no place, for the simple reason that in both these passages a fact, once for all in the past, and not often recurring, forms the object of the θαυμάζειν.) In our passage, if we were to reproduce the thought in its full logical completeness, another ὅτι μισεῖ, κ.τ.λ., would have to be supplied. "If the case occurs that the world hate you, wonder not (scil. at this, that the case occurs that the world hate you)."

It points to the declarations of our Lord, John xv. 18, 19, xvii. 14; Matt. x. 22, xxiv. 9; Mark xiii. 13; Luke xxi. 17. The Apostle addresses his readers as ἀδελφοί, when he directs to them this exhortation; not as if the word involved the idea of their being regenerate (compare, on the contrary, what was said upon ver. 10), but because he would at this moment bring to their minds that that Divine requirement of brotherly-love to all men, which was never fulfilled in the world, was actually fulfilled between himself and his readers. Thus, in the *idea* ἀδελφός as such there lies no specifically Christian element (compare ver. 12, "He slew his brother," which is quite parallel with "not loving his brother," ver 10); but, our ἀδελφός, ver. 13, serves for the address of the children of God in their antithesis to the κόσμος, because the idea of brotherly-relation, human in itself, is become in them, through the power of grace and the Spirit of Christ, an actual reality.

It is now in ver. 14 explained why the children of God should not marvel at the hatred of the world. "We know that we have passed from death to life, because we love the brethren; he that loveth not, abideth in death." St John places ἡμεῖς emphatically first. *We*—it is his purpose to say—*we* have the power to love our brethren; *all* cannot do that. But is that what he actually says? If it were his manner to demonstrate a proposition laid down only according to the rules of a mechanical logic, and if he had by "marvel not" intended nothing beyond the external and negative "deem it not incomprehensible," he would most assuredly have continued in another style. He would have been obliged to write, "We love the brethren, because we have passed from death unto life; but he that abideth in death, loveth not:" he would have been obliged to specify love as the *result* of receiving life, and hatred as the *result* of abiding in death. But, in the apostrophe, "Marvel not," he has more in his mind than that negative "think it not a wonder,"—more than the mere deeming it not an incomprehensible thing. When he appeals to them, "Marvel not," he arms them not only against a wondering of the understanding, but especially against a wondering and recoil of their spirit and temper, against such an internal abandonment and fear as might lead them astray from God; and therefore the negative $\mu\grave{\eta}$ $\theta\alpha\upsilon\mu\acute{\alpha}\zeta\epsilon\tau\epsilon$ includes in it the positive "but be strong and of good courage." Accordingly, ver. 14 is not constructed with the purpose of making it intelligible to their understanding how it should be that the world hateth the children of God; but with the purpose to impress upon their hearts the motives for courage and consolation. And therefore in ver. 14 he exhibits love, not as the consequence, but as the sign,[1] of their having received life: he does not say, "We love the brethren, because we have passed from a state of death to that of life;" but, "We know that we have passed from death to life, by this, that we love the brethren." The particle ὅτι does not depend upon $\mu\epsilon\tau\alpha\beta\epsilon\beta\acute{\eta}\kappa\alpha\mu\epsilon\nu$, but upon οἴδαμεν.

In the clause $\mu\epsilon\tau\alpha\beta\epsilon\beta\acute{\eta}\kappa\alpha\mu\epsilon\nu$, κ.τ.λ., the category of "light and darkness" is exchanged for the different, though related, category of θάνατος and ζωή, *death* and *life*. The "having passed from death unto life" must not be at once, and unconditionally, made identical with the "being born of God." The antithesis of ζωή and θάνατος is indeed correlative with that of Θεός and διάβολος; but not more so than that of φῶς and σκοτία. Each of these categories must be understood and apprehended according to the peculiar force which it contains in

---

[1] There is no propriety in the interpretation of the Romish and Socinian expositors, which regards the love, not as the sign, but as the cause, of the passing from death unto life. "By this, that we love, we know that we have passed from death to life."

itself. In his Gospel, St John inverts the order; he mentions, ch. i. 4, first the ζωή, then the φῶς. "In the Logos," he says, "was life;" not "the life," but "life." He takes a view of the whole multitude of things which had been made (ver. 3), and in which he may find life; but he finds life, true life, only in that eternal Word which was eternally essential to the nature of God—in that hypostatic, self-uttering act of God, who was from eternity, and apart from all creation of existing things, the speaking of God to God (πρὸς τὸν Θεόν), and by whom also the Father created all things that were created. In *Him* was life. For, as the Father (ch. v. 26) hath life in Himself, so hath He also given to the Son to have life in Himself; while, on the other hand, the creature hath its life, not as inherent in itself, but as dependent upon the will of God, which might withdraw the gift and leave the creature to become nothing again. Therefore St John can at once (ch. i. 4) call the Logos ἡ ζωή; and he adds to the new truth, "And the Life was the Light of men." How then are *light* and *life* related to each other? If we proceed from the principles of a mere empirical experience, all life might seem to be the elevation of a multiplicity of lower existences into a higher, simple, and indivisible existence, the factor of which lies not in that lower multiplicity, but in something without it. The elements, for example, of the living corporeal organism are chemical materials which, left to themselves, can do no other than decompose, according to chemical laws—"*verwesen*"—lose their nature, as we have seen in the corpse forsaken of life. Informed by soul, quickened by the principle of life, or by the living central-monad, they enter into combinations which could not be established in a chemical manner,—that is, according to the chemical laws which obtain in the macrocosm, in the inorganic world,—but which are brought into existence only by the living organism, the microcosm. The living organism assimilates the macrocosmical matter, and constrains it to enter into organic combinations. Chemistry may resolve these combinations in a chemical manner, and study their nature, but is powerless of itself to re-establish them. Chemistry is unable, by its own resources, to produce the smallest living vegetable cell, or living muscular fibre, not to say the living homunculus. Life is gendered only by the living; all the organic presupposes a living principle existing before it;

and thus the proposition of Jacobi (so abhorrent to Goethe, because so misunderstood), that all the living lives only through something independent of itself, maintains its perfect truth. Now, what the central-monad is in the individual organism, that the λόγος τοῦ Θεοῦ is in the universe, in the life of the macrocosm. But in stating this, we must not overlook the fact that the great organism of the universe does not consist merely of material elements, that is, chemical matter, like the microcosms of vegetable, animal, and human bodies; but that it is a living whole which bears in itself the powers of spiritual and moral life, as well as those of natural life, as its elements, through which therefore *history* is bound up with *the course of nature*.[1] And on that account the Logos is, as the *life*, so at the same time the *light*, of the world (concerning which, compare the observations upon ch. i. 5). As the life elevates a multiplicity of elements into a higher unity of *being*, so the light (even the physical light) elevates a multiplicity of actual existences to the higher unity of *being seen*. And thus the light is the intensest action of the life itself; that action by which living existences become existent *for one another*, reciprocally revealing their life. The Logos, who is the source of all creaturely *life*, is also the *original light* of the world, at the same time the eye and the sun. How fellowship with the Logos, as the Life and the Light, is not merely theoretical, but an essential religious fellowship, has been already shown upon ch. i. 5. Selfishness is the being sealed up in self, the opposite of light and shining; the lie is the opposite of the being penetrated by or admitting the light.

As the creature closes itself in selfishness and lie against Him who is the *light*, and therefore also the *love*, so also it rends itself asunder from Him who is its *life*, and in whom alone it has and can have life. Hence it is with the world sundered by sin from God, as it is with the corpse forsaken of the spirit: the harmonic union of the physical and spiritual elements which constitute the macrocosm ceases to exist, and there enters in a *bellum omnium contra omnes*, a disjunction or *decomposition* of

---

[1] In the misapprehension of this palpable fact lies the error of those who substitute a mere "*universal soul*," after the analogy of what may be regarded as the animal or vegetable soul, for the eternal, personal, and conscious Logos.

all. The unsaved κόσμος it is which in its μὴ ἀγαπᾶν exhibits this image of derangement, and proclaims itself thus "to be ἐν τῷ θανάτῳ, in death;" while, on the other hand, the children of God are, through the incarnate Logos being inborn into them, regenerated unto ἀγάπη, and declare by that self-renouncing love which gives itself to death, and which endures the hatred of the world in order to the saving of the world, that they are redeemed from that condition of death, and translated into the ζωή, the life.

It will appear as the obvious result of this, that, with the children of God, as with Christ Himself, the being delivered out of death takes effect only through the loving surrender to death. As Christ overcame death by enduring it, so analogously that love of the children of God which declares their "having passed into life" is such as patiently bears the hatred of the world. That this is involved also in the "because we love the brethren"—brethren, ἀδελφοί, being used in the most comprehensive meaning—is evident from what has been already observed on vers. 10 and 13. They exhaust St John's thought of its most profound and precious meaning, who would limit brotherly-love to the mutual love of the regenerate among themselves. The strongest counter-argument against this perverted view—which opposes the utterances of Christ, Matt. v. 44, etc., and all the doctrine of the Apostles, *e.g.*, 1 Cor. iv. 12 —is to be found in ver. 16.

The concluding words of our verse, ὁ μὴ ἀγαπῶν μένει ἐν τῷ θανάτῳ, are explained by the antithesis. But St John does not here, any more than elsewhere, specify the dry logical antithesis ("He that loveth not, *shows thereby* that he is still in death"); but he extends the thought to include the warning declaration that the not-loving, as it is a mark of the being still in death, so also it is a cause of the further abiding in death. For, as every sin, so especially this sin—that of not loving—shuts and seals the heart against the influences and operations of grace. All conversion begins with an opening of the heart to the judging light of God, and therefore with a feeling which abominates sin, and, of all sins, selfishness above all.

VER. 15. The new turn of the thought which enters at the end of ver. 14—that he who loveth not his brother is not only still in death, but on that account abideth in death, finds here in ver. 15 its further expansion and illustration. "He that hateth his brother is a murderer; and ye know that no murderer hath eternal life abiding in him." But we must take notice of the progression of the thought in ver. 14 *a*, ver. 14 *b*, and ver. 15: He that loveth not his brother (but hateth him) is, *a*, *not yet passed from death to life;* *b*, he *abideth* further in death; and, *c*, even supposing that he had had for a season the ζωὴ αἰώνιος in himself (which, however, according to ver. 9, is not possible in the fullest sense), yet it could not remain in him: he would, as the result of this μισεῖν, fall again out of the ζωή, thereby proved not to have been the true and real life.

Turning to the individual members of the paragraph by which the above proposition, stated in its third and most intense form, is established and proved, we note that the first clause, "Every one that hateth his brother is a murderer," is illustrated by its plain allusion backwards to the history of Cain, introduced in ver. 12. That was not merely an insulated example, but a history of a typical nature and character. In the conduct of Cain, that came out into distinct manifestation which is the very nature of all hatred generally. The mildest definition of the mildest form of hatred would be this, "The being unable to bear any one;" and what does this pregnant description of enmity mean, but that to A the existence of B is too much; that he cannot reconcile himself to it; and that, if it depended upon him, that existence would be done away with? The selfish negation of another's existence is the nature of all hatred: whether the person hated be put out of life, or only injured in life, matters not, as this may depend upon external circumstances; hatred as such is of itself a negation of another's existence—it is "murder in the heart" (Augustin),—*quem odimus vellemus periisse* (Calvin). Where hatred dwells in the heart, it is no merit of the hater that the appropriate fruit of murder does not ripen upon the tree of hate: it is all the same the specific and regular fruit of that tree. Thus, St John can write πᾶς ὁ μισῶν, κ.τ.λ., ἀνθρωποκτόνος ἐστί.[1] As to the words

---

[1] Manifestly opposed to the spirit of the context is the notion of Lyra and others, that St John calls the hater a murderer because he hurts his own soul. This idea follows in the second clause as an inference from the first, and cannot therefore give a reason for the first.

τὸν ἀδελφὸν αὐτοῦ, "his brother," the remarks hold good which were made upon ver. 10. The universal πᾶς of itself shows that St John does not speak merely of members of the Christian Church alone, but generally of all who hate their fellow-men. The second member of the statement runs, "And ye know that no murderer hath eternal life abiding in him." Düsterdieck is altogether wrong when he explains the declaration, οὐκ ἔχει ζωὴν αἰώνιον ἐν αὐτῷ μένουσαν, as "in its essential meaning perfectly corresponding with the μένει ἐν τῷ θανάτῳ," as he was also wrong in making this last equivalent to "he is still as yet in death." In this way we may make everything mean everything, and impose almost anything upon the meaning of St John. The Apostle rather intensifies, as we have already seen, the declaration, "He abideth in death," into the much more penetrating, "He hath not eternal life in himself as abiding." In appearance, this says less; in reality, it says much more. In appearance, the utmost is the denial that an ἀνθρωποκτόνος has eternal life *abiding* in him, while it is admitted that he may have it in him (in a certain sense) temporarily.[1] In reality, it is said most strongly and emphatically that a murderer, even admitting him to have ζωὴν αἰώνιον in himself, yet will and must fall again from this ζωή into the θάνατος.—St John designedly writes ζωὴν αἰώνιον without the article, because he (in harmony with ver. 9) cannot attribute "*the* eternal life," even temporarily, to one who is not, in the sense of ver. 9, an actual child of God. But such a man might have "eternal life"—that is, the powers of the world to come (compare Heb. vi. 4)—within him.

By οἴδατε ὅτι St John exhibits that which was said in the second member of the verse as a truth well known to all his readers. It has been asked, how it had become so well known to them. Grotius and Lücke thought that they received it from the Mosaic law, which affixed the punishment of death to murder: "For if the law of Moses could not tolerate such a

---

[1] Obviously only *may* have, not *have*. That πᾶς ἀνθρωποκτόνος has eternal life temporarily in him, St John could not reasonably say, and he does not say it. Logic teaches us that the negation of one thing does not involve any positive assertion of another. If, for example, I say that no murderer can have a happy future, I do not thereby assert that every murderer has had a happy past and present. But πᾶς οὐ is logically equivalent to οὐδείς.

man in terrestrial society, how much less would Christ tolerate him in the heavenly city!" (Grotius.) But, according to Matt. xxi. 31, Luke v. 31, this "for if—how much less" appears to be unjustifiable; and the question as to whom the Lord tolerates, and whom not, in His heavenly *societas*, is regulated not according to the Law, but by an altogether different principle. Still more inappropriate, if possible, is Lücke's reference to certain ordinances of ecclesiastical discipline that must have excluded murderers from the Christian community,—which, in the face of Luke xxiii. 43, is a bold assertion and argument. The Apostle does not appeal to any individual isolated teachings or ordinances, but to that which the conscience and Christian consciousness affirms to every living Christian as a self-evident truth. If death as such is the absolute opposite of the ζωή, it is evident of itself that the disposition which would diffuse death around—the mind of the μὴ ἀγαπᾶν, which, according to John viii. 44 and the twelfth verse of this chapter, is that of the πονηρός or διάβολος—cannot be reconciled in thought with the ἐν τῇ ζωῇ εἶναι. Either that temper of mind must end in a true and thorough conversion, or the rudiments of a ζωή which might have been present come to their end. Life and death, life and murder, cannot *abidingly* be reconciled in the same heart.

After this exposition, it is scarcely necessary to obviate the misunderstanding that whosoever has actually committed murder can never more be converted and attain to eternal life (against which Luke xxiii. 43 also speaks). It is plainly evident, from the first half of the verse, that it is not the external act of murder which St John describes by the word ἀνθρωποκτόνος, but the spirit and temper of not-loving, the condition of heart which hates. He who fosters this disposition is not yet in the ζωή; he abideth also (obviously as long as he nourishes it) in death, and falls again from the possible beginnings of a new heavenly life (that is, *then*, when he does not put an end to this disposition by earnest repentance, before it is too late). The notion that no man who had ever nourished this spirit of not-loving in his heart could ever be converted, most certainly St John does not mean to inculcate. For that would be to assert that no natural man could ever be converted; since all natural men as such are the children of the world, and bear in themselves that mind as their natural inborn σκοτία.

VER. 16. The turn of the thought introduced at the end of ver. 15 leads from the exhortation, that we *bear* the hatred of the world confidently and joyfully, to the exhortation that we should *repay it*, not with hatred, but with love. Ἐν τούτῳ ἐγνώκαμεν τὴν ἀγάπην, ὅτι ἐκεῖνος ὑπὲρ ἡμῶν τὴν ψυχὴν αὐτοῦ ἔθηκεν.

Τὴν ψυχὴν τιθέναι occurs again only in John x. 11 and 15 and 17, xiii. 37, xv. 13. In John xi. 17, 18 it stands in opposition to the πάλιν λαμβάνειν, and hence must indicate no other than the actual *giving up* of life—death itself. In the remaining passages the signification "venture life" would be suitable. Now, although this phraseology does in its meaning go beyond the Hebrew שׂוּם נפשׁו בכפו, yet it seems rather to have been derived from that Hebrew phrase, or at least from some reference to it, than to be illustrated by the Latin, where *ponere* is used for *deponere*, and where *vitam ponere* (Cic. ad Fam. 9, 24) occurs. Even the τίθησι τὰ ἱμάτια, John xiii. 4, offers no analogy, since by the τιθέναι there is simply expressed the "laying down," not the (essentially identical in meaning) "putting off." We assume that τιθέναι τὴν ψυχήν had originally the meaning of שׂוּם נפשׁ בכפו, "to pledge or offer the soul," and was then afterwards used in the intenser sense of "sacrificing the life." As it respects the construction, an οὖσαν must be supplied to the ἐν τούτῳ. This last cannot possibly depend upon ἐγνώκαμεν— "By this we have known or perceived love, that He"—for what would be the meaning of such a thought? Some explain it thus: We have known the love of Christ by this, that He gave His life for us; that is, by this, that He gave His life for us, we have known that He loveth us. But it is not true that St John, with the other disciples, perceived first by His dying that Christ loved them (compare, on the contrary, John xiii. 1); and, moreover, we cannot see what purpose would be served in this context by answering the question *in what* the disciples of Jesus had perceived love. Others (Luther, Bengel, etc.) explain: "By this, that He gave His life for us, we have first come to know what love is in its inmost nature, or what true love is." This is more tolerable and appropriate, but in such a form too modern. "What love in itself essentially is," could hardly be expressed by τὴν ἀγάπην. In the words τὴν ἀγάπην ἐγνώκαμεν the object does not appear as a *problem*, but as some-

thing known. Hence it is most natural to construe: "We have known love as that which consists in this, that He gave up His life for us." Ἐν τούτῳ forms the predicative idea to τὴν ἀγάπην, and ὅτι depends upon ἐν τούτῳ. It is true that classical Greek would have required this to be ἐν τούτῳ οὖσαν; but similarly classical Greek would have required in John iii. 25, μετὰ Ἰουδαίου τινός. It is entirely in conformity with St John's style that he *writes* ἐν τούτῳ, as if it belonged to ἐγνώκαμεν, while he *thinks* of it as the predicate to ἀγάπην.—Thus viewed, the thought now assumes its clear antithesis to ver. 15. It is not wherein we (subjectively) have perceived love, but in what (objectively) the nature of love consists, that St John purposed to say. The ἐγνώκαμεν, therefore, is just as introductory and subordinate as the οἴδαμεν in ver. 15.—Hatred in its inmost essence is *killing*, or a negation of another's life; love in its inmost essence is the voluntary sacrifice of one's own life. And, in fact, this love exists not merely *in abstracto* as an ideal requirement or object of contemplation, but it exists in concrete reality. He who is light and life *is* love; in the death of Christ that nature of love became a concrete act. As hatred became a concrete act in Cain, who took his brother's life; so love became a concrete act in Christ, who laid down His life for us.

But from the knowledge and perception that love consists ἐν τούτῳ, that Christ gave up His life for us, the ethical demand follows at once, that we—we who, according to ver. 11, etc., are under an internal obligation to exercise the ἀγαπή—" are bound, like Him, to lay down our lives also for the brethren." Here it is as clear as the light of day that the idea of ἀδελφός is not to be restricted to the idea of our brethren in salvation, our brethren in regeneration. The requirement, that we should be ready to lay down our life for our *brethren in Christ*, would point to but a wretched counterpart of the self-sacrificing love which Christ has shown to us. Christ died for us when we were yet enemies (Rom. v. 10), and only through His death have we *become the sons of God*. The Apostle Paul represented himself as having entirely to fill up τὰ ὑστερήματα τῶν θλίψεων τοῦ Χριστοῦ for the salvation of the sinful world yet to be saved. And can we suppose the Apostle John to restrict the obligation of loving surrender of life to the relation of the regenerate among themselves? No, ἀδελφός is used in the same broad sense as in vers. 10, 13, 14, 15, and designates the relation of *man to man*. We ought to behold in every *fellow-sinner* a *brother* to be saved. As far as the propitiatory virtue of the death of Christ extends, extends the obligation of this brotherly-love: its limit is not the fellow-regenerate, but the fellow-redeemed, among men; that is, it stretches to the whole human family. For the *world*, for the world under the slavery of the σκοτία and hating Himself, Christ laid down His life; and we therefore are bound, after Christ's example, and in His spirit, to love, with a love which would sacrifice life for those who hate us, the world which hateth both Him and ourselves (ver. 13). This, and nothing less than this, is the vast meaning of our verse. Every other view destroys the parallel between what Christ has done and what we must do.

And thus we have ample confirmation that it is not the general and vague notion of brotherly-love which St John treats of in this section, but the relation of the "sons of God" to those who are not "sons of God." They have the enmity of the world to endure; they must bear that enmity with confident joy, and recompense it by love which shrinks not from the sacrifice of life.

It is manifest how important ver. 16 was in those times of persecution, and in all similar times. The death of confessors is not only an act of faith and persevering profession, but equally an act of love. The martyr sacrifices his life willingly and cheerfully, knowing that from the seedtime of blood the harvest of the world's salvation grows.

VER. 17. Thus in the surrender of His own life for the salvation of the world consists the essence of ἀγαπή; *but*, he who should be deluded, in the contemplation of this highest and sublimest exhibition of love, into the imagination that love can show itself *only* in great actions and great sacrifices, and not in the most trifling matters of life, would altogether mistake the nature of *true* love. Such a love as would demonstrate itself only in great and heroical deeds, would be a proud love, and therefore no love at all. And it is in times of persecution and martyrdom that this dangerous error is imminent. Hence, St John appends to what had just been said in the previous verse, a warning, and in doing so uses the δέ. What had been said appears now to have relatively the force of a μέν: true, that the nature of love consists in this great sacrifice; but, how dwelleth the love of God in him who thinks he may omit the lesser duty of love?

The lesser matter which love must by no means omit, consists in the communication of *earthly* bread and the necessities of life. The greater matter consisted in this, that the children of God, having (according to vers. 14, 15) eternal life dwelling in them, seek to lead those who are still in death to the possession of the life—seek to communicate to them the "eternal life," and that (ver. 16), according to Christ's example, by the sacrifice of their own (earthly-bodily) life. The opposite to this heavenly-eternal possession of the ζωὴ αἰώνιος is now represented as the βίος τοῦ κόσμου. Ζωή is the life as an internal principle, as the sovereign power or energy; ζωή designates that dominant central-monad which rules, assimilates, reproduces the material elements: thus it is life as viewed in its sovereign ascendency and supremacy over macrocosmical matter, life as an internal principle and developed from itself. Hence this definition ἡ ζωή, in its highest and fullest sense, applies only to the λόγος τοῦ Θεοῦ as the source of all life (John i. 3, 4, compare John v. 26), and only in a derived and relative sense to those who partake of life from Christ. *Βίος*, on the other hand, is the organic bodily life in its conditionality, the life of the body as a finite and transitory state; hence the continuance of life as limitedly conceived. Then, in its derived meaning, it is what belongs to the prolonging of that life as dependent on external things, on nourishment. (Sept. Prov. xxxi. 3, 14; Cant. viii. 7; Mark xii. 44; Luke viii. 43, xv. 12, 30, xxi. 4; compare above on ch. ii. 16.) The ζωή in that higher sense, the ζωὴ αἰώνιος, the Christian has in common with Christ, and from Christ: the βίος he has in common with the κόσμος, and from the κόσμος; hence St John calls it βίος τοῦ κόσμου (Les biens de ce monde. Beza). Accordingly, it is self-evident that the Genitive τοῦ κοσμοῦ defines the βίος, not as sinful, but only as secular, earthly, and, in comparison with the ζωὴ αἰώνιος, worthless.—*And seeth his brother in need.* Θεωρεῖν signifies here, as everywhere, not the mere involuntary seeing, *conspicere*, in which the eye is merely passive, but the active beholding, or looking at. It is he who *can see before him* his brother (ἀδελφόν) as one who suffers distress, needy ($\chi\rho\epsilon ia$, as in Eph. iv. 28; Mark ii. 25, and elsewhere), and yet close his heart against him. $K\lambda\epsilon i\sigma\eta$ $\tau\grave{a}$ $\sigma\pi\lambda\acute{a}\gamma\chi\nu a$ $a\grave{v}\tau o\hat{v}$ $\grave{a}\pi'$ $a\grave{v}\tau o\hat{v}$: $\sigma\pi\lambda\acute{a}\gamma\chi\nu a$, in the Old-Testament meaning (רחמים), is equivalent to spirit or heart; and hence here is the object of the $\kappa\lambda\epsilon i\epsilon\iota\nu$, which figure would not suit the *figure* of $\sigma\pi\lambda\acute{a}\gamma\chi\nu a$. But we must not conceive the $\sigma\pi\lambda\acute{a}\gamma\chi\nu a$ as bearing its original meaning: it is not used figuratively, but as a metonymy, while $\kappa\lambda\epsilon i\epsilon\iota\nu$ is used figuratively. "To shut the heart" is to prevent the impression, which the beholding of an object of distress produces, from penetrating to the heart. $'A\pi'$ $a\grave{v}\tau o\hat{v}$ is pregnant in its sense: he closes his heart away from him; that is, so that he himself, as a consequence, turns away. (Compare $\grave{a}\pi'$ $a\grave{v}\tau o\hat{v}$, ch. ii. 28.) —*How dwelleth the love of God in him?* $`H$ $\grave{a}\gamma\acute{a}\pi\eta$ $\tau o\hat{v}$ $\Theta\epsilon o\hat{v}$ stands here in a different connection from that of ch. ii. 5: it is not connected with $\tau\epsilon\tau\epsilon\lambda\epsilon i\omega\tau a\iota$; in the present context the $\grave{a}\gamma\acute{a}\pi\eta$ is spoken of as a conduct *required of us*. By this, therefore, as also by the passage ch. iv. 20, we might be misled into one-sidedly understanding this $\grave{a}\gamma\acute{a}\pi\eta$ $\tau o\hat{v}$ $\Theta\epsilon o\hat{v}$ of our love to God. This, however, would be incorrect. For the words, "how abideth the love of God in him," are strictly parallel with "abideth in death," ver. 14, and "hath not eternal life abiding in him," ver. 15. And, even in ver. 16 the subject was not merely love as a deportment which *we* on our part are bound to exhibit, but love according to its substantial being, as substantively displayed in Christ and Christ's act of love. And therefore our present words can mean no other than that this substance of Divine love (having its source in God) cannot remain in him who does not practise love in lesser and earthly things. Such a man drives—that is, by the subtle pride which (as remarked above) is mingled with his love—the nature and spirit of the love of God out of himself.—The passage ch. iv. 20 does not furnish an argument against this explanation; since we have not to explain ch. iii. 17 by ch. iv., but simply to ask what is meant by the words themselves in ch. iii.

CONCLUSION OF THIS PART OF THE EPISTLE, VERS. 18-24. As St John closed the Second Part of the Epistle by directing, after the recapitulation addressed to the $\pi a\iota\delta ia$ (ch. ii. 26, 27), his final words to all his readers (vers. 28, 29), so now he ends our Third Part with a concluding address, which begins (after the analogy of ch. ii. 28) with τεκνία.

In ver. 18 he exhibits most prominently the *exhortation* which is the very essence of what has preceded (just as in ch. ii. 28 the analogous exhortation, " Abide in Him "). In ver. 19 he then recapitulates the general motive, which had been urged from ver. 7 onwards, that we possess in our conduct, as pleasing God, the mark that we are of the truth. And it is obvious that these words, as connected with what had been said from ver. 11 to ver. 17, describe the conduct which pleases God as ἀγαπᾶν, the manifestation of love.—From the close of the nineteenth verse to the twenty-second, this motive and reason is developed in its negative and in its positive side; and then in the close of ver. 22 the ἀγαπᾶν is extended (with a recapitulating return to the thought of ver. 4 seq., and ver. 7 seq.) to the τηρεῖν τὰς ἐντολάς. Finally, in vers. 23, 24 these previous considerations are in such a manner summed up in one as to present (after the analogy of ch. ii. 29) the germ-thought of the subsequent Fourth Part.

VER. 18. The exhortation runs: μὴ ἀγαπῶμεν λόγῳ μηδὲ τῇ γλώσσῃ, ἀλλ' ἐν ἔργῳ καὶ ἀληθείᾳ. The correctness of this reading, as attested by all the old codices, stands unquestionably firm against the Rec., which omits the τῇ before γλώσσῃ, and ἐν before ἔργῳ. The transition from the mere Dative λόγῳ and τῇ γλώσσῃ to ἐν with the Dative is thought by Lücke and others to be appropriate, inasmuch as the Datives describe the instruments by which the love produces its effect, while ἐν, on the other hand, introduces the elements in which the love moves. But this is contradicted by the fact that the two clauses are opposed to each other antithetically. Can we suppose St John to have meant to say, " Let us not approve the energy of our love with the instruments of word and tongue, but let our love move in the elements of deed and truth?" This would be a marvellous antithesis! De Wette perceived more correctly that the ἐν with the Dative is here equivalent to the simple Dative by itself. It is well known that St John often uses the ἐν in the Hebraizing sense of ב *instrumentale* (most strikingly in Rev. xiii. 10); and thus we have here nothing more than the Apostle's not unusual sinking down from the pure Greek into a Hebraizing phraseology.—Λόγος forms the antithesis to ἔργον, and, accordingly, signifies the mere word. Γλῶσσα enters in as an intensification. A man may love with words (without deeds), yet in such wise that the words are true and sincere; much worse is it, when the mere tongue chatters without the heart, and when, therefore, the very words are not sincerely meant. To this ἀλήθεια forms the antithesis.

VER. 19. The first member of the verse, "Hereby we know that we are of the truth," is easily understood. It is essentially the same thought which we have seen in ver. 14, viz., that love is the distinguishing *mark* of a state of grace. But here the state of grace, that is, the ἐκ Θεοῦ εἶναι (comp. ver. 9), is not viewed, as in ver. 14, according to the category of life and death, but according to that of ἀλήθεια and ψεῦδος, *truth* and *lie* (comp. ch. ii. 21); partly, because in ver. 18 the ἀλήθεια had just been opposed to the mere γλῶσσα, and partly because the Apostle has it already in his mind to return back, in the following Part, to the category of the ἀλήθεια, and the opposition between it and the Gnostic lie. Γνωσόμεθα is the reading of A.B.C. against the Rec. γινώσκομεν (which seems to have sprung from the notion of conforming the passage with ver. 24, ch. ii. 3 and 5, iv. 2 and 13, v. 5). The Future was not occasioned (as Huther thinks) by "the cohortative form of thought," as if we must supply, "If we observe this injunction, we shall thereby be able to know;" it simply serves to exhibit the declaration as a universally applicable *rule.* If γινώσκομεν stood in the text, the ἀγαπᾶν would then appear to be taken for granted as actually present : " Hereby—by the love which we are now enabled to exercise—we know;" it would be an *inference* drawn from the abiding continuance of something in the life. But, it seems the Apostle's purpose not to do that, but to lay down a general rule applicable to all cases. Ἐν τούτῳ, scil. τῷ ἀγαπᾶν, γνωσόμεθα, by our life we shall be able to know; the presence or the absence of the *love* will be ever and in all cases the distinguishing mark or test to ourselves, whether or not we be of the truth. That the words ἐν τούτῳ in this passage *look backwards*, is plain at the first glance, and is now pretty generally admitted ; that they cannot refer forward to ver. 20 (as if one of the two ὅτι, or both of them, depended upon the

R

ἐν τούτῳ), will be very plain from a closer consideration of what follows.

VERS. 19, 20, may be regarded as a difficult passage, inasmuch as expositors have always been widely at variance, both in their views of the whole and in their interpretation of the individual words, both as to the general meaning and the construction of the sentences. The points in question are these : (1) Whether καὶ ἔμπροσθεν αὐτοῦ begins a new and independent clause, so that the Future πείσομεν is co-ordinated with the Future γνωσόμεθα, or whether πείσομεν, like ἐσμέν, still depends upon ὅτι; and, in the former case, whether ἐν τούτῳ is to be referred merely to γνωσόμεθα, or also to πείσομεν. (2) Whether πείθειν means to *convince*, and has an object following; or, whether it means to *persuade*, " to persuade into pacification," and stands absolutely. (3) Whether ὅτι is generally a particle, and then also ἐάν a conditional particle, the second ὅτι being a resumption (epanalepsis) of the first ; or whether ἐάν stands for ἄν, and ὅ,τι must be read, in the sense of *quodcunque*. (4) Whether God is called μείζων because He is more merciful than our heart, or because He is more rigorous in His judgment upon us. (5) Whether, in ver. 21, by means of the words ἐὰν ἡ καρδία, κ.τ.λ., a second supposition is introduced in opposition to that contained in ver. 20 ; or whether, rather, this ἐάν stands in the sense of " if then now," and introduces a deduction from what is said in ver. 20.

Before these questions can be thoroughly examined and receive their answer, it is of great importance to settle the right reading. At the close of ver. 19 we must read the singular τὴν καρδίαν, with A. and B. (and Lachmann), against C., Vulg., and Rec.; since the authority of A. and B. is here perfectly decisive.[1] Manifestly, the plural was introduced here as a correction, the singular by the side of ἡμῶν not seeming correct.— In ver. 20 ὅτι is omitted before μείζων in Cod. A.; but it is vouched for by B. and C. The omission is easily accounted for : the recurrence of ὅτι after so short an intervening clause might appear to be superfluous. We have further to remark, that in ver. 22 ἐάν is sufficiently authenticated by B. and C., in opposition to the ἄν of A.

[1] In Cod. A. a later hand has inserted the plural.

And now we may simplify the investigation by removing out of the way certain interpretations which are generally acknowledged to be wrong. It is clear, at the outset, that πείσομεν does not, like ἐσμέν, depend upon ὅτι, but that it is independent and co-ordinate with the γνωσόμεθα. The only question that remains is, whether the ἐν τούτῳ still throws its influence upon the πείσομεν, or whether καὶ ἔμπροσθεν begins a perfectly independent reflection. Secondly, it may be regarded as settled that ὅτι before ἐάν cannot mean "for;" 1, because in that case the following ὅτι would be without an explanation, since only "that," and not "for," can be epanalectically repeated; and 2, because in that case there would be lacking some apodosis to ἐάν.[1] Thirdly, it may be considered as a settled point that we have no right arbitrarily to correct the last ὅτι (with Stephanus) into ἔτι, or the ὅτι ἐάν (with Andreä) into ὅτε ἄν or ὅταν; as also, that the latter ὅτι must not be taken (Beza) in the sense of δηλονότι, or (Calvin) in that of *certe*.

We begin then our investigation by a glance at ver. 21; that is, by giving its answer to the fifth of the questions mentioned above: it will be seen that this question is in reality independent, and may be decided with confidence, furnishing at the same time a firm basis for the explanation of ver. 20. Huther, like many other expositors, discerns in ver. 20 the reflection that, if or however much our heart may accuse us, we may pacify our heart on the ground that God is greater—to wit, greater in forgiveness and in grace—than our heart. For the present, we leave out of the question the correctness of the interpretation which, in view of ver. 20, leads to this result. The main point which concerns us now is only this, that Huther regards ver. 21 as a deduction from the premises laid down in ver. 20. It is not that to the *one* supposition, "that our heart condemn us," the other, "that it do not condemn us," is *opposed*; but the sense in his view is this: "If then, in consequence of that πείθειν, that purification obtained, our heart no longer condemn us, then (what follows is a necessary consequence, etc.)." But this explanation is verbally and

[1] Unless we agree with De Wette to find it in καὶ γινώσκει πάντα, translating καί by "also:" "For, if our heart accuse us, because God is greater than our heart, He also knoweth all things." But this will not commend itself by its clearness to any one.

grammatically untenable. Not only should we then expect μηκέτι καταγινώσκῃ, but, further, the particle ἐάν could not possibly serve to introduce an inference from a premiss actually presupposed as existing and real. This would have required εἰ with the Indicative. 'Ἐάν expresses the exact contrary; it introduces a condition, of which the future must decide whether it be or be not the case. 'Ἐάν does not mean, "If then, therefore;" but, "putting the case." And therefore we must regard it as absolutely indubitable, that the words of ver. 21, ἐὰν ἡ καρδία μὴ καταγινώσκῃ ἡμᾶς, are set over against the case assumed in ver. 20, ἐὰν καταγινώσκῃ, as the opposite case. In ver. 20 is expressed what would take place on the supposition that our heart condemns us; in ver. 21 is expressed what would take place on the contrary supposition, if our heart condemned us not.

And this leads us immediately to the decision of the third question. If in ἐὰν μὴ καταγινώσκῃ, ver. 21, the one supposition is laid down, ἐὰν καταγινώσκῃ in ver. 20 must lay down the opposite; that is, ἐάν must be a conditional particle. Hoogeveen and Huther would read ὅ,τι ἐάν in the sense of ὅ,τι ἄν ("of whatever our heart may at any time accuse us"); and Huther appeals to the fact, that many New-Testament codices have here and there the unclassical reading ἐάν instead of ἄν, and that even the union of ὅστις with such an ἐάν is not without example; for Lachmann and Tischendorf read ὅστις ἐάν in Gal. v. 10, and the latter ἥτις ἐάν in Acts iii. 23, and in Col. iii. 17 the preponderance of testimony is in favour of ὅ,τι ἐάν. This sets aside Düsterdieck's appeal to the dictum of Hermann (ad Vigerum, p. 835), which applies only to classical Greek; and, in fact, no one who is thoroughly acquainted with New-Testament Greek will deny the possibility of the combination ὅστις ἐάν (and καταγινώσκειν may certainly have the double Accusative of the person and the thing, though this construction never occurs in the New Testament, and but seldom in profane writers). But in *this* passage the reading ὅ,τι ἐάν, as equivalent to ὅτι ἄν, is not only very improbable (since immediately in ver. 22 ὃ ἐάν follows), but it is rendered flatly impossible by the antithetical relation of the two conditional propositions, ver. 20 and ver. 21.

Consequently, it is decisively settled that the latter ὅτι in ver. 20 can be only an epanalepsis of the preceding.

Now, when St John places in such sharp antithesis to each other the two opposite cases, 1. that of our hearts accusing us, and 2. that of our hearts not accusing us, we naturally and at once assume, after the analogy of many such examples of the Apostle's habit of antithesis (ch. i. 6 and 7, 8 and 9, ii. 4 and 5, 10 and 11, ch. iii. 3 and 4, 7 and 8), that here also he is opposing the ungodly deportment of those who are not at all, or are not truly, of God, to the godly and Christian deportment of those who are the genuine τέκνα Θεοῦ. That the 1 pers. pl. ἡμᾶς need not embarrass us, is plain from a glance at ch. i. 6–10.

But, in spite of this, Luther, Bengel, Morus, Spener, Olshausen, Düsterdieck, and others, have felt themselves under the necessity of regarding both sides of the matter as referring to one and the same class of true Christians, *both* of them finding their place within the limits of the same sincere Divine life. (The testing of this view will bring us to a decision concerning the first, second, and fourth of the five questions above-named.)

Those expositors (as also Huther, who admits generally no antithesis between ver. 20 and ver. 21) assume at the outset that ἐν τούτῳ must be referred to πείσομεν,—in opposition to Fritzsche and others, who regard καὶ ἔμπροσθεν, κ.τ.λ., as a perfectly independent and new thought. That reference has nothing grammatically against it, but nothing positively in its favour. In themselves, both interpretations are conceivable: " By this we shall know that we are of the truth, and (by this shall we) persuade or still our hearts;" and also the other, " By this shall we know, etc., and we shall persuade our heart, etc." Even Düsterdieck admits that it is the following train of thought which renders it necessary to refer ἐν τούτῳ also to πείσομεν. We regard this as still an open question, the decision of which must be given by what immediately follows.

But now we must further ask what the meaning of πείθειν is. Of course the word must be acknowledged to bear the two significations of *convince* and *persuade*. A third interpretation, that of stilling, pacifying, or *placare*, has been vindicated by Düsterdieck, following Luther; but it may be proved that it never bears this meaning: in Matt. xxviii. 14, for instance, it means simply no more than " persuade," the context showing

to what the Jews would persuade the Governor. So also with
1 Sam. xxiv. 8, where the Septuagint has translated the doubtful יְשַׁסַּע, which properly means *verbis lacerare, increpare*, by
ἔπεισε—not, indeed, to express the idea of *pacification*, but
simply to show the result, that David had so persuaded his fol-
lowers as that they should do his will. It is conceded also that
the meaning is not different in Joseph., Arch. vi. 5, 6. But
Huther, admitting that in our passage πείθειν means of itself
only to persuade, contends that the context requires the additional meaning of persuading or stilling to *repose*. For, πείθειν
stands here in an antithetical relation to καταγινώσκειν. But,
the question whether this be so or not, must be, after all, decided on other grounds. Considered in itself, one cannot see
why πείθειν should form a contrast with καταγινώσκειν: the
grammatical construction does not lead that way; for, πείθειν
is the finite verb of the governing proposition, and the words
μείζων ἐστὶ—καὶ γινώσκει πάντα rather would form a kind of
antithesis to the καταγινώσκειν of the conditional member of
the dependent proposition. Thus it must first be demonstrated
that the πείσομεν, in the ruling proposition, is in sense related to
the ὅτι μείζων, κ.τ.λ. But, far from being demonstrated, this
relation is opposed by the whole construction. That πείσομεν
was asserted absolutely and without any object, in a meaning
which the reader only after reading the twentieth verse would
discover, is in itself not very probable. He who read or heard
the word πείσομεν, together with the ὅτι which follows it, must
certainly have been disposed—since πείσομεν has no other
object stated, and since it expresses, as absolutely laid down, no
definite idea at all—to regard the clause with ὅτι as the object
of the πείσομεν; and, accordingly, to translate ὅτι, not by
"*because*," but by "*that*," taking πείθειν in the meaning of
convince. Huther, however, declares this explanation to be
untenable; "for, the consciousness that God is greater than
our heart, cannot be regarded as the result *of this*, that we know
ourselves by our love to be such as are of the truth." But who
does not see that this supposed objection holds good only on the
supposition that the ἐν τούτῳ is still referred to the πείσομεν, or
that between the two propositions, γνωσόμεθα and πείσομεν, a
relation of ground and consequence must be assumed? The
former, however, is not true; for we hold it established that ἐν

τούτῳ must be referred only to γνωσόμεθα; and of the latter we find no trace in the text. Thus Huther has refuted only those who translate πείθειν ὅτι by "convince that," and then at the same time would refer ἐν τούτῳ also to πείσομεν. The other acceptation, that ἐν τούτῳ belongs only to γνωσόμεθα, and that *then* πείθειν ὅτι means "convince that," he leaves entirely unrefuted. And unrefuted it will remain.

For, not only has πείσομεν no such meaning as "pacify;" not only does the interpretation "persuade," thus without an object, give no sense; not only does it require ὅτι, κ.τ.λ., as its object, and necessarily therefore bear the meaning of "convince;"—but the other acceptation is also wrecked on the words ὅτι μείζων, κ.τ.λ. If, with Lücke, we take πείσομεν in the sense of pacifying, and then refer μείζων to the greater *severity* of God, the following ideas rise: "By our love we know that we are of the truth, and by this we can pacify our heart, because, if our heart should accuse us (that is, of the want of love), then God is a still greater Judge than our heart, that is, an omniscient Judge (and therefore would still more condemn us)." But in what logical relation would this "because" stand to that which it is supposed to establish? From the fact, that if our own heart condemn us, the Omniscient would all the more condemn us, it cannot in fact follow that the consciousness of practising love it is which serves to pacify our heart. The matter of the clause with ὅτι would stand to the ἐν τούτῳ πείσομεν, at furthest, in the relation of an explanatory confirmation, not in that of a causal nexus; and ought, therefore, to be connected at least with γάρ, but not with the paratactic ὅτι, "for," certainly not with the syntactic ὅτι, "because."

Hence other expositors, who connect πείσομεν with ἐν τούτῳ, and take it in the sense of "pacify," have consistently sought to establish for the words ὅτι μείζων, κ.τ.λ., also another and perfectly opposite meaning. God is called μείζων, inasmuch as His forgiving grace is exalted above the fear of our self-condemning heart, and inasmuch as with *Him* there is the possibility of absolving us, even when to *us* there is no possibility of absolving ourselves. Nösselt has very ingeniously placed this in connection with the ἀγαπᾶν τὸν ἀδελφόν.

By this, that we practise love, we know that we are of the truth; by this we can pacify ourselves, and that on this ground, because if our heart (loving our neighbour, and consequently forgiving his trespasses) should accuse ourselves of any fault, God is still greater than our heart,—that is, will much more certainly forgive our sin than we could ever forgive our neighbour's sin. But however ingenious this may sound, the words of our passage cannot be made conformable to such an interpretation. The strength of such an interpretation is in what must be supplied. The element of the forgiveness of our neighbour, which of course is, in the nature of the case, contained in brotherly-love, had not been expressed in any form in the context: the idea of forgiveness must be forced upon the text, and that twice, first with regard to ourselves, and then afterwards with regard to God. If St John had had this idea in his mind, he would have written thus: ὅτι, εἰ ἡμεῖς τῷ ἀδελφῷ ἀφίεμεν τὰ παραπτώματα αὐτοῦ, πόσῳ μᾶλλον ὁ Θεὸς ἀφήσει ἡμῖν τὰ παραπτώματα ἡμῶν. But the main objection to this and every similar interpretation lies in the words καὶ γινώσκει πάντα. It is hard to see what the *omniscience* of God would have to do with the ὑπερπερισσεύειν of His grace. It must then be assumed that God, as knowing all things, might discover some excellencies in us which were concealed from our own modesty, and on account of those latent virtues would forgive our sin! Or, that He were better acquainted with our weakness than ourselves are, and therefore would not so severely reckon with our guilt (as if we were not of ourselves only too much inclined to excuse ourselves on these and other grounds!). We need not stay to demonstrate that both these acceptations are flatly opposed to scriptural teaching; that God does not forgive our sin because of our excellencies, or excuse it because of our weakness. The omniscience of God can therefore be no reason why He should be supposed to judge us more gently than we judge ourselves. But since the "knowing all things" is laid down in strictest connection with "is greater," the latter cannot intend the greater *mildness* of God.[1]

But neither can it signify this, viewed in itself. When God is called "greater," in comparison with our self-accusing heart, the heart which accuses us is called "less." This notion of

[1] Huther substitutes for "mildness" the vague idea of "glory;" but this is only disguising the matter. For this also really refers "is greater" to "forgiving love."

littleness cannot here be meant in any *laudatory* sense, since in that case some kind of disparagement would fall upon God's being greater. But it is manifest that our heart can be opposed to the "greater" God only in the sense either of positive blame, or at least of deficiency. But, according to this explanation, our heart can be the less, only *as far as it accuses us*. But it is quite incomprehensible how the self-accusation and self-condemnation could be represented as a defect, where there is no guilt. If indeed the thing intended were, that our heart in littleness of faith failed to apprehend aright the consolation of the forgiveness of sins, the matter would be quite different. In that sense, it might be said that God is greater than our heart; that is, that the superabundance of His grace covers the deficiency of our faith. But it is an exegetical violence to substitute this idea for the plain words, καταγινώσκῃ ἡμᾶς. We have not in the text of vers. 20 and 21 the antithesis between timorous littleness of faith and its joyful confidence, as if *in both cases* the heart were conscious of guilt,—in the one, however, appropriating forgiveness, and in the other not venturing to do so; but we have in ver. 20 the supposition that our heart *condemns us,* and in ver. 21 the supposition that our heart does *not* condemn us. This self-accusation of the heart can in no case be put to the account of its *being little* or *less;* any more than the forgiving fulness of God's grace can have its ground in the fact of His "knowing all things."

Thus we think we have shown that this entire view is at all points untenable; and shall now go on to set over against it that interpretation which alone we regard as correct and capable of perfect vindication.

After what has been already said, it must be assumed that the particle ἐάν, in the words ὅτι ἐάν, is a *conditional particle;* that the two clauses, ver. 20, ἐὰν καταγινώσκῃ, κ.τ.λ., and, ver. 31, ἐὰν μὴ καταγινώσκῃ, serve the purpose of setting over against each other two *opposite* suppositions; that πείσομεν means "to *convince;*" and that ὅτι introduces, with the signification "that," the objective proposition belonging to πείσομεν. —By no means, therefore, can we lower the reference of ἐν τούτῳ down to the πείσομεν; first, because this could be done only by means of a zeugma, for the assumption of which there is no occasion here; and, secondly, because, as we have already seen, a very inapposite thought would arise out of it. We regard, therefore, καὶ ἔμπροσθεν as the beginning of a new and perfectly independent clause.

St John has already said, in the preceding words, that we may always discern by our "loving" or "not loving" whether we are or are not of the truth. He now passes over to another and new reflection. "And before Him—לִפְנָיו, before God's face—shall we convince our hearts of this, that if our heart already condemns us, God is greater and knoweth all things." How far and in what sense God is greater, the words "and knoweth all things" declare. He penetrates by His knowledge all things. Now, if our heart, so inclined to self-deception and self-vindication (and *therefore* "little"), accuses us (that is, of not exercising love), God, the Omniscient, is greater than our heart; and we can therefore all the less stand before Him, all the less have the παῤῥησία. If we take μείζων in this sense (with Bullinger, Calvin, Beza, Grotius, à Lapide, Lücke, Neander, and many others), then the words "is greater," etc., form the purest, sharpest antithesis to the words "have confidence towards God," ver. 21, and all the details become perfectly clear. Then it becomes perfectly intelligible why St John writes ἔμπροσθεν αὐτοῦ πείσομεν. "And *before God's face* shall we convince ourselves," he says, in order by anticipation to remind us that we have not to do with ourselves and our own hearts alone, but that we stand before the all-searching eye of God; and, therefore, that it is not left to our own option whether we will or will not believe what is stated in the proposition with ὅτι. And certainly the ἔμπροσθεν αὐτοῦ must not be referred forward to the distant judgment—"when we one day stand before Him in judgment, we shall," etc. Πείσομεν τὴν καρδίαν ἡμῶν is not a simple paraphrase for πείσομεν ἡμᾶς αὐτούς: St John intends to lay the emphasis upon this, that the question is not of a mere conviction of the understanding, but that our heart, spirit, and conscience must be convinced of the truth that we can less escape God than we can ourselves. He uses the Future here, not to express by it a rule holding good for all supposed cases, but in order simply to express his own *expectation* of the truth of what is said. We cannot, in fact, see what form other than the Future he could have used here. An Imperative would have been too absolute; an insinuating Conjunctive, as a mere friendly injunction or challenge ("Let us, however, be convinced"), would have been insipid. He would neither command nor entreat: he would exhibit it as something which he decidedly expects, and which so necessarily and inevitably follows from the nature of the case itself, that he may expect it; therefore this precise and definite "before God's presence will we convince our hearts, that," etc. The words ἐὰν καταγινώσκῃ, κ.τ.λ., derive their fixed definiteness from the context. The question, whether we practise an active love or not, had preceded: in regard to this matter, our hearts can either accuse or acquit us. God is called "greater," as has been said, because He cannot be deceived; on the contrary, our hearts are "less," because we may suppose them liable to self-deception.

The whole thought, consequently, is closely bound up with the proposition laid down in the beginning of ver. 19. In the words ἐν τούτῳ γνωσόμεθα there was contained implicitly a challenge to self-examination. And the two opposite suppositions which are evolved by such a self-examination are more expressly referred to and described in vers. 20, 21. Of this we must be convinced in our heart and conscience, before God's presence, that, if the former of these suppositions be the true one with regard to us—if our own hearts *condemn* us in self-examination—assuredly we can stand before God with still less confidence than before our own hearts. That is, we shall then subjectively be able to attain to no παρρησία, and objectively shall not be acknowledged by Him as τέκνα, or as ἐκ τῆς ἀληθείας ὄντες. For how could He, who knoweth all things, acknowledge us "to be of Him," when our own hearts convict us of a lie?

The second supposed case is unfolded in VERS. 21, 22. What St John had to say touching the former part of the alternative he had introduced by the solemn appeal, "Before God's face shall we convince our heart, that;" but now he introduces what he has to say touching the second case by the graciously-confident address, "Beloved" (as in ch. ii. 7, iii. 2). He now takes for granted the existence of such a condition of things in regard to his readers; therefore he names them "his beloved,"—as they would present themselves to his mind, on the latter part of the alternative,—upon whom his glance may rest for a time with joyful love.

The conditional clause ἐάν, κ.τ.λ., has already received its explanation.[1] When the case occurs, that our heart sustains the application of the test prescribed in ver. 19, and does not accuse us, we discern that we "are of the truth," and " of God," and "children of God." This again resolves itself into a twofold consequence. First, παῤῥησίαν ἔχομεν πρὸς τὸν Θεόν (Cod. B. reads ἔχει instead of ἔχομεν, which is without any critical significance). Those who translate πείσομεν by "pacify" are now at great pains to establish a distinction between πείσομεν and παῤῥησίαν ἔχομεν. To us the παῤῥησίαν ἔχομεν seems to form the pure and simple antithesis to the idea contained in ὅτι μείζων, κ.τ.λ. We discern ourselves to be God's children; and therefore have that joy and confidence in our hearts which the children feel towards their father. The second point is καὶ ὃ ἐὰν αἰτῶμεν, λαμβάνομεν παρ' αὐτοῦ—the answer to prayer, of which the child of God (according to John xv. 7, etc.) may be fully assured. It is obvious, however, that here the child of God is supposed to pray *as such*—that is, "in the name of Jesus." And this includes everything: he asks in the spirit of Jesus, according to the pattern of our Lord's Prayer, in which there is one petition for daily bread, and all the rest supplicate heavenly blessings,—none being put up for earthly honour, or things too high for us; moreover, he asks in humility like that of which Jesus gave us an example in Gethsemane, in supplication far removed from the carnal presumption which would intrude into the secrets of the Divine government, and dictate what only the providence of the Almighty and All-wise can determine for the world's good and the good of each. But within these limits there is boundless room for the exercise of confidence in prayer; within these limits, even particular requests are permissible, and special petitions are granted, as the experience of every devout Christian can confirm by many examples.

The clause ὅτι τὰς ἐντολὰς αὐτοῦ τηροῦμεν, καὶ τὰ ἀρεστὰ

---

[1] As it regards the reading, the first ἡμῶν is wanting in A., the second is wanting in C., and in B. both are wanting. Probably both are genuine —the one or the other having been omitted simply for the sake of the sound.

ἐνώπιον αὐτοῦ ποιοῦμεν, does not give the reason *why* God *can* hear our prayers, for then it must have been said, ὅτι τὰ αὐτῷ ἀρεστὰ αἰτοῦμεν); nor does it belong only to the second clause, καὶ ὃ ἐὰν, κ.τ.λ., as if it specified the reason why God may grant our petitions (on account of our obedience); but it belongs to the whole sentence. We must not translate the ὅτι by "because," but rather by "for." We have confidence, and find hearing for our prayers; for we keep His commandments, and thereby approve ourselves to be His children. That this mediating thought must be supplied, and that our prayers must not be interpreted as *causa meritoria*, has been observed by most expositors. This is rendered indubitable by the previous chain of thought (comp. vers. 9, 14, 19); and the words in question are nothing but a recapitulation of that which had been more freely expanded above.[1] In fact, what had been expressed by "if our heart condemn us not" is now resolved into positive elements by the clause with ὅτι; and, indeed, in such a way as to refer the thought not to brotherly-love alone, but to the more general scope of the seventh verse. The antithesis of the ποιεῖν τὴν ἀνομίαν, ver. 4, and the ποιεῖν τὴν δικαιοσύνην, ver. 7, consists in the keeping of the *commandments* of God, and *consequently* in the doing what is in accordance with the Divine will and well-pleasing to the Divine Being.

VERS. 23, 24. But from this most general statement and view St John once more returns—again recapitulating—back to the specific mention of the ἀγάπη. But he inserts here an intermediate thought which had not occurred in the Third Part. "And this is His commandment, that we believe in the name of His Son Jesus Christ, and love one another." First and foremost, St John sums up the multitude of the ἐντολαί in the unity of the one ἐντολή. Of the legalist character stamped upon the Romish theology and Church he knows nothing. Even the "believing in Christ" and "loving one another" are not to him two commandments, but only one; because, where there is genuine and living faith there must be also love, as certainly as with the sun there must be light. God does not give us a

[1] It is obviously erroneous to separate, as the Romish expositors do, the ἀρεστὰ ποιεῖν from the τηρεῖν τὰς ἐντολάς, understanding the former of the *consilia evangelica*.

multitude of injunctions; but this one thing is His will, that we believe in Christ, and *consequently* love one another. It is by express design that St John here comprehends all piety in faith; that no man may pervert or misunderstand what he had said in ch. iii. But, at the same time, this mention of πίστις gives expression to a thought which paves the way for the next division of the Epistle. For he has it in view to return back once more to the contrast between the faith in Christ and the Gnostic false doctrine. Here he writes πιστεύειν τῷ ὀνόματι; elsewhere (ch. v. 13; John i. 12, ii. 23, iii. 18) εἰς τὸ ὄνομα. Düsterdieck thinks that the εἰς specifies the name of Jesus simply as the *object* of the faith, while the Dative case specifies the Person Himself with whom faith brings us into relation. But the converse is nearer the truth. Πιστεύειν εἴς τι means to repose confidence in anything; πιστεύειν τινί, to repose faith in an assurance. Hence, the construction with the Dative gives prominence rather to the *theoretical* aspect, the construction with εἰς rather to the experimental aspect, of faith.

The 24th verse is so entirely a recapitulation, that it needs no further explanation. Once more St John lays down the proposition: *he that keepeth His commandments, dwelleth in God and God in him* (comp. ch. ii. 24, John xv. 4, etc.); once more he adds the more definite intimation, *that the keeping of the commandments is not the efficient cause, but the mark of the μένειν of God in us.* Only the concluding words, ἐκ τοῦ πνεύματος οὗ ἡμῖν ἔδωκεν, are new. As it respects their grammatical arrangement and position, they form a free apposition to that which is contained in ἐν τούτῳ, so that we have to supply in thought γινώσκομεν again; but ἐν τούτῳ refers back. "By this (the keeping of the commandments) we know that He abideth in us—by the Spirit (we know it) whom[1] He hath given us." (To refer ἐν τούτῳ forward to ἐκ τοῦ πνεύματος is incompatible with the distinction between ἐν and ἐκ.) The Spirit given us by God is not specified as a second mark, simply distinguished from the keeping of the commandments (that would have required καὶ ἐκ τοῦ πνεύματος); but it is that one and the selfsame mark, which is here viewed and exhibited under another aspect. Moreover, it is self-evident, since a

---

[1] Οὗ stands here by attraction, and is not the *genitivus partitivus*.

mark is the matter in question, that the πνεῦμα here is not the power within which works obedience, but that it is regarded as a spirit manifesting its influence before men in an external holy life. This is made perfectly plain by reference to ch. iv. 1. St John shows throughout the whole of the next section how the true and genuine πνεῦμα, opposed to the false πνεῦμα of gnosis, is internally one with obedience and love (and, therefore, how dogmatic lie and moral error are closely connected). He prepares the way for this course of thought, when he places the possession of the true πνεῦμα in such direct apposition with the keeping of the ἐντολαί.—And this gives these concluding words the character, as it were, of an announcement of a new theme. The mention of πίστις in ver. 23 had paved the way for the chain of thought now commenced; and here, in the concluding words of ver. 4, St John makes a formal transition to it. And thus this verse contains (by means of the appositional juxtaposition of the πνεῦμα and the τηρεῖν τὰς ἐντολάς) the germ of the subjects unfolded in Part the Fourth; just as ch. ii. 29 had contained the germ of that of the Third.

PART THE FOURTH.

THE SPIRIT FROM GOD IS A SPIRIT OF TRUTH AND OF LOVE.

Ch. iv. 1–ch. v. 3.

WHEN we glance over the fourth chapter as a whole, we are involuntarily reminded of the two concluding verses of the third chapter. The Apostle has mentioned two kinds of God's commandment, by the fulfilment of which we may attain to know whether we dwell in God, and God in us: 1, that we *believe in the name of Jesus;* and, 2, that we *love one another.* Both these he then sums up, ver. 24, under the idea of the *Spirit of God.*

With this "*Spirit from God*" he begins at once the fourth chapter; that is, with the injunction to test the spirits, and to distinguish the Spirit of God from the spirit of πλανή. Now the first mark which he sets forth (vers. 2–6) is of a *dogmatic* nature; it is the confession that Jesus is come in the flesh. But then, in ver. 7, he springs as it were without any mediating thought to the exhortation, "Let us love one another," as being the second sign that we are of God. *These are manifestly the two marks which were mentioned in ch.* iii. 23, *and which here are further developed.* The second is unfolded in vers. 7–12. And then, in ver. 13, there is a recapitulation: "Hereby we know that we dwell in Him, and He in us, that is, by the *Spirit* which He hath given to us." Thus here also both sides are viewed together, and embraced under the one uniting idea of the *Spirit of God.*

But these are not to be externally distributed simply under one common head. St John will show the unity of the nature of the "Spirit from God," and demonstrate how those two aspects of it—sound faith and living love—are organically united in that one common nature, and in this sense one with each other. This has been already prepared for by the manner in which he had spoken, vers. 2–6 and vers. 7–12, of both elements; and now in vers. 14–16 the subject finds its full and express statement. In vers. 2–6, the coming of Jesus Christ into the flesh was exhibited as the object of true faith, in opposition to the πλανή of the Gnostics. In vers. 7–12 (specially vers. 9, 10), the same coming of Jesus Christ into the flesh, as the act of Divine love which precedes our love, was exhibited as the ground and root of all our love. And therefore St John can now, vers. 14–16, define the one and undivided nature of the "Spirit from God" as *faith in that love of God* which was manifested in the *sending of His only-begotten Son*, and from which it follows of itself *that we, in order to abide in God, must abide in love*.

These three explanatory groups of thoughts are now followed by a further and more hortatory expansion. It is now shown that, and in what manner, the presence of the Spirit of God may be known by these fundamental marks. Love is not simply an external mark of sonship; but *it is itself made perfect in confidence towards God*, since it has its root in the love *of God to us* (vers. 17–19):—thus it is itself παρρησία in its own nature. To this is attached the reflection, that he who hateth his brother, loveth not God. The same love which was, in its essence, a confidence in the previous love of God to us, assumes, by an internal necessity, the form of love to the brethren. Consequently, vers. 17–19 is parallel with the dogmatic view of the subject, vers. 2–6; but vers. 20, 21, with the ethical, vers. 7–12. And thus in ch. iv. 20–v. 2, the two sides—the faith that Jesus is the Christ, and the love to the brethren—are exhibited in *their mutual* inseparable dependence and connection; so that these two elements, faith and love, are shown to be, not only each in itself an evidence of the Spirit of God, but also mutually each as a mark of the other (ch. iv. 20, and v. 2). In ch. v. 3 a reflection is appended to this, which forms the transition to the final main section (concerning the world-overcoming power of faith).

This analysis of the scope of the section so entirely justifies itself (as seen by its reference to ch. iii. 23, and by the recurring collocation of the two leading topics in ch. iv. 13 and ch. v. 1), and it is so clear that the idea of the πνεῦμα ἐκ Θεοῦ (to which ch. iii. 24 formed the transition, which has its climax in ch. iv. 1, and recurs in ver. 13 as the uniting foundation of the two elements) is the *predominant idea* of this section, that it seems needless to refute the view of those who refer ch. iv. 1–6 to the preceding section, or of those who find here no organization at all, and refer back ch. iv. 1 to ch. ii. 29.

In VER. 1 the fundamental position of the section is laid down in the form of an injunction: " *Try the various spirits, whether they be of God.*" The exhibition of the marks by which the "Spirit from God" may be known—the dogmatic confession of the coming of Jesus into the flesh, and brotherly-love—forms the subject of the whole section.

On the address ἀγαπητοί, which serves to mark either a main or a subordinate section (here the former), compare above on ch. ii. 7, iii. 2 and 21.—Μὴ παντὶ πνεύματι πιστεύετε. Here there is presupposed a multiplicity of spirits: not merely a duality (the Spirit of God and the spirit of the lie), but many various spirits under each of the two heads. This is abundantly clear from the following words: " *Try the spirits,* whether they be of God;" which assumes that they may be demonstrated by the test to be spirits in their plurality coming from God. And so it is exhibited in ver. 2, " Every spirit that confesseth, etc.;" where again a plurality of spirits is referred to, each of which confesses Jesus. Hence, many expositors (Lyra, Calvin, Beza, Piscator, and others) have agreed that we must understand by πνεῦμα simply, and without qualification, the spirits of individual persons, that is, their personalities: the sense would then be—Prove the individual persons, the several teachers, who bring with them or represent any particular spirit. But we do not find in Holy Scripture πνεύματα used for the designation of men *qua* spiritual natures; nor could such a metonomy as would make " spirits" stand for the " bearers, or representatives, or instruments of a definite spirit," be justified. Others, on the contrary (à Lapide, Zwingli, Carpzov, Episcopius), take πνεύματα conversely, in its purely objective meaning, for *doctrinæ, dogmata*—which, however, is an equally indefensible interpretation of the phraseology. Düsterdieck, however, is not right when he reduces the Biblical idea of the πνεῦμα to the philosophical idea of "the superhuman *principle* which possesses the man;"[1] not right, even if he had spoken of a superhuman power or inspiration, instead of a superhuman principle. For this would be, among the children of the truth, no other than the power of God, that is, the Holy Spirit Himself; but this would be inconsistent with the representation of a *multiplicity* of the πνεύματα. Therefore, we must agree with Huther, so far as he does not understand by the πνεῦμα here any spirit higher than and distinguished from the human spirit. But he, on the other hand, is wrong when he takes the πνεῦμα to mean the human spirit itself *qua* the *organ* of a higher spirit. Bullinger discerned the true meaning (essentially, at least, though he wavers in the exhibition of it) when, appealing to 1 Cor. xiv. 32, he explained πνεῦμα as the *mens* and the *sensus* which came into existence or took effect through the influence and operation of a higher (Divine or ungodly) power in men.[2] It is not the *function* of the spirit, or the subjective spirit of man, as it stands in the relation of a receptive organ to higher influences, which is here spoken of; but the objective stamp or characteristic of spirit which obtains in man, the objective spirit which rules in him and assumes the character towards other men of a *power of doctrine*: spoken of, however, in such a way that every such spirit in the objective sense appears as produced and inspired by a higher Spirit; which, indeed, is plain from the very expression, ψευδοπροφῆται, as also from ver. 2. (To make this clear by examples: The spirits to be tested by us would not be the spirit of the individual Gaius, or that of the individual Titus, and so forth; but the spirits of Gnosticism, the spirit of Cerinthianism, of Valentinianism, and, on the other hand, the spirit of Paulinism, that of Petrinism, or, in later ages, the spirit of Augustinianism and Pelagianism, of Protestantism and Popery, of Pietism and Rationalism, and so forth.)

[1] Similarly Olshausen: "Here it is a pretended higher spirit which is spoken of, the representative of which gives himself out as a prophet."
[2] So, essentially, also Grotius: "Spiritum vocat prophetiam. Prophetia ejus, qui in ipsâ prophetiâ Jesum non pro Christo agnoscit, non est θεοπνευστός."

"Believe not every spirit:" that is, Believe not every formal exhibition of a higher spiritual influence and working, as soon as it appears before you in a compact and authoritative form, holding men by its power; "but prove the spirits, whether they be of God." Wherein the δοκιμάζειν consists (comp. 1 Thess. v. 21), how and by what tests, and in what respects, they are to be tried, will be unfolded in the following verses. But the reason *why* a δοκιμάζειν is necessary, lies in the fact that "many false prophets have gone out into the world." Ἐξέρχεσθαι εἰς τὸν κόσμον does not mean that they go forth from a place without or beyond the world,[1] and enter into the world; for, it is not evil spirits which are spoken of here, but human individuals, the false prophets themselves. We must simply connect with the going forth the additional phrase, "from their abodes." They went out in the absolute sense: they set forth to go up and down, *in publicum prodierunt;* and thus they went εἰς τὸν κόσμον,—which is not used here in opposition to heaven or hell, nor indeed in opposition to the kingdom of God, but simply denotes the world inhabited by men, the mass of mankind (not excluding the children of God, since they must be on their guard against the seduction of the false prophets).

When the Apostle thus urges his injunction to δοκιμάζειν upon *all* the "beloved," he takes away the very ground from under the Romish assumption, that the Papal See alone can finally decide what is true and what is heretical doctrine. The very πνεῦμα itself of that See must be solemnly tried by every Christian.

Vers. 2, 3. St John indicates how the (first) sign by which the Spirit from God may be known. Ἐν τούτῳ points forward, as is self-evident, to what is coming. Γινώσκετε is the best-authenticated reading; that of γινώσκεται (Minusc., Syr., Vulg.) has arisen from inadvertence. Τὸ πνεῦμα τοῦ Θεοῦ stands in the singular and with the definite article: it is not, therefore, one and the same with πᾶν πνεῦμα ὃ ὁμολογεῖ; it does not mark out the spirit of any one particular tendency or doctrine (well-pleasing to God), existing in some men, and through them exerting its influence upon others;—but that

---

[1] So Olshausen: "They go forth as sent apostles from the father of lies."

personal Spirit of God who approves Himself present in all the collective πνεύμασι ἃ ὁμολογεῖ, κ.τ.λ.—the *Holy Spirit*. The meaning is this : " Hereby ye know in which among the πνεύμασι, mentioned in ver. 1, the Spirit of God works; that is, which among these spirits are spirits (spirits from the Spirit of God) from God." Every spirit *that confesseth Jesus Christ as having come in the flesh*, is from God. Ἐν σαρκί cannot (as Piscator affirms) be simply and of itself equivalent to εἰς σάρκα. The Hebrew בְּ and לְ are rigorously distinguished; and therefore the author was not led, by involuntarily thinking in Hebrew, to the substitution of ἐν for εἰς. The assumption of a prolepsis—the resulting εἶναι ἐν being already conceived in connection with the ἔρχεσθαι εἰς—the sense of which would be the same as if it had been said, εἰς σάρκα ἐληλυθότα, is not at all more tolerable. It is true that verbs of rest occur with εἰς (as, for example, Mark ii. 1, Acts viii. 40, John i. 18, where the verb of rest, " be," involves the idea of movement effected, " having gone"); and, conversely, verbs which express movement are connected with ἐν, in as far as the verb of motion involves the result of the motion (as in Matt. x. 16; John iii. 35, v. 4; Rom. v. 5). But we cannot assume this in the case of such dogmatically-important distinctions of idea as that between ἔρχεσθαι εἰς σάρκα and ἔρχεσθαι ἐν σαρκί, more especially as St John elsewhere (for example, ch. v. 6) connects with the ἔρχεσθαι an altogether specific notion; and, generally, such a solution would be allowable only if the literal interpretation of the words afforded no appropriate sense. But the literal interpretation here gives a much more appropriate sense than the other. (So Olshausen.) The Cerinthic gnosis did not deny absolutely and simply that the Æon Christ had come " into the flesh ;" he was thought to have entered into the man Jesus at his baptism, and to have remained with him until the commencement of his sufferings;—but Cerinthus denied that Jesus Christ came *in the flesh*. When we take ἐν σαρκί literally, it does not denote the *terminus ad quem* of the coming, but the quality and condition of the state of Jesus as He came into the world; the ἐληλυθώς stands as an absolute idea, and bears the meaning, " having come into the world, and unto men." (The Perfect of itself shows that we cannot, with Socinus, interpret the ἔρχεσθαι in the sense of coming forward as a teacher, as in ver. 1, 2 John 10, etc.) Thus St John rigorously opposes to the Cerinthian doctrine—that Jesus was a mere man, dwelling upon earth; that Christ had entered into this man, but not as having come in the flesh to the earth—the truth that the Person, *Jesus Christ* (one and undivided), had *come*, and that in the flesh—ἐν σαρκί, being found and being manifested in the condition of σάρξ. Σάρξ naturally does not signify here, as in John i. 14, sinful human nature in its opposition to God, but it is used in that more primitive sense according to which בשׂר or בשׂר ודם denotes material, visible nature, in its *distinction* from God, and especially *human* nature as such (Gen. vii. 15 seq., viii. 17; Ps. lvi. 5; Jer. xvii. 5; 1 Tim. iii. 16; comp. Ps. lxv. 3, cxlv. 21; Isa. lxvi. 24; Joel ii. 28; Luke iii. 6; also Matt. xvi. 17; Gal. i. 16). The words therefore contain a twofold antithesis to the Cerinthian gnosis: first, that Jesus Christ is exhibited as one and the same person; and secondly, that He is acknowledged to have come " in the flesh," that is, in the form of existence of humanity upon earth. But, as it respects the construction, the words ὁμολογεῖ Ἰησοῦν Χριστὸν ἐν σαρκὶ ἐληλυθότα have not a force equivalent to ὁμολογεῖ, Ἰησοῦν Χριστὸν ἐν σαρκὶ ἐληλυθέναι; nevertheless, those expositors are in error who say that ἐληλυθότα is not of the nature of a predicate, but simply attributive in its character. " To confess Christ manifested in the flesh," would require in Greek, ὁμολογεῖν Ἰησοῦν Χριστὸν τὸν ἐν σαρκὶ ἐληλυθότα; as the words stand, they signify, " to confess Jesus Christ as one who was manifested in the flesh:" ἐληλυθότα without the article is not a mere attributive, but an apposition; and this apposition, referred to ὁμολογεῖ, involves the predicative idea. (So in 1 Cor. i. 23; 2 Cor. iv. 5). Hence, again, those are right who make Ἰησοῦν Χριστόν one and inseparable as the objective idea, not suffering Χριστόν to be an attribute, or in apposition. We must not translate, " He that confesseth Jesus, the Christ, come in the flesh;" but, " He that confesseth Jesus Christ as One come in the flesh." There is an antithesis to the Cerinthian rending asunder of Jesus and Christ in the whole clause; but the simple point of it is, that St John so strictly and unconditionally makes Ἰησοῦν Χριστόν *one* name.

In ver. 3 follows the negative member. Καὶ πᾶν πνεῦμα ὃ μὴ ὁμολογεῖ τὸν Ἰησοῦν, ἐκ τοῦ Θεοῦ οὐκ ἐστιν: thus read A.

and B.; Codex H. adds to the ’Ιησοῦν the words ἐν σαρκὶ ἐληλυθότα; later authorities further add Χριστόν; but it is clear (Griesbach, Lücke) that these variations owe their origin to an anxiety to conform ver. 3 to ver. 2. In ch. iii. 6 and 14, and ch. ii. 23, St John had, in an analogous way, repeated the idea to be repeated in a compressed form; and had taken for granted, just as here, that the readers would be able to explain the abbreviated form by the previous more expanded form. Never, on the contrary, does an instance occur in which St John, in the construction of these parallel members, had set literally or "symmetrically" the negative over against the positive. (Compare, on the contrary, ch. i. 6 and 7, 7 and 8, ii. 4 and 5; also below, ch. iv. 7, 8.) Another reading, πᾶν πνεῦμα ὃ λύει τὸν ’Ιησοῦν ἀπὸ Θεοῦ οὐκ ἐστιν, has certainly neither external authentication (since it occurs only in the Vulgate, and the Fathers of the fourth century; but is not found in a single manuscript) nor internal, being evidently only an interpreter's scholium.

The meaning of the words is explained by what was remarked upon ver. 2. It follows now: καὶ τοῦτό ἐστι τὸ τοῦ ἀντιχρίστου, ὃ ἀκηκόατε ὅτι ἔρχεται, καὶ νῦν ἐν τῷ κόσμῳ ἐστὶν ἤδη. Τοῦτο, scil. τὸ πνεῦμα. This τοῦτο naturally points backwards to the πᾶν πνεῦμα ὃ μὴ, κ.τ.λ.; yet in such a way that St John mentions, instead of this plurality of spirits which exert their influence among men, that one spirit who demonstrates his power and energy in those many spirits. "And this spirit (working in these spirits) is that of Antichrist." Thus this τοῦτο (τὸ πνεῦμα) is parallel with the πνεῦμα τοῦ Θεοῦ, ver. 2, and forms the antithesis to it. As the direct antithesis, however, one might indeed have expected πνεῦμα τοῦ διαβόλου; and certainly no other is meant by the "spirit of Antichrist" than the spirit of the prince of darkness. But, St John describes him in the specific form which he assumes in opposition to the kingdom of Christ—as the spirit of opposition to Christ, Antichrist. But, it is the *spirit*, not the *person*, of Antichrist that is spoken of. Concerning the *spirit* of Antichrist, which, independently of the person of Antichrist to be expected in the future, and before his manifestation, urges his work and career, St John says that his readers have heard from himself, that he would come into the world in the future, but was also already in the world.[1] This is made very plain by a comparison of all the other New-Testament prophecies concerning Antichrist. One day, in the future, that spirit was to come in concentrated form, exhibited emphatically in the *person of Antichrist;* but now already it is present, and manifests itself in the antichristian nature, demonstrating his energy in a multiplicity of πνεύματα. Thus our passage serves perfectly to confirm what was said upon ch. ii. 18.

Let us now once more glance over the general meaning of vers. 2 and 3. St John has primarily to do with the false teachers of *his* time: in opposition *to them*, he lays down the criterion of ver. 2, in the form of *this* specific formula of confession. Hence they do wrong who, on the one hand with a latitudinarian bias, declare all dogmatic errors to be unimportant which do not absolutely deny that Jesus Christ came in the flesh; as they do also, on the other, who take great pains to reduce all possible errors of another kind into the denial of the great point contained in ver. 2. True it is that the doctrines of the Christian faith are one organic whole; it may, indeed, be demonstrated that all those things, which in other passages of Scripture are stamped as errors in doctrine, do directly or indirectly offend against one or other of the points contained in the words ᾿Ιησοῦν Χριστὸν ἐν σαρκὶ ἐληλυθότα; yea, it may be admitted that St John here lays down the central-point or the foundation of all Christian faith, and so expresses it that "the testimony he bears, or the confession he requires, is broad enough to embrace all those who have in truth apprehended Christ by faith, and at the same time narrow enough to exclude all those who make any other than Christ the source of their life" (Düsterdieck). But, we must, on the other hand, admit that *this* mark, in the formula expressed in ver. 2, is *not* enough, and is not intended for the testing of all possible historically-manifested doctrine and false doctrine. For, it would be simply to open the door for all the most fearful abuses, if all imaginable controversies were to be brought to the decision of this passage of Scripture. Hence the Romish theologian Estius is quite right when he deems this present passage insufficient

---

[1] Grammatically, καὶ νῦν ἐστίν does not depend upon ἀκηκόατε ὅτι, but only upon ὅ. "Of whom ye have heard that he is in the future; and who is already in the world."

for the decision of all the various points of dogmatic controversy (though wrong in substituting the Pope, and the dogma of the Mass; instead of the word of God). God has given us not only the passage 1 John iv. 2, 3, but also His *entire* word of revelation; and by it and in it, the *entire* word of God, we must learn and test what is dogmatic truth, and what is error of doctrine. When, on the other hand, the question is not that of the definitive settlement of controversial points, but of the distinguishing between the Spirit of God and the spirit of Antichrist, our passage is for all ages the right criterion; and, the more plainly the Spirit of antichristianity and the antichristian kingdom unfolds itself in the world, the more manifestly does it exhibit itself as a spirit which denies the incarnation of the Son of God. For our own time, the passage teaches us that the spirits of those systems which exhibit as a redeemer, either a mere man Jesus who is not Christ and the Son of God, or a Christ-idea without any historical Christ, bear on themselves the essential signature of *anti*-Christianity, of open apostasy and unbelief.

VERS. 4–6. After St John had laid down a first criterion by which the spirits which are of God are to be distinguished from the antichristian spirits, he declares concerning his readers —not only his " affectionate supposition " (Düsterdieck)—but his full assurance of the fact, that *they* possessed the spirit which was of God. After he had specified *by what* and in what respects the spirits should be tried, he adds *that* his readers *are* in a condition to sustain this test, and to discern and overcome the spirit of Antichrist. For, only he who bears in himself the $\pi\nu\epsilon\hat{u}\mu\alpha$ $\Theta\epsilon o\hat{u}$, and therefore " is of God " (born of God), is able to test the two kinds of spirits, and know them, and distinguish them. The absolute " freedom from prepossession," or " impartiality," which should take its stand apart from and independent of the spirits both good and evil, and so be in a condition to test both,—is utterly unknown to the Apostle. There is no such position of neutrality and absolute indifference; no third position between the Christian and the not-Christian state of mind. " Ye are of God," $\dot{\epsilon}\kappa$ $\Theta\epsilon o\hat{u}$, is in itself a very comprehensive expression, which includes in itself the " having fellowship with God" (ch. i. 3 and 6), as well as the " having the love of God in him" (ch. ii. 15), and preeminently the being "a child of God," or "being born of God" (ch. iii. 1 and 9); but *here* it points back primarily to ver. 2, and is to be explained by the "having the Spirit which is of God,"—which however, in its essence, is obviously coincident with the "being born of God."—On τεκνία, *little children,* compare what was said ch. ii. 1, 12, 14, 18, 28, and ch. iii. 18.—" And have overcome them:" these words have been understood in two ways. As it regards the αὐτούς, indeed—that it does not refer to the *person of Antichrist* (Erasmus), but only to those *contemporary men* in whom the "spirit of Antichrist" already manifested itself in pseudo-prophetic "spirits," therefore to the "false prophets" of ver. 1 —is not open to much question, since ver. 5 sheds so clear a light upon it. On the other hand, the Perfect νενικήκατε has always divided the commentators. According to Bullinger and Calvin, St John's purpose is to invigorate his readers to the conflict by pointing to the fact that the victory, although not really gained, is nevertheless *ideally certain.* In harmony with this, Episcopius says that "the Perfect is used *propter futuritionis certitudinem;*" Neander, that "the victory of Christian truth, which will be seen in its actual process in time, is already taken for granted as already accomplished: Faith hastens on to the end of the great course of events;" Düsterdieck, that "in the midst of the hot conflict, the children of God know that the victory is already won." So also Lange, Rosenmüller, and many others, appealing to the Lord's declaration, John xvi. 33. —Others, on the contrary, as Zwingli, Grotius, Beausobre, and Huther, take the Perfect in an absolute and real sense: "St John might say ' *Ye have overcome* ' to his readers, not only as far as His power was mighty in them who had said, 'Be of good courage, I have overcome the world,' but also inasmuch as their opponents, with all their seductive arts, had already been put to shame by the Christians' fidelity, and had been obliged to yield" (Huther). This latter view we regard as most decisively correct. For, in ch. ii. 13, 14 this had been declared as a simple fact, concerning the young men, that they *had* overcome the wicked one; while in ver. 18 seq. the little children (of a coming generation) are armed for a *future* conflict. But it is there said also, in ver. 19, that "they went out from us;" by which we mark that a first stage of the conflict was already closed and completed in the past : *the church as a whole had withstood the Gnostics, and these had found themselves obliged to depart and constitute themselves a particular sect.* In ch. iv. 2, 3, the Apostle exhorts his people for the future also to prove the spirits (this is generally parallel with the exhortation of ch. ii. 18 seq.) ; but this very exhortation he grounds upon *what had been already accomplished* (vers. 4–6). His readers have ability for the application of that test, in the fact that they " are of God," and as such have maintained their place above the "false prophets " in a victory already achieved.

Wherein the power for this already-achieved victory, as of all other analogous victories, lies, is declared by the words ὅτι μείζων ἐστὶ ὁ ἐν ὑμῖν ἢ ὁ ἐν τῷ κόσμῳ. Ὁ ἐν ὑμῖν is ὁ Θεός (not ὁ Χριστός, as Augustin and Grotius explain : comp. ἐκ τοῦ Θεοῦ ἐστε, and in vers. 2 and 3 the contrasted τὸ πνεῦμα τοῦ Θεοῦ and τὸ τοῦ ἀντιχρίστου). Ὁ ἐν τῷ κόσμῳ is the prince of this world ; he from whom the πνεῦμα τοῦ ἀντιχρίστου proceeds. Thus, as St John in ch. ii. had gone forwards from the notion of the not-Christian and unchristian *world* (ch. ii. 15–17) to the notion of the specifically *anti*-Christian nature (ver. 18 seq.), so here, conversely, he goes backwards from the specific πνεῦμα τοῦ ἀντιχρίστου (iv. 3) to the more general notion of the κόσμος. In both cases there is the same fundamental fact at bottom, that the nature of the *un*-Christian " world " advances into *anti*-Christianity ; and, consequently, that the worldly mind and opposition to Christianity are most internally related to each other. Only he who overcomes the worldly mind can withstand the antichristian spirit (ch. ii. 15 seq.) ; only he who inwardly belongs to the world is in danger of being blended and taken captive by the pseudo-prophecy of antichristianity (ch. iv. 5); he who has God dwelling in himself is essentially above it (ch. iv. 4, " because," etc.).

Ver. 5 has received its explanation in what has just been said. Those pseudo-prophets are ἐκ τοῦ κόσμου, that is, children of the world, born of the world, and filled with *its* πνεῦμα ; what they bear in themselves is derived from the sinful, unregenerate world, unaffected by Christ. They are unregenerated in their inmost nature : although they give themselves out to be Christians, yea, that they are the Christians who have first penetrated into the true γνῶσις, still they are in truth only " of the world." (So in the present day the false prophets, who rend asunder the historical Jesus and the Christ, lay claim to the Christian name; but in the present day also holds good the apostolical verdict, ἐκ τοῦ κόσμου εἰσίν.) And therefore they speak ἐκ τοῦ κόσμου, they speak from out of the worldly nature; they speak not the word concerning repentance which judges and condemns, and brings sin to the light, but their doctrine is conversely framed so as to cloke sin, and to excuse it as not being from the will, but as an unavoidable consequence of matter, or as a necessary element in the development of the absolute spirit, or whatever other form these subtle evasions may assume. The essence of their teaching is always, instead of penitence, carelessness; instead of humility, pride; instead of love, ἐπιθυμία τῶν ὀφθαλμῶν; instead of renunciation of the world, ἀλαζονεία τοῦ βίου; instead of the crucifixion of the flesh, ἐπιθυμία τῆς σαρκός. And therefore, because the essence of their teaching is, in spite of all its Christian masks, so entirely and throughout "of the world," therefore "*the world heareth them:*" the world swallows these theories of wisdom as sweet morsels, and rejoices in being able to retain its worldly nature while it is secure at the same time of the double honour, first of the Christian name, and then of the highest Christian γνῶσις over and above. But, indeed, it is only the world which can be deceived by such fanatics.

Ver. 6. "We are of God: he that knoweth God heareth us; he that is not of God heareth not us." The meaning of the words is perfectly plain, after what has gone before. St John writes, ἡμεῖς ἐκ τοῦ Θεοῦ ἐσμέν, unconcerned about the probability that the ψευδοπροφῆται, with their dependents, may charge him on account of it with spiritual pride, as arrogating to himself alone the entire of true Christianity. There is a genuine spirit of opposition, in which the Christian not only has the right, but is under an obligation, to cry with the utmost decision, "*We* are of God, and *ye* are *not* of God."—Ἡμεῖς does not indicate, like the ὑμεῖς of ver. 4, the churches (Lücke), but the Apostle and teachers likeminded with himself (à Lapide, Calvin, etc.); for in the words ἀκούει ἡμῶν the "we" of the "speakers" is presupposed. But we must not connect this at once with an exclusive order of teachers, which did not yet exist; but all are meant who individually were called by position and opportunity to bear witness of their faith (Calvin, Spener).—" He that is of God, heareth our doctrine; he that is not of God, heareth not us :" here all that was said in vers. 2–5 is concentrated into a practical available sign. In the place of the *dogmatic* definition of ver. 2, we have now " our doctrine"—the apostolical or Johannæan words, in opposition to the doctrine or words of Cerinthus. He who hears it and receives it, approves himself thereby as ἐκ τοῦ Θεοῦ ὤν (not, that is, according to the weakening interpretation of Lücke and Neander, " as being endowed with an internal bias, drawing the heart to God;" but, as a child of God, as born of God, partaker of God's Spirit); he who rejects it, approves himself as μὴ ἐκ τοῦ Θεοῦ ὤν. And thus St John closes the section: By this, ἐν τούτῳ, we know the spirit of truth and the spirit of error." Ἐν τούτῳ refers back to the preceding words of our sixth verse (à Lapide, Calvin), and not to ver. 2 (Bengel, Lücke), which would rob the chain of thought of its appropriate climax and point. For that point lies in this, that the mark by which we may know (γινώσκομεν is to be referred generally to St John and his readers) who is of God and who is of the world, is exhibited as being the receiving of the doctrine laid down by St John and his disciples and his adherents.

The predestinarian question which Calvin and Düsterdieck force upon our text has really nothing to do with it. The distinction between " being of God " and " not being of God" is not a distinction of cause, but of result. Who co-operates to the end that a man becomes one ἐκ τοῦ Θεοῦ ὤν, or who is in fault that a man remains one μὴ ἐκ τοῦ Θεοῦ ὤν,—is not in the most distant way the subject; it only and merely lays down the acceptance or rejection of the apostolical doctrine concerning the incarnation of Jesus as *a mark* by which it may be known whether a man is—in the then disposition of his heart—a regenerate child of God or a child of the world.

But with this the Apostle has passed over from the testing of the πνεύματα, mentioned in ver. 1, to another and more general testing, to wit, the proving of the *state of heart of every individual*. Both tests are internally one, since for both the same criterion is applied. In ver. 1 the question is that of proving the spirits which come forward in doctrinal systems, and thus knowing whether they be of God; in ver. 6 the question is that of testing *persons*, whether they be children of God or children of the world. But that the two are not independent of each other is shown in vers. 4, 5. Only he who internally, in the posture of his heart, belongs to the world, *can* suffer himself to be taken captive by the spirits of antichristianity; he who is regenerate, rises superior to the temptation.—Consequently, the Spirit of God appears, from ver. 6 onwards, under another and new aspect of His self-demonstration. How the Spirit of God might be known, as ruling in *doctrinal systems* and tendencies, was shown, vers. 2, 3; ver. 6 speaks of the way in which He may be known as ruling in the *individuals*.

But here that first mark—the acceptance of the true doctrine, which evidences the $\pi\nu\epsilon\hat{\upsilon}\mu\alpha\ \tau\hat{\eta}s\ \dot{\alpha}\lambda\eta\theta\epsilon\acute{\iota}as$—is followed by a *second mark*. And of this the Apostle treats in the subsequent verses.

VERS. 7–12. He places this second mark at once, and without any medium of transition, by the side of the first,—indeed, in so unconnected a manner, that he seems as it were abruptly to pass at once, with a new address, "Beloved," to the requirement, "Let us love one another;" after that appending, in the words "for love is of God, and every one that loveth is born of God," the reflection that this *love* also is a *mark* of the $\epsilon\hat{\iota}\nu\alpha\iota\ \dot{\epsilon}\kappa\ \tau o\hat{\upsilon}\ \Theta\epsilon o\hat{\upsilon}$. But even in this is seen the internal unity of thought which pervades the two groups, vers. 1–6 and vers. 7–12. The idea of the marks by which the $\pi\nu\epsilon\hat{\upsilon}\mu\alpha\ \Theta\epsilon o\hat{\upsilon}$ may be known lies at the foundation of both; and in vers. 13–16 both marks are expressly combined in one, and exhibited in their *internal* connection and interchangeable character. To say, therefore (as De Wette and Neander do), that St John returns in ver. 7 "back to his earlier theme"—as if he had lost himself in a digression, from ver. 1 to ver. 6—is altogether to misunderstand as well the external construction as the internal organic connection of this entire section. De Wette finishes this unskilful exposition by declaring vers. 13, 14 afterwards to be "a short digression from the subject." Bengel and Düsterdieck see, at least approximately, the true organic connection; though the latter will have ver. 7 seq. to refer again to his imaginary "main proposition" of ch. ii. 29. It is not the general notion of the "being born of God" which rules our present section (ch. iv.);

but the specific notion of the *marks* by which the πνεῦμα Θεοῦ (to which in ver. 13 the love is as certainly referred as the true faith is in ver. 2 seq.) is to be distinguished from the spirit of darkness.

In the injunction, "Let us love *one another*," it is obvious that only the love of Christians towards each other is first of all meant; yet we see at once by the general reason given, in the great truth that God is love (ver. 8), and sent His Son εἰς τὸν κόσμον (ver. 9), that the universal love of all mankind is no more to be excluded here than it was excluded in ch. iii. 13 seq.

Love is ἐκ τοῦ Θεοῦ, and that does not mean well-pleasing to God (Grotius, Rosenmüller), nor *a Deo infusa* (Lyra); for the question is not here to be answered, whence the power to love may be gained by man: but this "*of* God" is strictly analogous, on the one hand, with "*of* God," ver. 2, and, on the other, with "*of* the world," ver. 5. Love as certainly springs from the nature *of God*, as the spirit which confesseth Jesus Christ to have appeared in the flesh springs from the nature *of God*; and as, on the other hand, the denial of the incarnation, as also hatred, and, according to ch. ii. 12, the lust of the flesh and the pride of life, spring from the nature of the κόσμος. That God's nature is ἀγάπη, and therefore that love also in us is a qualitative conduct derived from the nature of God,—*this* is the subject with which these words deal.

And on that very account the presence of love in a man is a *token* that he is born of God,—thus that he is born again. It is obvious that by ἀγάπη here is meant true, self-consecrating, self-devoting, self-sacrificing love, and not that natural pseudo-love which has its roots in the flesh, in self-seeking and subtle self-satisfaction, and which either puffs itself up with sentimentality, or strives to earn its approbation. *And knoweth God:* how the γινώσκειν τὸν Θεόν is connected with the γεννηθῆναι ἐκ τοῦ Θεοῦ, may be seen in ch. i. 5, ii. 3 (ἐγνώκαμεν αὐτόν), and the remarks upon those passages. (Düsterdieck refers incorrectly to ch. ii. 19 also, where an altogether different γινώσκειν is introduced.)

In ver. 8 follows the negative side; but here, as always, in a formal inversion (comp. the remark above on ver. 3). Instead of the Pres. οὐ γινώσκει stands the Aor. οὐκ ἔγνω (after the analogy of ch. iii. 1), because the Apostle will stamp the fact that such a man hath *not yet* known God, and still stands without the circle of the regenerate (not merely that he is not in a position to know God). And instead of the reason, "for love is of God," there follows here the more deeply penetrating, "for God is love."[1] Love is, as we have seen, therefore of God, because God's nature itself is love; and this last fundamental reason is now expressly uttered—God *is* love. But that does not mean that He is benevolent (Socinus, Grotius, Rosenmüller); nor is it said merely κατ' αὔξησιν that God is love, "sicut hominem prostitutæ impudentiæ appellamus impudentiam" (Bullinger); but (as Calvin rightly explains) it is *Dei natura* to love. This action of the loving self-communication of His nature is as essential to Him as that outbeaming of Himself in virtue of which He is called, ch. i. 5, φῶς; and in that passage we have seen how with the φῶς as well the ἀλήθεια as the ἀγάπη is internally connected. We must not, therefore, think merely of the love of God to the creature, but also of the inner-Divine Trinitarian love in God.[2]

In vers. 9, 10, the Apostle unfolds a thought which does not *merely* serve the purpose of exhortation to love, and quickening us in its exercise, but which at the same time is designed to set in a clear light the internal connection between the *second* mark, named in vers. 7, 8, of the πνεῦμα τοῦ Θεοῦ, that of love,

---

[1] That ὅτι here again introduces a *reason*, and must not merely be translated by "that," and made dependent upon ἔγνω, is evident from the parallelism with ver. 7, and from the repetition of the words ὁ Θεός.

[2] From the circumstance that Luther says, "Deus nihil est quam mera caritas," while Calvin says, "Dei natura est homines diligere," Dusterdieck takes occasion to make the remark that "the Reformed expositors, in contradistinction to the Lutheran," acknowledged no *nature* of love, but only *proofs* of love, in God, and consequently stood in the middle between the Lutherans and the Socinians. But every unbiassed reader will see that the restricted object *homines* is in Calvin accidental, and that all the emphasis lies upon the "natura," by which the act of loving is exhibiting as constituting the *nature* of God. Calvin is there defending the truth only against a false "philosophia," which *pantheistically* inferred from this passage that God's nature went forth in an obsure influence of love pervading the world, as if in these words the *essentia Divina* was defined on all sides, so that the attribute of *self-conscious will and knowledge* might be denied of God. *Against this* Calvin's words were directed, and *by this* his expressions must be understood.

and the *first* mark, named in vers. 2, 3, that of the confession of Christ's having come in the flesh. Certainly, a new exhortation to love is deduced in ver. 11 from what is said in vers. 9, 10; but for that alone the statement of ver. 9 would have been sufficient. The tenth verse goes beyond the design of giving a reason for ver. 11, and lays stress upon a point which was already contained in ver. 9,—in such a manner, too, as plainly to show that the Apostle already here purposes to prepare the way for the subsequent internal union and combination of the two marks in vers. 13–16.

Ἐν τούτῳ ἐφανερώθη ἡ ἀγάπη τοῦ Θεοῦ ἐν ἡμῖν: the first question here is, whether ἐν ἡμῖν belongs to ἐφανερώθη or to ἡ ἀγάπη. The latter is the view of Luther, Beza, Spener, Socinus, Episcopius, Grotius, Piscator, Beausobre, Bengel, Rosenmüller, Huther; this, however, is not only (in spite of the assurance of Huther) most certainly incorrect in grammar, since the article must have been repeated before ἐν ἡμῖν, but it is refuted by the simple fact that the words ἡ ἀγάπη τοῦ Θεοῦ ἐν ἡμῖν of themselves yield no clear idea. It is now generally admitted that ἐν ἡμῖν cannot stand for εἰς ἡμᾶς. Bengel explains the expression by a *prægnantia,* " amor Dei, qui nunc in nobis est;" but contradicting the context, which speaks, not of love as working in us, but of love as objectively revealed in Christ. Huther gives to ἐν ἡμῖν the signification "to us;" accordingly, ἡ ἀγάπη τοῦ Θεοῦ ἐν ἡμῖν would be the love manifesting itself in us: "it is not," he says, "the direction towards the end, but the tarrying in the end, which is made prominent, as in ver. 16." But in ver. 16 it is not the love of God, objectively manifested in the sending of Christ, which is alone spoken of, but also the μένειν of God in us; and therefore ἐν is there not *to,* but *in.* "Love of God *to* any one" is an expression which in itself cannot be used.—Hence we must refer (with Winer and others) the ἐν ἡμῖν to the verb ἐφανερώθη. But, thus connected, the ἐν ἡμῖν must be translated *to us*—a translation which now becomes *possible;* for, though we cannot speak substantively of the "love of God to any one," we may speak of God's *manifesting* His love *to* any one. Nor can we see any force in the objection of Huther, that the following clause with ὅτι introduces a difficulty. In this, that God hath sent His Son into the world, *that we might live,* His love hath been manifested

T

to us. But as this translation of ἐν by *to* is possible, so also it is *necessary;* for the signification *in* is not suitable, as the subject here is not the manifestation of the love of God in our inward nature.

Ἐν τούτῳ points forward to the words ὅτι τὸν υἱὸν αὐτοῦ, κ.τ.λ. The Apostle describes Him as the *Only-begotten,* that is, the Only (compare John i. 14 and 18, iii. 18), in order to make emphatic the greatness and the depth of the love of God, which gave up not only His own Son, but, over and above that, His *only* Son (only in number and in essence), in order to save us from death. On "sending into the world," compare John iii. 17 and 36, and xvii. 4 and 5 : the expression of itself involves the doctrine of Christ's pre-existence and divinity. "That we might live through Him :"—ζῆν is the comprehensive opposite of that θάνατος into which mankind had fallen through sin : compare ch. iii. 14 above, and our remarks. The first person points certainly to Christians, to believers; but the opposition to unbelievers is not emphasized; and the predestinarian doctrine, that Christ came into the world *finaliter* only for the elect, has no support in this passage. The stress rests only upon the "might live."

In ver. 10 St John lays the emphasis upon the truth that love consists in this—not that we have loved God, but that He loved us. First, we have to inquire, what the words mean, and how they are to be construed; then, what force they bear in this place. Ἡ ἀγάπη is spoken of here in the widest generality; and it is quite wrong and illogical to explain it here by " the love of God to us" (with Zwingli, Bullinger, Calvin, Grotius, Lücke, De Wette, and others). For the expression, " The love of God to us, consists not in our love to God, but in His love to us," would have been no better than an unmeaning truism. To what end could the Apostle have so formally stated what was so plainly self-understood ? No, he speaks quite generally of *the nature of love universally;* and expresses a thought of much importance in itself, and of much moment for what follows, viz., that all *loving* (by which, according to the context, we are to understand, as was shown upon ver. 7, only the true and perfectly unselfish loving) consists—that is, has its root— in this, not that we have loved God, but in this, that He hath loved us. *Love, according to its essence, has its source in God's love to us*, not in our love to God : that is the Apostle's thought. It is, in its nature, not a striving upward towards God which proceeds from *man*, but a flame which proceeds from God, and thereby enkindles men ; in its nature, therefore, it is divine, and flows from the essence of God. " Our love is nothing but the production and copy of the perfect love of God" (Düsterdieck) ; and, indeed, of that love which He hath manifested in the sending of His Son. The words ἐν τούτῳ ἐστίν are therefore already explained in this : "Love is therein, that, etc.," means, that " love has its essential existence (and also the source and root of its being) in this, that, etc." Οὐχ ὅτι does not stand instead of ὅτι οὐχ (Grotius, Lange) ; that would rob the passage of its sense and meaning, as if love should consist in this, that we have *not* loved God. And the antithesis, ἀλλ' ὅτι, shows of itself that οὐχ cannot belong to ἠγαπήσαμεν, but that the former ὅτι depends upon οὐχ. It is a still greater perversion to take (with v. Meyer and others) οὐχ ὅτι—τὸν Θεόν as a little clause by itself, which depends upon the ἀλλ' ὅτι, being placed first only for the sake of emphasis; in which case we should have to construe : " Herein is love, ὅτι—ὅτι οὐχ ἡμεῖς ἠγαπήσαμεν τὸν Θεόν—αὐτὸς ἠγάπησεν ἡμᾶς (that is, because, while we loved not God, He nevertheless loved us)." But what then is the meaning of the ἀλλά ? The sentence may, however, be construed without the least difficulty by supplying after οὐχ an ἐν τούτῳ, on which the first ὅτι may depend ; and, after ἀλλά, a second ἐν τούτῳ, on which the second ὅτι may depend. After the Apostle had begun to declare in what love positively consists, he breaks off, and says previously in what it does *not* consist. " Herein is love—not (in this) that we loved God, but (in this) that He loved us, and gave His Son to be the propitiation for our sins." Ἱλασμός is not " atonement," but " propitiation :" atonement, *reconciliatio*, is καταλλαγή ; while ἱλασμός is, on the other hand, *expiatio*—that by means of which it is rendered possible that God, who must manifest His ὀργή against unexpiated sin, should put an end to this ὀργή, and exhibit Himself as ἵλεως towards men. Compare the excursus above on ch. i. 9, and the remarks on ch. ii. 2.

And now it is easy to discern with what object and purpose St John has expanded and emphasized this thought in ver. 10 ;

to wit, that love, according to its essential being, has its root, not in our love to God, but in God's love to us. This serves to lay the foundation, and prepare the way, for the demonstration to be given in vers. 13–16, how the two distinguishing marks of the πνεῦμα Θεοῦ—the acknowledgment of the incarnation of Jesus Christ, and love—are internally and organically connected. Love is not something simply different from that confession, and which may be separated from it; love is, in its very nature, not something which has its root in the act, and conduct, and will of man in himself,—not something merely ethical which may be sundered from the religious element : it is rather in its nature an act of God, an outflowing of the *essence of God*, who in His nature is love (ver. 8) ; all (true) love has its root in the *love of God to us;* and this love of God to us, again, is not anything bodiless and vague, but has become incorporate, and concentrated, and manifested, in the sending of His only-begotten Son to be our propitiation. He who has not yet known and experienced this central-act of the love of God to us, has not yet known and experienced the love of God to us, and is not yet enkindled by it. And he who is not enkindled by the flame of this love of God to us, has, generally, no share in the nature of love ; for, to desire to love from *self* is a false and spurious love,—a love which has not its source in the love and act of the God of love, is not love at all. Thus has St John here already shown that true ἀγαπᾶν cannot at all exist without faith in the incarnation of Jesus Christ, and that he who denies this *can* have no share in ἀγάπη : that is, in other words, *that both those distinguishing marks do really most organically coincide; and that the latter of them, love, cannot possibly exist when the former is wanting.*

But, that the first also—faith in the love of God, as sending Jesus Christ—cannot exist without the second, he shows in vers. 11, 12 ; only that he here (conformably with the nature of the case) utters the theoretical demonstration of that in the form of an *obligation* (similarly as, in ver. 7, the introduction of the second mark had begun in the form of an *exhortation*). Hence also the affectionate address, ἀγαπητοί, is repeated; which accordingly serves not for the introduction of a new section (for ver. 11 is logically connected with ver. 9), but only of a new member of the train of thought.

Ver. 11 has the form of a logical inference. "If God hath loved us so much, we are bound to love one another." The middle-term between the premiss and the conclusion is omitted; not, however, that the reader may arbitrarily supply it, but because St John purposes to introduce it afterwards in ver. 12.

But this verse has been variously viewed. According to the opinion of Zwingli, Bullinger, à Lapide, Düsterdieck, and Huther, the words Θεὸν οὐδεὶς πώποτε τεθέαται (in which τεθέαται cannot mean the spiritual seeing or knowing, contrary to ver. 7, but only the bodily; so that only the invisibility of God is here expressed, and not that God cannot be known) occupy the place, and have the force, of a concessive clause. "*It is true* that God is invisible; but, if we love one another, He is *not the less* on that account in us." This logical relation of concession, however, would yield a good meaning only if it were easier, considered in itself, for a visible nature to dwell in us than for an invisible. Hence, we must decidedly give the preference to another view (that of Calvin and Lücke). St John will *illustrate* how, and to what extent, the love of God to us leads to our obligation of brotherly-love. God Himself in His own person is not visible to us, so that we might in act make known and demonstrate our love and gratitude to Him immediately: on that account, we have no other opportunity of demonstrating our love to Him than by exhibiting that love to those in whom God invisibly dwells; but in those He invisibly dwells, in whom His nature (and that is love) dwelleth. This then is the sentiment of our verse: *Because* (not *although*, but *because*) God is invisible, His abiding in us can be demonstrated only (not by a visible manifestation of God in us, but) by His nature (that nature which He manifested to us in the sacrifice of His Only-begotten) being exhibited in us, and our acts and dispositions—that is, by our showing forth this same self-sacrificing love. And thus is explained why (in ver. 10), from the love of God to us, the obligation follows that we should love *one another*: we can approve our return of love towards the *Invisible*, only by our manifesting (in the *visible* relation in which we stand, thus in relation to men) the reflection of that nature of God, or rather our being penetrated and pervaded by that nature. Καὶ ἡ ἀγάπη αὐτοῦ ἐν ἡμῖν τετελειωμένη ἐστίν is the reading of Cod. A., Vulg., and others; on the other hand,

Cod. B. places the words ἐν ἡμῖν before ἐστίν. The sense remains the same. The expression is to be explained as in ch. ii. 5. Ἡ ἀγάπη αὐτοῦ is not, 1, the love of God to us, onesidedly viewed. For, that love cannot *in itself* be perfected *by this means*, that we love one another; nor is it perfected under *the condition* that *we* love one another; for, according to ver. 10, the perfected love of God precedes all our love, for ever in itself imperfect, and lies at the foundation of it. Nor can, 2, the ἀγάπη αὐτοῦ be our love to God, again onesidedly viewed. For, in this case, the ἐν ἡμῖν would be superfluous, as it was in the former case unsuitable. But, 3, ἡ ἀγάπη αὐτοῦ here, as in ch. ii. 5, defines the *mutual relation of love between God and us*. (Zwingli : Est itaque certissimum *amicitiæ fœderis et conjunctionis Dei* signum dilectio et caritas Christiana mutua. Bullinger: Proinde spiritus ille caritatis utrumque conjunxit, homini Deum et Deo hominem ; caritas itaque Christiana certissimum signum est *gratiæ divinæ, amicitiæ et conjunctionis*.) And now the ἐν ἡμῖν has its own most important place. This *relation* of love between us and God is on the part of God perfected at the outset; but it will be and is perfected also in us, if we love one another. (Quite analogous with the sentiment of ch. ii. 5.)

In VERS. 13-16 the *two* marks—the confession of Jesus Christ appearing in the flesh, vers. 2, 3, and the love, ver. 7 seq.—are embraced together in their organic unity. Ἐν τούτῳ, ver. 13, does not point back—as the construction of the clauses itself shows—to what was said in vers. 11, 12, to love (in which case ver. 13 would be, moreover, a mere tautological repetition of ver. 12); but it points forward to the clause, ὅτι ἐκ τοῦ πνεύματος αὐτοῦ δέδωκεν ἡμῖν. *By this, that God hath given to us of His Spirit, we know that we abide in Him and He in us.* Here we perceive that the mark just mentioned, "if we love one another," is *substituted* by another, ὅτι ἐκ τοῦ πνεύματος, κ.τ.λ.; and it is thus indicated that the standing in love, or the exercise of reciprocal love, is a result, and consequently itself again a mark, of the πνεῦμα Θεοῦ. *And thus the second distinguishing mark, love, is declared to be as much a mark of the πνεῦμα Θεοῦ as in the first paragraph,* vers. 1-6, *the confession of the incarnation had been declared to be.* Only, as St John has thus placed the πνεῦμα Θεοῦ in connection with both marks—now with the second, as before with the first—he passes over at once, in ver. 14, to *exhibit the two marks in their relation to each other, and in their combined organic growth.* For this important point he had already, in vers. 9, 10, preparatorily laid the foundation.

In vers. 14, 15, he testifies that he had seen that the Father sent the Son as a Redeemer into the world; and repeats the statement of vers. 2, 3, that the *confession* that Jesus is the Son of God is the mark or sign of abiding in God (which, according to ver. 13, is identical with the mark of the possession of the πνεῦμα Θεοῦ). But immediately, in vers. 16, 17, he places this in internal relation to love. In this dwelling of God in those who acknowledge Christ, we have known and believed the love of God working in us; we have known that God is love, and thence it follows immediately that the abiding in love is a mark of abiding in God.

"And we," ver. 14, signifies, as the subject to "have seen and bear witness," the Apostle and his fellow-witnesses of the manifestation of Jesus Christ in the flesh. Θεᾶσθαι denotes, as in ver. 12, physical seeing; without, however, involving a designed reference back to ver. 12. On μαρτυροῦμεν compare the observations upon ch. ii. 1. The clause with ὅτι is clear: it is a condensed repetition of the thought of ver. 9. Μονογενῆ is not reproduced here; and the clause, "that we might live through Him," is summed up and included in the apposition, "the Saviour of the world." The κόσμος is mentioned as the object of the σώζειν (as in ver. 9), because the humanity which is *to be saved, to be redeemed,* is simply the *not-yet-redeemed* mankind, which still lies under the ban of sin and death; and therefore that which in the New Testament, and specifically in St John, is denoted by ὁ κόσμος. When the subject treated of is the general scope and design of the incarnation of Christ, and therefore redemption generally, the object to be redeemed must be simply exhibited as only *the unsaved world.* In other words, we cannot say with any propriety that Christ is the "Redeemer of the redeemed;" for, those who are *now* redeemed stood in need of a Redeemer as they were previously unredeemed, and therefore the κόσμος. The question, whether Christ came with the design to save all the individuals of this unredeemed world, or only a portion of them, does not in the most distant way enter into the text.

In ver. 15 the confession of vers. 2, 3 is recapitulated in a more compendious and concise form: ὅτι Ἰησοῦς ἐστιν ὁ υἱὸς τοῦ Θεοῦ. However, in this concise form the contrast and opposition to the Cerinthian gnosis comes out into more rigid expression. According to Cerinthus, neither was the man Jesus identical with the Æon Christ, nor was the Æon Christ acknowledged as the Son of God. Moreover, this briefer formula of the ὁμολογία is of great importance for our own time. We have in it an authentic interpretation of the method of formula in vers. 2, 3 : it goes, in the expression υἱὸς τοῦ Θεοῦ (which was prepared for by vers. 9 and 14), beyond the statement of vers. 2, 3; and we therefore see that those are deeply in error who, instead of interpreting vers, 2, 3 in the sense of ver. 15, first reduce the declaration of vers. 2, 3 to their own un-Johannæan meaning, and then deduce from those words the inference that it is by no means necessary to confess the Divinity of Jesus Christ, but that whosoever only confesses that Jesus Christ appeared *as man* for the salvation of the world, must be acknowledged to be a true Christian. According to St John, verily not so!

Ver. 16 is most strictly connected with ver. 15. It is wrong therefore, with Huther and others, to assert that the καὶ ἡμεῖς is perfectly parallel with the καὶ ἡμεῖς of ver. 14, and therefore includes only the Apostles. St John in ver. 14 by no means intended to set up any wall of partition between eyewitnesses and those who were not eyewitnesses of the life of Jesus; but all the emphasis lay upon the predicative idea, "*we have seen and bear witness*." The certainty of the truths of salvation is what he makes prominent ("we have *seen* and *testify*"), and not any distinction between the teachers and the taught (*we* have seen and bear witness : ye have not seen it yourselves, but must receive it on our testimony"). It appears as it were only involuntarily in ver. 14, from the (solely emphasized) predicative idea, that the subject "we" must be understood, as the nature of the case required, of the witnesses of the life of Jesus. Now, if St John introduced in ver. 4 no distinction between the teachers and the hearers, we cannot assume any such distinction down to ver. 16 ; else the ἡμεῖς of ver. 17 also must be understood of the eyewitnesses alone ! Rather does our καὶ ἡμεῖς derive its precision and meaning from the reference to ὃς ἄν, ver. 15. It is quite analogous to the ὑμεῖς, ver. 4, which follows the πᾶν πνεῦμα ὅ, ver. 2 and ver. 3. After the Apostle had in ver. 15 laid down the general proposition, that if any man confess Jesus, God abideth in him, so now he makes the declaration that with "us," that is, him and his readers, this was the case.

Thus this twofold truth, that "we acknowledge Jesus Christ as the Son of God, *and* that accordingly God dwelleth in us," has its reality in the "ἡμεῖς." But the Apostle expresses this twofold fact, ver. 16, in an altered form; that is, in the words, "We have known and believed the love which God hath ἐν ἡμῖν." It is here most weighty and significant, that that *confession of the Divinity of Christ* which involves or includes in itself the indwelling of God, now appears as the *having known the love which God hath in us.* Thus these two marks, the ὁμολογία, vers. 2, 3, and the ἀγάπη, ver. 7 seq., appear in their perfect identity and organic penetration. That confession of Jesus the Son of God is, according to vers. 1–6, and according to vers. 14, 15, not any theoretical dogmatizing, but altogether the result and the manifestation of the being and ruling of God in us. That confession, namely, presupposes, according to vers. 9, 10, and vers. 14, 15, our having vitally known the love of God manifested in the sending of Christ; but it is a *living and real* knowledge, that is, the being seized, and possessed, and kindled by that love. (Thus it is explained how, and how far, in ver. 15 that confession may be identified with the abiding of God in us.) Thus, the standing in that confession (that is, therefore, the having known the love of God, and the being enkindled by it, and consequently the being essentially penetrated by God abiding in us) is no other than (ver. 16) the "*having known the love of God;*" not merely the love which He objectively manifested, as a love to us, in the sending of Christ, but at the same time that love with which He hath enkindled ourselves, which He hath kindled *in us*, and by means of which, as being His own nature, He worketh *in us*. Therefore St John writes, "The love which God hath ἐν ἡμῖν." To interpret ἐν by *to* is, as we have seen, impracticable. In ver. 9 it was dependent upon ἐφανερώθη, and might be so translated; but here it depends upon ἔχειν, and cannot bear that sense. Ἐν ἡμῖν cannot, furthermore, have the meaning which would make the ἡμεῖς the *object* of the love of God (Luther, Calvin, Beza, Calovius, Grotius, etc.). St John had a good reason for choosing specifically this expression, and writing ἐν ἡμῖν. It is not his manner to arrange the individual links of his chain of thought in dialectic continuity, and thus logically to unfold his meaning; on the contrary, he selects his expressions so profoundly, and uses them with such plastic power, that in one single expression a whole series of preceding *intuitions* are as it were summed up and reflected. Thus, as we have shown above at length, the entire series of the intuitions developed, vers. 2, 3, vers. 9, 10, vers. 14, 15, are concentred and summed up in our expression, ἐγνώκαμεν καὶ πεπιστεύκαμεν τὴν ἀγάπην ἣν ἔχει ὁ Θεὸς ἐν ἡμῖν. In our knowing and having believed in Christ, the incarnate Son of God, we have known and believed the love of God; but, since this knowing and believing is no subjective theoretical action of ours, but an essential manifestation of God's nature in us—His working, ruling, and being in us,—we have known not merely, as it were, the love which God hath *to* us, but *His loving which He displays in us.* Ἡ ἀγάπη ἣν ἔχει ὁ Θεὸς ἐν ἡμῖν is no other than an exposition of the idea of the *relation* of love between God and us, with which we were met in ch. ii. 5, and again in ch. iv. 12. That is, this love-relation between God and us does not consist (as it would in the case of two men) in this, that God loveth man, and man again loveth God, both being reciprocally loving, and standing as it were independently; but in this (comp. ver. 10, and below, ver. 19), that God hath in fact and act manifested *in* us His nature, which is love, and thereby enkindled love *in* us: so that, if we love (Him and our brethren), it is in reality not we who love, but God who loveth *in us,* and in us τὴν ἀγάπην αὐτοῦ ἔχει.—The γινώσκειν and πιστεύειν belong inseparably to each other: the γινώσκειν is not that theoretical, theological knowledge, concerning which the proposition holds good, *fides præcedit intellectum ;* but it is, in the specific Johannæan sense (as in ch. ii. 3 and 13, iv. 7), that being penetrated, enlightened, and enkindled by the nature of God which simply coincides with the πιστεύειν, and is as much the root as the result of the πίστις. The Apostle might have been content to write only ἐγνώκαμεν; but he adds πεπιστεύκαμεν in order to make it prominent that the πιστεύειν, the receptive self-surrender to God, is not merely the primitive instrument, but on our side the abiding immanent foundation, of that relation of love between God and us.

" God is love; and he that dwelleth in love dwelleth in God, and God in him." These words at the conclusion make the idea of the ἀγάπη, ἣν ἔχει ὁ Θεὸς ἐν ἡμῖν, and the organic connection of the confession with the love, perfectly clear. To know the love which God hath towards and in us, includes two things : 1. to know (vers. 9 and 15) the act of Divine love in the mission of His Son; and, 2. ourselves to stand and abide in this nature of God, which is love. It is obvious that in *these* words not brotherly-love alone, but love absolutely, is spoken of. "To abide in love" does not mean merely to abide in the exercise of love, or to persevere in the *disposition* of love, but to abide in the *nature* of love ; and it includes both in itself—that we abide in the love of God to us, in the faith in God's love, and that we abide in the spirit of love to God and the brethren.—It is only when we apprehend the words in this generality of meaning, that we can attach to them ver. 17 without violence.

In vers. 17–19 begins the practical hortatory expansion of the subject: this goes on down to ch. v. 2 ; and then, without any direct interruption of the train, the Apostle passes on, by means of the transitional ideas of ver. 3, to the last section of this Part. St John now more fully unfolds, that, and in what precise manner, the presence of God's Spirit may be discerned in this double sign (the confession of Jesus the Son of God, and love). In vers. 17–19 the former and more dogmatic sign is considered; though no longer in its purely dogmatic form, as above, vers. 2, 3, but now in the relation to the ἀγάπη Θεοῦ which it has assumed in vers. 13–16. From ver. 20 to ch. v. 2 the Apostle dwells upon the second sign, love to the brethren.

Ver. 17. Ἐν τούτῳ τετελείωται ἡ ἀγάπη μεθ' ἡμῶν, κ.τ.λ. The first question here is, whether μεθ' ἡμῶν is to be connected with the verb, and the sense, " love is perfected *with* us ;" or whether μεθ' ἡμῶν belong to the noun ἡ ἀγάπη—which here, though not in ver. 7, would be grammatically tenable, because there is nothing intervening, to separate them in sense, between ἀγάπη and μετά. (Compare 2 Cor. vii. 7 ; Col. i. 4 and 8 ;

Eph. i. 15; Winer, Gram. § 19.) The former construction is altogether untenable. For, the preposition μετά has the meaning *inter, among;* and, consequently, specifies a multiplicity of objects or persons between and among whom something takes place; a signification which absolutely forbids its being connected with the verb τετελείωται. It yields no meaning to say, "Love is perfected among us, in our midst." If the Apostle had intended to express the idea that "*among* us, or *with* us"—that is, on our part—love is made perfect, then it would have been necessary that he should write ἐν. This signification of the μετά, that is *inter*, would be more appropriate, when we connect μεθ' ἡμῶν with the noun: the love which we have among us, that is, our reciprocal love, is made perfect, etc. But this does not suit the context; for reciprocal brotherly-love cannot be made perfect in confidence against the day of judgment.

The true explanation is given by Benson and Rickli, when they interpret, "the love (of God) with us," that is, the love which subsists between God and us; thus, that simple *relation* of love of which the Apostle had spoken in ver. 12, and just now again in ver. 16. We are perfectly justified in appealing to 2 Cor. xiii. 13, "The love of God be μεθ' ὑμῶν." And the objection, that "St John never combines together God and men in ἡμεῖς," does not affect our position in the least; since we interpret, "the love *of God* with *us*," and the ἡμῖν, therefore, refers only to men. The question, then, whether the love here bears the onesided meaning of the love of God towards us, or (which is not in harmony with the context) the onesided meaning of our love to God, or God and the brethren,—falls at once before a sound exposition.

The love-*relation* of God *with* us,—thus St John defines it expressly as a mutual relation. That relation, however, is especially viewed as having its basis and finding its origin in God; since it is not now ἐν that the Apostle uses, but μετά in the sense of 2 Cor. xiii. 13: thus this relation of love, viewed especially on the side of God, is perfected ἐν τούτῳ, ἵνα παρρησίαν ἔχωμεν ἐν τῇ ἡμέρᾳ τῆς κρίσεως. Bengel and others have referred ἐν τούτῳ, "in this," backwards to the closing words of ver. 16, καὶ ὁ μένων, κ.τ.λ. But this is not right; for the theoretical declaration that love is perfected by the "abiding in love," does not furnish any consolatory meaning; nor would the *telic clause* with ἵνα logically connect itself with this theoretical instruction. Beza, Socinus, and others referred the ἐν τούτῳ to the words ὅτι καθὼς κ.τ.λ.; but that would be to assume a hyperbaton quite alien to the style of St John. All these artifices are unnecessary; for St John in John xv. 8 lets a ἵνα follow an ἐν τούτῳ. All that need be said concerning this Johannæan ἵνα, has already been said above on ch. iii. 11 and 23. We have not to explain ἵνα by ὥστε (Bengel), or ὅταν; but must, after the analogy of the former passages, translate: "In this is the love (of God) with us perfected, that we *should have* confidence in the day of judgment." That means to say: In this—that the *will* of God, that we should have confidence in the day of judgment, is internally made known to us, and (already) approves itself in us as a power (of confidence)—the relation of love between God and us is demonstrated to be perfected. But we must not interpret: "Therein, that we should have (= shall have) confidence in the day of judgment, *will* one day the relation of love between God and us *be perfected;*" for the Perfect τετελείωται pleads against this. Concerning the ἡμέρα τῆς κρίσεως, compare ch. ii. 28.

The relation of love between God and us has been made perfect in this, that we know, feel, and by inward experience are already assured, that we shall stand before the judgment-seat of Christ, not with trembling, but with joyful confidence. Love is thus not merely an *external mark* of Divine adoption; but is also *itself* perfected in confidence towards God—in whom it no longer contemplates a Judge, but a reconciled Father—and towards Christ, in whom it beholds, not the Judge, but the σωτήρ.

To this is attached the elucidation or reason: ὅτι, καθὼς ἐκεῖνός ἐστιν, καὶ ἡμεῖς ἐσμὲν ἐν τῷ κόσμῳ. Ἐκεῖνος certainly refers (after the analogy of ch. ii. 6) not to God (Augustin, Calovius, Beza, Castalio), but to Christ. Ἐκεῖνος points back here to vers. 14, 15, as ch. ii. 6 does to ch. ii. 1. For the rest, these words present many and great difficulties to the expositor. It does not seem perfectly plain *how* they serve either for the establishment or for the illustration of what precedes. The first point to be settled is, whether the point of comparison between Christ and us lies in the words, "in this world"—that is, if we must interpret, "for as He is, so we are also, *in the world;*" equivalent to, "for as He is *in the world*, so we are *in the world.*" What makes against this explanation is, first of all, the verbal arrangement of the clause. We should expect, on that supposition, either that the words ἐν τῷ κόσμῳ τούτῳ would be found before ἐστίν, in the first member of the clause; or, secondly, that ἐστίν would be entirely omitted, and the sentence run : ὅτι, καθὼς ἐκεῖνος, καὶ ἡμεῖς ἐν τῷ κόσμῳ τούτῳ ἐσμέν. Yet this difficulty would disappear if only we consider ἐστίν to be unemphatic, and the words ἐν τῷ κόσμῳ τούτῳ to be placed *with emphasis* at the end of the sentence. A second obstacle to that interpretation is the inappropriateness of the thought which results. To take ἐστίν as used instead of ἦν would meet the difficulty; but we have no right to do that. In that case—or if the reading were ἦν—the very appropriate sentiment would be : "As Christ once was in the midst of an evil world, so we also are now in it; and therefore we look forward to the ἡμέρα κρίσεως, as the day of our deliverance, not with anxiety but with joyful confidence. The Judge, who will come, will come, not as our enemy, but as the world's enemy and our deliverer."— But the Present ἐστι appears to us to forbid this interpretation. "As He is," says the Apostle; but Christ, since His ascension, has been no longer in this visible world (Col. iii. 1, 2); the "being in the world," therefore, cannot possibly be adduced as the *tertium comparationis* between Christ and us. Grammatically considered, it must appear strange that St John does not follow the plain καθὼς by a οὕτως (οὕτως καὶ ἡμεῖς, κ.τ.λ.); but, in fact, even a καθὼς—οὕτως would not be sufficient to express that thought; St John would have needed to write, ὅτι οἷος ἐκεῖνός ἐστι, τοιοῦτοι καὶ ἐσμεν ἡμεῖς. (The addition ἐν τῷ κόσμῳ τούτῳ appears, on this view, almost superfluous and inharmonious.) And even then the passage would remain obscure and enigmatical enough. We should have expected that St John would make the quality, in which the *tertium comparationis* between Christ and us was to consist, specially emphatic by mentioning it (as he, *e.g.*, has done in ch. ii. 6, "As He *walked*, so we must *walk*); for in the context there is nothing specified by which we might discover what meaning St John attached to his words. And not only so: there is a second difficulty— that in fact we cannot conceive of any qualitative likeness between Christ and us which might serve to establish or give the reason for the proposition that love is perfected in our confidence against the judgment. To estimate this difficulty, we need only glance at the shifts of all the expositors. Luther explains: As Christ is in the world as a sufferer, so we also suffer; —but the ἐστίν does not suit that interpretation. Tirinus and Neander: As Christ is the Son of God, so we are the adopted sons of God. Sander: As Christ is (that is, *was*) *in* the world, without being *of* the world, so are we also. Düsterdieck, recurring to his notion of the main theme being righteousness (ch. ii. 29): As Christ is righteous, so we also are righteous (but in how different a sense!). Rickli: As Christ is temptable (*is?*), so we also are liable to temptation. Huther: As Christ is love, so love dwelleth in us also. Others, despairing of any definite view, find in the καθώς κ.τ.λ. merely the general notion of a relation of nature between Christ and us. But St John must have expressed this last otherwise than by the unusual adverbial καθώς; and, as it respects this and some of the other views, our confidence in prospect of the judgment cannot possibly be grounded upon our likeness to Christ, but only upon God's love manifested in Christ.

After all that has been said, we contemplate the words in question without any clear conception of their meaning: however easily they may be despatched by other expositors, they greatly embarrass me. One might be almost tempted to take refuge in the boldness of conjecture, and to read ΟΥΤΩΣ instead of ΕΣΤΙΝ! That, indeed, would remove at a stroke every difficulty. Then would the fatal Pres. ἐστίν be set aside, and the sense would supply an ἦν to the ἐκεῖνος: καθώς οὕτως would not indeed bear the meaning, "We are, *not less than* He, in the world," but the meaning, "We are, in the same *manner* as He was, in the world." This would yield the appropriate sentiment, that, because we find ourselves, as Christ did once, in this world (this wicked world)—even as He, that is, as not belonging to the world—we may look forward, not with terror, but with confidence, to His coming into judgment.—But, as such a conjecture will hardly be allowed by a criticism which scrupulously watches in the domain of Biblical exegesis, nothing remains but that we adopt one of two courses. We may either, 1. take ἐστίν in the sense of an historical Present, and regard

St John as having in his mind the humiliated state of Christ living upon the earth, but without consciously taking note of the difference between the Past and the Present (as in John v. 2), and laying all the stress upon the ἐκεῖνος,—the ἐστί being an emphasized and indifferent addition; or, 2. we may take ἐστίν as an actual Present, and refer the καθὼς ἐκεῖνός ἐστιν to this, that Christ is still in a certain sense—that is, in the Church, which is His body—in this wicked world. On the former supposition, the sense appears: "We look forward with confidence to the judgment. For, as Christ stands before us suffering, persecuted (before our eyes), so we also are in this evil world; and hence rejoice in the hope of our deliverance." On the latter supposition, the sense would be this: "We look forward with confidence to the judgment; for, as He (in His Church, and in the persons of His people) is persecuted still by the wicked world, we also are in this world (as sheep among wolves)." This last explanation seems to be opposed by the circumstance that *we*, ἡμεῖς, are nothing distinguished from the *Church of Christ*, and which might be compared with it, but that we are members and integral portions of that Church itself. St John's conception, lying at the basis of all this, is supposed to be: That which we have now to suffer in the world, is a persecution directed properly against Christ Himself; we are not otherwise in this wicked world than our Lord Himself is in us; we suffer with Him and for His sake; and, consequently, we all have reason to look forward with joyful confidence to His return in judgment upon this κόσμος.

In ver. 18 St John continues the leading thought which had been begun in ver. 17, that love is perfected in the παῤῥησία. *Fear is not in love*—ἐστίν as *verbum substantivum*—fear has in love, and the domain of love, no place. Ἀγάπη is said with its perfect *generality of meaning*: we must not limit it (with Calvin, Calovius, Spener) to the love of God to us, which in itself would be an inappropriate sense; nor to our love to God; nor to our love to the brethren. The Apostle utters the *altogether universal* judgment: Where love is, there is no fear; just as if He had said: Where men love one another, men fear not one another; where a relation is established through love, fear has no place. The two passions *generally*, according to their idea and essence, exclude each other: this is St John's declaration, and he lays it down as the ground of the special judgment which had been pronounced in ver. 17, that the relation of love subsisting between *us and God* is perfected in our παῤῥησία in relation to God's judgment. "*Perfect love casts out fear:*" here the proposition above is so far limited, that an imperfect grade of love is conceived as compatible with fear; while, on the other hand, a perfect and perfected love drives all fear out of the soul. This proposition also is to be apprehended as a *general judgment;* both these members of the general declaration form the foundation of what had been said in ver. 17. Because fear is not in love—that is, not in perfect love—therefore the τετελειοῦσθαι of the love which subsists between us and God shows itself in the absence and the positive contrary of fear—in the παῤῥησία.— Τελεία ἀγάπη does not denote a sentiment, or a perfection of love itself, as if it meant a "perfectly pure and perfectly holy love;" but love is here again contemplated as a *relation,* and a τελεία ἀγάπη may be regarded as existing between two persons, between whom there exists *nothing but* love—love undisturbed by the presence of wrath, or fear, or anything else that might qualify and abate its perfectness as a relation.

The general statement, "perfected love driveth out fear," is now on its own part established (ὅτι) by the little clause, ὁ φόβος κόλασιν ἔχει. The particle δέ shows that the following clause, ὁ δὲ φοβούμενος, κ.τ.λ., is not part of the reason assigned —that is, does not also depend upon ὅτι. The more sparing St John is of such particles, the more certain is it that, *when* he uses them, he connects a definite meaning with them. If the second clause, ὁ φοβούμενος—which is essentially identical with the judgment to be established, "perfect love casteth out fear" —were still dependent upon the ὅτι, it must have been introduced by οὖν, *ergo*. But since this is not the case, it is only the first clause which depends upon the ὅτι. The second, on the contrary, forms the independent antithesis to the words, "perfect love, etc."

Κόλασις certainly bears the meaning of chastisement or correction, not of torment or suffering. (Compare Matt. xxv. 46; Septuagint, Ezek. xliii. 11, xviii. 30; and Wisd. xi. 14; 2 Macc. iv. 38.) But we may not translate κόλασιν ἔχει by "*fear receives* (at the judgment) punishment, or is punished;"

nor by "*deserves* punishment" (De Wette). They simply signify, according to their literal etymological sense, "fear *hath* chastisement;" but this cannot again be understood as "fear bears its chastisement already in itself," or, "it carries with it the consciousness of punishment" (Calovius, Neander); for such a sentence could never serve for the proof or establishment of the proposition, that perfect love casts out fear: such a thought must have been connected with the preceding by δέ instead of ὅτι. We may rather say that in κόλασιν ἔχει that attribute of fear is expressed, in virtue of which it is incompatible with perfected love. Hence, although κόλασις means "chastisement," we must necessarily assume that we have *causa pro effectu* (Augustin, Luther, Bengel), and that κόλασις really signifies (as in Matt. xxv. 26) pain, torment, and anxiety. This sentiment or feeling, however, is altogether out of keeping and irreconcilable with the affection of love.

The final sentence, ὁ δὲ φοβούμενος, κ.τ.λ., is easily explained by what has gone before. It appears obviously to be the *antithesis* of the clause, ἡ δὲ τελεία, κ.τ.λ., but at the same time involves the simple and self-evident conclusion which follows from all that had been said.

In ver. 19 is repeated essentially the same thought as that of ver. 10. "We love (as well God as our brethren), because God hath first loved us." The love of God to us is the source of all our love. This clause is connected with the former, not by external dialectic conjunction, but by internal organic necessity. To the exhibition and establishment of general propositions in ver. 18, there follows once more (as in ver. 16 and ver. 4) a declaration concerning the actual relation in which the ἡμεῖς (St John and his readers) stand to these general propositions. Fear is not in love,—perfect love casteth out fear; because fear ever hath torment in it (anxious dread of punishment), which is irreconcilable with love. *Now we* have no fear: we live and move in love;[1] and that *because God hath first loved us* (in the sending of a Redeemer); consequently, we need not fear any future punishment. Thus St John once more shows how all our loving has its root in that love of God to us; and

---

[1] This connection, obvious as it is, is misapprehended by Luther, Grotius, and many others, who take this ἀγαπῶμεν as a Conjunctive of exhortation. Compare, on the contrary, Calvin, Bengel.

that it is capable of being a love perfected in us—a τελεία ἀγάπη—a love without fear—only *because* it is rooted in God's love to us; that is, in our having known and believed this love of God to us. So wonderfully are these truths interwoven,—so gloriously do the lights of Divine truth and Divine love sparkle and counterchange in this precious jewel,—that we may simply invert the deduction without robbing it of any of its truth. Love is perfected in confidence towards God, because it has its root in the love of God to us (ver. 17 in relation to ver. 18); and so it is itself, in its inmost nature, παῤῥησία, and incompatible with fear (ver. 18). And again, because all loving (ver. 18) is in its nature confidence, our loving (ver. 19) is founded upon God's love to us.

It is impossible that the conjunction and reciprocal action of faith in the incarnation of the Son of God, and love, should be more internally and organically exhibited.

In CH. IV. 20–CH. V. 2 follows a second portion of the practical hortatory development. It was shown, vers. 17–19, how love essentially has its root in our παῤῥησία of faith in Christ (ver. 19), and is again in that same παῤῥησία made perfect.—Hitherto the idea of the confidence has been kept in view, and with it the love of God displayed in Christ as its foundation; and the *first* of the two marks (vers. 2, 3) has been made matter of observation. Now the Apostle directs his view to the second mark, that of brotherly-love, ver. 7; and it is shown how and in what way it also practically approves itself to be a note of the πνεῦμα Θεοῦ.

Ver. 20. St John has laid it down as a fact, ver. 19, that *we* live in a state of *love* (and not in fear). In vers. 17–19, although the words of ver. 18 treat of *love generally as such*, the idea and nature of *loving*, our relation of love *to God*, had become the subject, as it had been already in vers. 12 and 16. St John had already demonstrated, on the practical ethical side, *that, and in what manner, love to God was organically connected with the believing confession of Jesus Christ.* But now it is his purpose to show further, *that, and in what manner, love to the brethren is organically and internally bound up with love to God.* He passes over to this in the way of obviating a possible misunderstanding. A man might have plainly perceived, from what had been said, that love must be bound up with a believing confession; but he might, at the same time, have fallen into the delusion that love to God was enough, and accordingly have suffered himself to continue in hatred to his brother. The Apostle now shows that he who does not love the brethren is not included in the declaration ἡμεῖς ἀγαπῶμεν, ver. 19. "If a man *say*, I love God, and hate his brother, he is a liar." The Apostle does not write ἐάν τις ἀγαπῇ τὸν Θεόν, κ.τ.λ., any more than St James (ch. ii. 14) writes ἐὰν πίστιν τις ἔχῃ. One passage serves for the elucidation of the other. As he who has not works actually has not faith, but only *says* he has it, so he who hates his brother cannot actually love God, but only *says* that he loves Him: this very assurance of his makes him a *liar*.

That is to say (so continues St John), it is quite *impossible* that any one *who hateth his brother should love God*. "For," he proceeds, "he that loveth not his brother, whom he hath seen, how *can* he love God, whom he hath not seen?" The *vis argumenti* does not lie in this (Huther), that it is *easier* to love a visible than to love an invisible being, and that he who has failed of the former will much more fail of the latter. For this is not true in itself: to love a person who stands visibly before me, and who it may be has injured me, is by no means easier than to love a person whom I have never seen, but of whose character I have heard nothing but good. In this argumentation of the Apostle the question is not of "easier" and "more difficult." Still less are we to assume, with some, that the Apostle presupposes no love generally to be possible without the object being seen; for it would follow from that, that we cannot love God (compare ver. 12). But the *vis argumenti* lies in what is said in ver. 12. Because we (such was the idea there) cannot behold God with our eyes, we have no other opportunity of demonstrating to Him our love in act than by showing our love to those *in whom He dwells*. And it is demonstrated that He dwells in us by this, that His nature, love, dwells in us, and that we exercise like Him self-renouncing (consequently, also, forgiving) love. Sander rightly observes on this verse: "He who will not discern, and does not honour, the image of God in his brother, despises thereby the antitype, God Himself." And so Calvin: "The Apostle here assumes that God offers

Himself to us in the persons of men, who bear His image engraven upon them. St John means no more than that he makes a vain boast, who professes to love God while he neglects God's image before his eyes." Thus we have not here a *conclusio a minori ad majus*—" He who cannot love his visible brother, can still less love the invisible God." The visibility of the one and the invisibility of the other do not come into view in order to make prominent the difference or distance between God and the brethren; but, inversely, the " hath seen" and " hath not seen" refer back to ver. 12, and serve to make emphatic the *relation* and *connection* between the invisible God and the visible images or representatives of God, in whom He presents to us the objects on which our love must be spent. And the sense is this: " He who loveth not his brother, whom he seeth, cannot be assumed to love God the Invisible; because he who should love God must necessarily love also God's nature when it is visibly presented before him."

By a delicate distinction, St John writes in the former half of the verse μισῇ, but in the latter μὴ ἀγαπῶν. In the former case, he would describe the actual position of one who says that he loves God, and nevertheless so far errs as to suffer himself to bear *hatred* to his brother in his heart. It was then needful to make the *contrast* sharp and express, and therefore to show the *uttermost* point to which an erring conscience may in this respect be misled. The Apostle speaks in presence of the experienced fact, that a man sometimes does utter his assurance that he loves God, while he nourishes in his heart hatred against his neighbour.—But in the latter case, where the Apostle is laying down a doctrinal position, the mere not-hating is insufficient; it is necessary that he should enforce the positive requirement that the Christian should *love* his brother. Hence he writes : " He that *loveth* not his brother, etc."

Ἀδελφός must, considered in itself, express nothing more here than it expressed above in ch. iii. 14, etc. The meaning of the Apostle is certainly not that we ought to love only our *fellow-Christians*, while we may hate those who are still unregenerate. How could the Apostle have forgotten the word of his Lord in Luke x. 30–37? But, having the church to which he writes before his eyes, the relation of Christians to Christians hovers specifically before his thoughts, since in this case a μισεῖν would be *doubly* to be reprobated. And this helps to explain the reason which follows in ch. v. 1.

In ver. 21 he emphatically points to the fact that we have an express commandment of the Lord, to the effect that he who loveth God, love his brother also. (Compare John xiii. 34, and especially Luke x. 27.)

In ch. v. 1 follows a further establishment of this point. And it is not to be explained simply on the presupposition that St John from ver. 20 onwards had in his view the relation generally between Christians and Christians. The latent limitation is to be accounted for by the kind of demonstration which the Apostle here adduces. It is his business now to exhibit the requirement of brotherly-love (like that of love to God, above, vers. 17–19) in its organic connection with *faith in the incarnation of the Son of God.*

Πᾶς ὁ πιστεύων, ὅτι Ἰησοῦς ἐστὶν ὁ Χριστός: this is, as compared with ch. iv. 2 seq., and 15, the third and shortest formula of the confession; it expresses, as opposed to the Cerinthian disjunction of the man Jesus from the Christ, simply and only the identity of Jesus and the Christ:[1] it was needless to repeat the further particulars, after the preceding passages had developed the individual critical points involved in the idea of the incarnation—that He is the only-begotten Son of God, who became man, vers. 9 and 15, and that He had come ἐν σαρκί, ver. 2. Now he that hath this faith—πιστεύειν being obviously taken in the sense of ch. iv. 16, and therefore not the mere theoretical acceptance of the proposition—is *born of God* (this is evident of itself from a comparison of ch. iv. 16 with ch. ii. 29 and ch. iii. 1 seq.); καὶ πᾶς ὁ ἀγαπῶν τὸν γεννήσαντα (that is τὸν Θεόν, of whom he is born, as had just been said; but not τὸν Χριστόν), ἀγαπᾷ καὶ τὸν γεγεννημένον ἐξ αὐτοῦ. That

---

[1] Huther erroneously maintains that Χριστός stands here for υἱὸς τοῦ Θεοῦ. It may rather be said that St John uses the expressions, "Jesus is the Son of God," and "Jesus is the Christ," promiscuously, because he would have both (the latter not excepted) understood in opposition to the Cerinthian gnosis; that is, because he does not, by the words "Jesus is the Christ," answer the general question which among the historical persons was the promised Messiah (whether Jesus, or John the Baptist, or Theudas, etc.), but designs to establish the identity of the man Jesus and the Χριστός come from heaven, against the Cerinthian sundering of the man Jesus from the Æon Christ.

the true believer loves God, had been laid down in ch. iv. 7–16, and 17–19; and we have shown, upon ch. iv. 20 seq., that it is taken for granted that the obligation of love to God is acknowledged and admitted even by him who may not love his brother: hence St John can, without any further mediate clause, as *e concessis*, connect with the major proposition, πᾶς ὁ πιστεύων, κ.τ.λ., the minor proposition, which is contained in the words πᾶς ὁ ἀγαπῶν, κ.τ.λ. The concluding clause then demonstrates its own necessity. He who believeth, is *born of God;* he then who, as a πιστεύων, loveth *God,* must also love *all believers*,[1] because these also are born of God, consequently bear in them the nature of God, and that the same nature which he himself bears as one who is born of God.

Ver. 2 offers now—when we have rightly perceived the turn in the process of thought introduced by ver. 1—not the slightest difficulty. St John has placed brotherly-love in strict connection with *faith in Christ;* he has shown that that love *has its root in this faith.* The natural and direct consequence therefore is this, *that a love of the brethren which does not rest upon this faith is not true love;* and therefore St John lays down the position: ἐν τούτῳ, κ.τ.λ.: *By this we know that we love the children of God, because we love God.* In ver. 20 seq. he had laid down the proposition that a true faith and the love of God never exist without brotherly-love, and that therefore brotherly-love is the sign (of faith and) of love to God: here, in ver. 2, he utters the declaration that true brotherly-love

---

[1] Huther entirely misapprehends the logical connection of these thoughts, when he suggests that there should be interposed between the first words, πᾶς ὁ πιστεύων, κ.τ.λ., and those which follow, πᾶς ὁ ἀγαπῶν, κ.τ.λ., the mediating clause, πᾶς ὁ γεγεννημένος ἐκ τοῦ Θεοῦ ἀγαπᾷ τὸν Θεόν. The major proposition, that every believer is born of God, does not serve merely for the establishment of the *subject-idea* in the concluding clause, but rather for the establishment of its *predicate*-idea. The chain of thought is not this: " He that believeth is born of God ; he that is born of God, loveth God ; he that loveth God, loveth also the children of God ;"—for then the third proposition would not follow from the first two, but stand co-ordinate with them as a new and undemonstrated proposition. But it is this: " He that believeth is born of God. (That the πιστεύων loveth God, and must love Him, is assumed as established and necessary.) He then who (as a πιστεύων) loveth God, the God of whom he is begotten, must consequently love *also the other* πιστεύοντας, because these like himself are *born of God;* therefore partakers of the same nature, ἀδελφοί in the highest sense."

cannot exist without the foundation of faith and the love of God, and that therefore faith and love to God (which is here presently defined as obedience to the ἐντολαί of God) is the sign of the genuineness of brotherly-love. As previously, in ch. iv. 2 seq., and ver. 7, each of the two elements—the confession of faith, and brotherly-love—had been exhibited as of itself a mark of the πνεῦμα Θεοῦ, so it is now shown that these two elements are reciprocally the sign one of the other. Where there is no brotherly-love, there can be no true faith and no true love of God; and, where the true faith and the true love of God (approving itself such by obedience to His commandments) are not, there can be no true brotherly-love. Faith without brotherly-love is dead faith, nothing better than a vain and lying babbling about faith; and a brotherly-love without faith, and without faithful fulfilment of the commandments of God, is no better than hypocritical,—it is not spiritual, but carnal in its inmost nature,—it is a love which seeks only its own subtle spiritual satisfaction, or its own honour.

Thus we do not find here Huther's " difficulty which needs solution;" to say nothing of the outrageous trajection of Œcumenius and Grotius, who would refer ὅτι to ἐν τούτῳ, and take the clause with ὅταν as the object of the γινώσκομεν.

In ver. 3 the Apostle himself declares that he had mentioned the τηρεῖν of the ἐντολαί as no other than the demonstration of *love to God*. But the thought into which this flows forms of itself the transition to a new and final division of the Epistle.

PART THE FIFTH.

FAITH OVERCOMETH THE WORLD.

Ch. v. 3–21.

THE Apostle is led by the nature of the case itself to substitute for love to God the keeping of His commandments: that is, by the consideration that *true* brotherly-love has no surer sign than its true and faithful fulfilment of all the commandments of God in relation to the brethren.

But this mention of the ἐντολαί serves him now, ver. 3, as the unforced transition to a new Part.

This Part of the Epistle certainly is not divided from the former by any such external demarcation as that which separates the fourth from the third, the third from the second, and this from the first; there is no formal commencement of a new subject; ver. 3, rather, forms, by the thought, " His commandments are not grievous," the bridge to the new theme which enters in ver. 4—" That which is born of God overcometh the world; and this is the victory which overcometh the world, even our faith." But there can be no hesitation in saying that this does form a *new theme*, and that consequently the matter of it begins a new Part. For, as from ch. iv. 1 onwards, all had revolved around the confession of Jesus Christ and brotherly-love, which two elements had been each first exhibited as in itself a mark of the Spirit of God and life in God, and then in their relation to each other and their organic interpenetration, and finally each as the mark or testing sign of the other; so now, from ch. v. 4 onwards to the close of the Epistle, all revolves round the idea of *faith as the victory over the world.* This faith is viewed, vers. 6–8, in its substance and objective nature; vers. 9–12, in its subjective assurance and power; and in the final section, vers. 13–21, in its result and effects.

VER. 3. The first words, which belong still to the former section, have been already explained. The new thought, "And His commandments are not heavy," forms the unforced transition to ver. 4. They are not grievously hard (to be fulfilled), because he who is born of God has in his faith the power to overcome the world :—first of all, the world in himself (the power of sin in his own flesh); but also all the temptations which come upon him from the world objectively considered, the world still untouched and unrenewed by Christ (ch. iv. 4). Hence, this connection makes it obvious that $\beta\alpha\rho\epsilon\hat{\iota}\alpha\iota$ $o\dot{\upsilon}\kappa$ $\epsilon\dot{\iota}\sigma\dot{\iota}$ does not refer to the *substance* of the commandments (Bengel), as if the New-Testament commandments were declared to be light in comparison of the yoke of the ceremonial law—a comparison which is quite foreign to the context; but that it refers to the *power* which dwells in those who are born of God in order to their fulfilment (Luther, Calvin, Grotius, Lücke, etc.).

VER. 4. What is said here in the first half of the verse, is connected by the $\ddot{o}\tau\iota$ (establishing the reason) with what was said in ver. 3. But this does not exclude the introduction of a *new main theme* in ver. 4. In the same manner St John had passed over, ch. iii. 24, to the idea of the $\pi\nu\epsilon\hat{\upsilon}\mu\alpha$, which then in ch. iv. 1 is introduced as the theme. It is a graceful form of transition, of which abundant examples are found in the literature of eloquence and homiletics, both of ancient and modern times.

After the Apostle has laid down the proposition as supporting his argument, $\ddot{o}\tau\iota$ $\pi\hat{\alpha}\nu$, $\kappa.\tau.\lambda.$ (where the neuter is used in the same sense as John iii. 6, vi. 37, xvii. 2; the matter of the proposition itself being fully explained by ch. ii. 13 seq., 27, iv. 4), he proceeds to assert the same thought independently, *as his formal theme*, and with such a modification as that position demanded. $K\alpha\grave{\iota}$ $\alpha\ddot{\upsilon}\tau\eta$ $\dot{\epsilon}\sigma\tau\grave{\iota}\nu$ $\dot{\eta}$ $\nu\dot{\iota}\kappa\eta$ $\dot{\eta}$ $\nu\iota\kappa\dot{\eta}\sigma\alpha\sigma\alpha$ $\tau\grave{o}\nu$ $\kappa\acute{o}\sigma\mu o\nu$, $\dot{\eta}$ $\pi\dot{\iota}\sigma\tau\iota\varsigma$ $\dot{\eta}\mu\hat{\omega}\nu$. Our *faith* is the victory, *which hath overcome the world*. Thus formularized, this proposition contains all the critical points which are to be developed in what follows. $'H$ $\pi\dot{\iota}\sigma\tau\iota\varsigma$ $\dot{\eta}\mu\hat{\omega}\nu$ must not be understood of faith in the subjective sense alone, of the *acting* or *spirit* of our faith; but it is our faith *as including its substance and object, Jesus Christ*. It is as well *that which*, or *Him in whom*, we believe (*our* faith, in opposition to Cerinthian superstition), as our believing *mind*, the spirit *in which* we believe. And thus the predicate ἐστὶν ἡ νίκη is by no means a metonomy; nor is it a breviloquence (Lücke) or concise form of expression,—the faith certainly being not itself the victory, but only the cause of the victory (the sense then being, "Faith, through which we become children of God, hath given us the victory over the world"). But it is faith, inclusive of its object—our πιστεύειν εἰς Ἰησοῦν Χριστόν, our embracing of Christ in faith—that *is* itself the action which conquers the world, and has already conquered it. This act of the acceptance of Jesus Christ, and His *Divine* light which overcometh the darkness, of His Divine life which overcometh death, in us (not merely in our hearts, but thereby in us as a part of humanity), *is* already the decisive victory over the κόσμος. As this victorious power of heaven streams into humanity, and is received by it—though at first by a very small fragment of it—and in consequence Christ's church has an existence; so, as the result, the deadly wound *is* already inflicted upon the κόσμος: the κόσμος as such is doomed, vanquished, and lost, however much it may seem still to thrive. The *head* of the serpent is bruised, and all the energetic contortions of its body are but symptoms of its mortal agony.

VERS. 5–8. How correct this *objective* exhibition of the πίστις is, the following verses will show. For here St John says in plain words, ver. 5, that he *who believeth that Christ is the Son of God* (as in ch. iv. 15), overcometh the world; and then he shows that it is *Christ Himself* who, as received in faith and as becoming an internal power in believers, overcometh the world.

What the power is in which Christ hath come, and what the consequent power is which He causes to work in us, and in the working of which true πιστεύειν consists,—*this* is unfolded in ver. 6. It is self-evident, when we consider it well, that ver. 6 serves as the confirmation of the main proposition of ver. 5, τίς ἐστιν ὁ νικῶν, κ.τ.λ., and not to the support of the lesser clause, ὅτι ὁ Ἰησοῦς ἐστιν ὁ υἱὸς τοῦ Θεοῦ. It is not necessary now that St John should establish the general proposition, that Jesus is the Son of God; for he has already in ch. iv. amply and comprehensively set forth the consistency and accord of this proposition with the principles of all knowledge of God. And that in fact the words of ver. 6 *cannot* serve for the establishment of the proposition, that Jesus is the Son of God, will be shown when we have examined carefully the meaning of ver. 6. Οὗτός ἐστιν ὁ ἐλθὼν δι' ὕδατος καὶ αἵματος, Ἰησοῦς ὁ Χριστός· οὐκ ἐν τῷ ὕδατι μόνον, ἀλλ' ἐν τῷ ὕδατι καὶ τῷ αἵματι. These, on the whole, easily intelligible words have been explained in the most various and strangest ways by different expositors. That we may not be embarrassed and delayed by needless examination of vapid interpretations,[1] we lay down at the outset the simple and true one, and leave such other renderings as deserve refutation to follow afterwards.

As it respects, first, the ἔρχεσθαι διά, it is evident from the parallel ἐν that διά is not to be taken as local (of the penetration by anything), but as instrumental. He came through water and blood, by means of water and blood, so far as water and blood were the instruments or *means* by which He wrought. So also ἐν is equivalent to ב. He came[2] (as the Conqueror over the world), not by means of water alone, but by means of water and blood. The thought of the passage is this: As the following section, ver. 9 seq., points plainly by means of its predominant idea of the μαρτυρία to John i. 7, 8, 15, 19–34, so our present passage also points to that passage, especially John i. 29 and 33 (compared with Matt. iii. 11). John the Baptist had come *with water*; he had summoned the Israelites, by means of the *symbol* of a water-baptism, to exhibit repentance, and to confess their desert of death (for the immersion into water was the type, not of cleansing, but of the being plunged into death; comp. Rom. vi. 3, 4; 1 Pet. iii. 20, 21). Thus John also brought the law, and led them to a knowledge of sin. But further than that he could not bring them. Christ, on the other hand,[3] came not with water alone: He did, indeed, institute a baptism of water, but He *baptized not merely with water*

---

[1] According to Grotius, the water signifies the pure holiness of Christ (the blood His death); Wahl makes the water the Divine voice at the baptism of Jesus; Stroth makes the blood the testimony of the Gentile centurion at the cross; Ziegler, the resurrection and ascension; Clemens Alexandrinus expounded the water as regeneration, but the blood as knowledge. And so on without end.

[2] Olshausen: "He appeared in the world."

[3] That Christ is set over against another *Person*, is evident from the words, οὗτός ἐστιν ὁ ἐλθών, "this is *He* who came."

(John i. 33; Matt. iii. 11); He came as the Lamb of God (John i. 29), and declared, when He suffered Himself to be symbolically baptized in the water by John, His readiness to sink into death for the sin of the world; He in due time suffered that death, and came (ἐλθών, Partic. Aor.) not merely with the water, the *sign*, but in the very reality of His *atoning blood*.[1] And hence it was that He (Matt. iii. 11; John i. 33) could baptize with the *Spirit* (comp. John xvi. 7, "If I go not away, the Comforter will not come unto you"). These are the profound views which St John connects together in these simple words, in a manner which every observant reader of his Gospel must be able to appreciate. The fundamental thought is therefore this, that in the love and grace of the self-sacrifice of Jesus to death lay the power through which He overcame the world;[2] and, consequently, that in us also faith must approve itself (comp. Heb. x. xi.) as a like readiness to sacrifice all the glory of this world, and life itself; and that this faith which renounces the visible (Heb. xi. 1, xii. 2) obtains the victory through suffering and patience.

By ὕδωρ is here primarily meant the water of John's baptism; by αἷμα, the atoning blood of Christ. But it is plain that in this antithesis ὕδωρ is at the same time also exhibited as the symbol of the preaching of the law and repentance connected with John's baptism; and, further, as the symbol of mere *doctrine* generally in opposition to *deed*, and also of the *sign* in opposition to the *thing*; consequently, of Christian water-baptism as such, so far as it is a sign. For, it is not said, "John came with water, Christ with blood;" but, "Christ came not merely (like John) with water, but with water and blood." Thus the "coming with water" is an element which holds good

---

[1] Olshausen seems (so far, indeed, as his brief, and here almost illegible, notes permit us to judge) to have held the same view. He writes: "Doctrine and baptism—death of Jesus;" and again, "Baptism and the blood of the cross."

[2] Huther erroneously presupposes that the coming by water and blood is adduced as evidence for the *Messiahship of Jesus*. Were that evidence the subject treated of, the construction must be adopted which makes δι' ὕδατος, κ.τ.λ., dependent, not upon ἐλθών but upon ἐστίν—a construction which Huther himself has rejected ("This is, by the water and blood, He who was to come").—But the Apostle rather shows, *by what Christ overcame the world*.

both of the Baptist *and* of Christ;[1] therefore it is what both *in common*,—that is, the institution of water-baptism as a visible sign, together with the preaching of repentance connected with it (Mark i. 15), and teaching generally. But Christ went beyond that which He had in common with the Baptist; He died also the death of atonement, and thus came, not with water only, but with water and blood.

This correct explanation is most nearly approached by the view of Wolf, Carpzov, and others, who interpret the water by (Christian) baptism, and the blood by the Lord's Supper. It is true that the ὕδωρ embraced, with John's baptism, Christian baptism also; but only as far as the latter was a visible sign, distinguished or distinguishable from the thing, forgiveness through the blood of Christ. Thus ὕδωρ signifies not the whole sacrament of baptism (consisting of sign and thing), but only the sign in the sacrament. It is true, further, that the atoning blood of Christ is one of the two *res cœlestes* in the Holy Supper, but it is only one. Had St John intended to describe the Lord's Supper in its antithesis to baptism, he must at least have conjoined the σῶμα with the αἷμα. And then this atoning blood is not anything peculiar to the Lord's Supper, but it is equally the foundation of the forgiveness of sins imparted with baptism. That explanation, therefore, is untenable, even apart from the consideration that there does not seem any reason in the context for the assertion that Christ instituted, not only baptism, but the Holy Supper also. For, such a remark could in the end be designed only to remind of the *death* of Christ, which lies at the foundation of the Supper—but equally also at the foundation of baptism.

[1] This important point has been overlooked by those who refer this either to Christian baptism alone (Dusterdieck), or to John's baptism alone. Huther supports the latter view by the assertion that ἐλθὼν δι' ὕδατος must signify a passive passing through water, an undergoing of baptism; thus the baptism of John *received* by Christ. Is then ἐλθὼν δι' αἵματος also a passing through blood?—It is manifest that ὕδωρ and αἷμα are exhibited only as the *means* by which Christ *works*, that is, overcometh the world; not as the things which He condemned. His *coming* into the world (according to the context, His victorious coming to conquer the world) was not merely by water, like that of John, but by water and blood; the institution (not the undergoing) of baptism and the shedding of blood, the sign *and the thing*, doctrine and deed.

Still more untenable is the explanation of Augustin, Vatablus, Bain, and others, that St John by ὕδωρ καὶ αἷμα referred to the water and blood which flowed from the side of Jesus after the piercing with the spear! Apart from the consideration that αἷμα stands first in that narrative,—apart, further, from the fact that this circumstance was mentioned by St John as an eyewitness, only for the establishment of the actual death of Christ, which resulted from it, and without any allegorical significance being connected with the water and blood,—it is in itself entirely incomprehensible why St John should so emphatically lay the stress upon this, that Jesus came not " with water alone." Did any one ever assert that from His body only water flowed? And what would be the meaning and force of this antithesis? And who would say, "He came *through* or *with* water and blood," in order to express that out of His body water and blood had flowed?

We therefore hold to the simple explanation, that Christ is therefore the Overcomer of the world, because He brought with Him not only (like John the Baptist) the water (the *sign* in order to *knowledge*), but also the blood (the *thing itself*, the deed of His love in self-consecration to death).

The Apostle now continues: καὶ τὸ πνεῦμά ἐστι τὸ μαρτυροῦν, ὅτι τὸ πνεῦμά ἐστιν ἡ ἀλήθεια. The exegetical question presented by these words is not whether ὅτι is to be rendered "that" or "because:" the most essential matter for the right apprehension of their meaning is to mark the relation in which the preceding words stand to ver. 5. We have already assumed above, that the sixth verse is intended to serve as a foundation or statement of the reason of the *main thought* of the fifth verse, "that which overcometh the world, is faith in Jesus the Son of God," and not merely of the words, "Jesus is the Son of God." This we must now more thoroughly establish. And, at the outset, it should be remembered that the proposition, that Jesus is the Son of God, has already received its proof and development in the previous section, ch. iv. 1-6, and 9, 10: an additional confirmation or demonstration of it, therefore, would be superfluous. But, further, we must bear in mind that the idea of νικᾶν τὸν κόσμον is predominant from ch. v. 4 onwards. St John's purpose is to demonstrate, not that Jesus is the Son of God, but that this our faith in the Divine Sonship of Jesus is the power that overcometh the world. And thus ver. 6 does not serve to show that Jesus is the Son of God, but rather to show, that in the act of the self-renouncing, self-sacrificing love of this Son of God—*who poured out His blood*—lay the world-overcoming power, as well of Himself, as of our faith in Him. But there is, moreover, a third reason, which is perfectly decisive. Supposing it assumed and granted that the sixth verse was intended to establish and support the words ὅτι Ἰησοῦς ἐστὶν ὁ Χριστός, the question arises—Can this verse serve the purpose of establishing that proposition? " *This is He* who cometh with water and blood, not (as John the Baptist) with water alone, but with water and blood"—might indeed bear the meaning which Düsterdieck and Huther find in them: " *This*, this *Jesus of Nazareth*, is the true Messiah, and no other is He, that is, not John the Baptist; for Jesus of Nazareth came not with the water of baptism, the sign, alone, but added to that the redeeming act of the shedding of His blood." And that indeed would establish the proposition, " that Jesus is the Son of God." But, was *this* the proposition which went before in ver. 5? Did the words of that verse bear the meaning that *Jesus, and no other,* had a right to be called the Son of God? Are they an answer to the question, *Who* (what *subject*) is to be acknowledged as the Son of God? Most certainly not! There existed no doubt among the disciples, or even among the opponents of St John, that Jesus, and not for example Theudas or Judas (Acts v. 36, 37), and not John the Baptist, was the Messiah and the Son of God; even Cerinthus, in common with all the Gnostics, held it as an assured fact, that Jesus of Nazareth was the historical personage with whom the Æon Christ united Himself.[1] The words ὅτι Ἰησοῦς, κ.τ.λ., have manifestly no other meaning than the same words have in ch. iv. 15 (comp. ch. iv. 2 seq., v. 1): they are not an answer to the question,

---

[1] That St John in this passage directs his polemic against *John's disciples*, and not against the Gnostics, is an altogether untenable supposition. Forty years earlier there were disciples of John in Ephesus (Acts xix. 1 seq , comp. ch. xviii. 25): they, however, did not hold John as the Messiah, but only knew not concerning Jesus ; and when they knew, were at once baptized unto Him. Nor can it be imagined how there should be, A.D. 96, a party extant which knew only the Baptist, and regarded him (in despite of his testimony) as the Messiah.

who is the Son of God, but to the question, *what* Jesus is; the emphasis falls, not upon the subject, but upon the predicate; St John lays it down as the essence of world-overcoming faith, not that *Jesus and no other* is to be acknowledged as the Messiah and the Son of God, but that Jesus is the *Son of God Himself* (and no mere man). Now, if all the emphasis lies upon the predicative idea, οὗτός ἐστι, ver. 6, cannot serve the purpose of repeating a definition of the subjective idea, which had not been found in ver. 5. The words, that this Jesus had come not with water alone, like the Baptist, might indeed have served as the foundation of the proposition, that *Jesus, and not the Baptist,* is the Son of God, but not of the proposition, that Jesus *is the Son of God;* and not therefore of the words ὅτι Ἰησοῦς ἐστὶν ὁ Χριστός containing this latter thought.

Thus it is demonstrated, that ver. 6 rather serves as the foundation or establishment of the *leading thought* in ver. 5. It is not that the "Messiahship of Jesus" is exhibited (Huther); but it is shown in what sense the faith, that Jesus is the Son of God manifested in the flesh (for the predicate ἐστὶν ὁ Χριστός is here again, as in ch. iv. 15, v. 1, only a concise summary of what had more copiously been said in ch. iv. 2 seq.), is that power by which alone (τίς ἐστιν—εἰ μή) the world is overcome. This Jesus is He (St John says) who brought with Him not merely the baptism of water—the symbol and symbolical *requirement* of regeneration, but the *power* also of regeneration, in the atoning offering of His *blood*. Thus here also, altogether as in ch. iv. 9, compared with vers. 2 and 15, the faith — the faith " that Jesus is the Christ," appears the same as the faith " that God sent his only-begotten Son into the world, that we might live through Him" (comp. ch. iv. 14 with ch. iv. 15).

This being so, it is self-evident that the following words, " and it is the Spirit that beareth witness," etc., do not add a third demonstration to the water and the blood, " that *this Jesus* is the Christ;" and, consequently, that the inquiry which springs out of that false assumption, to wit, whether ὅτι means " that" or " because," is a perfectly needless one. Düsterdieck assumes (with Zwingli, Calvin, Bengel, and others) that μαρτυροῦν stands absolutely, without an object, and that ὅτι must be translated by " because." He makes the imaginary object of μαρτυροῦν the proposition " that *this Jesus* is the Christ"—a

x

proposition which, as we have seen, does not occur in all the context.

Without pausing to examine all the various individual forms which this perverted interpretation has assumed in the hands of individual expositors, we shall proceed to give that exposition which appears, after what has been said, to be the only correct and the only possible one. The phrase οὗτός ἐστιν ὁ ἐλθών, with the emphasized οὗτος, referred back to the question τίς ἐστιν ὁ νικῶν. No man can overcome the world but he who believeth that Jesus is *the Son of God* (in the sense of ch. iv. 14, 15)—the Son of God who came into the world, and was manifest in the flesh. *This Jesus the Son of God* it is who hath brought, through the gracious act of the offering of His blood, the fulfilment of what was demanded, the thing in addition to the sign, the power as well as the requirement; and *the Spirit it is who* ——. St John does not write καὶ τὸ πνεῦμα μαρτυρεῖ; but τὸ πνεῦμά ἐστι τὸ μαρτυροῦν, which in its form is strictly parallel with οὗτός ἐστι ὁ ἐλθών, and, like this, must refer back to τίς ἐστι ὁ νικῶν. But τὸ πνεῦμα can be no other than the Spirit, whose nature had been unfolded in the previous section under its two aspects (ch. iv.): not the soul, which Jesus in death commended to the Father (Augustin); not the human nature of Jesus (Wetstein); not the doctrine of Jesus (Carpzov); not the spiritual man (Ziegler);—but the *Spirit of God,* so far as He is a power effectual in believers and their πνεύμασι (comp. above, ch. iv. 1–3), working in them, 1, *faith in* the love which brought the Son into the flesh, and offered an atoning sacrifice; and, 2, *love,* which in imitation of Christ, and as the shedding forth of His nature, similarly sacrifices itself. This makes the whole course of thought plain. It is to be shown how the believing in Christ the Son of God has the power to overcome the world. St John first declares that, and by what means, *He in whom we* believe, and who is the object and substance of our faith, Christ, possessed in Himself the world-overcoming power; and, secondly, he shows how, and in what way, *our faith in Him* is, in consequence of His power, and as receiving its virtue, itself a power that overcometh the world. He does not say, however, " and our faith it is that beareth witness," but, " the Spirit it is that, etc. :" first, because he would impress it upon his readers that our believing is not *our* subjective act, but a power and energy *of God* working in us; and, secondly, because the πνεῦμα (as he has shown in ch. iv.) embraces, with faith, that ἀγάπη also which reproduces in all points the world-overcoming act of Christ's love (compare Col. i. 24), which, by partaking of this self-sacrificing, patient, victorious mind of Christ, possesses power through the cross also to overcome the world.

Thus, finally, the predicative idea τὸ μαρτυροῦν is made clear. It must mark an act which in effect is identical with the act of the overcoming of the world. (And this is confirmed by what is said further in vers. 7-12 concerning the μαρτυρία: see below.) That testimony is meant, through which the hearts of all those who are susceptible are won to the Gospel, and consequently wrested from the world, and incorporated into the body of Christ. And it is simply this sacred proselytism (sit venia verbo!) by means of which the Church increases and the world decreases, the latter being therefore gradually overcome.

But it is, further, plain that μαρτυροῦν cannot stand without its object. Absolutely asserted, it gives us no definite idea. It will not do, as we have shown, to supply "that Jesus is the Christ" from ver. 5. Μαρτυροῦν, ver. 6, must have an object here; and all the more, because in ver. 7 it stands without one, which would be tolerable in the latter case if the object had been specified in ver. 6. We therefore take ὅτι τὸ πνεῦμά ἐστιν ἡ ἀλήθεια as an objective proposition. *The Spirit* (of God, who is effectual in us as the Spirit of faith and love) lays down His testimony (before the world) to this, *that the spirit* (this spirit of Christian faith and of Christian love) *is the truth.* The Spirit demonstrates Himself by His power and operation.—If ὅτι is taken as an explicative proposition, there arises the bald declaration, "The Spirit beareth witness (of what?); for the Spirit is truth." What would this in reality mean? Is it meant to be deduced, from the fact that the Spirit of God is truth, that He cannot possibly keep silence, but must bear testimony? The emphasis, however, does not rest here upon the predicative idea (it is not μαρτυρεῖ nor ἐστι μαρτυροῦν), but upon the subjective idea, τὸ πνεῦμά ἐστι τὸ μαρτυροῦν. Or is the thought to be this, that because the Spirit is truth, therefore what He testifies is stedfast and sure? But *that which* the Spirit testifies, has not yet been said. Consequently, it is manifest that ὅτι, κ.τ.λ., must be taken as an objective proposition, and the particle ὅτι must be translated by "that."

Vers. 7, 8. Ὅτι τρεῖς εἰσιν οἱ μαρτυροῦντες· τὸ πνεῦμα, καὶ τὸ ὕδωρ, καὶ τὸ αἷμα· καὶ οἱ τρεῖς εἰς τὸ ἕν εἰσιν. But the Textus Receptus has here the celebrated interpolation: ἐν τῷ οὐρανῷ· ὁ πατὴρ, ὁ λόγος, καὶ τὸ ἅγιον πνεῦμα· καὶ οὗτοι οἱ τρεῖς ἕν εἰσι. Καὶ τρεῖς εἰσι οἱ μαρτυροῦντες ἐν τῇ γῇ·—which is then followed by the words of the text: τὸ πνεῦμα, καὶ τὸ ὕδωρ, καὶ τὸ αἷμα· καὶ οἱ τρεῖς εἰς τὸ ἕν εἰσιν. The question of the genuineness or spuriousness of the words in question has been fiercely contested; but the view of most of the moderns (Griesbach, Lücke, Lachmann, Tischendorf, Düsterdieck, Huther) has been declared, not without a certain exaggerated emphasis, against their genuineness. There are some, however, such as Sander, Besser, and Mayer, who venture to defend it. If we go to the original sources, we are met by the fact, first, that as it respects the manuscript codices, not one Greek text with which we are acquainted, down to the sixteenth century, reads the words in question. Only four Greek codices of the sixteenth century contain the clause. But of these four, one (Cod. Bavianus) is a copy of the Complutensian Polyglot; another (34, or Cod. Britannicus) seems to have taken the words from the Vulgate, and that in a bad translation (πατὴρ, λόγος, καὶ πνεῦμα, without the article). Of Codd. 162 and 173 we may assume that they also received the interpolation from the Vulgate. Secondly, as it respects the *old versions* (Peschito, Arabic, Coptic, Æthiopic, and Latin, down to A.D. 600), they do not contain it, any more than the ancient codices. Thirdly, among the Fathers, none of the whole body of the ante-Nicene know the clause, save Cyprian;[1] and, what is of more moment, those very Fathers

---

[1] Tertullian is no exception. When he says (de Pudic. 21) that in the Church dwells *trinitas unius divinitatis, Pater, Filius, et Spiritus,* no thoughtful person would regard this as a reference to the interpolation in question. And when (adv. Praxeam, 25) he remarks upon John xvi. 15. *Ita connexus Patris in Filio et Filii in Paracleto tres efficit cohærentes alterum ex altero, qui tres unum sint, non unus, quomodo dictum est, Ego et Pater unum sumus* (John x. 30)—it must appear evident to every one, from the whole tenor of the words, that he had *not* before his eyes our present passage. No more does he refer to it in the *Introduction* of his book against Praxeas, where he copiously, and with almost scholastic exactness, develops his theory of the Trinity.

who in the Nicene controversy contended for the Nicene Creed, never appeal to these words, which would, however, have been their firmest and most welcome support; instead of that, they take pains to demonstrate the homoousia of the Son by other passages (for example, by the eighth verse of this very chapter). Cyprian is the only exception. In the Ep. ad Jubajanum, where he is speaking of the invalidity of the baptism of heretics, he asks what kind of a temple of God he would make who was baptized by a heretic. He could not be a *templum Creatoris*, who did not believe in a Creator; he could not be a temple of Christ, who denied Christ's divinity; nor could he be a temple of the Holy Ghost, for "*cum tres unum sint*, quomodo Spiritus placatus esse ei potest, qui aut Patris aut Filii inimicus est?" Meanwhile, here we have no other than the same dogmatical declaration which Tertullian had already made, and without the aid of 1 John v. 7, 8. More important, on the other hand, is another saying of Cyprian. He says (de Unit. Eccles.) : Dicit Dominus, Ego et Pater unum sumus (John x. 30), et *iterum* (thus in another passage) de Patre et Filio et Spiritu Sancto *scriptum est, et tres unum sunt*, et quisquam credit, hanc unitatem (that is, of the Church) de divinâ firmitate venientem, sacramentis cœlestibus cohærentem, scindi in ecclesiâ posse. Facundus, indeed (pro Defens. iii. 1, 3), supposed that Cyprian had here in view only the words τὸ πνεῦμα καὶ τὸ ὕδωρ καὶ τὸ αἷμα, καὶ οἱ τρεῖς εἰς τὸ ἕν εἰσι; having understood by the πνεῦμα the energy of the Holy Spirit in the Church, by the ὕδωρ the energy of the Father, and by the αἷμα that of the Son. But, although it might be *possible* that Cyprian so understood the words (and though, further, the Vulgate had translated εἰς τὸ ἕν εἰσι by *unum sunt*), yet between possibility and probability there is a difference, and Cyprian's words may be explained by the fact that in manuscripts which *he* had (of an old Latin version) the interpolation was already to be found. Thus was Cyprian's sentence viewed by Fulgentius Ruspensis (Responsio ad Arianos);[1] and, what is of more importance, Fulgentius him-

[1] "Quod etiam beatus martyr Cyprianus confitetur, dicens: qui pacem Christi et concordiam rumpit, adversus Christum facit; qui alibi præter ecclesiam colligit, Christi ecclesiam spargit. Atque ut unam ecclesiam unius Dei esse monstraret, hæc confestim testimonia de scripturis inseruit. Dicit Dominus" (then follow the words of Cyprian in question). I cannot,

self quotes the critically-questionable words as St John's, and therefore must have read them in *his* New Testament. (Fulgentius died A.D. 533.) But, before his time, towards the end of the fifth century, Vigilius (adv. Varim. Arian.) says: Johannes evangelista ad Parthos: tres sunt, inquit, qui testimonium perhibent in terra, aqua, sanguis et caro, et tres in nobis sunt, et tres sunt, qui testimonium perhibent in cœlo, Pater, Verbum et Spiritus, et hi tres unum sunt. We see that he had before him the passage in his New Testament in its corrupt form (aqua, sanguis *et caro*, et tres in *nobis* sunt); but also, that the gloss was already in the text, *and not merely in a single copy*, but that it was so widely diffused and acknowledged in the West as to be appealed to by him *bonâ fide* in his contest with his Arian opponents.[1] So also we find the citation in Cassiodorus, Etherius, and others: and Düsterdieck, therefore, goes too far when he says that we may "track the introduction of this interpolation into the text" by following Vigilius, Fulgentius, Cassiodorus, and others: these Fathers rather bear testimony to the fact, that the questionable clause had already, about A.D. 500, the character of a widely-extended *various reading*. Hence it may be explained, how in *later* times the words came to be written *in the margin* of individual Greek manuscripts.

If we clearly take into view this whole position of the matter, it will seem nothing less than inconceivable that Cyprian actually read the words in his text. The thought which he expresses there was by no means a strange one in the third century; it is to be found perfectly developed, for example, by Tertullian (from John x. 30, xvi. 15). If we only bear in

understand how Dusterdieck can doubt whether Fulgentius thought that the words of 1 John v. 7 were in Cyprian's mind. He says himself, "*He* (Cyprian) quotes this testimony *from the Scripture*, and so says Fulgentius, immediately after *he himself* had referred to the questionable words of the seventh verse as St John's." He must have read the words in *his* New Testament, and have regarded them as genuine. How could he then doubt that Cyprian also had these words in his mind?

[1] What weight such patristic notices have, even as opposed to the codd., we see strikingly evidenced by the passage, Matt. viii. 28, where the majority of the codd. have either inserted Γαδαρηνῶν as a correction from Mark and Luke, or read Γεργεσηνῶν, but where we find from Origen, in John (tom. vi. 24), that the old codd. of his time read Γερασηνῶν,—the reading Γεργεσηνῶν owing its origin to a conjectural correction of Origen himself.

mind how vague was the form of the oldest Latin versions, and how, in the fragments which we have of them, the text is sometimes freely handled, and sometimes corruptly given, it will appear by no means an impossibility that so early as the third century such a gloss as this could have slipped into the text.

Such a gloss we say. For, if we lay more stress upon this passage of Cyprian than some do, it is not for the purpose of maintaining the genuineness of the clause, but rather that we may contend against it on safer grounds. Granted, that Cyprian read the words in his text; what follows from that? That it was a very old reading, or possibly the original reading? By no means. This would be to confound all the first principles of a sound criticism of the text. Granted it not to be impossible that Greek codices may be yet discovered which shall contain the clause, we must direct our critical judgment by the evidence of the documents which we have, and not of those which we have not, and of the existence of which we as yet know nothing. And, accordingly, we are bound to say that the whole Greek-speaking East was not acquainted with the words in question, and in the Greek Church of the East the reading was known by none; otherwise, it would be found in some at least of the old codices, and it would have been employed in the controversy with the Arians. Assuming now, for argument's sake, that the words are genuine, in what but Arian interests could they have been thrown out of the text? And could this have been done without mention, or reprobation, or punishment? Would the orthodox Church have suffered such a theft to be committed without even observing the thief? Let him believe this who can! But how could this *spolium* have taken place at so late a date, since even the Peschito omits the words, and in all the East none is found who knew them?

On the internal arguments against the authenticity we do not lay any great stress. That St John—who wrote those passages in the Gospel, ch. i. 1, etc., x. 30, xvi. 15—*could* not have given expression to the thought that the Father, Son, and Spirit ἕν εἰσι, is no more than the untenable assertion of a subjective hypercriticism. That he, who elsewhere opposes Θεός to λόγος, and υἱός to πατήρ, should here insert between πατήρ and πνεῦμα the λόγος, involves no direct impossibility, though it is somewhat strange; as also is the attribute ἅγιον in connection with πνεῦμα, since from ch. iv. 1 downwards he has used the mere πνεῦμα, or πνεῦμα τοῦ Θεοῦ. As it regards the process of thought, there is nothing in the interpolation that directly conflicts with it, especially if we adopt the arrangement which is confirmed by the oldest citations in Vigilius, Fulgentius, Cassius, and Etherius: καὶ τρεῖς εἰσι οἱ μαρτυροῦντες ἐν τῇ γῇ· τὸ πνεῦμα, καὶ τὸ ὕδωρ, καὶ τὸ αἷμα· καὶ οἱ τρεῖς εἰς τὸ ἕν εἰσι. Καὶ τρεῖς εἰσι οἱ μαρτυροῦντες ἐν τῷ οὐρανῷ· ὁ πατὴρ, καὶ ὁ λόγος, καὶ τὸ πνεῦμα· καὶ οἱ τρεῖς ἕν εἰσιν. According to the correct interpretation of the μαρτυρία, which refers it, not to the demonstration that Jesus and no other is the promised Messiah, but to the testimony through whose might God overcometh the world, St John would first mention the three factors through which God works upon earth:—the *Spirit* of faith and love operating upon believers, and through them upon the world; then the *baptism of* water, instituted by Christ (as representative of the means and signs of grace); and then the *blood*, that is, that patient suffering unto death in which Christians have their Lord for a pattern and a forerunner. After these, he would introduce the Three-one God in heaven, who from heaven sustains the testimony of His Church, yea, Himself works from heaven in this testimony of His own upon earth,—as *Father*, who sent His Son; as *Word*, which came forth from the Father, and shineth as light in the darkness; and as *Spirit*, who worketh upon believers below, in order in them and through them to exert His power upon the world.[1] And, as the former triple energy of testimony on earth proceeds εἰς τὸ ἕν—that is, to one and the same end,—so also the Three Witnesses in heaven are ἕν, One Nature (compare John x. 30), and thus the witness tending to one end springs from one origin.

The *internal* arguments, therefore, would never be sufficient of themselves to determine any one in favour of or against the

[1] This, as the answer to Dusterdieck's question, as to how the testimony of the Spirit in heaven is to be distinguished from His testimony upon earth. Huther asserts that the trinity of the heavenly testimony would "enter without any preparation for it;" but we must remind him that in ver. 6 "Jesus Christ" and the "Spirit" had been for the first time mentioned together.

genuineness of the words in question. If, indeed, some old, unlooked-for Greek codex should be discovered, containing the passage, the critical question would take another aspect. However, as we do not make an appeal to codices which are not in our hands, but to those which we have and are acquainted with, nothing remains but to make the unambiguous confession that, according to all the sources at present in our hands, the clause in dispute is spurious.[1]

So much for the critical question. As it respects the exegesis, vers. 7 and 8 offer no difficulty, when ver. 6 is rightly understood. How those expositors who understand the μαρτυρεῖν of a testimony for the Messiahship of Jesus, must labour to torture the Spirit, the water, and the blood into a demonstration for that Messiahship, needs no remark of ours. Huther, in particular, who refers the ὕδωρ to the baptism of John, exclusive of the Christian baptism, and remarks upon ver. 7, "All these three expressions have here obviously the same meaning as before," must be embarrassed by the consideration that the Present Tense cannot well refer to John's baptism, as if it were still bearing witness.

Μαρτυρεῖν is to us, in ver. 7 as in ver. 6, that activity of testimony *by which the world is overcome.* It is the faith that Christ is the Son of God which (according to ver. 5) overcometh the world; and in what way, has been already said in ver. 6. He who constitutes the Object and Matter of that faith, Christ, came (as Conqueror) by means of this, that He did not, like the Baptist, bring a mere symbolical requirement of regeneration, but, through the sacrifice of His blood, the very power of regeneration. And the Spirit who now worketh in us faith in

---

[1] The Complutensian received the clause from the Vulgate, and so also the ante-Lutheran translations. Erasmus (first and second editions), Aldina (1518), (apito 1521–34) omitted it; but Erasmus restored it through fear of man (third edition, 1522). Beza, Stephanus, and the Text. Rec. retained it thenceforward. Luther and Bugenhagen declared it to be spurious; Zwingli omitted it in his annotations; Calvin was inclined to regard it as genuine, on the ground of the *Prologus galeatus,* which he held as coming from Jerome, and in which the omission of the clause is attributed to *infidelibus translatoribus.* The Zurich translation of the New Testament, 1529, contains it; but the succeeding editions are said to have inclosed it in brackets, though the copy in my possession (1561) has it without brackets. It was first received into Luther's translation in 1593.

this Christ, and at the same time that love which is derived from the nature of Christ, Himself testifies before the world that He (this Spirit of Christian faith and Christian love) is the truth. Ὅτι, St John continues; introducing, however, no reason, but only an explanation (like the Heb. כי so often, and St John thinks in Hebrew)—"that is to say," we might translate, "there are three that bear witness, the Spirit, and the water, and the blood." He names the Spirit first, not because the Spirit is "the only independent witness, not dependent on the water and the blood" (Düsterdieck)—for, without the act of the offering of the blood of Christ, the Spirit would not put forth His energy upon earth—but because the Apostle, after he had spoken in the beginning of ver. 6 of that with which Christ *had* come in the past, now purposes to speak of the witness by which the world *is* overcome in the present. As such, he has already, at the end of ver. 6, mentioned the πνεῦμα, which τὸ μαρτυροῦν ἐστι; and with this he now connects his words. But, this very testimony of the Spirit ruling in believers, works in such manner that those two instruments of victory with which Christ in the past appeared upon earth, are not laid aside, but continue their instrumentality, and are as it were continually reproduced anew. First, the *water*, which (according to ver. 6) was common to Him and to the Baptist; that is, *water-baptism* instituted by Christ, in its characteristic as an external institution, as a sign and symbol, and consequently as the representative of all the *means* of grace administered by men, especially in its connection with the preaching of the word, which is inseparable from baptism, and, according to the apostolical ordinance, preceded it. But then, also, the *blood*, the blood of Christ—that is, His atoning death, which ever continues its subduing power on the hearts of men. Not, however, the blood of Christ alone,—for St John writes generally that blood is a μαρτυροῦν,—but there must be added the power of the witnessing blood, which, for the testimony of Jesus, and in the spirit of Christ, in the spirit of self-sacrificing, suffering love, is still poured out continually by His people. And, as in ch. iv. the Spirit of God had been viewed under two aspects, as the Spirit of confession and as the Spirit of love, so we may say that in the water of baptism the confession is embodied which overcomes the lie of the world, but in the blood of testimony that love which overcomes the world's carnal power by suffering, even as Christ overcame death by dying.

In the concluding words, καὶ οἱ τρεῖς εἰς τὸ ἕν εἰσι, St John expresses the inseparable co-operation unto one end which is correlative with the unity of their origin in the one Spirit, who, as the Spirit of confession and the Spirit of suffering love, approves His Divine power. Εἰς τὸ ἕν does not mean "together" (Luther, *beisammen*), but " co-operating to one end;" not, however, with respect to the "leading clause, that Jesus is the Christ" (Düsterdieck), but to the overcoming of the world.

VERS. 9–12. How "our faith" (ver. 4), by means of its *object and substance* (Christ, who came with water and blood), as also in virtue of its *nature* (of the Spirit, ver. 6, who, ver. 7, still, in connection with baptism and self-renouncing suffering love, and in these, bears His testimony to Himself), has the power in itself to overcome the world—has been shown in vers. 5–8. Now, vers. 9–12, the other and subjective side of the matter is brought under consideration; it is shown, how this victory over the κόσμος takes effect in the individual man. The Apostle exhibits this to his readers, while he reminds them how they themselves had been brought to the *assurance* of faith by the "witness" dilated upon vers. 6–8. This, indeed, did not take place through external arguments directed to the understanding, but through the *power* of a new life which Christ and Christ's Spirit had manifested in them. Thus St John comes to speak, vers. 9–12, of the *assurance and power* of faith, and thus demonstrates and illustrates its world-conquering character.

Ver. 9. "If we receive the testimony of men:" this premiss (εἰ with the Indicative) lays down an admitted presupposition, from which an inference may and will be deduced. It is a known fact, that we (in human affairs, for example, before a tribunal) accept the testimony which is given by men, and give it its measured value. The first person plural serves to express the idea of the German "*man*." We, men, are wont to do so. (Not—*we Christians*). Granted, then, that we are accustomed to receive the testimony of men, how much more must we receive the testimony of God, this being obviously μείζων, greater in value, and dignity, and certainty! St John, however, expresses it so concisely as to omit the πόσῳ μᾶλλον λαβῶμεν. He says only, " God's testimony is greater ;" the complementary clause, " consequently, the rather to be received," was self-understood. Ὅτι αὕτη ἐστὶν ἡ μαρτυρία, ὅτι, κ.τ.λ. Instead of the second ὅτι the Rec. reads ἥν. (So De Wette and Sander.) But ὅτι is perfectly authenticated by Codd. A.B., Copt., Sahid., Armen., Vulg., and the Fathers (ἥν originated manifestly in the endeavour to conform ver. 9 to the following verse).—The first ὅτι may be taken either as a *causal* particle, or as an *explanatory* " for, that is." Lücke adopts the former, and supplies what is omitted before ὅτι thus : " But if we receive the testimony of God, we must believe that Jesus is the Christ ; for this is in truth the substance of His testimony." But such a completion of the thought is exegetically untenable ; it exhibits the same perversion which, from ver. 6 onwards, will think of nothing but " demonstration of the Messiahship of Jesus." Huther correctly sees that the clause with ὅτι serves to explain and define the previous idea, ἡ μαρτυρία τοῦ Θεοῦ, that is, to say what testimony must be here understood. But, even then, there are various views which may be taken. Either the second ὅτι may be translated by " for ;" in which case the αὕτη must necessarily refer back to ver. 8 (" that is to say, this—water, blood, and Spirit—is the testimony of God ; for He has testified it concerning His Son"). But this does not present any clear process in the thought ; we cannot see what the words ὅτι μεμαρτύρηκεν, κ.τ.λ., really mean to say in this case ; they would bear a definite meaning only if an αὐτός came before the μεμαρτύρηκεν, in order to emphasize that it was *God Himself* who gave this testimony. Or, the second ὅτι may be translated " that ;" in which case the clause ὅτι μεμαρτύρηκεν must be regarded as the explanation and substance of the αὕτη : " This, namely, is the testimony of God, that He has testified *concerning His Son.*" The emphasis then falls upon the words περὶ τοῦ υἱοῦ αὐτοῦ. In any case, the Apostle does *not* mean thereby (as Bengel and Lücke assume) *that* testimony which, according to vers. 7, 8, *still continuously goes on* through the Spirit, the water, and the blood ; certainly not the purely internal testimony which is treated of in ver. 11 : but he opposes to the continuous testimony which goes on through *man's* instrumentality, the immediately-*Divine*, *once-given* testimony (μεμαρτύρηκεν) ; and this must be conceived of as no other than that of John i. 33

(compare Matt. iii. 17, and the parallel passages, Mark ix. 7; John xii. 28). As the Apostle above, in ch. iv. 21, made it prominent that we have an express *commandment* of the Lord for the ἀγάπη, so similarly he points here, ch. v. 9, to the fact that we have an express *testimony* of God Himself on which our faith is founded. And the *words* περὶ τοῦ υἱοῦ αὐτοῦ plainly remind us of the *words* of Matt. iii. 17; Mark ix. 7.

Ver. 10. This testimony, however, as given in the past, does not altogether end the matter. He who believeth on this Son of God has the witness of God, not only externally to himself in the evangelical narrative, and as something belonging to the past, but internally and as an active and influential power. The like and selfsame testimony which was once uttered by God, "This is My beloved Son," approves itself as true in us, in believers, while it mightily demonstrates its power within us (as is afterwards shown, ver. 11).

He, on the other hand, who does not believe (and in whose inner soul, consequently, that testimony cannot demonstrate its power), is not excused (through this deficiency of a present mighty demonstration within him); but he remains under *this* guilt, that he believeth not that *historical and sure* testimony which God bore to His Son, and thereby "hath made God a liar," that is, has treated Him as a liar (compare ch. i. 10).

They who do not distinguish the Perfect in ver. 9, μεμαρτύρηκεν, from the Present in vers. 7, 8, are not in a position to view rightly the thought of ver. 10.

Vers. 11, 12 serve the purpose of explaining and unfolding the words "hath the witness in himself," ver. 10. Καὶ αὕτη cannot refer back to the "testimony which God hath testified," ver. 10; since in vers. 9, 10 the past historical testimony has been already clearly distinguished from the testimony which we bear in ourselves at the present. Rather must αὕτη go back to the commencing clause of ver. 10. This is confirmed by ver. 12; where it is said that the μὴ πιστεύων hath *not* life, consequently hath *not* received *this* testimony, ver. 11, which simply consists in the possession of the ζωή; consequently, it cannot be demanded of him that he should believe this *internal testimony*, nor can it be said of him that he maketh God a liar, because he believeth not this testimony which *hath not yet been borne within him.* It is therefore perfectly plain, that by the "witness which God hath given, μεμαρτύρηκεν," and by the not receiving of which the unbeliever maketh "God a liar," something other must be meant than the internal experience of the life-giving power of faith. This latter follows only upon faith itself. The μαρτυρία ἣν μεμαρτύρηκεν must, on the other hand, be something which the not-yet-believing man might and could already have perceived or rejected. Consequently, it *must* be the *objective, historical* testimony, by which God acknowledged Jesus as His Son. And, consequently, further, our words, ver. 11, καὶ αὕτη ἐστίν, κ.τ.λ., must refer, not to the second, but to the first, member of ver. 10.

The meaning of the words themselves furnishes no particular difficulty. "And this is the testimony (which we have), that God hath given to us (ἡμῖν) eternal life. And this life is in His Son." The believer has, as such, experienced the *power* of God in himself, the power which has awakened him from spiritual death, and given him the victory over the *I* of self, the power of a heavenly life. And in truth this heavenly life *is* and subsists in the Person of the Son of God. It is the death-overcoming power of Christ, the Son of God, which the believer has experienced, and experiences anew every day, upon and within his soul. With him, therefore, doubt upon that point is no longer possible; he can no more doubt of the Divinity and Divine power of Christ than a recovered blind man can doubt of the existence of the sun and of light. The Son of God, with His power overcoming the κόσμος, is to him a fact, a most proper and essential experience. This is the blessing which rests upon the belief of that objective historical μαρτυρία of God concerning His Son, that a man attains thereby to this internal experimental μαρτυρία of the living power of the Son of God overcoming the world and death.

"He that hath the Son, hath life; he that hath not the Son, hath not life:" these words develop and distribute the second member of ver. 11. That "this life *is* in His Son," approves itself in the fact that he who hath the Son hath life,—and conversely. (Grotius weakens the thought by saying: "He who hath the Son hath a *right* to *future* eternal life." St John says much more than this.)

VERS. 13–17. It has been maintained by De Wette and

others, against Spener, Bengel, and Lücke, that there is here no formal beginning of a final section, but that the chain of thought goes on continuously. This, however, does not follow from the mere fact that in ver. 13 the idea of the "eternal life" is resumed; for this idea is so profound, full, and comprehensive, as to justify us in thinking that St John, in the section ch. v. 4–12, had been gradually introducing it in all its fulness, in order to declare in his final section that this was the end of all his writing, to show them that *we have eternal life through faith in the Son of God*. This is the very end which he lays down, ch. xx. 31, as the final and consummate goal of his Gospel. —What speaks more strongly against the assumption that in ch. v. 13 there is the formal commencement of a final section in the *ordinary* sense, is the circumstance that the fundamental idea of the Fifth Part—*the world-overcoming power of faith*— still continues to stamp its impress upon the whole strain of the thought. Nevertheless, there is a sense in which vers. 13–21 actually form a concluding section. Not that the organic development of the thought comes to an end in ver. 12, a purely hortatory and final appendage now following; but the organic development of thought has now attained its all-comprehending crown or climax, so that the last strain of the last Part forms *at the same time* a conclusion of the whole matter, a conclusion which bears all the evident characteristics of being such.

That is to say, the words ταῦτα ἔγραψα ὑμῖν, ver. 13, by no means point back merely to vers. 10–12. How trivial would it be to say, "This (that he who hath the Son hath eternal life) have I written to you, that ye may know that he who believeth on the Son of God hath eternal life"—! "These things have I written" rather refer back (Bengel) to the ταῦτα γράφομεν of ch. i. 4. That which St John there announced at the outset, he has now fully accomplished. He has written this whole Epistle in order to bring his readers to this goal and topstone of knowledge, that they, if they believe on the name of the Son of God, have eternal life. To this same faith it was his design to lead them by his Gospel (John xx. 31): a new demonstration of the internal and external connection of the two documents.[1]

---

[1] Olshausen says on this passage: "The connection of the Epistle with the Gospel is here evident. In John xx. 31 St John lays down the very same end for his Gospel."

This concluding point he has now therefore reached. But even this last blessed result of faith, the "life eternal," he will still unfold in its *world-overcoming* power, and exhibit accordingly the πίστις also as in its *consequences* overcoming the world. But both these are exhibited in the *hearing and granting of prayer*. The believer is here represented as a man who, as it were, may place himself in command of the powers of God Himself. In the confidence of faith he may pray, and God heareth him. In the development of this thought it will be seen (vers. 16, 17) that St John has especially in view intercession for the *spiritual good* of other men, and for their *conversion* (and consequently, in this sense also, the proper overcoming of the world).

In ver. 14 we must read, with the Rec. and B., and in conformity with St John's style, ὅτι, ἐάν τι (against A. and Lachmann, ὅ,τι ἄν). "And this is the confidence which we have in Him, that,"—and so on. The παῤῥησία is connected, not with the idea of the ζωή (Düsterdieck), but with that of the πιστεύειν. The clause with ὅτι does not serve to explain the αὕτη, for *our παῤῥησία* cannot consist in that which *God doeth*. Ὅτι depends simply upon παῤῥησία, and only sets forth its matter or substance. "We have the confidence that He heareth us,"—this is the kernel of the thought; but, to make prominent how great and glorious a thing it is to be able to possess such confidence, St John uses, instead of the simple παῤῥησίαν ἔχομεν, the emphatic καὶ αὕτη ἐστὶν ἡ παῤῥησία ἣν ἔχομεν. Lücke is right therefore in saying that the logical completion of the clause would be thus: "And this is the confidence which we have: (we have the confidence) that he heareth us."

He (God) heareth us, "if we ask anything *according to His will*." Here is confirmed what was observed upon ch. iii. 22, that, in the doctrine concerning the granting of prayer, the petitioner is always assumed to live in the Holy Ghost and in the possession of a regenerate life; that, consequently, his supplication proceeds from a will which is in accordance with the Divine will, and which frames its desires according to the norm of God's Spirit and will; that, therefore, he never urges presumptuous requests, but prays only for that which Christ has taught us to ask for.

Ver. 15. If we know that God heareth our prayer (ἀκούει), we *have* already the thing prayed for (even though the fulfilment may not be plain to our own eyes at once). So rightly explain Episcopius, Lücke, and others (against Rickli, who finds in ver. 15 the simple declaration, that if God *hear* our prayer, He will also *grant* it. But the ἀκούειν τινός itself involves the granting; compare ver. 14). In the *knowing that* God heareth us, lies already the *possession* of what is asked, even though the fulfilment of our request may not be at once obvious to our eyes. This is the highest glory of the confidence of prayer, that the petitioner may at once, without doubt and with absolute assurance, regard the thing asked for as his own *possession*, even as he at first only *asked* God for it.—Instead of ἐάν with the Indicative, a pure Greek writer would have used εἰ with the Indicative (as in ch. iv. 11).

In vers. 16, 17 St John speaks of a *limit* which is placed to the world-overcoming power of prayer. If any petition might be supposed to be "according to the will of God," it would certainly be the petition for the *conversion and salvation of our neighbour*. This is indeed prayer, not for myself, but for him, and therefore springing from love; it is a prayer, not for earthly good, but for the salvation of a soul, and therefore for the extension and coming of the kingdom of God. Hence, one might be misled into the theoretical notion that *every* prayer for the conversion of a fellow-man *must* be heard and granted. The Apostle here obviates that erroneous inference. Conversion proceeds in a sphere of its own, which touches at all points the domain of human voluntary determination; and in this domain there is a point at which the human will may have so hardened itself against the converting influences of the grace of God, as that God cannot and will not any more save. When this point has been reached, intercession has no assurance of being heard.

It is plain, and indeed uncontested, that this is the general meaning of these words. The Apostle sets out with the presupposition that one sees his ἀδελφός sin the ἁμαρτίαν μὴ πρὸς θάνατον. Instead of the ἐάν, another author would have used εἰ with the Optative. How wide the idea of ἀδελφός is, we have

---

[1] Olshausen: "St John makes specially prominent the noblest application of prayer—Prayer for others."

already seen; and what St John in ver. 8 says concerning the witnessing, world-overcoming power of the αἷμα, that is, of the love which sacrifices its own life, shows us that he did not limit his meaning, any more than his Lord (Luke x. 30 seq.), to mere obligations towards our fellow-regenerate, exclusive of the obligations of love towards those who are still to be converted. First of all, we must think of the members of the Christian community, but not to the exclusion of those who are not Christians. To restrict the idea of ἀδελφός to the regenerate is altogether untenable, especially if the ἁμαρτία πρὸς θάνατον be the sin of apostasy, which, ch. ii. 19, the truly regenerate cannot commit.—He then who seeth his ἀδελφός (in the widest sense) sin—his sin not being yet the sin unto death—*should* (not *may*) pray for him; and God[1]—or he, the petitioner,[2] by his prayer—will *give him life*. This δώσει ζωήν of itself shows that it is not so much the commission of an individual sinful action which is meant by the ἁμαρτάνειν (in that case we should have expected as the answer of the prayer, "And God will forgive it to him"), as a *state* of sin which is to be removed by the impartation of a higher heavenly power of life. And this, therefore must define and limit the idea of the "sinning unto death." By this also cannot be meant an individual external action, deserving the punishment of death (as Morus, Lange, and the papal expositors suppose, with a false application of Num. xviii. 22); for θάνατος can be here only the antithesis of ζωή, and must not therefore be understood of bodily death. But πρὸς θάνατον he sins who has brought himself into such a posture and state of soul as renders impossible the conversion to πίστις and ζωή (Calvin, De Wette, Lücke).

The one and only point of difficulty in the whole passage is, whether and how it can be surely *known*, as to a third person, that the ἀδελφός has committed that sin of internal reprobation. That it is supposed to be possible to be known, is shown not so much by the ἐάν τις ἴδῃ (which refers primarily to the general ἁμαρτάνοντα), as by this, that the *repeated* restriction, ἁμαρτάνειν μὴ πρὸς θάνατον and τοῖς ἁμαρτάνουσι μὴ πρὸς θάνατον, *implicitly* requires the readers, *when* they see their brother sinning, to *test* whether the sin be or be not the "sin unto death." The

---

[1] So Beza, Socinus, Grotius, Spener, Bengel, Lucke.
[2] So Erasmus, Calvin, De Wette.

question then arises, how this mark of cognisableness may be reconciled with what is said besides concerning the "sin unto death;" or, in other words, what definite species of sin may be found in the case of which the mark that it may be known coincides with the other marks.

Düsterdieck lays down the following *norms* for the exposition of the idea of the ἁμαρτία πρὸς θάνατον : 1. That it may be known ; 2. That it can be committed only by a member of the Christian community ; 3. That for him who has committed it " there may not be prayer;" 4. That in and for itself it is not distinguished from every other sin, since every sin is in fact a sin unto death. Accordingly, he comes to the decision that the "sin unto death" cannot be the "sin against the Holy Ghost, Matt. xii. 31" (since this was committed by unbelievers); nor impenitence continued even unto (bodily) death (since it could never be known whether any man would continue his impenitence unto death) ;—but no other than shipwreck of faith, or apostasy.

However generally correct this may be, the question is left quite unsolved by it—how far this sin is *cognisable*. Düsterdieck was at first disposed to regard with some favour the notion of Grotius, who regarded excommunication from the Church as the *sure sign* of the commission of the sin unto death —as if that sin were to be known by what a man suffered, and not by what he did; and as if the Church might not be mistaken in the infliction of excommunication! He afterwards says, with Huther, that "a sin must be meant by which the internal abandonment of life in Christ is consummated and declared. But thus every grosser sin, murder, denial of Christ, adultery, may be such a sin unto death." We may reasonably doubt, however, whether the man who commits an act of adultery, must be therefore at once supposed to have finally and fully broken off all connection with Christ. Düsterdieck finally takes refuge in the assumption, that "the whole representation of the sin unto death must have been far less difficult to the first readers of the Epistle," and that apostasy to Gnosticism must necessarily have been its meaning to their minds. A miserable conclusion this, after eighteen pages of investigation! Were then the Cerinthian Gnostics the only men for whom prayer was not to be offered?

But these regulative principles for the exposition of the idea are, as a whole, partly incorrect, and partly inefficient. It is not correct to say that the sin here treated of could be committed only by the regenerate. If the sin unto death was apostasy to Gnosticism, then we are taught by ch. ii. 19, that those who committed this sin had never been truly regenerate. And it is an error to make ch. v. 1 prove that the idea of $ἀδελφός$ is limited to the fellow-regenerate: in our observations upon that passage, we have seen that, not the idea $ἀδελφός$, but the contextual process of the Apostle's thought, led him to the derivation of the $ἀγάπη$ there from the common fatherhood of God; and on ch. iii. 15, that the idea $ἀδελφός$, viewed in itself, embraces the whole relation of *man to man*. Accordingly, the first restriction falls to the ground. A "sin unto death" will *every* sin be through which man becomes incapable of any further conversion; therefore, both the "sin against the Holy Ghost," spoken of in Matt. xii. 31 seq., that is, unbelievers' decided hardening of themselves against the drawing of grace, and the sin of apostasy (comp. Heb. vi. 4) committed by members of the Christian community (though, according to ch. ii. 19, not internally and in the fullest sense regenerate), fall under the idea of the "sin unto death" alike.

Secondly, it is a perversion for him to maintain (misunderstanding a saying of Calvin, that every, the smallest sin, would *deserve* death) that every sin *in itself* is a sin unto death; and, therefore, that the question does not concern the objective quality of the sin, but only the subjective condition of heart in him who commits the sin. That would take away every vestige of the possibility of discerning and knowing the sin. But the Apostle says in ver. 18 just the reverse, that not every sin is a "sin unto death" in the sense of ver. 17.

Thirdly, it is a very incautious way of speaking, to lay down as a third mark, that for him who has committed the sin unto death "we are not to pray." St John speaks more cautiously; he does not forbid the praying,[1] but he says, $οὐ\ περὶ\ ἐκείνης\ λέγω\ ἵνα\ ἐρωτήσῃ$. Now, whether the $περί$ be connected with $ἐρωτήσῃ$ (as the majority of expositors think) or with $λέγω$ (which better suits the meaning of $περί$)—in

---

[1] Olshausen writes here erroneously, "Love forbids now to pray."

neither case is there any *prohibition* of prayer in the words; St John only takes this sin away from under the previous *commandment* to pray. (It is not—" For it I say that he may not pray;" the negation οὐ belongs decisively to the λέγω, not to ἐρωτήσῃ). But this is very important. For with it falls all that has been said by him concerning the cognisableness of this " sin unto death." If St John *forbids* a Christian to pray for the sinner unto death, he must presuppose that the having committed such a sin is in every case indubitably certain; but, taking the words of ver. 17 in their simple meaning, the only thing laid down and presupposed is this, *that a sin which is μὴ πρὸς θάνατον, not unto death, may be surely known as such*. And thus all the difficulties are solved. That any particular sin which another may commit, as also the general state in which he may be found, is *not πρὸς θάνατον*—that he may still repent and be converted—*this* may be easily and with the utmost confidence known. And *where* this is known with certainty, where there is no necessity for thinking another to be hardened and past salvation,—there *must* be prayer offered. Where, on the other hand, this certainty ceases, where there is reason to assume or suppose that another has committed the " sin unto death,"—there *this prayer ceases* (Grotius, Lange, Huther, Besser). Thus, in this latter case—that is, where there is room for much doubt (absolute assurance is never possible to any human eye)—the intercession is not *commanded;* neither is it *forbidden*, but left to the heart of the individual: only, that in such cases such assurance of the hearing of prayer as had been spoken of in ver. 14 seq. cannot have place.[1] The Christian is defended against the dangerous supposition, that unconditionally, and in every instance, prayer for the conversion of a third person *must* be granted.[2] There are cases, says St John, in

---

[1] The connection of thought, therefore, is not this Such an intercession remains unheard, because the intercession itself is a *forbidden one*, and *against* the will of God (Calvin, Bengel); but, conversely, Such an intercession is not *commanded*, because the assurance of hearing is not given.

[2] Bullinger's words on this point are very good : " Poterat autem aliquis pro impio aliquo contemtore Dei orare, Deumque ipsum, non auditus, arguere mendacii. Istud ut declinaret apostolus, notanter addidit : Impetrabis quidem, si ille Deum convertentem non contemserit. Pro eo, inquit, qui ad mortem peccat, rogari nolo, *i.e.* nolo quis exspectet se quidquam consecuturum, si oret pro perfidio et impio contemtore numinis."

which man has destroyed his own capacity of conversion (Matt. xii. 31 seq.; Heb. vi. 4 seq.); and, where it may be assumed that such a case is before us, intercession is *not commanded*: it may not reckon upon that acceptance and answer, simply because, whenever such a case occurs, the man has already fallen into spiritual θάνατος, into reprobation.

In ver. 17 follows the simple explanation that in fact every ἀδικία is sin, but that there is a ἁμαρτία οὐ πρὸς θάνατον. That ἔστι is the substantive verb, is plain from the arrangement of the words. (Luther was much in error when he took ἁμαρτία as the subject, in the sense of ἁμαρτία τις, ἐστίν as the copula, and οὐ πρὸς θάνατον as the predicate.)—The first words have an external resemblance to ch. iii. 4, but the likeness is only external. There, the matter of the idea ἁμαρτία was defined by ἀνομία; here, the comprehensiveness of the idea ἁμαρτία is defined by ἀδικία. There, the point was, that sin is in its nature a transgression of the *commandments* of God; here, the thought is that not merely the ἁμαρτία πρὸς θάνατον, but every ἀδικία, falls under the idea of ἁμαρτία, while there is within this range of the idea a sinning which is "not unto death." Ἀδικία is therefore an idea altogether different from ἀνομία. Ἀνομία serves for the *qualitative definition* of the idea ἁμαρτία; ἀδικία serves for its *qualitative limitation*. Ἀνομία is that which offends the specific commandments of God; and in ch. iii. 4 it is said that sin (all sin) offends against God's commandments. Ἀδικία is all that is opposed to the inmost, deepest idea of δικαιοσύνη (ch. i. 9 and ii. 29); and it is said in our passage that *every* deviation from the nature of Him who is righteous and maketh righteous, is of itself sin, but that not every sin is a sin unto death.

VERS. 18–20 form a proper conclusion. With a triple οἴδαμεν St John recapitulates three truths which he has dilated upon in the course of the Epistle. The *first*, that every man who is born of God sinneth not, but taketh heed and guardeth himself, and that Satan cannot touch him, had been unfolded, as to its general substance, in the first section (ch. i. 6, ii. 3 seq.); and, as to its foundation in sonship to God and regeneration, and the requirement of the τηρεῖν, in the third section (ch. iii. 3 seq.); and, as it respects the security against the πονηρός, in the second section (ch. ii. 13 and 20 seq., and 27), and also in the third. The *second* truth, that we are of God, while the world lieth in the evil one, had been prepared for in the first section, and then formed the foundation of the second section (ch. ii. 8 and 15 seq.), as also the second part of the third section (ch. iii. 13 seq.). The *third*, that Christ is come, and hath given us an understanding of the truth, had been copiously unfolded in the fourth and fifth sections, but had been before that touched upon in the second (ch. ii. 20 and 22).—Thus we see that St John does not here recapitulate the five main divisions, but *three main aspects and points of his teaching* which had pervaded more or less the various sections of his Epistle: our obligation and prerogative of holiness; our opposition to the world; our relation to the Person of Christ.

The first of these three thoughts connects itself immediately with the preceding verse. Not to obviate a perversion of his doctrine that there is a sin "not unto death" (Bengel)—for no occasion had been given for such a perversion—but as the simple appendage to his words, πᾶσα ἀδικία ἁμαρτία ἐστίν, and as a remembrancer of what had been taught throughout the Epistle, St John proceeds—Οἴδαμεν (with reference to his having said it before), *we know* that every one who is born *of God* sinneth not. These words have their full interpretation, as it respects the subject, in our remarks upon ch. ii. 9, and, as it respects the predicate, in our remarks upon ch. ii. 1 and 3, iii. 3, 4, 9.

But St John appends to the main thought two subordinate explanatory suggestions. First, he sets against the negative οὐχ ἁμαρτάνει the positive ἀλλ' ὁ γεννηθεὶς ἐκ τοῦ Θεοῦ τηρεῖ ἑαυτόν (where the Part. Aor. Pass. is employed to lay stress upon the contrast between the past and completed γεννηθῆναι and the idea of τηρεῖν, or of continuous preservation of grace); but he thus at the same time lays down the requirement of what the Christian has to do on his own part, in order to realize the "not sinning." Τηρεῖν ἑαυτόν, elsewhere with a predicate, as in 1 Tim. v. 22; James i. 27, "keeping oneself pure:" here we must either supplement the predicate, "keeps himself as one born of God," that is, preserves the new life and the state of grace; or, τηρεῖν αὐτόν is used in the sense of the (classical) Middle τηρεῖσθαι, "be on guard, taking heed" (that is, against sin). The latter explanation is the more natural. St John had occasion here to mention, not the result (that he remains a γεννηθεὶς ἐκ τοῦ Θεοῦ), but the means, that is, his guarding against sin. Moreover, he would have expressed in a clearer and less abstract way the thought that "he who is born of God keeps himself as one who has a new life."

But as he, in the words ἀλλ' ὁ, κ.τ.λ., has mentioned the *means* which we on our part must use, so in the concluding words of the verse, καὶ ὁ πονηρὸς οὐχ ἅπτεται αὐτοῦ, he gives the *ground of the confidence* which we may have in the contest with sin. God on His part suffers it not that Satan should touch us: Satan *may* not touch us (ἅπτεσθαι, as in the Sept., Ps. cv. 15, comp. Wisd. iii. 1); compare Luke xxii. 31, 32; Eph. vi. 11 seq.; 1 Cor. x. 13. "It is not meant, that temptation itself may be avoided" (on the contrary, comp. Eph. vi. 12; 1 John ii. 13), "but that the tempting attack shall be made hurtlessly, and be victoriously repelled" (Düsterdieck). A touching is signified which would wound us (our new man), and do us injury.

In ver. 19 the second main truth follows: *We know that we are of God.* In ver. 18 it was laid down as a universal judgment—He that is born of God sinneth not; in ver. 19 follows the specific judgment—We know that *we* are of God. But with this is presently contrasted the κόσμος, the antithesis of the "we." Καὶ ὁ κόσμος ὅλος ἐν τῷ πονηρῷ κεῖται. The predicate ἐν τῷ πονηρῷ κεῖται does not merely constitute the negative of ἐκ τοῦ Θεοῦ εἶναι, as if the sense were, "We know that we are of God, but the world is not of God;" and the idea of ἐν τῷ πονηρῷ κεῖσθαι is much weakened, if we regard (as is generally done) the "lying in the evil" as merely the "being in a miserable and wrong state generally." Ἐν πονηρῷ is not neuter, but, as the antithesis of ἐκ Θεοῦ, masculine. Κεῖσθαι ἐν τῷ πονηρῷ is, generally, parallel with the εἶναι ἐκ τοῦ Θεοῦ, but the Apostle must have had some reason why he did not write ἐκ τοῦ πονηροῦ ἐστιν (as in ch. iii. 10–12 and John viii. 4, comp. 1 John ii. 16); and this reason is to be sought in his habit of making the second member of an antithesis overpass the first[1]

---

[1] So fixed is this habit of St John, that even in ch. v. 12, where the second member does not in *fact* overpass the first, he introduces in the second member at least a *formal* change and advancement, that of τοῦ Θεοῦ added to τὸν υἱόν.

(compare above, ch. i. 6 and 7, and elsewhere). Concerning the world he says, not merely that it is " of the πονηρός," or has him for a father, and bears his nature, but also that it " lies in him," that is, lies in his bosom,—not, indeed, like an unborn child in the mother's womb (Spener, Steinhofer, after Isa. xlvi. 3), which would be only another form of being " of the evil one," and moreover would be an altogether inappropriate figure, —but like an infant on the bosom of a mother or a father, which is absolutely given up to its parents' power (Calvin, Bengel, Lücke). Consequently, St John speaks not only of the origin and nature of the world, but also of the destiny which it has to expect ; and thus these last words include at the same time a consolation for the ἡμεῖς which are ἐκ τοῦ Θεοῦ.

Ver. 20. The clause, ὅτι ἐκ τοῦ Θεοῦ ἐσμέν, leads naturally to the third great truth, to the person of Him through whose mediation we have become children of God. We know that the Son of God ἥκει, "has come" (compare ch. iv. 9 and 14), and hath given us[1] διάνοιαν ἵνα γινώσκωμεν τὸν ἀληθινόν. Διάνοια is not "knowledge" (Lücke), but the power of capacity of knowing (Luther, Bengel), compare Eph. iv. 18 ; 2 Pet. iii. 1 ; and, especially, the *facultas cognoscendi*, as it rests upon an ethical-religious basis (1 Pet. i. 13 ; Matt. xxii. 37 ; Eph. ii. 3 ; Heb. viii. 10, x. 16 ; Luke i. 51 ; Col. i. 21). It may therefore be appropriately translated " sense " or " discernment." As Christ has come (in the sense of ch. iv. 9), and through this act of love has kindled love in us (ch. iv. 10), thus communicating His nature to us, he has furnished us with the understanding which is necessary in order that we may know God. For God is, according to ch. i. 6, iv. 8, φῶς and ἀγάπη ; and only he who is penetrated by His *light*, and kindled by His *love*, can know Him.—But God is here termed the ἀληθινός, not as He who is the ἀλήθεια, and not as He who possesses the attribute of truth ; ἀληθινός forms here, as at the conclusion of this verse and John xvii. 3, the antithesis to *fictitious*, or false (Calvin, Huther, and most others). The true God stands in opposition to the imagined and vain gods, which are not φῶς and are not ἀγάπη.

In the concluding words which now follow—καί ἐσμεν ἐν

[1] That δέδωκεν has the same subject as ἥκει is clear, and has been admitted by all expositors with the exception of Bengel.

τῷ ἀληθινῷ, ἐν τῷ υἱῷ αὐτοῦ Ἰησοῦ Χριστοῦ· οὗτός ἐστιν ὁ ἀληθινὸς Θεὸς καὶ ζωὴ αἰώνιος—St John reaches in his recapitulation the same fundamental result, comprehending the crown and quintessence of all his teaching, which he had reached at the close of the development of the Fifth Section, ver. 12, and from which the final Section, ver. 13, had set·out. "We are in Him that is true" (God), not merely ἐκ τοῦ Θεοῦ, begotten of Him, born again of Him, but in virtue of that *being in Him* (compare John xvii. 23, and above, 1 John ii. 6 and 24). But *in Christ* we are in God; that is, because we are, and as long as we are, in Jesus Christ, we are in the Father. The words ἐσμὲν ἐν τῷ ἀληθινῷ constitute together one verbal idea, to which the words ἐν τῷ υἱῷ αὐτοῦ Ἰησοῦ Χριστοῦ are added as an explanatory definition. Our "being in the True" is the being found in Christ. Similarly, it was said in John xvii. 33, "I in them, and Thou in Me" (consequently, through My mediation, "Thou in them"). That ἐν τῷ υἱῷ, κ.τ.λ., are not in *apposition* to ἐν τῷ ἀληθινῷ (Vulg., Erasmus) is self-evident; for the Genitive αὐτοῦ refers to the ἀληθινῷ, and, consequently, the ἀληθινός is distinguished from "*His* Son."

But it does not by any means follow from this distinction between the ἀληθινός and "His Son" that οὗτος must in the closing words refer back to ἀληθινός (as Grotius and many others assume), and cannot point to υἱός. It is quite *possible* in itself, and very much in harmony with the style of St John's favourite *turns* of thought and expression, that he should, after having distinguished the ἀληθινός from His υἱός, simply say concerning the same Son, that He was Himself the ἀληθινὸς Θεός. (So Bullinger, Luther, Calvin, Beza, Bengel, Olshausen, Stier, and, generally, all orthodox expositors; even the Arminian Episcopius.) And this interpretation is the more *probable*, in comparison with the former. For, if it is referred to the Father, it would be a flat repetition, after the Father had been twice called ὁ ἀληθινός, to say now again, "This is the ἀληθινὸς Θεός." And, as it respects the second predicate, καὶ ζωὴ αἰώνιος, the Son had been in ver. 12 seq. with such precision exhibited as He in whom we have the ζωή,—this had been in ver. 12 so plainly laid down as the *final climax* of the whole development, and in ver. 13 as the *goal and consummate issue* of the whole Epistle,—that we here, at the close of the conclusion, might almost have naturally expected some such thought as that the Son is eternal life. Moreover, in the previous member of the verse, the proper predicate-idea lay in the words ἐν τῷ υἱῷ, κ.τ.λ.: these words declared, not that we are in God generally, but that our "being in God" has its basis in *Christ His Son;* and this also makes it more natural that οὗτος should be referred to υἱῷ.

The only thing which seems to oppose this view is the article before ἀληθινὸς Θεός. When St John, in the Gospel, ch. i. 1, etc., teaches the divinity of the Logos, he writes καὶ Θεὸς ἦν ὁ λόγος. This is correct. But it may be questioned whether it was the Apostle's design in this passage to attribute to the Son the *predicate of divinity*—that is, to say concerning Him that He was of a *Divine nature*. What would be the force of such a declaration here? It is St John's purpose to say, not *what* the Son of God is, but *who* He is. Not that He was more than mere man, and partaker of the Godhead, but that this Son, distinguished from the true God as His Son, was yet also the true God Himself—to say that, was strictly in keeping. For, thus writing, St John teaches us two things: that this υἱός is, on the one hand, identical with the ἀληθινὸς Θεός Himself; and, on the other, that He is for us the source of eternal life.—Now, in declaring *what* any one is, the predicate must have no article; in declaring *who* any one is, the predicate must have the article. Accordingly, Düsterdieck is wrong when he says that he must "maintain, with Lücke, that the Apostle could not have written more confusedly than to exhibit the Son of God, immediately after having distinguished Him from the true God, as being this true God Himself." There would have been confusion here, only if any reader had been in danger of misunderstanding the Apostle's οὗτος, κ.τ.λ., as placing the υἱός in *opposition to the* πατήρ as the ἀληθινὸς Θεός, and as declaring the πατήρ to be a false God. But there was no need to fear such a misunderstanding as that, more especially as St John had immediately before named the Father unconditionally the ἀληθινός. On the other hand, it would have been to our mind something like confusion, if the Apostle, who so plainly teaches in his Gospel the eternal divinity of the λόγος, should have done nothing more in the Epistle than *distinguish* the Son from the Father, and from the Father as *from the* ἀληθινός, without adding a single word as to their real identity of nature. Düsterdieck, indeed, seems to fear heterodoxy here: "the distinction between the Son and the Father would be obscured" by this exposition. That would be the case if St John had said of the Son, οὗτός ἐστιν ὁ πατήρ; but not when he says of the Son, οὗτός ἐστιν ὁ ἀληθινὸς Θεός. For ὁ ἀληθινὸς Θεός is simply no other than a definition of the Divine collective personality in opposition to the creature (and here in opposition to false gods); and One is called ὁ ἀληθινὸς Θεός, in such case as His internal trinitarian relation is out of view. That this Son, on whom our "being in the true God" rests, is *this true God Himself*, St John here says. We may say, in strictest scholastic orthodoxy, that the Son is ὁμοούσιος τῷ πατρί, and, *with the Father and the Spirit together*, is the Three-One God. But St John had not to speak the language of the schools, but the language of revelation.

Christ, as He is the true God Himself—that is, One with Him—is also ζωὴ αἰώνιος (the article before ζωή is wanting in A.B.; and St John never writes ἡ ζωὴ αἰώνιος, but always either ἡ αἰώνιος ζωή, or without the article ζωὴ αἰώνιος). He *is* eternal life; that is, he who hath Him hath life (ver. 12). It is worthy of notice that it is never said of God the Father that He *is* life, but only that He *hath* life (John v. 26, comp. ch. i. 4, xi. 25, xiv. 5). The Father as such is not life; but God Himself is the Eternal Living One as from eternity begetting the Son; and this Son Himself is "the Life" *for the creature*, in whom the creature "hath life."

VER. 21 is not (as many think) an "abrupt" final exhortation, but is clearly mediated by the idea of the ἀληθινὸς Θεός. If the Father, who hath revealed Himself in Christ, is the true God,—if the Son, in whom we have the Father, is the true God, —it follows that we must guard ourselves against all *idols*, that is, against all *false gods*.[1] This idea is a general, and very comprehensive one: it embraces all things and everything which may be opposed to the God revealed in Christ, and to His worship in πνεῦμα and in ἀλήθεια. Preeminently, therefore, it embraces the delusive and vain idols of the Cerinthian Gnosti-

---

[1] Olshausen "εἴδωλον is the antithesis of the true God."

cism, and infidelity, whether ancient or modern; but it includes also the idols and false mediators of superstition, to whom the confidence is transferred which is due only to God in Christ—be their name Madonna, or saints, or Pope, or priesthood, or pictures, or good works, or office, or church, or sacraments. The One Being in whom we have $τὴν ζωήν$ is *Christ*, who "is come not with water alone, but with water and blood;" and therefore our trust should never be reposed in the water alone—in the signs and institutions—but for ever in His atoning death, of which these signs are designed to remind us. And this Christ we possess through the *Spirit of God*, whose marks and tokens are not priestly vestments, but faith and love. In this meaning the Apostle's cry sounds forth through all the ages in the ears of all Christians: LITTLE CHILDREN, KEEP YOURSELVES FROM IDOLS!

TRANSLATION.

THAT which was from the beginning, which we have heard, which we have seen with our eyes, which we have beheld and our hands have handled—concerning the Word of life (and the Life was manifested; and we have seen, and bear witness, and declare unto you the Eternal Life, which was with the Father, and was manifested unto us),—That which we have seen and heard declare we unto you, that ye also may have fellowship with us, and that our fellowship (may be) with the Father, and His Son Jesus Christ. And *this* we write unto you, that our joy may be full.

This then is the message which we have heard of Him, and declare unto you, that God is light, and in Him is no darkness at all. If we say that we have fellowship with Him, and walk in darkness, we lie, and do not the truth; but if we walk in the light, as He is in the light, we have fellowship one with another, and the blood of Jesus His Son cleanseth us from all sin. If we say that we have not sin, we deceive ourselves, and the truth is not in us; but if we confess our sins, He is faithful and just to forgive our sins, and to cleanse us from all unrighteousness. If we say that we have not sinned, we make Him a liar, and His word is not in us.—My little children, this I write unto you, that ye may not sin. And if any man sin, we have an Advocate with the Father, Jesus Christ, who is righteous. And He is the propitiation for our sins; and not for ours alone, but for all the world.—And hereby we know that we have known Him, if we keep His commandments. He that saith, I have known Him, and keepeth not His commandments, is a liar, and the truth is not in him. But whoso keepeth His word in him the love of God is in truth perfected. Hereby know we that we are in Him. He that saith he abideth in Him, is bound, as He walked, so also himself to walk.

Beloved, I write no new commandment unto you, but an old commandment, which ye had from the beginning. The old commandment is the word which ye have heard. Again, a new commandment I write unto you, that which is true in Him and in you: *that the darkness is in act of passing, and the true light already shineth.* He that saith, he is in the light, and hateth his brother, is in darkness until now. He that loveth his brother abideth in the light, and there is no offence in Him. But he that hateth his brother is in darkness, and walketh in darkness, and knoweth not whither he goeth, because the darkness hath blinded his eyes.—I write unto you, little children, because your sins are forgiven you through His name. I write unto you, fathers, because ye have known Him that is from the beginning. I write unto you, young men, because ye have overcome the wicked one. I have written unto you, little children, because ye have known the Father. I have written unto you, fathers, because ye have known Him that is from the beginning. I have written unto you, young men, because ye are strong, and the word of God abideth in you, and ye have overcome the wicked one. Love not the world, neither the things that are in the world. If any man love the world, the love of God is not in Him. For all that is in the world, the lust of the flesh, and the lust of the eyes, and the pride of life, is not of the Father, but is of the world. And the world passeth away, and the lust thereof; but he that doeth the will of God abideth for ever.— Little children, it is the last hour: and as ye have heard that Antichrist shall come, even now there are many antichrists, whereby we know that it is the last hour. They went out from us, but they were not of us; for if they had been of us, they would have continued with us; but that they might become manifest, that they were not all of us. And ye have unction from the Holy One, and know all. I have not written unto you, because ye know not the truth, but because ye know it, and (know) that all that is lie is not of the truth. Who is the liar, but he that denieth that Jesus is the Christ? This is the Antichrist, who denieth the Father and the Son. Whosoever denieth the Son, hath not the Father: he that acknowledgeth the Son, hath the Father also. Let that abide in you which ye have heard from the beginning. If that which ye have heard from the beginning shall remain in you, ye also shall remain in the Son and in the Father. And this is the promise that He hath promised us, eternal life.—This have I written unto you concerning them that seduce you. And ye, "the anointing which ye have received from Him abideth in you," and "ye need not that any man teach you;" but as "the same anointing teacheth you concerning all things;" and "it is true and no lie," and "as it hath taught you, abide in it."—And now, little children, abide in Him; that, when He shall appear, we may have confidence, and not be ashamed before Him at His coming. If ye know that He is righteous, know that every one that doeth righteousness is born of Him.

Behold, what love hath the Father given unto us, in this, *that we should be called and are children of God! Therefore the world knoweth us not,* for it knew Him not.—Beloved, *now* are we children of God, and it hath *not yet* been revealed what we shall be. We know that, when it shall be revealed, we shall be like Him, for we shall see Him as He is. And every man that hath this hope towards Him, purifieth himself, even as He is pure. Whosoever committeth sin committeth also transgression of the law, and sin is transgression of the law; and ye know that He was manifested that He might take away sins, and in Him is no sin. Whosoever abideth in Him, sinneth not. Whosoever sinneth, hath not seen Him, nor known Him.—Little children, let no man deceive you. He that doeth what is right, is righteous, even as He is righteous: he that doeth what is sin, is of the devil; for the devil sinneth from the beginning. For this purpose the Son of God was manifested, that He might destroy the works of the devil. Whosoever is born of God committeth not sin; for His seed remaineth in him; and he cannot sin, because he is born of God. In this the *children of God* are manifest, and the children of the devil. Whosoever doeth not righteousness is not of God, neither he that loveth not his brother. For this is the message that ye heard from the beginning, that we should love one another; not as Cain was of that wicked one, and slew his brother. And wherefore slew he him? Because his own works were evil, and his brother's righteous.—Marvel not, brethren, *if the world hates you.* We know that we have passed from death unto life, because we love the brethren: he that loveth not, abideth in death. Whosoever hateth his brother is a murderer; and ye know that no murderer hath eternal life abiding in him. *In this* we have perceived love, that He laid down His life for us. And we are bound to lay down our lives for the brethren. But whoso hath this world's sustenance, and seeth his brother have need, and shutteth up his bowels from him, how dwelleth in him the love of God? — Little children, let us not love in mere word, nor in tongue, but in deed and in truth. Hereby shall we know whether we be of the truth. And before Him shall we convince our hearts, that if our heart condemn us, God is greater, and knoweth all things. Beloved, if our heart condemn us not, we have confidence towards God, and, whatever we may ask, we receive of Him; for we keep His commandments, and do that which is well-pleasing in His sight. And this is His commandment, That we should believe the name of His Son Jesus Christ, and love one another, as He gave us commandment. And he that keepeth His commandments dwelleth in Him, and He in him; and thereby know we that He abideth in us, by the Spirit which He hath given us.

Beloved, believe not every spirit, but *try the spirits, whether they be of God;* for many false prophets are gone out into the world. Hereby know ye the Spirit of God: Every spirit that confesseth Jesus Christ as having come in the flesh, is of God; and every spirit that confesseth not Jesus, is not of God; and this is that of Antichrist, whereof ye have heard that it should come, and even now already is it in the world. *Ye* are of God, little children, and have overcome *them;* because greater is He that is in you, than he that is in the world. *They* are of the world; therefore speak they of the world, and the world heareth them. *We* are of God: he that knoweth God, heareth us; he that is not of God, heareth not us. Hereby know we the Spirit of truth, and the spirit of seduction.—Beloved, let us love one another; for love is of God, and every one that loveth is born of God, and knoweth God. He that loveth not, hath not known God; for God is love. In this was manifested the love of God towards us, that God sent His Son, His Only-begotten, into the world, that we might live through Him. In this is love: not that we have loved God, but that He loved us, and sent His Son to be the propitiation for our sins. Beloved, if God so loved us, we are bound also to love one another. No man hath seen God at any time: if we love one another, God abideth in us, and His love is perfected in us. Hereby we know that we abide in Him, and He in us, *because He hath given us of His Spirit.* And we have seen, and do testify, that the Father sent the Son to be the Saviour of the world. Whosoever shall confess that Jesus is the Son of God, God dwelleth in him, and he in God. And we have known and believed the love which God hath in us: God is love; and he that abideth in love, abideth in God, and God in him.—Herein is love with us made perfect, that we have confidence in the day of judgment; for as He is, so are we also, in this world. There is no fear in love; but perfect love casteth out fear (for fear hath torment): but he that feareth is not perfected in love. *We* love, because He first loved us.—If a man say, "I love God," and hateth his brother, he is a liar; for he that loveth not his brother, whom he hath seen, how can he love God, whom he hath not seen? And this commandment have we from Him, That he who loveth God love his brother also. Whosoever believeth that Jesus is the Christ, is born of God; and every one that loveth Him that begat, loveth him also that is begotten of Him. By this we know that we love the children of God, when we love God and keep His commandments. For this is the love of God, that we keep His commandments; and His commandments are not grievous: for whatsoever is born of God *overcometh the world.*

And this is the victory which hath overcome the world: our faith. Who is he that overcometh the world, but he that believeth that Jesus is the Son of God? This is He that came by water and blood, Jesus the Christ; not with water only, but with water and blood. And it is the Spirit that beareth witness, that the Spirit is truth. For there are three that bear witness, the Spirit, and the water, and the blood; and these three tend to one.—If we receive the witness of men, the witness of God is greater: this is the witness of God, that He hath given testimony to His Son. He that believeth on the Son of God hath the witness in himself: he that believeth not God hath made Him a liar, because he hath not believed the witness that God hath borne concerning His Son. And this is the testimony, that God hath given to us eternal life; and this life is in His Son: he that hath the Son hath life; he that hath not the Son of God hath not life.—This have I written unto you, that ye may know that ye have eternal life, ye that believe in the name of the Son of God. And this is the confidence that we have towards Him, that, if we ask anything according to His will, He heareth us. And if we know that He heareth us, whatsoever we ask, we know that we *have* the petitions that we desired of Him. If any man see his brother sin a sin not unto death, he shall ask, and give him life,—to them that sin not unto death. There is a sin unto death: not concerning it do I say that we should pray. All unrighteousness is sin; but there is a sin not unto death.

We know: that whosoever is born of God sinneth not; but he that is born of God guardeth himself, and the wicked one toucheth him not.

We know: that we are of God, and the whole world lieth in the wicked one.

But we know: that the Son of God is come, and hath given us an understanding, that we may know Him that is true. And we are in Him that is true, in His Son Jesus Christ: this is the true God, and eternal life.

Little children, keep yourselves from idols!

THE

SECOND AND THIRD EPISTLES OF ST JOHN.

INTRODUCTION.

THE two documents which bear the name in our Canon of the Second and the Third Epistles of St John, are distinguished in a very marked manner, and in several ways, from the First Epistle; while, on the other hand, they may be regarded in a certain sense as very similar to it. They are distinguished from it, in the first place, by their *brevity*; in the second place, by their *object and character*,—neither of them being addressed to a church, but the former to a Christian woman named Kyria (2 John 1), and the latter to a man named Gaius (3 John 1),—both therefore to private persons; in the third place, by the fact that the author calls himself, somewhat mysteriously, ὁ πρεσβύτερος, *the Elder* (2 and 3 John, ver. 1); in the fourth place, and finally, by the circumstance that neither the *canonical character* of these Epistles, nor *the view held concerning their author*, was firmly established in patristic antiquity. On the other hand, the Second Epistle bears some resemblance to the First in respect to its doctrinal *matter*, which is the same, and its doctrinal *form*, which is similar, but not in respect to its *style*, which is different. (In regard to the second point, that of form, the passage, 2 John 5-7, and ver. 9, is so obviously a literal extract from the First Epistle, or direct allusion to it, that *on that very account*[1] the Second Epistle may be as naturally attributed to another author as to the Apostle himself.) In the Third Epistle we find no resemblance in style to the First. In ver. 11 occurs a turn of thought which may be explained (after the analogy of 2 John 5-7) as a close reminiscence of or allusion to the First Epistle; and this may be explained as the work of

[1] But, besides this passage, we are encountered by many specifically Johannæan ideas; *e. g.*, 2 John 12.

another author than the Apostle, just as in Polycarp we find allusions to the Apostolical Epistles. And in this very ver. 11 we have no less then four un-Johannæan expressions (τὸ κακόν, τὸ ἀγαθόν, ἀγαθοποιεῖν, κακοποιεῖν). The address ἀγαπητέ, ver. 4, is in any case irrelevant; for St John's employment of the address ἀγαπητοί, in addressing the Church in the First Epistle, does not exclude the possibility that another Christian might have addressed his friend and fellow-labourer as ἀγαπητέ. The word μαρτυρεῖν is in 3 John 3 and 12 used in a sense quite different from that of 1 John 1, 2, etc. But vers. 5-10 deviate so strikingly from all that we recognise as St John's style,[1] that any one who has any sense of stylistic distinctions and differences must feel himself decided. The construction of clauses, the turn of thought, the phraseology, all are different. Instead of the perfectly transparent and Hebraistic diction of the Apostle, we find a decidedly Greek diction; though not on that account pretending to beauty of style, but rather somewhat obscure, because closely condensed. The Apostle could write better Greek (less Hebraistic) than he was wont to do, when he took pains to do so; but here we seem to have to do with a writer who, when he takes his own free course, thinks and writes in Greek.

But now we are met by another striking fact. The Second and Third Epistles show so decisive a resemblance to each other, that there can be no doubt—there never has been any doubt—as to their coming from the same hand. Compare 2 John 1 with 3 John 1 (ἀγαπῶ ἐν ἀληθείᾳ); 2 John 4 with 3 John 3 (ἐχάρην λίαν); 2 John 12 with 3 John 13, 14 (διὰ μέλανος καὶ καλάμου γράφειν, and στόμα πρὸς στόμα λαλεῖν).

Now, if an author, who, like the author of the Third Epistle, writes in a style altogether different from the Apostle, nevertheless, in ver. 11, so plainly reproduces the language of St

---

[1] The expressions ὑγιαίνειν, εὐοδοῦσθαι, προπέμπειν ἀξίως τοῦ Θεοῦ, κοινωνεῖν, διδαχὴν φέρειν, περιπατεῖν κατὰ τὸ κακόν, τὸ ἀγαθόν, are simply such as St John never uses—expressions, instead of which he constantly uses others. And, though no one of these expressions would of itself have much weight, yet their concurrence to such an extent within the compass of so few verses, and verses, too, which have nothing in their matter specifically Johannæan, tells very heavily on the case. We may add also the large proportionate number of composite verbs, such as φιλοπρωτεύειν, ἀγαθοποιεῖν, κακοποιεῖν, εὐοδοῦσθαι.

John's First Epistle, ought not the appearances which meet us in the Second Epistle, vers. 5–7 and ver. 9, of resemblance in matter and phrase to that Epistle, to be explained in the same manner, that is, as allusions to it and intentional reminiscences? Even the remarkable reproduction of St John's style in 2 John 2 might be very well resolved into a reminiscence of the (written and *oral*) diction of the Apostle, and consequently into an *involuntary* imitation, without our being justified in saying, with De Wette, that "the author must have slavishly copied the style of the Apostle's thinking and writing." For 2 John 2 is the only passage in which there is a simple imitation of style (though even here not without some reference in the *matter* to Johannæan dicta; comp. 1 John ii. 24 and 27): all other resemblances in style are found *only* in such passages as designedly make allusion to definite sayings of the First Epistle (such as 3 John 11 to 1 John iii. 6; 2 John 5 to 1 John ii. 7; and 2 John 12 to 1 John i. 4), or where such sayings are almost expressly quoted (such as 2 John 6, 7, and 9, compared with 1 John v. 2, iv. 1, 3, ii. 23); and, even in one of *these* passages (2 John 10), we are met by the striking fact that the writer substitutes εἴ τις for the usual ἐάν τις of St John. It has been observed before, that in another passage (3 John 11) he reproduces St John's turn of *thought* in a form of *expression* which is not St John's.

Thus, if we had no other information concerning these two Epistles than that which they themselves furnish, their own peculiar character would lead us to the conclusion that they were written, not by the Apostle, but by a man who belonged to the circle of the Johannæan labours as a scholar and co-operator, who had read St John's writings, and who used and quoted these writings, especially the First Epistle, just in the same way as we find the Apostolical Epistles used and quoted by Polycarp and Clemens Romanus. 2 John particularly must have been written under the influence of the teaching of St John's First Epistle.

And if we turn to external testimonies, this view is not weakened, but on the contrary confirmed. We attach no importance to the fact that the two Epistles were entirely wanting for a considerable time in the canon of many churches. Tertullian and Cyprian do not mention them. But that the Syrian

Church did not receive them into its ecclesiastic version until the sixth century, may be sufficiently explained by three circumstances: first, that the two Epistles were merely private letters (though of a pastoral character); secondly, that one of them was even addressed to a woman; and, thirdly, that with the exception of what they have in common with (or rather what they derived from) the First Epistle of St John, they contain little that was specifically appropriate to the edification of the Church.—But that the Fragment of Muratori knew of the second only, and not the third, is no more true than that it "denied both Epistles to the Apostle" (Düsterdieck). We have proved in the Introduction to the Apocalypse that the words of the Fragment, "Epistola sane Judæ et superscripti Joannis duas (= δύας) in Catholica habentur," must refer, not to the first and second of John, but only to the second and third of John. The design of the Fragment was, in a purely practical interest, to instruct the reader what writings he must avoid as heretical, and what he might read as orthodox. The First Epistle of St John did not come into question at all; for it had been distinctly referred to in the Fragment as apostolical. The only purpose which the words above-quoted served, was to prevent the Epistle of St Jude and the second and third of John (which were received only by a part of the Church into the canon of Scriptures to be publicly read, and consequently were ἀντιλεγόμενα) from being regarded as heretical. And, when the Fragmentist immediately goes on to mention the "Sapientia, ab amicis Salomonis in honorem ipsius scripta," this collocation does not lead to the inference that he "intended to deny the Second and Third Epistle to St John," any more than his collocation of the Johannæan Apocalypse with the Petrine (an Antilegomenon) and the Pastor of Hermas (which was written *nuperrime temporibus nostris*) leads to the inference that he regarded the Apocalypse as spurious (which indeed he had already mentioned as genuine and apostolical).—In fact, the Fragment of Muratori tells us nothing at all decisive concerning the apostolical or non-apostolical origin of our two Epistles; we hear only that they were esteemed orthodox, and in no sense heretical, in the circle in which the author moved. For this and nothing else is concerned, as the connection shows, in the words *in Catholica habentur.*

INTRODUCTION. 363

But, that the two Epistles were wanting, not only in the canon of the Syrian Church, but in that of other churches also, is proved generally by the fact of their having been reckoned by Eusebius (iii. 25)[1] among the Antilegomena; for he does this by no means because it was doubtful whether they sprang from the Apostle or from another "John."[2] But to him those writings were Antilegomena—and Antilegomena, too, of the first class, in contradistinction to the subsequent "$νόθοις$," which he afterwards also reckons with the Antilegomena ($ταῦτα μὲν πάντα τῶν ἀντιλεγομένων ἂν εἴη$) because it is his design to oppose to both (to the Antilegomena in the stricter sense, as well as to the $νόθοις$) the *heretical* writings—those writings were Antilegomena, we repeat, which are "$ἀντιλεγόμεναι, ὅμως δὲ παρὰ πλείστοις τῶν ἐκκλησιαστικῶν γινωσκόμενα$," which therefore were admitted, not everywhere, but yet in the majority of churches, into the canon of Holy Scripture read publicly in Divine service. Thus, we learn from this canon of Eusebius, primarily, only—what the Peschito has already taught us, and what the canon of Muratori has led us to suppose—that these two Epistles were not everywhere admitted into the canon of the Scriptures publicly read;[3] a fact which is so manifestly to be accounted for, even on the supposition of their apostolical authorship, by the character of these Epistles as private documents, that it affords no ground of certain argument either against, or in favour of, their having been written by an Apostle.

But more important than this is a series of patristic passages, from which we gather that, in the very first centuries, and as soon as these Epistles were mentioned at all, it was regarded as an open question whether the Apostle or the Presbyter John was their author. That there was such a Presbyter John living at Ephesus, and a disciple of the Apostle, cannot, in the face of the

---

[1] $Τῶν δ' ἀντιλεγομένων, γνωρίμων δ' οὖν ὅμως τοῖς πολλοῖς, ἡ λεγομένη Ἰακώβου φέρεται καὶ ἡ Ἰούδα· ἥτε Πέτρου δευτέρα ἐπιστολή, καὶ ἡ ὀνομαζομένη δευτέρα καὶ τρίτη Ἰωάννου, εἴτε τοῦ εὐαγγελιστοῦ τυγχάνουσαι εἴτε καὶ ἑτέρου ὁμωνύμου ἐκείνῳ$.

[2] This addition, $εἴτε τοῦ εὐαγγελιστοῦ, κ.τ.λ.$, serves evidently rather for the elucidation of the word $ὀνομαζομένη$.

[3] Thus these Epistles were actually rejected by Theodor. Mopsu., and in the Homily on Matt. xxi. 23 attributed to Chrysostom, as uncanonical; and Theodoret does not mention them.

evidence of Papias, in Euseb. 3, 39, be doubted by anything but a hyper- or pseudo-criticism. The learned Origen, thoroughly acquainted with the earliest Christian literature, says (Euseb. 6, 25) : Ἰωάννης—κατελέλοιπε—ἐπιστολὴν πάνυ ὀλίγων στίχων· ἔστω δὲ καὶ δευτέραν καὶ τρίτην· ἐπεὶ οὐ πάντες φασὶ γνησίους εἶναι ταύτας. These words do indeed express a definite doubt as to the *apostolical authorship* (which indeed is not contained in their being merely numbered among the Antilegomena). So also Eusebius, in the passage quoted above (3, 25), besides the fact that he reckons these Epistles in respect to their *canonicity* among the Antilegomena, expresses a doubt in reference to their *author*, inasmuch as he speaks of an ὀνομαζομένη δευτέρα καὶ τρίτη Ἰωάννου, and leaves it undecided whether they had been composed by the Apostle or by another of the same name. So also Dionysius Alexandrinus (in Euseb. 7, 25) speaks of the δευτέρᾳ φερομένῃ Ἰωάννου καὶ τρίτῃ (compare the Appendix on the Catholic Epistles). Jerome, so thoroughly learned in all critical questions, writes (Catal. Script. Eccl., cap. 18, s. v. Papias) : Ex quo apparet ex ipso catalogo nominum (in Papias) alium esse Joannem, qui inter apostolos ponitur, et alium seniorem Joannem, quem post Aristionem enumerat. (Jerome refers here to the passage of Papias, preserved by Eusebius, 3, 39, in his λογίων κυριακῶν ἐξηγήσεις.) Hereupon Jerome proceeds : Hoc autem diximus propter superiorem opinionem, *quam a plerisque retulimus traditam*, duas posteriores epistolas Joannis non apostoli esse sed presbyteri. And in cap. ix. he had already written : Reliquæ autem duæ (epistolæ) quarum principium est : " Senior electæ dominæ et natis ejus," et sequentis : " Senior Cajo carissimo, quem ego diligo in veritate," Joannis presbyteri asseruntur, cujus et hodie alterum sepulchrum apud Ephesum ostenditur; et nonnulli putant duas memorias ejusdem Joannis evangelistæ esse, super qua re quum per ordinem ad Papiam auditorem ejus ventum fuerit, disserimus. Now, whether Jerome himself shared the view that the Second and Third Epistles sprang from the Presbyter, must appear very doubtful. In Ep. 2 ad Paulinum, he writes : Jacobus, Petrus, Joannes, Judas apostoli septem epistolas ediderunt; and in the Ep. ad Evagrium : Clangat tuba evangelica, filius tonitrui, quem Jesus amavit plurimum, qui de pectore Salvatoris doctrinarum fluenta potavit : " Presbyter electæ Domini," et in alia epistola : "Presbyter Caio." Indeed, Origen also says in his eighth homily on Joshua (where, addressing the Church, critical investigations would have been out of place) : Addit et Joannes tuba canere per *epistolas suas* — so that the similar sayings of Jerome in his (practical and hortatory) Epistles may probably be explained in the same way. In no case did the matter so stand that any one might have ventured confidently to maintain its composition by the Presbyter as an historically certain matter; the two Epistles were manifestly not dispersed (as their matter might imply) until a later period; the author does not mention his name, and all that consistent tradition held, from the time their first multiplication by copyists began, was, that they were " ἐπιστολαὶ 'Ιωάννου ;" and thus all were at first obliged to decide, from internal reasons, whether the Apostle or the Presbyter was the author. This presupposition explains all the facts which have reference to external testimony. Even the two passages in which Irenæus cites the Second Epistle lead to no other result. That is, these two passages would have the weight of positive historical, traditional witnesses for the apostolical composition, only if Irenæus *expressly testified* this apostolical composition, as in relation to the other writings of St John he does. But instead of this, we are met by the fact that, after he had previously (3, 16, 5) cited some passages from the *First* Epistle of St John (1 John ii. 18 seq.), he then continues (3, 16, 8) : quos et Dominus nobis cavere prædixit, et discipulus ejus Joannes *in prædicta epistola* fugere eos præcepit dicens : Multi seductores exierunt in hunc mundum, qui non confitentur Jesum Christum in carne venisse. Hic est seductor et antichristus. Videte eos, ne perdatis quod operati estis (2 John 7, 8). Et rursus in Epistola ait (and then follows 1 John iv. 1–3). Here it is quite plain that Irenæus quoted from a memory faithful to the words, and that under the erroneous supposition of their belonging to the First Epistle. That he ascribes them to the discipulus Domini has thus no weight in favour of the apostolical authorship of 2 John.—And even his second citation (1, 16, 3) loses through this circumstance its significance. He writes there : 'Ιωάννης δὲ, ὁ τοῦ κυρίου μαθητής, ἐπέτεινε τὴν καταδίκην αὐτῶν, μηδὲ χαίρειν αὐτοῖς ὑφ' ὑμῶν λέγεσθαι δουληθείς. Ὁ γὰρ λέγων αὐτοῖς, φησι, χαίρειν, κοινωνεῖ τοῖς ἔργοις αὐτῶν τοῖς πονηροῖς

(2 John 11). This passage also is cited from memory, and the singulars αὐτῷ and αὐτοῦ changed into the plural. But the question must be asked, whether the expression Ἰωάννης ὁ τοῦ κυρίου μαθητής obliges us to think of the *Apostle*? According to Papias, in Euseb. 3, 39, the Presbyter John was also a μαθητὴς τοῦ κυρίου. Nevertheless, as Irenæus elsewhere steadily gives the *Apostle* that predicate (*e.g.*, ii. 22, iii. 1 and 3), and never mentions a Presbyter John, it is not to be doubted that here also he had the Apostle in his thought. On the other hand, it may be questioned, after looking at that other citation, whether Irenæus was clearly aware to which of the two Epistles, the first or the second, the passage belonged; but, granted that he was clearly aware that the quotation was from 2 John, the manner of making it proves no more than this, that Irenæus was one of those who—whether with reason, or involuntarily— regarded these lesser " Epistles of John" (that he was acquainted with the third, however, is not expressly established by any sentence in his writings) as Epistles written by the Apostle. But, on the other hand, he gives us no authority whatever for believing that any traditional report of the apostolical authorship of 2 John had come down to Irenæus through Polycarp (as it had come to him concerning the Gospel, the Apocalypse, and First Epistle). And thus the other supposition is at least conceivable, that Irenæus, no more than Origen and Eusebius, had received nothing certain and positive from tradition concerning the person of this John, whose name tradition gave to both the Epistles; but that he shared (whether through conviction or unconsciously) the opinion of those who thought themselves bound to ascribe them both to the Apostle.

And how easily might the obvious similarity between 2 John 5–7, 9, 12, and passages of the First Epistle give rise to this opinion! It was not till a closer comparison was instituted between the Second and the Third Epistles, that it became clear that these passages did not proceed from the writer's own mind, but were reminiscences and citations. Certainly, the case does not stand, as some represent it, as if tradition spoke decidedly for the Apostle John, and internal grounds alone induced some to think of the Presbyter. Conversely, it might be maintained that only the (supposed) internal reason of the striking echoes of 1 John led to the precipitate opinion that 2 John also (and then 3 John, as in another way connected with 2 John by similarity of diction) proceeded from the Apostle,—while tradition referred the two Epistles generally to the Presbyter. In fact, it is remarkable that Jerome alludes to the latter view as the *older* and *traditional* opinion (in the words " quam a *plerisque* retulimus *traditam*," and " Joannis presbyteri *asseruntur*"—see above), while in his own time the apostolical origin was already predominantly held; so that he either shared in that belief himself, or in his hortatory letters at least did not venture to contradict it. Accordingly, one might be inclined to regard the presbyter-authorship as the view traditionally handed down, and the view of the apostolical authorship as one that arose later, and out of internal reasons.

Meanwhile, we would not venture to maintain this. As early as the time of Origen opinion suspiciously wavered; and Irenæus had no thought of the *difference* of the authors of the First, and Second, and Third Epistles. Accordingly, we can regard as confirmed only what has been laid down above. The two small private Epistles had been preserved in the families of Kyria and Gaius. Later, probably not till after the death of the receivers, attention was directed towards them. Copies were made; and gradually the Epistles became more widely known. Now, if there had been a definite report that the *Apostle* John had written the Epistles, it cannot be conceived how the opinion that the *Presbyter* John was their author could have arisen and found acceptance: the similarity of 2 John 5–9 to 1 John would have opposed such a conjecture; and the superscription ὁ πρεσβύτερος would not have been sufficient to give rise to such a notion, for St Peter also (1 Pet. v. 1) had appropriated to himself the name ὁ συμπρεσβύτερος. If we suppose only thus much to have been known, that " a John" had written these Epistles, it becomes perfectly plain, on the one hand, how some might have been misled by the Johannæan reproductions in 2 John to the assumption that St John must have been their author, and, on the other, how others—whether through a more correct judgment upon the superscription ὁ πρεσβύτερος, or through the un-Johannæan style of 3 John—were led to perceive that those echoes in 2 John 5 seq. were only *allusions* to 1 John, and that the Presbyter John wrote the Epistle.

Thus, external arguments do not avail at least to force us

from the above results; they afford no certain reasons for the hypothesis of an apostolical authorship.

But some critics think that this very description of himself by the author, as ὁ πρεσβύτερος, is a clear demonstration of the apostolical origin of these Epistles. They cannot indeed draw from the fact that the Apostle in his two writings (the Gospel and 1 John) does not mention himself by name (but in the Apocalypse he does), the strange conclusion that every letter whose author does not mention himself, must have been written by the Apostle John. But the other reason is therefore in their eyes all the stronger, that ὁ πρεσβύτερος, without the addition of a proper name, must have indicated a specific and very high dignity. A presbyter, in the common sense, who (like the Presbyter John) was a member of a presbytery, and thus one among many, would scarcely (they tell us) have ventured to mention himself as "*the* Presbyter." Granted that this were so, we reasonably ask, whether an Apostle would have been likely to do the same. And what meaning would this appellation in that case have? But at this point the critics widely diverge. Piscator, Lange, Olshausen, and others would take ὁ πρεσβύτερος in an adjectival sense: "the old man,"—whether St John appropriated this predicate because he was really advanced in years, or whether he would thereby intimate that "he had outlived all the other Apostles." But these assumptions are, besides being very strange, refuted by the fact that πρεσβύτερος, unless it occurs as an adjective joined to a substantive (as in Luke xv. 25), never throughout the New Testament bears the meaning of "the elder," not to say "the old man," but is the current and fixed term for the idea of the זקן (Elder of the Church). Therefore, other critics (Lyra, à Lapide, Lücke, etc.) think it necessary that πρεσβύτερος should be taken as an official designation. Some, however, think that "the Elder" κατ' ἐξοχήν signifies no less than a "primus totius Asiæ," or Episcopus primarius, Archiepiscopus (Lyra); others think that it was a title of honour, like *Monsignore* (à Lapide); others again (as Beza) understand the word in the sense of an Old-Testament Head of a tribe, or Arabian Sheik (which then would have to be taken in a figurative sense, we may suppose). Düsterdieck is less fanciful, for he refers to 1 Pet. v. 1, where St Peter names himself ὁ συμπρεσβύτερος; he forgets, however, that this is not there used as a title, but as a declaration. St Peter has previously addressed the πρεσβυτέρους of the churches; and now asserts of himself that he was a partaker of their office—the pastoral namely,—that of κυβέρνησις, ἐπισκοπή. Lücke is not more happy in his appeal to the fragment of Papias in Euseb. 3, 39, where Papias says that he would report ὅσα ποτὲ παρὰ τῶν πρεσβυτέρων καλῶς ἔμαθον καὶ καλῶς ἐμνημόνευσα; for he took no pleasure in the babblers, nor in those who delivered strange traditions and dogmas, but in those who delivered the precepts which the Lord handed down for faith, and which were rooted in truth. Εἰ δὲ πού—he then continues—καὶ παρηκολουθηκώς τις τοῖς πρεσβυτέροις ἔλθοι, τοὺς τῶν πρεσβυτέρων ἀνέκρινον λόγους· τί ᾿Ανδρέας ἢ τί Πέτρος εἶπεν ἢ τί Φίλιππος ἢ τί Θωμᾶς ἢ ᾿Ιάκωβος ἢ τί ᾿Ιωάννης ἢ Ματθαῖος ἤ τις ἕτερος τῶν τοῦ κυρίου μαθητῶν, ἅ τε ᾿Αριστίων καὶ ὁ πρεσβύτερος ᾿Ιωάννης οἱ τοῦ κυρίου μαθηταὶ λέγουσι. Lücke thinks he can gather from this passage that Apostles are mentioned in it " by the title of πρεσβύτεροι." But a single glance at the passage teaches us that Papias used the word πρεσβύτεροι simply in the adjectival sense of " the elder (men)," that is, those who lived before himself. For, he includes in the term as well the Apostles Andrew, Peter, John, etc., as the two who were not Apostles, Aristion and the " Presbyter John." And when he distinguishes this last from the Apostle John by means of the title ὁ πρεσβύτερος, he shows plainly enough that πρεσβύτερος could not have been a title of the Apostle.[1] Thus this attempt at explanation fails; and, after all, we cannot understand how the Apostle could possibly have described himself as " the Presbyter," while there was a college of presbyters in the Church, and he himself was not in the proper sense a presbyter at all. It is as if the rector of a gymnasium should sign himself in his letters " *the Professor.*" Far from being an act of humility, this act would rather have been a grievous and somewhat offensive one; as that Apostle would thereby either represent himself as the only, the proper, the true, and in his idea sufficient presbyter, or as uniting in himself all the vocations, and functions, and powers of the rest. In any case, his exhibition of himself as the exclusive Presbyter, would have made all

---

[1] So Irenæus (in Euseb. 5, 20) plainly sets the πρεσβύτεροι over against the ἀποστόλους.

others disappear and lose their distinctive prerogatives. (Lücke so far admits the force of this, as to say that the above explanation is by no means indubitable.) But, as this description of himself would have been on the part of St John ungraceful, so it would have been on the part of the readers unintelligible; for, how could Kyria and Gaius divine who the man was who introduced himself to them by the bare name of "the Presbyter?" They could, indeed, understand it very well if—but only if—the man who so wrote was one who, among themselves and in his intercourse with them, was customarily designated by this short appellative.

But if the application of the word πρεσβύτερος to the *Apostle* constrains us to such an assumption, there is no reason why the same assumption should not be pressed into the service of those who understand by the πρεσβύτερος the actual *Presbyter* John. Indeed, if this Presbyter John had written to any strange church, and to it had called himself "the Presbyter," it would have been a designation somewhat presumptuous and confusing. But how different it is, if we regard him as writing to two of his private and intimate friends, who not only heard from those who brought the Epistle who its writer was, and understood it from the contents of the Epistle, but who were also accustomed in their common life to mention this man briefly as "the Presbyter!" And how easily would such a designation have been brought into use for him as such! Not so, indeed, for the Apostle; for, as such a designation would have been on his part ungracious, so it would have been, on the part of the members of the Church, wanting in respect; moreover, it would have been in a double sense confusing, inasmuch as another John was living at Ephesus, who was generally distinguished from the Apostle as the *Presbyter*. But how obvious was it in confidential intercourse to call this "Presbyter John," in contradistinction to the Apostle, "the Presbyter" simply, omitting his proper name! The meaning of this designation, then, was not "he who is the only Presbyter *in the Church*," but, "he who of *the two Johns* is the Presbyter." (Just as "the Telamonian" would be enough to distinguish Ajax.) If this very natural appellation once became current, we can easily understand how the Presbyter John would, in his confidential, private Epistles, use it as such for his purpose. We need not seek further explanation of this by assuming (what, however, we *may* assume, and *must* assume), that the individual little churches of the district, which were then being formed—of which one had been formed around Kyria (2 John 1 and 4), another around Gaius, as well as in the residence of Diotrephes (3 John 9)— were assigned to *individual* members of the presbytery established in the mother-church of Ephesus for inspection and supervision;[1] and that among those daughter-churches, these (that of Kyria, and that of Gaius and Diotrephes) had been assigned to the Presbyter John, so that he occasionally visited them (3 John 10, ἐὰν ἔλθω), and in the intervals addressed his Epistles to the Church through its prominent members—thus being actually, in respect to these churches, "the Presbyter," even in his official character. (To the Apostle, on the other hand, it was impossible that any single isolated churches should have been thus assigned.)

And with this superscription of the two Epistles, pointing to the Presbyter John, we may associate finally the passage, 3 John 9, 10, where the writer complains of the contradiction of Diotrephes. From the beginning, the defenders of the Presbyter's authorship have rightly asserted it to be unimaginable that *such* an opposition should have been offered to an *Apostle*, and especially to this the last of the Apostles, whose age and whose entire character commanded reverence and awe. Düsterdieck passes over this argument very lightly: "The contradiction of that man to the Apostle John is certainly not more improbable than the same kind of opposition which St Paul met with in Corinth and in other places." But he forgets, 1. that the opposition of the Jewish Christians to St Paul rested on the basis of a more profound internal antithesis between them; and, 2. that those Jewish Christians strove, though wrongly, to oppose the authority of *Apostles* to that of St Paul the Apostle (Gal. ii. 4; 2 Cor. xi. 5), as if the latter, being no eyewitness of the life of Jesus, had not in their eyes the same authority with the rest. But, in the case of Diotrephes, none of these things existed. In the place of the contest between

[1] This must at least have been the natural process of the evolution: compare the relation of the later Chorepiscopi, Euseb. 7, 30 (καὶ οἱ λοιποὶ πάντες οἱ σὺν ἡμῖν παροικοῦντες τὰς ἐγγὺς πόλεις καὶ ἔθνη ἐπίσκοποι). Synod of Neocæsarea, ch. 13; Aneura, ch. 13; Antioch, ch. 8-10.

the Christianity of the Jews and that of the Gentiles, which lost its significance with the destruction of Jerusalem, there had entered in another contest—that between the Church and Gnosticism. But Diotrephes could not have been a Gnostic; for the Gnostics had been constrained by the energy of St John (1 John ii. 19) to go out from the Christian churches, while Diotrephes (3 John 9) is seen to be a prominent member of the Christian Church itself. He is not charged with any error of doctrine;[1] his only error was his φιλοπρωτεύειν. He would be the first in his ἐκκλησία, and that as opposed to the writer of 3 John; for his φιλοπρωτεύειν showed itself in this, that he οὐκ ἐπιδέχεται him. Now, whether this means merely that he rejected his *letters and commandments,* or that he "despised and thought nothing of" his person generally, or, finally, that the "not receiving *us,*" ver. 9, finds its explanation in the "not receiving *the brethren,*" ver. 10,—in which case it would involve an interdiction of ecclesiastical communion,—in any and every case, it must be perfectly unintelligible how any member of a newly-established Church should have in any such manner rebelled against *the Apostle St John.* For such a rebellion would indeed have absolutely deserved the name of mad and infatuated! Moreover, we are told that Diotrephes "prateth against us with malicious words" (ver. 10), that he slandered the author of 3 John with wicked babbling, denied hospitable brotherly reception to those who were sent to him, and thus cut the bond of all Christian fellowship. But even the worst Galatian and Corinthian Judaizers never ventured to treat St Paul thus.

How entirely different is the matter, and how intelligible all becomes, if we regard the *Presbyter* John as the author of this Epistle! Let us endeavour to make present to our mind the whole position of the case and its relations. In certain places around Ephesus, nearer or more distant, Christian communities were in process of being formed. They were as yet too small,

---

[1] Olshausen: "Probably Diotrephes belonged to the great party which St John withstands in his Epistles." But there is not the slightest trace of anything which might lead to such a conclusion; on the contrary, everything is against it. If Diotrephes had been a Gnostic, our author would certainly not have complained merely that he prated against himself, but his charge would have mainly been that he denied *Christ.*

and internally and externally too weak, to be organized each into an independent Church, overlooked by its own separate presbytery. In one of them was an (elderly) woman, who stood at the head of the little circle of newly-converted (2 John 1 and 4). Another of these rising Churches seems to have been distributed through several neighbouring places; that is, 3 John 9, 10 indicates that Gaius did not live in the same place with Diotrephes: nevertheless the author, ver. 9, speaks of "*the* Church"—manifestly that to which Gaius belonged,[1] while the following verses show that Diotrephes was a prominent member of it. Probably Diotrephes lived in the same place which was the chief seat of this Church, but Gaius lived in a χώριον, or a *village* in the neighbourhood.—Now, both these Churches were committed to the Presbyter John for ἐπισκοπή and oversight: it was his duty now and then personally to visit them; under his guidance and direction stood all those persons, such as Kyria, Diotrephes, and Gaius, who in his absence had the interim management of affairs, and conduct of the worship of the church,—they being the most prominent members in it. The Presbyter John was then really the πρῶτος in each of these churches. But Diotrephes, an ambitious man, would no longer endure this subjection to an Ephesian presbyter: he would himself be the πρῶτος (φιλοπρωτεύει); he would make his little church independent, and reduce it under his own sway. Consequently, he withstands the directions of the Presbyter John; oppresses those Christians living round him who were faithful to the Presbyter; vindicates his own conduct by saying all manner of evil concerning him, seeking to degrade and vilify him in the eyes of the Church; and, when the Presbyter sent to him certain members of the Church with an Epistle (ver. 9), Diotrephes refused them (induced perhaps by fear, lest his slanders should be revealed and refuted) the reception of brotherly hospitality, and would not allow other members of the Church to receive them. However reprobate this conduct was, it is as imaginable and to be accounted for, as a similar rebellion against the *Apostle* John would have been unimaginable and

---

[1] Else the Apostle would hardly have been able to say, "I have written something to the Church," but must have said, "I have written to the Church in such a place," in order to distinguish it from the Church of Gaius.

unaccountable. Indeed, we should prefer to assume that all this took place after the Apostle's death.

What is it, then, that the Presbyter John does? First, he had written an Epistle, but Diotrephes had not received "$ἡμᾶς$;" that is (according to ver. 10), the $ἀδελφοί$ who carried his Epistle (and consequently the Epistle itself). Now he turns to a member of the same Church, who, however, lived not in its capital city, but in another place, and who therefore was not under the influence of the despotism which Diotrephes, according to ver. 10, already exercised over the members of the Church where he lived. He communicates to him what had passed, and adds the exhortation that Gaius should not imitate this $κακόν$. Against this danger the previous conduct of Gaius had given him every warrant. For Gaius *had* already (ver. 3) received and treated hospitably those $ἀδελφοί$ who had been cast out by Diotrephes, and who (ver. 7) were unwilling to take anything of the Gentiles. The design of the Presbyter John is, on the one hand, to thank him for this (vers. 3–8), but, on the other hand, to exhort him (ver. 11) that he should continue to refuse to be led away into compliance with the views of Diotrephes. At the same time, he gives him notice that he would find in Demetrius (who probably also lived in another place than Diotrephes) a man like-minded, and a great help (ver. 12).—The Presbyter John, therefore, primarily aims only to take measures against the further spread of the schism now beginning. To suppress it altogether would be the work of his own visit to the place where Diotrephes lived (ver. 10, $ἐὰν$ $ἔλθω$): he would annihilate him in the eyes of the Church, and deprive him of his false consideration, by showing him the groundlessness and wickedness of his slanderous reproaches, and the unchristian character of his acts ($ὑπομνήσω$).[1]

Thus the whole posture of matters becomes perfectly plain,

---

[1] Strange that Düsterdieck should say, "The authority of which the writer is conscious, in his conduct towards Diotrephes, is scarcely comprehensible, unless the *Apostle* is regarded as the writer." But of what authority is he conscious? No other than what perfect right on his side gives him. All that he would do was to expose to Diotrephes his slanders, and represent to him and all the Christians of his party the unchristian wickedness of their doings. Surely it needed not an Apostle to do this! How otherwise would Titus have acted among the Corinthians?

when we regard the matter treated of here as the endeavour of an ambitious man to sever a daughter-church from her relation of dependence upon the mother-church, and to set herself up as an independent society. On the other hand, the entire Epistle would be a riddle, if we regarded it as dealing with the rebellion of an individual against the Apostle John.

The earlier defenders of the view which we hold appealed further to the passage, 2 John 10 seq., as being opposed to the spirit of love which reigned in St John: but in this they were decidedly wrong. Such a prohibition might very well have come from that Apostle who left the bath when he saw that Cerinthus was there (see Introduction to 1 John). The "love" of the Apostle John was not a soft universal sentiment towards all; to him, indeed, the idea of brotherly-love embraces love to *all* men (see above on 1 John iii. 15, v. 1 and 6), but a love which took no pleasure in souls but for their salvation;[1] hence it met sin, not with servile or gentle connivance, but with firm maintenance of truth, and rigorous discipline of correction. It was said by the Spirit of God that, with men who decisively oppose the truth, and deny Jesus the Christ, we must break off all conventional intercourse and friendship; because the forms and ceremonies which that requires become a lie, when the fundamental conditions of a specifically friendly and profitable relationship are wanting. Hence we must hold fast, in relation to 2 John 10 seq., that the Presbyter John wrote these words under the inspiration of the Spirit of His Lord Jesus Christ, and in harmony with the teaching of his master, the Apostle.

This passage, therefore, cannot be pressed into the service of the authorship of the Presbyter John. But the demonstrations given above constrain us with the utmost decision to adhere to that opinion which was in the earliest centuries held by one-half of the Christian Church, and which since the Reformation has been maintained by Erasmus, Grotius, Dodwell, Harenberg,

---

[1] We must not forget that the sentiment of love to our fellow-saved forms with St John (as generally in Christendom) the basis on which universal love (to those to be saved) rests, or out of which it grows. By no means is a vague love of all the world the basis, as if love to our fellow-Christians were only a species and special direction of that vague humanitarian love (comp. 2 Pet. i. 7).

Beck (and waveringly by Lücke and Reuss); to wit, that the *Presbyter John was the author of these two Epistles.*

But we must strongly protest against the way in which some critics exhibit this question as one concerning the "genuineness or spuriousness" of these two Epistles. We hold them to be the genuine Epistles of the Presbyter John, as certainly as they hold the Gospel of St Luke to have been the genuine production of St Luke, notwithstanding he was not an *Apostle*. But how can the question of "genuineness or spuriousness" be intelligently introduced here? This question can arise only in the case of a document, the author of which either mentions himself, or, if he conceals his name (as St John in his Gospel and Epistle), is testified to have been the author by the unanimous witness of ancient tradition, and by its own internal intimations (*e.g.*, that he had been an eyewitness of the life of Christ, John xix. 35; 1 John i. 1). Neither of these is the case here. The question here is the same as in relation to the Epistle to the Hebrews, the author of which does not name himself; and with respect to whose apostolical authorship, or otherwise, the declarations of antiquity are divided; and in which certainly the style and other considerations are decisive against an apostolical authorship. Now, as it cannot be reasonably objected to those who ascribe the Epistle to the Hebrews to St Luke, the helper of the Apostle (as, for example, Delitzsch and myself), that they declare the Epistle to be "spurious," so it cannot be reasonably objected against those who hold the Second and Third Epistles to have been written by the Presbyter John, that they deny the "genuineness" of these Epistles.

Still less is the *canonicity* of these Epistles invaded by this general view and conviction. The Epistle to the Hebrews furnishes here a perfect analogy. In the case of those writings, the authors of which are not named by themselves, or established clearly by patristic tradition, their canonicity does not depend upon the question of this or that authorship. These two Epistles approve themselves divinely-inspired to every one who is born of the Spirit, by the spirit which reigns in their words. And, that they were more slowly dispersed through the churches, and in some of them were long unknown, may be sufficiently explained by their nature as private Epistles, and by their more occasional design.

The question as to the Readers, the Design, and the Period of composition, has been already considered above, in its relation to the Third Epistle. As to the Second Epistle, it may be said that Κυρία cannot be held equivalent to *Curia* (as if this again were equivalent to *ecclesia !*)—as Hammond thought—nor can it be a symbolical description of a church, or the Church, as the "bride of the Κύριος." For, while the Church is, as related to the Bridegroom, the bride,—as related to the "Lord," she is not the "lady," but an obedient handmaid. Further, Κυρία cannot have (as Michaelis divined) the signification of "the Church to be assembled at the day of the Lord in behalf of the service of God." Nor is it very probable that the author would have addressed any beloved woman as a "chosen lady" and sister (Luther, Beza, etc.), or as "Lady Eclecta" (Wetstein, Grotius, who take Ἐκλεκτή as a proper name). We may also dismiss the quaint investigation (à Lapide) whether this "chosen lady" was named Drusia, or whether she was Martha the sister of Lazarus, or even Mary the mother of our Lord (in which case Κυρία must be most fittingly translated *Madonna*). As to this last view, the author (whether St John or the Presbyter) would have needed rather to call himself ὁ νεώτερος, when addressing a woman who must have lived—about the year 94 or 96 ær. Dion.[1]—at least a hundred and thirty years.

Leaving all these subtle points of investigation to themselves, we hold Κυρία—following in the wake of Benson, Bengel, Olshausen, and many others—to be the proper name of a woman who, with her children, had been converted to Christianity. As ver. 4 speaks of these children as walking in the truth, we must suppose these not to have been little children, but adult sons and daughters. Thus they indicate a little collection of Christian households which, with the aged mother at the head, formed one of those small daughter-churches that have been mentioned above. The sister's children of this Kyria lived, according to ver. 13, in Ephesus.

When, therefore, the Presbyter writes in ver. 4 of his rejoicing that *some of her children* walk in the truth, and then follows it with an exhortation (ver. 5) to love, and (ver. 7) to a firm maintenance of the confession of Jesus Christ, and then

---

[1] As 2 John plainly refers to 1 John, it is clear that it could not have been written *before* the years 94–96.

proceeds to say, "Take heed that ye lose not what ye have wrought," and then (ver. 10) adds the specific injunction to break off all personal intercourse with the Gnostic false teachers, and particularly not to receive them into the house—we see the whole occasion and scope of the Epistle lying before our eyes. There were manifestly others of the children of Kyria, who in their houses had failed of that decided opposition to the seduction of the Gnostics; the bond of love between them and the former had already been relaxed; and the danger of apostasy was at hand. Against that, this Epistle was a warning; from that it would restrain them, until the Presbyter should find time to pay them a personal visit. But he addresses his exhortations in such a form as designedly to remind them of the important Epistle which the Apostle had written, and which he presupposes Kyria and her children to be acquainted with; and thus he supports his own requests and exhortations by the authority of the highly esteemed (then probably deceased) Apostle.

Thus, these two Epistles preserve to us a beautiful, instructive, and profitable picture of the personality and faithful work of a helper and disciple of the Apostles; and give us at the same time a living insight into the relations of the pastoral influence in the early Churches, and the work of the individual members of a presbytery of the apostolical time. Thus a man, in the person of the *Presbyter John*, takes his rank among the writers of the New Testament, who approves himself, in the few lines which he has left behind him, one full of faith and of the Holy Ghost—an illustrious type and example of a Christian presbyter.

THE SECOND EPISTLE OF ST JOHN.

VERS. 1–3. *Address and Greeting.*—It is necessary at the outset to establish the true reading, as the readings here waver much. In ver. 1, Cod. B. reads καὶ οὐκ ἐγὼ μόνος; Cod. A., on the contrary, οὐκ ἐγὼ δὲ μόνος; and in Cod. G. we have the combination, καὶ οὐκ ἐγὼ δὲ μόνος. This last form, manifestly a mere combination, has least to be said in its favour. According to Huther, etc., καί was the genuine reading, and δέ the correction of a copyist, who aimed to strengthen the contrast. But, as Cod. A. throughout the whole of the First Epistle of St John has never corrected the oft-recurring Hebraistic adversative καί into δέ, it is not very probable that it has done it here; but it is more obvious to suppose that the copyist of Cod. B. has corrected an original δέ into καί, in order to make the Second Epistle conform to the First—an endeavour of which we shall find several more examples.—In ver. 2, Cod. A. reads τὴν ἐνοικοῦσαν, and with it we find also in some later manuscripts τὴν οὖσαν; Cod. B., on the other hand, has τὴν μένουσαν, also reproduced in the Vulgate, which, it is well known, was largely influenced by Cod. B. Düsterdieck thinks that μένουσαν is vindicated by its being the Johannæan expression; but it is this very echo of St John's style which makes it suspicious. How any transcriber could have corrected a μένουσαν into ἐνοικοῦσαν, is altogether, in fact, incomprehensible; it is much more probable that an original ἐνοικοῦσαν was corrected into μένουσαν—partly, in order to establish a conformity with 1 John ii. 14 and 24, iii. 9, iv. 16, and partly because the meaning of the following words, "and shall be with you," was to be interpreted into it. But the very tautology which would result from the μένουσαν by the side of ἔσται εἰς τὸν αἰῶνα, speaks decisively against the reading μένουσαν. Some later Codd. have, instead of μεθ' ἡμῶν, the reading μεθ' ὑμῶν; but the ὑμῶν was manifestly derived from ver. 3, either through neglect, or from a false zeal to produce conformity. When, on the other hand, Cod. A. omits in ver. 3 the words ἔσται μεθ' ὑμῶν (so also the Syr.), this evidently took place through an application of the false principles of Alexandrian criticism. It was thought that there was a want of beauty in the sudden recurrence of the phrase εἶναι μετά, and therefore it was left out the second time as superfluous. But, the very fact of the inversion of the order of the words (ver. 2, μεθ' ἡμῶν ἔσται; ver. 3, ἔσται μεθ' ὑμῶν) shows that the words were not repeated merely through inadvertence, but are genuine and original. And in this inversion of the order there is a delicate turn. The author designedly attaches his benediction in ver. 3 to what was said in the close of ver. 2. The word κυρίου before Jesus is wanting in A.B., Syr., Erp., Æth., Vulg., and is decidedly spurious.

We read therefore: Ὁ πρεσβύτερος ἐκλεκτῇ Κυρίᾳ καὶ τοῖς τέκνοις αὐτῆς, οὓς ἐγὼ ἀγαπῶ ἐν ἀληθείᾳ, οὐκ ἐγὼ δὲ μόνος, ἀλλὰ καὶ πάντες οἱ ἐγνωκότες τὴν ἀλήθειαν, διὰ τὴν ἀλήθειαν τὴν ἐνοικοῦσαν ἐν ἡμῖν, καὶ μεθ' ἡμῶν ἔσται εἰς τὸν αἰῶνα· ἔσται μεθ' ὑμῶν χάρις, ἔλεος, εἰρήνη παρὰ Θεοῦ πατρός, καὶ παρὰ Ἰησοῦ Χριστοῦ τοῦ υἱοῦ τοῦ πατρός, ἐν ἀληθείᾳ καὶ ἀγάπῃ.

Concerning ὁ πρεσβύτερος, as well as concerning Κυρία and her children, all that is needful has been said in the Introduction. Ἐκλεκτή the latter is called, in the sense of 2 Tim. ii. 10; 1 Pet. i. 1, ii. 9, etc.; that is, in the sense of ἅγιος, holy. Every Christian is an ἐκλεκτός, because he is chosen out of the profane world into the sanctified company of the Church of God.

The relative clause, οὓς ἐγὼ, κ.τ.λ., must be construed in such a way as to supply an ἀγαπῶσι to the second subject, ἀλλὰ καὶ πάντες, κ.τ.λ.—thus making the words διὰ κ.τ.λ., ver. 2, depend upon these verbs ἀγαπῶ and ἀγαπῶσιν. Ἐγὼ is not without its specific force, being used on account of the following antithesis, οὐκ ἐγὼ δὲ μόνος, ἀλλὰ, κ.τ.λ. The Elder says, first, that *he* loved Kyria and her children; and then, that they were likewise loved by *all who have known the truth.* Thus Kyria was, in the estimation of all who knew her, a woman highly to be esteemed, a very eminent Christian. The words οὓς ἀγαπῶ have the clause ἐν ἀληθείᾳ added. This appendage cannot have been intended merely to mark the sincerity of the love;

for it manifestly refers to what is subsequently said concerning the ἀλήθεια. But we are not warranted, on the other hand, in interpreting, " Whom I love on the basis of the objective Christian truth" (Bengel, Lücke, Olshausen); for, that would have required ἐν τῇ ἀληθείᾳ. In the first interpretation, this much is correct, that it is not the objective foundation, but the kind and manner of the " loving," which was to be indicated; but it is wrong in regarding " truth" here as merely in the human sense opposed to falsehood. When the Presbyter says that he " loved her *in truth*," he does not mean that he loved her " truly and sincerely," but that he loved her with that love which was a *love in truth* (so that the idea of the " truth" as a moral, substantial idea, is co-ordinated with the moral idea of love, as in the converse order ἀληθεύειν ἐν ἀγάπῃ). His love was such as approved itself in perfect truth and truthfulness of conduct: thus it was not blind to the faults and sins of the object beloved; it did not spare from a false delicacy and sense of propriety; but it had its existence in the sphere of truth, that is, of the ἀληθὴς εἶναι, the being true. Thus the " loving in truth" forms an antithesis to that perverted friendship with the deniers of Christ, against which vers. 7-11 give warning. Ἀλήθεια accordingly designates here, not truth in the objective sense (revealed truth), but truth as the subjective Christian-moral characteristic of the spirit, and temper, and being. Thus viewed, ἀλήθεια is not the same in signification with that which is afterwards mentioned as ἡ ἀλήθεια, though it does indeed stand in close actual relation with it. For, he who has known the objective truth of the revelation of God in Christ (ἐγνωκότες τὴν ἀλήθειαν), has dwelling in him the truth *quà* the nature of God (compare above on 1 John ii. 4); and, for the sake of this truth, which dwells in him as well as in those who are to be loved (διὰ τὴν ἀλήθειαν τὴν ἐνοικοῦσαν ἐν ἡμῖν), he will love these also ἐν ἀληθείᾳ, that is, within the sphere of this subjective spirit of love which is regulated by this objective indwelling truth.

Why the author here describes the being converted to Christianity as " the having known the truth," is clear from what has been just said; so also is the meaning of the introductory words of ver. 2.—Ἡμῖν is naturally used in common; equivalent to " in me as in them (the τέκνοις)."—The question whether the author meant by πάντες all Christians of all lands (Beda, Lyra, Düsterdieck, Huther), or all those Christians who came into any sort of contact with Kyria (Grotius, Carpzov, De Wette, Lücke), must manifestly be decided in favour of the latter interpretation. In the *word* πάντες there is indeed no limitation, but there is in the *situation*.

In the words καὶ μεθ' ἡμῶν ἔσται εἰς τὸν αἰῶνα we are not to find a continuation of the attribute τὴν ἐνοικοῦσαν ἐν ἡμῖν— as if it were simply "through the truth, which dwelleth in you, and shall be with you for ever." But, in these words the Presbyter passes over to a substantially new leading thought. He utters his *wish:* "And may this truth (which dwelleth in us) be with us for ever." That our ἔσται is not to be taken as an affirmation (Bengel), but as a wish, is manifest from this, that the following invocation adheres strictly to the same form: "(Yea) may grace, mercy, peace, be with you." In fact, the occasion and the whole object of the letter was the fact that some of the children of Kyria were in danger of falling from the truth. On that account the Presbyter places so emphatically the invocation of blessing at the outset,—the wish and hope that the truth, which dwelleth in us, may abide with us. In the words ἔσται μεθ' ὑμῶν χάρις, κ.τ.λ., this general wish, which at first included all, is prominently referred to *Kyria and her children.*

The benediction or greeting of ver. 3 needs scarcely any explanation. *Grace* is the most universal source of all our salvation and new life; but it approves itself as *mercy* in relation to our specific sins and unfaithfulness, and the misery in which we have thus involved ourselves; and the *peace* of heart with God is the fruit of this merciful demonstration of grace in us. Grace comes from God the Father; and it comes through the mediation of Jesus Christ, the Son of the Father (as He is here already termed, not without reason, in opposition to the seducers and false teachers to be mentioned in ver. 10). This grace, this mercy, this peace, is to be μεθ' ὑμῶν ἐν ἀληθείᾳ καὶ ἀγάπῃ: and thus it is shown by what fruits God's grace, operating in us, must declare its presence. As the author himself, and every true Christian, "loveth in truth" (ἀγαπᾷ ἐν ἀληθείᾳ), and "in love is true" (ἀληθεύει ἐν ἀγάπῃ), so must it also be in those who are here addressed. But the Presbyter has, further, a specific reason for giving prominence to these two points. For, these are the two exhortations which he will urge in what follows,—that they should be stedfast in ἀγάπη, as well as in that subjective ἀλήθεια which manifests itself in the holding fast of the objective truth. The words ἐν ἀληθείᾳ καὶ ἀγάπῃ thus contain, at the same time, a reference to the contents of the whole Epistle.

Now, that the Presbyter could not obviate the danger of his hearers being deceived by Gnostic false teachers, without involuntarily thinking of the Epistle of his teacher the Apostle, and showing that he thought of it, is naturally to be supposed. Nor could he do this without in some way referring those readers to that Epistle. The very combination of the two main elements, *truth* and *love*, plainly enough reminds them of the two main points of the Fourth Section (and chapter) of the apostolical Epistle of St John. But all the more significant on that account is the *perfectly independent manner* in which the Presbyter here, vers. 1–3, introduces these two main elements, setting out from the *subjective* statement, ἀγαπῶ ἐν ἀληθείᾳ.

VERS. 4–6. *First exhortation, to love.*—Ver. 4 begins the proper substance of the Epistle: "I have greatly rejoiced" (we must reproduce the Aorist by our Perfect) "that I found among thy children those who walk in *truth,* as we have received a commandment from the Father." The partitive ἐκ (with τινὰς to be supplied) is not a Hebraism, but genuine Greek (comp. Aristoph. Nub. 1089). The qualitative idea does not lie in the clause with καθώς, so that ἐν ἀληθείᾳ would be merely an adverbial appendage ("who truly walk as we have received commandment"); but it is ἐν ἀληθείᾳ which contains the qualitative idea—the kind of walking. "To walk in *truth*" is to be interpreted after the analogy of "loving *in truth,*" ver. 1, and is closely connected with the closing words of the third verse. The article perhaps would have been used by ourselves, since "in truth" has the adverbial meaning of *revera*. But the author did not employ the article, because he did not mean to be understood as referring to objective dogmatic truth, but to that subjective nature of the ἀληθὴς εἶναι which is imparted by God to man.—"To walk in the truth" is the general expression which includes all sides of the Christianly-called and Christianly-sanctified life; and must not be referred, as some refer it, simply to brotherly-love alone. That Christian walks in ἀληθείᾳ who is a Christian not merely in name but in nature, in whom the nature of Him who is the substantial ἀλήθεια has become a living reality. The clause with καθώς cannot be a qualitative limitation, by the addition of which a particular species of walking in truth is made prominent—"who so walk in truth as we have received *commandment*,"—for that would require us to assume a kind of walking in truth which is opposed to the commandment of the Father. The clause with καθώς might be regarded as, on the one hand, *appositional* (explicative), so that the idea of "walking in truth" would be explained by the idea of "walking as we have received commandment" ("who walk in truth, that is, so as we have received commandment"); but that would assume καθὼς ἐντολὴν ἐλάβομεν to be used instead of κατ᾽ ἐντολὴν ἣν ἐλάβομεν. Or, on the other hand, that clause may be regarded as *argumentative* (καθώς being "as we then," "as we indeed"); and this is the simpler view, being in accordance with the use of καθώς in ver. 6. The thought would then be as follows: "I have found among thy children those who walk in truth; as we also (in fact) have a commandment from the Father (*that we* should walk in the truth)"; that is, as this indeed is the will of God. It is wrong to refer the ἐντολή to the commandment of love following in ver. 5. Ver. 4 is not to be explained by ver. 5. He who reads ver. 4 simply, could certainly refer the ἐντολή only to the commandment to walk in the truth (Matt. xxi. 28 seq.; John xiv. 15, etc.).

The Presbyter found *among* the children of Kyria such as walked in truth. While he expresses his joy on that account, he tenderly intimates that he could not assign that praise to all her children. But it does not by any means follow from this, that the remaining children were still heathens: it does follow, however, that the Presbyter had not found them altogether walking in the truth. And it is this fact which explains the succeeding exhortations and warnings. It is strange that Düsterdieck and others should violate this most obvious connection between ver. 4 and the following verses, substituting the supposition that the author spoke of *some* children of Kyria only because "he had not yet become acquainted" with the remainder. According to the opinion of these expositors, the occasion and design of his writing was not to point the attention of Kyria to the spiritual danger which threatened one part of her family, and thus to influence the children's minds through their mother; but "the Apostle had become acquainted with some of the children of Kyria who were earnest Christians," and wrote to testify his joy on that account. All the other exhortations and warnings were added fortuitously, without any *special* occasion! But thus the Epistle is robbed of all its pith and sinews. The assertion that the author must have written $\tau o\grave{v}\varsigma\ \pi\epsilon\rho\iota\pi\alpha\tau o\hat{v}\nu\tau\alpha\varsigma$ if he had intended to express that he "had found among her children *some* walking in the truth," is based upon a pure delusion. The article might indeed have been prefixed; but the sentence, *without* that article, can mean, grammatically, no other than this: "I have found among thy children those walking in the truth." Hardly would any one derive from the absence of the article the meaning that the writer had come to know only the children who walked in the truth, and did not know the others. On the contrary, the failure of the article gives more distinctness and prominence to the idea of "some."

It is through the tenderness of his manner, that the Presbyter conceals the blame which he has to express under the form of limitation of his praise. And it has its reason in this, that he does not address his letter to the children themselves who were in danger of error, but to the aged and venerable matron. He would not at once begin with a word which might cause her grief: "I have rejoiced to find among thy children those who walk in truth. And now I beseech thee, Kyria—that we love one another," and so on. This was speaking plainly enough for such an one as Kyria was.

The question whether the writer made the discovery accidentally, or after a special examination, that some of the children of Kyria walked in the truth, will appear to be a needless one, when we look at the position of the whole matter. Some of her children he had found walking in the truth, and others not: that is, he had heard concerning the latter, that they had entered into some kind of fellowship with false teachers, and that their love to the Church and to the children of God had grown cold; while he had with joy heard concerning the former, that they remained stedfast and true in faith and love.

In ver. 5 he attaches, by καὶ νῦν, his *request* to the *observation* communicated in ver. 4. That νῦν is not to be taken in the sense of time (in opposition to the Aorist ἐχάρην), but belongs to καί, has been established by Düsterdieck, against Lücke, De Wette, and others. Καὶ νῦν is a *logical* connecting word; not connecting, however, with the thought, that by a Divine commandment the walk of Christians is regulated, but with the *main fact* stated in ver. 4, that *of* the children of Kyria, some were walking in the truth. This being so,[1] he prays her that *mutual love may be maintained.* That he does not command or exhort, but request, is another trait of that delicacy and humility which was perfectly appropriate in relation to this aged matron.[2] (Of any " official" prerogative, before which all pure human relation must sink into the dust, the New Testament knows nothing at all.) But when a person is prayed ἵνα ἀγαπῶμεν ἀλλήλους, there must be some *lack* in that person's circle of this ἀγαπᾶν ἀλλήλους.

"Not as though I wrote a new commandment unto thee, but that which we had from the beginning," is interposed as a parenthesis; and it merely suggests a remembrancer, that the commandment to love one another was one long and well known to Kyria; that he therefore required of her nothing new, and as it were unfamiliar, but only that he was obliged *anew* to ask a request, the ground and justification of which she would, without any question, acknowledge. This is the meaning, as the context shows. It is only in their *form* that these words remind us of the passage, 1 John ii. 7; and this indeed is not accidental. The Presbyter really intends, in ver. 6 seq., to refer to the matter also of that apostolical document; and, therefore, he gives *his own independent thought* a *form* which is similar to that passage of the Epistle, which in itself contained a *somewhat different* (although analogous) idea. We have seen that the ἐντολή which the *Apostle* lays down as not a new one, but given

[1] The distinction which Düsterdieck seeks to establish, in 1 John v. 16 and 2 John 5, between ἐρωτᾶν and αἰτεῖν, is altogether groundless. He makes ἐρωτᾶν the request among equals, and αἰτεῖν the request of a superior. Hence Jesus always calls His asking an ἐρωτᾶν. But in 1 John v. 16, our praying to God is mentioned as an ἐρωτᾶν. The truth is, that ἐρωτᾶν originally meant *interrogare*, then *rogare*; but αἰτεῖν originally, to " demand" (hence αἰτία, suit, *causa*), and then generally *petere*, " seek."

[2] On the age of Kyria, see the remarks in the Introduction.

from the beginning, was no other than this, that "God is light (and we therefore must walk in light);" and that he sets over against this ἐντολὴ παλαιά the new ἐντολή of ver. 8, "that the light already shineth." Our passage bears a similarity only to ver. 7, but not to ver. 8. As there the Apostle John had said it was not a new commandment, but that which was given from the beginning, that God is light, and we should walk in light; so *similarly*, and with allusion to that passage (but also to John xiii. 34), the Presbyter John here says that it is not a new commandment, but one given from the beginning (by Christ Himself, John xiii. 34), that we should love one another. The *end* for which he says this is one altogether different here: as already observed, he strengthens and confirms his request by reminding Kyria that he asks not anything new, but only asks anew for something, the necessity of which she had long known and acknowledged. We saw, when upon 1 John ii. 7, how wrong it was to explain that passage (the whole context of which says nothing about ἀγάπη) by the present one; but not less improper is it to explain this passage by that. Each of the two places has its own independent meaning, approved by the context; it is only the *form* of this matter which the Presbyter here, *remembering* and *alluding to* St John's passage, has shaped with reference to its model. He says, concerning the specific commandment of mutual love, that which the Apostle had said concerning the general commandment of walking in the light.

In ver. 6 the Presbyter now appends two thoughts, which —combined together with this brevity and want of connection —would be very mysterious and perplexing were they not *specific allusions* to the Epistle of the Apostle, presupposed to be well-known to Kyria.

"And this is love, that we walk after His commandments." He first declares that love itself is nothing isolated, but that it consists generally in the keeping of the commandments. And this makes it perfectly intelligible how he can transfer, in ver. 5, that which the Apostle had said concerning the universal walk in light to the demand and requirement of mutual love. But, at the same time, he declares thereby what he understands by the ἀγαπῶμεν ἀλλήλους; that is, not an effeminate, self-seeking, self-complacent love to our neighbour, but a love which manifests itself in the steady discharge of every obligation. Ἡ ἀγάπη is employed generally, and not limited to the love of our neighbour alone; but, if it holds good of love generally, that it consists in a περιπατεῖν κατὰ τὰς ἐντολάς, it must also hold good of the love of our neighbour, that it consists in the fulfilment of the Divine commandments which regulate our relations to our neighbour. But the Presbyter is led to lay down the thought in this *generality of expression*, by the circumstance that he is not speaking here in his own name, but reproduces an utterance of the Apostle. It is the passage 1 John v. 3 : "This is the love of God, that we keep His commandments." He naturally omits the words τοῦ Θεοῦ, since he has just been speaking of the ἀγαπᾶν ἀλλήλους : thus he generalizes the thought, but cites (only with the unessential change of τηρεῖν into περιπατεῖν, which also better suited the reference to brotherly-love) the essential components of that apostolical utterance, and that so literally, as to retain the entire form, αὕτη ἔστιν ἡ ἀγάπη ἵνα.

But the Apostle in that passage had placed in juxtaposition the two thoughts :—that love to God shows itself in brotherly-love; and, again, that brotherly-love shows itself in the keeping of the commandments of God. After the Presbyter has quoted the latter, he is naturally led to add something that shall be analogous to the former also. But, as he has not now to do with the two ideas—the love of God and brotherly-love—but with brotherly-love and the keeping of God's commandments, his second thought takes the following form : αὕτη ἡ ἐντολή ἐστιν, καθὼς ἠκούσατε ἀπ' ἀρχῆς, ἵνα ἐν αὐτῇ περιπατῆτε. The words καθὼς, κ.τ.λ., are parenthetically inserted, and it cannot be denied that καθώς here means "as indeed, truly." But the words ἐν αὐτῇ do not refer back to ἐντολή, but to ἀγάπη. "This is (as ye have heard from the beginning) the commandment, that ye should walk in love."—The form suggests 1 John iv. 21; the matter, 1 John iv. 7 and 11. But the whole sharply-defined and entirely unmediated antithesis of the two thoughts rests upon the section 1 John iv. 1–v. 3 (the concluding verse of which is literally cited); and we see as plainly as can be that the writer is thus brief, simply because he can take it for granted that the whole section is perfectly familiar to Kyria. As a superfluous intimation, καθὼς κ.τ.λ. declares that he here refers to what was well known.

VERS. 7–11. *Second exhortation:* viz., *the warning against Gnosticism.* The mention that many πλάνοι had come to the world is closely connected by ὅτι with what precedes; and this shows that the writer regarded the existence of these πλάνοι as the reason which had made the preceding exhortation to love so necessary. *The declension of their love had its cause in the relation of these* τέκνα *to the* πλάνοις. (It is needless and untenable, with Lücke, to make ὅτι grammatically dependent upon ἐρωτῶ σε.)

Our seventh verse, again, is no other than a citation—a full citation, as far as unessentials go—of the passage 1 John v. 1–3, with a reminiscence of 1 John v. 6, and ii. 22. The Apostle writes, ὅτι πολλοὶ ψευδοπροφῆται ἐξεληλύθασιν εἰς τὸν κόσμον; and the Presbyter writes, taking up also the idea of the πλάνη in 1 John v. 6, ὅτι πολλοὶ πλάνοι εἰσῆλθον εἰς τὸν κόσμον. (The reading ἐξῆλθον, or ἐξῆλθαν, Cod. A., may be regarded as a conjectural emendation after 1 John ii. 19, iv. 1. How Cod. B. reads is uncertain. Ἐξῆλθον is the reading of Codd. G. and I., Theoph., Œcum., and others.) The substance and matter of the πλάνη itself the Presbyter sums up literally according to 1 John v. 2 ("he that confesseth that Jesus Christ is come in the flesh"), in the words, "who confess not that Jesus Christ is come in the flesh." He then closes, with a manifest reminiscence of 1 John ii. 22 ("this is Antichrist"), by the words, "This is the deceiver and the Antichrist;" but, referring back to the introductory words of our verse, he takes up and includes the "deceiver."

The *meaning* of all these words has been already elucidated in the observations upon 1 John iv. 1 seq. Their *scope* is clear enough here, and in ver. 8 it is more fully developed. The Presbyter reminds Kyria briefly but plainly of that which the Apostle had written concerning these false teachers, and especially of what he had said as to their *anti*-Christian character. Bearing this well in mind, she would never think it a thing indifferent that such poison might possibly be insinuated into her family.

In ver. 8, Cod. B. reads ἀπολέσητε—εἰργασάμεθα—ἀπολάβητε. On the other hand, Cod. A. reads thrice the 2d person plural (the Text. Rec. has thrice the 1st person plural, following lesser authorities). Lachmann and Tischendorf follow rightly the Codex B. How easily might the copyists have yielded to the suggestion that εἰργασάμεθα must be corrected into εἰργάσασθε, since they who are in danger of losing must be the same who were to work out what they are in danger of losing! And the reading of the Text. Rec. would arise with equal facility, as soon as ἀπολεσητε and ἀπολάβητε were corrected to harmonize with εἰργασάμεθα.—Reading, then, εἰργασάμεθα, all those explanations vanish which refer this "working" to that which believers, through the labour of repentance and the fight of faith, have "wrought out" for themselves—that is, have won by effort—whether as reward (μισθον πλήρη), or as the fellowship and grace of God, or as good works, and the like. This ἐργάζεσθαι rather signifies the work and labour of the ministers of the Gospel, through which those who were addressed had been brought to conversion and furthered in their Christian course to the present time; and by ἃ εἰργασάμεθα, "the things which we have wrought," we are to understand that stage of salvation to which, through those labours, Kyria and her children had attained. She, with all hers (the exhortation βλέπετε is addressed to all, though especially to those of her "children" of whom the "walking in truth," ver. 4, did *not* hold good), were to take good heed that that (life in Christ) should not be subverted which had been wrought in them by the ministry of the Presbyter John, and their other pastors and teachers, but that they should rather bear away the full reward. Βλέπετε ἑαυτούς, as in Mark xiii. 9, is to look well at themselves—that is, to give heed to their own heart and conduct. By "full reward" cannot be understood the fruits of apostolical labour already obtained below; for it is not the reward obtained by the teachers for their work that is spoken of, but that which Kyria with her children were to receive (ἀπολαμβάνειν, as in Matt. x. 41; Luke xvi. 25; Gal. iv. 5; Col. iii. 24).

Μισθός rather signifies here, as in Luke vi. 23, 1 Cor. iii. 14, and elsewhere, everlasting happiness as the prize of victory (as a "reward reckoned of grace," assigned by grace, comp. Rom. iv. 4). But the question arises as to what we must understand to be the opposite of the μισθὸς πλῆρης—the *full* reward. One would suppose that he who should lose and trifle away the ἐργαζόμενον would receive, not simply an imperfect reward, but none at all. Moved by this consideration, Aretius and Grotius explained it rightly, that eternal life is described as a *full* reward, in contradistinction to the manifold reward of grace which believers receive in the present life. (We must not, however, with Grotius, think of Luke x. 7, but of the foretaste of blessedness and peace of conscience, and the experience of religious joy.) Bengel refers it to the "different degrees of glory;" but when the thing concerned is the preserving or the perfecting of the state of grace, it is not the various degrees of glory which we must think of, but the question whether we shall or shall not receive, in addition to the reward already received, the full reward of eternal salvation.

In ver. 9 the Presbyter quotes yet another saying of the apostolical Epistle, and a saying which forms the logical link of connection between the required *abiding in a state of grace*, ver. 8, and the required *maintaining the confession of Jesus Christ as come in the flesh*, ver. 7. It is the declaration, namely, "He that abideth in this διδαχή hath the Father and the Son." This declaration occurs in 1 John ii. 23; and it is quoted here in a manner so simple—without any preface, or reason, or development—that we cannot but plainly mark the writer's intention to utter no new reflection of his own, but rather to *remind* them of an already well-known doctrinal saying of the Apostle, and to make his *appeal* to that.

The citation is made in the same free manner as that in which ver. 6 quotes the passage 1 John v. 3. Πᾶς ὁ προάγων καὶ μὴ μένων ἐν τῇ διδαχῇ τοῦ Χριστοῦ, Θεὸν οὐκ ἔχει—he writes—ὁ μένων ἐν τῇ διδαχῇ, οὗτος καὶ τὸν υἱὸν καὶ τὸν πατέρα ἔχει. So read A.B., Copt., Sah. The Text. Rec. has, instead of προάγων, the word παραβαίνων (after G. and I.), which is manifestly an accommodating conjectural interpretation. As it respects, first of all, its relation to 1 John ii. 23, the Presbyter begins, as there, with πᾶς ὁ; he reproduces the meaning of οὐδὲ τὸν πατέρα ἔχει by the words Θεὸν οὐκ ἔχει; and then, as there, opposes to the negative a positive member. But the deviations are not accidental and arbitrary; they all reduce themselves to this, that, in conformity with *his* context, the writer has not to do here with the two ideas of "confession of the *Son*" and "having of the Father," but with the related though somewhat differently modified pair of ideas, "the *confession* of Christ" and the "*having* of the Father and the Son."

Therefore he does not place the "denial of *the Son*" and the "having of *the Father*" in opposition to each other, as subject and predicate; but he lays down the "not abiding *in the doctrine* of Christ" as the subject-idea, and the "*having* God" as the predicate-idea. As, therefore, his chief emphasis rests upon the "having," and the antithesis between "Father" and "Son" retires, it was altogether more appropriate to use the more general expression "God." The positive counter-member of the clause must naturally then be constructed after the analogy of the preceding negative member: here also the "abiding in the doctrine" must form the subject-idea, and the "having the—" the predicate-idea. But yet the influence of the passage, 1 John ii. 23, is so plainly upon him, that he takes up into his predicate the double-idea which had been prominent in the foreground there—πατήρ and υἱός, and also the thought of 1 John ii. 23, "he that confesseth *the Son* hath *the Father* also," —and therefore writes, "hath both the Father and the Son." (This is the reading of B.: Cod. A. places υἱόν first; but, according to the context, the πατέρα must be emphatically first.) Thus here also the writer uses the quotation with perfect freedom and independence; the reference and appeal to the apostolical expression, the reminiscence of the train of thought in 1 John ii. 23, appears undeniably to every eye. More was not necessary: as to details, the Presbyter, himself a holy man of God, inspired by the Holy Ghost, might as freely reconstruct the saying for the purposes of his context as the Apostle himself might have done.[1]

On the thought itself nothing more need be said, as it has been already explained upon 1 John ii. 23. As it regards the words, the Genitive τοῦ Χριστοῦ with the διδαχή is not the *Gen. Subjecti*, but, as must appear from the relation to 1 John ii. 23, the *Gen. Objecti* (Bengel, Lücke). As it respects that προάγων which precedes the "and abideth not," it means in

[1] Hence this freedom of treatment is no argument for the apostolical composition of this Epistle. On the other hand, these visible references to 1 John are not *in themselves* arguments against the apostolical composition. But, having to do simply with citations, the argument which they have been supposed to furnish as to the similarity of style between the 1 John and this Epistle is of no account. It is not when the author is speaking his own words, but only when he is referring to passages in 1 John, that we find specifically Johannæan expressions and turns of thought.

itself *præcedere*, going forward, progressing; but the "not abiding" defines its meaning in the present case. He who in such a sense goes forward in knowledge as not to abide in the doctrine of Christ, hath not God. It is undeniable that reference is here made to the pretensions of the Gnostics, who always represented their doctrine as a constant progression in knowledge. There is a progress (the Presbyter would say) which forsakes the first principles which have been established; and such a progress is apostasy. In all (true) progression of knowledge there must ever be a firm adherence to the unchangeable *root* or foundation of knowledge.

In vers. 10, 11, the Presbyter founds a purely practical exhortation upon what was said in vers. 7-9. Εἴ τις and not ἐάν τις is used, because there are not two cases supposed, one of which will be *found* to be the fact (whether or not such a τις will come); but a *possible* event is assumed, in order to lay down a rule of conduct for its occurrence. It does not say, "in case one should come," but "if (when, as oft as) one comes:" ἐάν corresponds with the Norwegian *huis*, εἰ to the Norwegian *naar*. But we must not forget (as Düsterdieck does) that the Apostle John uses ἐάν even in such cases (compare 1 John v. 15 and 16, and the remarks on the passage); and therefore our εἴ τις is one of the instances in which the style of 2 and 3 John differs from the style of 1 John.

"If any man cometh unto you, and bringeth not this doctrine." Οὐ is closely connected with the idea of φέρει, not with εἰ. The meaning is not, "*unless* a man bring this doctrine," but, "if any man *bring not*, that is, deny, this doctrine:" hence it is not μή, but οὐ. Φέρειν signifies, primarily, only "bear with one," which then indeed passes over into the "presenting," as its result. The ἔρχεσθαι πρός is explained by the exhortation, "Receive him not into your house." The case is supposed that one of those false teachers mentioned in ver. 7 laid claim to the hospitality of their dwelling; but this presupposes a relation of personal friendship and intercourse already established. This very exhortation, therefore, seems to intimate, as also the subsequent, "and bid him not God speed," that in the family circle of Kyria there had been some tendency to error in this direction.

And how often in the present day is there failure on this

point! and how needful among ourselves this exhortation of the Presbyter! Among those who actually possess Christian faith and Christian knowledge, how many are there who, under the influence of a secret vanity, think they must play a magnanimous part, and exhibit at once the firmness of their faith and the largeness of their charity, and therefore do not seek to avoid personal intercourse with notorious enemies of the Christian faith! *They* are so firmly grounded that they can venture on this without fear of being perverted! They stand so spiritually high, and their views are so broad and free, that there is no danger for themselves, but much advantage to those with whom they hold this fellowship! But this is a soul-imperilling delusion. A Christian man should have to do with these deniers of Christ only for the one sole end of their conversion: as soon as he sees that his great object is spurned, he has nothing more to do with them. Any compromise, which would let them think in their own way, and nevertheless continue personal intimate fellowship, is altogether of evil; it is a denial of the Lord, who will not have His light put under a bushel. And those who think themselves so secure, will surely take harm to their own faith; for, while they habituate themselves to *assume* argumentatively an impartial and indifferent relation to the great confession of Christ manifest in the flesh, they end by *becoming* indifferent. They lose the ἀκμή of their ὁμολογία: it is not love for sinners' souls, but sheer vanity, which makes them take pleasure in the society of these strong spirits; their secret heart is already estranged from the Lord; and therefore it cannot fail but that through these breaches the influence of the false teachers should gradually, surely, and deeply penetrate, making them more and more internally indifferent to the " doctrine of Christ," more and more disposed to acknowledge the ingeniousness and the plausibility of the opposite doctrine, and to resent with impatience and warmth the interference of those who would warn them (the ἀγάπη growing cold),—until in the end they glide by imperceptible stages into the camp of the enemies. Therefore in this matter the rule is—*principiis obsta*. The vain and aimless *friendly intercourse* with such liars must be broken off at once. And this is what the words mean—καὶ χαίρειν αὐτῷ μὴ λέγετε. The significance of this prescription is altogether misapprehended by those who (like Bengel, Lücke, etc.)

think that not every kind of greeting is meant, but that the prohibition refers to the use of the specific Christian brotherly salutation in regard to such teachers of error. They might indeed be greeted with the customary formulas of life, but "grace, mercy, and peace" was not to be invoked upon them. But this solution is, in the first place, literally untenable, since χαίρειν λέγειν does by no means indicate the specifically Christian greeting of brotherhood and peace: it is no other than the classical-Greek phrase of the conventional greeting of courtesy, which had its origin in heathenism, and was therefore quite general (compare Odyss. xxiv. 402, xi. 248, xiii. 229; Il. 9, 197; Pindar, Pyth. 2, 57: χαίρειν was also the standing salutation in the superscription of heathen letters). And, in the second place, this explanation takes all the force and pith from the exhortation of our verse. With such a false teacher the Christian is not even to stand upon the footing of mere acquaintanceship; he is not only not to continue any such fellowship, he is not to enter into it. This was the Presbyter's meaning, and no other; and in this he was perfectly right.

He specifies the reason in ver. 11. He who greeteth such a false teacher, that is, he who is in the habit of personal intercourse with him, κοινωνεῖ τοῖς ἔργοις αὐτοῦ τοῖς πονηροῖς. It does not mean that he becomes partaker of the *guilt* of his evil works, but that he becomes a sharer in *his evil works themselves;* he will soon, by means of that familiar and personal fellowship, be involved in the same evils and drawn into the same course of action as the false teacher. How then? That has been already shown above.

Vers. 12, 13. Conclusion.

The construction with the Participle is quite Greek in its conception, and altogether foreign to St John's style. (It is here used as the Partic. Imperfecti.) "Having had much to write unto you, I would not (write it) with paper and ink, but hope to be with you and speak to you face to face." The antithesis to writing with paper and ink is evidently not "spiritual writing" (B.-Crusius), but the oral intercourse which he hoped soon to enjoy. "With paper and ink" is only a more definite designation of the "writing." The point is, "Though I might have much to write to you, I will not *write* it all to you, but say it unto you when we meet."—'Ἀλλὰ ἐλπίζω is guaranteed by B.G.I. and others (against ἐλπίζω γάρ of A.); and it is also logically more appropriate. So also is γενέσθαι (taken in the pregnant sense) by A.B., Vulg., and others, against the Rec. ἐλθεῖν, which is evidently a conjectural emendation on account of the preceding πρός. ("To be to you or with you" = "to have come unto you.") Στόμα πρὸς στόμα, of *speaking*, like πρόσωπον πρὸς πρόσωπον (1 Cor. xiii. 12) of *seeing*. The former phrase is found in the Septuagint, Num. xii. 8; Jer. xxxix. (xxxii.) 4.—Χάρτης is the Egyptian paper, and probably of the finer kind: compare Hug's Introduction.

Thus the Presbyter would say orally and in person what he had further to say. His Epistle was designed only to interpose a temporary check to the danger which was imminent, while at the same time it would announce and prepare them for his coming. (But ver. 12 is by no means, as Huther thinks, an apology for the brevity of his Epistle.)

In the words ἵνα ἡ χαρὰ, κ.τ.λ., he again plainly alludes to 1 John i. 4. His visit would have no other end than to re-establish that state of soul between Kyria and her children, to introduce which had been the end of the Apostle and his work. That blessed object was to be attained which the Apostle had aimed to attain by his Epistle. Thus, in these few words, he most significantly declares that *his* endeavour and *his* exhortation rested entirely upon the authority of the Apostle St John.

The greeting of ver. 13 is self-understood. The sister's children of Kyria must have been living at Ephesus (the sister herself must either have lived elsewhere, or have been already deceased, since no greetings come from her). For the rest, this greeting is not without practical significance. If those sister's children had charged the Presbyter with their greetings to Kyria, he must have told them *that*, and indeed *why*, he was writing to her. (It is probable that it was through these sister's children he received intelligence how matters stood in the house of Kyria.) But thus there lay in the simple reference to these near relatives a hortatory element of some force. These relatives shared, too, the care, and had their parting request, of the Presbyter.—The ἀμήν at the close is decidedly spurious.

THE THIRD EPISTLE OF ST JOHN.

VER. 1. GREETING.—The greeting is the same as 2 John 1, only that the point contained in the words ἐν ἀληθείᾳ is not here developed any further, because there was no occasion for it. That he loved in (the) truth, the Presbyter declares to each: what that means, and how this love is distinguished from a false, carnal friendship with the unworthy, it was necessary that he should unfold only to Kyria.

As it respects the person of Gaius, we find three of that name in the New Testament: 1. Gaius of Corinth, Rom. xvi. 23; 1 Cor. i. 15; 2. Gaius of Derbe, Acts xx. 4; and 3. Gaius of Macedonia, Acts xix. 29. There is no reason for assuming the identity of our Gaius with either of these; he was a fourth man of this name. (Olshausen and most expositors.)

VERS. 2-4. Each of the three sections of the Epistle begins with the affectionate address ἀγαπητέ. Περὶ πάντων belongs to εὐοδοῦσθαι, and περί is used in the same meaning as Matt. iv. 6; Mark i. 44—*in relation to, concerning.* Thus περὶ πάντων forms an antithesis to ἡ ψυχή. The Presbyter wishes for Gaius that he may, in respect of *all* things, prosper and be well, as his soul (already) prospered. It is altogether wrong (with Beza) to refer περὶ πάντων to εὔχομαι, and to insinuate into περί the meaning of πρό—a meaning which it has in composition, as for instance in περιγίγνεσθαι, but never when it stands alone as an independent preposition. And we can scarcely think that the writer would have uttered the thought that he, "before all things," wished Gaius *bodily* wellbeing.

Thus he wishes for him that in all respects he might prosper and be in health, as indeed (καθώς as in 2 John 4 and 6) his soul prospers (and is in health). This, however, does not justify the conclusion that Gaius must necessarily have been sick in body. The περὶ πάντων (rightly understood) gives the εὐοδοῦσθαι καὶ ὑγιαίνειν an altogether universal reference to every kind of earthly wellbeing; although the addition of ὑγιαίνειν gives to health a special prominence.—By health of soul is naturally meant spiritual soundness in the soul's condition and experience.

The third verse serves, as the γάρ (omitted only in the Vulgate and some later codd.) shows, to explain wherein Gaius' health of soul had been demonstrated, how it had been noted by the writer. Ἐχάρην λίαν as in 2 John 4.—Μαρτυρεῖν τινι is used for bearing testimony to a matter; ver. 6 and John v. 33, xviii. 17. The Genitive σου depends upon τῇ ἀληθείᾳ. What is meant by this "truth," is explained by the addition, "as thou walkest in the truth." The καθώς, however, does not serve for *definition*, as if the clause which it begins bore to τῇ ἀληθείᾳ the relation of an explicative apposition : " They bore testimony to thy truth, that is, (they bore testimony) how thou walkest in the truth." But καθώς is employed, as in 2 John 4 and 6, 3 John 2, with a *confirmative* meaning: " As thou (in deed) dost walk in the truth." As to the idea of " walking in truth," see above on 2 John 4. As to who these " brethren " were, see below on ver. 5 seq.

The general idea of ver. 4—serving for the explanation, confirmation, and strengthening of the "rejoiced greatly"— needs no comment. As to the phraseology, it is to be noted that comparatives like μειζότερος occur in classic Greek as well as in the New Testament (Eph. iii. 8); and then, that τούτων (well vouched for, against the softer reading ταύτης of some lesser codd.) is to be taken as the Genitive of the neuter ταῦτα, on which neuter idea the explanatory clause ἵνα, κ.τ.λ., depends. "I have no greater joy than *this*, that I may hear that my children walk in (the) truth," equivalent to "There is for me no greater joy, etc." The ἵνα involves the idea of a wish. (In strict technical precision, εἰ or ὅτι ought to have been used.)— Τέκνα μου—my children—might be used by the *Presbyter* John concerning the members of his Church. According to Papias (Euseb. 3, 39), he had been a personal disciple of Jesus, and therefore must have been advanced in years.

VERS. 5–10. After the generally laudatory acknowledgment,

the writer approaches the object which gave him occasion to write this Epistle. Concerning ἀγαπητέ, see above on ver. 2.— Πιστὸν ποιεῖς ὃ ἐὰν ἐργάσῃ εἰς τοὺς ἀδελφοὺς καὶ τοῦτο ξένους. Ἐργάσῃ is established by B.C.G.I. against the ἐργάζῃ of A.; and so is τοῦτο, by A.B.C., Vulg., and others, against the Rec. εἰς (G.C.).—Πιστὸν ποιεῖς does not mean, "Thou doest what is worthy of a πιστὸς ἀνήρ" (Beza, Lücke); nor, "Thou doest what correspondeth with expectation" (Bengel); nor is πιστόν "faithfully" (De Wette: "Thou dealest faithfully in all, etc."). But πιστὸν ποιεῖν is essentially identical with the classic phrase πιστὸν ποιεῖσθαι (Med.), where πιστόν is to be regarded as a substantial neuter, and equivalent to πίστις (see Passow). The usual meaning of the phrase is "to give a pledge of fidelity."—Ὃ ἐάν = ὃ ἄν. Καὶ τοῦτο as in Phil. i. 28; Eph. ii. 8; 1 Cor. vi. 6:—"Thou givest a pledge of thy true mind in all that thou hast done towards the brethren, and, moreover, towards strangers." Τοὺς ἀδελφούς the author writes, because he had already spoken of them in ver. 3. Ξένοι they were in relation to Gaius; because they were not at home when in his house and Church, but had come there as travellers. And thus he had evidenced his fidelity, not only by general kindness, but by the hospitable reception of these. Hence the heightened καὶ τοῦτο.

His conduct towards them is more closely described in ver. 6: Οἳ ἐμαρτύρησάν σου τῇ ἀγάπῃ ἐνώπιον ἐκκλησίας. That they gave testimony concerning him, had been already stated in ver. 3. But there it was more generally said that they bore testimony to his walk in the truth; here it is more specific, that they bore testimony to the love which he manifested towards them. Ἐνώπιον ἐκκλησίας depends on ἐμαρτύρησαν, not upon ἀγάπῃ. By the ἐκκλησία we must naturally understand the Ephesian Church.

Wherein these proofs of love consisted, the following words declare: οὓς καλῶς ἐποίησας προπέμψας ἀξίως τοῦ Θεοῦ. The reading wavers. The Text. Rec. has ποιήσεις προπέμψας; in which, however, the Future and the Aor. Part. do not seem to accord. Codex C. reads ποιήσας προπέμψεις; some lesser codices, ποιεῖς προπέμψας. Luther and Grotius conjectured ἐποίησας, which may illustrate also how the reading in Cod. C. originated. The reading ποιήσεις might easily arise from misunderstanding the meaning to be, that an exhortation for the future is here added ("Thou wilt do well, if thou sendest them on provided for worthily of God"). So also the modern expositors, following the Text. Rec., take the words as an exhortation for the future. They take it for granted that these "brethren" had come, and that as converters of the Gentiles, from some distant place to the dwelling of Gaius; that they had found a hospitable reception at his hands; that they had then come to Ephesus, were now on the point of returning home, and in their return homewards would call at the house of Gaius again. But we can hardly imagine anything more strange than that the members of a strange and distant Church, who were purposing to convert the Gentiles, should come to Ephesus and its neighbourhood, where there was already a centre of Christianity, and where their labours would be perfectly superfluous. But, as below in ver. 10, equally with ver. 5, οἱ ἀδελφοί with the definite article are mentioned as already known, it cannot be doubted that we must understand by them, not converters of the Gentiles from a distant Church, but those *Ephesian* members of the Church whom the Presbyter had sent to Diotrephes, and who, rejected by Diotrephes and his Christian companions in that place, turned to the dwelling-place of Gaius—because they would not lay claim to the hospitality of the Gentiles (ver. 7) —and from him received a hospitable reception. These had now returned to Ephesus, and had borne witness that Gaius— unlike Diotrephes—"walked in the truth," and what love he had shown towards themselves.—But, how these same brethren could have been sent *again* to Gaius, we cannot discover.

An exhortation to future hospitality cannot, therefore, on any account, be regarded as contained in the words οὓς καλῶς, κ.τ.λ. If we do not conjecture, with Luther and Grotius, ἐποίησας, then we must of necessity, constrained by the Aor. Part. connected with it, assume that this Future is used in the same way as in Luke i. 37, οὐκ ἀδυνατήσει παρὰ τῷ Θεῷ πᾶν ῥῆμα, "nothing is impossible with God;" 1 Cor. xv. 29, τί ποιήσουσι, κ.τ.λ., "what will they then do," etc. ?—that is, the Future would not here express the future of time, but, just as the German Future, a mere general sense of *probability and plausibility*, the so-called Attic supposition. "It will indeed be right and praiseworthy, that thou hast sent them forward in a worthy manner." Thus ποιήσεις would be an urbane form of ποιεῖς or ἐποίεις. However, even thus viewed, the Future would not grammatically accord with the Aorist Participle: therefore it is better to read ἐποίησας. How easily might the reading ποιήσεις have arisen, through error or misunderstanding, out of an original ἐποίησας,—the misunderstanding being naturally caused by ver. 8.[1]

Προπέμπειν, *send on*, is the term for the *provident* dismissal of a guest, whom we provide with what is needful for his further journey (Tit. iii. 13; Rom. xv. 24; 1 Cor. xvi. 6, 11). Ἀξίως τοῦ Θεοῦ has its explanation in ver. 7.

Ὑπὲρ γὰρ τοῦ ὀνόματος ἐξῆλθον, scil. τοῦ ὀνόματος τοῦ Θεοῦ (Bengel); not τοῦ Χριστοῦ (Grotius, Lücke), which in this connection, where τοῦ Θεοῦ immediately precedes, seems forced. The expression—whether Θεοῦ or Χριστοῦ be supplied—indicates generally this, that they made their journey, not for their own occasions and earthly interests, but in the interest of the kingdom of God. Viewed in themselves, the words would permit us to think of a mission to convert the Gentiles, or of a flight through persecution (in which case we must, with Beza, Bengel, and Olshausen, force ἀπὸ τῶν ἐθνικῶν into dependence upon ἐξῆλθον); but they do not constrain us to any such supposition, and the context of the whole Epistle leads to a different conclusion. For, it is evident from ver. 10, that "*the* brethren" spoken of from ver. 3 onwards had been sent by the author to Diotrephes with an Epistle, and that they had been refused reception and hospitality. Thus the words, " receiving nothing from the Gentiles," obtain a specific meaning. Among the Christians in the place where Diotrephes dwelt, they found no hospitable reception; lay claim to the hospitality of the Gentiles dwelling there, they *would* not: then they turned to the (not very distant) dwelling-place of Gaius; and thus what Gaius did to them was done " worthily *of God*," that is, done in a manner worthy of God, in whose service they had made the journey, and in whose honour they had declined all fellowship with the Gentiles.

[1] If we suppose the E to have been overlooked, we have the reading ποιήσας of Cod. C. But, as the two Participles without a finite verb yielded no sense, it would be natural to correct this again into ποιήσεις (Rec.),—especially as ver. 8 was supposed to contain an exhortation for the future.

But now it becomes perfectly clear, that the words οὓς καλῶς, κ.τ.λ., *cannot* contain any exhortation for the future, but *must* be referred to the past. For, that which is said in ver. 7 in explanation of "worthy of God," was among the transactions that had taken place.

In ver. 8 the author utters the general proposition, "We are bound to receive such," in order to exhibit the conduct of Diotrephes, who received them not, as an unrighteous and self-condemned procedure, directly contrary to this ὀφείλομεν. Overlooking this transitional point between the praise of Gaius, vers. 5–7, and the blame of Diotrephes, vers. 9, 10, it has been thought that ver. 8 contained *a silent hint for Gaius;* and hence, in ver. 6, the ποιήσας, which slipped in, instead of the original ἐποίησας, was changed into a ποιήσεις.

We (universally: all Christians) are bound to receive such persons (persons of such a mind as these, according to ver. 7, had approved themselves by acts to possess), that we may be fellow-labourers for the truth. Ὑπολαμβάνειν, occurring only here in the New Testament, means in profane Greek both to receive and to support. The context here decides for the former meaning. Συνεργοὶ (comp. 1 Thess. iii. 2; 2 Cor. viii. 21; Col. iv. 11) γίγνεσθαι τῇ ἀληθείᾳ *might,* viewed in itself, be understood of a co-operation in the service of the conversion of the Gentiles, if the context were speaking of this matter. But it means only to become fellow-labourers of the τοιοῦτοι who were for the ἀλήθεια; and, according to the context, those ἀδελφοί were in *this* way active in serving the truth, that they brought a letter and oral exhortations to Diotrephes, in order to obviate the threatening schism. (Compare the Introduction.)

Ver. 9. The writer goes on without any pause or interruption: "I wrote something to the Church, but, etc." It is a needless assumption, that from ver. 9 onwards another circumstance is suddenly entered upon, different from what is supposed to occupy the previous part.

While the context establishes that the "Church" above in ver. 6 meant the Ephesian Church, here the words imply that that Church is meant to which Diotrephes belonged. And, as that is called simply "the Church," we may infer—as also from the circumstance that those brethren whom Diotrephes rejected were able (on the same day or evening) to repair to Gaius, who thus must have dwelt in the neighbourhood of Diotrephes—that Gaius also was a member of the same Church. (See the Introduction.)

Ἔγραψά τι is the reading of A.B.C. But the writer does not intend by this expression to intimate—as Düsterdieck strangely thinks—that his Epistle was an "insignificant" (!) one, the slender results of which he himself foresaw. It is far better to regard this τι as a most significant aposiopesis. " I had written something to the Church,"—something which, if it had been publicly read, would not have failed of its effect; " but Diotrephes, who will be the first among them" (see the Introduction), " receiveth us not." What the conduct was which is meant by this expression, is explained, 1. by the antithesis to " I wrote," which the " but" establishes (a not-receiving of the Epistle) ; and 2. by ver. 10 (a rejection of the brethren who brought the Epistle). In not receiving the Epistle, and in denying hospitality to those who brought it themselves, he receiveth ἡμᾶς—the Presbyter John himself *with* the messengers —not. To assign to ἐπιδέχεσθαι the vague meaning of " reckon, or hold valid" (Lücke), is to weaken the definite sense attached to it by ver. 10.

Thus it was the purpose of Diotrephes no longer to receive any instructions from that member of the Ephesian Presbytery to whom his (young, commencing) Church had been hitherto submissive : he would govern it *himself;* and that Church was, under his direction, to assume the position of an *independent* Church.

In ver. 9 the writer makes very brief allusion to something which had been no doubt more explicitly narrated to Gaius by those brethren who, rejected by Diotrephes, had received his hospitality. But he nevertheless touches these circumstances here, in order to express to Gaius in what light these things appeared to him (the Presbyter), and to exhibit to him the unwarrantable shamelessness of the conduct of Diotrephes. In the word φιλοπρωτεύειν he unveils his sinful motive ; in the words " receiveth *us* not," he suggests to Gaius, that Diotrephes had outraged, not only these brethren, but himself, the Presbyter also. And both he says, in order that Gaius may all the more carefully guard against being involved in, or inveigled into, his schismatical proceedings.

To the same end, he tells him in ver. 10 that he purposes

himself to come, and to detect Diotrephes and expose him. Hence he enters upon the individual aspects of his wickedness. Ὑπομνήσω must not be translated by *puniam, arguam*, unless we are willing to sacrifice all the delicacy of the expression. It is a great thought, that only to mention that which Diotrephes had done would be sufficient to annihilate him. Φλυαρέω is a word of contempt: it does not mean "slander," λοιδορέω, but (according to Eustathius on Iliad 21, 361) τὸ ἐν οὐ δέοντι λόγους προιέναι, to speak nought, "babble and prate," *plaudern*, as Luther well hits it off. Here it stands with the Objective Accusative, equivalent to "prate at any one." In the addition λόγοις πονηροῖς lies the wickedness, in the φλυαρῶν the wretched nullity, of the words which Diotrephes spoke against the Presbyter.

The following words need no explanation; as to the fact itself, see the remarks in the Introduction. Τοὺς ἀδελφούς is, as in ver. 5, "*the* brethren," those mentioned above. Ἐκ τῆς ἐκκλησίας ἐκβάλλει is to be understood of the excommunication which Diotrephes threatened against those who had been ready to receive with hospitality those "brethren," and by means of which they had been restrained from doing so.—In order to avoid the worst evil, a schism within the Church, they had for the time receded.—But still the categorical ἐκβάλλει seems to show that the excommunication actually took effect on some who did not *at once* accommodate themselves. Compare also below on ver. 12.

In VERS. 11, 12 follows the main exhortation, which contains the scope of the whole Epistle. Gaius must not imitate the κακόν described in vers. 9, 10 (the wickedness of Diotrephes, *and* the weakness of those who succumbed to his terrors); he must not be persuaded to go over to the party of Diotrephes; but he must imitate that which is good. And, as a pattern of the "good," Demetrius is in ver. 12 set before him,—who, therefore, was by no means a member of the Ephesian Church, and a bearer of the letter, but a man of Diotrephes' own Church, who firmly withstood him in all his pretensions.

Before, however, Gaius is referred to the example of this Demetrius, the writer grounds his exhortation, "Follow not, etc," on the general proposition, "He that doeth good, etc.," which contains an undeniable allusion to 1 John iii. 6. The *thought* is there the same: that he who is a child of God sinneth not, but purifieth himself (consequently, he who doeth good approves himself as "being of God"); on the other hand, he who sinneth hath not seen Him. But, in harmony with the context, in which had occurred τὸ ἀγαθόν—τὸ κακόν, the Presbyter employs here the words ἀγαθοποιεῖν and κακοποιεῖν. Thus he treats the passage 1 John iii. 6 just in the way in which he had treated the individual passages of the apostolical Epistle in his own Second Epistle.

Ver. 12. "To Demetrius (good) testimony is given of all" (that is, of all the ἀδελφοῖς, vers. 3, 5, 10), "and of the truth itself." But what does this mean? The truth in the objective sense, the Christian doctrine, cannot be intended. Huther and Düsterdieck think that "the good testimony of the πάντες is represented as one not having its foundation in their human judgment, but in the testimony given them by the ἀλήθεια dwelling in them." But αὐτὴ ἡ ἀλήθεια, in opposition to the πάντες, cannot possibly be the truth which uttered itself in the testimony of the "all." B.-Crusius refers it to the truth of Christianity, which had been advanced by the earlier labours of Demetrius; but his earlier missionary activity could scarcely bear testimony to his present deportment, apart from the harshness of the metonymy which this explanation requires. Lücke expounds that the truth itself would bear testimony to him, if it were asked (that is, if it could speak). Beausobre, Grotius, etc., think of the truth which manifested itself as a living power in the *life* of Demetrius. And this is the only correct interpretation; though we must not limit it to the "truth" which manifested itself generally in his life, but think of the truth which, in these days, in his conduct towards Diotrephes, had so mightily shown its power. Doubtless for its sake he had suffered wrong, and had been content to submit to ill-treatment and persecution (probably the excommunication mentioned in ver. 10). Thus it might be said that the truth (ἐν ᾗ περιπατεῖ, comp. ver. 4) bore testimony in his behalf.

Finally, the Presbyter appends his own testimony for him; and it was needful to explain on what it was founded. It is enough to utter his "αὐτὸς ἔφα," and he writes, "And thou knowest that our testimony is true."

VERS. 13–15. CONCLUSION.—The idea of vers. 13, 14 is perfectly like that of 2 John 12, but the expression differs from it in certain minute points: Πολλὰ εἶχον γράψαι σοι is the reading of A.B.C. and others, in opposition to the Text. Rec. γράφειν, which is slenderly authenticated by G.I., and doubtless owed its origin to the wish to conform it with 2 John 12. On the other hand, we have in Cod. A. a similarly originating various reading, οὐκ ἐβουλήθην, instead of the correct Text. Rec. οὐ θέλω, which is authenticated by B.C. and others. At the close of the verse we must read σοι γράφειν (B.C.).

Thus the distinction between this and 2 John 12 lies in this, first, that the writer does not employ the participial construction (πολλὰ ἔχων), but two clauses (εἶχον—ἀλλ' οὐ θέλω) are opposed to each other; secondly, he uses εἶχον as Imperfect (comp. Acts xxv. 22; Rom. ix. 3), and accordingly employs the Inf. Aor. γράψαι; thirdly, with οὐ θέλω the verb γράφειν is repeated; and, fourthly, he attaches the clause ἐλπίζω, κ.τ.λ., by δέ. ('Αλλά would here have been unsuitable; rather γάρ, but no codex inserts that.) Thus δέ has the meaning of "on the other hand."

The idea itself has been explained, partly on 2 John 12, and partly in the Introduction.—Huther erroneously thinks an ἄν wanting to εἶχον. Εἶχον ἄν would mean, "I should have had much to write (scil. unless);" but the writer would say, "I had much to write."

The final salutation, ver. 14, begins with the specific Christian wish of peace (instead of the profane ἔρρωσο), with which we may compare Gal. vi. 16, Eph. vi. 23, 1 Pet. v. 14, 2 Thess. iii. 16, and others, including 2 John 3. Then the writer sends Gaius salutations from the friends, and charges him to greet "the friends *by name*,"—which latter commission, as well as the expression φίλοι ("friends," in opposition to enemies), is to be explained by the existing relations between Gaius and Diotrephes. Gaius was to greet every one from the Presbyter by name, who had kept aloof from the schism and wickedness of Diotrephes, and thus confirm them in their fidelity.

TRANSLATION OF THE TWO EPISTLES.

I.

THE Presbyter to Kyria, the elect, and her children, whom I love in truth; and not I only, but also all they that have known the truth: for the truth's sake which dwelleth in us; and it will be with us for ever. Grace, mercy, and peace be with you from God the Father, and from Jesus Christ the Son of the Father, in truth and love.

I rejoiced greatly that I found among thy children those who walk in (the) truth, as we have received a commandment from the Father. And now I beseech thee, Kyria (not as though I wrote a new commandment unto thee, but that which we had from the beginning), that we love one another. And this is love, that we walk after His commandments: this is His commandment, as ye have heard from the beginning, that ye should walk in it.—For " many deceivers are entered into the world, who confess not that Jesus Christ is come in the flesh." " This is the deceiver and the Antichrist." Look to yourselves, that ye lose not what we have wrought, but that ye may receive a full reward. Whosoever transgresseth, and abideth not in the doctrine of Christ, hath not God: he that abideth in the doctrine, he hath both the Father and the Son. If there come any unto you, and bringeth not (with him) this doctrine, receive him not into your house, and greet him not. For he that greeteth him is partaker of his evil deeds.

Having many things to write unto you, I would not (write) with paper and ink; but I trust to come unto you, and speak face to face, " that your joy might be full." The children of thy elect sister greet thee.

II.

The Presbyter unto the well-beloved Gaius, whom I love in (the) truth.

Beloved, I wish that in every respect thou mayest prosper and be in health, even as thy soul doth prosper. For I rejoiced greatly when brethren came and testified of thy truth, even as thou walkest in (the) truth. I have no greater joy than to hear that my children walk in truth.

Beloved, thou givest token of thy fidelity in whatsoever thou hast done to the brethren, and that to strangers, who have borne witness of thy charity before the Church; and in regard to whom thou hast done well that thou hast sent them forward on their journey in a way worthy of God. Because for His name's sake they went forth, and took nothing from the Gentiles. We therefore ought to receive such, that we might be fellow-helpers to the truth. I wrote something to the Church; but Diotrephes, who will be first among them, receiveth us not. Wherefore, when I come, I will remind him of the works which he doeth, prating against us with malicious words: and, not content therewith, neither doth he himself receive the brethren, and forbiddeth them that would, and casteth them out of the Church.

Beloved, follow not the evil, but the good. He that doeth good, is of God: he that doeth evil, hath not seen God. Demetrius hath good report of all men, and of the truth itself: but we also bear record; and thou knowest that our testimony is true.

I had many things to write; but I will not with ink and pen write unto thee: however, I hope I shall shortly see thee, and we shall speak face to face. Peace be to thee. Our friends salute thee. Greet the friends by name.

APPENDIX

ON

THE CATHOLIC EPISTLES.

THE seven Epistles in the New-Testament canon which were distinctively not Pauline—that is, the Epistle of St James, two of St Peter, three of St John, and that of St Jude—were in the time of Eusebius (ii. 23) already wont to be collected together under the name of the "Catholic Epistles." But it is doubtful what the precise meaning was which this expression was meant to convey; and that meaning can be found only by a specific and close investigation. The word, derived from καθ' ὅλου, means of itself *generalis, general, universal*: used concerning an Epistle, it may be designed to express that the Epistle *was written by many authors in common;* or, that *it was directed to several Churches in common;* or, finally, that it was *universally acknowledged as canonical*. Each of these three interpretations of the expression καθολικαὶ ἐπιστολαί has had its defenders.

But the first of them at once declares itself to be inappropriate. If the designation, αἱ καθολικαὶ ἐπιστολαί, were applied only to the whole Collection of the seven Epistles, it must of course be presumed that that Collection was called "Catholic" because as a whole it sprang not from one, but from a community of authors,—in opposition to the Collection of Pauline Epistles, which sprang from one author alone. But, even in that case, the expression would be somewhat strange and inexact. For it would necessarily point to a *common* production of the whole; whereas the several authors did not by any means co-operate to a common authorship of a compilation of Epistles which aimed at unity as a whole,[1] but every one of them wrote his own Epistle apart from the rest, with its own specific aim, and on its own specific occasion, and the whole were collected together into one only after the death of the individual writers. And, in fact, we find that it was not merely the *Collection* which bore the name "Catholic," but that, as we shall presently see, each of the *individual* Epistles was itself designated a καθολικὴ ἐπιστολή. At most, we should have to assume that the name "Catholic," after it had once become firmly established for the *Collection* as such, was afterwards also transferred to its *individual component parts* (so that καθολικὴ ἐπιστολή would be equivalent to "an Epistle belonging to the Collection of the Catholic Epistles"). But such an assumption contradicts the reality of history. For we find the designation "Catholic" applied *first* to the individual Epistles—to wit, by Dionysius Alexandrinus (in Eusebius 7, 25), Origen (Select. in. Ps. 3; Comment. on John, concerning 1 Peter; de Orat. and Comm. on John, concerning 1 John, and elsewhere concerning the Epistle of Jude)—*before* it was transferred by Eusebius (2, 23; 6, 13) to the *entire Collection*.—But, generally speaking, the expression "Catholic" never occurs, throughout the whole of patristic literature, as the designation of the conjoint work of many several authors. The only exception seems to be the passage in Clemens Alexandrinus, Strom. 4, where the Epistle in Acts xv. is mentioned in the words κατὰ τὴν ἐπιστολὴν τὴν καθολικὴν τῶν ἀποστόλων ἁπάντων;[2] but here an Epistle is referred to which was actually decreed and accepted by a whole assembly. But how, on the other hand, the seven Epistles in question could have been termed "Catholic" in *this* sense—as the common production of several authors *together*,—and how each of these Epistles could have been

---

[1] Just as when several writers combine in a common work, *e.g.*, an encyclopædia; in which case we should certainly describe this encyclopædia as their "joint work."

[2] Even here the word might bear the elsewhere customary signification of *encyclical* (directed to several Churches); nevertheless, the juxtaposition of καθολικός and τῶν ἀποστόλων ἁπάντων makes it more natural to refer the former to the common co-operation of the *authors*.

termed "a joint production," we cannot understand. Hence, we must regard the view of Hug and others, who refer καθολικός to the community of several *authors*, as altogether set aside.

It is not so easy to determine the question, whether the expression "Catholic" was applied to our Epistles by the Fathers in the sense of *encyclical*, or of *acknowledged canonical*.[1] The former predicate seems at the first glance too narrow for them; since, while it suits the Epistle of St James, and the First of St John, the First and Second of St Peter, and that of St Jude, it does not suit the Second and Third Epistles of St John. The latter predicate seems, on the one hand, too broad, since there were many other Epistles besides these seven which were certainly held to be canonical; and, on the other, it does not seem properly suitable, since 2 Peter, 2–3 John, Jude, and even James, were not found originally in the catalogues (or κάνονες) of *all* Churches, and on that account were termed ἀντιλεγόμεναι. Meanwhile, it is only a more exact investigation which will lead to any certain result.

Dionysius of Alexandria (in Euseb. vii. 25) attempted to establish that the Apocalypse must have been written by another John, and not the Apostle, because the Apostle does not mention his name in his writings. After appealing to the Gospel, he goes on, ὁ δὲ εὐαγγελιστὴς οὐδὲ τῆς καθολικῆς ἐπιστολῆς προέγραψεν ἑαυτοῦ τὸ ὄνομα; and, after having quoted the beginning of 1 John, he proceeds, ἀλλ' οὐδὲ ἐν τῇ δευτέρᾳ φερομένῃ Ἰωάννου καὶ τρίτῃ, καίτοι βραχείαις οὔσαις ἐπιστολαῖς, ὁ Ἰωάννης ὀνομαστὶ πρόκειται. It would seem here obvious enough that καθολικός must be taken as the antithesis of φερόμενος. Hug indeed thinks that the particle ἀλλά standing between the two words makes it impossible to regard καθολικός and φερόμενος as antithetical ideas. Kirchhofer goes so far as to maintain that Dionysius, "by the word φερόμενος, distinguishes the Second and Third Epistles from the First, because these were not addressed to several Churches; but not because he wished to describe them as only by report assigned to St John, for he held St John as their author." Dionysius nowhere says that he positively held St John to be author of 2 and 3 John: he takes care not to write

[1] The latter is the view of Nosselt, Hammond, and others; the former, that of Grotius, Wolf, and Wetstein.

ἀλλ' οὐδὲ ἐν τῇ δευτέρᾳ φερομένῃ καὶ τρίτῃ προέγραψεν ἑαυτοῦ τοῦ ὄνομα, but discreetly says, ἀλλ' οὐδὲ——ὁ Ἰωάννης ὀνομαστὶ πρόκειται; and again, further on, συνᾴδουσι μὲν γὰρ ἀλλήλοις τὸ εὐαγγέλιον καὶ ἡ ἐπιστολή (not ἐπιστολαί). But, that φερόμενος should bear the meaning of "not addressed to several Churches," is an absurdity which needs no refutation. When Dionysius applies the predicate φερομένη to the Second and Third Epistles, he clearly and unambiguously declares that for his own part he was very far from being convinced of their apostolical origin. But that did not prevent his turning these two Epistles to the account of his assertion. Granted, he would say, that these Epistles *were* apostolical (or, that the readers held them for apostolical), even then the proposition, that the Apostle did not mention himself by name, would be unaffected. Thus we see also (against Hug) that καθολική may be logically used as the antithesis to φερομενή. It was quite logical to write: "The Apostle, even in his acknowledged genuine document, did not prefix his name, but began without preliminaries with the mystery of the Divine revelation, etc. But also in the *supposed* Second and Third Epistles, John is not mentioned by name." Καθολικός, therefore, *may* here form the antithesis of φερόμενος.

Not that it *must*, however, form any such antithesis. The two expressions are divided by too great an interval to allow of our saying that καθολικός must here be viewed as the antithesis of φερόμενος. It is quite as conceivable that καθολικός is used here in that meaning of *encyclical* which, as we shall presently see, was its common meaning in the more ancient patristic period. The First Epistle of St John was an encyclical document addressed to the Church of Ephesus, and to the surrounding Churches of Asia Proconsularis. Dionysius may therefore *either* have applied to it the *epitheton naturale* of "Catholic," as the only Epistle of St John which he regarded as genuine, just as Origen does in passages where he has no thought of any antithesis to καθολικός,[1]—*or* he might have had this inten-

---

[1] *E. g.*, Selecta in Ps 3: Καὶ τὰ λεγόμενα ἐν τῇ καθολικῇ ἐπιστολῇ παρὰ τῷ Πέτρῳ (then follows 1 Pet. iii. 19). Here, the First Epistle of St Peter is not called encyclical that it might be opposed to another not encyclical; for the Second Epistle of St Peter was encyclical. But καθολικός is here simply *epitheton naturale*.

tion, to say that the Second and Third Epistles of St John, apart from the doubtful question of their apostolical origin, were in all cases, and indubitably, not encyclical documents. But it was not necessary that he should express more positively this antithesis to encyclical (*if* he had it in view); it was understood of itself. Now, when he applies to the Second and Third Epistles the predicate φερόμενος, he does not take up again that antithesis between encyclical and not-encyclical; but he intends to express the new and independent thought, that he did not confidently hold these Epistles to be apostolical. This view of the καθολικός is logically tenable. It was strictly logical for Dionysius to write: "Even to his encyclical *writing* [on *writing* the emphasis lies] the Evangelist did not prefix his name, but without any preliminary began with the mystery of the Divine revelation. That which was from the beginning, he says, that which we have heard, that which we have seen with our eyes. For, on account of this revelation, the Lord pronounced Peter blessed: Blessed art thou, Simon Barjona, for flesh and blood hath not revealed it unto thee, but My Father in heaven. But also in the supposed *Second and Third* Epistles [on 'Second and Third' lies the emphasis], the name John is not mentioned." The full citation of the passage shows that we are not constrained to regard καθολικός as the antithesis of φερόμενος.

Thus, this much-contested passage of Dionysius establishes no more than this, that καθολικός *may* be taken, as well with the meaning "acknowledged as apostolical," as with the meaning "encyclical." Nothing more definite can be derived from this passage, but must be looked for elsewhere.

And now, at the outset, it is remarkable that in none of the old canons does the word occur in the sense of κανονικός or ἐνδιάθηκος. Cassiodorus (de Instit. Div. lect. c. 8) was the first to describe the Epistles, 1 Pet., 1 and 2 John, 2 Pet., 3 John, and James, as *epistolæ canonicæ;* whence it has been rightly argued (as Cassiodorus could not have held 2 Pet., 3 John, and Jude as apocryphal) that he had in his mind the collection of the *seven* Epistles, and took the current word καθολικός in the sense of κανονικός. Similarly, Theophylact explains καθολικός as the antithesis of ἀπόκρυφος.

In the more ancient patristic period, on the other hand, we

never meet with this use of καθολικός as equivalent to κανονικός. It is not right to appeal to Euseb. 3, 3. Here we read: Πέτρου μὲν οὖν ἐπιστολὴ μία ἡ λεγομένη αὐτοῦ πρότερα ἀνωμολόγηται· ταύτῃ δὲ καὶ οἱ πάλαι πρεσβύτεροι ὡς ἀμφιλέκτῳ ἐν τοῖς σφῶν αὐτῶν κακεκέχρηνται συγγράμμασι· τὴν δὲ φερομένην αὐτοῦ δευτέραν οὐκ ἐνδιάθηκον μὲν εἶναι παρειλήφαμεν· ὅμως δὲ πολλοῖς χρήσιμος φανεῖσα μετὰ ἄλλων ἐσπουδάσθη γραφῶν. Τὸ γὲ μὴν τῶν ἐπικεκλημένων αὐτοῦ πράξεων, καὶ τὸ κατ' αὐτὸν ὠνομασμένον εὐαγγέλιον, τὸ δὲ λεγόμενον αὐτοῦ κήρυγμα, καὶ τὴν καλουμένην ἀποκάλυψιν οὐδ' ὅλως ἐν καθολικαῖς ἴσμεν παραδεδομένα, ὅτι μήτε ἀρχαίων μήτε τῶν καθ' ἡμᾶς τις ἐκκλησιαστικὸς συγγραφεὺς ταῖς ἐξ αὐτῶν συνεχρήσατο μαρτυρίαις. It is customary to supply γραφαῖς to καθολικαῖς—needlessly, however, for ἐκκλησίαις might as well be supplied; but even then, καθολικός does not stand simply and as such in the sense of "canonical." They are called "catholic writings," as the clause with ὅτι shows, because use was made of them in the καθολικὴ ἐκκλησία.

But this usage—*if* indeed ἐκκλησίαις is not to be supplied—stands almost isolated, and must simply be explained by the context. Where, on the other hand, a single New-Testament document receives the predicate ἡ καθολική (*e.g.*, ἐπιστολή), this predicate stands in the Fathers decidedly in the sense of *encyclical*. This is manifestly the fact; for, five of the seven Epistles which were customarily called καθολικαί were no other than those concerning which the "οὐκ ἐνδιαθήκους αὐτὰς παρειλήφαμεν" held good. But it would have been exceeding strange, if those very writings which, being the majority, were not yet universally acknowledged as canonical, had been described as "universally acknowledged," in opposition to the remainder. And then, Eusebius places the ideas ἀντιλεγόμενα and καθολικά even in strict juxtaposition, when he (6, 14) writes concerning Clemens Alexandrinus: ἐν δὲ ταῖς Ὑποτυπώσεσι, ξυνελόντα εἰπεῖν, πάσης τῆς ἐνδιαθήκου γραφῆς ἐπιτετμημένας πεποίηται διηγήσεις, μηδὲ τὰς ἀντιλεγομένας παρελθών, τὴν Ἰούδα λέγω καὶ τὰς λοιπὰς καθολικὰς ἐπιστολάς. Thus, he comprises the Epistle of St Jude, with the other "Catholic" Epistles, among "the *not* universally acknowledged"—a plain proof that καθολικαὶ ἐπιστολαί had not to him the meaning of "universally-acknowledged Epistles." So also he speaks (3,

23) of the Epistle of St James as the πρώτη τῶν ὀνομαζομένων καθολικῶν, and adds ἰστέον δὲ ὡς νοθεύεται.[1]

To these negative arguments (that καθολικός did not mean "canonical") may be added the following positive arguments (that it had the meaning of "encyclical"). Apollonius (in Euseb. 5, 18) relates of the Montanist Themisus: ἐτόλμησε μιμούμενος τὸν ἀπόστολον, καθολικήν τινα συνταξάμενος ἐπιστολὴν κατηχεῖν τοὺς ἄμεινον αὐτοῦ πεπιστευκότας. Themisus could not have written an Epistle made up of several, nor an Epistle acknowledged canonical, but only a circular-letter meant for the several Phrygian Churches. To the same interpretation we are led by the words of Eusebius himself (4, 23): (Διονύσιος) χρησιμώτατον ἅπασιν ἑαυτὸν καθιστὰς ἐν αἷς ὑπετυποῦτο καθολικαῖς πρὸς τὰς ἐκκλησίας ἐπιστολαῖς. We see what was the meaning which was universally at that time connected with the expression καθολικὴ ἐπιστολή. Thus also Œcumenius (Prolegomena in Epist. Jac.) explains the current designation of our seven Epistles in the following way: καθολικαὶ λέγονται αὗται, οἱονεὶ ἐγκύκλιοι· οὐ γὰρ ἀφορισμένως ἔθνει ἑνὶ ἢ πόλει, ὡς ὁ θεῖος Παῦλος τοῖς Ῥωμαίοις ἢ Κορινθίοις προσφωνεῖ ταύτας τὰς ἐπιστολὰς ὁ τῶν τοιούτων τοῦ Κυρίου μαθητῶν θίασος, ἀλλὰ καθόλου τοῖς πιστοῖς, ἤτοι Ἰουδαίοις τοῖς ἐν τῇ διασπορᾷ, ὡς καὶ ὁ Πέτρος, ἢ καὶ πᾶσι τοῖς ὑπὸ τὴν αὐτὴν πίστιν χριστιανοῖς τελοῦσιν. When Origen (cont. Cels. i. 63) calls the Epistle of Barnabas a καθολικὴ ἐπιστολή—so terming it, obviously, as intending to designate it an *encyclical* Epistle, for it could not be his wish to represent it as canonical—we see plainly in what sense he terms the First Epistles of St Peter and St John "Catholic Epistles," in the passages above quoted. Just as they were wont to quote thus, "St Paul says in his Epistle *to the Romans*," so, in the case of an Epistle which had no specific designation, they quoted by the formula, "St John says in his *general* (that is, encyclical) writing." This was the origin of the term: first, they denominated the First Epistle of St John, the First and Second of St Peter, those of St James and St Jude, "Catholic Epistles;" then this designation was

---

[1] Whoever reads the passage in its connection, and without bias, will see plainly that this remark is not made with the design to limit the idea of καθολικός, or to annul it,—that, in other words, ὀνομαζόμενος is not used in the pregnant sense of "*only so called*, but not actually *being*."

applied to the *collection as such,* although in the meantime the two small Epistles, addressed to private persons, had been received into the number—which, however, obviously could not prevent the whole collection from being *a potiori* designated as the Encyclical Epistles. It was not until the Arian and subsequent controversies had brought into more frequent and more definite use the distinction between the καθολικὴ ἐκκλησία and the αἱρετικοῖς, that the old signification of καθολικός, as equivalent to encyclical, vanished entirely from the minds of men. *Then* they began (Theodoret, Cassiodorus) erroneously to understand the word, even when found as the predicate of an Epistle or collection of Epistles, in the sense "of being acknowledged orthodox and canonical by the Catholic Church." This could not have been possible till a time when the remembrance of the *antilegomenon* character of five among the "Catholic Epistles" had passed away.[1]

[1] The first who recognised this *change* in the signification of καθολικός was Bertholdt (Einleitung, I. S. 221). But he erroneously refers that change of signification to a period as early as the end of the third century. That καθολικός originally meant "encyclical," and only afterwards obtained the meaning of "canonical," has been assumed, after Bertholdt, by De Wette and Olshausen, and most of the moderns.

INDEX.

I. GREEK WORDS AND PHRASES EXPLAINED.

	Page		Page
Ἀγάπη,	287	Ἔγραψά τι,	403
Ἀγάπη αὐτοῦ, ἡ,	294	Εἰ μή,	190
Ἀγάπη τοῦ Θεοῦ, ἡ,	165	Ἐκλεκτή,	380
Ἀγγελία,	77	Ἐν ἡμῖν and εἰς ἡμᾶς,	289
Ἁγνίζειν and ἁγιάζειν,	216, 217, 218	Ἐντολαί, αἱ,	128
		Ἐντολή,	135
Ἁγνός and ἅγιος,	217	Ἐπιθυμία,	167
Ἀδελφός and ἀδελφοί,	238, etc. 337	Ἔργα τοῦ διαβόλου,	232
		Ἔρχεσθαι διά,	316
Ἀδικία and ἀνομία,	110	Ἔρχεσθαι πρός,	393
Αἴρειν,	224	Ἐρωτᾶν and αἰτεῖν,	386
Αἰών and εἰς τὸν αἰῶνα,	175	Ἐσχάτη ὥρα,	178, etc.
Ἀκούειν τινός,	337		
Ἀλαζονία,	169	Ἥτις,	60
Ἀλήθεια,	381		
Ἀληθῶς,	129	Ζωή,	55, 64, 254
Ἁμαρτία πρὸς θάνατον,	338, etc.		
Ἁμαρτίαν ἔχειν,	97	Θεωρεῖν,	254
Ἀνομία,	110		
Ἀντίχριστος,	181	Ἱλασμός,	121, 122, 291
Ἀπ' ἀρχῆς,	139, 140	Ἵνα,	102, 301
Ἀποκαλύπτεται,	106		
Ἀρχή,	49	Καθαρίζειν,	93, 110
		Καθαρισμός,	94
Βίος,	169, 254	Καθολικὴ ἐπιστολή,	410
Βλέπετε ἑαυτούς,	390	Καθ' ὅλου,	409
		Καταλλαγή,	291
Γεγεννῆσθαι ἐκ Θεοῦ,	208	Κόλασις,	305
Γράφω and ἔγραψα,	159	Κόσμος,	162, 164, 295
		Κόσμου, τὰ τοῦ,	162, 163
Διάνοια,	345	Κόσμῳ, πᾶν τὸ ἐν τῷ,	165
Δικαιοσύνη Θεοῦ,	105, etc.		
Δικαιοσύνην, ποιεῖν τήν,	201	Λόγος,	53, 54
Δίκαιος,	104, 109, 120, 230, 331	Λόγος αὐτοῦ,	112, 128
		Λόγου τῆς ζωῆς, περὶ τοῦ,	52
Ἐάν,	88	Μετά,	300
Ἐγνώκαμεν,	126	Μισθός,	390

2 D

INDEX.

	Page
Ξένοι,	399
Ὁ ἦν ἀπ' ἀρχῆς,	46
Οἱ Ἰουδαῖοι,	35
Ὅμοιος,	214
Ὁμολογεῖν,	101, 193, 194
Ὀργή,	106, 122
Ὅς and ὅστις,	61
Παιδία,	154, 176, 177, 178
Παράκλητος,	120
Πατέρα οὐκ ἔχειν,	192
Περιπατεῖν,	89
Περιπατεῖν ἐν τῇ σκοτίᾳ,	97
Πιστὸν ποιεῖν,	399
Πλάνη, πλάνος, πλανάω,	99
Πνεῦμα,	275
Ποταπός,	205
Πρεσβύτερος,	368
Προάγων,	392
Προπέμπειν,	401
Σαρκί, ἐν,	277
Σάρξ,	168, 278
Σκάνδαλον,	149
Σκότει, ἐν τῷ,	89
Σκοτία and ἡ σκοτία,	98

	Page
Σπέρμα,	233, 234
Σπλάγχνα,	255
Τέκνα Θεοῦ,	207
Τεκνία,	116
Τηρεῖν ἑαυτόν,	343
Υἱόν,	192
Ὑπολαμβάνειν,	402
Φανεροῦσθαι,	58, 212
Φανερωθῆναι,	211
Φέρειν,	393
Φερόμενος,	412
Φλυαρέω,	404
Φῶς,	79
Φωτί, ἐν τῷ,	147
Χαίρειν,	395
Χαρά,	75
Χάρτης,	396
Χρίσμα,	186
Ψευστὴν ποιοῦμεν αὐτόν,	112
Ψεύστης, ὁ,	189
Ψυχὴν τιθέναι, τὴν,	251

II. PASSAGES OF SCRIPTURE INCIDENTALLY ILLUSTRATED OR EXPLAINED.

	Page
Luke i. 37,	400
i. 78,	144
xxiv. 39,	48
John i. 1,	49; 62, 64
i. 3,	20
i. 4,	245
i. 9, 10,	21
i. 14,	21
i. 17, 18,	21
i. 18,	63
i. 29,	224
i. 32,	21
iii. 13, 14,	22
iii. 16,	163, 164
v. 26,	245
vi. 40,	208
vi. 51,	71
viii. 44,	167, 232
xi. 17, 18,	251

	Page
John xvii. 21,	70
xx. 27,	48
xx. 31,	20
xxi. 22,	179
Acts viii. 9,	17
xxiv. 15,	216
Romans i. 17,	105–109
1 Corinthians xiv. 32,	275
xv. 29,	400
2 Corinthians iii. 18,	214
2 Thessalonians ii. 1, etc.,	182
Hebrews vi. 4,	234
James i. 17,	80

III. PRINCIPAL MATTERS.

Abiding in love, 299.
Advent of Christ, expected by the Apostles in the immediate future, 179, etc.
Advocate with the Father, our, 118, 120.
Anointing, the, which believers receive, 185, 186, 198.
Antichrist, and many Antichrists, 180–183, 191, 192 ; the spirit of, 279.
Antithesis, the, between the children of God and the children of the devil, 229, 230.

Beginning, that which was from the, 46.
Beginning, from the, 139, 140.
Believing in God's love, 298.
Blinding the eyes, darkness, 150, etc.
Blood of Christ, its cleansing power, 93, 95, 96.
Blood, and water, which Jesus came by, 316–319.
Born of God, 311 ; he that is, sins not, 232, 235
Bowels, to shut up the, 255.
Brethren, 146.
Brother, hatred of one's, inconsistent with love to God, 308, etc.
Brotherly-love, 237.

Cain, 240, 241.
Calling, the, of John, 14, etc.
Catholic, meaning of the term, 409 ; how applied to the Epistles so called —the question investigated, 409–416.; origin of the term, 415, 416.
Cerinthic Gnosis, the, 277, 288, 296.
Cerinthus, the most ancient, actual Gnostic, 17 ; the doctrines of, 17, etc. ; the God of, 85 ; the lie of, 191, 277.
Children, 154, 176, 177, 178.
Children of God, and children of the devil, 229, 230, 236.
Children, little, 116.
Christ, that Jesus is the, the kernel of all truth, 188, 189 ; the rationalistic and pantheistic, 191 ; denying that Jesus is the, 191, 193 ; the confession of, 193, etc. ; became incarnate to take away sin, 223–225 ; without sin, 225 ; manifested to destroy the works of the devil, 232 ; the true God, 348.
Coming of Christ, expected by the Apostles as at hand, 179.
Commandment, the old and the new, 134, etc., 138, etc.
Commandments, God's, a standard to regulate the believer's walk and spirit, 125 ; their nature, 128.
Confession of Christ, 193, etc., 297.
Confession of sin, 96, 101, 102.
Construction and style of John's Gospel and Epistle, 6, etc.
Conversion, true, 227.

Darkness, none in God, 83, etc.
Darkness, walking in, 89, 149, 150 ; blinding the eyes, 150.
Darkness, passing away, 144.
Death, passing from, unto life, 244.
Death, a sin unto, 337–342.
Demetrius, 404, 405.
Denying the Father and the Son, 192 ; that Jesus is the Christ, 191, 193.
Diotrephes, 404, 405.
Devil, the, 232 ; the works of, 232 ; the children of, 229, 230, 236.

INDEX.

Ebionitism, 15, etc.
Epistle, the First, of St John,—is it an Epistle? 1; addressed to specific readers, 2; is, in essence, not in form, an Epistle, 3; why all greeting and benediction are absent from it, 5, etc.; never doubted to be the production of John, 6; style and construction the same as of the Gospel, 6; circle of ideas also the same, 7, etc.; dogmatic views of both the same, 8, etc.; genuineness of, 11, etc.; relation of, to the Gospel, 14, etc.; belongs to the same time as the Gospel, 25, etc.; rests upon the Gospel, 26, etc.; time and place of its composition, 34, etc.; patristic tradition respecting its having been written in Patmos, 37; readers of, 38; Augustine's assertion, that it was written to the Parthians, and ground of the mistake, 38, 39; diction and tone of, 40; literature of, 41, 42.
Epistle, Second and Third, of John, 359; how distinguished from the First, 359; internal evidence in relation to its authorship, 359, 360, 361; external evidence, 361, etc.; investigation of the claims of John the Presbyter to the authorship of, 363–376; canonicity of, 376; readers, 377, 378.
Eternal Life, the, 56, 60.
Evil One, the, toucheth him not, 344; the world lying in the, 344.
EXCURSUS on Rom. i. 17, 105–109.
Eye, lust of the, 167, etc.

Faith, the victory of, 311, etc.
Faith *inamissibilis*, 184.
Faithful and just to forgive sin, God is, 102–105.
Fall, can the regenerate ever? 234.
False teachers, how to act towards them, 393–395.
Father, denying the, 192; to have the, 192, 193; the love of the, 205, etc.
Fathers, 160.
Fear, none in love, 304; has torment, 305.
Fellowship, 72.
Fellowship with God, 88, 92.
Flesh, denying that Jesus is come in the, 277.
Flesh, lust of the, 166, etc.
Forgiveness, 104; upon confession, 155.

Gaius, 397.
Genuineness of the First Epistle of John, 11, etc.
Gnosis, the true, 18, etc.
Gnosis, the Cerinthic, 277, 278, 296.
Gnosticism, 16, etc.; John's opposition to, 18–23, 189, 229.
God is light, 79, etc.; in the light, 91, etc.; is love, 288; no man hath seen, at any time, 293; how to demonstrate our love to, 293; His love to us, 297; the true, 347, 348.
God speed, not to be addressed to false teachers, 393, etc.
Gospel of St John, the style and construction of, the same as those of his First Epistle, 6; circle of ideas of, the same, 7; personality of, the same, 7; directly referred to in the First Epistle, 28, 29.
Grace, mercy, and peace, 382.

Handling of the Word of Life, 48.
Hatred, and love, 252.
Hatred of one's brother, 149, 248; inconsistent with the love of God, 308.
Hatred, the world's, of believers, 243, etc.
Heart, our, condemning, 259, etc.; God greater than our, 263, 266.

INDEX. 421

Hebraizing idiom in the use of ἵνα, 102.
Hope, the purifying influence of Christian, 215.
Hour, the last, 178.

In God, 131.
Incarnation of Christ to take away sin, 223, etc ; its object in respect to the κοσμός, 295.
Intercession of Christ, 121.

Jesus is the Christ,—the kernel of all truth, 188, 189 ; denying that, 191, 193.
John the Apostle, his calling, 14, etc.
John, the First Epistle of—is it an Epistle? 1 ; addressed to specific readers, 2 ; in essence, but not in form, an Epistle, 3, etc. ; why all greeting and benediction are wanting in it, 5 ; the style and construction the same as those of the Gospel, 6 ; circle of ideas the same, 7 ; dogmatic views the same, 8 ; genuineness of, 11, etc. ; its relation to the Gospel, 14, etc. ; belongs to the same time as the Gospel, 25, etc ; rests upon the Gospel, 26 ; time and place of writing, 34, etc. ; readers of, 38 ; diction and tone, 40 ; literature, 41, 42.
John, the Second and Third Epistles of,—internal evidence as to their authorship, 359–361 ; external evidence, 361–363 ; claims of John the Presbyter to the authorship of, investigated, 363–376.
John the Presbyter, 363.
Joy, full, 74, 75.

Keep oneself, to, 343.
Knowing God, 126.
Knowing all things, 186, 187.
Knowing and believing in God's love, 298.
Kyria, to whom the Second Epistle of John was addressed, 377, 380, 384.

Last hour, the, 178.
Liar, who is the, 188, 190.
Lie, the, 188, 189, 190.
Life, the, was manifested, 55, 62 ; the eternal, 56, 60 ; the Son of God called, 64, 65.
Life, passing from death unto, 244, etc. ; and light, how related, 345.
Life, to lay down one's, 251.
Light, God is, 79, 80–83, 85 ; God is in the, 91.
Light, the, 80–83 ; walking in the, 87, 90, 91 ; shineth, 146 ; dwelling in the, 147 ; and life, how related, 245.
Likeness to Christ, 213, 214.
Little children, 116.
Logos, the, 49 ; with the Father, 62.
Love, God is, 288 ; source of, 287, 290, 291 ; no fear in, 304 ; perfect, 305.
Love of God, the, meaning of the phrase, 128, 130, 165, 294.
Love of the Father, 205, etc.
Love to God, how to prove it, 293, 311, etc. ; to abide in, 299.
Love of one's brother, 238, etc. ; bound up in love to God, 307, etc.
Love of the world, 163, etc.
Love and hatred, 252.
Love-relation, the, between God and us, 298, 300, etc.
Loving in the truth, 380, 381.
Lusts of the flesh, and of the eye, 166–169.
Luxury, 170, 171.

Man of Sin, the, 182.
Manifestation of the children of God, 211.
Manifestation of Christ in the flesh, 223.
Manifested, the Life was, 223.
Meritum de congruo, 104.
Message, the, which John received, 77, 78.
Murderer, he who hates his brother is a, 248.

Nazarene element, the, of Christianity, 15.
New commandment, the, 138, etc.

Old commandment, the, 134, etc., 138, etc.
Only Son, and Only-begotten, 290.

Pantheistic Christ, the, 191.
Paraclete, 120.
Parthians, Augustine's assertion that the First Epistle of John was addressed to the, 39.
Patmos, the patristic tradition which refers the writing of John's Gospel to the Isle of, 37; date of John's exile to, 38.
Perfect love, 305.
Perseverance of the saints, 234, 235.
Personality of the Gospel and First Epistle of John, the same, 7.
Plural, the use of the, by John in his First Epistle, 45.
Prayer, the efficacy of, when according to God's will, 336; for one who has not sinned unto death, 337, etc.
Predestination, and semi-Pelagianism, 115, note; absolute, 235.
Presbyter John, the, 363; the author of the First and Second Epistles of John, 363-384.
Progress, true and false, 393.
Propitiation for the sin of the world, Christ the, 121, 122.
Purification, self-, produced by Christian hope, 216, etc., 218, 220.

Rationalistic Christ, the, 191.
Regenerate, the, cannot sin, 235.
Regeneration, 208.
Reward, a full, 390.
Righteous, who is, 230.
Righteous, Jesus Christ the, 120, etc.
Righteousness, to do, 201.
Righteousness of God, the, 105-109.

Seed of God, the, 233, etc.
Self-deception, 99.
Simon the magician, the first exhibition of the gnostic nature seen in, 17.
Sin, 221; committing, 221, 222, 223; the incarnation of Christ designed to take away, 223, 225; none in Christ, 225; the man born of God does not commit, 226, renounced by the converted soul, 227.
Sin, the confession of, 96, to have, 97, 98.
Sin not unto death, 337-342.
Son, the Only-begotten, 290.
Son, denying the Father and the, 192.
Sons of God, 207.
Spirit, the biblical idea of, 275.
Spirit of Antichrist, 279.
Spirit of God, the, marks by which it may be known, 276, 292.
Spirit, the, and the water, and the blood, 330.

Spirits, the injunction to try the, 274, etc.
Stumbling, 148, etc.
Style of John's First Epistle and his Gospel, 6, etc.

Taking away sin, 225.
Teachers, false, how to act towards them, 393–395.
Testimony of God, the, 331, 334.
Torment, fear has, 305.
Toucheth not him that is born of God, the Evil One, 344.
True, He that is, 346; God, 347.
Truth, the, 187, 188.
Truth, doing and speaking the, 89, etc.; loving in the, 380, 381; walking in the, 383.

Victory, faith the, which overcometh the world, 311.
Vocation, the, of John, 14, etc.

Walking as Christ walked, 132.
Walking in darkness, 89.
Walking in the light, 87, 90, 91.
Walking in the truth, 383.
Water and blood, Jesus came by, 316, etc., 319.
Water, the, and the spirit, and the blood, 330, etc.
Will of God, the blessedness of doing the, 174.
Witness of the Spirit, 319, etc., 322.
Witnesses, the three heavenly, 324–329.
Word of God, the, 112, 113.
Word of Life, the, 28, 52.
Works of the devil, the, 232.
World, the, 162; things of, 162, 163; love of the, 163, 165; passeth away, 173, etc., 176; knows not Christ nor His people, 209, etc.; its hatred of the children of God, 243, etc.; as the object of salvation, 295; as Christ is, so are we in the, 302, etc.; the victory over, 314, etc.; lieth in the Wicked One, 344.
Wrath of God revealed, 105, etc.

Young men, 160.

THE END.

www.ingramcontent.com/pod-product-compliance
Lightning Source LLC
Chambersburg PA
CBHW071138300426
44113CB00009B/1007